D1026866

THE ROYAL DESCENT

OF

MRS. SAMUEL F. LEIB,

OF "LIEBHEIM," SAN JOSÉ, CAL.

ALFRED THE GREAT, King of England=Lady Ethelbith.

Edward the Elder, King of England=Lady Edgiva.

Edmund I., King of England=Lady Elgiva.

Edgar the Peaceful, King of England=Lady Elfrida.

Ethelred the Unready, King of England=Lady Elgifa.

Edmund Ironsides, King of England=Lady Algita.

Prince Edward the Exile, of England=Lady Agatha.

Princess Margaret, of England=Malcolm III., King of Scotland.

Princess Matilda, of Scotland=Henry I., King of England.

Maud, Empress of Germany=Geoffrey, Count of Anjou.

Henry II., King of England=Lady Eleanor of Aquitaine.

John, King of England=Lady Isabel de Taillefer.

Henry III., King of England=Lady Eleanor of Provence.

Edward I., King of England=Lady Eleanor of Castile.

Princess Elizabeth of England=Humphrey, Earl of Hereford and Essex.

Sir William, Earl of Northampton, K. G.=Lady Elizabeth de Badlesmere.

Lady Elizabeth de Bohun=Sir Richard, Earl of Arundel, K. G.

Lady Elizabeth Fitzalan=Sir Robert Goushill, of Hault Hucknall.

Lady Joan Goushill=Sir Thomas, Baron Stanley, K. G.

Lady Elizabeth Stanley=Sir Richard Molineux, of Sefton.

Sir Thomas Molineux, of Sefton=Lady Anne Dutton.

Sir William Molineux, of Sefton=Lady Jane Rigge.

Sir Richard Molineux, of Sefton=Lady Eleanor Ratcliffe.

Lady Margaret Molineux=John Warren, of Pointon, Cheshire.

Sir Edward Warren, of Pointon=Lady Anne Davenport.

John Warren, of Pointon=Anne Ognal.

Edward Warren, of Pointon=Margaret Arderne.

Humphrey Warren, of "Frailty," Charles Co., Md.=Eleanor (second wife).

Thomas Warren, of " Frailty," Charles Co., Md.=Mary Barton (first wife).

Barton Warren, of " Frailty," Charles Co., Md.=Elizabeth ———.

Mary Warren (widow of Harrison Musgrave)=John Stone, of Charles Co., Md.

Rev. Barton Warren Stone, 1772–1844=Elizabeth Campbell (first wife).

Mary Ann Harrison Stone=Charles Chilton Moore, of Fayette Co., Ky.

Hannah A. Ransdell Moore=John de Lafayette Grissim, M.D., Georgetown, Ky.

Lida Campbell Grissim, a member of the Va.=Judge Samuel Franklin Leib,
and Cal. Societies of the Colonial Dames of   of " Liebheim," San José, Cal.
America, Society of Daughters of the Ameri-
can Revolution, the Order of the Crown, *etc.*
(*See* p. 319.)

| Lida Campbell Leib, member of the Order of the Crown. | Elna Warren Leib. | Franklin Allen Leib. | Roy Chilton Leib. | Earl Warren Leib. |

Some
"Colonial Dames"
of Royal Descent

Pedigrees Showing the Lineal Descent from Kings of
Some Members of the National Society of the
Colonial Dames of America, and of the
Order of the Crown

Charles Henry Browning

HERITAGE BOOKS
2010

HERITAGE BOOKS

AN IMPRINT OF HERITAGE BOOKS, INC.

Books, CDs, and more—Worldwide

For our listing of thousands of titles see our website
at
www.HeritageBooks.com

A Facsimile Reprint
Published 2010 by
HERITAGE BOOKS, INC.
Publishing Division
100 Railroad Ave. #104
Westminster, Maryland 21157

International Standard Book Numbers
Paperbound: 978-0-7884-1997-3
Clothbound: 978-0-7884-8361-5

COLONIAL DAMES OF ROYAL DESCENT.

* A member of the Order of the Crown.

---

* A member of the Order of the Crown.

* A member of the Order of the Crown.

* A member of the Order of the Crown.

THE ROYAL DESCENT

OF

MRS. L. MONTGOMERY BOND, JR.,

OF ELIZABETH, N. J.

LOUIS VIII., King of France⫤Blanche, daughter of Alphonso VIII. of Castile.

Robert, Count of Artois⫤Lady Matilda of Brabant.

Blanche, widow of Henry I., King of Navarre⫤Edmund, son of Henry III., King of England.

Henry, Earl of Lancaster⫤Lady Maud de Chaworth.

Lady Maud Plantagenet⫤Sir William de Burgh, Earl of Ulster.

Lady Elizabeth de Burgh⫤Lionel, Duke of Clarence.

Lady Philippa Plantagenet⫤Edmund de Mortimer, Earl of Marche.

Lady Elizabeth de Mortimer⫤Sir Henry de Percy, K. G., "Hotspur."

Henry, Earl of Northumberland⫤Lady Eleanor de Neville.

Henry, Earl of Northumberland⫤Lady Eleanor Poynings.

Lady Margaret de Percy⫤Sir William Gascoigne, of Gawthrope.

Lady Elizabeth Gascoigne⫤Gilbert de Talboys, of Kyme.

Sir George de Talboys, of Kyme⫤(Name unknown.)

Lady Anne de Talboys⫤Sir Edward Dymoke, of Scrivelsby, Lincolnshire.

Lady Frances Dymoke⫤Thomas Windebank, of Haines Hill, Berkshire.

Lady Mildred Windebank⫤Robert Reade, Linkenholt Manor, Southampton.

Col. George Reade, of Gloucester Co., Va.⫤Elizabeth Martian, of York Co., Va.

Mildred Reade⫤Col. Augustine Warner, Jr., of "Warner's Hall."

Mildred Warner⫤Lawrence Washington, of "Bridge's Creek," Va.

Augustine Washington, of Stafford Co., Va.⫤Mary Ball, of "Epping Forest," Va.

Col. Samuel Washington, of Va., (a brother of⫤Anne Steptoe (fourth wife).
President Washington)

George Steptoe Washington, of "Harewood,"⫤Lucy Payne (sister of Dolly, wife of President
Jefferson Co., W. Va.   Madison).

Samuel Walter Washington, M.D., of "Hare- Louisa Clemson.
wood"

Lucy Washington⫤John Bainbridge Packett, of "Harewood."

Frances H. Washington Packett, of Elizabeth,⫤L. Montgomery Bond, Jr., of Philadelphia.
New Jersey, a member of the N. J. Society of
the Colonial Dames of America, the Order of
the Crown, etc.

William de Hertburne Washington Bond.   Mary Carolena Washington Bond.

COLONIAL DAMES OF ROYAL DESCENT.

PEDIGREE I.

LOUIS VIII., **King of France**, *m.* Blanche of Castile, and had:

ROBERT, Earl of Artois, *k.* 1247, who had by his wife Matilda, daughter of Henry, Duke of Brabant:

LADY BLANCHE (widow of Henry, King of Navarre, *d.* 1274), who *m.*, secondly, Edmund Plantagenet (son of **Henry III.**, **King of England**), Earl of Leicester, Lancaster, and Chester; lord high steward of England, who *d.* 1295, and had:

HENRY PLANTAGENET, third Earl of Leicester, *d.* 1345, who *m.* Lady Maud, daughter of Sir Patrick de Chaworth, and had:

LADY ELEANOR PLANTAGENET, widow of John, second Baron Beaumont, *d.* 1342, who *m.*, secondly (his second wife), Sir Richard Fitz-Alan, K.G., ninth Earl of Arundel and seventh Earl of Surrey, *d.* 1375, and had:

JOHN FITZ-ALAN, Lord Maltravers, second son, *d.* 15 December, 1379, who *m.* Lady Eleanor, *d.* 10 January, 1405, granddaughter and heiress of John, Lord Maltravers (Lord and Lady Maltravers's wills are given in Nicolas's "Testamenta Vetusta"), and had:

JOHN FITZ-ALAN de Arundel, eldest son, *d. v. p.*, who had:

SIR THOMAS FITZ-ALAN, Knt., younger son (his will given in Nicolas's "Testamenta Vetusta"), (brother of John Fitz-Alan, twelfth Earl of Arundel), who *m.* Lady Katherine, daughter of Sir John Dynham, and sister of Sir John Dynham, K.G., Baron Dynham, and had:

LADY ELEANOR FITZ-ALAN, who *m.* Sir Thomas Browne, Knt., treasurer of the household to King Henry VI., and had:

SIR ANTHONY BROWNE, standard-bearer to Henry VII., who had:

LADY ELIZABETH BROWNE, who *m.* Henry Somerset, second Earl of Worcester, *d.* 26 November, 1549, also of Royal Descent, and had:

(9)

SIR WILLIAM SOMERSET, K.G., third Earl of Worcester, *d.* 21 February, 1589, who *m.* Lady Christian, daughter of Edward, Lord North, and had:

SIR EDWARD SOMERSET, K.G., fourth Earl of Worcester, *d.* 3 March, 1627–1628, who *m.* Lady Elizabeth, daughter of Francis Herbert, Earl of Huntingdon, and had:

LADY CATHRINE SOMERSET, who *m.*, 8 November, 1596 (Dugdale's "Baronage"), William, second Baron Petre, of Writtle, *b.* 24 June, 1575, *d.* 5 May, 1627, and had:

THOMAS PETRE (brother of Robert, third Lord Petre, *d.* 1638, Dugdale's "Baronage"), who *m.* Ursula, daughter of Richard (or Walter) Brooke, of Lapsley Hall, Suffolk, and had:

WINIFRED PETRE, *d.* 1771, who *m.* George Atwood, of Beverlyin, *d.* 1794, and had:

GEORGE ATWOOD, who *d.* at Warburton Manor, Maryland, 1744; *m.* Anne Petre, and had:

ANNE ATWOOD, who *m.*, 3 June, 1739, William Digges, of Warburton Manor, Maryland, also of Royal Descent, and had:

GEORGE DIGGES, of Warburton Manor, who *m.* and had:

WILLIAM DUDLEY DIGGES, of Warburton Manor, who *m.* Eleanor Carroll, also of Royal Descent, and had:

NORA DIGGES, who *m.*, 1854, James Ethelbert Morgan, M.D., of Washington City, and had:

ADA MORGAN, a member of the Maryland Society of the Colonial Dames of America, who *m.*, 1889, Richard Smith Hill, of Prince George county, Maryland, and had: *Nora Digges* and *Elizabeth Snowden*, twins, and *Ada Morgan*.

PEDIGREE II.

CHARLEMAGNE, Emperor of the West, King of the Franks, had by his third wife, Lady Hildegarde, *d.* 783, daughter of Childebrand, Duke of Suabia:

PEPIN, KING OF LOMBARDY and Italy, who *m.* Lady Bertha, daughter of William, Count of Thoulouse, and had:

BERNARD, KING OF LOMBARDY, who had by his wife, Lady Cunegonde:

PEPIN, COUNT OF VERMANDOIS and Peronne, 840, who had:

HERBERT I., COUNT DE VERMANDOIS, *d.* 902, who had:

HERBERT II., COUNT DE VERMANDOIS, *d.* 943, who had:

ALBERT I., THE PIOUS, COUNT DE VERMANDOIS, *d.* 987, who *m.* Princess Gerberga, daughter of Louis IV., King of France, and had:

HERBERT III., COUNT DE VERMANDOIS, who had:

OTHO, COUNT DE VERMANDOIS, 1021–1045, who had:

HERBERT IV., COUNT DE VERMANDOIS, 1045–1080, who *m.* Lady Hildebrante, Countess of Valois and Amiens, heiress, and daughter of Raoul III., Count de Valois, and had one child:

ADELHEID, COUNTESS OF VERMANDOIS, 1080–1117, who *m.* (his third wife) Hugh Magnus, Duke of France and Burgundy, Marquis of Orleans, Count of Paris, Valois and Vermandois, son of Henry I., King of France, grandson of Hugh Capet, King of France, and had:

LADY ISABEL DE VERMANDOIS (also called Elizabeth), *d.* 1131 (widow of Robert de Beaumont, Earl of Mellent and Leicester, *d.* 1118), who *m.*, secondly, William de Warren, second Earl of Surrey, *d.* 113–, also of Royal Descent, and had:

WILLIAM DE WARREN, third Earl of Surrey, *d. s. p. m.* in 1148. He *m.* Lady Adela, *d.* 1174, daughter of William de Talvas III., Count of Alençon and Ponthieu, also of Royal Descent, and had:

LADY ISABELLA DE WARREN, Countess of Surrey, *d.* 1199 (widow of William de Blois, *d.* 1160), who *m.*, secondly, 1163, Hameline Plantagenet, fifth Earl of Warren and Surrey, *d.* 1202, and had:

LADY ISABELLA PLANTAGENET DE WARREN, who *m.* (his first wife) Roger Bigod, created Earl of Norfolk in 1189, steward of England, a surety for the Magna Charta, also of Royal Descent, *d.* 1220, and had:

HUGH BIGOD, second Earl of Norfolk, one of the sureties for the Magna

Charta, *d.* 1225; *m.* Lady Maud Marshall, daughter of William, Earl of Pembroke, protector of England during the nonage of Henry III. and his wife Lady Isabel de Clare, also of Royal Descent, and had:

SIR RALPH BIGOD, KNT., third son, who *m.* Lady Berta de Furnival, and had:

LADY ISABEL BIGOD (widow of Gilbert de Lacie, Lord of Meath, *d.* 1241), who *m.*, secondly, John Fitzgeoffrey, of Barkhampstead and Kirtling, sheriff of Yorkshire, 1234, justiciary of Ireland in 1246, son of Geoffrey Fitz Piers, Earl of Essex, justiciary of England, and had:

JOHN FITZJOHN, chief justice of Ireland, 1258, father of:

MAUD FITZJOHN (widow of Gerard de Furnival, of Sheffield, *d.* 1280), who *m.*, secondly, William de Beauchamp, of Elmley, created Earl of Warwick, *d.* 1298, also of Royal Descent, and had:

LADY SARAH DE BEAUCHAMP, who *m.* Richard, sixth Baron de Talbot, of Goodrich, *d.* 1306, also of Royal Descent, and had:

LADY GWENTHELLEAN DE TALBOT, who *m.* Sir Payne de Turberville, custos of Glamorganshire, 134–, and had:

SARAH DE TURBERVILLE, who *m.* William de Gamage, sheriff of Gloucestershire in 1325, and had:

GILBERT DE GAMAGE, of Rogiad, who *m.* Lettice, daughter of Sir William Seymour, of Penhow, and had:

SIR WILLIAM GAMAGE, of Rogiad and Coyty, who *m.* Mary, daughter of Sir Thomas de Rodburg, and had:

SIR THOMAS GAMAGE, of Rogiad and Coyty, who *m.* Matilla, daughter of Sir John Dennis, and had:

JANE GAMAGE, who *m.* Roger ap Arnold ap Arnholt-Vychan, of Llanthony Manor, in Monmouthshire, also of Royal Descent, and had:

THOMAS ARNOLD, eldest son, succeeded to Llanthony Manor. He *m.* Agnes, daughter of Sir Richard Wairnstead (or Warnstead), and had: JOHN, eldest son and heir, who owned Hingham Manor, Churcham parish, Gloucestershire; *d.* 15 September, 1545, and

RICHARD ARNOLD, second son, who resided in Street parish, Somersetshire. He *m.* Emmote, daughter of Pearce Young, of Damerham, Wiltshire, and had:

RICHARD ARNOLD, eldest son, who resided on Bagbere Manor, in Middleton parish, Dorsetshire, before 1549. His will, dated 15 May, 1593, was proved 9 July, 1595. He owned, besides Bagbere—the old Bagbere Manor house was demolished in 1870—the manors of Alton Pancras, Buckland Newton, Cheselbourne and Melcombe Horsey, all in Dorsetshire. He was buried in July, 1595, in the Milton Church. He was twice married, and of his children by his first wife, whose name has not been preserved, JOHN, eldest son and heir, and

THOMAS ARNOLD,* named in his father's will. He resided on Melcombe Horsey Manor, in Dorsetshire (Subsidy Rolls, 1598), and removed to Cheselbourne Manor, in this county. He *m.*, first, Alice, *b.* 29 September, 1553, daughter of John Gully, of Northover Manor, in Tolpuddle parish, Dorset; the name of his second wife has not been preserved (*See* H. Q. Somerby's Arnold pedigree, "compiled in 1870 from the Herald's Visitations, Inqui. P. M., Subsidy Rolls, parish registers," *etc.* N. E. His. Geneal. Register, October, 1879, and the Family Records kept by the immigrant William Arnold and his son, N. E. His. Gen. Reg., vol. 33, p. 427). By his first wife he had:

WILLIAM ARNOLD, *b.* 24 June, 1587. He was appointed 23 November, 1616, guardian of the children of his brother John, of Cheselbourn, 1585–1616. He sailed from Dartmouth with his wife and four children Friday, 1 May, 1635, and arrived in New England 24 June, 1635; came to Providence, Rhode Island, 20 April, 1636, and to Newport 19 November, 1651. He had many grants of land and filled important offices of trust in the Colony of Rhode Island. He was one of the thirteen original proprietors of the Province Plantations; was a signer of the agreement for a form of government in the colony in 1640, and was commissioner for Providence to the Court of Commissioners in 1661 (see Austin's "Genealogical Dictionary of Rhode Island"). He *d.* about 1676, having issue by his wife, Christian, *bapt.* 15 February, 1583, daughter of Thomas Peake, of Muchelney, Somersetshire, of whom:

    1.—ELIZABETH ARNOLD, *b.* 23 November, 1611, *d.* in 1683; *m.* William Carpenter, of Providence, *d.* 7 September, 1685, and had:

        I.—BENJAMIN CARPENTER, of Providence, *m.* Mary, daughter of Pardon and —— (Butterworth) Tillinghast. She was *b.* October, 1661, and *d.* 1711 (about). Their son:

            BENJAMIN CARPENTER, *b.* 1673, *d.* 16 December, 1766; *m.* Prudence, daughter of Nathaniel and Christian (Cole) Kingsley. She was *b.* 23 August, 1714, and *d.* 29 July, 1801. Their son:

            OLIVER CARPENTER, *b.* 1 September, 1739, *m.* Susanna, daughter

---

* The following ladies, members of the National Society of the Colonial Dames of America, are also of Royal Descent through Thomas Arnold:

MRS. LEWIS T. HOYT, New York State Society.

MRS. CHARLES S. SARGEANT, Massachusetts State Society.

MRS. S. VAN R. THAYER, Massachusetts State Society.

MRS. GEORGE V. CRESSON, Pennsylvania State Society.

MRS. B. JONES TAYLOR, Maryland State Society.

MRS. D. GIRARD WRIGHT, Maryland State Society.

MRS. A. L. DANIELSON, Rhode Island State Society.

MRS. LEWIS BUCKNER, Kentucky State Society.

Miss Julia Montrose Angell, Michigan State Society. (R.J.)

of Benjamin and Jemima (Williams) Potter. She was *b.* 3 July, 1755. Their daughter:

CHARLOTTE CARPENTER, *m.* Allen Gladding, son of Jonathan and Susanna (Cary) Gladding, of Bristol, Rhode Island. He was *b.* 14 November, 1764, and *d.* 22 May, 1837. Their daughter:

SUSAN CARY GLADDING, *m.* John Holden Ormsbee, son of John and Barbara (Holden) Ormsbee. He was *b.* 1780 and *d.* 5 September, 1860. Their daughter:

CHARLOTTE BARBARA ORMSBEE, *m.* Alexander Farnum, and had:

MARGARET BARBARA FARNUM, a member of the Rhode Island Society of the Colonial Dames of America, who *m.* Charles Warren Lippitt, of Providence, former Governor of Rhode Island, and had: *Charles Warren* (deceased); *Alexander Farnum* (deceased); *Jeanie Barbara* (deceased); *Charles Warren, Jr., Alexander Farnum,* and *Gorton Thayer.*

II.—TIMOTHY CARPENTER, of Providence, *d.* 19 August, 1726, who *m.* Hannah, daughter of William and Hannah (Wickes) Burton, and had:

ELIZABETH CARPENTER, who *m.* Peleg Williams, *d.* 1766, and had:

FREELOVE WILLIAMS, 1713–1791, who *m.,* 1732, Daniel Fiske, 1710–1804, also of Royal Descent, and had:

DANIEL FISKE, 1753–1810, who *m.,* 1785, Freelove Knight, and had:

CELIA FISKE, 1787–1859; *m.,* 1815, Stephen Burlingame, *d.* 1837, and had:

COLONEL STEPHEN BURLINGAME, 1819–1890; *m.,* 1841, Elsie Maria Tillinghast, 1820–1884, and had:

SARAH MARIA BURLINGAME, a member of the New Hampshire Society of the Colonial Dames of America, who *m.,* 12 December, 1877, Prentiss Webster, of Lowell, Mass., 1851–1898, and had: *Susan H., Adeline B., Prentiss B., Helen B.,* and *Dorothy P.*

2.—BENEDICT ARNOLD, of Providence, *b.* 21 December, 1615. Governor of the Rhode Island Colony, 1663–1678; *d.* 19 June, 1678; *m.,* 17 December, 1640, Damaris Westcott, of Stukeley, and had:

CAPTAIN JOSIAH ARNOLD, of Jamestown, Rhode Island, *b.* 22 December, 1646, *d.* 26 December, 1724–1725; *m.,* first, 14 September, 1683, Sarah Mills, 1665–1704, and had by her:

ABAGAIL ARNOLD, *b.* 14 December, 1685, *d.* 14 December, 1705–1706; *m.,* 14 February, 1704–1705, Governor Jonathan Law, *b.* Milford, Connecticut, 6 August, 1674; chief justice of Connecticut 1725–

1741, governor of the Connecticut Colony, 1741–1750, *d.* 6 November, 1750, and had:

JONATHAN LAW, JR., *b.* Milford, 5 December, 1705–1706, *d.* 24 September, 1790; *m.*, 11 January, 1737, Eunice Andrew, *b.* 16 August, 1720, *d.* 2 March, 1762, a descendant of the Rev. John Eliot, the celebrated apostle to the Indians; of Governor William Brenton, of Rhode Island; of Rev. Samuel Andrew, of Milford, Connecticut, a founder and second president of Yale College; of Governor Robert Treat, of Connecticut, *etc.*, and had:

BENEDICT ARNOLD LAW, *b.* Milford, 20 December, 1740, *d.* at North Milford, 19 November, 1819; *m.*, 4 January, 1770, Sarah, *b.* 24 April, 1749, *d.* 26 November, 1785, daughter of Captain Richard Bryan, of Milford, and had:

SARAH BRYAN LAW, *b.* North Milford, 9 November, 1785, *d.* at Philadelphia, Pennsylvania, 19 February, 1854; *m.*, 14 January, 1808, Ebenezer Johnson, Jr., *b.* 30 April, 1774, *d.* 8 July, 1863, and had:

CHARLOTTE AUGUSTA JOHNSON, *b.* New Haven, Connecticut, 5 July, 1823, who *m.*, 27 August, 1846, Dewitt Clinton Morris, of Philadelphia, Pennsylvania, *b.* 1821, *d.* 28 July, 1868, a descendant of Lewis Morris, chief justice of New York; governor of New Jersey, and had:

CHARLOTTE JOHNSON MORRIS, of Brunswick, Maine, a member of the New York and Maine Societies of the Colonial Dames of America, who *m.*, at New Haven, Connecticut, 11 July, 1876, Professor William Addison Houghton, of Bowdoin College, and had: *William Morris, Charles Andrew Johnson,* and *Harriet Cecil.*

3.—JOANNA ARNOLD, *b.* 27 February, 1617, *d.* 1692; *m.*, first, 1646, Zachariah Rhodes, of Providence, 1603–1665, a signer of the Compact of 3 July, 1644; was constable 1660, deputy 1664, town treasurer 1665, a town councilman 1665, *etc.;* will proved 29 May, 1666, and had: *Mary,* (see below) and

I.—REBECCA RHODES, *d.* 1727 (widow of Nicholas Power), who *m.*, secondly, 2 December, 1676, Daniel Williams, of Providence, *b.* February, 1642, *d.* 14 May, 1712, and had:

MARY WILLIAMS, *d.* after 1740, who *m.* Epenetus Olney, of Providence, *b.* 18 January, 1675, *d.* 18 September, 1740, and had:

JAMES OLNEY, of North Providence, *d.* 10 February, 1770; *m.*, 1 March, 1733, Hannah Winsor, of Providence, *b.* 26 August, 1711, *d.* 27 December, 1777, and had:

EMOR OLNEY, of Johnston, Rhode Island, *b.* 28 November, 1741, *d.* 29 March, 1830; *m.*, 1760, Amy Hopkins, 1742–1782, and had:

PARIS OLNEY, *b.* 18 October, 1770, *d.* 1850; *m.* Mercy Winsor, *b.* 31 August, 1769, and had:

MARY ANN OLNEY, *b.* 21 June, 1803, *d.* 11 September, 1878; *m.*, 25 December, 1822, Clark Sayles, of Pawtucket, *b.* 18 May, 1797, *d.* 8 February, 1885, and had:

WILLIAM FRANCIS SAYLES, of Pawtucket, *b.* 20 September, 1824, *d.* 7 May, 1894; *m.*, 30 October, 1849, Mary Wilkinson Fessenden, also of Royal Descent, and had:

MARY FESSENDEN SAYLES, a member of the Rhode Island Society of the Colonial Dames of America, who *m.*, 21 May, 1872, Roscoe Stetson Washburn, of Providence, and had: *Maurice King, Roscoe Clifton, William F. S.* (deceased), and *John Fessenden* (deceased).

II.—JOHN RHODES, of Warwick, Rhode Island, *b.* 1658, *d.* August, 1716; *m.,* first, 12 February, 1685, Waite, 1668–1711, daughter of Resolved Waterman, 1638–1670, and his wife Mercy, 1640–1705, daughter of Roger Williams, 1599–1683, the founder of the Rhode Island and Providence Plantations, and had:

PHEBE RHODES, *b.* 30 November, 1698, *d.* 1761, who *m.*, first, Anthony Holden, *d.* 13 May, 1720, and had:

CATHARINE HOLDEN, only child, *b.* 13 October, 1717, *d.* 4 May, 1807; *m.*, 2 January, 1736, Christopher Lippitt, *b.* 29 November, 1712, *d.* 7 December, 1764, and had:

I.—CHARLES LIPPITT, *b.* 2 March, 1754, *d.* 17 August, 1845; *m.*, 12 January, 1783, Penelope, *b.* 5 February, 1758, *d.* 27 August, 1839, daughter of John Low, and had:

    1.—JULIA LIPPITT, *b.* 29 January, 1784, *d.* 22 March, 1867; *m.*, 9 September, 1814, Joseph Sweet, *b.* 5 December, 1782, *d.* 9 January, 1878, and had:

        I.—JULIA SWEET, a member of the Rhode Island Society of the Colonial Dames of America, who *m.*, 7 June, 1849, John Henry Weir, of Providence, Rhode Island, *b.* 27 August, 1819, *d.* 12 September, 1858.

        II.—CATHARINE SWEET, a member of the Rhode Island Society of the Colonial Dames of America.

    2.—WARREN LIPPITT, *b.* 25 September, 1786, *d.* 22 January, 1850, who *m.*, 7 July, 1811, Eliza Seamans, *b.* 20 February, 1792, *d.* 7 April, 1881, and had:

        HENRY LIPPITT, *b.* 9 October, 1818, *d.* 5 June, 1891, who *m.*, 16 December, 1845, Mary Ann Balch, *b.* 7 October, 1823, *d.* 31 August, 1889, and had:

I.—JEANIE LIPPITT, *b.* 6 January, 1852, a member of the Rhode Island Society of the Colonial Dames of America, who *m.*, 18 April, 1893, William Babcock Weeden, of Providence, Rhode Island. *No issue.*

II.—MARY BALCH LIPPITT, *b.* 14 July, 1858, a member of the Rhode Island Society of the Colonial Dames of America, who *m.*, 7 January, 1892, Charles John Steedman, of Philadelphia. Issue: *Charles Richard, b.* 31 July, 1897.

III.—ABBY FRANCES LIPPITT, *b.* 31 October, 1861, a member of the Rhode Island Society of the Colonial Dames of America, who *m.*, 24 January, 1893, Duncan Hunter. Issue: *Mary L., Frances G.,* and *Janet Malise.*

II.—COLONEL CHRISTOPHER LIPPITT, *b.* 28 October, 1744, *d.* 17 June, 1824; *m.*, 23 March, 1777, Waite Harris, *b.* 1775, *d.* 8 September, 1836, and had:

WILLIAM LIPPITT, *b.* 21 November, 1786, *d.* 8 October, 1872; *m.*, 1 January, 1809, Rhobey Sheldon, *b.* 19 October, 1790, *d.* 3 January, 1865, and had:

SARAH WILLIAMS LIPPITT, *b.* 7 February, 1832, who *m.*, 15 June, 1859, John Tyler Mauran, *b.* 20 November, 1826, *d.* 23 December, 1882, and had:

JULIA LIPPITT MAURAN, of Providence, Rhode Island, *b.* 25 June 1860, a member of the Rhode Island Society of the Colonial Dames of America.

4.—STEPHEN ARNOLD, of Pawtuxet, *b.* 22 December, 1622, *d.* 15 November, 1699. He was a deputy to the general court for thirteen years, and governor's assistant nine years. He *m.*, 24 November, 1646, Sarah, 1629–1713, daughter of Edward Smith, of Newport, *d.* 1675, governor's assistant six years, commissioner to the court of commissioners two years and deputy to the general court seven years, and had:

I.—PHŒBE ARNOLD, 1670–173—, who *m.*, 25 December, 1691, Benjamin Smith, Jr., of Warwick, Rhode Island, son of Benjamin Smith, 1631–1713, governor's assistant nineteen years, deputy to the general court eight years, and his wife Lydia, also of Royal Descent, daughter of William Carpenter, *d.* Providence, 1685 (and his wife Elizabeth, a daughter of the aforesaid William Arnold, 1587–1676), one of the thirteen original proprietors of the Providence Plantations, commissioner, deputy, assistant, *etc.*, and had:

PHŒBE SMITH, *b.* 5 December, 1699, who *m.* James Cargill, Jr., of North Kingston, Rhode Island, and had:

LUCY CARGILL, who *m.* Nathan Arnold, of Cumberland, Rhode Island, a descendant of Thomas Arnold, *d.* 1674, and had:

CAPTAIN NATHAN ARNOLD, of Cumberland, who *d.* from wound received in battle 29 August, 1778; *m.* Esther Slack Darling, also of Royal Descent, and had:

SETH ARNOLD, of Smithfield, Rhode Island, who *m.* Mrs. Belinda (Mason) Streeter, a descendant of Captain Roger Williams, the founder of Rhode Island and the Providence Plantations, and president of the Colony, and had:

FRANCES ARNOLD, who *m.* William Henry Hathaway, of Dighton, Massachusetts, also of Royal Descent, and had:

BELINDA OLNEY HATHAWAY, a member of the Rhode Island Society of the Colonial Dames of America, Society Daughters of the American Revolution, Order of the Crown, *etc.*, who *m.* Joshua Wilbour, of Bristol, Rhode Island.

II.—ESTHER ARNOLD, *b.* 22 September, 1647, *d.* 1688. She *m.*, first, 1671, James Dexter, *d.* 1676, and *m.*, second, 30 October, 1680, William Andrews, by whom she had an only child:

MARY ANDREWS, who *m.* Simon Smith, son of Benjamin Smith, 1631–1713, and his wife, Elizabeth (Lydia), *d.* 1 October, 1711, daughter of William Carpenter, of Providence, Rhode Island, *d.* 7 September, 1685, and his wife, Elizabeth, 1611–1683, a daughter of the aforesaid William Arnold, and had:

SIMON SMITH, who *m.*, 23 March, 1766, Freelove, *b.* 13 July, 1743, daughter of Arthur Fenner, 1699–1788, and had:

SIMON SMITH, 1710–1753, who *m.* Elizabeth Turpin, and had:

SARAH SMITH, *b.* 28 May, 1780, who *m.*, 25 June, 1803, John Carpenter Bucklin, *d.* 1842, and had:

JEANNETTE BUCKLIN, *b.* 1814, *d.* 25 June, 1854, who *m.*, February, 1849, George Davis, *b.* 5 April, 1811, *d.* 14 October, 1895, and had:

MARY DAVIS, *b.* 9 June, 1851, a member of the Rhode Island Society of the Colonial Dames of America, who *m.*, 23 January, 1873, George Corlis Nightingale, of Providence, Rhode Island, and had: *Jeannette Davis, Mary Greene, George Corlis,* and *Alice Bucklin.*

III.—ISRAEL ARNOLD, *b.* 30 October, 1649, *d.* 15 September, 1716, who *m.*, 16 April, 1677, Mary (widow of Elisha Smith), *d.* 19 September, 1723, daughter of James Barker, of Newport, 1623–1702, one of those named in the Royal Charter, 1663; was ensign, 1648; commissioner for three years, assistant for nine years, deputy for twelve years and deputy governor, 1678–1679, and had:

SARAH ARNOLD, *d.* Warwick, Rhode Island, 26 November, 1727, who *m.*, 21 December, 1708, Silas Carpenter, Jr., of Providence, Rhode Island, *b.* 27 July, 1709, *d.* 13 June, 1751, also a descendant of the aforesaid William Arnold, and had:

MARY CARPENTER, *b.* 14 February, 1714, who *m.*, 29 April, 1733, Benjamin Westcott, 3d, of Providence, *b.* 1716, and had:

JAMES WESTCOTT, of Providence, *b.* 25 March, 1740, *d.* 17 March, 1814; *m.*, 1767, Martha, *b.* 9 September, 1747, *d.* 18 August, 1790, daughter of William and Lydia (Harris) Tillinghast, of Providence, and had:

JAMES WESTCOTT, JR., of Providence, *b.* 28 June, 1773, *d.* 2 June, 1853; *m.*, 23 August, 1795, Mary Dewer, *b.* Providence, 1776, *d.* 2 June, 1853, and had:

STEPHEN T. WESTCOTT, *b.* 22 November, 1799, *d.* West Roxbury, Massachusetts, 13 June, 1874; *m.*, 22 June, 1826, Mary Smith Barker, *b.* Salem, Massachusetts, 23 December, 1800, *d.* West Roxbury, 29 September, 1860, and had:

EMMA WESTCOTT, a member of the Rhode Island Society of the Colonial Dames of America and the Order of the Crown, who *m.*, 23 December, 1868, Jonathan Russell Bullock, of Bristol, Rhode Island, and had:

EMMA RUSSELL BULLOCK, only child, who *m.*, 6 May, 1897, Albert Stanton Cheseborough, of Bristol, Rhode Island.

IV.—ELIZABETH ARNOLD, *b.* 2 November, 1659, *d.* 5 June, 1728; *m.*, 16 December, 1680, Peter Greene, of Warwick, Rhode Island, *b.* 7 February, 1654-5, *d.* 12 August, 1723, and had:

WILLIAM GREENE, *b.* 29 July, 1690, *d.* 17 March, 1766; *m.*, 14 February, 1712-13, Sarah Medbury, of Rehoboth, Massachusetts, b. 27 April, 1689, *d.* 6 April, 1763, and had:

JAMES GREENE, *b.* 1713, *d.* 30 May, 1792; *m.*, 15 June, 1738, Desire Slocum, of Warwick, *b.* 14 January, 1720, *d.* 22 November, 1794, and had:

JAMES GREENE, *b.* 26 October, 1754, *d.* 14 October, 1825; *m.*, 17 November, 1782, Rebecca Pitman, *b.* 11 March, 1763, *d.* 7 July, 1806, and had:

ELIZA GREENE, *b.* 1 August, 1791, *d.* 23 March, 1820; *m.*, 3 December, 1809, Stephen Harris, of Warwick, *b.* 29 October, 1786, *d.* 10 October, 1858, and had:

CYRUS HARRIS, *b.* 16 October, 1812, *d.* 23 June, 1887; *m.*, 26 August, 1836, Abby Spalding, of Centreville, Rhode Island, *b.* 12 November, 1816, *d.* 21 November, 1888, and had:

ABBY GREENE HARRIS, *b.* 31 December, 1851, a member of the Rhode Island Society of the Colonial Dames of America, who *m.*, 28 February, 1876, Samuel Ames, of Providence, Rhode Island, *b.* 10 April, 1849. *No issue.*

THE ROYAL DESCENT

OF

MRS. JONATHAN R. BULLOCK,

OF BRISTOL, R. I.

HUGH CAPET, King of France=Lady Adela of Aquitaine.

Princess Hedewige=Ranigerus V., Count of Hainault.

Lady Beatrix d'Hainault=Eblo I., Count de Reimes de Rouci.

Adela, Countess de Rouci=Hildwin, Count de Montdider de Rouci.

Lady Margaret de Rouci=Hugh, Count de Clermont.

Lady Adeliza de Clermont=Gilbert, 2d Earl of Clare.

Lady Adeliza de Clare=Alberic de Vere.

Lady Juliana de Vere=Hugh Bigod, Earl of Norfolk.

Roger Bigod, Earl of Norfolk=Lady Isabella de Warren.

Hugh Bigod, Earl of Norfolk=Lady Maud Marshall.

Sir Ralph Bigod, Knt.=Lady Berta de Furnival.

Lady Isabel Bigod=John Fitz-Piers Fitz-Geoffrey.

John Fitz-John=(Name unknown).

Lady Maud Fitz-John=William, Earl of Warwick.

Lady Sarah de Beauchamp=Richard de Talbot, of Lintone.

Lady Gwenthellean de Talbot=Sir Payne de Turberville, of Glamorganshire.

Lady Sarah de Turberville=William de Gamage, of Gloucestershire.

Gilbert de Gamage=Lady Lettice Seymour.

Sir William Gamage=Mary de Redburg.

Sir Thomas Gamage=(Name unknown).

Lady Jane Gamage=Roger ap Arnholt, of Llanthony.

Thomas Arnold, of Llanthony=Agnes Wairnstead.

Richard Arnold, of Somersetshire=Emmote Young, of Wiltshire.

Richard Arnold, of Dorsetshire=(First wife, name unknown).

Thomas Arnold, of Dorsetshire=Alice Gully, of Dorsetshire.

William Arnold, of Providence, R. I.=Christian Peake.

Stephen Arnold, of Pawtuxet, R. I.=Sarah Smith.

Israel Arnold=Mary Barker.

Sarah Arnold=Silas Carpenter, of Providence.

Mary Carpenter=Benjamin Westcott, 3d, of Providence.

James Westcott, of Providence=Martha Tillinghast, of Providence.

James Westcott, of Providence=Mary Dewer.

Stephen T. Westcott, West Roxbury, Mass.=Mary Smith Barker.

Emma Westcott, member of the National So-=Jonathan Russell Bullock, of Bristol, Rhode Island.
ciety of the Colonial Dames of America

Emma Russell Bullock=Albert S. Cheseborough, of Bristol, Rhode Island.

PEDIGREE III.

ROBERT BRUCE, King of Scotland, had by his first wife, Lady Isabel, daughter of Donald, Earl of Marr:

PRINCESS MARGERY BRUCE, *d.* 1315–16, who *m.*, 1315 (his second wife), Walter, lord high steward of Scotland, 1293–1326, and had, only child:

ROBERT II., King of Scotland, *b.* 2 March, 1315–16, who had by his first wife, Lady Elizabeth, daughter of Sir Adam Mure, of Rowallan:

PRINCESS CATHERINE STUART, who *m.* Sir David Lindsay, of Glenesk, created, in 1389, Earl of Crawford, *d.* before 1412, and had:

LADY MARJORY LINDSAY, sister of Alexander, second Earl of Crawford, who *m.* Sir William Douglas, of Lochlevan and Lugton, and had:

SIR HENRY DOUGLAS, of Lochlevan and Lugton, who *m.* Lady Elizabeth, daughter of Sir Robert Erskine, of that Ilk, *d.* 1453, and had:

ROBERT DOUGLAS, of Lochlevan and Kincross, *k.* at Flodden, who had by his first wife, Elizabeth, daughter of David Boswell, of Balmuto:

SIR ROBERT DOUGLAS, Knt., of Lochlevan, only son, who *m.* Margaret, daughter of David Balfour, of Burleigh, and had:

THOMAS DOUGLAS, of Lochlevan, only son, *d. v. p.*, who *m.* Elizabeth, daughter of Archibald Boyd, son of Sir Robert, first Lord Boyd, of Kilmarnock, regent of Scotland 1466, justiciary and lord high chamberlain, and had:

ELIZABETH DOUGLAS, third daughter (sister of Sir Robert Douglas, of Lochlevan, *k.* at Pinkie, 1547, father of Sir William Douglas, seventh Earl of Morton, and Robert Douglas, Earl of Buchan), who *m.*, before 26 August, 1529, Alexander Alsynder (or Alexander), of Menstrie, *d.* 1545 (see Wood's " Douglas Peerage of Scotland," ii., 536–39; Brown's " Genesis of the United States," p. 813; Roger's " House of Alexander," *American Heraldic Journal,* iv., p. 59; Hewlett's " Scotch Dignities," p. 160), and had:

ANDREW ALEXANDER, of Menstrie, eldest son, *d.* before 26 August, 1529, father of:

JOHN ALEXANDER, of Gogar, 1541, second son (only uncle of William Alexander, created Earl of Stirling, who had descendants), father of:

(21)

ALEXANDER ALEXANDER, of Millnab, only son, father of:

DAVID ALEXANDER, of Muthill, second son, father of:

JAMES ALEXANDER,* *b.* 1691, second son, who came to America in 1716, and became surveyor-general of New Jersey in 1714. He was for many years a member of the King's council and attorney-general, and auditor-general of New Jersey and New York, *d.* in 1756, and had by his wife, Mary, *d.* 1760, daughter of John Sprott, of Wigton, in Scotland, and widow of Samuel Prevost or Provost:

1.—MARY ALEXANDER, *b.* 16 October, 1721, *d.* 24 April, 1767, who *m.*, 1739, Peter Van Brugh Livingston, of New York, a son of Philip Livingston, second lord of Livingston Manor, New York, and had:

I.—CATHERINE LIVINGSTON, 1743–1798, who *m.*, 20 April, 1762, Nicholas Bayard, of New York, and had:

  1.—KATHERINE ANNE BAYARD, who *m.* Robert Charles Johnson, of New York, and had:

  KATHERINE ANNE JOHNSON, who *m.* Thomas Pollock Devereux, and had:

  JOHN DEVEREUX, who *m.* Margaret Mordecai, and had:

  ELLEN DEVEREUX, a member of the North Carolina Society of the Colonial Dames of America, the Order of the Crown, *etc.*, who *m.* John Wetmore Hinsdale, of Raleigh, North Carolina, and had: *Margaret*, wife of John Cotton Engelhard; *Samuel Johnson, Elizabeth Christophers, John Wetmore, Ellen Devereux*, and *Annie Devereux*.

  2.—ELIZA BAYARD, *d.* 1846, who *m.*, 30 April, 1791, John Houston McIntosh, of Darien, Georgia, also of Royal Descent, and had:

  I.—JOHN HOUSTON MCINTOSH, *b.* Cumberland Island, Georgia, 7 June, 1802, *d.* 4 May, 1852; *m.*, 13 September, 1832, Mary Randolph, daughter of Joseph and Elizabeth Higbee, of Trenton, New Jersey, and had:

  MARY RANDOLPH MCINTOSH, a member of the Ohio Society of the Colonial Dames of America, who *m.*, 12 March, 1861, John Kilgour, of "The Pines," Mt. Lookout, Cincinnati, Ohio, and had: *Charles, Bayard Livingston, Elizabeth, Louise,* and

  I.—MARY KILGOUR, a member of the New York Society of the Colonial Dames of America, who *m.*, 16 April, 1890,

---

* MRS. WALTER KENNEDY, a member of the Tennessee State Society of the National Society of the Colonial Dames of America is also of Royal Descent, through James Alexander.

Edmund E.Miller, of Cincinnati and New York, and had:
Mary Kilgour, b. Cincinnati, 4 April, 1891.

II.—CHARLOTTE KILGOUR, a member of the New York
Society of the Colonial Dames of America, who *m.*, 21
April, 1896, Captain Ashton B. Heyl, M.D., United States
Army, and had: *John Kilgour, b.* 2 March, 1897, at Fort
Riley, Kansas.

II.—ELIZA BAYARD MCINTOSH, who *m.* Duncan L. Clinch,
United States Army, and had:

ELIZA BAYARD CLINCH, who *m.* General Robert Anderson,
United States Army, and had:

ELIZA MCINTOSH CLINCH ANDERSON, a member of the New
York Society of the Colonial Dames of America, who *m.* James
M. Lawton, of New York City.

II.—SARAH LIVINGSTON, who *m.* Major John Ricketts, of Jamaica,
and had:

MARIA ELIZA RICKETTS, *m.* William Palmer, of Suffolk, and had:

SARAH JULIA PALMER, *m.* William Fisher, of Philadelphia, and had:

ELIZABETH FISHER, a member of the Society of the Colonial Dames
of America, who *m.* Edward King, of New York City. *Issue.*

2.—ELIZABETH ALEXANDER, who *m.* John Stevens, of Perth Amboy,
New Jersey, and had:

JOHN STEVENS, of Hoboken, New Jersey, who *m.* Rachel Cox, and
had:

EDWIN AUGUSTUS STEVENS, who *m.*, secondly, Martha Bayard Dod,
and had by her:

CAROLINE BAYARD STEVENS, a member of the Society of the Colonial
Dames of America, who *m.* Archibald Alexander, of New York City.
Issue.

3.—CATHERINE ALEXANDER, who *m.* (his first wife) Major Walter Rutherfurd, of the British Army, and had:

JOHN RUTHERFURD, of Edgarstown, New Jersey, *b.* 1760, *d.* 23 February, 1840, United States Senator from New Jersey, 1791–1798, who
m., 1781, Magdalene, daughter of General Lewis Morris, chief justice
and governor of New Jersey, a member of the Continental Congress
and a signer of the Declaration of Independence, and had:

ROBERT WALTER RUTHERFURD, of New York, 1778–1851, who *m.* his
cousin, Sabina E., daughter of Colonel Lewis Morris, Jr., and had:

JOHN RUTHERFURD, of New York, *d.* 1871, who *m.* Charlotte, daughter
of James Kane Livingston, of New York, and had:

HELENA RUTHERFURD, a member of the New York Society of the Colonial Dames of America, who *m.* Alfred Ely, of Newton, Massachusetts.

4.—WILLIAM ALEXANDER, *b.* 1726, major-general in the American Army; surveyor-general of New Jersey; he assumed the title " Earl of Stirling," as under Scottish law and custom he inherited it, according to a decision of the Chancery Court of Scotland in 1759, which declared him the nearest heir-male to the last Earl of Stirling (see sketch of General Alexander, by his grandson, Judge Duer, in " Proceedings of the New Jersey Historical Society," 1847), but was denied the right to it, and forbidden by the English House of Lords to use it. Before his case was argued, 10 March, 1762, " Lord Stirling " *d.* in Albany, New York, 15 January, 1783, leaving issue by his wife Sarah, daughter of Philip Livingston, second lord of the Manor of Livingston, New York:

CATHERINE ALEXANDER, 1755–1826, who *m.*, first, 27 July, 1779, at " Basking Ridge," New Jersey, Colonel William Duer, of the New York Line, Continental Army, and had:

I.—JUDGE WILLIAM ALEXANDER DUER, of New York, 1780–1858, president of Columbia College, 1829–1842, who *m.*, 1806, Marie, daughter of William Denning, of New York, and had:

ELIZABETH DENNING DUER, *b.* 1821, a member of the Society of the Colonial Dames of America, who *m.*, 1845, Archibald Gracie King, of New York, and had:

MARIA DUNNING KING, a member of the Society of the Colonial Dames of America, who *m.*, 4 October, 1871, John King Van Rensselaer, of New York. *Issue.*

2.—SARA GRACIE KING, a member of the Society of the Colonial Dames of America, who *m.*, 1 December, 1875, Frederic Bronson, of New York City. *Issue.*

II.—MARIE THEODORA DUER, 1789–1837, who *m.*, 1816, Beverly Chew, of New Orleans, Louisiana, and had:

ALEXANDER LAFAYETTE CHEW, of Geneva, New York, who *m.* Sarah Augusta Prouty, also of Royal Descent, and had:

KATHERINE ADELAIDE CHEW, a member of the New Jersey Society of the Colonial Dames of America, who *m.* Samuel Winship, of Morristown, New Jersey. Issue: *Theodora Augusta.*

PEDIGREE IV.

CHARLEMAGNE, King of France and Emperor of the West, *d.* 814, had by his third wife, Hildegarde, *d.* 783, daughter of Childebrand, Duke of Suabia:

PEPIN, KING OF LOMBARDY and Italy, second son, who *m.* Lady Bertha, daughter of William, Count of Thoulouse, and had:

BERNARD, KING OF LOMBARDY, who had by his wife, Cunegonde:

PEPIN, Count of Vermandois and Peronne, a lay abbot, 840, father of:

PEPIN DE SENLIS DE VALOIS, Count Berengarius, of Bretagne, father of:

LADY POPPA DE VALOIS, who *m.* (his first wife) Rollo the Dane, founder of the royal House of Normandy and England, first Duke of Normandy, 912, *d.* 932, also of Royal Descent (see Anderson's "Royal Genealogies"), and had:

WILLIAM THE LONGSWORD, second Duke of Normandy, father of:

RICHARD I., third Duke of Normandy, father of:

GODFREY, Count of Eu and Brion, in Normandy, father of:

GISLEBERT-CRISPIN, Count of Eu and Brion, father of:

BALDWIN DE BRION, who accompanied his relative, William of Normandy, to England, and became high sheriff of Devonshire. He *m.* Lady Albreda, daughter of Richard-goz d'Abrancis, Viscount d'Auveranchez (who accompanied the Conqueror and was granted the Earldom of Chester, in 1086), and his wife, Lady Emme, half-sister of King William the Conqueror, and had:

RICHARD D'AUVERANCHE de Redvers, Baron of Oakhampton, created Earl of Devon, *d.* 1137; *m.* Lady Adeliza, daughter of William Fitz-Osborne, Count of Bretoille, lieutenant and steward in Normandy, created Earl of Hereford, and had:

BALDWIN DE REDVERS, second Earl of Devon, *d.* 1155; *m.* Lady Lucia, daughter of Dru de Balm, and had:

WILLIAM DE REDVERS de Vernon, who succeeded as sixth Earl of Devon, *d.* 1216. He had by his wife, Lady Mabel de Bellomont, also of Royal Descent, daughter of Robert the Consul, Earl of Mellent and first Earl of Gloucester, *d.* 1147:

LADY MARY DE REDVERS (widow of Robert de Courtenay, of Oakhampton, *d.* 1242), who *m.*, secondly, Peter Prouz, of Eastervale, Devonshire (see Vivian's "Devonshire Visitations"), and had:

2 (25)

WILLIAM PROUZ, father of:

WALTER PROUZ, who had by his wife, a daughter of Baron Dinham:

WILLIAM PROUZ, who had by his wife, daughter and heiress of Giles de Gidley, in Devonshire:

SIR WILLIAM PROUZ, Knt., Lord of Gidley, m. Alice, daughter and heiress of Sir Fulke Ferners, of Throwleigh, and had:

WILLIAM PROUZ, of Orton, Devonshire, m. Alice, daughter of Sir Hugh de Widworthy, and had (see Vivian's "Devonshire Visitations"):

LADY ALICE PROUZ, who m. Sir Roger Moels, Knt., and had:

LADY JOAN MOELS, who m. John Wotton, of Widworthy, in Devonshire, and had:

JOHN WOTTON, of Widworthy (see Westcote's "Devonshire Pedigrees"), who m. Engaret, daughter of Walter Dymoke, and had:

ALICE WOTTON, who m. Sir John Chichester, Knt., b. 1385, who was in the retinue of Le Sieur de Harrington at Agincourt, son of Sir John Chichester, of Treverbin, Cornwall, and had:

RICHARD CHICHESTER, b. 1424, sheriff of Devonshire, 1469, 1475, d. 25 December, 1496; m. Margaret, daughter of Sir Nicholas Keynes, of Winkleigh, and had:

NICHOLAS CHICHESTER, b. 1447, who m. Christian, daughter of Sir William (or Nicholas) Pawlet, and had:

JOHN CHICHESTER, of Rawleigh, Devon, b. 1472, d. 22 February, 1537–8; m., secondly, Joan, daughter of Robert Bright, or Brett, and had:

AMIAS CHICHESTER, of Arlington, Devon, b. 1527, d. 4 July, 1577; m. Jane Giffard, will proved 16 April, 1596; daughter of Sir Roger Giffard, of Brightley, d. 1 May, 1547, and had:

FRANCES CHICHESTER, (see N. E. His. Gen. Reg., April, 1897), who m. John Wyatt, bapt. Braunton, Devon, 27 November, 1558; admitted to the Inner Temple in 1576, son of Philip Wyatt, steward and town clerk of Barnstaple, Devon, 1562–3, d. 1592, and had:

MARGARET WYATT, who m. at Braunton, 2 February, 1626, Matthew Allyn,* bapt. Braunton, 17 April, 1605; came to New England, resided at Cambridge, 1632; at Hartford, 1637; at Windsor, 1648. He was a representative to the general court of Massachusetts, 1636; was excommunicated at Hartford; was deputy and assistant in the Connecticut

---

* MRS. HENRY GILBERT HART, a member of the New York State Society of the National Society of the Colonial Dames of America, is also of Royal Descent, through Matthew Allyn and Margaret Wyatt.

Colony, 1648–67; a commissioner to the United Colonies, 1660, 1664; *d.* 1 February, 1670–71, and had:

LIEUTENANT-COLONEL JOHN ALLYN, *bapt.* Braunton, 24 February, 1630; came to New England with his father; was cornet of troop, 1657–58; town clerk of Hartford, 1659–96; deputy, 1661; magistrate, 1662; secretary of Connecticut, 1663–65, 1667–95; *d.* 16 November, 1696. (See the pedigree chart of his ancestry, compiled by Messrs. Waters, F. Olcott Allen, Jeremiah Allyn, and Bolton, 1898.) He *m.*, 19 November, 1651, first, Ann, daughter of Henry Smith, and granddaughter of Colonel William Pynchon, treasurer of the Massachusetts Colony, *etc.*, and had:

MARY ALLYN, 1657–1724; *m.*, 6 October, 1686, William Whiting, *b.* 1659, and had:

CHARLES WHITING, 1692–1738; *m.*, 10 January, 1716–1717, Elizabeth Bradford, 1696–1777, and had:

WILLIAM BRADFORD WHITING, 1731–1796; *m.*, 24 July, 1757, Amy Lathrop, 1735–1815, and had:

DANIEL WHITING, 1768–1855; *m.*, 19 January, 1804, Elizabeth Gilbert Powers, 1782–1859, and had:

HENRY LAURENS WHITING, 1821–1897; *m.*, 3 November, 1851, Anna Frances Johnson, *b.* 1830, and had:

VIRGINIA WHITING, *b.* Philadelphia, Pennsylvania, 20 March, 1857, a member of the California Society of the Colonial Dames of America, who *m.* (his second wife), 20 July, 1882, Edwin White Newhall, of San Francisco, California, and had: *Edwin White, b.* 21 April, 1883; *Virginia Whiting, b.* 20 March, 1889, and *Frances Henrielle, b.* 2 October, 1890.

PEDIGREE V.

HENRY I., **King of France**, had, by his third wife, Anne of Russia:

HUGH-MAGNUS, Duke of France and Burgundy, Marquis of Orleans, Count of Paris, Valois and Vermandois, who had, by his third wife, *m.*, 938, Adelheid (or Hadwid), daughter of Herbert IV., Count of Vermandois:

LADY ISABEL DE VERMANDOIS, third daughter (called also Elizabeth), *d.* 1131. She *m.*, first, 1096, Robert de Beaumont, Earl of Mellent and first Earl of Leicester, *d.* 1118, and *m.*, secondly, William de Warren, second Earl of Surrey, *d.* between 1131 and 1138, and had:

LADY GUNDREDA DE WARREN, who *m.*, first, Roger de Bellomont de Newburgh, second Earl of Warwick, *d.* 1153, and had:

WALERAN DE NEWBURGH, fourth Earl of Warwick, *d.* 1205, who had, by his second wife, Alice, daughter of John de Harcourt and widow of John de Limesi:

LADY ALICE DE NEWBURGH, who *m.* William, Baron Mauduit, of Hanslape, heritable chamberlain of the exchequer, *d.* 1256, and had:

LADY ISABEL DE MAUDUIT, *d.* before 1268 (sister of William Mauduit, seventh Earl of Warwick, *d. s. p.* 1268), who *m.* William, fifth Baron Beauchamp, of Elmley Castle, will 7 January, 1268, and had:

WILLIAM DE BEAUCHAMP, Baron Beauchamp, created Earl of Warwick, *d.* 1298, who *m.* Maud, daughter of John Fitz-John, chief justice of Ireland, in 1258, and widow of Gerard de Furnival, and had:

GUY DE BEAUCHAMP, second Earl of Warwick, 1275–1315, who *m.* Lady Alice, daughter of Ralph de Toni, and widow of Thomas de Leyburne, and had:

LADY MATILDA DE BEAUCHAMP, who *m.* Geoffrey, second Baron de Say, admiral of the King's Fleet, *d.* 1359, and had:

LADY IDONES DE SAY, who *m.* Sir John Clinton, of Mantoch, third Baron Clinton, 1326–1397, and had:

LADY MARGARET CLINTON, who *m.* Sir Baldwin de Montfort, and had:

SIR WILLIAM DE MONTFORT, *d.* 1453, who *m.* Margaret Peche, and had:

SIR BALDWIN DE MONTFORT, *b.* 1445, *d.* 1475, who *m.* Joanna Vernon, and had:

ROBERT MONTFORT, of Bescote, Staffordshire, who had:

(28)

KATHERINE MONTFORT, who *m.* Sir George Booth, *d.* 1483, son of Sir William Booth, sheriff of Chester, and had:

SIR WILLIAM BOOTH, *d.* 1519, who *m.* Ellen, daughter of Sir John Montgomery, and had:

JANE BOOTH, who *m.*, secondly, Sir Thomas Holford, of Chester, and had:

DOROTHY HOLFORD, who *m.* (his second wife) John Bruen, of Bruen-Stapleford, Cheshire, *b.* 1510, *d.* 14 May, 1580 (see Ormerod's " History of Cheshire," ii., 322), and had:

JOHN BRUEN, of Stapleford, *b.* 1560, *d.* 18 January, 1625, buried at Tarvin, who had, by his third wife, Margaret:

MARY BRUEN, *bapt.* 14 June, 1622, came to New England with her half-brother, Obadiah Bruen, who *m.*, 1653 (his second wife), John Baldwin, Sr., one of the founders of Milford, Connecticut, *d.* 1681 (see " The Baldwin Family History," Pond's " Old Milford Tombstones," Caulkin's " History of New London "), and had:

HANNAH BALDWIN, *b.* 20 November, 1664, who *m.*, 17 January, 1682, Dr. John Fiske, of Milford, Connecticut, *b.* 12 December, 1654, *d.* 1715, and had:

BENJAMIN FISKE, *b.* 1683, *d.* 14 February, 1765; *m.*, 24 July, 1701, Abigail Bowen, and had:

DANIEL FISKE, *b.* 16 December, 1710, *d.* 27 June, 1804; *m.*, 24 December, 1732, Freelove Williams, *b.* 13 November, 1713, *d.* 20 April, 1791, also of Royal Descent, and had:

DANIEL FISKE, *b.* 28 April, 1753, *d.* 5 May, 1810; *m.*, 13 April, 1785, Freelove Knight, *b.* 21 January, 1766, *d.* 20 May, 1819, and had:

CELIA FISKE, *b.* 17 February, 1787, *d.* 7 May, 1859; *m.*, 16 November, 1815, Stephen Burlingame, *b.* 2 October, 1789, *d.* 20 August, 1837, and had:

COLONEL STEPHEN BURLINGAME, *b.* 3 December, 1819, *d.* 15 November, 1890; *m.*, 30 October, 1841, Elsie Maria Tillinghast, *b.* 3 January, 1820, *d.* 20 May, 1884, and had:

SARAH MARIA BURLINGAME, *b.* 10 February, 1855, a member of the New Hampshire Society of the Colonial Dames of America, and of the Massachusetts Society of the Descendants of Colonial Governors, who *m.*, 12 December, 1877, Prentiss Webster, of Lowell, Massachusetts, *b.* 24 May, 1851, *d.* 26 October, 1898, and had: *Susan Hildreth, Adeline Burlingame, Prentiss Burlingame, Helen Burlingame,* and *Dorothy Prentiss.*

PEDIGREE VI.

CHARLEMAGNE, Emperor of the West, King of the Franks, had by his third wife, Lady Hildegarde, daughter of Childebrand, Duke of Suabia:

PEPIN, KING OF LOMBARDY, who *m.* Lady Bertha, daughter of William, Count of Thoulouse, and had:

BERNARD, KING OF LOMBARDY, who had by his wife, Lady Cunegonde:

PEPIN, Count of Peronne and Vermandóis, father of:

PEPIN DE SENLIS, Count Berengarius, of Bayeux and Valois, father of:

LADY POPPA, who *m.* (his first wife) Rollo the Dane, first Duke of Normandy, *d.* 932, son of Rognvald the Mighty, Jarl of Möre, in Upland, Norway, and of the Isles of Orkney and Shetland Isles (see "Royal House of Sweden," in Anderson's "Royal Genealogies"), and had:

WILLIAM (LONGUE-EPEE), second Duke of Normandy, who had:

RICHARD I. (Sanspeur), third Duke of Normandy, who had:

RICHARD II. (le Bon), fourth Duke of Normandy, who had:

RICHARD III., fifth Duke of Normandy, who had by Lady Adela, daughter of Robert the Pious, King of France:

LADY ALICE (half-sister of Queen Maud of England), who *m.* Radulfe, Viscount of Bayeux, and had:

RANULF DE BRISQUESART, de Meschines, *b. ante* 1066, Viscount of Bayeux, created, 1119, Earl Palatine, of Chester, *d.* 1128; *m.* Lady Maud (or Margaretta), sister of Hugh (lupus), Earl of Chester, and daughter of Rubard, Viscount de Auveranches, created, 1086, Earl of Chester, and his wife, Lady Margaret (Emme), a half-sister of King William the Conqueror (see Banks's "Extinct Peerages" and Doyle's "Official Baronage"), and had:

RANULF DE MESCHINES DE GERNON, *b. ante* 1109, fifth Earl Palatine, of Chester, *d.* 1153; *m.* Lady Maud, daughter of Robert the Consul, Earl of Gloucester and Mellent (see Planche's "The Conqueror and His Companions"), and had:

HUGH DE KYVELIOC, Earl Palatine of Chester, *d.* 1181, who had by his wife, Lady Bartred, daughter of Simon, Earl of Evereux, in Normandy:

(30)

LADY DE MESCHINES, sister of Ranulph, Earl of Chester and Lincoln, who *m.* (see Banks's "Baronage" and "Stemmata Anglicana," and Edmondson's "Baronagium Genealogicum) Reginald Bacun, son of Robert, son of Roger, son of George de Bacunsthorp, in Norfolk (see Kimber's "Baronetage," 1771; *Notes and Queries*, First Series, and Blomefield's "Norfolk"), and had:

RICHARD BACUN, benefactor of Bury Abbey and founder of the Priory of Roucester, Staffordshire, who *m.* Alice de Multon, and had:

SIR ROBERT BACON, of Bacunsthorp, who *m.* daughter of Sir Richard d'Ingham, and had:

SIR THOMAS BACON, who *m.* Elizabeth ——, living 1249, and had:

SIR HENRY BACON, 1270 (brother to Sir Bartholomew Bacon, a justice itinerant, Sir Stephen Bacon, and "Friar Bacon"), who had:

SIR HENRY BACON (brother to John Bacon, chamberlain to the Exchequer and secretary to the King; master of the Rolls, etc.), who *m.* Margaret Ludham, and had:

SIR ROGER BACON (brother to Sir John Bacon, justice itinerant), a celebrated commander in the wars of Edward II. and III., who *m.* Felicia Kirton, and had:

BEATRICE BACON, heiress, who *m.* Sir William Thorpe (see "New England His. and Geneal. Register," April, 1883), and had:

WILLIAM THORPE, who *m.* (see Playfair's "British Family Antiquity") Margery, daughter of John Quadladde (or Quadlop), and had:

JOHN THORPE, whose daughter and heiress:

MARGERY THORPE, *m.* (according to Playfair) John Bacon, of Drinkstone, son of John, son of John Bacon, of Hessett and Bradfield, Suffolk, and had:

EDMUND BACON, of Drinkstone, who *m.* Elizabeth Crofts, and had:

JOHN BACON, of Drinkstone, *d.* 1500, who *m.* Agnes, daughter of Thomas Cockfield (or Cokefield), and had:

ROBERT BACON, of Drinkstone (*bur.* at Hessett, with his wife), who *m.* Isabel, daughter of John Cage, of Pakenham, Suffolk, and had:

JAMES BACON, alderman of London, *d.* 15 June, 1573, *bur.* St. Dunstan's, East London (a brother of Sir Nicholas Bacon, Lord Keeper of the Great Seal, 1509–1579, whose son was the celebrated Sir Francis, Lord Bacon), who *m.*, secondly, Margaret, daughter of William Rawlings, of London, and widow of Richard Gouldston, and had by her:

SIR JAMES BACON, Knt., of Friston Hall, Suffolk, *d.* London, 17 January, 1618; *m.* Elizabeth, daughter and heiress of Francis and Anne (Drury) Bacon, of Hessett (see Cullome's "History of Hawstead") and had:

Rev. James Bacon, rector of Burgatt, Suffolk, *d.* 9 November, 1649, will probated 23 January, 1649-1650, who *m.* Martha Honeywood, *d.* 25 August, 1670, and had:

Martha Bacon (sister of Colonel Nathaniel Bacon, *b.* 1620, member of the Virginia Council for forty years, *d.* in York county, Virginia, 1692—see his will in New England His. Geneal. Reg., vol. xxxvii., p. 194), who *m.*, *ante* 1652, Anthony Smith, of Colchester, Virginia, *d.* 1667, and had:

Abigail Smith, *b.* 11 March, 1656, *d.* 12 November, 1692, who *m.* (his first wife) Major Lewis Burwell, of White Marsh, Gloucester county, Virginia, and had :

1.—Joanna Burwell, 1674-1727; *m.*, 1693, Colonel William Bassett, Jr., of "Eltham," New Kent county, Virginia, 1670-1723, a member of the Virginia Council, son of Captain William Bassett (see Henning's "Virginia Statutes," ii., 220, and Keith's "Ancestry of Benjamin Harrison") and his wife, Bridget, daughter of Miles Cary, of Virginia, and had :

Colonel William Bassett, of "Eltham," *b.* 8 July, 1709, *d.* 174-, burgess in 1743, who *m.*, 1729, Elizabeth, daughter of William Churchill, of "Barkby Park," Middlesex county, Virginia, a member of the Virginia Council, 1705, and had :

Hon. Burwell Bassett, of "Eltham," *b.* 1734, member of the house of burgesses, of the Virginia convention of 1788, *etc.*, *d.* 4 January, 1793; *m.*, secondly, 7 May, 1757, Anna Maria Dandridge, *b.* 30 March, 1739, *d.* 17 December, 1777, sister of Mrs. George Washington, and daughter of John Dandridge, of New Kent county, Virginia, and had:

John Bassett, Jr., of "Eltham" and "Farmington," Hanover county, Virginia, *b.* 30 August, 1765 (second son, and heir to his elder brother, Burwell), *d.* 1826; *m.*, 12 September, 1786, Betty Carter, daughter of William Burnet Browne, of "Elsing Green," King William county, Virginia, also of Royal Descent, and had :

George Washington Bassett, of "Eltham," *b.* 23 August, 1800, *d.* 28 August, 1878 (he was a grandnephew of Mrs. George Washington, who was his godmother), who *m.* his cousin, Betty Burnet, daughter of Robert Lewis (a nephew and private secretary of General Washington), also of Royal Descent, and his wife, Judith Walker Browne, also of Royal Descent, and had:

I.—Anna Virginia Bassett, who *m.* Major John Hayes Claiborne, of Richmond, Virginia, also of Royal Descent, and had :

Delia Claiborne, a member of the Virginia Society of the Colonial Dames of America, who *m.*, 10 June, 1885, General

Simon B. Buckner, of "Glen Lily," Hart county, Kentucky, former Governor of Kentucky, and had:

SIMON BOLIVAR BUCKNER, *b.* 18 July, 1886.

II.—ELLA BASSETT, a member of the Virginia Society of the Colonial Dames of America, *d.* 1898, who *m.* Lewis William Washington. *Issue.*

2.—NATHANIEL BURWELL, who *m.* Elizabeth Carter, also of Royal Descent, and had:

I.—LEWIS BURWELL, of "White Marsh," who *m.* Mary Willis, and had:

REBECCA BURWELL, who *m.* Jacqueline Ambler, and had:

ANNE AMBLER, who *m.* George Fisher, and had:

ELIZA JACQUELINE AMBLER, who *m.* Thomas Marshall Colston, and had:

RALEIGH COLSTON, who *m.* Gertrude Powell, and had:

JANE COLSTON, a member of the Virginia Society of the Colonial Dames of America, who *m.*, 12 September, 1871, Conway Robinson Howard, of Richmond, Virginia, and had: *Mary Eloise, m.* Francis Elliott Sharp; *Gertrude, Jeanie C.,* and *Conway R.*

II.—ELIZABETH BURWELL, who *m.* William Nelson, of Yorktown, president of the Virginia Colony, and had:

ROBERT NELSON, who *m.*, secondly, Susan Robinson, and had:

PEYTON RANDOLPH NELSON, who *m.* Sallie Berkeley Nicolson, also of Royal Descent, and had:

WILLIAM WILMER NELSON, who *m.* Sally Browne Catlett, and had:

SALLY BERKELEY NELSON, of Richmond, Virginia, a member of the Virginia Society of the Colonial Dames of America, who *m.* William Todd Robins, Colonel Confederate States Army. Issue: *Ruth Nelson, Elizabeth Todd, Augustine Warner, Wilmer Nelson,* and *Sally Berkeley Nicolson.*

III.—CARTER BURWELL, who *m.* Lucy Grymes, and had:

NATHANIEL BURWELL, who *m.* Lucy (Page) Baylor, also a descendant of Robert Carter, 1663–1732, and had:

GEORGE H. BURWELL, who *m.* Agnes Atkinson, and had:

ISABELLA DIXON BURWELL, who *m.* Peter H. Mayo, and had:

AGNES ATKINSON MAYO, a member of the Virginia Society of the Colonial Dames of America, who *m.* Thomas Nelson Carter, of Richmond, Virginia, also a descendant of Robert Carter, 1663–1732, and had: *Isabelle Burwell.*

IV.—COLONEL ROBERT CARTER BURWELL, of Isle of Wight county, Virginia, *m.* Sarah Nelson, and had:

FRANCES BURWELL, who *m.* Governor John Page, of "Rosewell," also of Royal Descent, and had:

FRANCES PAGE, who *m.*, secondly, Dr. Carter Berkeley, of "Edgewood," and had:

CATHERINE FANNY BERKELEY, who *m.* Lucius Horatio Minor, of "Edgewood," also of Royal Descent, and had:

MARY WILLIS MINOR, of Baltimore, a member of the Maryland Society of the Colonial Dames of America.

3.—MARTHA BURWELL, seventh child, *b.* November, 1685, who *m.* Colonel Henry Armistead, of Gloucester county (son of John Armistead, a Virginia councillor—see *William and Mary Quarterly*, July, 1898, p. 445; Keith's "Harrison Pedigree," pp. 36–37), and had:

WILLIAM ARMISTEAD, will probated 30 December, 1755, who *m.*, 1739, Mary, daughter of James Bowles, *d.* 1728, and his wife, Rebecca, daughter of Colonel Thomas Addison, and had:

COLONEL JOHN ARMISTEAD, who *m.*, 1764, Lucy, daughter of Colonel John and Lucy (Walker) Baylor, and had:

GENERAL WALKER KEITH ARMISTEAD, United States Army, who *m.* Elizabeth, daughter of John and Elizabeth (Wright) Stanly, and had:

CORNELIA ARMISTEAD, who *m.* Major Washington I. Newton, United States Army (son of Thomas Newton, of Norfolk, Virginia, M. C., 1801–1833), and had:

ELIZABETH STANLY NEWTON, a member of the California Society of the Colonial Dames of America, who *m.* Pedro Merlin Lusson, of San José, California, and had:

CORNELIA ARMISTEAD NEWTON LUSSON, a member of the Virginia Society of the Colonial Dames of America, who *m.* George A. Crux, of Portland, Oregon.

4.—ELIZABETH BURWELL, *d.* 1734, who *m.* Benjamin Harrison, of "Berkeley," 1673–1710, colonial treasurer and attorney-general of Virginia (see Keith's "Ancestry of Benjamin Harrison"), and had:

BENJAMIN HARRISON, of "Berkeley," high sheriff, burgess, *etc., d.* 1744, who *m.*, 1722, Anne, daughter of Robert Carter, of "Carotoman," also of Royal Descent, and had:

I.—BENJAMIN HARRISON, of "Berkeley," 1726–1791, member of the Continental Congress, a signer of the Declaration of Independence, governor of Virginia, *etc.*, who *m.* Elizabeth, *b.* 1730, daughter of Colonel William Bassett, Jr., of "Eltham," son of Colonel William Bassett, of

"Eltham," New Kent county, Virginia, member of the Virginia council, and his wife, Joan Burwell, aforesaid.

GENERAL WILLIAM HENRY HARRISON, of Ohio, 1773–1841, President of the United States, who *m.* Ann Tuthill, daughter of Judge John Cleves Symmes, of Ohio, and had:

1.—JOHN SCOTT HARRISON, of Cleves, Ohio, 1804–1878, *m.*, 1831, ELIZABETH IRWIN, and had:

GENERAL BENJAMIN HARRISON, of Indiana, President of the United States, who *m.*, first, Caroline Scott, and had by her:

MARY SCOTT HARRISON, a member of the Virginia Society of the Colonial Dames of America, who *m.*, 5 November, 1884, James Robert McKee, of Indianapolis, Indiana, and had: *Benjamin Harrison* and *Mary Lodge.*

2.—LUCY SINGLETON HARRISON, 1800–1826, who *m.* (his first wife) Judge David Kirkpatrick Este, of Cincinnati, also of Royal Descent, and had:

LUCY ANN HARRISON ESTE, who *m.* Joseph F. Reynolds, of Hagerstown, Maryland, and had:

ANNA HARRISON REYNOLDS, who *m.* John Law Crawford, and had:

LUCY ESTE CRAWFORD, a member of the Maryland Society of the Colonial Dames of America, who *m.* George C. Woodruff, of Litchfield, Connecticut. *No issue.*

II.—NATHANIEL HARRISON, a member of the Virginia State Senate, 1780, who *m.* Mary, daughter of Edmund Ruffin, of Prince George county, Virginia, and had:

EDMUND HARRISON, of Amelia county, Virginia, 1761–1826, who *m.* Martha Wayles Skipwith, also of Royal Descent, and had:

WILLIAM HENRY HARRISON, of Amelia county, 1812–1884, who *m.* Lucy A. Powers, and had:

PROF. EDMUND HARRISON, of Louisville, Kentucky, who *m.* Kate Steger, and had:

1.—LELIA SKIPWITH HARRISON, a member of the Virginia Society of the Colonial Dames of America, who *m.* Howard D. Hoge, of Richmond.

2.—LULIE HARRISON, a member of the Virginia Society of the Colonial Dames of America, who *m.* Dana Henry Rucker, of Richmond, Virginia, and had: *Edmund Harrison, b.* 18 February, 1898.

3.—JENNIE HARRISON, a member of the Virginia Society of the Colonial Dames of America, who *m.* Charles H. Chalkley, of Hopkinsville, Kentucky.

III.—CARTER HENRY HARRISON, of " Clifton," who married Susan, daughter of Isham Randolph, of " Dungeness," and had:

ROBERT CARTER HARRISON, who *m.*, Anne Cabell, and had by her :

MARY HOPKINS HARRISON, who *m.* Samuel Q. Richardson, and had :

ROBERT CARTER RICHARDSON, who *m.* Marie Louise Harris, and had :

MARY CABELL RICHARDSON, of Covington, Kentucky, a member of the Virginia Society of the Colonial Dames of America, founder of the Order of Colonial Governors, etc.

PEDIGREE VII.

EDWARD I., King of England, had by his first wife, m. 1254, Princess Eleanor, only child of Ferdinand III., King of Castile and Leon:

PRINCESS JOAN PLANTAGENET D'ACRE, d. 1305, who was the second wife of Gilbert, ninth Earl of Clare, seventh Earl of Hertford, and third Earl of Gloucester, d. 1295, also of Royal Descent, by whom she had:

LADY MARGARET DE CLARE (widow of Piers de Gravestone, Earl of Cornwall), who m., secondly, Hugh, second Baron d'Audley, created, in 1337, Earl of Gloucester, d. 1347-1349, and had:

LADY MARGARET D'AUDLEY, heiress, who m. (his first wife) Sir Ralph de Stafford, K.G., second Baron de Stafford, created, in 1351, Earl of Stafford, d. 1372, and had:

SIR HUGH DE STAFFORD, K.G., second Earl of Stafford, 1344-1386, who m. Lady Phillippa, daughter of Sir Thomas de Beauchamp, K.G., third Earl of Warwick, 1313-1369, also of Royal Descent, and had:

LADY MARGARET DE STAFFORD, d. 9 June, 1370, who m. (his first wife) Sir Ralph de Neville, K.G., fourth Baron de Neville, of Raby, created, in 1397, Earl of Westmoreland; Earl Marshal of England, d. 1425, and had:

LADY MARGARET DE NEVILLE, d. 1463, who m., first, Richard, third Baron Scrope, of Bolton, d. at Rouen, 29 August, 1420, also of Royal Descent, and had:

SIR HENRY LE SCROPE, fourth Baron Scrope, of Bolton, d. 1459, who m. Lady Elizabeth, daughter of John, Baron Scrope, of Masham and Upsal, and had:

LADY MARGARET LE SCROPE, who m. John Bernard, of Abingdon, Northamptonshire, 1437-1485, and had:

JOHN BERNARD, of Abingdon, 1469-1508; m. Margaret, daughter of John Daundelyn, and had:

JOHN BERNARD, of Abingdon, 1491-1549; m. Cicely, daughter of John Muscote, of Earls Barton, and had:

FRANCIS BERNARD, of Abingdon, 1530-1609; m. Alice, daughter of John Hazlewood, of Maidwell, and had:

FRANCIS BERNARD, of Kingsthorpe, Northamptonshire, bur. 21 November, 1630, who m. Mary, daughter of Anthony Woodhouse, of Glasswell, and had:

COLONEL WILLIAM BERNARD, of Nansemond County, Virginia, member of the Virginia Council, 1642–1659, d. 31 March, 1665, who m. Lucy, daughter of Captain Robert Higginson (she m., second, Major Lewis Burwell, and m., third, Colonel Philip Ludwell), and had:

LUCY BERNARD (see *Virginia Mag. of His. and Biog.*, vi., 409), who m. Dr. Edmund Gwynne, of Gloucester county, Virginia, will dated 10 March, 1683, and had:

LUCY GWYNNE, who m. Thomas Reade, of Gloucester county, Virginia, will 4 January, 1694, also of Royal Descent, and had:

I.—MILDRED READE (see *Virginia Mag. of His. and Biog.*, iv., 204), who m. Major Philip Rootes, and had:

ELIZABETH ROOTES, who m. (his second wife) Rev. John Thompson, of St. Mark's parish, Culpeper county, Virginia, will proved 16 November, 1772, and had by her:

PHILIP ROOTES THOMPSON, of Culpeper,Virginia, M.C., 1801–1807; m., secondly, Sally, daughter of Robert Slaughter, of " The Grange," Culpeper county, Virginia, and had by her:

JUDGE R. AUGUSTUS THOMPSON, of San Francisco, who had by his first wife:

—— THOMPSON, a member of the Virginia Society of the Colonial Dames of America, who m. S. C. Hine, of San Francisco, and had:

SALLIE HELENA HINE, a member of the Virginia Society of the Colonial Dames of America, who m. her cousin, William Thompson.

JUDGE R. AUGUSTUS THOMPSON had by his second wife, Elizabeth Jane Early:

1.—RUTH HOUSTON THOMPSON, a member of the Virginia and California Societies of the Colonial Dames of America, who m. William Craig, of San Francisco, California.

2.—ROBERTA THOMPSON, of San Francisco, a member of the Virginia and California Societies of the Colonial Dames of America.

II.—MARY READE, who m. Captain Mordecai Throckmorton, of Virginia, 1696–1768, also of Royal Descent, and had:

LUCY THROCKMORTON, who m., 16 June, 175–, Robert Throckmorton, J. P., of Culpeper county, Virginia, b. 20 November, 1736, son of Major Robert Throckmorton (brother of the aforesaid Captain Mordecai Throckmorton), and his wife, Mary Lewis, also of Royal Descent, and had:

FRANCES THROCKMORTON, *b.* 29 February, 1765, who *m.*, 20 December, 1783, General William Madison, of "Woodbury Forest," Madison county, Virginia (see Hayden's "Virginia Genealogies," p. 257–259), and had:

REBECCA CONWAY MADISON, *b.* at "Montpelier," Orange county, Virginia, 31 March, 1785, *d.* March, 1860, who *m.*, 1803, Reynolds Chapman, *b.* at "Chericoke," King William county, Virginia, 22 July, 1778, *d.* at "Berry Hill," Orange county, Virginia, 184–, and had:

JUDGE JOHN MADISON CHAPMAN, *b.* at "Berry Hill," 1810, *d.* 31 March, 1879; *m.*, 3 August, 1841, Susannah Digges Cole, also of Royal Descent, and had:

1.—SUSIE ASHTON CHAPMAN, *b.* 18 December, 1845, a member of the Tennessee Society of the Colonial Dames of America, the Order of the Crown, *etc.*, who *m.*, 3 October, 1878, Calvin Perkins, of Memphis, Tennessee, and had: *Blakeney, b.* 4 April, 1880; *Belle Moncure, b.* 7 October, 1881; *Ashton Chapman, b.* 27 January, 1883; *Mamie Anderson, b.* 11 April, 1884; *Louis Allen, b.* 10 April, 1885, and *William Alexander, b.* 23 March, 1886.

2.—BELLE CHAPMAN, *b.* November, 1858, a member of the Virginia Society of the Colonial Dames of America, the Order of the Crown, *etc.*, who *m.*, 12 November, 1878, William Moncure, of Richmond, Virginia, and had: *William, b.* Orange County, Virginia, 1 October, 1880; *Belle Perkins, b.* Richmond, Virginia, 17 November, 1882, and *Vivienne Daniel, b.* Franklinton, North Carolina, 17 February, 1885.

3.—ASHTON ALEXANDER CHAPMAN, *b.* Orange county, Virginia, 22 August, 1867; *m.*, 23 January, 1895, Nannie Eaton, daughter of Colonel Roger O. Gregory, of Oxford, North Carolina.

THE ROYAL DESCENT

OF

MISS MARGARET VOWELL SMITH,

OF ALEXANDRIA, VA.

EDWARD I., King of England⳦Lady Eleanor of Provence.

Princess Joan Plantagenet⳦Gilbert de Clare, Earl of Gloucester and Hertford.

Lady Margart de Clare⳦Hugh de Audley, Earl of Gloucester.

Lady Margaret de Audley⳦Sir Ralph de Stafford, K. G., Earl of Stafford.

Sir Hugh de Stafford, K. G., Earl of Stafford⳦Lady Philippa de Beauchamp.

Lady Margaret de Stafford⳦Sir Ralph de Neville, K. G., Earl of Westmoreland.

Ralph de Neville, of Oversley, Warwickshire⳦Lady Mary de Ferrers.

John de Neville, of Wymersley, Yorkshire⳦Lady Elizabeth de Newmarch.

Joan de Neville⳦Sir William Gascoigne, of Gawthrope, Yorkshire.

Sir William Gascoigne, of Gawthrope, York⳦Lady Margaret de Percy.

Lady Elizabeth Gascoigne⳦Gilbert de Talboys, of Kyme.

Sir George de Talboys, of Kyme⳦(Name unknown.)

Lady Anne de Talboys⳦Sir Edward Dymoke, of Scrivelsby, Lincolnshire.

Lady Frances Dymoke⳦Thomas Windebank, of Haines Hill, Berkshire.

Lady Mildred Windebank⳦Robert Reade, Linkenholt Manor, Southampton.

Col. George Reade, of Gloucester Co., Va.⳦Elizabeth Martian.

Mildred Reade⳦Col. Augustine Warner, Jr., of "Warner's Hall."

Mary Warner (m. 17 February, 1680)⳦John Smith, of "Purton," Gloucester Co., Va.

Augustine Smith, of "Purton," 1687–1756⳦Sarah Carver.

John Smith, of "Shooters' Hill," Va., 1715–1771⳦Mary Jacqueline.

Augustine Smith, of "Shooters' Hill," 1738–1774⳦Margaret Boyd.

Mary Jacqueline Smith, 1773–1846⳦John Cripps Vowell, of Alexandria, Va.

Sarah Gosnelle Vowell, member of the National Society of the Colonial Dames of America⳦Francis Lee Smith, of Fauquier Co., Va.

Margaret Vowell Smith, of Alexandria, Va., member of the National Society of the Colonial Dames of America, the Order of the Crown, etc.

PEDIGREE VIII.

ROBERT BRUCE, King of Scotland, had by his second wife, Lady Elizabeth de Burgh, daughter of Richard, Earl of Ulster:

PRINCESS MARGARET BRUCE, sister of King David II., who *m.*, 1344 (his first wife), William, Earl of Sutherland, *d.* 1370, and had:

JOHN, sixth Earl of Sutherland, only son, *d.* 1389, who *m.* Lady Mabilla Dunbar, daughter of Patrick, tenth Earl of March, and had:

NICHOLAS, eighth Earl of Sutherland, second son, *d.* 1399, who *m.* Elizabeth, daughter of John Macdonald, Lord of the Isles, and had:

ROBERT, ninth Earl of Sutherland, *d.* 1442, who *m.* Lady Mabilla, daughter of John, second Earl of Murray, and had:

ALEXANDER SUTHERLAND, of Dunheath, third son, who had:

LADY MARGARET SUTHERLAND, *m.* William Sinclair, third Earl of Orkney, and Earl of Caithness, and had:

LADY MARJORY SINCLAIR, who *m.* Andrew, Lord Leslie, who *d. v. p.*, 1502, son of George Leslie, first Earl of Rothes, and had:

WILLIAM LESLIE, third son, third Earl of Rothes, who *m.* Lady Margaret, daughter of Sir Michael Balfour, of Mountquhanie, and had:

GEORGE, fourth Earl of Rothes, *k.* in France, in 1558, who had by his third wife, Margaret Crichton:

LADY HELEN LESLIE, second daughter, widow of Gilbert de Seton the younger, who *m.* Mark Ker, Abbot, or Commendator of Newbottle, 1546, extraordinary lord of session, *d.* 1584, second son of Sir Andrew Ker, of Cessford, and Agnes, daughter of William, Lord Crichton, and had:

MARK KER, eldest son, succeeded his father in office, was made a baron 28 July, 1587, and created, 10 February, 1606, Earl of Lothian, *d.* 8 April, 1609. He *m.* Lady Margaret, daughter of John, fourth Lord Maxwell, and Lord Herries, in right of his wife, Agnes, daughter of William, Lord Herries, and had:

LADY JEAN KER, who *m.*, first, the Hon. Robert Boyd, Master of Boyd, *d. v. p.*, eldest son of Thomas, fifth Lord Boyd, and his wife Margaret, daughter of Sir Matthew Campbell, of Loudon, and had:

JAMES, eighth Lord Boyd, of Kilmarnock, second son, *d.* 1654, who *m.* Catherine, daughter of John Craik, of York City, and had:

WILLIAM, ninth Lord Boyd, created Earl of Kilmarnock, 7 August, 1661, *d.* 1692, who *m.*, 25 April, 1661, Lady Jean Cunningham, daughter of William, ninth Earl of Glencairn, chancellor of Scotland, and had:

ROBERT BOYD, of Kilmarnock, fourth son, *b.* 6 August, 1689, *d.* 1761; *m.* Margaret Thompson, by whom he had:

JAMES BOYD, *b.* in Kilmarnock, 3 May, 1732, *d.* 30 September, 1798. In 1756 he came to America with a patent from George II. for sixty thousand acres in New Brunswick. During the Revolution he sided with the Colonies, and thereby forfeited his grant. He *m.*, 11 August, 1757, Susannah, daughter of Colonel Joseph Coffin, of Newburyport, and had:

1.—ROBERT BOYD, *b.* October, 1758, *d.* 18 January, 1827; *m.*, 1 November, 1791, Ruth, daughter of David Smith, of Portland, and had:

WILLIAM BOYD, *b.* 16 December, 1800, graduated at Harvard 1820, *d.* Portland, Maine, 10 May, 1875. He *m.*, 10 September, 1832, Susan Dayton, daughter of Charles Harrod, of New Orleans, Louisiana, and his wife Hannah Dayton, granddaughter of Major-General Elias Dayton, of Elizabethtown, New Jersey, and had:

MAJOR CHARLES HARROD BOYD, of Portland, Maine, a member of the Military Order of the Loyal Legion, and the societies of the Grand Army of the Republic, Sons of the American Revolution and the Colonial Wars, *b.* 4 July, 1833, *m.*, 1 September, 1858, Annette Maria, daughter of Colonel Greenlief Dearborn, United States Army, who served in the War of 1812 and in the Florida War, and great-granddaughter of Major-General Henry Dearborn, secretary of war under Jefferson, commander-in-chief of the army under Madison, and minister to Portugal under Monroe, and had:

I.—ANNIE FRANCES HARROD BOYD, a member of the Maine Society of the Colonial Dames of America, the Order of the Crown, *etc.*

II.—AUGUSTA DEARBORN; III.—JULIA WINGATE; IV.—EMILY DEARBORN.

2.—JOSEPH COFFIN BOYD, of Portland, Maine, *b.* Newburyport, 23 July, 1760, *d.* 12 May, 1823; *m.*, 24 January, 1796, Isabella, daughter of Judge Robert Southgate, of Scarboro', Maine, and had:

JUDGE SAMUEL STILLMAN BOYD, of Natchez, Mississippi, *b.* 27 May, 1807, *d.* 21 May, 1869; *m.*, 15 November, 1838, Catherine Charlotte Wilkins, of Natchez, and had:

ANNA MARIA WILKINS BOYD, *b.* 10 March, 1859, a member of the Pennsylvania and Mississippi Societies of the Colonial Dames of America, the Order of the Crown, *etc.*, who *m.* William Benneville Rhodes, of Natchez, and had: *Catherine Charlotte Boyd, b.* 1890, and *Dorothy Marie, b.* 1894.

PEDIGREE IX.

HUGH CAPET, King of France, 987, had by his wife, Lady Adela, daughter of William, Duke of Aquitaine:

PRINCESS HEDEWIGE, who m. Raginerus IV., Count of Hainault, and had:

LADY BEATRIX, who m. Eblo I., Count of Rouci and Reimes, and had:

ADELA, Countess de Rouci, who m. Hildwin IV., Count de Rouci and Montdider, and had:

LADY MARGARET DE ROUCI, who m. Hugh, Count de Clermont and de Beauvais, and had:

LADY ADELIZA DE CLERMONT, who m. Gilbert de Tonsburg, in Kent, second Earl of Clare, and had:

LADY ADELIZA DE CLARE, who m. Alberic, second Baron de Vere, appointed by Henry I. great high chamberlain of England, and had:

ALBERIC DE VERE, third Baron, created, in 1135, Earl of Oxford and great high chamberlain, d. 1194; m., secondly, Lady Lucia, daughter of William, third Baron d'Abrancis, and had by her:

ROBERT DE VERE, third Earl of Oxford; one of the twenty-five Barons selected to enforce the Magna Charta; m. Lady Isabel, daughter of Hugh, second Baron de Bolbec, and had:

HUGH DE VERE, fourth Earl of Oxford, great high chamberlain, d. 1263; m. Lady Hawise, daughter of Saher de Quincey, Earl of Winchester, one of the twenty-five Magna Charta Barons, and had:

ROBERT DE VERE, fifth Earl of Oxford, d. 1296; m. Lady Alice, daughter of Gilbert, Baron Saundford, chamberlain in fee to Eleanor, Queen of Henry III., and had:

ALPHONSO DE VERE, second son, who m. Lady Jane, daughter of Sir Richard Foliot, Knt., and had:

JOHN DE VERE, seventh Earl of Oxford, killed at Rheims, who m. Lady Maud, daughter of Bartholomew, first Baron Badlesmere, executed in 1322, and widow of Robert Fitz-Payn, and had:

AUBREY DE VERE, second son (uncle of Robert, ninth Earl of Oxford, and Duke of Dublin, declared a traitor to King Richard, and outlawed and attainted, and d. in exile, 1292), who was restored to the honors, titles and estates of Oxford, and was the tenth Earl of Oxford; m. Lady Alice, daughter of John, Lord Fitz-Walter, and had:

RICHARD DE VERE, eleventh Earl of Oxford, *d.* 1417; *m.* Lady Alice, daughter of Sir John Sergeaux, Knt., of Cornwall, and had:

ROBERT DE VERE, second son, who *m.* Lady Joan, daughter of Sir Hugh Courtenay, Knt., also of Royal Descent, and had:

JOHN DE VERE, who *m.* Alice, daughter of Walter Kelrington, and had:

SIR JOHN DE VERE, K.G., who succeeded as fifteenth Earl of Oxford; great lord high chamberlain of England, *d.* 1539, who *m.* Elizabeth, daughter of Sir Edward Trussel, of Cublesdon, and had:

LADY ANNE DE VERE, who *m.* Edmund Sheffield, created Lord Sheffield, of Butterwicke, in 1547, killed in battle, 1548–49, and had:

JOHN, second Lord Sheffield, who *m.* (her first husband) Lady Douglas, daughter of William, Lord Howard, of Effingham, and had:

SIR EDMUND SHEFFIELD, K.G., third Lord, a celebrated naval officer, who for the part he took in the defeat of the Armada was made a Knight of the Garter, and Governor of Brill, and in 1626 created Earl of Mulgrave, *d.* 1646, aged 80 years; *m.*, first, Lady Ursula, daughter of Sir Robert Tirwhit, of Ketleby, and had:

LADY FRANCES SHEFFIELD, who *m.* Sir Philip Fairfax, Knt., of Stenton, and had:

SIR WILLIAM FAIRFAX, of Stenton, 1610–1692, who *m.* Frances, daughter of Sir Thomas Chalomer, chamberlain to Prince Henry; *k.* in 1644, at Montgomery Castle, and had:

ISABELLA FAIRFAX, *bapt.* at Stenton, 16 August, 1637; *d.* 25 October, 1691; who *m.* Nathaniel Bladen, of Hemsworth, Yorkshire, councillor, *etc.; bapt.* at Bolton Percy, son of Rev. Dr. Thomas Bladen, dean of Oxford, and had:

WILLIAM BLADEN,* 1670–1718, clerk of the Maryland House of Burgesses 1497, clerk of the Prerogative Office 1699 and commissary-general of Maryland 1714, who had by his first wife, Letitia, daughter of Judge Dudley Loftus, LL.D., deputy judge advocate in Leinster, Ireland, in 1651; a master in chancery, and vicar-general of Ireland till his death in 1695:

ANNE BLADEN, who *m.* Benjamin Tasker, of Annapolis, 1690–1768,

---

* The following ladies, members of the National Society of the Colonial Dames of America, are also of Royal Descent through William Bladen:

MISS LIZINKA C. BROWN (deceased), Maryland State Society.

MRS. EDWARD S. BEALL, Maryland State Society.

MISS LOUISA OGLE BEALL, Maryland State Society.

MRS. CHARLES S. SHAWHAN, Maryland State Society.

MISS MARY WINN, Maryland State Society.

president of the council for thirty-two years, and deputy-governor of the Province of Maryland 1752, commissioner to Pennsylvania 1752, a delegate to the Colonial Congress at Albany, New York, 1754, *etc.*, and had:

1. REBECCA TASKER, who *m.* Daniel Dulany, mayor of Annapolis 1764, member of the council from 1757, and secretary of State of Maryland from 1761, *b.* 1721, *d.* 19 March, 1797, and had:

COLONEL BENJAMIN TASKER DULANY, of Virginia, who *m.*, 1773, Elizabeth, daughter of Daniel French, of "Clairmont," Fairfax county, Virginia, and had:

I.—DANIEL FRENCH DULANY, of Virginia, who *m.* Sarah, daughter of Commodore Thomas Tingey, United States Navy, and had:

MARY DULANY, who *m.* Mottrom Ball, of Virginia, and had:

REBECCA BALL, a member of the Virginia Society of the Colonial Dames of America, who *m.* John Addison, of Richmond, Virginia.

II.—BENJAMIN TASKER DULANY, who *m.* Miss Rozier, of "Notley Hall," Prince George county, Maryland, and had:

MAJOR ROZIER DULANY, United States Army, who *m.* Fannie Carter, of "Sabine Hall," Virginia, also of Royal Descent, and had:

REBECCA DULANY, who *m.* Colonel Richard H. Dulany, of "Welbourne," Virginia, and had:

FRANCES ADDISON CARTER DULANY, a member of the Maryland Society of the Colonial Dames of America, who *m.* J. Southgate Lemmon, of Baltimore.

2.—ELIZABETH TASKER, who *m.* Christopher Lowndes, and had:

CHARLES LOWNDES, 1765–1846, who *m.* Eleanor, *d.* 18 August, 1805, daughter of Edward Lloyd, of "Wye," Governor of Maryland, and had, besides other children: *Lloyd*, and

RICHARD LOWNDES, 1801–1844, who *m.*, 22 March, 1832, Louisa Black, and had:

1.—ELOISE LOWNDES, who *m.*, 11 July, 1864, J. Philip Roman, and had:

I.—ELOISE LOWNDES ROMAN, a member of the Maryland Society of the Colonial Dames of America, who *m.*, 25 September, 1894, Ernest St. George Lough.

II.—LOUISA LOWNDES ROMAN, a member of the Maryland Society of the Colonial Dames of America, who *m.* at Annapolis, 15 June, 1899, Arthur J. Hepburn, United States Navy.

III.—J. PHILIP ROMAN, *m.*, 15 November, 1899, Mary Katherine Clark.

2.—ELIZABETH TASKER LOWNDES, a member of the Maryland Society of the Colonial Dames of America, who *m.*, 2 December, 1869, her first cousin, Lloyd Lowndes, Governor of Maryland, son of the aforesaid Lloyd Lowndes, and had: I. *Elizabeth T., d. inf.;* II. *Lloyd, m.*, 23 November, 1899, Mary Campbell Quinn; III. *Richard T., m.*, 22 October, 1896, Mary McDowell, and had: *Richard Tasker;* IV. *Charles Thomas;* V. *William Bladen;* VI. *Upshur, d. inf.;* VII. *Elizabeth;* VIII. *Tasker Gantt.*

3.—ANNE TASKER, who *m.* Samuel Ogle, 1704–1762, thrice Governor of the Province of Maryland, and had:

ANNE OGLE, who *m.* John Tayloe, of " Mt. Airy," King George county, Virginia, and had:

ANNE OGLE TAYLOE, who *m.* Henry Howell Lewis, United States Navy, and had: *Henry Grosvenor, Theodorick Napier, Anne Ogle, d.*, and

VIRGINIA TAYLOE LEWIS, of Baltimore, a member of the Maryland Society of the Colonial Dames of America.

PEDIGREE X.

EDWARD I., **King of England**, had by his first wife, Princess Eleanor, daughter of Ferdinand III., King of Castile and Leon :

PRINCESS ELEANOR PLANTAGENET, who *m.* Henri, Comte de Barr, and had :

LADY ELEANOR DE BARR, who *m.* Llewelyn ap Owen, and had :

THOMAS AP LLEWELYN, who *m.* Lady Eleanor, daughter of Philip ap Iver ap Cadivor, and had :

ELEANOR V. PHILIP, who *m.* Griffith Vychan (or Vaughn), Lord of Glyndyfrdwy, and had :

LOWRY VAUGHN (sister of Owen Glendower), who *m.* Robert Puleston, of Emral, and had :

JOHN PULESTON, of Emral, who *m.* Angharad, daughter of Griffith de Hanmer, and had :

MARGARET PULESTON (see Dunn's " Visitations of Wales "), who *m.* David ap Ievan ap Einion, constable of Harlech Castle in 1468, and had :

EINION AP DAVID, of Coyniarth, in Edermon, who had :

LLEWELYN AP EINION, who had :

GRIFFITH AP LLEWELYN, who *m.* Mary, daughter of Howell ap Harry, and had :

CATHERINE V. GRIFFITH, who *m.* Edward ap Ievan, of Llanwddyn parish, Monmouthshire, and had :

ELLEN V. EDWARD, who *m.* Lewis ap Griffith, of Yshute, Denbigshire, 1525–1600, and had :

ROBERT AP LEWIS, of Rhiwlas, Merionethshire, 1555–1645, who *m.* Gwyrrll, daughter of Llewelyn ap David, of Llan Rwst, in Denbigshire, and had :

EVAN AP ROBERT AP LEWIS, of Rhiwlas and Vron Gôch, Merionethshire, 1585–1662, who had :

OWEN AP EVAN, of Vron Gôch farm, near Bala, Merionethshire, *d.* 1669, who *m.* Gainor John, *d.* 14 December, 1678, and had :

ELLEN EVANS, who *m.* Cadwalader Thomas ap Hugh, of Kiltalgarth, Llanvawr, Merionethshire, who suffered persecution and imprisonment because he was a Quaker, and had by him, who *d. ante* February, 1682–

(47)

1683 (see Glenn's "Merion in the Welsh Tract," and Keith's "Provincial Councillors of Pennsylvania"):

JOHN CADWALADER,* *b.* 1677–1678, came to Pennsylvania 1697, and was admitted a freeman of Philadelphia, in July, 1705; elected to the Common Council, 1718–1733; member of the Provincial Assembly, 1729–1734; *d.* 23 July, 1734, intestate. He *m.* at Friends' Meeting, Merion, Pennsylvania, 29 December, 1699, Martha, *d.* 16 April, 1747, daughter of Dr. Edward Jones, of Merion, and'his wife, Mary, daughter of Dr. Thomas Wynne, of Philadelphia, and had:

1.—THOMAS CADWALADER, M.D., of Philadelphia, a member of the Common Council, 1751–1774; of the Provincial Council, 1755–1776; medical director of the army hospitals, 1776; *d.* at his country-seat, "Greenwood," Mercer county, New Jersey, 14 November, 1779, aged 72 years. He *m.*, 18 June, 1738, Hannah, *d.* 1786, aged 74, daughter of Thomas Lambert, of Trenton, New Jersey, and had:

I.—COLONEL LAMBERT CADWALADER, of Philadelphia and Trenton, a member of the constitutional convention; a deputy to the Continental Congress; member of Congress from New Jersey, 1789–1795; *d.* at "Greenwood," 13 September, 1813, aged 81 years. He *m.*, in 1793, Mary, daughter of Archibald McCall, of Philadelphia, and had:

MAJOR-GENERAL THOMAS CADWALADER, of "Greenwood," *b.* 11 September, 1795, *d.* 22 October, 1873. He *m.*, 27 December, 1831, Maria C., daughter of Nicholas Grosverneur, of New York, and had:

MARIA CADWALADER, a member of the Society of the Colonial Dames of America, who *m.*, 29 April, 1880, John Hone, of New York City, and had: *Hester.*

II.—GENERAL JOHN CADWALADER, of Philadelphia, *b.* January, 1742, *d.* 10 February, 1786; *m.*, first, Elizabeth, *d.* 15 February, 1776, daughter of Edward Lloyd, of "Wye House," Talbot county, Maryland, and had:

ELIZABETH MCCALL, *b.* 1773, *d.* October, 1824, who *m.*, 1792, Archibald McCall, of Philadelphia, *d.* 1843 (son of Archibald McCall and his wife, Judith, daughter of Peter Kemble, president of the Provincial Council of New Jersey), and had:

COLONEL GEORGE ARCHIBALD MCCALL, United States Army, of

---

* The following ladies, members of the National Society of the Colonial Dames of America, are also of Royal Descent through John Cadwalader :

MISS MARTHA MORRIS BROWN, Pennsylvania State Society.

MRS. SAMUEL CHEW, Pennsylvania State Society.

MRS. WILLIAM PEARSALL, Pennsylvania State Society.

" Belair," Pennsylvania, *b.* 16 March, 1802, *d.* 26 February, 1868; *m.*, 1853, Elizabeth, daughter of William McMurtrie, and had:

ELIZABETH McCALL, a member of the Pennsylvania Society of the Colonial Dames of America, who *m.* Edward Fenno Hoffman, of Philadelphia, and had: *Edward F., b.* 27 July, 1888; *John C., b.* 18 Dec., 1889, *d.* 3 March, 1890; and *Phœbe White, b.* 3 Feb., 1894.

2.—HANNAH CADWALADER, *b.* 15 April, 1715, *d.* 15 December, 1787; *m.*, 29 April, 1737, Samuel Morris, of Philadelphia, *b.* 21 November, 1711, *d.* April, 1782. He was commissioned to settle the Braddock expedition accounts, 1756; was a member Common Council of Philadelphia, 1756–1766; vice-president council of safety, and afterwards of the board of war during the Revolution; a founder of the Pennsylvania Hospital, 1752; register of wills, Philadelphia, 1777; a founder of the Philadelphia Library, 1742; justice court of common pleas, 1745, and of the orphans' court, 1747; high sheriff of Philadelphia county, 1752, and had by his wife, Hannah Cadwalader:

ANTHONY CADWALADER MORRIS, of Philadelphia, *d.* 28 September, 1798; *m.*, 12 April, 1770, Mary, daughter of William Jones, and had:

1.—HANNAH MORRIS, *d.* 26 January, 1832, who *m.*, 24 November, 1791, Nathaniel Mitchell, of Laurel, Sussex county, Delaware, *b.* 1753, *d.* 21 February, 1814. He was adjutant of a Delaware battalion under Colonel John Dagworthy, 1775; captain second Delaware battalion, under Colonel Samuel Patterson, 1776–1777; captain in Colonel Grayson's regiment of Virginia line, 1777–1779; major in Colonel Nathaniel Gist's regiment of Virginia and Maryland line, 1779–1781; brigade major and inspector to General Muhlenburg, 1780–1781; prisoner of war on parole, July 18, 1782; member of Delaware Society of the Cincinnati; delegate to first Colonial Congress from Delaware, 1786–1788; Governor of Delaware, 1805–1808, and had by his wife, Hannah Morris:

THEODORE MITCHELL, *b.* 7 January, 1804, *d.* 26 September, 1884; *m.*, 6 June, 1837, Rebecca Ann Earp, *d.* 1 July, 1893, and had:

EMILIE REBECCA MITCHELL, *b.* 22 July, 1850, who *m.*, 7 April, 1869, Robert Edgar Hastings, of Philadelphia, *b.* 12 November, 1843, and had:

I.—FLORENCE HASTINGS, *b.* 11 May, 1870, *d.* 31 July, 1870.

II.—MABEL HASTINGS, *b.* 10 October, 1871, a member of the Pennsylvania Society of the Colonial Dames of America, who *m.*, 2 June, 1898, Henry Burnett Robb, of Philadelphia, and had: *Henry Burnett, b.* 12 February, 1899.

III.—THEODORE MITCHELL HASTINGS, *b.* 16 July, 1876, a member of the Delaware Society of the Cincinnati.

2.—FRANCES MORRIS, 1791–1864; *m.*, 1809, Nathaniel Stout Allison, M.D., 1786–1817, and had:

ELIZABETH ALLISON, 1812–1844; *m.*, 1836, Oliver Spencer Janney, 1810–1861, and had:

FRANCES MORRIS JANNEY, *b.* 7 December, 1839, a member of the Pennsylvania Society of the Colonial Dames of America, who *m.*, 5 November, 1857, John Steinmetz, of Philadelphia, *b.* 22 September, 1830, *d.* 30 July, 1877, and had:

I. OLIVER JANNEY STEINMETZ, *b.* July 24, 1858, *d.* August 15, 1858.

II. ELIZABETH MORRIS STEINMETZ, *b.* May 22, 1859, *m.* 27 November, 1383, S. Bevan Miller, and had: *Francis Morris, b.* December 4, 1884; *Elise Bevan, b.* December 22, 1886, and *Allison Janney, b.* January 20, 1891.

III. FRANCES ALLISON STEINMETZ, *b.* October 3, 1860, *d.* July 17, 1866.

IV. SPENCER JANNEY STEINMETZ, *b.* July 3, 1863.

V. and VI. JOHN E. W. and DANIEL C., twins, *b.* 21 August, 1864; *d. inf.*

VII. MARY ELEANOR STEINMETZ, *b.* December 7, 1865.

VIII. EDITH ALLISON STEINMETZ, *b.* July 14, 1867.

IX. JOSEPH ALLISON STEINMETZ, *b.* March 22, 1870.

X. ANITA MAY, *b.* May 9, 1874, *m.*, January 27, 1897, Roland L. Taylor, and had: *Anita Marjory, b.* November 26, 1897.

PEDIGREE XI.

EDWARD I., **King of England**, had by his first wife, Princess Eleanor of Castile:

PRINCESS JOAN D'ACRE, d. 1307, who m., first (his second wife), Gilbert de Clare, Earl of Hertford and Gloucester, d. 1295, and had:

LADY MARGARET DE CLARE (widow of Piers de Gavestone, Earl of Cornwall), who m., secondly, Hugh d'Audley, Earl of Gloucester, d. 1347, and had:

LADY MARGARET D'AUDLEY, who m. (his first wife) Sir Ralph de Stafford, K.G., created, in 1351, Earl of Stafford, d. 1372, and had:

SIR HUGH DE STAFFORD, K.G., second Earl of Stafford, d. 1386, who m. Lady Philippa, daughter of Sir Thomas de Beauchamp, K.G., Earl of Warwick, also of Royal Descent, and had:

LADY MARGARET DE STAFFORD, who m. (his first wife), Sir Ralph de Neville, K.G., created, in 1399, Earl of Westmoreland, d. 1425, and had:

LADY MARGARET DE NEVILLE, who m. Richard le Scrope, d. 1420, and had:

HENRY LE SCROPE, fourth Baron le Scrope, of Bolton, d. 1459, m. Lady Elizabeth, daughter of John le Scrope, Lord of Masham and Upsal, and had:

LADY ELIZABETH LE SCROPE, who m. Oliver St. John, of Lydiard-Tregoze, Wilts, d. 1497, also of Royal Descent, and had:

SIR JOHN ST. JOHN, of Lydiard-Tregoze, only son, knighted by Henry VIII., d. at sea, 1512, who m. Lady Jane, daughter of Sir John Ewarby, K.B., of Farley, Hants, also of Royal Descent, and had:

JOHN ST. JOHN, of Lydiard-Tregoze, m. Lady Margaret, daughter of Sir Richard Carew, of Bedington, Surrey, and had:

NICHOLAS ST. JOHN, of Lydiard-Tregoze, m. Lady Elizabeth, daughter of Sir Richard Blount, of Mapledurham, Oxford, and had:

SIR JOHN ST. JOHN, of Lydiard-Tregoze (second son, brother and heir of Oliver, Viscount Grandison), who m. Lady Lucy, daughter of Sir Walter Hungerford, of Farley Castle, Wilts, and had:

SIR JOHN ST. JOHN, of Lydiard-Tregoze, knighted in 1608, created a

Baronet in 1611. He *m.*, first, Lady Anne, daughter of Sir Thomas Leighton, of Feckingham, Wilts, also of Royal Descent, and had:

LADY ANNE ST. JOHN, *b.* 5 November, 1614, who *m.*, first, Sir Francis Henry Lee, second Baronet, of Quarendon, *d.* 26 July, 1639, and had:

FRANCIS HENRY LEE, second son (see Foster's "Royal Descents," p. 162), father of:

SIR EDWARD HENRY LEE, of Ditchley, Oxford, third baronet, *d.* 1716, who was elevated to the peerage in 1674, as Baron of Spellesburg, Viscount Quarendon and Earl of Litchfield, which titles became extinct with the death of the fourth Earl, in 1778. He had by his wife, Lady Charlotte Fitz-Roy, a natural daughter of Charles II., King of England, by Lady Barbara Villiers, Duchess of Cleveland:

LADY CHARLOTTE LEE, who *m.*, 2 June, 1698, Benedict Leonard Calvert, fifth Lord Baltimore, of Baltimore, county Longford, Ireland, M.P. for Harwich, who *d.* 16 April, 1715, son of Charles, fourth Lord Baltimore, Governor of the Province of Maryland, 1661 (see Foster's "Yorkshire Pedigrees"), and had:

BENEDICT LEONARD CALVERT, M.P. for Harwich, Governor of the Province of Maryland, *b.* 1700, *d.* 1751–52; *m.*, 20 July, 1730, Lady Mary, daughter of Sir Thomas Jansen, Bart., and had:

ELEANOR CALVERT, *d.* 28 April, 1811, who *m.*, first, 3 February, 1774, John Parke Custis, of "Abingdon" (the stepson of President Washington), *b.* at "The White House," on the Pamunky River, New Kent county, Virginia, 1753, *d.* at "Eltham," 5 November, 1781, son of Daniel Parke Custis (and his wife, Martha Dandridge, who *m.*, secondly, President Washington), and had:

MARTHA PARKE CUSTIS, *b.* at General Washington's "Mt. Vernon," 31 December, 1777, *d.* at "Tudor Place," 13 July, 1854; *m.* at "Hope Park," Fairfax county, Virginia, 6 January, 1795, Thomas Peter, of "Tudor Place," Georgetown, District of Columbia, *b.* 4 January, 1769, at "Peter's Square," Georgetown, *d.* at "Tudor Place," 16 April, 1834, and had:

BRITANNIA WELLINGTON PETER, President of the District of Columbia Society of the Colonial Dames of America, *b.* at "Tudor Place," 28 January, 1815, who *m.*, 8 December, 1842 (his second wife), Commodore Beverley Kennon, United States Navy, also of Royal Descent, accidentally *k.* by the bursting of a gun on the United States Frigate "Princeton," 28 February, 1844, and had:

MARTHA CUSTIS KENNON, *b.* at "Tudor Place," 18 October, 1843, who *m.* at "Tudor Place," 23 April, 1867, Armistead Peter, M.D., of Georgetown, and had: *Armistead.*

PEDIGREE XII.

HUGH CAPET, King of France, had, by his wife Lady Adela, daughter of William, Duke of Aquitaine:

ROBERT THE PIOUS, KING OF FRANCE, who had, by his second wife, Lady Constance, daughter of William, Count of Provence :

PRINCESS ADELA (widow of Richard III., Duke of Normandy), who *m.*, secondly, 1027, Baldwin V., Count of Flanders, *d.* 1067, and had:

BALDWIN VI., COUNT OF FLANDERS and Artois, *m.* Countess Richildis, daughter and heiress of Raginerus V., Count of Hainault, and had:

GILBERT DE GAUNT (nephew of Queen Maud of England), who had:

LADY EMMA, *m.* Alan de Percy, the Great, second Baron Percy, and had :

WILLIAM DE PERCY, third Baron, who *m.* Lady Alice, daughter of Richard Fitz-Gilbert de Tonebridge de Clare, of county Suffolk, created Earl of Clare, justiciary of England, *d.* 1090, and had:

LADY AGNES DE PERCY, who *m.* Josceline de Louvaine, Baron de Percy, son of Godfrey, Duke of Brabrant, Louvain and Lother, d. 1140, also of Royal Descent, and had:

HENRY DE PERCY, eldest son, *d. v. p.*, who *m.* Lady Isabel, daughter of Adam de Brus, and had:

WILLIAM DE PERCY, sixth Baron Percy, *d.* 1245; *m.* Lady Eleanor, daughter of Lord Bardolf, and had:

HENRY DE PERCY, seventh Baron Percy, *d.* 1272; *m.* Lady Margaret de Warren, also of Royal Descent, and had:

HENRY DE PERCY, tenth Baron Percy, *d.* 1315; *m.* Lady Eleanor Fitz-Alan, also of Royal Descent, and had :

HENRY DE PERCY, eleventh Baron Percy, of Alnwick, *d.* 1352 ; *m.* Lady Imania (or Ida), daughter of Robert, Baron de Clifford, of Appleby, *k.* at Bannockburn, 1313, and his wife, Lady Maud de Clare, both of Royal Descent, and had:

LADY MAUD DE PERCY, who *m.* (his first wife) Sir John de Neville, K.G., third Baron Neville, of Raby, *d.* 17 October, 1389, and had :

SIR RALPH DE NEVILLE, K.G., fourth Baron, created in 1399, Earl of Westmoreland, Earl Marshal of England for life, *d.* 1425, who had, by his second wife, Lady Joane de Beaufort, also of Royal Descent, widow of Sir Robert de Ferrers:

SIR EDWARD NEVILL, K.G., BARON BERGAVENNY, fourth son, *d.* 18 October, 1476, who *m.*, first, 1435, Lady Elizabeth Beauchamp, 1415–1447, only child of Richard, first Earl of Worcester, and his wife, Lady Isabel de Despencer, a descendant of King Edward III., and had:

SIR GEORGE NEVILL, Knt., 1440–1492, second Baron Bergavenny, who *m.*, first, Margaret, *d.* 1485, daughter of Sir Hugh Fenne, sub-treasurer of England, and had:

SIR GEORGE NEVILL, K.B., third Baron Bergavenny, who had, by his third wife, Lady Mary Stafford, daughter of Edward, Duke of Buckingham, who was beheaded on Tower Hill:

LADY URSULA NEVILL, who *m.* (his first wife) Sir Warham St. Leger, Knt., of Ulcombe, sheriff of Kent, 1560; chief-governor of Munster, 1566; member of the Privy Council, 1585 (see Lodge's " Peerage of Ireland," 1754, vol. iii.). He was a bitter foe of the Irish, and he and Hugh Maguire, Prince of Farmagh, killed each other in a battle while heading their forces, 4 March, 1599. Sir Warham and Lady Ursula had:

SIR ANTHONY ST. LEGER, Knt. (see Berry's " Kent Pedigrees," Foster's " Royal Descents "), of Ulcombe, *m.* Mary, daughter of Sir Thomas Scott, and had:

SIR WARHAM ST. LEGER, of Ulcombe, *d. ante* 1632; *m.* Mary, daughter of Sir Rowland Hayward, lord mayor of London, *d.* 1593, and had:

URSULA ST. LEGER, 1600–1672, who *m.* Rev. Daniel Horsmanden, D.D., rector of Ulcombe, Kent, removed by Parliament, 1643, *d.* 1654, and had:

COLONEL WARHAM HORSMANDEN,* of Purleigh, Essex, came to Virginia in 1649, but returned to England and *d.* there, who had:

MARIA HORSMANDEN, *d.* 9 November, 1699, who *m.* Colonel William Byrd, *b.* 1652, who came to Virginia in 1674 from London, son of John and Grace (Stegg) Byrd, and *d.* 1704 (see Munsell's " Byrd MSS.," Dr. Page's " Page Family History," Neill's " Virginia Carolorum," Brown's " Genesis of the United States "), and had:

I.—COLONEL WILLIAM BYRD, 2d, of "Westover," Charles City county, Virginia, 1674–1744, president of H. M. Council in Virginia, *etc.; m.*, first, Lucy, daughter of Colonel Daniel Parke, and had by her:

WILHELMINA BYRD, who *m.* Thomas Chamberlayne, of New Kent county, Virginia, and had:

EDWARD PYE CHAMBERLAYNE, who had by his second wife, Mary Bickerton Webb:

---

* The following ladies, members of the National Society of the Colonial Dames of America, are also of Royal Descent, through Colonel Horsmanden:

MISS EVELYN B. McCANDLISH, Maryland State Society.

MRS. ARTHUR E. POULTNEY, Maryland State Society.

MRS. ALEX. B. RANDALL, Maryland State Society.

Lucy Parke Chamberlayne, who *m.* Robert Carter Williamson, of Brook Hill, Henrico county, Virginia, and had:

Mary Amanda Williamson, a member of the Virginia Society of the Colonial Dames of America, who *m.* John Stewart, of Bute, Scotland, and had:

    1.—Mary Amanda, *d.* 1889, wife of Thomas Pinckney. Issue: *Charles Cotesworth.*

    2. Isobel Lamont Stewart, a member of the Virginia Society of the Colonial Dames of America, who *m.* Joseph Bryan, of Richmond, Virginia, and had: *John Stewart, Robert Coalter, Jonathan Randolph, St. George Tucker,* and *Thomas Pinckney.*

    3. Marion McIntosh, wife of Rt. Rev. George W. Peterkin, D.D., Bishop of West Virginia. Issue: *Mary Stewart.*

    4. Lucy Williamson; 5. Anne Carter; 6. Norma; 7. Elizabeth Hope.

Colonel William Byrd, 2d, of "Westover"; *m.,* secondly, Maria, daughter of Thomas Taylor, of Kensington, England, and had by her:

    I.—Maria Byrd, who *m.* (his second wife) Colonel Landon Carter, of "Sabine Hall," Richmond county, Virginia, also of Royal Descent, and had:

Landon Carter, of Pittsylvania county, Virginia; *m.* Judith Fauntleroy, also of Royal Descent, and had:

Wormeley Carter, *m.,* 1787, Sarah Edwards, and had:

Wormeley Carter, 1792–1821; *m.,* 1815, Lucinda Washington Alexander, and had:

Judge William Alexander Carter, 1818–1881; *m.,* 1848, Mary Eliza Hamilton, and had:

Mary Ada Carter, a member of the Pennsylvania Society of the Colonial Dames of America, who *m.,* 1874, Joseph K. Corson, M.D., surgeon United States Army, also of Royal Descent, and had: *Mary Carter,* 1876–1890, and *Edward Foulke, b.* 1883.

    II.—Anne Byrd, who *m.* Charles Carter, of "Cleve," also of Royal Descent, and had:

    1.—Maria Carter, who *m.* William Armistead, and had:

Eleanor Bowles Armistead, who *m.* Judge William McMechen, of Baltimore, Maryland, and had:

Sidney Jane McMechen, who *m.* John Charles Van Wyck, of Baltimore, Maryland, and had:

Sidney McMechen Van Wyck, *b.* 6 April, 1830, *d.* at San Francisco, California, 27 April, 1887; *m.* Nannie Churchill Crittenden, also of Royal Descent, and had:

LAURA SANCHEZ VAN WYCK, of San Francisco, a member of the California Society of the Colonial Dames of America, the Order of the Crown, *etc.*

2.—LANDON CARTER, of "Cleve," *m.* Mildred Willis, also of Royal Descent, and had:

LUCY LANDON CARTER, *m.* General John Minor, of Fredericksburg, Virginia, and had:

LUCIUS HORATIO MINOR, of "Edgewood"; *m.* Catherine Francés Berkeley, also of Royal Descent, and had:

MARY WILLIS MINOR, of Baltimore, a member of the Maryland Society of the Colonial Dames of America.

III.—JANE BYRD, who *m.*, 1746, John Page, of "North End," Matthews county, Virginia (son of Mann Page, of "Rosewell"), a member of the Virginia Council, and had:

1.—JUDITH Page, who *m.*, 1775, Colonel Hugh Nelson, of Yorktown, Virginia (son of William Nelson, president of the Virginia Council), and had:

JANE BYRD NELSON, who *m.*, 1798, Francis Walker, of "Castle Hill," Albemarle county, Virginia, M.C., 1793–1795, and had:

JUDITH PAGE WALKER, 1802–1882; *m.*, 24 March, 1820, William Cabell Rives, of "Castle Hill," Albemarle county, 1793–1868, United States Senator, United States Minister to France, *etc.*, and had:

ALFRED LANDON RIVES, of Mobile, Alabama; *m.*, 1859, Sadie McMurdo, of Richmond, Virginia, and had:

AMÉLIE LOUISE RIVES, a member of the Virginia Society of the Colonial Dames of America, who *m.*, first, John Armstrong Chanler, of New York City, and *m.*, secondly, P. Troubetskoy.

2.—LUCY PAGE, who *m.*, 1792, Francis Nelson, of "Mt. Air," Hanover county, Virginia, son of Governor Thomas Nelson, of Yorktown, Virginia, and had:

JUDITH NELSON, who *m.* (first wife) Mann Page, of Greenland, Virginia, and had:

FRANCIS NELSON PAGE, United States Army, *d.* near Fort Smith, Arkansas, 25 March, 1860; *m.* Susan Duval, and had:

LUCY NELSON PAGE, a member of the Virginia Society of the Colonial Dames of America, who *m.* William A. Hardaway, M.D., of St. Louis, Mo., and had: *Augusta, b.* 29 October, 1877, *d.*

12 December, 1882; *Page, b.* 17 June, 1881, *d.* 8 June, 1890, and *Francis Page, b.* 26 April, 1888.

IV.—Colonel William Byrd, 3d, of "Westover," 1728–1777, who *m.*, first, Elizabeth Hill, daughter of Colonel John Carter, of "Shirley," King's counsel, *etc.*, also of Royal Descent, and his wife Elizabeth, daughter of Edward Hill, King's counsel, and had by her:

Thomas Taylor Byrd, who *m.* Mary Anne, daughter of William Armistead, of "Hesse," Gloucester county, Virginia, and his wife Maria, daughter of Colonel Charles Carter, of "Cleve," also of Royal Descent, and his second wife, Ann, daughter of Colonel William Byrd, Jr., aforesaid, and had:

Maria Carter Byrd, who *m.* Judge Philip Narbonne Nicholas, of Richmond, Va., also of Royal Descent, and had:

Elizabeth Byrd Nicholas, of Washington, D. C., a member of the District of Columbia Society of the Colonial Dames of America, and national treasurer of the general society.

Colonel William Byrd, 3d, of "Westover," *m.*, secondly, 29 January, 1761, Mary, 1740–1814, daughter of Charles and Ann (Shippen) Willing, of Philadelphia, Pennsylvania, and had by her:

Maria Horsmanden Byrd, *b.* 26 November, 1761, *m.*, 1784, John Page, of "Broadneck," *b.* 29 June, 1760, *d.* 17 September, 1838, also of Royal Descent, and had:

1.—Abby Byrd Page, *b.* 1798, *d.* April, 1888, who *m.* John Hopkins, of Winchester, Virginia, also of Royal Descent, and had:

William Evelyn Hopkins, Commodore United States Navy, *b.* 10 January, 1821, *d.* 25 October, 1894; *m.*, 8 March, 1852, Louise Kimball, *b.* March, 1832, and had:

Maria Byrd Hopkins, a member of the Virginia and California Societies of the Colonial Dames of America, *b.* 2 February, 1853, who *m.*, at Mare Island, California, 30 April, 1873, Colonel Stuart Selden Wright, of Fresno, California, also of Royal Descent, and had:

Louise Kimball Wright, *b.* 6 December, 1874, a member of the Virginia and California Societies of the Colonial Dames of America, who *m.*, 7 June, 1895, John Mannen McClure, of Oakland, California, and had: *Mannen Wright, b.* 7 April, 1896.

2.—Sarah Walker Page, *m.*, 1815, Major Thomas M. Nelson, United States Army, member of Congress from Virginia, 1816–1819, and presidential elector, 1829 and 1833, and had:

Maria Byrd Nelson, who *m.* William Gray Woolfolk, of Columbus, Georgia, and had:

4

Rosa Woolfolk, a member of the Maryland Society of the Colonial Dames of America, who *m.* Robert Ober, of Baltimore, and had: *Gustavus* and *Maria Byrd Nelson.*

II.—Anne Ursula Byrd, who *m.* Robert Beverley, of " Beverly Park," Drysdale parish, King and Queen county, Virginia, and had:

Colonel William Beverley, only son, of " Beverley Manor," Essex county, and " Blandfield," Virginia, member of the House of Burgesses, 1748, *d.* 1756; *m.* Elizabeth Bland (sister of Colonel Richard Bland, of the Virginia Line), and had:

Robert Beverley, only son, of " Wakefield," Culpeper county, Virginia, *d.* 1800; *m.* Maria Carter of " Sabine Hall," Virginia, also of Royal Descent, and had:

Evelyn Byrd Beverley, *m.*, first, George Lee, and, secondly, Patrick Hume Douglas, M.D., of Leesburg, Loudoun county, Virginia, *d.* 1837, and had:

I.—William Byrd Douglas, *b.* at Leesburg, 8 December, 1815, *d.* Nashville, Tennessee, 13 December, 1882; *m.*, first, Martha Rebecca Bright, and had by her:

Mary Margaret Douglas, a member of the Virginia Society of the Colonial Dames of America, who *m.*, first, James R. Buckner, of Nashville, and had:

James R. Buckner, Jr., of Nashville; *m.* Louise Eve, and had : *Edward Richards, b.* 1 February, 1892, and *Jane Eve, b.* 9 May, 1893.

Mary Margaret Douglas, *m.*, secondly, Edward D. Richards, of Nashville, and had:

Evelyn Byrd Richards, *m.* Owen H. Wilson, M.D., of Nashville.

William Byrd Douglas, of Nashville, 1815–1882; *m.*, secondly, Mrs. Hannah (Underwood) Cook, and had by her: *Bruce, m.* Ella Kirkman, and had issue, and

Ellen Douglas, a member of the Virginia Society of the Colonial Dames of America, who *m.* Dr. G. A. Baxter, of Chattanooga, Tennessee (son of Judge John Baxter, of Knoxville, Tennessee), and had : *Byrd Douglas* and *Bruce Beverley.*

II.—Hugh Douglas, who *m.* Nancy Hamilton, and had:

Evelyn Beverley Douglas, a member of the Virginia Society of the Colonial Dames of America, who *m.* John Sergeant Wise, of New York City, and had: *John S., d.; Hugh D., Henry Alexander, John S., Hamilton, d.; Eva Douglas, Jennings C., Margaretta,* and *Byrd Douglas.*

PEDIGREE XIII.

EDWARD I., King of England, had by his first wife, Princess Eleanor, daughter of Ferdinand III., King of Castile:

PRINCESS ELIZABETH PLANTAGENET, widow of John de Vere, who *m.*, secondly, 1306, Humphrey de Bohun, fourth Earl of Hereford and Essex; lord high constable of England, *k.* 16 March, 1321, and had:

LADY ELEANOR DE BOHUN, who *m.*, 1327, James Butler, lord butler of Ireland and second Earl of Carrick, and Earl of Ormond, and had:

JAMES BUTLER, second Earl of Ormond; lord butler and lord justice of Ireland 1331–1382, who *m.* Lady Elizabeth, daughter of Sir John d'Arcy, first Baron d'Arcy, of Platten, County Meath; lord justice of Ireland, and had:

LADY ELEANOR BUTLER, *d.* 1392, who *m.*, 1359, Gerald Fitz-Maurice Fitz-Gerald, fourth Earl of Desmond, lord justice of Ireland, murdered in 1397, and had:

JAMES FITZ-GERALD, seventh Earl of Desmond; Governor of Limerick, Waterford, Cork and Kerry, who *m.* Lady Mary, daughter of Ulick Burke Mac William-Iachter, a chieftain in Connaught, and had:

LADY HONORA FITZ-GERALD, who *m.* Thomas Fitz-Maurice, eighth Lord of Kerry, *d.* 1469 (see Lodge's "Peerage of Ireland," 1754, Vol. I.), and had:

LADY JOAN FITZ-MAURICE, *m.* (his first wife) Turlogh-donn O'Brien, prince of Limerick and Thomond, *d.* 1528, a descendant of King Brian Boru, and had:

MURROUGH O'BRIEN, third son, created Earl of Thomond for life, 1 July, 1543, and Baron Inchiquin, *d.* 1551; *m.* Eleanor, daughter of Thomas Fitz-Gerald, Knight of the Valley, and had (see Lodge's "Peerage of Ireland," 1754, Vol. IV., page 12, and 1789, Vol. III., page 417, and O'Hart's "Irish Landed Gentry," page 128):

LADY HONORIA O'BRIEN, *m.* Sir Dermod O'Shaughnassie, Knt., of Gortinshigorie (or Gort), County Galway (see his royal descent in O'Hart's "Irish Pedigrees," 3d edition, pages 393–5, and see Blake-Foster's "The Irish Chieftains," 1872, and Hardiman's "West Connaught"), and had:

LADY MAUD O'SHAUGHNASSIE, who *m.*, about 1560, Edmund Bermingham, fifteenth Baron of Athenry (see Lodge's "Peerage of Ireland," 1754, Vol. IV.), and had:

RICHARD BERMINGHAM, sixteenth Baron of Athenry, 1570–1635; who *m.* " a daughter of the family of Tuite," and had :

EDWARD FITZ-RICHARD BERMINGHAM, seventeenth Baron of Athenry, *d.* 1640; *m.* Mary, daughter of Sir Festus Burke, of Donamon and Glinsk, County Galway, and had :

LADY ANNE BERMINGHAM, who *m.* The O'Connor-Duinn, of Ballintober, Roscommon (see " The O'Connor-Don " family, O'Hart's " Irish Pedigrees "), and had :

CLARE O'CONNOR-DUINN, who *m.* Charles O'Carroll, of Ely, O'Carroll, Kings county, Ireland (see "Stemmata Carrollana," in the Journal of the Royal His. and Arch. Asso. of Ire., Oct. 1883, also O'Ferrell and Betham's O'Clery's " Linea Antiqua," O'Hart's " Irish Land Gentry," *etc.*), and had :

DR. CHARLES CARROLL,* *b.* 1691, who removed to Annapolis, Maryland, about 1737, and was the representative of Annapolis in the Maryland Assembly. He *m.* Dorothy, daughter of Henry Blake and his wife Henrietta Maria, daughter of Philemon Lloyd, speaker of the Lower House of the Assemblies of Maryland in 1681, and granddaughter of Edward Lloyd, a member of the Privy Council and General Assembly of Maryland, and one of the commissioners, under the Lord Protector in 1654, for the governing of the affairs of Maryland, *d.* 29 September, 1755, and had : *Charles*, called the barrister, *b.* 22 March, 1722, *d. s. p.* 28 May, 1783; member of Congress from Maryland, and

MARY CLARE CARROLL, *b.* 13 May, 1727, who *m.*, 21 July, 1747, Nicholas Maccubbin, of Maryland, *d.* 1787, and had : *Mary Clare* and

I.—JAMES MACCUBBIN-CARROLL, who assumed the surname Carroll, under the will of his uncle Charles Carroll, barrister, who *d. s. p.* 28 May, 1783. He *m.* Sophia Dorsey Gough, and had :

1.—JAMES CARROLL, who *m.* Achsah Ridgely, of Hampton, and had :

JAMES CARROLL, of Baltimore, Maryland, who *m.* Mary Wethered Ludlow, and had :

SALLY W. CARROLL, of Baltimore, a member of the Maryland Society of the Colonial Dames of America.

---

* The following ladies, members of the National Society of the Colonial Dames of America, are also of Royal Descent through Dr. Charles Carroll :

MRS. ETHAN ALLEN (deceased), Maryland State Society.

MRS. EDWARD S. BEALL, Maryland State Society.

MISS LOUISE OGLE BEALL, Maryland State Society.

MRS. J. ALEX. PRESTON, Maryland State Society.

MISS MARY WINN, Maryland State Society.

MRS. JOHN O. TURNBULL, Maryland State Society.

2.—CHARLES RIDGELEY CARROLL, *m.* Rebecca Pue, and had:

REBECCA CARROLL, who *m.* Carroll Spence, son of Commodore Robert Trail Spence, United States Navy, and his wife Mary Clare, sister of the aforesaid James Maccubbin-Carroll, and had:

KATE STYLES SPENCE, a member of the Maryland Society of the Colonial Dames of America, who *m,* Charles W. Washburn, of Baltimore.

II.—CHARLES MACCUBBIN, of Maryland, *b.* 1 January, 1757, *d.* 20 June, 1799; *m.* 12 May, 1793, Sarah Allen, *b.* 22 April, 1774, and had:

ELEANOR MACCUBBIN, *b.* 11 May, 1795, *d.* 9 December, 1858; *m.,* 27 October, 1812, her cousin, George Mackubin, *b.* 9 March, 1789, *d.* 11 January, 1853, treasurer of Maryland, 1826–1843, and had:

1.—CHARLES NICHOLAS MACKUBIN, of Annapolis, Maryland, *m.* Ellen Fay, of Boston, Massachusetts, and had:

FLORENCE MACKUBIN, of Baltimore, *b.* at Florence, Italy, a member of the Maryland Society of the Colonial Dames of America.

2.—RICHARD CREAGH MACKUBIN, of "Strawberry Hill," Anne Arundel county, Maryland, *b.* 8 August, 1815, *d.* 18 November, 1865; *m.,* 31 October, 1839, Hester Ann Worthington, *b.* 28 November, 1818, *d.* 22 February, 1848, and had:

ELEANOR MACKUBIN, a member of the Maryland Society of the Colonial Dames of America, who *m.,* 14 June, 1866, Charles Baltimore Calvert, of "Riversdale" and "Mac Alpine," Prince George county, Maryland, and had:

I.—ELEANOR CALVERT, *m.,* 14 June, 1892, William Gibson Carey, and had: *Charles Baltimore Calvert, b.* Lynn, Massachusetts, 8 November, 1893, and *William G., b.* Schenectady, New York, 3 July, 1896.

II.—HESTER VIRGINIA CALVERT, *m.,* 20 September, 1899, Henry Walter Lilly, M.D.

III.—CHARLOTTE AUGUSTA; IV. CHARLES BENEDICT (dead); V. RICHARD CREAGH MACKUBIN; VI. GEORGE HENRY; VII. ROSALIE EUGENIA STIER; VIII. CHARLES BALTIMORE; IX. ELIZABETH STEUART.

THE ROYAL DESCENT

OF

MRS. FRANCIS LEE SMITH,

OF ALEXANDRIA, VA.

EDWARD I., King of England⸗Princess Eleanor of Castile.

Princess Joan Plantagenet⸗Gilbert de Clare, Earl of Gloucester and Hertford.

Lady Margart de Clare⸗Hugh de Audley, Earl of Gloucester.

Lady Margaret de Audley⸗Sir Ralph de Stafford, K. G., Earl of Stafford.

Sir Hugh de Stafford, K. G., Earl of Stafford⸗Lady Philippa de Beauchamp.

Lady Margaret de Stafford⸗Sir Ralph de Neville, K. G., Earl of Westmoreland.

Ralph de Neville, of Oversley, Warwickshire⸗Lady Mary de Ferrers.

John de Neville, of Wymersley, Yorkshire⸗Lady Elizabeth de Newmarch.

Joan de Neville⸗Sir William Gascoigne, of Gawthrope, Yorkshire.

Sir William Gascoigne, of Gawthrope, York⸗Lady Margaret de Percy.

Lady Elizabeth Gascoigne⸗Gilbert de Talboys, of Kyme.

Sir George de Talboys, of Kyme⸗(Name unknown.)

Lady Anne de Talboys⸗Sir Edward Dymoke, of Scrivelsby, Lincolnshire.

Lady Frances Dymoke⸗Thomas Windebank, of Haines Hill, Berkshire.

Lady Mildred Windebank⸗Robert Reade, Linkenholt Manor, Southampton.

Col. George Reade, of Gloucester Co., Va.⸗Elizabeth Martian.

Mildred Reade⸗Col. Augustine Warner, Jr., of " Warner's Hall."

Mary Warner (m. 17 February, 1680)⸗John Smith, of " Purton," Gloucester Co., Va.

Augustine Smith, of " Purton," 1687–1756⸗Sarah Carver.

John Smith, of " Shooters' Hill," Va., 1715–1771⸗Mary Jacqueline.

Augustine Smith, of " Shooters' Hill," 1738–1774⸗Margaret Boyd.

Mary Jacqueline Smith, 1773–1846⸗John Cripps Vowell, of Alexandria, Va.

Sarah Gosnelle Vowell, member of the National   Francis Lee Smith, of Fauquier Co., Va.
Society of the Colonial Dames of America. *Issue.*

PEDIGREE XIV.

ETHELRED II., King of England, 978–1016, *m.*, first, Lady Elgiva, or Elgifa, *d.* 1003, daughter of Earl Thorad, and had by her:

PRINCESS ELGIVA (sister of King Edmund Ironsides), who *m.* Uthred, Prince of Northumberland, and had:

LADY ALDIGITHA, who *m.* Maldred (brother of King Duncan I., murdered by his nephew, Macbeath, in 1041), eldest son of Crynan, Lord of the Western Isles and Archthane of Dul Argyle, and his wife Lady Beatrice, daughter of Malcolm II., King of Scots, and had:

COSPATRICK, Earl of Northumberland and Dunbar, who had:

LADY GUNILDA (sister of Cospatrick, first Earl of Dunbar), who *m.* Orme, feudal Baron of Seaton, and had:

COSPATRICK, first feudal Baron of Workington, *d.* 1179, who had:

THOMAS DE WORKINGTON, *d.* 7 December, 1152, who had:

PATRICK DE CURWEN, of Workington, second son, *d.* 1212, who had:

GILBERT DE CURWEN, of Workington, who had:

GILBERT DE CURWEN, of Workington, eldest son, *d.* 1278, who *m.* Edith Harrington, *d.* 1353, and had:

GILBERT DE CURWEN, of Workington, eldest son, *d.* 1370, who had:

GILBERT DE CURWEN, of Workington, *b.* 1403; *m.* Alice Lowther, of Lowther, and had:

WILLIAM DE CURWEN, of Workington, who had by his second wife, Margaret, daughter of Sir John Croft, Knt. :

CHRISTOPHER CURWEN, of Workington (see Cumberland Visitations, 1615), *m.* Elizabeth Hudleston, of Millum, and had:

THOMAS CURWEN, of Workington Hall, Cumberland (see Burke's "Royal Descents," Ped. 37, and Jackson's "Cumberland Pedigrees," p. 288), who *m.* Anne, daughter of Sir Robert Lowther, Knt., and had:

ELIZABETH CURWEN, who *m.* John Cleburne, of Cleburne Hall and Bampton, Westmoreland, *d.* 8 August, 1489 (see O'Hart's "Irish Pedigrees," third series, and O'Hart's "Irish Landed Gentry"), and had:

THOMAS CLEBURNE, of Cleburne Hall, *b.* 1467, who had:

ROBERT CLEBURNE, of Cleburne Hall and Killesby, York, who *m.* Emma, daughter of George Kirkbride, of Kirkbride, Northumberland, and had:

EDMUND CLEBURNE, of Cleburne Hall and Killesby, who *m.* Anne Layton, of Dalemain, Cumberland, and had:

RICHARD CLEBURNE, of Cleburne Hall and Killesby, *d.* 4 January, 1607, who *m.* Eleanor, daughter of Launcelot Lancaster, of Stockbridge and Barton, Westmoreland, and had:

EDMOND CLAIBORNE, of Cleburne Hall, who *m.*, 1 September, 1576, Grace, daughter of Allan Bellingham, of Helsington and Levins, and had:

CAPTAIN WILLIAM CLAIBORNE, of "Romancoke," King William county, Virginia, *b.* 1587. He settled in Virginia in 1621, and was secretary and treasurer of the Virginia Colony, and surveyor-general of the "Old Dominion." Grants of twenty-five thousand acres of land are of record in his name in the Virginia land office. He *m.*, in 1638, in London, Jane Buller, and, dying before 1680, had issue:

I.—LIEUTENANT-COLONEL WILLIAM CLAIBORNE, of "Romancoke," Virginia, who had:

WILLIAM CLAIBORNE, *d.* 1705, who had:

WILLIAM CLAIBORNE, *m.* Elizabeth Whitehead, and had:

PHILIP WHITEHEAD CLAIBORNE, of "Liberty Hall," King William county, Virginia, who *m.* Elizabeth Dandridge, also of Royal Descent, and had:

PHILADELPHIA CLAIBORNE, who *m.* Abner Waugh, and had:

SARAH SPOTSWOOD WAUGH, *m.* James Lyons, and had:

LUCY LYONS, *m.* John Hopkins, and had:

JOHN HOPKINS, *m.* Abby Byrd Page, also of Royal Descent, and had:

WILLIAM EVELYN HOPKINS, *m.* Louise Kimball, and had:

MARIA BYRD HOPKINS, *m.* Stuart Selden Wright, also of Royal Descent, and had:

LOUISE KIMBALL WRIGHT, a member of the Virginia Society of the Colonial Dames of America, who *m.* John M. McClure, of Oakland, California. *Issue.*

II.—LIEUTENANT-COLONEL THOMAS CLAIBORNE, of "Romancoke," *b.* 17 August, 1647, *d.* 7 October, 1683; *bur.* at "Romancoke." He had by his wife, Sarah, whose surname has not been preserved (she *m.*, secondly, Captain Thomas Bray):

CAPTAIN THOMAS CLAIBORNE, of "Sweet Hall," King William county, *b.* 16 December, 1680, *d.* 16 August, 1732, *bur.* at "Sweet Hall." He *m.*, thirdly, Anne, *b.* 20 May, 1684, *d.* 4 May, 1733, daughter of Henry Fox, of King William county, and his wife, Anna West, also of Royal Descent, and had by her:

1.—COLONEL NATHANIEL CLAIBORNE, of "Sweet Hall"; *m.* Jane, daughter of William Cole, of Warwick county, Virginia, and had:

WILLIAM CLAIBORNE, of Manchester, Virginia, *d.* 29 September, 1809, *m.* Mary, daughter of Ferdinand Leigh, of King William county, and had:

NATHANIEL HERBERT CLAIBORNE, *b.* Surrey county, Virginia, 14 November, 1777, *d.* Franklin county, Virginia, 15 August, 1859. He was for many years a member of both branches of the Virginia Legislature, and a member of the council during the war of 1812; member of Congress, 1825–1837, *etc.* He *m.*, 1815, Elizabeth Archer Binford, of Goochland county, Virginia, and had:

I.—ELIZABETH HERBERT CLAIBORNE, 1829–1855, *m.*, 1851, James Coleman Otey, of Bedford county, Virginia, and had:

LULIE LEIGH OTEY, a member of the Virginia and California Societies of the Colonial Dames of America, who *m.*, 1870, Hervey Darneal, of Alameda, California, and had: *Susan Cole, Herbert Claiborne,* and *Hervey Otey.*

II.—NATHANIEL CHARLES CLAIBORNE, of "Rocky Mount," Franklin county, Virginia, who *m.* Mildred Kyle Morris, and had:

JENNIE CLAIBORNE, *b.* 5 September, 1853, at "Rocky Mount," a member of the Missouri Society of the Colonial Dames of America, who *m.*, 21 October, 1874, Robert McCormick Adams, of St. Louis, Missouri, and had: *Hugh Claiborne, b.* 6 September, 1875; *Mildred Kyle, b.* 20 October, 1877, *d.* 20 October, 1886; *Amanda McCormick, b.* 26 August, 1880; *Nathalie, b.* 19 October, 1882; *Virginia Claiborne, b.* 3 August, 1885; *Robert McCormick* and *Marian Kyle,* twins, *b.* 17 June, 1890, and *John Alan Bellingham, b.* 7 February, 1896.

2.—SARAH CLAIBORNE, who *m.* Joseph Thompson, and had:

COLONEL ROGER THOMPSON, who had:

JOSEPH THOMPSON, who *m.* Elizabeth James, and had:

MARY THOMPSON, who *m.* Burr Harrison McCown, and had:

ANNIE McCOWN, who *m.* Alexander Craig, and had:

LOUISE CRAIG, a member of the Virginia and Kentucky Societies of the Colonial Dames of America, who *m.* Samuel A. Culbertson, of Louisville, and had: *William Stuart,* and *Alex. Craig.*

3.—COLONEL AUGUSTINE CLAIBORNE, of "Windsor," King William county, Virginia, *b.* 1721, *d.* 3 May, 1787, an eminent attorney and member of the house of burgesses and State Senate; *m.*, Mary, daughter of Buller Herbert, of "Puddlecock," Dinwiddie county, Virginia, and had:

I.—HERBERT CLAIBORNE, of "Chestnut Grove," New Kent county, Virginia, *b.* 7 August, 1746. He had by his second wife, Mary Burnet Browne, also of Royal Descent:

HERBERT AUGUSTINE CLAIBORNE, of Richmond, Virginia, 1784–1841, *m.* Delia, daughter of James Hayes, of Richmond, and had:

JOHN HAYES CLAIBORNE, of Richmond, Virginia, Major Confederate States Army, who *m.* Anna Virginia, daughter of George Washington Bassett, of "Eltham," New Kent county, Virginia, and had:

DELIA CLAIBORNE, a member of the Virginia Society of the Colonial Dames of America, who *m.*, 10 June, 1885, Simon B. Buckner, of "Glen Lily," Hart county, Kentucky, Lieutenant-General Confederate States Army and Governor of Kentucky, and had: *Simon Bolivar, b.* 18 July, 1886.

II.—MARY CLAIBORNE, *b.* 1744, who *m.*, 1763, General Charles Harrison, of "Berkeley," Virginia, an officer in the Virginia line, Continental Army, *d.* 1796, and had:

ELIZABETH RANDOLPH HARRISON, who *m.* General Daniel Claiborne Butts, also of Royal Descent, and had:

DANIEL CLAIBORNE BUTTS, who *m.* Ariadne Smith, and had:

MARIE ELOISE BUTTS, who *m.* Robert Dunlop, and had:

1.—AGNES DUNLOP, a member of the Virginia Society of the Colonial Dames of America, who *m.* William H. Wight, of Cockeysville, Baltimore county, Maryland, and had: *Robert Dunlop.*

2.—MARIE DUNLOP, a member of the Virginia Society of the Colonial Dames of America, who *m.* Warner Moore, of Richmond, Virginia, and had: *Marie Jean,* and *Warner.*

III.—ANNE CLAIBORNE, *b.* 1749, who *m.*, 1768, Richard Cocke, and had:

BULLER COCKE, who *m.* Elizabeth Barron, and had:

ELIZABETH M. COCKE, who *m.* Louis Trezevant, M.D., and had:

ELIZABETH COCKE TREZEVANT, a member of the Virginia Society of the Colonial Dames of America, who *m.* George de Benneville Keim, of Philadelphia, and had:

1.—JULIA MAYER KEIM, of Philadelphia, a member of the Pennsylvania Society of the Colonial Dames of America.

2.—SUSAN DOUGLASS KEIM, of Philadelphia.

PEDIGREE XV.

HENRY I., King of France, had by his third wife, Anne of Russia:

HUGH THE GREAT, Duke of France and Burgundy, who had by his third wife, *m.* 938, Lady Adelheid, daughter of Herbert IV., Count of Vermandois:

LADY ISABEL DE VERMANDOIS, *d.* 1131 (widow of Robert, Earl of Mellent, *d.* 1118), who *m.*, secondly, William de Warren, second Earl of Surrey (see Watson's "Ancient Earls of Warren and Surrey"), and had:

WILLIAM DE WARREN, third Earl of Surrey, *d. s. p. m.* 1148. He *m.*, before 1143, Lady Alice de Talvace, also of Royal Descent (or Talvas, see Doyle's "Official Baronage"), *d.* 1174, and had:

LADY ISABELLA DE WARREN, heiress, *d.* 1199 (widow of William de Blois, *d. s. p.* 1160), who *m.*, secondly, 1163, Hameline Plantagenet de Warren, fifth Earl of Surrey, *d.* 1202, and had:

LADY ISABEL DE WARREN, who *m.* Roger, Baron le Bigod, created, 1189, Earl of Norfolk; lord high steward of England, and had:

HUGH, second Earl of Norfolk, *d.* 1225; *m.* Lady Maud Marshall, daughter of William le Marshal, Earl of Pembroke, the celebrated Protector during the nonage of Henry III., and had:

SIR HUGH BIGOD, second son, appointed, 22 June, 1257, chief justice of England, resigned in 1260, *d.* 1266 (see Foss's "Lives of the Chief Justices"), who *m.*, first, Joan, daughter of Robert Burnet, and had:

SIR JOHN BIGOD, Knt., younger brother of Roger, the last Earl of Norfolk, *d. s. p.* 1306, and father of

ROGER BIGOD, Knt., of Settington, youngest son, father of

JOAN BIGOD, who *m.*, 1358, Sir William de Chauncy, Knt., last Baron of Skirpenbeck, Yorkshire, which he sold in 1399, and purchased Stepney in Middlesex, and had:

JOHN CHAUNCY, of Stepney, *d.* 1444–1445, who *m.* Margaret, daughter of William Gifford, of Gedleston, and had:

JOHN CHAUNCY, of Sawbridgeworth, Herts, *d.* 7 May, 1479, who *m.* Anne, daughter of John Leventhorp, of Shingey Hall, and had:

JOHN CHAUNCY, of Sawbridgeworth, *d.* 8 June, 1510, who *m.* daughter of Thomas Boyce, and had:

JOHN CHAUNCY, of Pishobury Manor, *d.* 4 June, 1546, who *m.* Elizabeth Proffit, widow of Richard Mansfield, and had:

(67)

HENRY CHAUNCY, of New Place Gifford's, second son and heir, *d.* 14 April, 1587; *m.*, Lucy ——, and had:

GEORGE CHAUNCY, of Yardley-Bury, Hertfordshire, second son, *d.* 1627, whō had by his second wife, Anne, daughter of Edward Welsh, of Great Wymondley, and widow of Edward Humberston (see " Chauncy Pedigree," compiled by Stephen Tucker, Somerset Herald in Ordinary; Chauncy pedigree in Sir Henry Chauncy's " History of Hertfordshire," Fowler's " Chauncy Memorials," *etc.*) :

REV. CHARLES CHAUNCY, D.D., second President of Harvard College, *b.* 5 November, 1592, *d.* Cambridge, Massachusetts, 19 February, 1671; *m.*, 17 March, 1630, Catherine, *b.* 1601, *bapt.* 2 November, 1604, *d.* 23 June, 1667; daughter of Robert Eyre, of New Sarum and Chilhampton, Wilts, a barrister, *bur.* at St. Thomas's, 8 August, 1638, aged 69, and his first wife, Anne, daughter of Rt. Rev. John Still, D.D., bishop of Bath and Wells in 1592, *d.* 26 February, 1607, and his first wife, Anne, daughter of Thomas Arblaster (or Alabaster), of Hadley, Suffolk (see Somersetshire Visitations, 1623; Wiltshire Visitations, 1623; Bliss's Wood's " Athenæ Oxonienses," ii., 829, and Burke's " Commoners," iv., 538), and had:

1.—REV. ISAAC CHAUNCY, M.D., eldest son, *b.* Ware, Eng., 23 August, 1632, educated at Harvard College, was minister at Woodborough, Wiltshire, and was ejected by the Act of Uniformity, in 1662; *d.* London, 28 February, 1712. He had by his wife, Jane, whose surname has not been preserved:

CHARLES CHAUNCY, of Boston, Massachusetts, *d.* 4 May, 1781; *m.* Sarah, daughter of Judge John Walley, who commanded the land force in the expedition of Sir William Phipps against Canada, and had:

MARY CHAUNCY, 1707–1776; *m.* Jacob Cushing, of Hingham; representative for twelve years to the general court, and had:

CHARLES CUSHING, 1744–1809, a representative and member of the Massachusetts Senate; *m.* Hannah Croade, and had:

PRISCILLA CUSHING, *b.* 1779; *m.* Thomas Stearns, and had:

THOMAS STEARNS, *m.* Charlotte Blood, and had:

CHARLOTTE CHAMPE STEARNS, a member of the Massachusetts Society of the Colonial Dames of America, who *m.* Henry Ware Eliot, of St. Louis, Missouri, and had: *Ada, Margaret Dawes, Charlotte C., Marian Cushing, Henry Ware,* and *Thomas Stearns.*

2.—REV. ISRAEL CHAUNCEY, *b.* 1644, *d.* at Stratford, Connecticut, 1703, had by his first wife, Mary Nichols:

REV. ISAAC CHAUNCEY, *b.* 1670, *d.* at Hadley, Conn., 1745; had by his first wife, Sarah, *d.* 1720, daughter of Richard and Abigail (Hudson) Blackleach :

ABIGAIL CHAUNCEY, *b.* 1701, who *m.* (his second wife) Rev. John Graham, *b.* at Edinburgh, 1694; graduate University of Glasgow; came to New England in 1718; *d.* at Woodbury, 1774, and had:

SARAH GRAHAM, who *m.* Gideon Hurd, and had :

LOVE HURD, who *m.* Phineas Chapin, of Salisbury, and had :

MARY CHAPIN, *b.* 1791, *d.* at Milwaukee, Wisconsin, 1860; *m.*, first, at Chapinville, Connecticut, 25 November, 1810, Ezra Jewell, *b.* 27 January, 1786, *d.* at Lyons, New York, 10 October, 1821, and had :

HENRY CHAPIN JEWELL, *b.* at Salisbury, Connecticut, 1 December, 1811 ; *m.*, 1 October, 1833, Mary Anne Elizabeth Russell, *b.* Salisbury, Connecticut, 23 December, 1813, and had :

MARY ELEANOR JEWELL, *b.* Canaan, New York, 3 July, 1842, a member of the Wisconsin Society of the Colonial Dames of America, who *m.*, at Oshkosh, Wisconsin, 18 October, 1864, Edgar Philetus Sawyer, *b.* Crown Point, New York, 4 December, 1842, and had :

1.—MARIA MELVINA SAYWER, *b.* Fond du Lac, Wisconsin, 18 July, 1865, a member of the Massachusetts Society of the Colonial Dames of America, who *m.*, 2 June, 1886, Charles Curry Chase, of Oshkosh, Wisconsin, and had : *Jewell Sperry*, *b.* 28 August, 1888; *Mary Henrietta*, *b.* 2 September, 1892, *d.* 7 September, 1892; *Prescott Sawyer*, *b.* 20 April, 1899, *d.* 1 Feb. 1900.

2.—PHILETUS HORACE SAWYER, *b.* 25 October, 1874 ; *m.*, at Madison, Wisconsin, 12 November, 1896, Caroline, daughter of Governor W. H. Upham, and had : *Kathryn Upham*, *b.* 3 October, 1899.

MARY CHAPIN (widow of Ezra Jewell) *m.*, secondly, John Ashley Dutcher, of Salisbury, Connecticut, and had:

JOHN ASHLEY DUTCHER, JR., *b.* at Salisbury, *d.* at Milwaukee ; *m.* Annette, daughter of Pierpont Edwards, of Kent, Connecticut, and had :

CORNELIA FRANCES DUTCHER, a member of the Massachusetts Society of the Colonial Dames of America, who *m.* Henry Belcher Goodrich, of Milwaukee, Wisconsin, and had : *Cornelia Frances* and *John Dutcher.*

3.—REV. NATHANIEL CHAUNCY, of Hatfield, Massachusetts, *b.* 1639, *d.* 4 November, 1685; *m.*, 12 November, 1673, Abigail, 1645–1704, daughter of John Strong, of Northampton, Massachusetts, and had :

I.—SARAH CHAUNCY, 1683–1767 ; *m.*, 1712, Rev. Samuel Whittelsey, of Wallingford, 1686–1752, and had:

Rev. Chauncy Whittelsey, of New Haven, 1717–1787; *m.*, 1745, Elizabeth Whiting, 1717–1751, and had:

Chauncey Whittelsey, of Middletown, 1746–1812; *m.*, 1770, Lucy Wetmore, 1748–1826, and had:

Lucy Whittelsey, 1773–1856; *m.*, 1797, Joseph Wright Alsop, of Middletown, 1772–1844, and had:

Charles Richard Alsop, of Middletown, 1802–1865; *m.*, 1833, Margaret Elinor Armstrong, 1814–1897, and had:

Catherine Beatty Alsop, a member of the New York Society of the Colonial Dames of America, who *m.* Rev. Christopher S. Leffingwell, of Bar Harbor, Maine, and had: *Alsop, Mary Mütter, Douglas, Christophea, Aimée G.*, and *Alice G.*

II.—Rev. Nathaniel Chauncy, of Durham, Connecticut, *b.* 21 September, 1681, *d.* 1 February, 1756; he was the first graduate of Yale College; *m.*, 12 October, 1708, Sarah, daughter of Captain James Judson, of Stratford, and had:

1.—Rev. Elnathan Chauncy, of Durham, Connecticut, *b.* 10 September, 1724, *d.* 14 May, 1796; *m.*, 6 February, 1760, Elizabeth, 1733–1793, widow of Colonel Samuel Gale, and daughter of Rev. William and Temperance (Gallup) Worthington, of Saybrooke, and had:

Catherine Chauncy, *b.* 6 August, 1765, *d.* 12 April, 1841; *m.*, 14 March, 1790, Reuben Rose Fowler, of Durham, 1763–1844, and had:

Prof. William Chauncey Fowler, LL.D., of Durham, Connecticut, *b.* 1 September, 1793, *d.* 15 January, 1881; author of "The Memorials of the Chaunceys," *etc.*, who *m.*, 21 July, 1825, Harriet, *d.* 30 March, 1844, widow of Edward Cobb, and daughter of Noah Webster, LL.D., the celebrated lexicographer, and had:

Emily Ellsworth Fowler, *b.* 26 August, 1826, *d.* 23 November, 1893; *m.*, 16 December, 1853, Gordon Lester Ford, and had:

1.—Rosalie Greenleaf Ford, *b.* 28 September, 1858, a member of the New York Society of the Colonial Dames of America, who *m.*, 27 May, 1880, William Rufus Barr, of New York City, and had: *Honor Ellsworth, b.* 7 July, 1881; *Rufus Gordon, b.* 12 November, 1884; *Gillian Webster, b.* 12 August, 1886, and *Lester Stacy, b.* 6 March, 1894, *d.* 29 October, 1895.

2.—Emily Ellsworth Ford, a member of the New York Society of the Colonial Dames of America, who *m.* Roswell Skeel, Jr., of New York City. *No issue.*

2.—Colonel Elihu Chauncy, of Durham, *b.* 24 March, 1710, *d.* 10 April, 1791; commanded a regiment in the French War; chief justice of the County Court, and member of the Connecticut Legislature for thirty-nine years; *m.*, 28 March, 1739, Mary, daughter of Samuel Griswold, of Killingworth, and had:

CATHERINE CHAUNCY, *b.* 11 April, 1741, *d.* 8 April, 1830; *m.*, 1 February, 1759, Rev. Elizur Goodrich, D.D., of Durham, 1734–1797, and had:

I.—JUDGE ELIZUR GOODRICH, LL.D., of New Haven, Connecticut, *b.* 24 March, 1761, *d.* 1 November, 1849. He was member of Congress from Connecticut, 1799; mayor of New Haven, 1803–22; professor at Yale College; collector of the port of New Haven; chief justice of New Haven County Court for thirteen years, judge of the Probate Court for seventeen years, *etc.* He *m.*, 1 September, 1785, Anne Willard, *d.* 1818, daughter of Daniel and Esther (Colton) Allen, of Great Barrington, Massachusetts, and had:

NANCY GOODRICH, *b.* 1 January, 1793, *d.* 15 January, 1847; *m.* Henry L. Ellsworth, of Lafayette, Indiana, 1790–1858, commissioner for Indian affairs under President Jackson; chief of the United States Patent Office, *etc.*, and had:

ANNIE GOODRICH ELLSWORTH, a member of the New York Society of the Colonial Dames of America, who *m.*, 1852, Roswell Smith, of New York City, *b.* 30 March, 1829, *d.* 19 April, 1892, and had: *Julia Goodrich Smith, m.*, 21 April, 1879, George Innis, Jr., of New York, and had: *Elizabeth, Julia,* and *George Ellsworth.*

II.—REV. SAMUEL GOODRICH, of Ridgefield, Connecticut, *b.* 12 January, 1763, *d.* 19 April, 1835; *m.*, 29 July, 1784, Elizabeth, *b.* 22 February, 1764, *d.* aged 72 years, daughter of Colonel John Ely, M.D., and his wife Sarah Worthington, of Pachog, and had:

1.—SARAH WORTHINGTON GOODRICH, *b.* 7 August, 1785, *d.* 14 September, 1842, who *m.*, first, 5 February, 1805, Amos Cook, of Danbury, Connecticut, and had:

ELIZABETH COOK, who *m.*, 31 August, 1824, Richard Wayne Stiles, and had:

ELIZABETH WOLCOTT STILES, who *m.*, 15 September, 1847, Cortlandt Parker, of New Jersey, and had:

MARY FRANCES PARKER, a member of the Massachusetts Society of the Colonial Dames of America, who *m.*, 21 August, 1890, Henry Parkman, of Boston, and had: *Mary Elizabeth, b.* 1891; *Edith Wolcott, b.* 1892; *Henry, b.* 1894; *Penelope, b.* 1896, and *Francis, b.* 1898.

SARAH WORTHINGTON GOODRICH, *m.*, secondly, 21 June, 1815, Frederick Wolcott, of Litchfield, Connecticut, and had:

I.—MARY WOLCOTT, who *m.* Theodore Frothingham, and had:

MARY GOODRICH FROTHINGHAM, a member of the Pennsylvania Society of the Colonial Dames of America, who *m.* Charles A. Brinley, of Philadelphia. *Issue.*

II.—CHARLES MOSELEY WOLCOTT, *b.* 20 November, 1816, *d.* 20 November, 1889; *m.*, 26 November, 1849, Katharine A. Rankin, and had:

1.—KATHARINE RANKIN WOLCOTT, *b.* 29 April, 1855, president of the New York Society of the Colonial Dames of America, who *m.*, 8 April, 1896, Samuel Verplanck, of Fishkill-on-Hudson, New York. *No issue.*

2.—HENRY GOODRICH WOLCOTT, *b.* 16 July, 1853, *m.*, 22 May, 1879, Julia S. Hutchins, and had: *Oliver, b.* 14 March, 1880, *d.* 26 December, 1893; *Charles Moseley, b.* 11 August, 1882; *Henry Goodrich, b.* 2 March, 1884, *d.* 10 August, 1885; *Elizabeth Ellsworth, b.* 8 September, 1886; *Katharine Rankin, b.* 16 August, 1888, *d.* 7 December, 1893, and *Julia Hutchins, b.* 1 July, 1892.

3.—ANNETTA RANKIN WOLCOTT, *b.* 29 June, 1857.

2.—CATHARINE GOODRICH, *b.* 2 December, 1792, *d.* 15 October, 1873; *m.*, 12 September, 1817, Daniel Dunbar, of Berlin, Connecticut, *b.* 28 March, 1774, *d.* 1841, and had:

MARGARET ELIZABETH DUNBAR, *b.* 28 May, 1828, a member of the New York Society of the Colonial Dames of America, who *m.*, 4 September, 1849, Homer H. Stuart, of New York, *b.* 1 April, 1810, *d.* 5 October, 1885, and had:

I.—KATHARINE DUNBAR STUART, a member of the New York Society of the Colonial Dames of America, *b.* 22 October, 1852, *m.*, 29 September, 1884, John G. Dunscomb, and had: *Margaret Stuart, b.* 1886; *Cecil, b.* 1887, *John C., b.* 1889, and *Godefroi, b.* 1893.

II.—HOMER HINE STUART, JR., *b.* 30 January, 1855, *m.*, 3 October, 1888, Margaret Beckwith Kenney, and had: *Homer Howland, b.* 5 July, 1890.

III.—INGLIS STUART, of New York, *b.* 24 March, 1859.

PEDIGREE XVI.

OWEN GWYNEDD, Prince of North Wales, had :

IEVAN AP OWEN GWYNEDD, whose daughter,

LADY GWENLLIAN, *m.* Hwfa ap Kendrig ap Rhywalon, lord of Christion-ydol-Cynrig and Maelor Cynraig, of the tribe of Tudor Trevor, lord of Hereford, and had :

LADY ANGHARAD, who *m.* Kendrig ap Iorwerth, lord of Brynffenigl and Llansadwrn, a descendant of Brochwel Ysgithrog, Prince of Powys, and had :

EDNYFED VYCHAN ap Kendrig, lord of Brynffenigl and Krigeth, chief chancellor and chief justice to Llewelyn ap Iorwerth, King of North Wales and a commander in the army of Llewelyn in his war with King John, of England. He had by his second wife, Gwenllian, daughter of Rhys ap Griffith, lord of South Wales, and representative of the Sovereign Princess of South Wales (*see* Burke's " Ancestry of the Royal House of Tudor ") :

GRIFFITH AP EDNYFED VYCHAN, of Henglawdd, who had by his second wife, Gwenllian, daughter of Howell ap Trehearn, lord of Brecknock :

SIR HOWELL AP GRIFFITH, Knt., who *m.* Tanghost, daughter of David Goch ap Howell, and had :

GRIFFITH AP SIR HOWELL, who had by his second wife :

ROBERT AP GRIFFITH, of Einmal, who had :

RHYS AP ROBERT, from whom derived, sixth in descent (*see* Burke's " Royal Families," vol. ii., p. 39) :

MEREDITH AP JOHN, who had :

RT. REV. GEORGE LLOYD, D.D., sixth son, bishop of Sodor and Man, 1600–04, and bishop of Chester, 1604–16, who *m.* Anne, daughter of John Wilkinson, of Norwich, and had :

ANNA LLOYD, who *m.* (his second wife) Theophilus Eaton, first Governor of the New Haven Colony, New England, son of Rev. Richard and Elizabeth Eaton, vicar of Great Polworth, Cheshire, whose will, 11 July, 1616, proved 14 January, 1616–17 (*see* " N. E. His. Gen. Reg." October, 1899), and had :

HANNAH EATON, who *m.*, 4 July, 1659, William Jones, Deputy-Governor of the New Haven Colony, Connecticut, and had :

ELIZABETH JONES, who *m.*, 1689, Captain John Morgan, and had :

WILLIAM MORGAN, who *m.*, 3 July, 1716, Mary Avery, and had:

WILLIAM MORGAN, JR., who *m.*, 4 July, 1744, Temperance Avery, and had:

CHRISTOPHER MORGAN, who *m.*, 16 February, 1768, Deborah Ledyard, and had:

CHRISTOPHER MORGAN, JR., who *m.*, 15 July, 1805, Nancy Barber, and had:

EDWIN BARBER MORGAN, who *m.*, 23 September, 1829, Charlotte F. Wood, and had:

1.—LOUISE F. MORGAN, a member of the New York Society of the Colonial Dames of America, who *m.*, 28 June, 1865, Nicholas Lansing Zabriskie, of Aurora, New York.

2.—KATHARINE MORGAN, a member of the New York Society of the Colonial Dames of America, who *m.* William Brookfield of New York City.

PEDIGREE XVII.

EDWARD III., **King of England**, had by his wife, Lady Philippa, daughter of William, Count of Hainault, also of Royal Descent:

SIR EDMUND PLANTAGENET DE LANGLEY, K.G., Duke of York, Earl of Cambridge, *etc.*, fifth son, *d.* 1402, who had by his first wife, Princess Isabel, daughter and heiress of Peter, King of Castile and Leon:

LADY CONSTANCE PLANTAGENET, who *m.* Thomas, Baron le Despencer, created in 1337 Earl of Gloucester, beheaded in 1400, also of Royal Descent, and had:

LADY ISABEL LE DESPENCER, who *m.*, first, Richard de Beauchamp, created in 1421 Earl of Worcester, also of Royal Descent, and had:

LADY ELIZABETH DE BEAUCHAMP, heiress, 1415–1447, who *m.* 1435 (his first wife), Sir Edward de Neville, K.G., Baron Abergavenny, *d.* 1476, also of Royal Descent, and had:

SIR GEORGE DE NEVILLE, second Baron Abergavenny and Lord Latimer, 1440–1492, who *m.*, first, Lady Margaret, *d.* 1485, daughter and heiress of Sir Hugh Fenne, sub-treasurer of England (*see* Foster's " Royal Descents," p. 5), and had:

SIR GEORGE DE NEVILLE, K.B. and K.G., third Baron Abergavenny, *d.* 1535–36; *m.*, thirdly, Lady Mary, daughter of Edward Stafford, Duke of Buckingham, beheaded on Tower Hill, 17 May, 1521, and had by her:

LADY URSULA DE NEVILLE, who *m.* (his first wife) Sir Warham St. Leger, of Ulcombe, Kent, high sheriff, 1560; chief governor of Munster, Ireland, 1566; member of the Privy Council, 1585; *k.* in battle in Ireland 4 March, 1599, (*see* Lodge's " Peerage of Ireland," 1754, iii., and Berry's " Kent Pedigrees "), and had:

LADY ANNE ST. LEGER, *bur.* in St. Mary's, Chilham, 20 January, 1636–37, aged 81. She *m.* Thomas Digges, of Digges Court, in Kent, mustermaster general of the English Army in the Low Countries, and had by him, who *d.* 24 August, 1595:

SIR DUDLEY DIGGES, Knt., master of the rolls in 1619, who erected Chilham Castle, in Kent. (*See* Bridge's " Topographer," February, 1791.) He was a member of the London Company for colonizing Virginia, and dying 18 March, was buried in St. Mary's, Chilham, 23 March, 1638. He *m.* Lady Mary, daughter of Sir Thomas Kempe, Knt., of

Olantigh, Kent, and had by her, who was *bur.* in St. Mary's 5 May, 1631 :

EDWARD DIGGES,* third son, *bapt.* 29 March, 1621. He had an interest in the Virginia London Company, and served as Governor of the Virginia Colony, 30 March, 1655, to 13 March, 1658, and was a member of the Governor's Council from 22 November, 1654, till his death, 15 March, 1675. (*See* Brown's " Genesis of the United States," 990). He *m.* Elizabeth Braye (or Page), and had :

1.—COLONEL WILLIAM DIGGES, *b.* at Chilham Castle, came to Maryland in 1679, *m.* Elizabeth Seawell, and had :

CHARLES DIGGES, of Charleston and Warburton Manor, now the site of Fort Washington, who *m.* (Miss Dulany ?), and had :

I.—WILLIAM DIGGES, of Warburton Manor, who *m.*, 3 June, 1739, Anne, daughter of George Atwood, Jr., *d.* at Warburton Manor, 1744, also of Royal Descent, and had :

GEORGE DIGGES, of Warburton Manor, who had :

WILLIAM DUDLEY DIGGES, of Warburton Manor and Green Hill, near Washington City, who *m.* Eleanor, daughter of Daniel Carroll, of Duddington Manor, now a part of Washington City, also of Royal Descent, and had :

NORA DIGGES, who *m.*, 1854, James Ethelbert Morgan, M.D., of Washington City, and had :

ADA MORGAN, the youngest of seven children, a member of the Maryland Society of the Colonial Dames of America, who *m.*, 1889, Richard Smith Hill, of Prince George county, Maryland, and had : *Nora Digges* and *Elizabeth Snowden*, twins, and *Ada Morgan.*

II.—ANNE DIGGES, who *m.* Dr. George Steuart, *d.* 1780, commissioner of the Maryland Land Office, 1753–57, mayor of Annapolis, 1759–63, *etc.*, and had :

DR. JAMES STEUART, *m.* Rebecca Sprigg, and had :

---

* The following ladies, members of the National Society of the Colonial Dames of America, are also of Royal Descent, through Edward Digges :

MRS. MARY J. BAUGHMAN, Maryland State Society.

MRS. H. B. DENMAN (deceased), Maryland State Society.

MRS. GEORGE ALONZO JONES, Maryland State Society.

MRS. ALEXANDER B. RANDALL, Maryland State Society.

MRS. EMORY SPEER, Georgia State Society.

MRS. L. McLEAN TIFFANY, Maryland State Society.

MRS. CHARLES P. WILLIAMS, Maryland State Society.

GENERAL GEORGE H. STEUART, *m.* Anne Jane Edmondson, and had:

DR. JAMES HENRY STEUART, *m.* Ellen L. Duvall, and had:

1.—MARY ELIZABETH STEUART, of Baltimore, a member of the Maryland Society of the Colonial Dames of America.

2.—HENRIETTA STEUART, of Baltimore, a member of the Maryland Society of the Colonial Dames of America.

2.—DUDLEY DIGGES, of "Bellefield," *b.* about 1663, *d.* 18 January, 1710, councillor and auditor of the Virginia Colony; *m.* Susannah, daughter of Colonel William Cole, of "Denbigh," Warwick, Virginia (and his first wife, Susan Croft), and had by her, who *d.* 9 December, 1708, aged 34 years:

COLONEL COLE DIGGES, of "Bellefield," eldest son, *b.* 1691, *d.* 1744; president of the Virginia Council, *etc.* He *m.* Elizabeth, daughter of Dr. Henry and Mary (Folliott) Power, and had:

1.—DUDLEY DIGGES, of "Bellefield," a member of the Virginia Committee of Correspondence, 1773–74; of the Colonial Convention, 1776, *etc.* He had by his first wife, Martha Armistead:

MARTHA DIGGES, who *m.* Captain Nathaniel Burwell, of the Virginia Line Continental Army, a member of the Virginia Society of the Cincinnati, and had:

THOMAS NELSON BURWELL, who *m.* Elizabeth, daughter of Andrew Nicholson and Judith Wormeley, daughter of Dudley Digges, of "Bellefield," and his second wife, Elizabeth Wormeley, and had:

LUCY CARTER BURWELL, a member of the Virginia Society of the Colonial Dames of America, who *m.* Peterfield Trent, M.D., of Richmond, Virginia, and had: *William Peterfield Trent, M.A., LL.D.,* who *m.* Alice, daughter of Frederick Lyman, of East Orange, New Jersey, and had: *Lucia.*

DUDLEY DIGGES, of "Bellefield," Virginia, member of the Virginia Committee of Correspondence, 1774; of the Convention of the Colonies, 1776, *etc.*, *m.*, secondly, Elizabeth Wormeley, of "Rosegill," and had:

ELIZABETH DIGGES, who *m.* Robert Nicolson, and had:

SALLY BERKELEY NICOLSON, who *m.* Peyton Randolph Nelson, also of Royal Descent, and had:

WILLIAM WILMER NELSON, *m.* Sally Browne Catlett, and had:

SALLY BERKELEY NELSON, of Richmond, Virginia, a member of the Virginia Society of the Colonial Dames of America, who *m.* William Todd Robins, colonel Confederate States Army, and had: *Ruth Nelson, Elizabeth Todd, Augustine Warner, Wilmer Nelson,* and *Sally Berkeley Nelson.*

2.—MARY DIGGES, *d.* 12 November, 1744, aged 27 years, *m.* (his first

wife), 23 August, 1739, Nathaniel Harrison, Jr., of " Brandon," Prince
George county, Virginia, *d.* 1 October, 1791, aged 78 years, and had :

ELIZABETH HARRISON, *b.* 30 July, 1737, who *m.*, 31 January, 1760,
Major John Fitzhugh, and had :

ANNA FITZHUGH, who *m.* George May, and had:

HENRY MAY, M.D., of Petersburg, Virginia, *b.* 30 March, 1804, *d.* 27
December, 1886; *m.* Julia Jones, and had :

SALLY MAY, a member of the Virginia Society of the Colonial
Dames of America, the Order of the Crown, *etc.*, who *m.* James H.
Dooley, of Richmond, Virginia.

3.—MAJOR WILLIAM DIGGES, of " Denbigh," Warwick county, Virginia, who *m.* Frances, daughter of Major Anthony and Diana (Starkey)
Robinson, and had :

SUSANNAH DIGGES, who *m.* William Cole, 3d, of Albemarle county, Virginia, descended from Colonel William Cole, secretary of the Virginia
Colony and member of the Council, and his wife Martha, daughter of
Colonel John Lear, a member of the Council, and had :

WILLIAM COLE, 4th, of " Swynard," Orange county, Virginia, who *m.*
Mary Frances, daughter of Colonel Gerard Alexander, of " Effingham,"
Prince William county, Virginia, and had :

SUSANNAH DIGGES COLE, *b.* 25 December, 1824, who *m.*, 3 August, 1841,
Judge John Madison Chapman, of Orange county, Virginia, 1810–1879,
also of Royal Descent, and had :

1.—SUSIE ASHTON CHAPMAN, a member of the Tennessee Society of
the Colonial Dames of America, the Order of the Crown, *etc.*, who *m.*
Calvin Perkins, of Memphis, Tennessee, *b.* Columbus, Miss. *Issue.*

2.—BELLE CHAPMAN, a member of the Virginia Society of the Colonial
Dames of America, the Order of the Crown, *etc.*, who *m.*, 12 December,
1878, William Moncure, of Richmond, Virginia. *Issue.*

3.—ASHTON ALEXANDER CHAPMAN.

PEDIGREE XVIII.

LOUIS VI., King of France, had by his second wife, Lady Adelaide, daughter of Humbert II., Count de Piedmont, *d.* 1103 :

Peter of France, Lord of Courtenay, Gastinois, fifth son, who *m.* Lady Alice, daughter of Sir Reginald de Courtenay, first Baron Oakhampton, *d.* 1194, and had :

Lady Alice de Courtenay (sister of Peter, Emperor of Constantinople, 1217), who *m.* Aymer de Taillefer, Count de Angoulême, and had :

Lady Isabel de Taillefer, *d.* 1246, second wife and widow of John, King of England, *d.* 1216, who *m.*, secondly, Hugh le Brun, Earl of Marche, in Poictou, and had :

Lady Alice le Brun, who *m.* John Plantagenet de Warren, seventh Earl of Surrey, *d.* 1304 (*see* Watson's " Earls of Warren and Surrey "), and had :

William de Warren, *d. v. p.*, 15 December, 1286, who *m.* Lady Joan de Vere, daughter of Robert, fifth Earl of Oxford, *d.* 1296, and had :

Lady Alice de Warren, who *m.*, 1305, Sir Edmund Fitz-Alan, K.B., eighth Earl of Arundel, beheaded in 1326, and had :

Sir Richard Fitz-Alan, K.G., ninth Earl of Arundel and seventh Earl of Surrey, *d.* 1375, who *m.*, secondly, Lady Eleanor Plantagenet, daughter of Henry, third Earl of Lancaster, also of Royal Descent, and had by her :

Lady Alice Fitz-Alan, who *m.* Sir Thomas de Holland, Earl of Kent, *d.* 1397, also of Royal Descent, and had :

Lady Margaret de Holland, *d.* 1440, who *m.*, first, John de Beaufort, Earl of Somerset, Marquis of Dorset, Lord High Admiral and Lord Chamberlain, *d.* 1410, also of Royal Descent, and had :

Sir Edmund de Beaufort, K.G., Duke of Somerset, *etc.*, Regent of France, Lord High Constable of England, *k.* 1455, who *m.* Lady Alianore, widow of Thomas de Roos and daughter of Sir Richard de Beauchamp, K.G., Earl of Warwick and Albemarle, Lord High Steward, guardian of Henry VI., Lieutenant-General of Normandy and France, also of Royal Descent, *d.* 1439, and had :

Henry de Beaufort, beheaded in 1463, father of :

Charles de Somerset, Baron Herbert in right of his wife, created, in

1514, Earl of Worcester, d. 1526, who had by his wife, Lady Elizabeth, heiress and daughter of William de Herbert, Earl of Huntingdon :

HENRY DE SOMERSET, second Earl of Worcester, d. 26 November, 1549, who m. Elizabeth, daughter of Sir Anthony Browne,,standard-bearer to Henry VII., also of Royal Descent, and had:

LADY ELEANOR DE SOMERSET, m. Sir Roger Vaughan, Knt., of Porthaml, Talgarth, and had:

WATKIN VAUGHAN, of Talgarth, who had by his wife, Joan v. Evan ap Gwilim Ychan, of Peytyn Gwyn:

SIR WILLIAM VAUGHAN, of Porthaml, d. 1564, m. Catherine v. Jenkin Havard, of Tredomen, and had:

CATHERINE VAUGHAN, who m. David ap Evan, of Neath, high sheriff of Glamorganshire, in 1563, and had:

MARY DAVID EVAN, widow of Edward Turberville, of Sutton, who m., secondly, Thomas Basset, of Miscin, and had :

CATHERINE BASSET, who m. Richard ab Evan, of Collonna, Glamorganshire, and had :

JANE EVANS, who m. Evan ab John, of Treverigg, Llantrisant parish, Glamorganshire, d. ante 165—, and had :

JOHN AB EVAN, alias " John Bevan, Senior,"* b. about 1646. He m., about 1665, Barbara, probably daughter of William Awbrey, of Pencoed, and removed from Treverigg in 1683, with his family, to Pennsylvania, and settled in Merion and became a large landholder (see Glenn's " Merion in the Welsh Tract "). He was a member of the Assembly, 1687–1700, a justice in Philadelphia county 1685 and in Chester county 1689, and dying at Treverigg in 1726 (his will proved in Glamorganshire, 21 October, 1726), had by his wife, Barbara, who d. 26 January, 1710:

JANE BEVAN, d. 12 December, 1703, who m., 1 December, 1687, John Wood, of Darby, Pennsylvania, a member of the Assembly, 1704–1717, son of George Wood, a member of the Assembly, 1682–1683, and had :

ABRAHAM WOOD, of Makefield township, Bucks county, Pennsylvania, b. 2 March, 1702, d. September, 1733, who m. Ursula, 1701–1778, daughter of Philip Taylor, of Oxford, Philadelphia county (see Glenn's " Merion in the Welsh Tract "), and had :

ANN WOOD, b. 24 January, 1734, d. Lancaster, Pennsylvania, 8 March, 1799; m., 1756, William Henry, b. Chester county, Pennsylvania, 19

---

* The following ladies, members of the National Society of the Colonial Dames of America, are also of Royal Descent through John Bevan, Sr. :

MRS. DUNCAN L. BUZBY, Pennsylvania State Society.

MRS. THOMAS MCKEAN, Pennsylvania State Society.

May, 1729, *d.* 15 December, 1786, justice of the peace, 1758, 1770, 1777, associate justice of courts of common pleas and quarter sessions in 1780, and in 1776 elected a member of the Assembly, and in 1777 of the council of safety ; treasurer of Lancaster county, Pennsylvania, from 1777 till his death, in 1786 (his wife, Ann, acted as county treasurer for twelve years after his death), and had :

WILLIAM HENRY, *b.* 12 March, 1757, *d.* 21 April, 1821 ; associate justice of the Northampton county courts, 1788–1814 ; *m.*, 21 November, 1781, Sabina Schropp, and had :

ELIZABETH HENRY, *b.* 15 October, 1782, *d.* 15 December, 1844 ; *m.*, 23 August, 1804, John Jordan, *b.* 1 September, 1770, Hunterdon county, New Jersey, and had :

ANTOINETTE JORDAN, *b.* 10 January, 1813, *d.* 22 December, 1880 ; *m.*, 18 January, 1849, John Thomas Bell, *b.* 26 August, 1804, *d.* 4 March, 1882, and had :

EMILY BELL, of Philadelphia, a member of the Pennsylvania Society of the Colonial Dames of America.

THE ROYAL DESCENT

OF

MISS ALICE HUMPHREYS,

OF SAN FRANCISCO, CAL.

EDWARD I., King of England⹋Princess Eleanor of Castile.

Princess Elizabeth Plantagenet⹋Humphrey de Bohun, Earl of Hereford.

William de Bohun, Earl of Northampton⹋Lady Elizabeth de Badlesmere.

Lady Elizabeth de Bohun⹋Richard Fitz-Alan, K.G., Earl of Arundel.

Lady Elizabeth Fitz-Alan⹋Sir Robert Goushill, of Hault Hucknall, Derby.

Lady Joan Goushill⹋Sir Thomas Stanley, K.G., Lord Stanley.

Lady Margaret Stanley⹋Sir William Troutbeck, of Prynes Castle, Cheshire.

Lady Jane Troutbeck⹋Sir William Griffith, of Penrhyn Castle.

Sir William Griffith, of Penrhyn Castle⹋Jane Puleston of Carnarvon.

Lady Sibill Griffith⹋Owen ap Hugh, of Bodeon.

Jane Owen⹋Hugh Gwyn, of Penarth.

Sibill Gwyn⹋John Powell, of Llanwddyn.

Elizabeth Powell⹋Humphrey ap Hugh, of Llwyn-du.

Samuel ap Humphrey, of Port Neven⹋Elizabeth ———.

Daniel Humphreys, of Pennsylvania⹋Hannah Wynne, of Pennsylvania.

Joshua Humphreys, of Darby, Pennsylvania⹋Sarah Williams, of Blockley, Pennsylvania.

Joshua Humphreys, of Ponta Reading, Pa.⹋Mary Davids, of Philadelphia.

Samuel Humphreys, of Georgetown, D. C.⹋Letitia Atkinson.

William Penn Humphreys, United States Navy⹋Mary Stencon.

Alice Humphreys, of San Francisco, member of the National Society of the Colonial Dames of America, the Order of the Crown, etc.

PEDIGREE XIX.

HENRY I., King of France, had by his third wife, Anne of Russia:
HUGH THE GREAT, Duke of France and Burgundy, who had by his
third wife, *m.* 938, Lady Adelheid, daughter of Herbert IV., Count of
Vermandois:

LADY ISABEL DE VERMANDOIS, *d.* 1131 (widow of Robert, Earl of Mellent, *d.* 1118), who *m.*, secondly, William de Warren, second Earl of Surrey (*see* Watson's "Ancient Earls of Warren and Surrey"), and had:

WILLIAM DE WARREN, third Earl of Surrey, *d. s. p. m.* 1148. He *m.*,
before 1143, Lady Alice de Talvace, also of Royal Descent (or Talvas,
see Doyle's "Official Baronage"), *d.* 1174, and had:

LADY ISABELLA DE WARREN, heiress, *d.* 1199 (widow of William de
Blois, *d. s. p.* 1160), who *m.*, secondly, 1163, Hameline Plantagenet de
Warren, fifth Earl of Surrey, *d.* 1202, and had:

LADY ISABEL DE WARREN, who *m.* Roger, Baron le Bigod, created, 1189,
Earl of Norfolk; lord high steward of England, and had:

HUGH, second Earl of Norfolk, *d.* 1225; *m.* Lady Maud Marshall,
daughter of William le Marshal, Earl of Pembroke, the celebrated Protector during the nonage of Henry III., and had:

SIR HUGH BIGOD, second son, appointed, 22 June, 1257, chief justice
of England, resigned in 1260, *d.* 1266 (*see* Foss's "Lives of the Chief
Justices"), who *m.*, first, Joan, daughter of Robert Burnet, and had:

SIR JOHN BIGOD, Knt., younger brother of Roger, the last Earl of Norfolk, *d. s. p.* 1306, and father of

ROGER BIGOD, Knt., of Settington, youngest son, father of

JOAN BIGOD, who *m.*, 1358, Sir William de Chauncy, Knt., last Baron
of Skirpenbeck, Yorkshire, which he sold in 1399, and purchased Stepney in Middlesex, and had:

JOHN CHAUNCY, of Stepney, *d.* 1444–1445, who *m.* Margaret, daughter
of William Gifford, of Gedleston, and had:

JOHN CHAUNCY, of Sawbridgeworth, Herts, *d.* 7 May, 1479, who *m.*
Anne, daughter of John Leventhorp, of Shingey Hall, and had:

JOHN CHAUNCY, of Sawbridgeworth, *d.* 8 June, 1510, who *m.* daughter
of Thomas Boyce, and had:

JOHN CHAUNCY, of Pishobury Manor, *d.* 4 June, 1546, who *m.* Elizabeth Proffit, widow of Richard Mansfield, and had:

(83)

HENRY CHAUNCY, of New Place Gifford's, second son and heir, d. 14 April, 1587 ; m., Lucy ——, and had :

GEORGE CHAUNCY, of Yardley-Bury, Hertfordshire, second son, d. 1627, who had by his second wife, Anne, daughter of Edward Welsh, of Great Wymondley, and widow of Edward Humberston (see " Chauncy Pedigree," compiled by Stephen Tucker, Somerset Herald in Ordinary ; Chauncy pedigree in Sir Henry Chauncy's " History of Hertfordshire," Fowler's " Chauncy Memorials," etc.) :

REV. CHARLES CHAUNCY, D.D.,* second President of Harvard College, b. 5 November, 1592, d. Cambridge, Massachusetts, 19 February, 1671 ; m., 17 March, 1630, Catherine, b. 1601, bapt. 2 November, 1604, d. 23 June, 1667 ; daughter of Robert Eyre, of New Sarum and Chilhampton, Wilts, a barrister, bur. at St. Thomas's, 8 August, 1638, aged 69, and his first wife, Anne, daughter of Rt. Rev. John Still, D.D., bishop of Bath and Wells in 1592, d. 26 February, 1607, and his first wife, Anne, daughter of Thomas Arblaster (or Alabaster), of Hadley, Suffolk (see Somersetshire Visitations, 1623; Wiltshire Visitations, 1623; Bliss's Wood's " Athenæ Oxonienses," ii., 829, and Burke's " Commoners," iv., 538), and had :

SARAH CHAUNCY, b. 13 June, 1631, at Ware, England, d. 3 June, 1699, Wethersfield, Connecticut; m., 26 October, 1659, at Concord, Massachusetts, Rev. Gershom Bulkeley (son of Rev. Peter and Grace Chetwode Bulkeley), b. 6 December, 1636, at Concord, d. 2 December, 1713, at Glastonbury, a member of the Massachusetts Assembly, 1679, and had :

1.—EDWARD BULKELEY, b. 1673, d. 27 August, 1748, Wethersfield ; m., 14 July, 1702, at Wethersfield, Dorothy, b. 31 March, 1681, Concord, d. 1748, Wethersfield, daughter of Jonathan and Elizabeth (Hoar) Prescott, and had :

I.—CHARLES BULKELEY, b. 27 March, 1703, Wethersfield; m., 28 May, 1724, Mary, b. 9 April, 1699, Middletown, d. 24 January, 1771, Wethersfield, daughter of John and Hannah (Starr) Sage, and had :

1.—SARAH BULKELEY, b. 20 April, 1733, Wethersfield, d. 10 December, 1802, Rutland, Vermont; m., 5 August, 1756, at Wethers-

---

* The following ladies, members of the National Society of the Colonial Dames of America, are also of Royal Descent through Charles Chauncy :

MISS ELIZABETH C. WILCOX, Massachusetts State Society.

MRS. JOHN E. THAYER, Massachusetts State Society.

MISS ELLEN R. NYE, New York State Society.

MRS. WILLIAM B. BEEKMAN, New York State Society.

MRS. ETIENNE ST. GEORGE, New York State Society.

field, Cephas Smith, son of Noah and Mary (Johnson) Smith, and had:

CEPHAS SMITH, JR., *b.* 21 October, 1760–1761, Suffield, Connecticut, *d.* 24 January, 1815, Rutland; *m.*, 9 November, 1794, at Preston, Connecticut, Mary, *b.* 25 December, 1775, Preston, *d.* 30 April, 1842, Salem, N. Y., daughter of Nathaniel and Esther (Tyler) Gove, and had:

MARY PAGE SMITH, *b.* 3 June, 1805, Rutland, *d.* 1 April, 1838, Pittsford, Vermont; *m.*, 5 December, 1827, at Rutland, Chester, *b.* 5 July, 1797, Sandisfield, Massachusetts, *d.* 30 January, 1879, Pittsford, son of Simeon and Phœbe (Couch) Granger, and had:

WILLIAM SMITH GRANGER, *b.* 18 September, 1834, Pittsford; *m.*, 12 June, 1871, at Providence, Rhode Island, Caroline, *b.* July 4, 1846, Providence, daughter of John Talbot and Caroline (Richmond) Pitman, and had:

MARY ALICE GRANGER, of Providence, a member of the Rhode Island Society of the Colonial Dames of America.

2.—BRIG.-MAJOR EDWARD BULKELEY, *b.* about 1736, *d.* 30 June, 1787, a member of the Society of the Cincinnati; *m.*, 27 October, 1771, Rachel Lyman Pomeroy, also of Royal Descent, and had:

ROXA LYMAN BULKELEY, *b.* 25 October, 1772, *m.*, 25 February, 1793, Colonel Selah Francis, and had:

ROXA BULKELEY FRANCIS, *b.* 4 July, 1796, *d.* 1868; *m.*, 4 May, 1815, Judge Jesse Booth, who was commissioned Quartermaster in the War of 1812, in the regiment raised by his father-in-law, under Brigadier-General Farrington. He held important offices in State and county, and was a member of the New York Legislature, and also served as judge a number of years, and had:

ELLEN CORDELIA BULKELEY BOOTH, a member of the Connecticut Society of the Colonial Dames of America, who *m.*, 21 November, 1864, Byron Coleman Dick, of Oakland, California. *No issue.*

3.—BENJAMIN BULKELEY, who had:

HANNAH BULKELEY, who *m.* Amos Woodruff, and had:

RUSSELL WOODRUFF, *m.* Maria Smith, and had: *Franklin Amos, Morgan Lewis, Charles Russell, Joseph Bulkeley,* and *H. Estelle,* of New York City.

II.—DOROTHY BULKELEY, *b.* 11 September, 1716, *d.* 7 December,

1801; *m.*, 8 January, 1741, Thomas Curtis, of Wallingford, Connecticut, *b.* 8 October, 1710, *d.* 6 November, 1789, and had:

HEPHZIBAH CURTIS, *b.* 1757, *d.* 4 January, 1807; *m.*, 7 July, 1784, Jason Boardman, of Rocky Hill, Connecticut, *b.* 16 January, 1762, *d.* 10 February, 1844, and had:

RHODA BOARDMAN, *b.* 11 May, 1787, *d.* 10 December, 1852; *m.*, 2 January, 1811, Sabin Colton, of Longmeadow, Massachusetts, *b.* 18 August, 1783, *d.* 10 November, 1857, and had:

SABIN WOOLWORTH COLTON, *b.* 20 February, 1813, at Longmeadow, *d.* 3 May, 1890, in Philadelphia, Pennsylvania; *m.*, 4 August, 1835, Susanna, *b.* 25 December, 1812, daughter of Captain William Beaumont, of Argyleshire, Scotland, and his wife, Euphemia McCall, and had:

JULIA COLTON, *b.* 13 April, 1844, a member of the Pennsylvania Society of the Colonial Dames of America, who *m.*, 29 December, 1869, Harrison Allen, M.D., of Philadelphia, *b.* Philadelphia, 17 April, 1841, *d.* 14 November, 1897, and had: *Harrison, b.* 26 February, 1875, *d.* 30 March, 1899, and *Dorothea W., b.* 6 December, 1879.

III.—SARAH BULKELEY, *m.* Joseph Stow, and had:

SARAH STOW, *m.* Josiah Savage, and had:

REBECCA SAVAGE, *m.* Richard Dowd, and had:

REBECCA DOWD, *m.* Enoch Cornwall Roberts, and had:

EBENEZER ROBERTS, *m.* Clarissa Root Bancroft, and had:

FLORENCE ROBERTS, a member of the Connecticut Society of the Colonial Dames of America, who *m.* William Converse Skinner, of "Woodleigh," Hartford, Connecticut, and had: *Marjorie Roberts, Roberts Keney,* and *William Converse.*

2.—REV. JOHN BULKLEY, of Colchester, Connecticut, *d.* June, 1731; *m.*, 1701, Patience, daughter of Captain John and Sarah Prentice, of New London, Connecticut, and had:

I.—COLONEL JOHN BULKLEY, of Colchester, *b.* 19 April, 1705, Judge of the Supreme Court of Connecticut, 1745–1753, Commissioner to England, 1745, *d.* 21 July, 1753; *m.*, 29 October, 1738, Mary, widow of John Gardiner, of New London, drowned in 1735, and daughter of Rev. Eliphalet Adams, of New London, and had:

1.—CAPTAIN CHARLES BULKLEY, of Colchester, *b.* 1752, who *m.* Betsy Taintor, and had:

I.—SOLOMON TAINTOR BULKLEY, of Williamstown, Massachusetts, who *m.* Mary Welk, and had:

SARAH TAINTOR BULKLEY, who *m.* George W. Pleasants, and had:

NANNIE BUELL PLEASANTS, a member of the Virginia Society of the Colonial Dames of America, who *m.* Samuel Adams Lynde, of Chicago, Illinois.

II.—ESTHER BULKLEY, *m.* Jesse Sabin, and had:

SARAH ELIZABETH SABIN, *m.* Robert McClelland, and had:

AUGUSTA McCLELLAND, *b.* Monroe, Michigan, 1865, a member of the Massachusetts Society of the Colonial Dames of America, who *m.* George Nexsen Brady, of Detroit, Michigan, and had:

1.—ROBERT McCLELLAND BRADY, *m.* Mary Belle Holland.

2.—MARY AUGUSTA BRADY, a member of the Michigan Society of the Colonial Dames of America, *m.* Robert Mallory Berry, United States Navy.

2.—COLONEL ELIPHALET BULKELEY, *b.*, Colchester, Connecticut, 8 August, 1746, *d.* Wilkes-Barre, Pennsylvania, 11 January, 1816; captain Twelfth Regiment, 1773–76, and lieutenant-colonel Twenty-fifth Regiment, Connecticut militia; *m.*, 16 September, 1767, Anna Bulkeley, and had:

JOHN CHARLES BULKELEY, *b.* Colchester, who *m.* Sally Taintor, and had:

ELIPHALET ADAMS BULKELEY, *b.* Colchester, June, 1803, *m.* Lydia Smith Morgan, and had:

WILLIAM HENRY BULKELEY, *b.* East Haddam, Connecticut, 2 March, 1840, *m.*, September, 1863, Emma Gweney, of Brooklyn, and had:

SARAH TAINTOR BULKELEY, *b.* Hartford, Connecticut, 7 November, 1876, a member of the Massachusetts Society of the Colonial Dames of America, who *m.*, 7 November, 1895, Richard Henry Macauley, of Detroit, Michigan, and had: *Richard Bulkeley, b.* 28 August, 1896; *Frances Gweney, b.* 1 February, 1898, and *Sally, b.* 11 January, 1899.

COLONEL ELIPHALET BULKELEY, *d.* Wilkes-Barre, Pennsylvania, 1816, aforesaid, was the ancestor of

FRANCES BULKELEY, a member of the Pennsylvania Society of the Colonial Dames of America, who *m.* Asa R. Brundage, of Wilkes-Barre, Pennsylvania, and had:

MARY GILLETTE BRUNDAGE, of Wilkes-Barre, a member of the Pennsylvania Society of the Colonial Dames of America.

II.—CAPTAIN GERSHOM BULKELEY, of Colchester, *b.* 4 February, 1709, *m.*, 28 November, 1733, Abigail Robbins, and had:

SARAH BULKELEY, *b.* 10 January, 1735, who *m.*, 23 November, 1758, John Taintor, of Colchester, *b.* 23 February, 1725–26, *d.* 1798, and had:

JOHN TAINTOR, of Wyndham, Connecticut, *b.* 23 September, 1760, *d.* 29 March, 1825, who *m.*, 1786, his cousin, Sarah, *b.* 12 June, 1770, *d.* 29 October, 1856, daughter of Enos Hosford (or Horseford), and his wife Abigail, daughter of Ichabod Lord, and his wife Patience Bulkeley, aforesaid, and had:

1.—ABBIE LOUISE TAINTOR, who *m.* William Gibbons, and had:

SARAH TAINTOR GIBBONS, who *m.* Ward McAllister, of New York City, and had:

LOUISE WARD MCALLISTER, of New York City, a member of the Pennsylvania Society of the Colonial Dames of America.

2.—SARAH TAINTOR, *b.* 1787, *d.* 6 June, 1827, who *m.*, 20 February, 1815, Israel Foote, of New York City, *b.* 19 January, 1783, *d.* 21 September, 1871, and had:

JOHN TAINTOR FOOTE, of Morristown, New Jersey, *b.* 27 May, 1819, *m.* Jordena Cannon, *b.* 1827, *d.* 2 November, 1853, daughter of Horatio Turpin Harris, United States Navy, of Newport, Kentucky, 1799–1855, and his wife Keturah L., daughter of General James Taylor, of Newport, Kentucky, and had:

KATHARINE JORDENA FOOTE, a member of the New Jersey Society of the Colonial Dames of America, and Society of the Daughters of the Cincinnati, who *m.* Philip H. Cooper, captain United States Navy, and had: *Dorothy B.,* *b.* 9 March, 1889, and *Leslie B.,* *b.* 24 March, 1894.

PEDIGREE XX.

EDWARD I., King of England, had by his wife, Princess Eleanor, daughter of Ferdinand III., King of Castile and Leon:

PRINCESS ELIZABETH PLANTAGENET, 1289–1316, who *m.*, secondly, 14 November, 1302, Humphrey de Bohun, constable of England, Earl of Hereford and Essex, *k.* in 1321, and had:

LADY MARGARET DE BOHUN, will dated 28 January, 1390–1, who *m.*, 1325, Sir Hugh Courtenay, K. G., second Earl of Devon, *d.* 1377 (*see* notice of Courtenay Royal Descent from Gibbons's "Decline and Fall of the Roman Empire," in Bridge's "Topographer," June, 1789), and had:

LADY MARGARET COURTENAY, who *m.* John, third Baron Cobham, and had:

LADY JOANE COBHAM, who *m.* Sir John de la Pole, Knt., and had:

LADY JOANE DE LA POLE, who *m.* Sir Reginald Braybrooke, and had:

LADY JOANE BRAYBROOKE, who *m.* Sir Thomas Brooke, Lord Cobham, and had:

SIR EDWARD BROOKE, Lord Cobham, *d.* 1464, who *m.* Lady Elizabeth, daughter of James, Lord Audley, and had:

JOHN BROOKE, Lord Cobham, *d.* 1511–12, who *m.*, first, Lady Margaret, daughter of Sir Edward Neville, K.G., Baron Bergavenny, also of Royal Descent, and had by her:

THOMAS BROOKE, Lord Cobham, *d.* 1529, who *m.*, first, Dorothy, daughter of Sir Henry Heydon, Knt., and had by her:

LADY ELIZABETH BROOKE, who *m.*, 1520, Sir Thomas Wyatt, of Allington Castle, Kent, 1503–1544, poet-laureate to Henry VIII., and had:

SIR THOMAS WYATT, of Allington Castle, executed 11 April, 1554, on Tower Hill (*see* Brown's "Genesis of the United States," p. 996), who *m.*, 1536–1537, Lady Jane, daughter of Sir William Hawte, of Bishop Bourne, Kent, and had:

LADY JANE WYATT, who *m.* Charles Scott, of Egerton, Kent, *d.* 1617, also of Royal Descent, and had:

THOMAS SCOTT, of Egerton, 1567–1635, who *m.*, secondly, 1604, Mary, *d.* 1616, daughter of John Knatchbull, of Mersham Hatch (*see* Berry's "Kent Pedigrees," p. 169), and had by her:

DOROTHEA SCOTT, *bapt.* 22 September, 1611, who came to Oyster Bay,

6 (89)

Long Island, New York, in 1680, with her children by her first husband
(*m.* about 1636), Major Daniel Gotherson, of Cromwell's army, who *d.*
1666 (*see* Scull's " Life of Dorothea Scott ") ; of these:

DOROTHEA GOTHERSON, *m.*, 1680, John Davis, of Oyster Bay. They removed to Pilesgrove township, Salem county, New Jersey, in 1705, and
had :

JUDGE DAVID DAVIS, of Salem county, New Jersey, *d.* aged 90 years,
who *m.* Dorothy Cousins, *d.* 1789, aged 96 years, and had:

1.—AMY DAVIS, who *m.*, 1741, John Gill, of Haddonfield, New Jersey,
and had :

JOHN GILL, who *m.*, first, 17 January, 1788, Anna Lovett Smith, and
had :

JOHN GILL, of Camden, New Jersey, 1795–1874 ; *m.*, 6 August, 1817,
Sarah Hopkins, and had :

WILLIAM HOPKINS GILL, 1832–1873 ; *m.*, 6 July, 1858, Phœbe Shreve,
and had :

MARY R. GILL, a member of the Pennsylvania Society of the Colonial Dames of America, who *m.*, 30 December, 1885, Johns Hopkins, of Baltimore, and had : *Johns* and *William Gill.*

2.—HANNAH DAVIS, *b.* 1728, who *m.* Richard Wood, of Salem county,
New Jersey, *b.* 18 March, 1727, and had :

RICHARD WOOD, of Haddonfield, New Jersey, *b.* 2 July, 1755, who *m.*,
secondly, 6 November, 1793, Elizabeth, 1776–1826, daughter of Job
Bacon, and had :

1.—RICHARD DAVIS WOOD, of Philadelphia, *b.* 29 March, 1799, *d.* 1
April, 1869; *m.*, at the North Meeting, Philadelphia, 16 October, 1832,
Julianna Randolph, of Philadelphia, *b.* 21 October, 1810, *d.* 15 March,
1884, and had :

GEORGE WOOD, of Philadelphia, *b.* 31 July, 1842, who *m.*, at the
Twelfth Street Meeting, Philadelphia, Mary Sharpless Hunn, of
Philadelphia, *b.* 23 August, 1844, and had :

LYDIA HUNN WOOD, *b.* 23 March, 1867, a member of the Pennsylvania
Society of the Colonial Dames of America, who *m.*, at the Haverford
Meeting, 23 April, 1892, Charles Winter Bailey, of Philadelphia, *b.* 1
December, 1866, and had : *Mary Hunn Wood,* b. 12 July, 1896.

2.—CHARLES S. WOOD, of Philadelphia, who *m.*, 5 June, 1834, Juliana,
daughter of George FitzRandolph, and had :

ELIZABETH WOOD, a member of the Pennsylvania Society of the
Colonial Dames of America, who *m.*, 3 June, 1858, John Hooker
Packard, M.D., of Philadelphia, and had, besides other children :

ELIZABETH DWIGHT PACKARD, of Philadelphia, a member of the
Pennsylvania Society of the Colonial Dames of America.

PEDIGREE XXI.

EDWARD I., **King of England**, had by his first wife, *m.*, 1254, Eleanor, *d.* 1290, daughter of Ferdinand III., King of Castile and Leon :

PRINCESS ELIZABETH PLANTAGENET, 1282–1316, widow of Sir John de Vere, who *m.*, secondly, 14 November, 1302, Humphrey de Bohun, Earl of Hereford and Essex, lord high constable, *k.* at Boroughbridge in 1321, of Royal Descent, and had :

SIR WILLIAM DE BOHUN, K.G., fifth son, created, 1337, Earl of Northampton, *d.* 1360; who *m.* Lady Elizabeth, *d.* 1356, daughter of Bartholomew, Baron de Badlesmere, executed in 1322, and had :

LADY ELIZABETH DE BOHUN, who *m.* (his first wife) Sir Richard Fitz-Alan, K.G., tenth Earl of Arundel, beheaded in 1398, also of Royal Descent, and had :

LADY ELIZABETH FITZ-ALAN, *d.* 8 July, 1425, who *m.*, first, 1378, Sir William Montacute, *k. s. p.*, 6 August, 1383; *m.*, secondly, 1386, his second wife, Thomas, Lord Mowbray, Earl Marshal of England, first Duke of Norfolk and Earl of Nottingham, *d.* 22 September, 1399; and *m.*, thirdly, Sir Robert Goushill, Knt., lord of Hault Hucknall Manor, county Derby, and had by him, who had been an esquire to the first Duke of Norfolk (she *m.*, fourthly, Gerard de Ufflete, Knt., of Wighill, York, *see* Glover's " History of Derby," ii., 78) :

LADY ELIZABETH GOUSHILL, who *m.*, first, Sir Robert Wingfield, Knt., of Letheringham, Suffolk, *d.* 1431 (*see* Lodge's " Peerage of Ireland," 1754, iii., and Camden's " Huntingdonshire Visitations ") : and had :

SIR HENRY WINGFIELD, of Orford, Suffolk, younger son, will dated 21 February, 1483. He *m.*, first, Alice —— , and *m.*, secondly, Lady Elizabeth, daughter of Sir Robert Rook, or Rowks, and had :

SIR ROBERT WINGFIELD, of Orford and Upton, Northants, who was present at the memorable interview between Henry VIII. and Francis I. in 1520; *m.* Margery, daughter of John Quarles, of Ufford, Northants, and had :

ROBERT WINGFIELD, of Upton, M. P., *d.* 31 March, 1580 (*see* the " Tinwell Parish Register," Rutland), who *m.* (her first husband) Elizabeth, daughter of Richard Cecil, of Burleigh, sheriff of Northamptonshire and custodian of Windsor Castle, and sister to the lord high treasurer Cecil, and had :

DOROTHEA WINGFIELD (*see* Lodge's " Peerage of Ireland," iii., 347), *d.* 7 November, 1619 (*see* Marshall's "Genealogist," iii., 327), who *m.*, at St. George's, Stamford, 30 September, 1587 (his first wife), Adam Claypoole, Esq., of Latham, Lincolnshire, and Narborough (*see* "Rutland Visitations," 1618), and had:

SIR JOHN CLAYPOOLE, Knt., of Narborough, Northants, third son, clerk of the Hanaper, knighted by Cromwell (*see* Waylen's "House of Cromwell"), who *m.*, 8 June, 1622, Marie Angell, of London, and had by her, who *d.* 1661:

JAMES CLAYPOOLE, of Philadelphia, *b.* 6 October, 1634, *d.* 1687. He arrived in Pennsylvania in the "Concord," 8 June, 1683, and was a merchant and treasurer of the "Free Society of Traders of Pennsylvania,"—so elected in London, 29 May, 1682 (*see* Graff's "Claypoole Family " and " Pa. Mag.," x.). He *m.*, at Bremen, in Germany, by Conradus Lelius, a Calvin minister, 12 December, 1657, Helen Merces (or Mercer), who *d.* in Philadelphia, in 1688, and had:

JOSEPH CLAYPOOLE, of Philadelphia and Mt. Holly, N. J., *b.* in Scots' Yard, London, 1677, *d.* 1744. He came to Philadelphia with his father, and was high sheriff of Philadelphia county. He *m.*, first, 20 July, 1703, Rebecca Jennings, at Charleston, South Carolina, and *m.*, secondly, 10 April, 1716, Edith Ward, who *d.* 1715.

JOSEPH CLAYPOOLE, had by his first wife:

I.—GEORGE CLAYPOOLE, 1706–1770 ; *m.*, first, Hannah ——, *d.* 1744, and had by her:

GEORGE CLAYPOOLE, *b.* 1733, who *m.*, 1756, Mary Parkhouse, and had:

WILLIAM CLAYPOLE, M.D., of Wilmington, North Carolina, 1758–1792; *m.*, 1790, Mary Wright (a sister of Judge Joshua Wright, of Cape Fear), and had:

ANNE CLAYPOLE, 1791–1838; *m.*, 1809–10, William Henry Hill, of Wilmington, North Carolina, *d.* 1814, and had:

ELIZA ANN HILL, *b.* 13 May, 1813, *d.* 6 December, 1896 ; *m.*, 1830, William Augustus Wright, of Wilmington, North Carolina, and had:

1.—ANN CLAYPOLE WRIGHT, *b.* 8 September, 1836, *d.* 27 November, 1887, who *m.* Walker Meares, and had :

I.—WILLIAM AUGUSTUS, *d.* 1858; II. WALKER, *d.* 1862; III. JOSHUA ; IV. SUSAN KIDDER ; V. GEORGE MORDECAI, *d.* 1876; VI. CLAYPOLE, *d.* 1882.

VII.—ADELAIDE SAVAGE MEARES, of Wilmington, North Carolina, a member of the North Carolina Society of the Colonial Dames of America.

VIII.—ELIZA ANN HILL MEARES, a member of the North Carolina Society of the Colonial Dames of America, who *m.* William C. Munds, of Wilmington, North Carolina, and had: *Annette Claypole,* and *William Capers.*

IX.—MARGARET ENGELHARD MEARES, a member of the North Carolina Society of the Colonial Dames of America, who *m.*, 1897, William Bennett Thorpe, and had: *William B., b.* 1898.

2.—WILLIAM AUGUSTUS WRIGHT, *m.* Louisa Holmes, and had: *Alice, William A.,* and *Sallie.*

3.—FLORENCE WRIGHT, 1849–1884, who *m.*, first, 1869, William Fotterall Potter, and *m.*, secondly, 1881, Colonel John W. Atkinson, and had:

I.—ELIZA POTTER, *b.* 1871, a member of the North Carolina Society of the Colonial Dames of America, who *m.*, 1897, Thomas Settle, of Greensboro, North Carolina. *No issue.*

II.—SARAH POTTER, *b.* 1874, a member of the North Carolina Society of the Colonial Dames of America, the Order of the Crown, *etc.,* who *m.*, 1898, Tench C. Coxe, of Asheville, North Carolina, and had: *Franklin, b.* Sept., 1899.

II.—REBECCA CLAYPOOLE,, *b.* 26 November, 1711, *d.* 1 August, 1762, who *m.*, 1 May, 1729, Henry Pratt, of Philadelphia, *b.* 30 April, 1708, *d.* 31 January, 1748, and had:

1.—MATTHEW PRATT, of Philadelphia, an artist, who *m.* ——, and had:

HENRY PRATT, of "The Hills," Philadelphia county, Pennsylvania, who *m.* Elizabeth Dundas, also of Royal Descent, and had:

SARAH CLEMENTINA PRATT, 1791–1836; *m.*, 1809, Thomas McKean, Jr., of Philadelphia, 1779–1852, and had:

I.—SARAH ANN McKEAN, *m.*, 1833, George Trott, and had:

SARAH McKEAN TROTT, *m.*, 1857, James W. Hazlehurst, and had:

ELIZABETH BORIE HAZLEHURST, a member of the Pennsylvania Society of the Colonial Dames of America, who *m.*, 1887, Daniel Lammot, of Philadelphia, also of Royal Descent.

II.—CLEMENTINA SOPHIA McKEAN, *m.*, 1843, Charles Louis Borie, and had:

1.—ELIZABETH McKEAN BORIE, a member of the Pennsylvania Society of the Colonial Dames of America, who *m.*, 1872, John Thompson Lewis, of Philadelphia. *Issue.*

2.—EMILY BORIE, a member of the Pennsylvania Society of the Colonial Dames of America, *m.*, 1871, James Mauran-Rhodes, of Philadelphia. *Issue.*

3.—SARAH CLEMENTINA McKEAN BORIE, a member of the Pennsylvania Society of the Colonial Dames of America, who *m.*, 1886, George C. Mason, of Philadelphia.

2.—HANNAH PRATT, *b.* 3 April, 1732, who *m.*, 3 May, 1755, her cousin, Enoch Hobart, of Philadelphia, who *d.* 27 October, 1776, and had:

RT. REV. JOHN HENRY HOBART, D.D., of Auburn, New York, *b.* 14 September, 1775, *d.* 12 September, 1830; consecrated P. E. Bishop of New York in 1811; *m.*, 6 May, 1800, Mary Goodin, *d.* 4 April, 1847, daughter of Rev. Thomas Bradbury and Jane (Emote) Chandler, and had:

ELIZABETH CATHERINE HOBART, *b.* 27 January, 1810, *d.* 26 May, 1883; *m.*, 22 June, 1830, Rev. George Emlen Hare, D.D., LL.D., *b.* 4 September, 1808, *d.* 15 February, 1892, and had:

CHARLES WILLING HARE, of Philadelphia, *b.* 31 August, 1835, *m.* Mary S. Widdifield, and had:

CHRISTINE SINGER HARE, a member of the Pennsylvania Society of the Colonial Dames of America, who *m.* Newberry Allen Stockton, of Bethayres, Montgomery county, Pennsylvania.

JOSEPH CLAYPOOLE, 1677–1744, had by his second wife:

I.—EDITH CLAYPOOLE, *b.* 1723, *d.* 27 February, 1800, who *m.*, first, 1744, David Chambers, of Philadelphia, *d.* 1759, and had:

REBECCA CHAMBERS, *b.* 2 September, 1751, *d.* 1834, who *m.*, 3 March, 1768, Robert Wallace, of Pennsylvania, and had:

REBECCA WALLACE, *b.* 23 August, 1778, *d.* 1867, who *m.*, 2 January, 1800, Judge Jacob Burnet, of Cincinnati, a United States senator and son of Dr. William Burnet, a delegate to the Continental Congress from New Jersey, and the first surgeon-general, United States Army, and had:

ELIZABETH BURNET, *b.* 23 June, 1818, *d.* 5 April, 1889, who *m.*, 1 November, 1837, Hon. William Slocum Groesbeck, of Cincinnati, *b.* 24 July, 1815, *d.* 7 July, 1897, and had:

JULIA GROESBECK, a member of the New York Society of the Colonial Dames of America, who *m.*, 1 June, 1876, Robert Ludlow Fowler, of New York City, and had: *William S. G., Mary Powell, Robert L.,* and *Elizabeth Burnet Groesbeck.*

II.—JAMES CLAYPOOLE, of Philadelphia, *b.* 22 January, 1720; sheriff of Philadelphia county, Pennsylvania, 1777; *m.*, first, 24 May, 1742,

Rebecca White; *m.*, secondly, Mary, daughter of Dr. David Chambers.
By his second wife he had:

CAPTAIN ABRAHAM GEORGE CLAYPOOLE, of Philadelphia and Chillicothe, Ohio, an officer in the Pennsylvania Line, Continental Army, and one of the original members of the Pennsylvania Society of the Cincinnati, *b.* 1756, *d.*, Philadelphia, 10 February, 1827. He *m.*, secondly, in New York, November, 1795, Elizabeth Steele, *d.* 4 November, 1818, and had by her:

1.—JANE BYRNE CLAYPOOLE, *b.* at Trenton, New Jersey, 7 March, 1797, *d.* 2 July, 1864, who *m.*, at Chillicothe, 21 June, 1819 (his second wife), Thomas James, of Chillicothe, *b.*, Maryland, 5 November, 1776, *d.* 13 June, 1856, and had:

> WILLIAM JAMES, of St. James, Missouri, *b.* 30 March, 1823, who *m.*, 2 July, 1846, Lucy Ann, *b.* 21 August, 1822, daughter of Robert Dun, of Glasgow, Scotland, and his wife, Lucy Wortham Angus, of Petersburg, Virginia (*see* "Americans of Royal Descent," fourth edition, p. 864), and had:

> I.—THOMAS JAMES, of Kansas City, Missouri, *b.* Chillicothe, 21 August, 1847; *m.*, 2 July, 1873, Octavia Ann, *d.* 4 November, 1894, daughter of William Hearst Bowles, M.D., of Maries county, Missouri, and his wife, Augusta Glanville, and had: *Lucy Wortham, b.* St. Josephs, Missouri, 13 September, 1880.

> II.—LUCY JAMES, *b.* Chillicothe, 29 December, 1848, a member of the Pennsylvania Society of the Colonial Dames of America, a member of the Order of the Crown, *etc.*, who *m.*, first, 15 November, 1871, Colonel William Alexander Rucker, United States Army, *b.* at Grosse Isle, Michigan, 17 March, 1831, *d.* at Chicago, 22 January, 1893, and had: *William James*, only child, *b.* St. James, Missouri, 25 April, 1873, and *m.*, secondly, 31 October, 1899, James Dun.

> III.—JANE JAMES, a member of the Maryland Society of the Colonial Dames of America, *b.* Maramec Iron Works, Missouri, 4 October, 1851; *m.*, 31 October, 1881, Captain George Hamilton Cook, United States Army, *d.* 4 October, 1889, and had: *Lucy James, b.* 13 December, 1882; *Elizabeth Graham, b.* 28 January, 1884; *Jane James, b.* 15 July, 1885, and *Frances Swayne, b.* 13 December, 1887.

2.—ALICE ANNE CLAYPOOLE, *b.* 7 December, 1798, *d.* 30 September, 1822, who *m.* Major David Gwynne, United States Army, *d.* at "Fair Hope," Jefferson county, Kentucky, 21 August, 1849, and had:

> ABRAHAM EVAN GWYNNE, of Cincinnati, Ohio, who *m.* Cettie Moore, daughter of Henry Collins Flagg, mayor of New Haven, Connecticut, 1836–41, *d.* 18 March, 1863, and had:

> I.—ALICE CLAYPOOLE GWYNNE, a member of the New York Society

of the Colonial Dames of America, who *m.*, 1870, Cornelius Vanderbilt, of New York City, *b.* 27 November, 1843, *d.* 12 September, 1899 (son of William Henry, 1821–1885; and grandson of Cornelius Vanderbilt, 1794–1877), and had : *William H., b.* 21 December, 1870, *d.* 22 May, 1892; *Cornelius, Gertrude, Alfred,* and *Gladys.*

II.—Cettie Moore Gwynne, a member of the New York Society of the Colonial Dames of America, who *m.* William Edgar Shepherd, of New York City. *Issue.*

3.—Sarah Claypoole, *b.* 9 February, 1801, *d.* 31 January, 1870, who *m.*, 8 June, 1825, William David Lewis, of Philadelphia, 1792–1881, collector of the port, Philadelphia, 1851, and had :

Sarah Claypoole Lewis, a member of the Pennsylvania Society of the Colonial Dames of America, who *m.*, 11 October, 1849, Thomas Neilson, of Philadelphia, and had :

I.—William Delaware Neilson, of Philadelphia.

II.—Robert Henry Neilson, *d.* 10 November, 1887 ; *m.* Emily Souder Lemiard, *d.* 22 March, 1894, and had : *Dorothy Lewis, b.* 27 April, 1892.

III.—Sarah Neilson, *d.* 10 July, 1892.

IV.—Thomas Rundle Neilson, *m.*, 12 January, 1898, Louise Fotterall.

V.—Lewis Neilson, *m.*, 6 February, 1893, Clara Augusta Rosengarten, and had : *Henry Rosengarten, b.* 8 December, 1693, and *Sarah Claypoole, b.* 28 March, 1897.

VI.—Emma Florence ; VII.—Mary Alice Lewis ; VIII. Frederick Brooke.

PEDIGREE XXII.

ROBERT BRUCE, King of Scotland, had by his first wife, Lady Isabel, daughter of Donald, Earl of Mar:

LADY MARJORY BRUCE, m. Walter, the lord high steward, and had:

ROBERT II., King of Scotland, had by his first wife, Lady Elizabeth, daughter of Sir Adam Mure, of Rowallan, Knt.:

ROBERT STUART, Duke of Albany, Regent of Scotland, who had by his first wife, Lady Marjory, Countess of Menteith:

LADY MARJORY STUART, who m. (his first wife) Sir Duncan Campbell, of Lochow, created Lord Campbell in 1445, d. 1452, and had:

SIR COLIN CAMPBELL, of Glenurchy, third son, 1400–1478. He had by his second wife, Lady Margaret Stuart, daughter of John, Lord Lorn:

SIR DUNCAN CAMPBELL, of Glenurchy, eldest son, who was slain at Flodden, in 1513, leaving issue by his second wife, Lady Margaret Moncrieffe, daughter of the laird of Moncrieffe, in Perthshire:

LADY ANNABELLA CAMPBELL, who m., by dispensation obtained 9 October, 1533, Alexander Napier, laird of Merchiestoun, b. 1509, k. at battle of Pinkie, 1547, only son of Sir Alexander Napier, k. at Flodden, and had:

SIR ARCHIBALD NAPIER, laird of Merchiestoun and Edinballie, eldest son, b. before 1535, master of the Mint of Scotland in 1587, d. 1608, who had by his first wife, Lady Janet, d. 1563, daughter of Sir Francis Bothwell, a lord of Sessions, and sister of Adam Bothwell, Bishop of Orkney:

JOHN NAPIER, laird of Merchiestoun, eldest son, b. 1550, d. 1617. He was an author of many valuable books, librarian of Merchiestoun, and well known as the inventor of the table of logarithms. (*See* Playfair's "Family Antiquity," iii., 606, and "Life of John Napier," by David Stewart, Earl of Buchan, 1787.) He had by his second wife, Agnes, daughter of James Chisholme, of Cromlix, Perthshire:

ADAM NAPIER, of Blackstoun, in Renfrewshire, fifth son, half-brother of Sir Alexander Napier, created Baron Napier. He had:

A DAUGHTER (*see* Wood's Douglas's "Peerage of Scotland," ii., 282–292), who m. William Craik, of Arbigland, Dumfries, and had:

ADAM CRAIK, of Arbigland, who m. Lady Maria, daughter of Sir Colin Campbell, of Ardkinglass, created a baronet in 1679, and his wife, who was a daughter of the above Adam Napier and a sister of William Craik's wife, and had:

WILLIAM CRAIK, of Arbigland, *b.* 1703, who had by his first wife:

DR. JAMES CRAIK, the physician and intimate friend of President Washington, *b.* at Arbigland, 1730, came to Virginia in 1750, surgeon-general of the Continental Army, a member of the Maryland State Society of the Cincinnati, and *d.* at his home in Fairfax county, Virginia, in 1814. He *m.*, 13 November, 1760, Marianna, *b.* 1740, daughter of Charles Ewell, of Prince William county, Virginia, and his wife, Sallie Ball, a cousin of President Washington, and had:

SARAH CRAIK, *b.* 11 November, 1764, *m.*, 25 January, 1785, Daniel Jenifer, Jr., M.D., 1756–1809, surgeon in the Continental Army till 1782, member of the Maryland State Society of the Cincinnati, and had:

COLONEL DANIEL JENIFER, *b.* 15 April, 1791, *d.* 18 December, 1855, a member of Congress from Maryland, 1831–33, 1835–41, and United States minister to Austria. He *m.* Eliza Trippe Campbell, of Charles county, Maryland, and had:

NANNIE O. JENIFER, who *m.* William Stone Triplett, of Virginia, and had:

1.—EMILY LOUISA TRIPLETT, a member of the Virginia Society of the Colonial Dames of America, who *m.* Meredith F. Montague, of Richmond, Virginia, and had: *Nannie Jenifer Triplett, William Triplett, Meredith,* and *Emily Triplett.*

2.—ELIZABETH TRIPLETT, a member of the Virginia Society of the Colonial Dames of America, who *m.* Thomas R. Price, of New York City, and had: *Elizabeth.*

PEDIGREE XXIII.

DAVID I., King of Scotland, *m.* Lady Maud, daughter of Waltheof, Earl of Northumberland and Northampton, and had:

HENRY, Earl of Huntingdon and Northumberland, eldest son, *d. v. p.* 1152, *m.*, 1139, Lady Adeline de Warren, daughter of William, second Earl of Surrey, and his wife, Lady Isabel, daughter of Hugh the Great, son of Henry I., King of France, and had:

DAVID, Earl of Huntingdon, *m.* Lady Maud de Meschines, daughter of Hugh, Earl of Chester, and had:

LADY ISABEL DE HUNTINGDON, who *m.* Robert de Brus, or Bruce, Earl, or Lord, of Annandale, *d.* 1245, and had:

ROBERT BRUCE, Earl of Annandale, 1210–1295, a claimant to the crown of Scotland, 1290, as nearest kin to Alexander III.; *m.*, first, 1244, Lady Isabel, daughter of Gilbert de Clare, Earl of Hertford and Gloucester, and had:

ROBERT BRUCE, Earl of Annandale and Carrick, *d.* 1304, who *m.*, 1271, Marjory, Countess of Carrick, widow of Adam de Kilconcath, *d.* 1270, and daughter and heir of Neil, second Earl of Carrick, *d.* 1256, and had:

LADY MATILDA BRUCE (sister of Robert I., King of Scotland), who *m.* (his second wife) Hugh, fifth Earl of Ross, and had:

WILLIAM, sixth Earl of Ross, who had by his second wife, a daughter of Sir David Graham, of Montrose:

LADY MARGARET LESLIE, who *m.* Sir David Hamilton, of Cadyou, *d.* 1375 (*see* Riddell's "Stewardiania," p. 76), also of Royal Descent, and had:

SIR DAVID HAMILTON, of Cadyou, *d. ante* 14 May, 1392, *m.* Lady Johannetta, daughter of Sir Robert de Keith, Great Marshal of Scotland, 1324, and had:

SIR JOHN DE HAMILTON, of Cadyou, *d.* before 28 July, 1397, who *m.* Lady Janet, daughter of Sir James Douglas, Lord of Dalkeith and Liddisdale, *d.* 1420, by his first wife, Lady Agnes, daughter of Patrick Dunbar, Earl of Dunbar and Marche, also of Royal Descent, and had:

SIR JAMES HAMILTON, of Cadyou, one of the hostages for the ransom of King James I. in 1424, and a member of His Majesty's Privy Council, who *m.*, before 20 October, 1422, Lady Janet, daughter of Sir Alexander

Livingston, of Callendar, who was appointed governor to young King James II., and justice-general of Scotland in 1449, and ambassador to England, *d.* 145-, and his wife, a daughter of Dundas, of Dundas, and had:

GAVIN HAMILTON, fourth son, provost of the Collegiate Church of Bothwell, who *m.* Jean Muirhead, "the Fair Maid of Lechbrunnock," descended from the House of Lauchope (*see* Wood's Douglas's "Peerage of Scotland," i., pp. 311, 695), and had:

JOHN HAMILTON, of Orbiston, who *m.* Jean, daughter of Hamilton, of Woodhall, and had:

GAVIN HAMILTON, of Orbiston and Raplock, 1512–1540, commendator of Kilwinning, who *m.* Helen, daughter of Wallace, of Cairnhill, and had:

JOHN HAMILTON, of Orbiston, *k.* in the battle of Langsyde, who *m.* Margaret, daughter of Hamilton, of Haggs, and had:

MARJORY HAMILTON, who *m.* David Dundas, of Duddingston (*see* Burke's "Landed Gentry," 1858), and had:

GEORGE DUNDAS, of Manor, 1628; *m.* Margaret, daughter of William Livingston, of West Quarter, and had:

JOHN DUNDAS, of Manor, who *m.* Elizabeth, daughter of Hamilton, of Kilbrackment, and had:

RALPH DUNDAS, of Manor, who *m.* Helen, daughter of Sir Thomas Burnet, M.D., physician to King William and Queen Anne, of England, and had:

JOHN DUNDAS, of Manor, who had by his first wife, Anne, daughter of John Murray, of Polnaise: THOMAS, of Philadelphia, whose grandson succeeded to the estates of Manor, and

JAMES DUNDAS, *b.* at Manor, 1734, removed to Philadelphia, 1757, *d.* 1788; *m.* Elizabeth, *d.* 1787, daughter of James Moore, and had:

ELIZABETH DUNDAS, *b.* 28 January, 1764, *d.* 15 September, 1793, who *m.*, 27 October, 1785, Henry Pratt, of "The Hills," Philadelphia, also of Royal Descent, and had:

SARAH CLEMENTINA PRATT, *b.* 29 December, 1791, *d.* 31 December, 1836; *m.*, 14 September, 1809, Thomas McKean, Jr., of Philadelphia, *b.* 20 November, 1779, *d.* 5 May, 1852; adjutant-general of Pennsylvania, 1808–1811 (son of Thomas McKean, LL.D., member and President of the Continental Congress, from Delaware, chief justice and Governor of Pennsylvania, a signer of the Declaration of Independence, and his second wife, Sarah Armitage, of New Castle, Delaware), and had:

1.—HENRY PRATT McKEAN, of Philadelphia and "Fernhill," *b.* 3 May, 1810; *m.*, 8 July, 1841, Phœbe Elizabeth, daughter of Stephen and Martha Cornell (Mabbett) Warren, of Troy, New York, and had:

Thomas McKean, of Philadelphia and " Fernhill," *b.* 28 November, 1842; *m.*, 24 September, 1863, Elizabeth Wharton, a member of the Pennsylvania Society of the Colonial Dames of America, also of Royal Descent.

2.—Sarah Ann McKean, *b.* 10 August, 1811; *m.*, 5 November, 1833, George Trott, of Boston and of Philadelphia, and had :

Sarah McKean Trott, *b.* 8 December, 1835; *m.*, 2 December, 1857, James W. Hazlehurst, of Philadelphia, and had :

Elizabeth Borie Hazlehurst, a member of the Pennsylvania Society of the Colonial Dames of America; *m.*, 1 June, 1887, Daniel Lammot, of Philadelphia, also of Royal Descent.

3.—Elizabeth Dundas McKean, *b.* 2 March, 1815, *d. s. p.* 29 March, 1886; *m.*, 23 May, 1839, Adolphe Edward Borie, of Philadelphia, Secretary of the Navy under President Grant, *d.* 5 February, 1880.

4.—Clementina Sophia McKean, *b.* 27 May, 1829; *m.*, 23 May, 1843, Charles Louis Borie, of Philadelphia, *b.* 7 January, 1819, *d.* 7 November, 1886, and had :

I.—Elizabeth McKean Borie, *b.* 4 March, 1844, a member of the Pennsylvania Society of the Colonial Dames of America, who *m.*, 11 December, 1872, John Thompson Lewis, of Philadelphia, and had : *Charles Borie, Phœbe Morris,* and *Elizabeth Borie.*

II.—Beauveau Borie, of Philadelphia, *b.* 9 May, 1846; *m.*, 3 December, 1868, Patty Duffield Neill. *Issue.*

III.—Emily Borie, *b.* 9 April, 1851, a member of the Pennsylvania Society of the Colonial Dames of America, who *m.*, 5 January, 1871, James Mauran-Rhodes, of Philadelphia and Ardmore, Pennsylvania, *b.* Providence, Rhode Island, 25 December, 1848, and had : *Clementina Borie, m.* Edward T. Hartshorne; *Mary Aborn, James Mauran, Frank Mauran, Elizabeth McKean, Emily Borie, d.* 1881 ; *Emily Beauveau, Charles Borie, Sophia Beauveau,* and *Lawrence Mauran.*

IV.—Sarah Clementina McKean Borie, *b.* 2 February, 1853, a member of the Pennsylvania Society of the Colonial Dames of America, who *m.*, 12 October, 1886, George Champlin Mason, Jr., of Philadelphia and Ardmore, Pennsylvania, *b.* Newport, Rhode Island, 8 August, 1849. *No issue.*

THE ROYAL DESCENT

OF

MRS. WILLIAM E. STRONG,

OF NEW YORK CITY.

HENRY III., King of England⊤Lady Eleanor of Provence.

Edmund, Earl of Lancaster⊤Lady Blanche of Artois.

Henry, Earl of Lancaster⊤Lady Maud de Chaworth.

Lady Maud Plantagenet⊤Sir William de Burgh, Earl of Ulster.

Lady Elizabeth de Burgh⊤Lionel, Duke of Clarence.

Lady Philippa Plantagenet⊤Edmund de Mortimer, Earl of Marche.

Lady Elizabeth de Mortimer⊤Sir Henry de Percy, K. G., "Hotspur."

Henry, Earl of Northumberland⊤Lady Eleanor de Neville.

Henry, Earl of Northumberland⊤Lady Eleanor Poynings.

Lady Margaret de Percy⊤Sir William Gascoigne, of Gawthrope.

Lady Elizabeth Gascoigne⊤Gilbert de Talbois, of Kyme.

Sir George de Talbois, of Kyme⊤(Name unknown.)

Lady Anne de Talbois⊤Sir Edward Dymoke, of Scrivelsby, Lincolnshire.

Lady Frances Dymoke⊤Thomas Windebank, of Haines Hill, Berkshire.

Lady Mildred Windebank⊤Robert Reade, Linkenholt Manor, Southampton.

Col. George Reade, of Gloucester Co., Va.⊤Elizabeth Martian.

Mildred Reade⊤Col. Augustine Warner, Jr., of "Warner's Hall."

Mary Warner (*m.* 17 February, 1680)⊤John Smith, of "Purton," Gloucester Co., Va.

Augustine Smith, of "Purton," 1687-1756⊤Sarah Carver.

John Smith, of "Shooters' Hill," Va., 1715-1771⊤Mary Jacquelin.

Augustine Smith, of "Shooters' Hill," 1738-1774⊤Margaret Boyd.

Mary Jacquelin Smith, 1773-1846⊤John Cripps Vowell, of Alexandria, Va.

Sarah Gosnell Vowell, member of the National⊤Francis Lee Smith, of Fauquier Co., Va.
Society of the Colonial Dames of America

Alice Corbin Smith, member of the National⊤William Everard Strong, of New York City.
Society of the Colonial Dames of America

Francis Lee Strong. *d.*   Anne Massie Strong.   Alice Everard Strong.

PEDIGREE XXIV.

EDWARD I., King of England, had by his second wife, Princess Margaret, daughter of **Philip III., King of France:**

EDMUND PLANTAGENET, Earl of Kent, beheaded in 1330, who had by his wife, Lady Margaret, daughter of John, Baron de Wake, also of Royal Descent:

LADY JOAN PLANTAGENET, "the Fair Maid of Kent," divorced from William de Montacute, Earl of Salisbury. She *m.*, secondly, Sir Thomas de Holland, K.G., Earl of Kent, Captain-General of Brittany, France and Normandy, *d.* 1360 (she was the mother of King Richard II. by her third husband, Edward the Black Prince), and had:

SIR THOMAS DE HOLLAND, K.G., second Earl of Kent, marshal of England, *b.* 1397, who had by his wife, Lady Alice Fitz-Alan, daughter of Sir Richard, Earl of Arundel and Surrey, *d.* 1375, and his second wife, Lady Eleanor Plantagenet, also of Royal Descent:

LADY MARGARET DE HOLLAND, *d.* 31 December, 1440, who *m.*, first, Sir John de Beaufort, K.G., Earl of Somerset, Marquis of Dorset, lord high admiral and chamberlain, *d.* 16 March, 1410, also of Royal Descent, and had:

EDMUND DE BEAUFORT, K.G., fourth Duke of Somerset, Marquis of Dorset, Regent of France; *k.* at St. Albans, in 1455. He *m.* Lady Alianore Beauchamp, daughter of Richard, Earl of Warwick, and had:

LADY JOANE DE BEAUFORT, who *m.*, first, Sir Robert St. Lawrence, fifteenth Baron Howth, lord chancellor of Ireland, and had:

LADY ANNE ST. LAWRENCE, who *m.* Thomas Cusack, of Gerardstown, and had:

ELIZABETH CUSACK, who *m.*, 1563, Patrick Delafield, son of Sir Thomas Delafield, of Fieldstown, county Kildare (*see* Burke's "History of the Commoners," i., 544), also of Royal Descent, and had:

JOHN DELAFIELD, who *m.* Anne de la Bere, and had:

JOHN DELAFIELD, who *m.*, 1610, Elizabeth, daughter of Thomas Hampden, of Hampden, in Bucks, and had:

JOHN DELAFIELD, who *m.*, 1636, Elizabeth Brooke, and had:

JOHN DELAFIELD, *b.* 1637. For distinguished military services at the battle of Zenta, he was created a Count of the Holy Roman Empire, in 1697, with remainder of the title to his descendants, male and female, of his name. His eldest son:

John Delafield, *b.* 1656, *m.* Mary, daughter of James Heanage (or Headage), and had:

John Delafield, *b.* 1692, who *m.* Sarah, daughter of James Goodwin, and had:

John Delafield, eldest son, *b.* 1720, *d.* 1763; *m.* Martha, *b.* 1719, *d.* 1761, daughter of John Dell, of Aylesbury, in Bucks, and had:

John Delafield, of New York City, a Count of the Holy Roman Empire, as inherited from his great-grandfather; *b.* in England, 16 March, 1748. He *m.*, 4 December, 1784, Anne, *b.* 24 February, 1766, *d.* 6 March, 1839, daughter of Joseph Hallett, of New York, and dying, 3 July, 1824, had:

1. Count John Delafield, of New York, eldest son, *b.* 22 January, 1786, *d.* 22 October, 1853. He *m.*, first, in England, 22 January, 1817, Mary, daughter of John Roberts, of London, and had by her four children, of whom the eldest son, John, *b.* 1812, succeeded his father as a Count of the Holy Roman Empire, and dying, in 1866, was succeeded in the title by his eldest surviving son, Wallace Delafield, of St. Louis, Missouri, *b.* 1 May, 1840. He *m.*, secondly, 27 November, 1821, Harriot Wadsworth, daughter of Benjamin Tallmadge, of Litchfield, Connecticut, and had: *Harriot, Clarence,* and

I.—Mary Floyd Delafield, *b.* 11 May, 1834, a member of the Maine Society of the Colonial Dames of America, who *m.*, 4 November, 1858, Henry Adams Neely, of Portland, Maine, and had: *Harriot D.*, *b.* 2 January, 1862, *d.* 25 August, 1863, and *Albert Delafield, b.* 23 August, 1863, *d.* 26 December, 1890.

II.—Tallmadge Delafield, of Brooklyn, New York, who *m.*, 2 October, 1850, Anna Andrews Lawrence, and had *Tallmadge, Harriot,* and

Cornelia Delafield, a member of the Maine Society of the Colonial Dames of America, who *m.*, 31 October, 1877, in Aurora, New York, Theodore Clarence Woodbury, of Portland, Maine, and had: *Edith White, b.* 3 February, 1880, and *Lawrence Delafield, b.* 25 May, 1883.

2.—Major Joseph Delafield, of New York City, *b.* 22 August, 1790, *d.* 12 February, 1875; *m.*, 12 December, 1833, Julia, *b.* 15 September, 1801, *d.* at Rhinebeck, New York, 23 June, 1882, daughter of Maturin Livingston, of Stadsburgh, New York, and his wife Margaret, daughter of Governor Morgan Lewis, a son of Francis Lewis, of New York, a signer of the Declaration of Independence, and had: *Lewis Livingston,* 1834–1883, *Maturin Livingston, b.* 1836, and

Julia Livingston Delafield, of New York City, a member of The Colonial Dames of America Society.

PEDIGREE XXV.

EDWARD I., King of England, had by his first wife, Princess Eleanor, only child of Ferdinand III., King of Castile:

PRINCESS ELIZABETH PLANTAGENET, 1282–1316, widow of John de Vere, who *m.*, secondly, 14 November, 1302, Humphrey de Bohun, fourth Earl of Hereford and Essex; lord high constable of England, *k.* at Boroughbridge 1321, and had by him:

LADY MARGARET DE BOHUN, *d.* 16 December, 1391, who *m.*, 1325, Sir Hugh de Courtenay, K.G., second Earl of Devon, *d.* 1377, also of Royal Descent, and had:

EDWARD COURTENAY, of Goderington, Devon, second son, *d. v. p.*, who *m.* Emeline, daughter and heiress of Sir John d'Auney, of Modeford Terry, Somerset, and had:

SIR HUGH COURTENAY, of Haccomb, Devon, second son, brother of Edward Courtenay, third Earl of Devon, who *m.*, thirdly, Maud, daughter of Sir John Beaumont, of Sherwill, Dorset, *d.* 1468, and had:

LADY MARGARET COURTENAY, who *m.* Sir Theobald Grenville, of Stowe, Cornwall, and had:

SIR WILLIAM GRENVILLE, of Bideford, Cornwall, *m.* Lady Philippa, daughter of Sir William Bonville, K.G., Baron Bonville, of Chuton, and had:

THOMAS GRENVILLE, of Stowe, Cornwall, sheriff of Gloucestershire, *m.* Elizabeth, sister to Sir Theobald Gorges, Knt., of Devonshire, and had:

SIR THOMAS GRENVILLE, of Stowe (*see* Edmondson's " Baronage "), *m.* Elizabeth (or Isabella), daughter of Sir Otis Gilbert, of Compton, sheriff of Devonshire, 1474, *d.* 1494, and had:

SIR ROGER GRENVILLE, of Stowe and Bideford, *m.* Margaret, daughter of Richard Whitleigh, of Efford, Devon, and had:

AMY GRENVILLE, *m.* John Drake, of Ashe, Musbury and Exmouth, sheriff of Devonshire, 1561–62, and had:

ROBERT DRAKE, of Wiscombe Park, Devon, *m.* Elizabeth, daughter of Humphrey Prideaux, of Thewborough, Devon, *d.* 1550, and had:

WILLIAM DRAKE, of Wiscombe Park, *m.* Philippa, daughter of Sir Robert Dennys, of Holcombe, Devonshire, *d.* 1592, and had:

JOHN DRAKE, *b.* at Wiscombe, 1585, came to New England 1630 and settled at Windsor, Connecticut, in 1635, *d.* 17 August, 1659; *m.* Elizabeth Rodgers, *d.* 7 October, 1681 (*see* Stiles' "History of Windsor," N. Y. His. Geneal. Record, ii., 102, and Salisbury's "Genealogies,"—this Drake pedigree is registered in the College of Heralds, London), and had:

1.—SERGEANT JOB DRAKE, of Windsor, Connecticut, *d.* 6 August, 1689, *m.*, 25 June, 1646, Mary, *d.* 11 September, 1689, daughter of Henry Wolcott, of Galdon Manor, Tolland, Somersetshire, England, and Windsor, 1578–1655, and had:

LIEUTENANT JOB DRAKE, of Windsor, 1652–1711; *m.*, 13 September, 1677, Mrs. Elizabeth Cook, 1651–1729, daughter of Daniel Clarke, of Windsor, 1623–1710, and had:

SARAH DRAKE, *b.* 10 May, 1686, *d.* 21 January, 1747, who *m.*, 3 December, 1702, Major-General Roger Wolcott, Governor of Connecticut, *etc.*, *d.* 17 May, 1767, and had:

I.—URSULA WOLCOTT, 1724–1788, who *m.* Judge Matthew Griswold, of Lyme, governor, chief justice, *etc.*, of Connecticut, 1714–1799, and had:

JOHN GRISWOLD, of Lyme, Connecticut, 1752–1812; *m.* Sarah, 1748–1802, daughter of Rev. Stephen Johnson, of Lyme, 1724–1786, and had:

URSULA GRISWOLD, 1775–1811, who *m.* Richard McCurdy, of Lyme, 1769–1857, and had:

JUDGE CHARLES JOHNSON McCURDY, LL.D., of Lyme, who *m.* Sarah Ann, 1799–1835, daughter of Richard Lord, of Lyme, 1752–1818, also of Royal Descent, and had:

EVELYN McCURDY, a member of the Connecticut Society of the Colonial Dames of America, who *m.* Prof. Edward Elbridge Salisbury, of New Haven, Connecticut. *No issue.*

II.—ALEXANDER WOLCOTT, M.D., *b.* 7 January, 1712, *m.*, 1745 (his third wife), Mary Richards, of New London, *d.* 25 March, 1795, and had:

ALEXANDER WOLCOTT, *b.* 15 September, 1758, *d.* 26 June, 1828, in Boston, Massachusetts; *m.*, 1 September, 1785, Frances Burbank, of Springfield, Massachusetts, and had:

FRANCES WOLCOTT, *b.* 9 August, 1786, *m.*, 1803, secondly, Arthur W. Magill, of Middletown, Connecticut, and had:

JULIETTE A. MAGILL, *b.* 11 September, 1806, *m.*, 9 August, 1829, John H. Kinzie, of Chicago, Illinois, *d.* 15 September, 1870, and had:

ELEANOR LYTLE KINZIE, president of the Georgia and second vice-president of the National Societies of the Colonial Dames of America, *b.* 18 June, 1835, who *m.*, 21 December, 1857, William Washington Gordon, of Savannah, Georgia, who graduated at Yale in 1854, served with General Lee, General Hood, General Joseph E. Johnston and General Hugh Mercer in the Civil War; was, by special appointment of President McKinley, Brigadier-General commanding 2d Brigade, 1st Division, 7th Army Corps United States Army, in the Spanish War; was appointed commissioner to Porto Rico with General Brooke and Admiral Schley, to arrange for the evacuation of that island, and had:

I.—ELEANOR KINZIE GORDON, *b.* 27 September, 1858, *m.*, 2 January, 1884, Richard Wayne Parker, of Newark, New Jersey, and had: *Alice Gordon, b.* 27 January, 1885; *Eleanor Wayne, b.* 21 March, 1887; *Elizabeth Wolcott, b.* 19 November, 1889; *Wayne, b.* 29 September, 1892, *d.* 1 April, 1899, and *Cortlandt, b.* 5 February, 1896.

II.—JULIETTE MAGILL GORDON, *b.* 31 October, 1860, a member of the Georgia Society of the Colonial Dames of America, who *m.*, 21 December, 1886, William Mackay Low, of Wellesbourne House, Warwickshire, England. *No issue.*

III.—SARAH ALICE GORDON, *b.* 7 August, 1863, *d.* 30 December, 1880.

IV.—WILLIAM WASHINGTON GORDON, JR., *b.* 16 April, 1866, *m.*, 2 March, 1892, Ellen Buchanan Screven, also of Royal Descent, a member of the Georgia Society of the Colonial Dames of America, and had: *William Washington III., b.* 4 March, 1893, and *Ellen Buchanan, b.* 1 June, 1895, *d.* 21 May, 1897.

V.—MABEL MCLANE GORDON, *b.* 28 October, 1870, a member of the Georgia Society of the Colonial Dames of America, who *m.*, 31 October, 1899, Hon. Rowland Charles Frederick Leigh, of Stoneleigh Abbey, Warwickshire, England.

VI.—GEORGE ARTHUR GORDON, *b.* 30 August, 1872.

2.—JOHN DRAKE, JR., of Windsor, *d.* 7 July, 1688–89; *m.*, 30 November, 1648, Hannah Moore, and had:

LYDIA DRAKE, *b.* 26 January, 1661, *d.* May, 1702; *m.*, 10 April, 1681, Joseph Loomis, of Windsor, and had:

CAPTAIN JOSEPH LOOMIS, *b.* 8 October, 1684, *d.* 30 May, 1748; *m.*, 28 June, 1710, Mary Cooley, of Springfield, Massachusetts, and had:

MARY LOOMIS, *b.* 12 January, 1720–21, *d.* 5 May, 1744; *m.*, 28 October, 1742, Elijah Fitch, and had:

MARY FITCH, *b.* 25 April, 1744, *d.* 11 November, 1774, *m.*, 6 December, 1759, Ebenezer Reed, and had:

DR. ELIJAH FITCH REED, of Windsor, *b.* 13 May, 1767, *d.* South Windsor, 9 September, 1847; *m.*, 6 June, 1792, Hannah, daughter of Alexander and Joanna (Smith) McLean, and had:

Rev. Julius Alexander Reed, D.D., *b.* at Windsor 16 January, 1809, *d.* 27 August, 1890, at Davenport, Iowa; *m.*, at Jacksonville, Illinois, 2 December, 1835, Caroline Blood, also of Royal Descent, and had:

Mary Reed, *b.* Fairfield, Iowa, 9 February, 1843, a member of the Massachusetts and Iowa Societies of the Colonial Dames of America, who *m.*, 7 August, 1863, Samuel Francis Smith, of Davenport, Iowa, and had: *Anna Reed, b.* 15 September, 1870.

3.—Elizabeth Drake, who *m.* first, 14 November, 1644, (*see* Stiles's "History of Windsor,"), William Gaylord, of Windsor, Connecticut, *d.* 14 December, 1656, and had:

Nathaniel Gaylord, *b.* September 3, 1656, who *m.*, 17 October, 1678, Abigail Bissell, *b.* 23 November, 1658, *d.* 23 September, 1723, and had:

Josiah Gaylord, *b.* 24 February, 1686, who *m.*, 7 May, 1713, Naomi Burnham, *b.* 3 June, 1688, *d.* January, 1762, and had:

Nehemiah Gaylord, *b.* 15 June, 1722, *d.* 1801, who *m.*, 10 May, 1748, Lucy Loomis, *b.* 5 August, 1727, *d.* 2 September, 1800, and had:

Lucy Gaylord, *b.* 14 April, 1749, *d.* 4 July, 1837, who *m.*, 1769, Zachariah Mather, of Stockbridge, Massachusetts, *b.* 22 September, 1743, *d.* 21 August, 1816, and had:

Lucy Mather, *b.* 2 June, 1770, *d.* 29 March, 1862, who *m.*, 4 February, 1788, John Field Fitch, of East Windsor, Connecticut, *b.* 7 February, 1766, *d.* 1819, and had:

Augustus Fitch, M.D., of Columbia, South Carolina, *b.* 30 October, 1794, *d.* 26 August, 1857, who *m.*, 1 May, 1821, Abigail Putnam, *b.* 26 April, 1797, *d.* 31 July, 1834, and had:

Julia Ann Fitch, who *m.*, 30 January, 1851, Augustus Horatio Jones, of Charleston, South Carolina, and had:

Annie Vane Jones, of Savannah, Georgia, a member of the Georgia Society of the Colonial Dames of America, the Order of the Crown, *etc.*

PEDIGREE XXVI.

EDWARD I., King of England, had by his first wife, Princess Eleanor, daughter of Ferdinand III., King of Castile and Leon :

PRINCESS JOAN D'ACRE, *d.* 1307, who *m.*, first (his second wife), Gilbert de Clare, Earl of Clare, Hertford and Gloucester, *d.* 1295, also of Royal Descent, and had :

LADY MARGARET DE CLARE, widow of Piers de Gavestone, who *m.*, secondly, Hugh, second Baron d'Audley, created, in 1337, Earl of Gloucester, *d. s. p. m.*, 1347, and had :

LADY MARGARET D'AUDLEY, who *m.* Sir Ralph, second Baron Stafford, K.G., one of the founders of the Order of the Garter, created, in 1351, Earl of Stafford, *d.* 1372, and had :

LADY JOANE DE STAFFORD, who *m.* John, second Baron de Cherleton, lord of Powys, Wales, chamberlain to King Edward III., and had :

SIR EDWARD DE CHERLETON, K.G., fourth Baron de Cherleton, lord of Powys, second son, elected a Knight of the Garter, 1406–07, *d. s. p. m.*, 14 March, 1420; who *m.* Lady Eleanor de Holland, daughter of Thomas, second Earl of Kent, also of Royal Descent, and had :

LADY JOANE DE CHERLETON, who *m.* Sir John de Grey, K.G., created, in 1418, Earl of Tankerville, *k.* 22 March, 1420, also of Royal Descent, and had :

SIR HENRY DE GREY, second Earl of Tankerville, *d.* 1449, who *m.* Lady Antigone Plantagenet, daughter of Humphrey, Duke of Gloucester, and had :

LADY ELIZABETH DE GREY, *m.* Sir Roger Kynaston, Knt., *d.* 1517, also of Royal Descent, and had :

LADY MARY KYNASTON, *m.* Howell ap Ievan, of Yns-y Maen-Gwyn, and had :

HUMPHREY AP HOWELL, *m.* Anne, daughter of Sir Richard Herbert, Knt., of Colebrook, and had :

JANE VCH. HUMPHREY, *m.* Griffith ap Howell, of Nannau, Merionethshire, *temp.* 1541 (*see* Dwnn's " Visitations of Wales," ii., 226), a descendant of Bledhyn ap Cynfyn, a prince of Powys, and had :

JOHN AP GRIFFITH, of Nannau, second son, who *m.* Elizabeth, daughter of David Lloyd, of Trawsfynedd, and had :

(109)

LEWIS AP JOHN, of Dyffrydan township, 1654, *m.* Ellen, daughter of Howell ap Gruffydd, and had:

OWEN AP LEWIS, who *m.* Mary, daughter of Tudor Vaughan, of Caer y Nwch, Merionethshire, and had:

ROBERT AP OWEN, who *m.* Margaret, daughter of John ap Lewis, and had:

LEWIS AP ROBERT, (*see* P. S. P. Conner's "Lewis Pedigree," and Glenn's "Merion in the Welsh Tract"), who *m.* Mary, and had:

ELLIS LEWIS, *b.* in Wales about 1680, came from Ireland to Pennsylvania (he was a Quaker, and his "Certificate of Removal" is dated at Mt. Mellick, Queen's county, Ireland, 25 May, 1708), and settled in Kennett township, Chester county, *d.* 31 August, 1750, will proved 29 October, 1750. He had by his first wife, *m.*, at Concord Meeting, Chester county, in 1713, Elizabeth, *b.* 3 March, 1687–88, daughter of Nathaniel Newlin, of Newlin township, Chester county, member of the Provincial Assembly, 1698; justice of the county, 1703; commissioner of property, *etc.*, and had:

ROBERT LEWIS, of Philadelphia, *b.* 21 March, 1714, member of the Assembly, 1745, *d.* 1790; *m.*, at Concord Meeting, 23 May, 1733, Mary, 1714–1782, daughter of William Pyle, of Chester county, a member of the Assembly and a justice, and had:

ELLIS LEWIS, of Philadelphia, 1734–1776, who *m.*, secondly, 16 June, 1763, Mary, daughter of David Deshler, of Philadelphia, and had:

PHEBE LEWIS, 1767–1845, who *m.*, 10 October, 1787, Robert Waln, Jr., 1765–1836, and had:

REBECCA WALN, 1802–1846, who *m.* Jeremiah Fisher Leaming, of Philadelphia, 1795–1888, and had:

REBECCA LEAMING, 1836–1888, who *m.*, 1869, Charles Pendleton Tutt, M.D., 1832–1866, son of Colonel Charles P. and Ann Mason (Chichester) Tutt, and had: *Charles Leaming*, and

REBECCA WALN TUTT, a member of the Virginia Society of the Colonial Dames of America, who *m.*, first, Edward Gray Pendleton, and had: *Maud Pendleton, d.*, and *m.*, secondly, Franc Ogilvy-Wood, of Colorado Springs, Colorado, and had: *Guy Catlin Wood, d.*

PEDIGREE XXVII.

HENRY I., King of France, had by his third wife, Anne of Russia:

HUGH THE GREAT, Count de Vermandois, Duke of France, *etc., m.*, thirdly, Lady Adela, or Adelheid, 1080–1117, daughter and heiress of Herbert IV., Count de Vermandois, 1045–1080, also of Royal Descent, and had by her:

LADY ISABEL DE VERMANDOIS, *d.* 1131, who *m.*, first, 1096, Robert, Baron de Bellomonte, Earl of Mellent and Leicester, *d.* 1118, and had:

ROBERT DE BELLOMONTE, second Earl of Leicester, justice of England, *d.* 1168, who had by his wife, Lady Aurelia, or Amicia, daughter of Ralph de Waer, Earl of Norfolk, Suffolk and Cambridge, which earldoms he forfeited in 1074:

ROBERT DE BELLOMONTE, third Earl of Leicester, steward of England, *d.* 1196, who had by his wife, Lady Petronella, daughter of Hugh de Grentesmaismill:

LADY MARGARET DE BELLOMONTE, who *m.* Sairer, Baron de Quincey, of Bushby, created Earl of Winchester, one of the sureties for King John's Magna Charta, *d.* 1219, and had:

ROGER DE QUINCEY, second Earl of Winchester, constable of Scotland, *d.* 1264, who had by his second wife, Lady Helen, daughter of Alan Macdonal, lord of Galloway:

LADY ELIZABETH DE QUINCEY, who *m.* Alexander, second Baron Cumyn, first Earl of Buchan, and had:

LADY —— CUMYN (sister of Alexander, second Earl, *d.* 1289), who *m.* Sir John de Keith, great marshal of Scotland, and had:

ADAM DE KEITH, rector of Keith-Marischall, 1292, *k.* in 1336, father of:

JOHANNA KEITH, who *m.* Sir Alexander Stewart, of Derneley and Cambusnethan, Knt., third son of Sir Alan Stewart, of Dreghorn, who was *k.* at Hallidon Hill, 1333, and had:

LADY JANET STEWART, who *m.* Thomas, first Lord Somerville, *d.* 1445, and had:

LADY MARGARET DE SOMERVILLE, who *m.*, first, Sir Roger Kyrkepatrick, laird of Klyosebern, Dumfrieshire, and had:

ALEXANDER KYRKEPATRICK, second son, laird of Kirkmichael, whose son:

WILLIAM KIRKPATRICK, of Kirkmichael, obtained, in 1565, from the vicar of the parish of Garrel, the church-lands and glebe of the parish, though, just previous to this, he was " under scandal with the Reformers for allowing mass to be celebrated within his bounds." He was summoned to Parliament in 1548, and was father of:

SIR ALEXANDER KIRKPATRICK, Knt., of Kirkmichael, eldest son, who *m.* Margaret Chateris, and had:

WILLIAM KIRKPATRICK, of Kirkmichael, eldest son, father of:

WILLIAM KIRKPATRICK, of Kirkmichael, who sold his estate, and *d.* 9 June, 1686. His eldest son (*see* Wood's Douglas's " Peerage of Scotland "):

GEORGE KIRKPATRICK, of Knock, in Kirkmichael parish, had Thomas (an ancestor of Eugenie, former Empress of France), and

ALEXANDER KIRKPATRICK, younger son, whose son

ALEXANDER KIRKPATRICK, *b.* in Watties Neach, Dumfrieshire, removed to Belfast, Ireland, about 1725, and then to America in 1736, and settled finally in Somerset county, New Jersey, where he *d.* 3 June, 1758, leaving issue by his wife, Elizabeth (*see* " Kirkpatrick Genealogy "):

DAVID KIRKPATRICK, *b.* Watties Neach, 17 February, 1724, *d.* Mine Brook, Somerset county, New Jersey, 19 March, 1814; *m.*, 31 March, 1748, Mary McEowen, and had:

ANNE KIRKPATRICK, who *m.* Captain Moses Este, of Morristown, New Jersey, and had:

JUDGE DAVID KIRKPATRICK ESTE, of Cincinnati, who *m.*, first, 1819, Lucy Singleton, daughter of General William Henry Harrison, President of the United States, also of Royal Descent, and had by her:

LUCY ANN HARRISON ESTE, who *m.* Joseph Reynolds, of Baltimore and Hagerstown, Maryland, and had:

ANNA HARRISON REYNOLDS, who *m.* John Law Crawford, and had:

LUCY ESTE CRAWFORD, a member of the Maryland Society of the Colonial Dames of America, who *m.* George ·C. Woodruff, of Litchfield, Connecticut. *No issue.*

PEDIGREE XXVIII.

ROBERT II., King of Scotland, had by his first wife, Lady Elizabeth, daughter of Sir Adam Mure, of Rowallan:

PRINCESS CATHERINE STEWART, who *m.* Sir David Lindsay, Knt., of Glenesk, created, in 1389, Earl of Crawford, and had:

.ALEXANDER LINDSAY, second Earl of Crawford, *k.* 13 January, 1445–46, who *m.* Lady Mariotta, daughter of Sir David Dunbar, of Cockburn, son of George, Earl of Dunbar and Marche, and had:

SIR WALTER LINDSAY, of Kinblethmont, Edzell and Bewfort, third son, who *m.* Lady Isabel, daughter of William, Lord Livingston, or Sophia, daughter of Livingston, of Saltcoats, and had:

SIR DAVID LINDSAY, Knt., of Bewfort and Edzell, *d.* 1527, who had by his first wife, Catherine Fotheringham, of Powrie:

WALTER LINDSAY, of Edzell, eldest son, *k. v. p.*, at Flodden, 1513, who *m.* a daughter of Erskine, of Dun, and had:

SIR DAVID LINDSAY, of Edzell and Glenesk, eldest son, *d.* 1558. His relation, David Lindsay, seventh Earl of Crawford, "having been used by his sons with unnatural barbarity, disponed, in 1541, his estates and honors" in favor of this Sir David Lindsay, who became eighth Earl of Crawford, who subsequently conveyed back the estates and title to the grandson of the seventh Earl, reserving only during his lifetime the title of Earl of Crawford. He had by his second wife, Lady Catherine, daughter of Sir John Campbell, of Calder:

SIR DAVID LINDSAY, of Edzell, eldest son, one of the lords of Session, *d.* 1610; *m.*, first, Lady Helen Lindsay, daughter of David, ninth Earl of Crawford, and had by her:

LADY MARGARET LINDSAY, who *m.* David Carnegy, of Kinniard, created Lord Carnegy and Earl of Southesk, *d.* 1658, and had:

LADY CATHERINE CARNEGY, who *m.* Sir John Stuart, created Lord Stuart, of Traquier, and Earl of Traquier, Lord Linton and Cabarston; lord high treasurer of Scotland in 1635, *d.* 1659, and had:

JOHN STUART, second Earl of Traquier, 1622–1666; *m.*, secondly, 2 April, 1654, Lady Ann Seton, daughter of George, Earl of Winton, and had by her:

CHARLES STUART, fourth Earl of Traquier, 1659–1741; *m.* Lady Mary Maxwell, 1671–1759, daughter of Robert, Earl of Nithesdale, and had:

(113)

JOHN STUART, sixth Earl of Traquier, 1698–1779; *m.*, 1740, Lady Christiana, 1702–1771, daughter of Sir Peter Anstruther, Bart, and widow of Sir William Weir, Bart, and had:

LADY CHRISTINA STUART, who *m.*, at Traquier House, the seat of her father, in 1769 (*see* "Am. Historical Register," July, 1895), Judge Cyrus Griffin, of Williamsburg, Virginia, president of the last Continental Congress, *b.* 1749, *d.* 1810, and had:

MARY GRIFFIN, *m.* Major Thomas Griffin, of Yorktown, and had:

MARY BERKELEY GRIFFIN, who *m.* William Waller, of Williamsburg, Virginia, and had:

WILLIAM NEVISON WALLER, of Williamsburg, who had by his first wife, *m.*, 1 February, 1842, Elizabeth, daughter of John Tyler, President of the United States of America:

MARY STUART WALLER, a member of the Georgia Society of the Colonial Dames of America, who *m.*, 25 April, 1867, Captain Louis G. Young, of Savannah. *No issue.*

PEDIGREE XXIX.

ROBERT BRUCE, King of Scotland, had by his wife, Lady Elizabeth de Burgh, of Royal Descent:

LADY MATILDA BRUCE, who *m.* Thomas Isaac, Esq., and had:

JOANNA ISAAC, who *m.* John d'Ergadia, lord of Lorn, and had:

ISABEL D'ERGADIA, who *m.* Sir John Stewart, of Innermeath, and had:

SIR JAMES STEWART, "the Black Knight of Lorn," third son, who *m.*, 1439, Lady Joan de Beaufort, also of Royal Descent, widow of James I., King of Scotland, and had:

SIR JOHN STEUART, of Balveny, lord of Lorn, created, in 1457, Earl of Athol, *d.* 19 September, 1512, uterine brother of King James II. He *m.*, secondly, Lady Eleanor, daughter of William Sinclair, Earl of Orkney and Caithness, also of Royal Descent, and had:

LADY ISABEL STEWART, who *m.* (his second wife, *see* Wood's Douglas's "Peerage of Scotland," i., 141 and 549), Alexander Robertson, fifth Baron of Strowan, and had:

JOHN ROBERTSON, first laird of Muirton, in Elgin, second son, who *m.* Margaret Crichton (possibly a daughter of Sir James Crichton, of Fendraught, eldest son of William, third Lord Crichton, who forfeited, 24 February, 1483–84), and had:

GILBERT ROBERTSON, of Muirton, heir, who *m.* Janet, daughter of John Reid, of Ackenhead, and had:

DAVID ROBERTSON, of Muirton, heir, who *m.* —— Innes, and had:

WILLIAM ROBERTSON, of Muirton, heir, who *m.* Isabel Petrie, and had:

WILLIAM ROBERTSON, of Gladney, who *m.* —— Mitchell, and had:

REV. WILLIAM ROBERTSON, of Edinburgh, (*see* Burke's "Royal Families," ii., Ped. 190), who *m.* a daughter of Pitcairn, of Dreghorn, and had: WILLIAM ROBERTSON, Royal Historiographer (*see* Lord Brougham's account of the Robertsons), and:

JEAN ROBERTSON, who *m.* Alexander Henry, of Aberdeen, and had:

COLONEL JOHN HENRY,* who came to Virginia in 1730, and was seated at "Studley" and "The Retreat," in Hanover county. He *m.* Sarah, widow of Colonel Syme, and daughter of Isaac Winston, and had:

---

* MRS. WILLIAM L. ROYALL, a member of the Virginia State Society of the National Society of the Colonial Dames of America, is also of Royal Descent through John Henry.

1.—PATRICK HENRY, of " Red Hill," Charlotte county, Virginia, 1736–1799, first Governor of Virginia; *m.*, first, 1754, Sarah Shelton, of Hanover, Virginia, and had by her:

ELIZABETH HENRY, who *m.* Philip Aylett, of Virginia, also of Royal Descent, and had :

MARY MACON AYLETT, who *m.* Philip Fitzhugh, and had :

LUCY FITZHUGH, who *m.* John Redd, and had :

LUCY REDD, a member of the Indiana Society of the Colonial Dames of America, the Order of the Crown, *etc.*, who *m.* William Jacqueline Holliday, of Indianapolis, Indiana, also of Royal Descent, and had :

I.—ARIANA AMBLER HOLLIDAY, a member of the Indiana Society of the Colonial Dames of America, who *m.* Henry W. Bennett, of Indianapolis.

II.—JAQUELINE S. HOLLIDAY, *m.* Florence Baker.

III.—LUCY FITZHUGH HOLLIDAY, *m.* George E. Hume.

GOVERNOR PATRICK HENRY, *m.*, secondly, Dorothea Dandridge, also of Royal Descent, and had by her:

JOHN HENRY, who *m.* Elvira Bruce McClelland, and had :

WILLIAM WIRT HENRY, of Richmond, Virginia, who *m.* Lucy Gray Marshall, a member of the Virginia Society of the Colonial Dames of America, and had :

I.—LUCY GRAY HENRY, a member of the Virginia Society of the Colonial Dames of America, who *m.* Matthew Bland Harrison, of Richmond, Virginia.

II.—ELIZABETH HENRY, a member of the Virginia Society of the Colonial Dames of America, who *m.* James Lyons, of Richmond, Virginia.

2.—ANNE HENRY, *m.* Colonel William Christian, removed to Jefferson county, Kentucky, an officer in the Virginia Line, Continental Army, and had :

PRISCILLA CHRISTIAN, who *m.*, October, 1785, Colonel Alexander Scott Bullitt, *b.* Prince William county, Virginia, 1761, *d.* Jefferson county, Kentucky, 13 April, 1816; member and speaker of Kentucky State Senate, and was the first lieutenant-governor of the State, 1800, and had :

WILLIAM CHRISTIAN BULLITT, of Louisville, Kentucky, *m.*, 1819, Mildred Ann, daughter of Joshua and Reachy (Walker) Fry, and had :

JOHN CHRISTIAN BULLITT, of Philadelphia, Pennsylvania, *b.* 10 February, 1824, *m.*, 1850, Therese C. Langhorne, and had :

THERESE LANGHORNE BULLITT, of Philadelphia, a member of the Pennsylvania Society of the Colonial Dames of America, who *m.*, 1874, John W. Coles, M.D., surgeon United States Army, and had : *Therese Pauline.*

PEDIGREE XXX.

HUGH CAPET, King of France, had by his wife, Lady Adela (or Alisa), daughter of William, Duke of Aquitaine, and his wife, Princess Adelheid, daughter of Otto I. the Great, Emperor of Germany, 936–973 (and his second wife, Adelheid, widow of Lothary, King of Italy):

PRINCESS HAVIDE, or Hedewige, who *m.* Ranigerus IV., eleventh Count of Hainault, 977, and had:

LADY BEATRIX, who *m.* Eblo I., Count of Rouci and Reimes, and had:

LADY ADELA, Countess de Rouci, who *m.* Hildwin IV., Count of Montdider and Rouci, and had:

LADY MARGARET DE ROUCI, who *m.* Hugh de Clermont, Count de Beauvois, and had:

LADY ADELIZA DE CLERMONT, who *m.* Gilbert de Tonsburg, Kent, second Earl of Clare, and had:

LADY ADELIZA DE CLARE, who *m.* Alberic de Vere, the first great high chamberlain of England, *k.* 1140, and had:

LADY JULIANA DE VERE, who *m.* Hugh, third Baron Bigod, lord high steward, created in 1140 Earl of Norfolk, *d.* 1177, and had:

ROGER BIGOD, created in 1189 Earl of Norfolk, lord high steward, one of the sureties for the observance of the Magna Charta, *d.* 1220. He *m.*, first, Lady Isabel de Warren, also of Royal Descent, daughter of Hameline Plantagenet, Earl of Surrey, and had:

HUGH BIGOD, Earl of Norfolk, a surety for the Magna Charta, *d.* 1225, who *m.*, Lady Maud, daughter of William le Marshal, Earl of Pembroke, protector of England, and had:

SIR RALPH BIGOD, third son, who *m.* Lady Berta de Furnival, and had:

LADY ISABEL BIGOD, who *m.*, first, Gilbert de Lacy, and had:

LADY MAUD DE LACY, who *m.* Geoffrey, Baron de Genevill, of Trim, *d.* 1306–07, and had:

PETER DE GENEVILL, second son and heir, Baron de Genevill, *m.* Lady Joan, daughter of Hugh le Brune, Earl of Angoulême, and had:

LADY JOAN DE GENEVILL, who *m.* Sir Roger, Baron de Mortimer, of Wigmore, created Earl of Marche, executed for treason in 1330, also of Royal Descent, and had:

LADY MAUD DE MORTIMER, who *m.* John, second Baron de Cherlton, of Powys, chamberlain to Edward III., *d.* 1360 (*see* Jones's " Feudal Barons of Powys "), and had :

LADY JANE DE CHERLETON, who *m.* John, sixth Baron le Strange, of Knockyn, *d.* 1397 (*see* Lloyd's " History of Powys Fadog," iv., 118), also of Royal Descent, and had :

LADY ELIZABETH LE STRANGE, who *m.* Gruffydd ap Madoc Vychan, of Rhuddalt, third Baron of Glyndyfrdwy (*see* Burke's " Royal Families," chart pedigree, vol. ii., p. lxi.), and had :

LADY ISABEL, who *m.* Goronway ap Gruffith ap Madoc, and had :

TUDOR AP GRUFFITH AP GORONWAY, of Penllyn, father of:

HOWEL AP TUDOR, father of:

DAVID-LLWYD, father of:

LADY GWENHWYFAR, who *m.* David ap Evan-Vaughn, of Llanuwchllyn, and had :

DAVID-LLWYD AP DAVID, of Llandderfel, Penllyn, 1500, who *m.*, first, Annesta Griffith, and had by her :

ROBERT AP DAVID-LLWYD (or Lloyd), of Nantfreur, Penllyn, *d.* before 1592, who had by his wife, Mary v. Reynold :

THOMAS AP ROBERT, of Gwern y Brechtwn, *b.* before 1520, *d.* May, 1612, *bur.* in the Church of Llandderfel, who had, by his wife Catherine Robert Griffith :

EVAN AP THOMAS, of Nant y Friar, 1555–1640, who *m.* Dorothea Evans, *d.* 1619, and had :

THOMAS AP EVAN, 1579–1649, sheriff of Merionethshire, 1623, *m.* Catherine, daughter of William ap David, of Llandderfel, and had:

FFOULKE AP THOMAS, *bapt.* 14 April, 1623, who *m.* Lowry, daughter of ᵢ Edward ap David, of Llanvor, Merionethshire, and had :

EDWARD AP FFOULKE, *b.* 1651, *d.* 1741; *m.* Eleanor, *d.* 1733, daughter of Hugh ap Cadwalader ap Rhys, of the parish of Spytu, Denbighshire. He lived at Coed-y-foel, and left for Pennsylvania, 2 February, 1698, with his wife and nine children, where they arrived 17 June, 1698, and purchased seven hundred acres in Gwynedd township, Montgomery county, Pennsylvania (*see* Jenkins's " History of Gwynedd," and Glenn's " Merion in the Welsh Tract "). Their son :

THOMAS FOULKE, of Gwynedd, Pennsylvania, had :

WILLIAM FOULKE, of Gwynedd, who had :

AMOS FOULKE, of Philadelphia, 1740–1791 ; *m.*, 1779, Hannah Jones, 1749–1829, also of Royal Descent, and had :

EDWARD FOULKE, of Gwynedd, 1784–1851 ; *m.*, 1810, Tacy Jones, and had, besides other issue :

1.—ANN JONES FOULKE, 1811–1888; *m.*, 1833, Hiram Corson, M.D., of Conshohocken, and had:

SUSAN FOULKE CORSON, a member of the Pennsylvania Society of the Colonial Dames of America, who *m.*, 26 November, 1868, Jawood Lukens, of Conshohocken, Pennsylvania. *No issue.*

2.—PRISCILLA FOULKE, 1821–1882; *m.*, 22 April, 1849, Thomas Wistar, Jr., of Philadelphia, and had:

SUSAN FOULKE WISTAR, a member of the Pennsylvania Society of the Colonial Dames of America, who *m.*, 27 May, 1872, Howard Comfort, of Philadelphia, and had: *William Wistar, b.* 27 May, 1874.

3.—REBECCA JONES FOULKE, *b.* 18 May, 1829, a member of the Pennsylvania Society of the Colonial Dames of America; *m.*, 8 October, 1857, Robert R. Corson, of New Hope, Pennsylvania. *No issue.*

THE ROYAL DESCENTS

OF

MRS. THOMAS SETTLE,

AND

MRS. TENCH C. COXE.

EDWARD I., King of England⹀Princess Eleanor of Castile.

Princess Elizabeth Plantagenet⹀Humphrey de Bohun, Earl of Hereford.

William de Bohun, Earl of Northampton⹀Lady Elizabeth de Badlesmere.

Lady Elizabeth de Bohun⹀Richard Fitz-Alan, Earl of Arundel.

Lady Elizabeth Fitz-Alan⹀Sir Robert Goushill, of Hault Hucknall.

Lady Elizabeth Goushill⹀Sir Robert Wingfield, of Letheringham.

Sir Henry Wingfield, of Orford⹀Elizabeth Rowks.

Sir Robert Wingfield, of Upton⹀Margery Quarles.

Robert Wingfield, of Upton⹀Elizabeth Cecil.

Dorothea Wingfield⹀Adam Claypoole, of Latham, Lincolnshire.

Sir John Claypoole, of Latham⹀Marie Angell.

James Claypoole, of Philadelphia⹀Helen Merces.

Joseph Claypoole, of Philadelphia⹀Rebecca Jennings.

George Claypoole, of Philadelphia⹀Hannah ———.

George Claypoole⹀Mary Parkhouse.

William Claypole, M.D., Wilmington, N. C.⹀Mary Wright.

Ann Claypole⹀William Henry Hill, Wilmington, N. C.

Eliza Ann Hill⹀William Augustus Wright, Wilmington, N. C.

Florence Wright⹀William Fotterall Potter.

| Eliza Potter, member of the National Society of the Colonial Dames of America, the Order of the Crown, etc. *No issue.* | =Thomas Settle, of Greensboro, N. C. | Sarah Potter, member of the National Society of the Colonial Dames of America, the Order of the Crown, etc. | =Tench C. Coxe, of Asheville, N. C. Franklin Coxe, *b.* Sept., 1899. |

PEDIGREE XXXI.

EDWARD I., King of England, had by his second wife, Princess Margaret, daughter of Philip III., King of France:

PRINCE EDMUND, of Woodstock, Earl of Kent, who *m.* Lady Margaret, daughter of John, Baron Wake, also of Royal Descent, and had:

PRINCESS JOAN PLANTAGENET, the Fair Maid of Kent, who *m.*, first, William de Montacute, Earl of Salisbury; *m.*, secondly, Sir Thomas de Holland, K.G., Earl of Kent, captain-general of Brittany, France and Normandy, also of Royal Descent, and *m.*, thirdly, Edward the Black Prince, son of King Edward III., and had by him King Richard II. By her second husband she had:

SIR THOMAS DE HOLLAND, K.G., second Earl of Kent, earl marshal of England, *d.* 1397, who *m.* Lady Alice, daughter of Sir Richard Fitz-Alan, K.G., Earl of Arundel and Surry, *d.* 1375, also of Royal Descent, and had:

LADY ALIANORE DE HOLLAND, widow of Roger de Mortimer, Earl of Marche, who *m.*, secondly, Sir Edward de Cherleton, K.G., fourth Lord Cherleton, of Powys, elected a Knight of the Garter, 1406–07, *d.* 14 March, 1420, also of Royal Descent, and had:

LADY JOANE DE CHERLETON, who *m.* Sir John de Grey, K.G., also of Royal Descent, created, in 1418, Earl of Tancarville, in Normandy. He was slain in the battle of Baugy Bridge, 22 March, 1420, and had by Lady Joane:

SIR HENRY DE GREY, Knt., second Earl of Tankerville, *d.* 1449, who *m.* Lady Antigone, daughter of Humphrey Plantagenet, Duke of Gloucester, regent of France, and had:

LADY ELIZABETH DE GREY, who *m.* Sir Roger Kynaston, Knt., *d.* 1517, also of Royal Descent (*see* Jones's " Feudal Barons of Powys "), and had:

HUMPHREY KYNASTON, of Morton, Salop, *d.* 1534, who *m.* Elizabeth, daughter of Meredith ap Howel, of Lansilin, Denbighshire, also of Royal Descent, and had:

MARGARET KYNASTON (*see* Burke's " Royal Families," I., Ped. 47), who *m.* John Lloyd Wynn, of Dyffryn, also of Royal Descent, and had:

HUMPHREY LLOYD WYNN, of Dyffryn, who had:

KATHERINE LLOYD, who *m.* her kinsman, John Lloyd, of Dolobran Hall, *b.* about 1575, *d.* after 1639, also of Royal Descent (*see* Glenn's

" Merion in the Welsh Tract," p. 336; Smith's " Lloyd and Carpenter Families," and Foster's " Royal Descents "), and had:

CHARLES LLOYD, of Dolobran Hall, *b.* 1613, *bur.* 17 August, 1657; a magistrate for Montgomeryshire, who *m.* Elizabeth, daughter of Thomas Stanley, of Knockyn, Salop, son of Sir Edward Stanley, Knt., and had :

THOMAS LLOYD,* *b.* Dolobran, 17 February, 1640, *d.* 10 September, 1694. He was educated at Jesus College, Oxon, and was William Penn's agent in Pennsylvania, and the first Deputy Governor and President of the Provincial Council of Pennsylvania, 1664–93. He *m.*, first, 9 September, 1665, Mary, daughter of Roger Jones, of Welshpool, Montgomeryshire, and had by her, who *d.* 1680:

1.—DEBORAH LLOYD, 1682–172–; *m.*, 12 September, 1704, Dr. Mordecai Moore, of Anne Arundel county, Maryland, his second wife, and had:

DEBORAH MOORE, 1705–1751; *m.*, 9 February, 1720–21, Dr. Richard Hill, of Hill's Point, Maryland, *b.* 1698, *d.*, Funchal, 1762, and had:

I.—MARGARET HILL, 1737–1816; *m.*, 21 September, 1758, William Morris, of Philadelphia, 1732–1766, and had:

1.—JOHN MORRIS, M.D., of Philadelphia, 1759–1793; *m.*, 16 October, 1783, Abigail Dorsey, *d.* 1793, and had:

MARGARET MORRIS, 1792–1832, who *m.*, 4 October, 1810, Isaac Collins, Jr., of Philadelphia, and had:

FREDERIC COLLINS, of Philadelphia, *b.* 21 January, 1820, *d.* 27 November, 1892; *m.*, 28 August, 1844, Laetitia P. Dawson, and had: *Annie Morrison, b.* 26 July, 1849, *m.*, 10 April, 1890, Morris Earle, and

ELIZABETH DAWSON COLLINS, a member of the Pennsylvania Society of the Colonial Dames of America, *b.* 23 January, 1847, who *m.*, 3 June, 1869, Charles F. Hulse, of Philadelphia (son of Charles Hulse, of Nottingham, England), *d.* 28 August, 1876, and had:

I.—LAETITIA COLLINS HULSE, a member of the Pennsylvania Society of the Colonial Dames of America, who *m.*, 28 April, 1892, Samuel Bowman Wheeler, of Philadelphia, also of Royal Descent, and had: *Samuel B., b.* 22 February, 1893; *Frederic C., b.* 30 March, 1894, and *Elizabeth Dawson, b.* 7 May, 1897.

II.—MARGARET MORRIS HULSE, *b.* 22 April, 1873, who *m.* 2 November, 1898, Burnet Landreth, Jr., of Philadelphia.

---

* The following ladies, members of the National Society of the Colonial Dames of America, are also of Royal Descent, through Thomas Lloyd :

MRS. JOHN LOWELL, JR., Massachusetts State Society.

MRS. JAMES A. LOWELL, Massachusetts State Society.

2.—GULIELMA MARIA MORRIS, *b.* 18 August, 1766, *d.* 9 September, 1826; *m.*, 8 April, 1784, John Smith, of Philadelphia, *b.* 3 November, 1791, *d.* 18 April, 1803, also of Royal Descent, and had:

> JOHN JAY SMITH, of "Ivy Lodge," Philadelphia, *b.* 16 May, 1798, *d.* 23 September, 1881, who *m.*, 1821, Rachel C., daughter of Robert Pearsall, of Flushing, Long Island, and had:

>> ELIZABETH PEARSALL SMITH, of Germantown, Philadelphia, a member of the Pennsylvania Society of the Colonial Dames of America.

3.—RICHARD HILL MORRIS, of Philadelphia, 1762–1841; *m.*, secondly, 25 October, 1798, Mary, daughter of Richard S. Smith, of Burlington, New Jersey, and had by her, who *d.* 1848:

I.—EDMUND MORRIS, of Burlington, New Jersey, 1804–1874; *m.*, 1827, Mary P., *d.* 1876, daughter of William Jenks, of Bucks county, Pennsylvania, and had:

> MARY ANN MORRIS, a member of the Pennsylvania Society of the Colonial Dames of America, the Order of the Crown, *etc.*, who *m.*, 5 November, 1863, Alexander C. Fergusson, of Philadelphia, and had:

>> EDMUND M. FERGUSSON, *m.*, 1898, Mary F. Huber.

>> AGNES M. FERGUSSON, *m.*, 1893, Charles Edwin Noblit.

>> HENRY A. FERGUSSON, *m.*, 1892, Jessie M. Dysart.

>> MARY M. FERGUSSON, *d.* 1876.

>> ALEXANDER C. FERGUSSON, JR., *m.*, 1895, Linda W. Cook.

>> HELEN FERGUSSON.

II.—CHARLES MOORE MORRIS, 1810–1883; *m.*, 12 October, 1831, Ann Jenks, *d.* 1870, and had:

WILLIAM JENKS MORRIS, *b.* 27 August, 1832, *m.*, 26 December, 1858, Ann W. Humphreys, 1831–1886, and had:

> GERTRUDE R. MORRIS, a member of the Pennsylvania Society of the Colonial Dames of America, who *m.*, 28 January, 1891, James Smith Merritt, of Philadelphia, and had: *Morris Hill, b.* 28 December, 1891, and *James Smith, b.* 31 May, 1896.

II.—RACHEL HILL, 1735–1796, who *m.*, 17 April, 1759, Richard Wells, of Philadelphia, and had:

MARY WELLS, 1761–1819, who *m.*, 24 November, 1785, Benjamin W. Morris, of Philadelphia, 1762–1825, and had:

SARAH MORRIS, who *m.*, 5 August, 1804, Jacob Shoemaker Waln, of Philadelphia, *d.* 4 April, 1850, and had:

I.—Edward Waln, of Philadelphia, who *m.*, Ellen, daughter of Henry Nixon, of Philadelphia, and his wife, Maria, daughter of Robert Morris, of Philadelphia, and had :

> Ellen Waln, a member of the Pennsylvania Society of the Colonial Dames of America, Society Daughters of the American Revolution, *etc.*, who *m.* Charles Custis Harrison, of Philadelphia, Provost of the University of Pennsylvania, and had : *George Leib, Edward W., d.* 1872; *Ellen Nixon, Charles Custis, Henry Waln,* and *Esther Waln.*

II.—Mary Waln, who *m.* Richard Vaux, recorder, 1841–47, and mayor of Philadelphia, 1856–60, member of Congress, 1872, and had :

> Meta Vaux, of Philadelphia, a member of the Pennsylvania Society of the Colonial Dames of America.

2.—Mary Lloyd, youngest daughter, *m.*, 1694, Judge Isaac Norris, of " Fair Hill," Germantown, Philadelphia. Isaac Norris settled in Philadelphia in 1693, and at his death, in 1735, was a member of the Colonial Assembly of Pennsylvania. He was mayor of the city, presiding judge of the Common Pleas Court, and member of the Governor's Council for over thirty years. He had by Mary Lloyd :

> I.—Isaac Norris, of " Fairhill," *b.* 1701, *d.* 1764. He was elected to succeed his father in the Assembly, and was almost perpetual speaker till 1759, when he resigned. He *m.*, 1739, Sarah, daughter of James Logan, of " Stenton ;" 1674–1751, chief justice of Pennsylvania, also of Royal Descent, and had :
>
> > Mary Norris, 1740–1803, who *m.*, 1770, Brigadier-General John Dickinson, 1732–1808, president of the Supreme Executive Council of Pennsylvania, 1782, member of the first Continental Congress, *etc.*, and had :
> >
> > Maria Dickinson, 1783–1854, who *m.*, 1808, Albanus Charles Logan, M.D., of " Stenton," 1783–1854, also of Royal Descent, and had :
> >
> > Gustavus George Logan, of " Stenton," Philadelphia, 1815–1876; *m.*, 1846, Anna, daughter of William Armatt, of London, England, and had :
> >
> > Frances Armatt Logan, a member of the Pennsylvania Society of the Colonial Dames of America, *d.* 8 May, 1898.

> II.—Charles Norris, of " Fairhill," Philadelphia county, Pennsylvania, 1712–1766; *m.*, secondly, 1759, Mary, daughter of Joseph Parker, of Chester, Pennsylvania, deputy register, and had by her, who *d.* 1799:

JOSEPH PARKER NORRIS, of "Fairhill," *b.* 5 May, 1763, *d.* 22 June, 1841; *m.*, 20 May, 1790, Elizabeth Hill, *d.* January, 1861, daughter of Joseph Fox, of Philadelphia, speaker of Pennsylvania Assembly, and had:

I.—ISAAC NORRIS, of Philadelphia, *b.* 21 February, 1802, *d.* 1890; *m.* 18 May, 1830, Mary, daughter of George Pepper, of Philadelphia, and had:

> MARY PEPPER NORRIS, *b.* 7 October, 1837, a member of the Pennsylvania Society of the Colonial Dames of America, who *m.*, 30 April, 1857, Travis Cochran, of Philadelphia, *b.* 7 March, 1830, and had: *Mary Norris, John T., d.* 23 March, 1882; *Isaac N., Elizabeth Travis, d.* 4 December, 1870, and *Fanny T.*

II.—MARY PARKER NORRIS, *b.* 19 June, 1791, who *m.*, 11 November, 1813, William Fishbourne Emlen, of Philadelphia, and had:

> GEORGE EMLEN, of Philadelphia, *b.* 25 September, 1814, *d.* 7 June, 1853, who *m.*, 6 May, 1840, Ellen Markoe, and had *George*, p. 126, and ELLEN EMLEN, of Philadelphia, *b.* 13 February, 1850, a member of the Pennsylvania Society of the Colonial Dames of America.

3.—THOMAS LLOYD, JR., *b.* 15 September, 1675, *d.* Goodmansfield, London, before 1718; *m.* Sarah Young, *b.* 2 November, 1676, *d.* in Philadelphia, and had:

THOMAS LLOYD, 3d, of Philadelphia, *d.* 14 May, 1754; *m.* Susanna, *d.* 8 April, 1740, widow of Dr. Edward Owen, and daughter of Philip Kearny, of Philadelphia, and had:

I.—SUSANNAH LLOYD, *d.* 24 October, 1772, who *m.*, 4 November, 1762 (his first wife), Thomas Wharton, Jr., of Philadelphia, member of the Pennsylvania Committee of Safety, 1775–76, president of the Council of Safety, 1776, president of the Supreme Executive Council, 1777–78, *d.* 23 May, 1778, at Lancaster, Pennsylvania, and had:

> WILLIAM MOORE WHARTON, of Philadelphia, *b.* 24 June, 1768, *d.* 14 August, 1816. He had by his second wife, Deborah Shoemaker:

> 1.—DANIEL CLARK WHARTON, of Philadelphia, *b.* 9 July, 1808, *d.* 11 May, 1876; *m.* Ann Waln, daughter of Thomas W. and Hannah (Griffitts) Morgan, and had:

>> I.—MARY MORGAN WHARTON, of Philadelphia, a member of the Pennsylvania Society of the Colonial Dames of America.

>> II.—ANNE ROTCH WHARTON, a member of the Pennsylvania Society of the Colonial Dames of America, who *m.*

Charles J. Churchman, of Philadelphia, and had: *Mary W., Agnes, Charles W., Clark W.,* and *Waln Morgan.*

III.—HELEN ROTCH WHARTON, a member of the Pennsylvania Society of the Colonial Dames of America, who *m.*, 2 April, 1874, George Emlen, Jr., of Philadelphia, *b.* 27 November, 1843, also of Royal Descent, and had: *Annie Wharton, d.* 17 July, 1875; *Ellen Markoe,* and *Dorothea.*

2.—ELIZABETH SHOEMAKER WHARTON, *b.* 16 June, 1813, who *m.* William J. McCluney, United States Navy, and had:

ARABELLA MCCLUNEY, a member of the Pennsylvania Society of the Colonial Dames of America, who *m.*, 7 February, 1877, Stiles Huber, of Philadelphia, and had: *Wharton McC.*

II.—SARAH LLOYD, *d.* 1788, who *m.*, 1757, Judge William Moore, of Philadelphia, *d.* 1793, president of the Supreme Executive Council of Pennsylvania, 1781, and had:

ROBERT KEARNY MOORE, *d.* 1807 on his estate opposite Louisville, Kentucky; *m.*, 5 May, 1806, Catharine, *b.* 27 May, 1775, *d.* 22 March, 1863, daughter of Jonas and Catharine (Walker) Allen, of Virginia, and had:

SARAH LLOYD ROBERT MOORE, only child, *b.* Louisville, Kentucky, 24 February, 1807, *d.* 4 August, 1833; *m.*, 29 April, 1823, Urban Épenetus Ewing, M.D., of Louisville, *d.* 23 December, 1874, and had, besides other issue: *Mary L., m.* Thomas Eaches (and had: *Urban E. Eaches,* of Louisville), and

SARAH LLOYD MOORE EWING, a member of the Kentucky Society of the Colonial Dames of America, and Kentucky State Regent of the Daughters of the American Revolution Society. She *m.*, first, Nathaniel Burwell Marshall, M.D., of Louisville, Kentucky, also of Royal Descent, a grandson of Chief Justice Marshall, and had:

1.—SALLIE MOORE EWING MARSHALL, *m.* William Jarvis Hardy, Jr., of New York City, and had: *William J., Marshall Burwell,* and *Ewing Lloyd.*

2.—CLAUDIA BURWELL MARSHALL, *m.* James Bruce Morson, of Birmingham, Alabama, and had: *Sallie Marshall, Claudia Hamilton,* both accidentally drowned, 26 August, 1891, and *Thomas Seddon.*

3.—BURWELL KEITH MARSHALL, of Louisville, *m.* Lizzie Veech, and had: *Richard Veech, Elizabeth, Mary Louisa, Sallie Ewing,* and *Burwell.*

4.—EWING MARSHALL, M.D., of Louisville, *m.* Martha Snead, and had: *Alice Snead, Mary Lloyd,* and *Evelyn.*

5.—MARY LLOYD EWING MARSHALL, *m.* Philip Trapnill Allin, of Louisville. *No issue.*

SARAH LLOYD MOORE EWING, *m.*, secondly, Henry Lewis Pope, of Louisville, and had:

HENRY EWING POPE, of Louisville, only child.

4.—RACHEL LLOYD, *b.* 20 January, 1667–68, who *m.*, first, 6 July, 1688 (his first wife), Samuel Preston, of Philadelphia, Pennsylvania, *b.* Pautuxent, Maryland, 1665; mayor of Philadelphia, 1711; Colonial treasurer, 1714; Provincial councillor, 1708, *etc., d.* 10 September, 1743 (*see* Keith's "Provincial Councillors of Pennsylvania," and Glenn's "Colonial Mansions"), and had:

I.—MARGARET PRESTON, *b.* 1689, who *m.*, 27 May, 1709, Dr. Richard Moore, of Anne Arundel county, Maryland (son of Dr. Mordecai Moore and his first wife), will proved in September, 1734, and had:

RICHARD MOORE, of Anne Arundel county, Maryland, *d.* 1760, who *m.* Mary West, of "The Wood Yard," on the Eastern Shore, Maryland, and had:

HANNAH MOORE, *d.* 22 May, 1805, who *m.* Hugh Roberts, *b.* 1744, *d.* 25 June, 1825, also of Royal Descent, and had:

ELIZABETH ROBERTS, who *m.*, 10 July, 1794, John Davis, of Philadelphia, and had:

LUCELLA DAVIS, *d.* 30 May, 1881, who *m.* John Pennington, of Philadelphia, *b.* Monmouth county, New Jersey, 1 August, 1799, *d.* 18 March, 1867, and had:

ELIZABETH DAVIS PENNINGTON, a member of the Pennsylvania Society of the Colonial Dames of America, who *m.* Henry Carey Baird of Philadelphia, *b.* 10 September, 1825, son of Captain Thomas J. Baird, United States Army, and Elizabeth, daughter of Matthew Carey, of Philadelphia, and had:

HELENA LAWRENCE BAIRD, *m.* William Howard Gardiner, of Boston, and had: *William Howard, b.* 24 March, 1875; *John Pennington, b.* 18 June, 1876, and *Edward Carey, b.* 14 November, 1878.

II.—HANNAH PRESTON, 1693–1772, who *m.*, 25 May, 1711, Samuel Carpenter, Jr., son of Samuel Carpenter, of Philadelphia, Provincial councillor and treasurer, and had:

1.—HANNAH CARPENTER, *d.* 1766, who *m.*, 8 April, 1746 (his first wife), Samuel Shoemaker, mayor of Philadelphia, 1769–71, *d.* 1800, son of Samuel Shoemaker, mayor of Philadelphia, 1743, 1752 and 1760, and had:

BENJAMIN SHOEMAKER, of Philadelphia, 1746–1808, who *m.*, 1773, Elizabeth, daughter of Edward and Anna (Coleman) Warner, and had:

ANNA SHOEMAKER, 1777–1865, who m., first, 5 May, 1796, Robert Morris, Jr., of Philadelphia, son of Robert Morris, of Philadelphia, the financier of the American Revolution, and had:

ELIZABETH ANNA MORRIS, d. 24 December, 1870, who m., first, 7 June, 1821, Sylvester Malsan, and had:

HENRY MORRIS MALSAN, m., 25 September, 1848, Sarah E. White, of Whitesboro', New York, and had:

1.—ANNA LOUISE MALSAN, b. 4 April, 1850, a member of the New York Society of the Colonial Dames of America, who m. Charles E. Smith, of Whitesboro', New York, and had: Adrian L., Claude Malsan, and Bertha Bulkley.

2.—JULIA PAULINE MALSAN, b. 12 June, 1852, a member of the New York Society of the Colonial Dames of America, who m., 8 October, 1878, M. A. C. Ludwig Wilhelmi, of New York City, and had: Frederick William, b. 7 September, 1879, and Julia White, b. 12 November, 1881, d. 3 March, 1888.

2.—JUDGE PRESTON CARPENTER, of Salem, New Jersey, b. 28 October, 1721, d. 20 October, 1785, had by his first wife, m., 17 October, 1742, Hannah, b. 1723, daughter of Samuel Smith, of Salem, and had:

I.—ELIZABETH CARPENTER, who m., 1767, Ezra Firth, of Salem county, New Jersey, and had:

HANNAH FIRTH, b. 26 September, 1778, d. 24 January, 1854, who m., 20 April, 1797, Isaac C. Jones, of Philadelphia, b. 9 December, 1769, d. 26 January, 1865, and had:

LYDIA JONES, b. 24 October, 1804, d. 19 February, 1878, who m., 8 June, 1825, Caspar Wistar, M.D., of Philadelphia, b. 5 June, 1801, d. 4 April, 1867, and had:

MARY WALN WISTAR, b. 8 June, 1829, who m., 5 September, 1855, Moses Brown, of Germantown, Philadelphia, and had:

MARY WALN WISTAR BROWN, b. 23 November, 1862, a member of the Pennsylvania Society of the Colonial Dames of America, who m., 9 February, 1888, Thomas S. K. Morton, M.D., of Philadelphia, and had: Samuel George, b. 2 December, 1888, d. 31 January, 1889; Mary Waln Wistar, b. 26 November, 1889; Thomas George, b. 17 October, 1891, d. 10 September, 1892; Helen Kirkbride, b. 13 May, 1893, d. 20 February, 1895, and Sarah Wistar, b. 27 November, 1895.

II.—THOMAS CARPENTER, of Carpenter's Landing, Gloucester county, New Jersey, 1742–1847; he served as adjutant of Colonel Dick's regiment of New Jersey militia, and as paymaster and quartermaster of Gloucester and Salem counties' troops in the Revolutionary War; m., 13 April, 1774, Mary, daughter of Edward Tonkin, of Burlington county, New Jersey, and had:

EDWARD CARPENTER, of Glassboro', New Jersey, 1772–1813, *m.*, 5 September, 1799, Sarah, daughter of James Stratton, M.D., of Swedesboro', New Jersey, and had:

1.—MARY TONKIN CARPENTER, 1804–1893; *m.*, 1830, Richard W. Howell, of Camden, New Jersey, 1799–1859, and had:

ANNA HOWELL, a member of the Pennsylvania Society of the Colonial Dames of America, who *m.*, 1869, Malcolm Lloyd, of Philadelphia, and had: *Howell, b.* 1871, *m.*, 1897, Emily Innes; *Malcolm J., b.* 1874; *Stacy B., b.* 1876; *Francis Vernon, b.* 1878; *Anna Howell, b.* 1880; *Esther, b.* 1882, and *Mary Carpenter, b.* 1887.

2.—EDWARD CARPENTER, JR., of Philadelphia, 1813–1889, who *m.*, 16 November, 1837, Anna Maria, daughter of Benjamin M. Howey, of Gloucester county, New Jersey, and had:

SARAH CAROLINE CARPENTER, a member of the Pennsylvania Society of the Colonial Dames of America, who *m.*, 18 July, 1865, Andrew Wheeler, of Philadelphia, and had: *Andrew, Jr., m.* Mary Wilcox Watson (*issue: Sophia Wilcox* and *Eleanor Ledlie*); *Annie, d.* young; *James May, d.* young; *Samuel Bowman, m.* Laetitia C. Hulse, also of Royal Descent (see p. 122); *Arthur Ledlie, Walter Stratton* and *Herbert.*

III.—MARGARET CARPENTER, *b.* 26 August, 1756, *d.* 3 October, 1821; *m.*, 1776, James Mason Woodnutt, of Salem, New Jersey, and had:

HANNAH WOODNUTT, *b.* 12 October, 1784, *d.* 185–, who *m.*, 1799, Clement Acton, of Salem county, New Jersey, *d.* 21 January, 1820, and had:

1.—MARGARET WOODNUTT ACTON, who *m.* John D. Griscom, M.D., of Philadelphia, and had:

CLEMENT A. GRISCOM, of Philadelphia and Haverford, who *m.* Frances Canby Biddle, a member of the Pennsylvania Society of the Colonial Dames, Society Daughters of the American Revolution, *etc.*, also of Royal Descent, and had: *Clement A., Rodman E., Lloyd C., Francis C.*, and

HELEN BIDDLE GRISCOM, a member of the Pennsylvania Society of the Colonial Dames of America, who *m.* Samuel Bettle, of Philadelphia.

2.—CLEMENT JAMES ACTON, of Cincinnati, Ohio, *b.* 1817, *d.* 6 July, 1875, who *m.*, 1846, Mary, *b.* 24 April, 1823, daughter of Colonel John Noble, of Columbus, Ohio, and had: *Margaret W.*, wife of Augustus W. Durkee, of New York, and

ELIZA NOBLE ACTON, *b.* 26 May, 1852, a member of the Pennsylvania and the Ohio Societies of the Colonial Dames of

America, who *m.*, 1878, Frank N. Hickok, of New York, *b.* 23
October, 1847, and had: *Margaret Acton, b.* 9 April, 1880.

IV.—HANNAH CARPENTER, *b.* 1743, *d.* 1820 ; *m.*, first, 1768, Charles
Ellet, of Salem, New Jersey (his second wife), and had by her:

JOHN ELLET, of Salem county, New Jersey, *b.* 1769, *d.* 1824 ; *m.*, first,
1792, Mary, daughter of William Smith, of Salem, New Jersey, and
had by her:

HANNAH CARPENTER ELLET, *b.* 1793, *d.* 1862; *m.*, first, 1813, George
Wishart Smith, of Princess Anne county, Virginia, *d.* Philadelphia,
Pennsylvania, 1821, and had by him :

CHARLES PERRIN SMITH, of Trenton, New Jersey, *b.* 1819, *d.* 1883;
m., 1843, Hester A., daughter of Colonel Matthew Driver, of Caroline county, Maryland, and had : *Ellen Wishart, Charles P., Florence
Burman,* and

ELIZABETH ALFORD SMITH, of Trenton, New Jersey, a member of the
New Jersey Society of the Colonial Dames of America.

PEDIGREE XXXII.

HENRY III., King of England, 1206–1272; *m.*, 1236, Eleanor of Provence, *d.* 1291, and had by her:

PRINCE EDMUND, Earl of Leicester, Lancaster and Chester, high steward of England, 1245–1295. He had by his second wife, Blanche, widow of Henry I., King of Navarre, *d.* 1274, and daughter of Robert, Earl of Artois, son of **Louis VIII.**, **King of France**, by his wife, Blanche of Castile:

HENRY PLANTAGENET, third Earl of Lancaster, *d.* 1345; *m.* Maud, *b.* 1280, daughter of Patrick de Chaworth, 1253–1282, and had:

LADY ELEANOR PLANTAGENET, widow of John, second Baron Beaumont, *d.* 1342, who *m.*, secondly (his second wife), Sir Richard Fitz-Alan, K.G., ninth Earl of Arundel and seventh Earl of Surrey, *d.* 1375, and had by her:

JOHN FITZ-ALAN, Baron Maltravers, who *m.* Lady Eleanor, the heiress and granddaughter of John, Baron Maltravers, and had:

JOHN FITZ-ALAN, Lord Maltravers, lost at sea, in 1380, who had:

LADY JOAN FITZ-ALAN, *m.* Sir William Echyngham, *d.* 1412, and had:

SIR THOMAS ECHYNGHAM, Knt., *d.* 1444, who had:

THOMAS, Baron Echingham, *d.* 1482, who had:

LADY MARGARET ECHINGHAM, who *m.* William Blount, *d. v. p.*, eldest son of Sir Walter le Blount, K.G., *d.* 1474; treasurer of Calais, 1461; created Lord Montjoy, and his wife, Lady Anne Nevill, also of Royal Descent, and had:

ELIZABETH BLOUNT, who *m.* Sir Andrews, Baron Wyndsore, of Stanwell and Bardsley Abbey, *d.* 1549, also of Royal Descent, and had:

LADY EDITH WYNDSORE, who *m.* George Ludlow, of Hill Deverill, high sheriff of Wiltshire, 1567, *d.* 1580 (*see* Keith's "Ancestry of Benjamin Harrison"), and had:

THOMAS LUDLOW, of Dinton, *d.* 1607, who *m.* Jane, daughter of Thomas Pyle, of Bopton, Wilts, and had:

GABRIEL LUDLOW, *bapt.* 10 February, 1587, called to the Bar, 1620, *d.* 1639; *m.* Phyllis ———, and had:

SARAH LUDLOW, *d.* about 1668, who *m.* (his fourth wife) Colonel John Carter, of "Carotoman," Lancaster county, Virginia, who came to Virginia about 1643, probably from Middlesex, and became a member of

the Virginia House of Burgesses from Lower Norfolk county in 1643–44;
county justice and a member of the Governor's Council, 1657, *d.* 10
June, 1669, and had:

COLONEL ROBERT CARTER,* of "Carotoman," 1663–1732, only son by
Sarah Ludlow, a member and speaker of the House of Burgesses, 1695–
99; treasurer of the Colony, 1704–32, *etc.* (*see* Keith's "Ancestry of Benjamin Harrison "). He *m.*, first, 1688, Judith, *d.* 1699, daughter of John
Armistead, of "Hesse," Gloucester county, Virginia, and *m.*, secondly,
1701, Elizabeth, daughter of Thomas Landon, of Middlesex county, Virginia, and widow of —— Willis. From his wealth and authority in
the colony he became known as "King Carter" (*see* Glenn's "Some
Colonial Mansions").

COLONEL ROBERT CARTER had by his first wife:

1.—ELIZABETH CARTER, 1680–1721, who *m.*, first, Nathaniel Burwell,
of Gloucester county, Virginia, also of Royal Descent, and had:

I.—LEWIS BURWELL, of "White Marsh," who *m.* Mary Willis, and
had:

REBECCA BURWELL, who *m.* Jacqueline Ambler, and had:

ANNE AMBLER, who *m.* George Fisher, and had:

ELIZA JACQUELINE FISHER, who *m.* Thomas Marshall Colston,
and had:

RALEIGH COLSTON, who *m.* Gertrude Powell, and had:

JANE COLSTON, a member of the Virginia Society of the Colonial
Dames of America, who *m.*, 12 September, 1871, Conway Robinson Howard, of Richmond, Virginia, and had: *Mary Eloise,*
wife of Francis Elliott Shoup; *Gertrude, Jeanie Colston,* and *Conway Robinson.*

II.—ELIZABETH BURWELL, who *m.* William Nelson, of Yorktown,
president of the Virginia Colony, and had:

---

* The following ladies, members of the National Society of the Colonial Dames of
America, are also of Royal Descent through Colonel Robert Carter :

MRS. BENJAMIN O'FALLON, Missouri State Society.

MISS MARGARET GORDON, Maryland State Society.

MRS. R. CURZON HOFFMANN, Maryland State Society.

MRS. THOMAS C. MCLEAN, Maryland State Society.

MISS CARY ANN NICHOLAS, Maryland State Society.

MISS ELIZABETH CARY NICHOLAS, Maryland State Society.

MRS. WILLIAM C. PAGE, Maryland State Society.

MRS. ALEX. B. RANDALL, Maryland State Society.

MISS ANNIE N. SANDERS, Pennsylvania State Society.

MRS. ARTHUR E. POULTNEY, Maryland State Society.

ROBERT NELSON, *m.*, secondly, Susan Robinson, and had by her:

PEYTON RANDOLPH NELSON, *m.* Sally Berkeley Nicolson, also of Royal Descent, and had:

WILLIAM WILMER NELSON, *m.* Sally Browne Catlett, and had:

SALLY BERKELEY NELSON, of Richmond, Virginia, a member of the Virginia Society of the Colonial Dames of America, who *m.* William Todd Robins, Colonel Confederate States Army, and had: *Ruth Nelson, Elizabeth Todd, Augustine Warner, Wilmer Nelson,* and *Sally Berkeley Nicolson.*

III.—CARTER BURWELL, who *m.* Lucy Grymes, and had:

NATHANIEL BURWELL, who *m.* Mrs. Lucy (Page) Baylor, also a descendant of the aforesaid Robert Carter, 1663–1732, and had:

GEORGE H. BURWELL, who *m.* Agnes Atkinson, and had:

ISABELLA DIXON BURWELL, who *m.* Peter H. Mayo, and had:

AGNES ATKINSON MAYO, a member of the Virginia Society of the Colonial Dames of America, who *m.* Thomas Nelson Carter, of Richmond, Virginia, also a descendant of Robert Carter, 1663–1732, aforesaid, and had: *Isabelle Burwell.*

IV.—COLONEL ROBERT CARTER BURWELL, of Isle of Wight county, Virginia, *m.* Sarah Nelson, and had:

FRANCES BURWELL, who *m.* Governor John Page, of "Rosewell," also of Royal Descent, and had:

FRANCES PAGE, who *m.*, secondly, Dr. Carter Berkeley, of "Edgewood," also of Royal Descent, and had:

CATHERINE FRANCES BERKELEY, who *m.* Lucius Horatio Minor, of "Edgewood," also of Royal Descent, and had:

MARY WILLIS MINOR, of Baltimore, a member of the Maryland Society of the Colonial Dames of America.

ELIZABETH CARTER, aforesaid widow of Nathaniel Burwell, *m.*, secondly, Dr. George Nicholas, R. N., of Williamsburg, Virginia, and had:

JUDGE ROBERT CARTER NICHOLAS, of Hanover county, Virginia, 1725–1788, treasurer of Virginia and first presiding judge of the Court of Appeals of Virginia. He *m.* Ann, daughter of Colonel Wilson Cary, of "Rich Neck" and "Ceeleys," and had:

I.—JUDGE PHILIP NARBORNE NICHOLAS, of Richmond, Virginia, who *m.* Maria Carter Byrd, also of Royal Descent, and had:

ELIZABETH BYRD NICHOLAS, of Washington, a member of the District of Columbia Society of the Colonial Dames of America and national treasurer of the General Society, member of the Order of the Crown, *etc.*

II.—Judge George Nicholas, of Kentucky, who *m.* Margaret Smith, of Maryland, and had :

> Judge Samuel Smith Nicholas, of Kentucky, who *m.* his cousin, Mary M., daughter of General John Spear Smith, of Baltimore, Maryland, and had :
>
> > Cary Anne Nicholas, a member of the Virginia Society of the Colonial Dames of America, who *m.* Rudolph Fink, of Crescent Hill, Jefferson county, Kentucky, a native of Germany, and had : *Albert, Mary Nicholas, Margaret Carter, Henry,* and *Cary.*

III.—Wilson Cary Nicholas, of Albemarle county, Virginia, Governor of Virginia and United States Senator from Virginia. He *m.* Margaret, daughter of General Samuel Smith, of Baltimore, Maryland, and had :

> Robert Carter Nicholas, of Louisiana, 1793–1856, United States Senator from Louisiana. He *m.*, in 1840, Susan Vinson, of Louisiana, and had :
>
> > Caroline Nicholas, a member of the Virginia Society of the Colonial Dames of America, who *m.* William Gerald Müller, of " Albemarle Farm," Hammond, Louisiana, and had :
> >
> > > 1.—Gretchen Müller, who *m.* Y. L. Bayne, of Alabama, and had : *Y. L., Jr.,* and *William Müller.*
> > >
> > > 2.—Sue Müller, who *m.* Harlie Short, of Nebraska, and had : *Harlie, Jr.,* and *Victor Burthe.*

2.—Judith Carter, who *m.*, 1718 (his second wife), Mann Page, of " Rosewell," Gloucester county, Virginia, 1690–1730, and had :

> I.—Mann Page, *b.* 1719, member of Congress from Virginia in 1777; *m.*, first, 1743, Alice, daughter of John Grymes, of Middlesex county, Virginia, and had :
>
> > John Page, of " Rosewell," *b.* 17 April, 1744, *d.* 11 October, 1808, Governor of Virginia ; *m.*, first, 1765, Frances, daughter of Robert Carter Burwell, of the Isle of Wight county, Virginia, also of Royal Descent, and had by her, who *d.* 1784 :
> >
> > > Frances Page, *b.* 1777 (widow of Thomas Nelson, Jr.), who *m.* secondly, Dr. Carter Berkeley, of " Edgewood," and had :
> > >
> > > > Catharine Frances Berkeley, who *m.* Lucius Horatio Minor, of " Edgewood," also of Royal Descent, and had :
> > > >
> > > > > Mary Willis Minor, of Baltimore, a member of the Maryland Society of the Colonial Dames of America.
>
> II.—Robert Page, of " Broadneck," *m.*, 20 January, 1750, Sarah Walker, and had :
>
> > 1.—John Page, of " Pagebrook," who *m.* Maria Horsmanden Byrd, also of Royal Descent, and had :

SARAH WALKER PAGE, who *m.*, 1815, Major Thomas M. Nelson, United States Army, *d.* 1853, member of Congress from Virginia, 1816–19 ; a presidential elector, 1829 and 1833, and had :

MARIA BYRD NELSON, who *m.* William Gray Woolfolk, of Columbus, Georgia, and had :

ROSA WOOLFOLK, a member of the Maryland Society of the Colonial Dames of America, who *m.* Robert Ober, of Baltimore, and had : *Gustavus* and *Maria Byrd Nelson.*

2.—CATHARINE PAGE, who *m.* Benjamin C. Waller, and had :

WILLIAM WALLER, of Williamsburg, Virginia, *m.* Mary Berkeley Griffin, also of Royal Descent, and had :

WILLIAM NEVISON WALLER, of Williamsburg, who *m.*, first, 1 February, 1842, Elizabeth, daughter of John Tyler, President of the United States, and had :

MARY STUART WALLER, a member of the Georgia Society of the Colonial Dames of America, who *m.*, 25 April, 1867, Captain Louis G. Young, of Savannah, Georgia. *No issue.*

3.—JOHN CARTER, of " Carotoman," *b.* 1690, secretary of the Virginia Colony, 1722 ; member of the Council, 1726, *etc.*, *d.* 30 April, 1743, who *m.*, 1723, Elizabeth, daughter of Colonel Edward Hill, of " Shirley," Charles City county, Virginia, and had :

I.—EDWARD CARTER, of " Blenheim," Albemarle county, Virginia, member of the House of Delegates, *etc.*, who *m.* Sarah, daughter of Colonel John Champe, of Fredericksburg, Virginia, and had :

1.—ROBERT CARTER, of " Redlands," who *m.* Mary, daughter of John Coles, of Albemarle county, and had :

ROBERT HILL CARTER, of " Redlands," who *m.* Margaret, daughter of General John Spear Smith, of Baltimore, Maryland, and had :

MARY COLES CARTER, of St. Timothy's, Catonsville, Baltimore county, Maryland, a member of the Maryland Society of the Colonial Dames of America.

2.—ELIZABETH CARTER, who *m.* William Stanard, of Roxbury, Charles City county, Virginia, and had :

VIRGINIA STANARD, who *m.* (his second wife) Samuel Slaughter, of Culpeper county, Virginia, and had :

COLUMBIA SLAUGHTER, who *m.* William Green, LL.D., of Richmond, Virginia, and had :

ELIZABETH TRAVERS GREEN, who *m.* James Hayes, of Richmond, Virginia, and had :

ANNE SOMERVILLE HAYES, a member of the Kentucky Society of the Colonial Dames of America, who m., 31 March, 1891, Urban Ewing Eaches, of Louisville, Kentucky, also of Royal Descent, and had: *Katharine Moore Ewing* and *Elizabeth Travers Green.*

3.—JANE CARTER, who m., first, Samuel Kellett Bradford, of Virginia, and had:

SAMUEL KELLETT BRADFORD, JR., of Culpeper county, Virginia, m., 27 July, 1816, Emily, daughter of Samuel Slaughter, of Culpeper, by his first wife, Miss Banks, and had:

LOUISA M. BRADFORD, who m., August, 1842, General Horatio G. Wright, United States Army, and had:

MARY HILL WRIGHT, of New York City, a member of the New York Society of the Colonial Dames of America, who m., 21 February, 1867, Edwin H. Wootton, of Kent county, England, and had: *Hubert Wright, Mary Isabel,* wife of Charles H. Richardson, and *Moray Nairne.*

II.—CHARLES CARTER, of "Shirley," 1732–1806, who m., first, 1756, his cousin, Mary Walker, daughter of Colonel Charles Carter, of " Clevʋ " (and his first wife, Mary Walker), son of Colonel Robert Carter, 1663–1732, aforesaid, and his second wife, Mrs. Elizabeth (Landon) Willis, and had:

ELIZABETH HILL CARTER, 1764–1832, who m. Colonel Robert Randolph, of "Eastern View," Fauquier county, Virginia, 1760–1825, also of Royal Descent, and had:

CAPTAIN CHARLES CARTER RANDOLPH, of " The Grove," who m. Mary Ann Fauntleroy Mortimer, of Fredericksburg, Virginia, and had:

LANDONIA RANDOLPH, who m. Robert Dabney Minor, United States Navy, of Fredericksburg, Virginia, and had:

LANDONIA RANDOLPH MINOR, a member of the Virginia Society of the Colonial Dames of America, who m. William Sparrow Dashiell, of Richmond, Virginia, and had: *Robert Minor* and *Thomas Grayson.*

PEDIGREE XXXIII.

LOUIS VIII., **King of France,** had by his wife, Princess Blanche of Castile, also of Royal Descent:

ROBERT, COUNT OF ARTOIS, third son, *k.* 1247, who *m.*, 1237, Matilda, *d.* 1249, daughter of Henry, Duke of Brabant, and his wife, *m.*, 1207, Mary, *d.* 1239, daughter of Philip of Swabia, Emperor of Germany, *d.* 1208, and had:

LADY BLANCHE, of Artois, widow of Henry, King of Navarre, *d.* 1274, who *m.*, secondly, Edmund Plantagenet, Earl of Leicester, Lancaster, and Chester; lord high steward of England, son of Henry III., King of England, 1245–1295, and had:

HENRY PLANTAGENET, third Earl of Leicester, *d.* 1345, who *m.* Lady Maud, *b.* 1280, daughter of Sir Patrick de Chaworth, 1253–1282, and his wife, Isabel, daughter of William de Beauchamp, first Earl of Warwick, and had:

LADY ELEANOR PLANTAGENET, widow of John, second Baron Beaumont, who *m.*, secondly (his second wife), Sir Richard Fitz-Alan, K.G., ninth Earl of Arundel and seventh Earl of Surrey, *d.* 1375, and had:

JOHN FITZ-ALAN, Lord Maltravers, second son, who *m.* Lady Eleanor, granddaughter and heiress of John, Lord Maltravers, and had:

JOHN FITZ-ALAN, eldest son, *d. v. p.,* who had by his second wife, Katherine, widow of William Stafford, of Frome, and daughter and co-heir of Sir John Chideock, heir to the barony of Fitz-Payne:

"SIR THOMAS ARUNDEL, *alias* FITZ-ALAN," Knt. (brother of John, Earl of Arundel), his will, 3 October, 1485, given on p. 378, Nichols' "Testamenta Vetusta," who had by his wife, Katherine, daughter of Sir John Dynham, and sister and co-heiress of Sir John, Baron Dynham, K.G.:

LADY ELEANOR FITZ-ALAN, who *m.* Sir Thomas Browne, Knt., treasurer of the household to King Henry VI., and had:

SIR GEORGE BROWNE, Knt., of Beechworth Castle, county Surrey, second son, who had:

SIMON BROWNE, of Browne Hall, Lancastershire, who had:

THOMAS BROWNE, of Brandon, *d.* 1 May, 1608, who had by Margaret, his wife, who *d.* 1 May, 1605:

FRANCIS BROWNE, of Weybird Hall, Brandon, county Suffolk, *d.* 9 May, 1626, who had:

9

WILLIAM BROWNE, *b.* 1608, who came from London, where he was a member of the Fishmongers' Company, to Salem, Massachusetts, in 1634–5. He *m.*, first, in London, Mary, *d.* 1635, sister of Rev. Mr. Young, of Long Island, New York, and *m.*, secondly, Sarah, daughter of Samuel Smith, of Yarmouth, and *d.* 25 January, 1687, leaving issue by his second wife:

MAJOR WILLIAM BROWNE,* of Salem, Massachusetts, *d.* 1716; member of Governor Andros's council and of the council of safety (*see* Salisbury's "Genealogies," Savage's "Genealogical Dictionary," and the *American Heraldic Journal*, vol. ii). He *m.*, first, Hannah, daughter of George Curwen, and had:

1.—COLONEL SAMUEL BROWNE, of Salem, *d.* 1731; justice of court of common pleas, member of His Majesty's council, who *m.*, secondly, 1705, Abigail, daughter of John Keatch, of Bristol, England, and had:

WILLIAM BROWNE, of Beverley, Massachusetts, 1709–1763, who *m.*, 14 November, 1737, Mary, daughter by his second wife of William Burnet (son of Rt. Rev. Bishop Gilbert Burnet), Provincial Governor of New York and Massachusetts, and had:

WILLIAM BURNET BROWNE, of " Elsing Green," King William county, Virginia, *b.* 7 October, 1738, who *m.*, first, Judith Frances Carter, of " Cleve," also of Royal Descent, and had Betty Carter, Judith Walker, and

MARY BURNET BROWNE, who *m.* (his second wife) Herbert Claiborne, of " Chestnut Grove," New Kent county, Virginia, *b.* 1746, also of Royal Descent, and had:

HERBERT AUGUSTINE CLAIBORNE, 1784–1841; *m.* Delia, daughter of James Hayes, of Richmond, Virginia, and had:

MAJOR JOHN HAYES CLAIBORNE, of Richmond, Virginia, who *m.* Anna Virginia, daughter of George W. Bassett, of " Eltham," New Kent county, Virginia, son of John Bassett (also of Royal Descent) and his wife, Betty Carter, daughter of the aforesaid William Burnet Browne, and had:

DELIA CLAIBORNE, a member of the Virginia Society of the Colonial Dames of America, who *m.*, 10 June, 1885, Simon Bolivar Buckner, of " Glen Lily," Hart county, Kentucky, Lieutenant-General Confederate States Army, Governor of Kentucky, *etc.*, and had: *Simon Bolivar, b.* 18 July, 1886.

2.—MARY BROWNE, who *m.*, 1699, Chief Justice Benjamin Lynde, of Salem, Massachusetts, 1665–1744, also of Royal Descent, and had:

---

* MRS. LEWIS W. WASHINGTON (deceased), a member of the National Society of the Colonial Dames of America, was also of Royal Descent through Major William Browne.

CHIEF JUSTICE BENJAMIN LYNDE, JR., of Salem, 1700–1781, who *m.* Mary Goodrich Bowles, and had:

LYDIA LYNDE, who *m.* Rev. William Walter, and had:

HARRIET LYNDE WALTER, who *m.* John Odin, and had:

ESTHER ODIN, who *m.* Rev. Benjamin Dorr, D.D., and had:

1.—MARY WARREN DORR, a member of the Pennsylvania Society of the Colonial Dames of America, who *m.* William L. Schäffer, of Philadelphia.

2.—HARRIET ODIN DORR (deceased), a member of the Pennsylvania Society of the Colonial Dames of America, who *m.* Major James Edward Carpenter, of Philadelphia, also of Royal Descent. *Issue.*

3.—ESTHER ODIN DORR, a member of the Pennsylvania Society of the Colonial Dames of America, who *m.* William Hewitt Webb, of Philadelphia, and had:

ANNE GRISCOM WEBB, a member of the Pennsylvania Society of the Colonial Dames of America, who *m.* Albert Ripley Leeds, of Hoboken, N. J.

THE ROYAL DESCENTS

OF

MRS. WILLIAM D. BETHELL,

AND

MRS. JOHN M. GRAY.

EDWARD I., King of England⹏Princess Eleanor of Castile.

Princess Joan Plantagenet⹏Gilbert de Clare, Earl of Gloucester and Hereford.

Lady Margaret de Clare⹏Hugh de Audley, Earl of Gloucester.

Lady Margaret de Audley⹏Sir Ralph de Stafford, K. G., Earl of Stafford.

Sir Hugh de Stafford, K. G., Earl of Stafford⹏Lady Philippa de Beauchamp.

Lady Margaret de Stafford⹏Sir Ralph de Neville, K. G., Earl of Westmoreland.

Ralph de Neville, of Oversley, Warwickshire⹏Lady Mary de Ferrers.

John de Neville, of Wymersley, Yorkshire⹏Lady Elizabeth de Newmarch.

Joan de Neville⹏Sir William Gascoigne, of Gawthrope, Yorkshire.

Sir William Gascoigne, of Gawthrope, York⹏Lady Margaret de Percy.

Lady Elizabeth Gascoigne⹏Gilbert de Talboys, of Kyme.

Sir George de Talboys, of Kyme⹏(Name unknown.)

Lady Anne de Talboys⹏Sir Edward Dymoke, of Scrivelsby, Lincolnshire.

Lady Frances Dymoke⹏Thomas Windebank, of Haines Hill, Berkshire.

Mildred Windebank⹏Robert Reade, Linkenholt Manor, Southampton.

Col. George Reade, of Gloucester Co., Va.⹏Elizabeth Martian.

Mildred Reade⹏Col. Augustine Warner, Jr., of "Warner's Hall."

Elizabeth Warner⹏Col. John Lewis, Gloucester Co., Va.

Col. Charles Lewis⹏Mary Howell.

Anne Lewis⹏Edmund Taylor, Caroline Co., Va.

Francis Taylor⹏Rev. Nathaniel Moore, Granville Co., N. C.

Anne Lewis Moore⹏Edward Washington Dale, Columbia, Tenn.

Elvira H. Dale⹏Jerome Bonaparte Pillow, of Tenn.

Cynthia Pillow⹏William Decatur Bethell, of Denver, Col.　　Elvira Pillow⹏John Maffitt Gray, of Nashville, Tenn.

Bessie⹏Dr. John M.　Jennie⹏John P.　William D.⹏Helen　Annie⹏Dr. J. W.　John M.⹏Rebecca
Bethell.　Foster.　Bethell.　Edrington.　Bethell.　Worden.　Gray.　Madden.　Gray.　Wilson.

Bethell Pinckney John M.　Bethell　Cynthia　John P.　William D. Charles W.　Annie G.　Rebecca
Foster.　Foster.　Foster.　Edrington. Edrington. Edrington. Bethell.　Bethell.　Madden.　Gray.

PEDIGREE XXXIV.

HENRY I., King of France, *m.* Anne, daughter of Jaroslaus, Grand Duke or Czar of Russia, 1015–1051, and had:

HUGH THE GREAT, Duke of France and Burgundy, Count de Vermandois, who *m.*, thirdly, 938, Lady Adelheid, 1080–1117, daughter of Herbert, fourth Count de Vermandois and Troyes, 1045–1080, also of Royal Descent (*see* Anderson's " Royal Genealogies "), and had:

LADY ISABEL DE VERMANDOIS, *d.* 1131 (*see* Planche's " The Conqueror and His Companions " for a sketch of this lady), who *m.*, first, Robert de Beaumont, first Baron de Bellomont by tenure, and Earl of Mellent, created Earl of Leicester, and had by him, who *d.* 1118:

ROBERT-BOSSU DE BELLOMONT, second Earl of Leicester, lord justice of England, *d.* 1168, who *m.* Lady Amicia, daughter of Ralph de Waer, Earl of Norfolk, Suffolk and Cambridge, and had:

GERVASE PAGANEL, Baron of Dudley, Staffordshire, who *m.* Lady Felice, daughter and heiress of Athelstan Dodo, son of Geoffrey, son of Athelstan Dodo, who built Dudley Castle, and had:

LADY HAWYSE PAGANEL, Baroness of Dudley, heiress, who *m.* John de Someri, in Cambridge, Baron of Dudley, in right of his wife, and had:

RALPH DE SOMERI, Baron of Dudley, eldest son, *d.* 1210, who *m.* Margaret ———, and had:

WILLIAM PERCEVAL DE SOMERI, Baron of Dudley, eldest son, *d.* 1221, who had:

ROGER DE SOMERI, second son, *d.* 1272, who *m.*, secondly, Lady Amabel, daughter of Robert de Chaucumbe, and widow of Gilbert, third Baron de Segrave, who *d.* 1254, and had by her:

LADY MARGARET DE SOMERI (widow of Urian St. Pierre), who *m.*, secondly, Ralph Baron Basset, lord of Drayton, Staffordshire (a grandson of Richard Basset, justice of England, son of Ralph Basset, justice of England, *d.* 1120), and had:

RALPH, BARON BASSET, of Drayton, who *m.* either Lady Joan, daughter of John de Grey, justice of Chester, *d.* 1265 (*see* Burke), or Lady Joan, daughter of Reginald de Grey, *d.* 1308, son of John, the justice of Chester (*see* Dugdale), and had:

SIR RALPH, BARON BASSET, of Drayton, K.B., *d.* 1343, who *m.* Lady

Joan, daughter of Thomas Beauchamp, third Earl of Warwick, also of Royal Descent, and had:

LADY JANE BASSET, who *m.* John de Stourton, of Preston, Wilts, *d.* 1364, and had:

WILLIAM DE STOURTON, steward of Wales in 1402, who *m.* Elizabeth, daughter of John Moyne (or Moigne), of Moddenton, Wilts, and had:

SIR JOHN DE STOURTON, created Baron Stourton in 1448, *d.* 1462, who *m.* Lady Margery, daughter of Sir John Wadham, of Merrifield, Somerset, and had:

WILLIAM, SECOND BARON STOURTON, *d.* 1478, who *m.* Lady Margaret, daughter of Sir John Chidoke, or Chidiock, also of Royal Descent, and had:

LADY JOAN DE STOURTON, who *m.* Tristram Fauntleroy, of Mitchell's Marsh, Hants, (*see* Dugdale's "Baronage"), will dated 25 July, 1539, *d.* 1539 (son of John Fauntleroy, of The Marsh, at Alvestop, Dorset, and brother of Agnes Fauntleroy, wife of Edward, fifth Lord Stourton, *d.* 1536 (*see* Wallace's "Historical Magazine," July, 1891; Hutchin's "Dorsetshire,"), and had:

JOHN FAUNTLEROY, of Crandall, Hampshire, *d.* February, 1598, who *m.* Margaret ——, *d.* April, 1613, and had:

WILLIAM FAUNTLEROY, of Crandall, *d.* February, 1625, who *m.* Frances ——, *bur.* at Hedley, in 1638, and had:

JOHN FAUNTLEROY, of Crandall and Hedley, Hampshire, only son, *bapt.* at Crandall, 3 January, 1588; *bur.* at Hedley, 11 March, 1644; *m.*, at Hedley, 5 September, 1609, Phœbe Wilkinson, *bur.* at Hedley, 29 September, 1629, and had:

COLONEL MOORE FAUNTLEROY,* second son, came to Virginia and had grant of land in Upper Norfolk in 1643. He had a confirmation of arms issued to him, 1633, by Borough, Garter King at Arms; he was an extensive land-owner in Virginia, and a burgess, 1644–1659, and justice of Rappahannock county (*see* an account of him and family in "Virginia Historical Magazine," July, 1891). He *m.*, first, in England, 26 December, 1639, Dorothy, daughter of Thomas Colle, of Liss, Hampshire, and *m.*, secondly, in Virginia, Mary Hill, marriage contract dated 1648. He *d.* before 1665, having issue by second wife:

---

* The following ladies, members of the National Society of the Colonial Dames of America, are also of Royal Descent through Moore Fauntleroy:

MRS. THOMAS F. SCREVEN, Georgia State Society.

MRS. WILLIAM W. GORDON, JR., Georgia State Society.

MISS FRANCES M. SCOTT, Arkansas State Society.

MISS LIZZIE C. MILLER, North Carolina State Society.

COLONEL WILLIAM FAUNTLEROY, of Rappahannock county, Virginia, a county justice, 1680–95, who *m.*, 1680, Katharine (will proved 1728), daughter of Colonel Samuel Griffin, of Northumberland county, Virginia, and had:

1.—COLONEL MOORE FAUNTLEROY, of Richmond county, Virginia, *d.* 1739, who *m.* Margaret, daughter of Paul Micou, of "Port Micou," Essex county, Virginia, and had:

I.—JUDITH FAUNTLEROY, who *m.* Landon Carter, of Pittsylvania county, Virginia, also of Royal Descent, and had:

WORMLEY CARTER, who *m.* Sarah Edwards, and had:

WORMLEY CARTER, who *m.* Lucinda Washington Alexander, and had:

JUDGE WILLIAM ALEXANDER CARTER, 1818–1881, who *m.*, 1848, Mary Eliza Hamilton, and had:

MARY ADA CARTER, a member of the Pennsylvania Society of the Colonial Dames of America, who *m.*, 1874, Joseph K. Corson, M.D., surgeon United States Army, also of Royal Descent, and had: *Mary Carter, b.* 1876, *d.* 1890, and *Edward Foulke, b.* 1883.

II.—ELIZABETH FAUNTLEROY, who *m.* Colonel William Brockenbrough, of Richmond county, and had:

JOHN BROCKENBROUGH, M.D., a signer of the Westmoreland Association, who *m.* Sarah, daughter of William Roane, and had:

JUDGE WILLIAM BROCKENBROUGH, of the Virginia Court of Appeals, who *m.* Judith, daughter of Rev. John White and his wife, Mary Braxton, also of Royal Descent, and had:

SARAH JANE BROCKENBROUGH, who *m.* Colonel Edward Colston, of Berkeley county, Virginia, and had:

ELIZABETH MARSHALL COLSTON, who *m.* R. Alfred Williams, of Richmond, Virginia, and had:

ROSALIE BELL WILLIAMS, a member of the Maryland Society of the Colonial Dames of America, who *m.* William C. Page, of Baltimore, and had: *Rosalie Braxton, Ellen West,* and *Virginia Dandridge.*

2.—COLONEL WILLIAM FAUNTLEROY, of "Naylor's Hole," Richmond county, Virginia, *b.* 1684, burgess, 1736–1772; *m.* Apphia, daughter of John Bushrod, of Westmoreland county, Virginia, and had:

COLONEL WILLIAM FAUNTLEROY, of "Naylor's Hole," 1713–1793, who had by his second wife, Margaret, daughter of Jeremiah Murdock, a justice in King George county, Virginia, 1728–1752:

I.—JOSEPH FAUNTLEROY, of "Greenville," Frederick (Clark) county, Virginia, 1754–1815; *m.* Elizabeth Foushee, daughter of Bushrod Fauntleroy, and had:

ROBERT HENRY FAUNTLEROY, 1807–1850, United States Coast Survey; *m.* Jane Dale, daughter of Robert Owen, of New Harmony, Indiana, and had:

ELEANOR FAUNTLEROY, a member of the California Society of the Colonial Dames of America, who *m.* Professor George Davidson, of United States Coast Survey.

II.—JOHN FAUNTLEROY, of Richmond county, Virginia, 1745–1798; a member of the House of Delegates, 1784, who, *m.* Judith, widow of Leroy Griffin, a daughter of Colonel James and Lettice (Lee) Ball, of "Bewdley," and had:

LETTICE LEE FAUNTLEROY, *d.* 1820, who *m.* Austin Brockenbrough, M.D., of Richmond county, Virginia, and had:

COLONEL JOHN FAUNTLEROY BROCKENBROUGH, *d.* 1865, who *m.* Frances Ann Carter, and had:

ELLA BROCKENBROUGH, who *m.* John Watrus Beckwith, and had:

ELLA STANLEY BECKWITH, a member of the Georgia Society of the Colonial Dames of America, who *m.* Alexander Rudolf Lawton, of Savannah, and had: *Alexander Rudolf* and *John Beckwith.*

PEDIGREE XXXV.

EDWARD III., King of England, *m.*, 1327, Lady Philippa, daughter of William, Count of Hainault and Holland, and his wife, Joanna, daùghter of Charles de Valois, younger son of **Philip III.**, **King of France,** and had :

EDMUND PLANTAGENET, Earl of Cambridge and Duke of York, who *m.*, first, Lady Isabel, daughter of **Peter, King of Castile and Leon,** and had by her:

RICHARD PLANTAGENET, Earl of Cambridge, beheaded in 1415, who *m.* Lady Anne, daughter of Edward de Mortimer, Earl of March, and his wife, Lady Philippa, daughter of Lionel, Duke of Clarence, second son of **Edward III., King of England,** and had :

RICHARD PLANTAGENET, Earl of Cambridge and Duke of York, the Protector, starter of the War of Roses, *k.* in the final battle of Wakefield, 1460. He *m.* Lady Cecily, daughter of Ralph de Nevill, Earl of Westmoreland, also of Royal Descent, and had:

SIR GEORGE PLANTAGENET, K.G., Duke of Clarence (brother of Kings Richard III. and Edward IV., father of King Edward V. and Richard, Duke of York, both murdered in the Tower of London, and Elizabeth, consort of King Henry VII.), who *m.* Lady Isabel de Nevill, daughter of Richard, Earl of Salisbury and Warwick, also of Royal Descent (her sister, Anne, *m.*, first, Edward, only son of King Henry VII., and *m.*, secondly, King Richard III.). He was attainted of treason and drowned in a butt of Malmsey wine in the Tower of London, in 1477, and his honors were forfeited. His only daughter :

LADY MARGARET PLANTAGENET, Countess of Salisbury, beheaded for high treason, when 72 years old, 27 May, 1541 (sister of Edward, " the last of the Plantagenets," who was executed in 1499 on London Tower Hill), *m.* Sir Richard Pole, K.G., and had :

SIR HENRY POLE, first Lord Montagu, beheaded in 1539, on London Tower Hill, for high treason. He *m.* Lady Jean, daughter of George Neville, Lord Abergavenny, also of Royal Descent, and had :

LADY KATHERINE POLE, who *m.* Sir Francis Hastings, K.G., second Earl of Huntingdon, also of Royal Descent, and had :

LADY CATHERINE HASTINGS, who *m.* Sir Henry, tenth Baron Clinton, K.B., second Earl of Lincoln, also of Royal Descent, and had :

THOMAS CLINTON, third Earl of Lincoln, *d.* 15 January, 1619; *m.* Elizabeth, daughter of Henry Knyvett, of Charlton, Wilts, and had:

LADY SUSAN CLINTON, who *m.* " John Humfrey, Esq.," 1595–1661, a lawyer, of Dorchester, in Dorsetshire. Mr. Humfrey was one of the six gentlemen to whom the council of Plymouth, England, in March, 1627–8, sold that part of New England " between three miles north of the Merrimac and three miles south of the Charles," for the Massachusetts Bay Company, of London; John Winthrop, Governor, and John Humfrey, Deputy-Governor. Mr. Humphrey came to New England, with Lady Susan, in July, 1634, and made his home on his farm of five hundred acres at Swampscott (Lynn), Massachusetts, and entered upon his duties as assistant, and was one of the founders of Lynn. In 1640 he was a member of the Ancient and Honorable Artillery Company; in 1641 was appointed to the command of the militia with the rank of Sergeant Major-General. He and his wife, Lady Susan, returned to Sandwich, Kent, England, 26 October, 1641, having sold his farm to Lady Deborah Moody. Their daughter:

ANNE HUMPHREY, *b.* 1621, who *m.*, first, at Salem, Massachusetts, William Palmer (or Palmes?), of Ardfinan, in Ireland, and had:

SUSAN PALMER, *b.* 1665 ("New England Historical Genealogical Register, vol. xxxi., p. 307), who *m.* Samuel Avery, of New London, Connecticut, *d.* 1 May, 1723, son of Captain James Avery, 1620–1700, from whom are descended:

1.—ALICE GERRY, a member of the Maryland Society of the Colonial Dames of America, who *m.* David Stewart, of Baltimore.

2.—CLARA JENNESS, a member of the Maryland Society of the Colonial Dames of America, who *m.* W. T. Hamilton, of Hagerstown.

ANNE HUMPHREY *m.*, secondly, Rev. John Myles, a pioneer Baptist, who was driven away from Swansea and took refuge in New England, in 1663, and in 1670 was one of the founders of Swansea, Massachusetts, and *d.* in 1683, aged 62 years. Their descendant:

ESTHER SLACK DARLING, *m.* Captain Nathan Arnold, of Cumberland, Rhode Island, who died from wounds and exposure after the battle of Rhode Island, 29 August, 1778, also of Royal Descent, (p. 18), and had:

SETH ARNOLD, of Smithfield, Rhode Island, who *m.* Belinda Mason Streeter, daughter of Jonathan and Patience (Mason) Mason, and a descendant of Roger Williams, the founder of Rhode Island, and had:

FRANCES ESTHER ARNOLD, 1820–1896, who *m.*, 1 August, 1837, William Henry Hatheway, of Dighton, Massachusetts, 1814–1875, and had:

BELINDA OLNEY HATHEWAY, a member of the Rhode Island Society of the Colonial Dames of America, the Order of the Crown, *etc.*, who *m.* Joshua Wilbour, of Bristol, Rhode Island, United States Consul at Dublin. *No issue.*

PEDIGREE XXXVI.

Henry I., **King of France,** had by his third wife, Anne of Russia:

HUGH THE GREAT, Duke of France and Burgundy, Marquis of Orleans, and Count of Paris and Vermandois, who *m.*, thirdly, 938, Lady Adelheid, daughter of Herbert, Count of Vermandois, and had by her:

LADY ISABEL DE VERMANDOIS, who *m.*, first, Robert, Earl of Mellent, first Baron de Bellomont, created Earl of Leicester, and had:

ROBERT DE BELLOMONT, second Earl of Leicester, justiciary of England, *d.* 1168, who had by his wife, Lady Amicia, daughter of Ralph de Waer, Earl of Norfolk:

ROBERT DE BELLOMONT, third Earl of Leicester, high steward of England, *d.* 1190, who had by his wife, Lady Petronella, daughter of Hugh Grentemaisnill, high steward of England:

LADY MARGARET DE BELLOMONT, who *m.* Saier de Quincey, created, 1207, Earl of Winchester, *d.* 1219 (*see* "The Magna Charta Barons and their American Descendants"), and had:

ROGER DE QUINCEY, second Earl of Winchester, constable of Scotland, *d.* 1264, who *m.* Lady Helen, daughter of Alan McDonal, Lord of Galloway, also of Royal Descent, and had:

LADY ELIZABETH DE QUINCEY, who *m.* Alexander, Baron Cumyn, second Earl of Buchan, *d.* 1289, also of Royal Descent, and had:

LADY AGNES CUMYN, who *m.* (*see* Wood's Douglas's "Peerage of Scotland," i., 62, and Dugdale's "Baronage of England," i., 504) Gilbert de Umfraville, eighth Earl of Angus, *d.* 1307-8, and had:

ROBERT DE UMFRAVILLE, ninth Earl of Angus, 1274-1326, who had by his second wife, Lady Alianore:

SIR THOMAS DE UMFRAVILLE, of Harbottle Castle, Northumberland, second son, who *m.* Joane, daughter of Adam de Rodam, of Northumberland, and had:

SIR THOMAS DE UMFRAVILLE, Lord of Riddesdale and Kyme, second son, who had by his wife, Lady Agnes:

LADY JOANE DE UMFRAVILLE (sister of Gilbert d'Umfraville, titular Earl of Kyme, *k.* 1422), who *m.* Sir William Lambert, of Owlton, Durham, and Harbottle, Northumberland (*see* Douglas's "Peerage of Scotland," i., 64, 456; Burke's "Dictionary of the Peerage"), also of Royal Descent, and had:

ROBERT LAMBERT, of Owlton (or Owton), father of:

HENRY LAMBERT, of Ongar, Essex, living in 1447, who had:

ELIZABETH LAMBERT, heiress, who *m.*, about 1488, Thomas Lyman, of Navistoke, Essex, *d.* 1509, son of John Lyman, a London merchant, who purchased the estate of Navistoke, and had:

HENRY LYMAN, of Navistoke and High Ongar, Essex, 1517, who *m.* Alicia, daughter of Simon Hyde, of Westersfield, Essex, and had:

JOHN LYMAN, of High Ongar, eldest son, *d.* 1587, at Navistoke, who had by his wife, Margaret, daughter of William Gérard, of Beauchamp, St Paul, Essex:

HENRY LYMAN, of High Ongar, eldest son, *d.* 1609, who *m.*, secondly, Phillis, daughter of John Scott, of Navistoke, and had by her, who was living, widow of Ralph Green, of High Ongar, in 1629:

RICHARD LYMAN,* *bapt.* 20 October, 1580, at High Ongar, came to Charlestown, Massachusetts, in 1631, and *d.* August, 1640, at Hartford, Connecticut, of which he was one of the original proprietors. He *m.*, before 1617, Sarah Osborne, *b.* Halsted, Kent, *d.* Hartford, 1640, and had:

1.—RICHARD LYMAN, *d.* at Northampton, Massachusetts, 3 June, 1662: *m.* Hepzibah, daughter of Thomas Ford, and had:

JOHN LYMAN, *b.* 1655, *d.* Northampton, 13 October, 1727; *m.*, December, 1694, Abigail, daughter of John Holton, and had:

ABNER LYMAN, of Northampton, *b.* 1 February, 1701, *d.* 25 January, 1774; *m.*, 3 May, 1739, Sarah, *b.* 11 January, 1708, daughter of Ichabod Allis, and widow of Joseph Miller, and had:

SARAH LYMAN, *b.* 11 April, 1740; *m.*, 7 December, 1758, Joseph Allen, *b.* at Northampton, 12 October, 1735, *d.* at Charlotte, Vermont, 17 June, 1810, and had:

EUNICE ALLEN, *b.* 25 February, 1775, at Pittsfield, Massachusetts, *d.* 19 July, 1843, at Pittsford, Vermont, who *m.*, 1791, Remembrance Hitchcock, of Pittsford, Vermont, *b.* 1770, *d.* 17 August, 1849, and had:

---

* The following ladies, members of the National Society of the Colonial Dames of America, are also of Royal Descent through Richard Lyman:

MRS. CHARLES H. ANSON, Massachusetts State Society.

MISS AMELIA DE PAU FOWLER, Maryland State Society.

MISS BESSIE H. LYMAN, Massachusetts State Society.

MISS EMILY R. LYMAN, Pennsylvania State Society.

MRS. CHARLES H. BURBANK, New Hampshire State Society.

MRS. GEORGE W. CROCKETT, Massachusetts State Society.

MRS. ROBERT P. LISLE, Pennsylvania State Society.

HENRY HITCHCOCK, of Rutland, Vermont, *b.* Pittsford, 22 August, 1805, *d.* 28 August, 1871 ; *m.*, 23 June, 1837, Hannah Lucy Hulett, also of Royal Descent, and had :

ABIGAIL JANE HITCHCOCK, *b.* at Clarendon Springs, Vermont, 3 May, 1843, a member of the Massachusetts Society of the Colonial Dames of America, of the Order of the Crown, *etc.*, who *m.*, 15 February, 1866, Horace Hoxie Dyer, of Rutland, Vermont, and had : *Horace Edward, b.* 16 April, 1870; *m.* 6 December, 1893.

2.—LIEUTENANT JOHN LYMAN, of Northampton, Massachusetts, *b.* High Ongar, 16 September, 1623, *d.* 20 August, 1690 ; *m.*, 12 January, 1655, Dorcas, daughter of John Plum, of Branford, Connecticut, *d.* 1648, and had :

I.—MOSES LYMAN, of Northampton, *b.* 20 February, 1662–3, *d.* 25 February, 1701 ; *m.* Ann ——, and had :

1.—MARY LYMAN, *d.* 18 January, 1776, who *m.*, 18 June, 1719, Captain Samuel Dwight (" Dwight Genealogy," i., pp. 272–288, and " Lyman Genealogy," pp. 33, 318, *etc.*), and had :

MARY DWIGHT, *b.* 2 March, 1721, *d.* 21 January, 1809; *m.*, March, 1738, Daniel Hall, Jr., of Middletown, Connecticut, and had :

MARY HALL, *b.* 3 November 1742, *d.* 10 January, 1833; *m.*, 3 December, 1765, Judge Eliphalet Terry (" Terry Genealogy," pp. 10–38), and had :

ELIPHALET TERRY, of Hartford, Connecticut, *b.* 26 December, 1776, *d.* 8 July, 1849 ; *m.*, 5 June, 1817, Lydia Coit (" Coit Genealogy," p. 131), and had :

MARY HALL TERRY, *b.* 3 June, 1820, a member of the New York Society of the Colonial Dames of America, the Order of the Crown, *etc.*, who *m.*, 1 September, 1840, Charles Collins, *b.* 2 April, 1817, *d.* 30 November, 1891, also of Royal Descent (see p. 152), and had :

I.—LYDIA COIT COLLINS, a member of the New York Society of the Colonial Dames of America, who *m.*, 8 June, 1864, William Platt Ketcham, of New York, and had :

1.—ARTHUR COLLINS KETCHAM, *m.*, 7 April, 1890, Bruce Allen, and had : 1. *William Tredwell, b.* 27 February, 1891 ; *Margaret Bruce, b.* 25 February, 1892; and *Archer Collins, b.* 5 April, 1893.

2.—MARY VAN WINKLE KETCHAM, *m.*, 1 December, 1890, Thomas Hunt Talmadge, *d.* 29 November, 1895, and had : *Thomas Hunt,* b. 9 December, 1894, and *Lillian, b.* 3 April, 1896.

3.—ETHEL MIRIAM KETCHAM, *unm.*

II.—CLARENCE LYMAN COLLINS, of New York, a member of the Society of the Colonial Wars, *etc.*, who *m.* Marie Louise, daughter of Horace F. Clark, and his wife, Marie Louise, daughter of Commodore Cornelius Vanderbilt, of New York, and had:

> EDITH LYMAN COLLINS, Comtesse Czaykowska, a member of the Order of the Crown, who *m.*, in Paris, France, 7 January, 1897, Richid Bey, Comte Czaykowska, councillor of State and first secretary to the Turkish embassy at Rome, and had:
>
> > 1.—COUNT VLADIMIR CLARENCE LADISLAS MICHEL, *b.* at Rome, 10 October, 1897.
> >
> > 2.—CHEVALIER STANISLUS MICHEL FREDERIC MARIE, *b.* at The Hague, 20 June, 1899.

III.—LOUISE TERRY COLLINS, a member of New York Society of the Colonial Dames of America, the Order of the Crown, *etc.*, who *m.*, 4 October, 1884, William Allen Butler, Jr., of New York, and had:

> 1.—WILLIAM ALLEN BUTLER, 3D, *b.* 7 January, 1886.
>
> 2.—LYMAN COLLINS BUTLER, *b.* 2 January, 1888.
>
> 3.—CHARLES TERRY BUTLER, *b.* 20 September, 1889.
>
> 4.—LYDIA COIT BUTLER, *b.* 19 November, 1891.
>
> 5.—LOUISE TRACY BUTLER, *b.* 23 October, 1894.

2.—CAPTAIN MOSES LYMAN, of Northampton, *b.* 27 February, 1689, *d.* 24 March, 1762; *m.*, 13 December, 1712, Mindwell Sheldon, 1692–1780, and had:

1.—REV. ISAAC LYMAN, of York, Maine, *b.* 25 February, 1724–25, *d.* 1810; *m.*, 24 April, 1750, Ruth Plummer, of Gloucester, Massachusetts, 1730–1824, and had:

> THEODORE LYMAN, of Boston, *b.* 8 January, 1755, *d.* Waltham, Massachusetts, 24 May, 1839; *m.*, secondly, 24 January, 1786, Lydia Williams, of Marlboro, Massachusetts, and had by her:
>
> > GEORGE WILLIAM LYMAN, of Waltham, Massachusetts, *b.* 4 December, 1786. He *m.*, first, 31 May, 1810, Elizabeth Gray, 1791–1824, daughter of Harrison Gray Otis, of Boston, and had:
> >
> > > GEORGE THEODORE LYMAN, of Bellport, Long Island, *b.* 23 December, 1821; *m.*, 17 April, 1845, Sally, *b.* 4 October, 1825, daughter of James W. Otis, of New York, and had:
> > >
> > > > ALICE LYMAN, *b.* 14 January, 1852, a member of the Pennsylvania Society of the Colonial Dames of America, who *m.* William Platt Pepper, of Philadelphia.

GEORGE WILLIAMS LYMAN, *m.*, secondly, 3 May, 1827, Anne, *b.* 9 May, 1798, daughter of William Pratt, of Boston, and had:

SARAH PRATT LYMAN, *b.* 5 February, 1835, a member of the Massachusetts Society of the Colonial Dames of America, who *m.*, 23 April, 1862, Philip H. Sears, of Boston, and had: *Annie Lyman, Mary Pratt, Richard, Francis Philip*, and *Evelyn*.

2.—PHŒBE LYMAN, 1719–1802, who *m.* Caleb Strong, of Northampton, 1701–1776, and had:

MARTHA STRONG, 1749–1827, who *m.*, 1773, Rev. Ebenezer Moseley,· 1741–1825, and had:

SOPHIA MOSELEY, 1773–1821, who *m.* John Abbot, of Westford, Massachusetts, 1777–1854, and had:

JOHN WILLIAM PITT ABBOT, of Westford, *b.* 27 April, 1806, *d.* 16 August, 1862; *m.*, 18 July, 1833, Catharine Abbot, *b.* 18 March, 1808, *d.* 14 April, 1891, and had:

JOHN WILLIAM ABBOT, of Westford, *b.* 14 April, 1834, *d.* 10 November, 1897 ; *m.*, 21 October, 1857, Elizabeth Rowell Southwick, *b.* 8 September, 1838, and had:

I.—CATHARINE MABEL ABBOT, *b.* 28 January, 1861 ; *m.* 15 September, 1881, Abbot L. Kebler, 1856–1888, and had : *Catharine Abbot, b.* 22 June, 1885 ; *d.* 1. August, 1896, and *Elizabeth Abbot, b.* 31 October, 1888.

II.—EMMA SOUTHWICK ABBOT, *b.* 17 July, 1864, a member of the Massachusetts and Colorado Societies of the Colonial Dames of America, who *m.*, 5 June, 1888, Julian A. Kebler, of Denver, Colorado.

III.—LUCY KEBLER ABBOT, *b.* 26 March, 1870; *m.* 22 June, 1893, Julian Abbot Cameron, and had: *Alexander Abbot, b.* 5 August, 1895.

IV.—JOHN CAMERON ABBOT, *b.* 25 February, 1872 ; *m.* 12 January, 1898, Anna M. Fletcher, and had: *John Fletcher, b.* 28 November, 1898.

3.—MOSES LYMAN, of Goshen, Connecticut, *b.* 13 October, 1713, *d.* 1768; *m.*, 24 March, 1742, Sarah Heighton (or Hayden), and had: COLONEL MOSES LYMAN, of Goshen, *b.* 20 March, 1743, *d.* 29 September, 1829, and had by his second wife, Mrs. Mary Buel Judd, who *d.* 1835:

MARY LYMAN, *b.* 27 June, 1787, *d.* 8 May, 1870; *m.*, 30 April, 1811, Amos Morris Collins, of Hartford, and had:

I.—WILLIAM LYMAN COLLINS, of Hartford, *b.* 10 February, 1812, who *m.* Harriet Rierson Collins, and had:

ELLEN COLLINS, a member of the Connecticut Society of the Colonial Dames of America, the Order of the Crown, *etc.*

II.—CHARLES COLLINS, *b.* 2 April, 1817, *d.* 30 November, 1891, who *m.*, 1 September, 1840, Mary Hall Terry, also of Royal Descent, and had issue as above.

III.—ERASTUS COLLINS, who *m.*, 1848, Mary Sarah Atwood, and had:

CAROLINE LYMAN COLLINS, a member of the Connecticut Society of the Colonial Dames of America, the Order of the Crown, *etc.*, who *m.*, 1886, Charles Whitney Page, of Middletown, and had: *Atwood Collins, b.* 12 November, 1887; *Charles Whitney, b.* 27 January, 1890, and *Ruth Whitney, b.* 6 May, 1890.

II.—LIEUTENANT BENJAMIN LYMAN, of Northampton, *b.* 10 August, 1674, *d.* 14 October, 1723; *m.*, 27 October, 1698, Thankful Pomeroy, and had:

1.—MARY LYMAN, who *m.*, 22 November, 1750, Lieutenant Oliver Pomeroy, and had:

RACHEL LYMAN POMEROY, *b.* 15 September, 1754, *d.* 14 August, 1774; *m.*, 27 October, 1771, Brigadier-Major Edward Bulkeley, an original member of the Society of the Cincinnati, also of Royal Descent, and had:

ROXA LYMAN BULKELEY, *b.* 25 October, 1772, *m.*, 25 February, 1793, Colonel Selah Francis, and had:

ROXA BULKELEY FRANCIS, *b.* 4 July, 1796, *d.* 1868; *m.*, 4 May, 1815, Judge Jesse Booth, quartermaster in the War of 1812, in the regiment of his father-in-law, and also held important offices in State and county. He served in the New York Legislature, and also served as judge for a number of years. Their daughter:

ELLEN C. BULKELEY BOOTH, a member of the Connecticut Society of the Colonial Dames of America, who *m.*, 21 November, 1864, Byron Coleman Dick, of Oakland, California. *No issue.*

2.—CAPTAIN WILLIAM LYMAN, of Northampton, *b.* 12 December, 1715, *d.* 13 March, 1774; *m.* Jemima Sheldon, and had:

GENERAL WILLIAM LYMAN, *b.* Northampton, 7 December, 1755, *d.* Colchester, England, 22 September, 1811, *bur.* in Gloucester Cathedral, 30 September, 1811. He *m.*, 11 June, 1803, Jerusha Welles, and had:

MARTHA LYMAN, *b* 29 February, 1792, *d.* 14 April, 1831; *m.*, 4 August, 1818, John Cox, and had:

JAMES SITGREAVES COX, *b.* 13 February, 1823; *m.*, 25 June, 1857, Mary Fullerton, *b.* 15 January, 1836, daughter of Erskine and Mary (Fullerton) Hazard, and had:

MARTHA LYMAN COX, *b.* 17 May, 1860, a member of the Massachusetts Society of the Colonial Dames of America, who *m.*, 1 September, 1887, William Sohier Bryant, of Longwood, Massachusetts, and had: *Mary Cleveland, Elizabeth Sohier, Alice, Julia Cox, Gladys,* and *William Sohier.*

3.—AARON LYMAN, *b.* 1 April, 1705, *d.* 12 June, 1788; *m.*, 12 December, 1733, Eunice Dwight, *d.* 28 March, 1760, and had:

SUSANNAH LYMAN, *b.* 16 November, 1734, *d.* 1 February, 1770; *m.*, 9 November, 1763, Major Elihu Kent, *b.* 1 June, 1733, *d.* 12 February, 1814, and had:

SUSAN KENT, *b.* 20 September, 1768, *d.* 29 December, 1839; *m.*, 5 October, 1788, Judge Hezekiah Huntington, *b.* 30 December, 1759, *d.* 27 May, 1842, and had:

JULIA ANN HUNTINGTON, *b.* 10 December, 1790, *d.* 24 January, 1849; *m.*, 12 October, 1814, Judge Leicester King, *b.* 1 May, 1789, *d.* 19 September, 1856, and had:

CATHERINE BRINDLEY KING, *b.* 8 July, 1832; *m.*, 19 September, 1855, William Kimbrough Pendleton, *b.* 8 September, 1817, *d.* 1 September, 1899, and had:

CLARINDA HUNTINGTON PENDLETON, *b.* 25 August, 1856, a member of the Georgia Society of the Colonial Dames of America, who *m.*, 30 January, 1879, Joseph Rucker Lamar, of Augusta, Georgia, and had: *Philip Rucker, b.* 16 June, 1880; *William Pendleton, b.* 5 October, 1882, and *Mary Lamar, b.* 15 April, *d.* 11 July, 1885.

THE ROYAL DESCENT

OF

MRS. GEORGE M. CONARROE,

OF PHILADELPHIA, PA.

EDWARD I., King of England⊤Princess Eleanor of Castile.

Princess Elizabeth Plantagenet⊤Humphrey de Bohun, Earl of Hereford.

William de Bohun, Earl of Northampton⊤Lady Elizabeth de Badlesmere.

Lady Elizabeth de Bohun⊤Richard Fitz-Alan, K.G., Earl of Arundel.

Lady Elizabeth Fitz-Alan⊤Sir Robert Goushill, of Hault Hucknall, Derby.

Lady Joan Goushill⊤Sir Thomas Stanley, K.G., Lord Stanley.

Lady Margaret Stanley⊤Sir William Troutbeck, of Prynes Castle, Cheshire.

Lady Jane Troutbeck⊤Sir William Griffith, of Penrhyn Castle.

Sir William Griffith, of Penrhyn Castle⊤Jane Puleston of Carnarvon.

Lady Sibill Griffith⊤Owen ap Hugh, of Bodeon.

Jane Owen⊤Hugh Gwyn, of Penarth.

Sibill Gwyn⊤John Powell, of Llanwddyn.

Elizabeth Powell⊤Humphrey ap Hugh, of Llwyn-du.

Owen Humphrey, of Llwyn-du⊤Jane ———.

Rebecca Humphrey⊤Robert Owen, of Fron Gôch, d. Philadelphia, 1697.

Owen Owen, of Philadelphia⊤(Name unknown).

Sarah Owen⊤John Biddle, of Philadelphia.

Col. Clement Biddle, of Philadelphia⊤Rebekah Cornell.

Ann Wilkinson Biddle⊤Thomas Dunlap, of Philadelphia.

Nannie Dunlap, a member of the National So-—George Mecum Conarroe, of Philadelphia.
ciety of the Colonial Dames of America.

PEDIGREE XXXVII.

HENRY III., King of England, had by his wife (*m.* 1236), Lady Eleanor, daughter of Raymond de Berenger, Count of Provence :

PRINCE EDMUND, 1245–1295, Earl of Leicester, Lancaster, and Chester, lord high steward of England, who had by his second wife, Blanche, widow of Henry I., King of Navarre, and daughter of Robert, Earl of Artois, son of Louis VIII., King of France :

HENRY PLANTAGENET, Earl of Lancaster and Leicester, *d.* 1345, who *m.* Lady Maud, daughter of Patrick de Chaworth, 1253–1282, and his wife, Lady Isabel, daughter of William de Beauchamp, first Earl of Warwick, also of Royal Descent, and had :

LADY ELEANOR PLANTAGENET, widow of John de Beaumont, who *m.*, 1346, secondly (his second wife), Sir Richard Fitz-Alan, K.G., Earl of Arundel and Surrey, *d.* 24 January, 1375–6, and had :

SIR RICHARD FITZ-ALAN, K.G., tenth Earl of Arundel, *b.* 1346, beheaded in 1397, who *m.*, first, Lady Elizabeth de Bohun, also of Royal Descent, and had :

LADY ELIZABETH FITZ-ALAN, who *m.*, thirdly, Sir Robert Goushill, Knt., of Hault Hucknell Manor, Derby, and had :

LADY JOAN GOUSHILL, who *m.* Sir Thomas Stanley, installed 14 May, 1457, K.G., Lord Stanley, *d.* 12 January, 1458–59, and had :

LADY MARGARET STANLEY (sister of Sir William Stanley, who crowned Henry VII. on Bosworth Field), who *m.*, first, Sir John Butler, of Bewsey, Knt., and *m.*, secondly, Sir William Troutbeck, of Prynes Castle, Werrall, Cheshire, slain at Bloreheath, and had :

LADY JANE TROUTBECK, who *m.*, first, Sir William Boteler, and *m.*, secondly, Sir William Griffith, K.B., of Penrhyn Castle, Carnarvonshire, chamberlain of North Wales, and had :

SIR WILLIAM GRIFFITH, of Penrhyn, chamberlain of North Wales, who *m.*, secondly, Jane, daughter of John Puleston, of Carnarvon Castle, also of Royal Descent, and had by her :

LADY SIBILL GRIFFITH, who *m.* Owen ap Hugh, of Bodeon, high sheriff of Anglesea in 1563 and 1580, *d.* 1613, and had :

JANE OWEN, who *m.* Hugh Gwyn, of Penarth, high sheriff of Carnarvonshire in 1600, and had :

SIBILL GWYN, who *m.*, *ante* 20 September, 1588, John Powell (John ap Howell Gôch), of Gadfa, Llanwddwn township, Montgomeryshire, who was buried in the church at Llanwddyn, 24 July, 1636, and had:

ELIZABETH POWELL, who *m.* Humphrey ap Hugh ap David ap Howel ap Grono ap Einion, of Llwyn-du, Merionethshire, and had by him, who *d.* 1664–5:

1.—SAMUEL AP HUMPHREY, of Portheven, Merionethshire, who had by his wife, Elizabeth:

DANIEL HUMPHREYS, who removed in 1682 to Haverford township, in the " Welsh Tract," Pennsylvania (*see* Glenn's " Merion in the Welsh Tract," " The Humphreys Family History," *etc.*). He *m.*, 1695, Hannah, daughter of Dr. Thomas Wynne, of Merion, Pennsylvania, speaker of the first three general assemblies of Pennsylvania, and had:

JOSHUA HUMPHREYS, of Darby, 1710–1793; *m.*, at Merion Meeting House, 1742, Sarah, daughter of Edward Williams, of " Blockley," Philadelphia county, Pennsylvania, and had:

JOSHUA HUMPHREYS, of Ponte Reading, Pennsylvania, 1751–1838. He was the first naval constructor and master shipbuilder to the Government, 1774. He *m.* Mary Davids, of Philadelphia, 1757–1805, and had:

I.—SAMUEL HUMPHREYS, *b.* 1798, chief naval constructor to the Government, 1826–46; *d.* at Georgetown, District of Columbia, 16 August, 1846. He *m.*, 1808, Letitia, daughter of Andrew Atkinson, of " Cavan Garden," county Donegal, Ireland, and of Florida, and his wife, Lady Jane, daughter of Sir Archibald Murray, of Black Barony, in Scotland, and had:

WILLIAM PENN HUMPHREYS, United States Navy, of San Francisco, California, *m.*, 1870, Mary Stencon, and had:

ALICE HUMPHREYS, of San Francisco, a member of the California Society of the Colonial Dames of America, the Order of the Crown, *etc.*

II.—SARAH HUMPHREYS, 1780–1854, who *m.* Henry Hollingsworth, of Philadelphia, and had:

HANNAH HOLLINGSWORTH, 1813–1881, who *m.* Thomas Stewardson, M.D., of Philadelphia, 1807–1878, and had:

MARY HOLLINGSWORTH STEWARDSON, of Philadelphia, a member of the Pennsylvania Society of the Colonial Dames of America.

2.—OWEN HUMPHREY, of Llwyn-du, parish of Llangelynin, Talybont, Merionethshire, eldest son, 1625–1699, a justice under Cromwell, who had by his wife, Jane:

REBECCA HUMPHREY,* who *m.*, 1678 (marriage certificate extant), Robert Owen, of Fron Gôch, Merionethshire, *b.* 1657, *d.* Merion township, Philadelphia county, Pennsylvania, 1697. He removed to Pennsylvania in 1690, and was a justice of the peace for Merion township, and a member of the provincial assembly (*see* Glenn's "Owen of Merion," *Pennsylvania Magazine,* vol. xiii., part 2; Glenn's "Merion in the Welsh Tract," p. 112, *etc.*, for the Welsh families connected with this pedigree), and had issue:

1.—ROBERT OWEN, of Philadelphia, *m.* Susannah, daughter of Judge William Hudson, mayor of Philadelphia, and had:

HANNAH OWEN, 1720–1791, who *m.*, first, John Ogden, of Philadelphia, and *m.*, secondly, 7 June, 1752 (his second wife), Joseph Wharton, of "Walnut Grove," Philadelphia, and had by him, who *d.* 1776, aged 69 years:

RACHEL WHARTON, 1762–1836, who *m.*, 13 December, 1781, William Lewis, of Philadelphia, 1746–1801, and had:

HANNAH OWEN LEWIS, *b.* 6 June, 1795, *d.* 24 January, 1857, who *m.*, 23 June, 1824, Richard Wistar, Jr., of Philadelphia, *b.* 3 October, 1790, *d.* 3 November, 1863, and had:

FRANCES ANNA WISTAR, who *m.*, 23 June, 1857, Lewis Allaire Scott, of Philadelphia, also of Royal Descent, and had:

HANNAH LEWIS SCOTT, of Philadelphia, a member of the Pennsylvania Society of the Colonial Dames of America.

2.—OWEN OWEN, high sheriff and coroner of Philadelphia county, father of:

SARAH OWEN, who *m.*, 3 March, 1736, John Biddle, of Philadelphia, son of William Biddle, of "Mt. Hope," Burlington county, New Jersey, and had:

I.—OWEN BIDDLE, of Philadelphia, *b.* 1737, a delegate to the Provincial Congress, 1775; member of the Pennsylvania committee of safety and of the council of safety; delegate to the constitutional convention, 1776, *etc.*, who *m.*, 29 September, 1760, Sarah, daughter of Thomas Parke, Jr., of Chester county, Pennsylvania, and had:

CLEMENT BIDDLE, *b.* 6 August, 1778, *d.* 10 February, 1856; *m.*, first, 1810, Mary, daughter of William Canby, and had by her:

1.—WILLIAM CANBY BIDDLE, *b.* 25 September, 1816, *d.* 22 December, 1887; *m.*, 21 February, 1838, Rachel Miller, and had:

---

* The following ladies, members of the National Society of the Colonial Dames of America, are also of Royal Descent through Rebecca Humphrey:

MRS. EUGENE BLACKFORD, Maryland State Society.

MRS. ARTHUR E. POULTNEY, Maryland State Society.

I.—FRANCES CANBY BIDDLE, *b.* 11 August, 1840, a member of the Pennsylvania Society of the Colonial Dames of America, who *m.*, 18 June, 1862, Clement Acton Griscom, of Philadelphia and Haverford, also of Royal Descent, and had: *Clement A., Rodman E., Lloyd C., Francis C.,* and

> HELEN BIDDLE GRISCOM, *b.* 9 October, 1866, a member of the Pennsylvania Society of the Colonial Dames of America, who *m.*, 20 June, 1889, Samuel Bettle, of Philadelphia, and had: *Griscom, b.* 19 February, 1890.

II.—MARY BIDDLE, *b.* 17 December, 1849, a member of the Pennsylvania Society of the Colonial Dames of America, who *m.*, 28 January, 1869, Howard Wood, of Philadelphia, and had: *Biddle, Helen B., Alan Wood, 3d; Howard, Clement B., Owen B., d.* 20 February, 1882; *Rachel Biddle, Marion Biddle,* and *Dorothy, d.* 9 April, 1887.

III.—HANNAH NICHOLSON BIDDLE, *b.* 18 April, 1855, a member of the Pennsylvania Society of the Colonial Dames of America, who *m.*, 18 October, 1877, Charles Williams, of Philadelphia and Haverford, and had: *William Biddle, Frances Biddle,* and *Eleanor Poultney Biddle.*

2.—ROBERT BIDDLE, of Philadelphia, who *m.* Anna, daughter of Daniel L. and Hannah (Nicholson) Miller, and had:

> HANNAH MILLER BIDDLE, *b.* 24 August, 1850, a member of the Pennsylvania Society of the Colonial Dames of America, who *m.*, 5 January, 1882, John C. W. Frishmuth, of Riverton, N. J., and had: *Edna Helen, John Whitney, Robert Biddle,* and *Clarice.*

II.—COLONEL CLEMENT BIDDLE, of Philadelphia, *b.* 10 May, 1740, *d.* 14 July, 1814. He was a distinguished officer in the Continental army; *m.*, secondly, Rebekah, daughter of Gideon Cornell, lieutenant-governor and chief justice of the Rhode Island Colony, and had by her:

1.—ANN WILKINSON BIDDLE, *b.* 12 June, 1791; *m.*, 2 June, 1822, Thomas Dunlap, of Philadelphia, and had:

> NANNIE DUNLAP, *b.* 21 November, 1830, a member of the Pennsylvania Society of the Colonial Dames of America, who *m.* George Mecum Conarroe, of Philadelphia.

2.—COLONEL CLEMENT CORNELL BIDDLE, Philadelphia, third son, *b.* 24 October, 1784, captain of the State Fencibles and colonel of First Regiment Volunteer Light Infantry of Pennsylvania in the War of 1812. He *m.* Mary Searle, daughter of John Barclay, mayor of Philadelphia, 1791, a native of Ballyshannon, Ireland, and had:

John Barclay Biddle, *b.* 3 January, 1815, who *m.*, 7 November, 1850, Caroline, daughter of William Phillips, and had:

Anna Clifford Biddle, a member of the Pennsylvania Society of the Colonial Dames of America, who *m.*, in 1881, Clement Stocker Phillips, of Philadelphia.

3.—Thomas Biddle, of Philadelphia, *b.* 4 June, 1776, *m.*, 12 February, 1806, Christine, daughter of General Jonathan Williams, and had:

I.—Colonel Henry Jonathan Biddle, of Philadelphia, *b.* 16 May, 1807, adjutant-general of Pennsylvania Volunteers, *d.* from wound received at New Market Cross-Roads, 30 June, 1862; *m.*, 1 June, 1854, Mary Deborah, daughter of Samuel Baird, of Philadelphia, and had:

Lydia McFunn Biddle, *b.* 9 April, 1857, a member of the Pennsylvania Society of the Colonial Dames of America, who *m.* Moncure Robinson, Jr., of Philadelphia.

II.—Alexander Biddle, of Philadelphia, *b.* 29 April, 1819; *m.*, 11 October, 1855, Julia Williams, a member of the Pennsylvania Society of the Colonial Dames of America, daughter of Samuel Rush, M.D., of Philadelphia, and had:

Marianne Biddle, of Philadelphia, a member of the Pennsylvania Society of the Colonial Dames of America.

4.—Rebekah Cornell Biddle, *b.* 7 November, 1782, *m.*, 1 September, 1808, Professor Nathaniel Chapman, of Philadelphia, and had:

George William Chapman, of Philadelphia, *b.* 10 December, 1816, *m.* Emily, daughter of John Markoe, of Philadelphia, and had:

I.—Mary Randolph Chapman, a member of the Pennsylvania Society of the Colonial Dames of America, who *m.* John Borland Thayer, of Philadelphia, and had: *George C., Henry C., John B., Walter, Mary, Sidney,* and *Farnum.*

II.—Elizabeth Camac Chapman, a member of the Pennsylvania Society of the Colonial Dames of America, who *m.* William Davis Winsor, of Philadelphia, and had: *Louise Brooks* and

Emily Chapman Winsor, a member of the Pennsylvania Society of the Colonial Dames of America, who *m.* William R. Philler, of Philadelphia and Haverford.

III.—Rebecca Chapman, a member of the Pennsylvania Society of the Colonial Dames of America, who *m.* James Davis Winsor, of Philadelphia and Haverford, and had: *Henry, James, Davis, Rebecca, Ellen,* and

Mary Winsor, of Haverford, a member of the Pennsylvania Society of the Colonial Dames of America.

3.—GAINOR OWEN, *b.* 26 October, 1688, who *m.*, at Merion Meeting House, 4 October, 1706, Jonathan Jones, of Merion, Pennsylvania, 1680–1770 (son of Dr. Edward Jones, of Merion, *d.* 1737, and his wife, Mary, daughter of Dr. Thomas Wynne, of Sussex, Delaware county, Pennsylvania, who came with William Penn, in the "Welcome"), and had:

I.—OWEN JONES, of Merion, Pennsylvania, *b.* 19 November, 1711, *d.* 10 October, 1793, the last colonial treasurer of Pennsylvania, who *m.*, 30 May, 1740, Susannah, 1719–1801, daughter of Hugh Evans, of Merion, 1682–1772, also of Royal Descent, and had:

    1.—LOWRY JONES, *b.* 1743, *d.* 15 April, 1804, who *m.*, 5 July, 1760, Daniel Wister, Philadelphia, *b.* 4 April, 1738, *d.* 2 December, 1805, son of John and Catherine Wister, and had:

       I.—CHARLES JONES WISTER, of Philadelphia, *b.* 12 April, 1782, *d.* 23 July, 1865 ; *m.*, 15 December, 1803, Rebecca, daughter of Joseph Bullock, of Philadelphia, and had:

         WILLIAM WYNNE WISTER, of Philadelphia, *b.* 25 March, 1807, *d.* 17 December, 1898 ; *m.* Hannah Lewis, daughter of Alexander and Rachel Wilson, and had:

         RACHEL WILSON WISTER, *b.* 22 January, 1835, *m.*, 12 November, 1862, William Barton Rogers, son of James B. and Rachel Rogers, and had:

         MABEL ROGERS, a member of the Pennsylvania Society of the Colonial Dames of America, who *m.*, 15 April, 1896, Edgar W. Baird (son of Matthew Baird), of Philadelphia and Merion, and had: *Edgar W.*, *b.* 5 April, 1897, and *Gainor Owen*, *b.* 27 October, 1898.

       II.—JOHN WISTER, of Germantown, Philadelphia, *b.* 20 March, 1776, *d.* 10 December, 1862, who *m.*, 1798, Elizabeth, daughter of Thomas Harvey, of Bucks county, Pennsylvania, and had:

         LOUIS WISTER, of "St. Mary's," near Ardmore, Pennsylvania, *m.*, 3 July, 1850, Elizabeth Emlen, daughter of Dr. Jacob and Sarah Emlen (Physick) Randolph, and had by her, who *d.* 25 December, 1891 : *Sara Edythe*, and

         ELIZABETH HARVEY WISTER, a member of the Pennsylvania Society of the Colonial Dames of America, who *m.*, 18 December, 1883, Charles Penrose Keith, of Philadelphia. *No issue.*

    2.—HANNAH JONES, *b.* 28 December, 1749, *d.* 1829, who *m.*, 1779, Amos Foulke, of Philadelphia, also of Royal Descent, and had: EDWARD FOULKE, of Gwynedd township, Montgomery county, Pennsylvania, *b.* 17 November, 1784, *d.* 17 July, 1851 ; *m.*, 11 December, 1810, Tacy, daughter of Isaac and Gainor Jones, of Montgomery county, Pennsylvania, and had, besides other issue:

I.—ANN JONES FOULKE, 1811–1888; *m.*, 1833, Hiram Corson, M.D., of Conshohocken, and had:

> SUSAN FOULKE CORSON, a member of the Pennsylvania Society of the Colonial Dames of America, who *m.*, 26 November, 1868, Jawood Lukens, of Conshohocken. *No issue.*

II.—PRISCILLA FOULKE, 1821–1882; *m.*, 22 April, 1849, Thomas Wistar, Jr., of Philadelphia, and had:

> SUSAN FOULKE WISTAR, a member of the Pennsylvania Society of the Colonial Dames of America, who *m.*, 27 May, 1872, Howard Comfort, and had: *William Wistar, b.* 27 May, 1874.

III.—REBECCA JONES FOULKE, *b.* 18 May, 1829, a member of the Pennsylvania Society of the Colonial Dames of America, who *m.*, 8 October, 1857, Robert R. Corson, of New Hope, Pennsylvania.

II.—REBECCA JONES, *b.* 20 February, 1709, *d.* 8 January, 1779. She *m.*, at Merion Meeting House, 4 June, 1733, John Roberts, *b.* 26 June, 1710, *d.* Merion 13 January, 1776, and had:

LIEUTENANT-COLONEL ALGERNON ROBERTS, *b.* 24 November, 1750, *d.* at Merion in 1815. He *m.*, 18 January, 1781, Tacy, daughter of Colonel Isaac Warner, of Blockley, Philadelphia county, Pennsylvania, and had:

1.—ALGERNON SYDNEY ROBERTS, *b.* 29 March, 1798, *d.* 14 September, 1865; *m.*, 10 April, 1823, Elizabeth, 1802–1891, daughter of Captain Anthony and Mary (Ogden) Cuthbert, of Philadelphia, and had:

> I.—ALGERNON SYDNEY ROBERTS, JR., of Philadelphia, *b.* 24 October, 1827, who *m.*, 7 November, 1850, Sarah, daughter of James and Sarah Carstairs, and had:
>
> > ELIZABETH CUTHBERT ROBERTS, a member of the Pennsylvania Society of the Colonial Dames of America, who *m.*, 28 December, 1882, Walter Scott Wyatt, of Ohio, United States Army.
>
> II.—ELIZABETH CUTHBERT ROBERTS, of Philadelphia, a member of the Pennsylvania Society of the Colonial Dames of America.

2.—EDWARD ROBERTS, of Philadelphia, *b.* 29 June, 1800, *d.* 3 November, 1872; *m.*, in May, 1825, Mary Elizabeth Reford, 1801–1862, and had:

> I.—ANNA FRANCES ROBERTS, *b.* 7 November, 1827, *d.* 13 October, 1890; *m.* Edward Browning, of Philadelphia, and had:
>
> > MARY ROBERTS BROWNING, a member of the Pennsylvania Society of the Colonial Dames of America, who *m.* Arthur Vincent Meigs, M.D., of Philadelphia, also of Royal Descent, and had: *Edward Browning* and *John Forsythe.*
>
> II.—ADELAIDE ROBERTS, a member of the Pennsylvania Society of the Colonial Dames of America, who *m.* Daniel Francis Shaw, M.D.

THE ROYAL DESCENT

OF

MRS. WILLIAM J. HOLLIDAY,

OF INDIANAPOLIS, IND.

ROBERT BRUCE, King of Scotland, had:

Margery, *m.* Walter, High Steward, and had:

Robert II., King of Scotland, who had:

Catherine, *m.* Sir David Lindsay, and had:

Alexander, 2d Earl of Crawford, who had:

Walter Lindsay, of Beaufort, who had:

Sir David Lindsay, of Edzell, who had:

Walter Lindsay, of Edzell, who had:

Alexander Lindsay, of Edzell, who had:

Rev. David Lindsay, Bishop of Ross, who had:

Rachel, *m.* Rev. Dr. John Spottiswood, and had:

Sir Robert Spottiswood, of New Abbey, who had:

Dr. Robert Spotswood, of Tangier, who had:

Gen. Alexander Spotswood, of Va., who had:

Anne, *m.* Col. Bernard Moore, of Va., and had:

Bernard Moore, of "Chelsea," Va., who had:

Elizabeth, *m.* Col. James Macon, and had:

Mary, *m.* Col. William Aylett, and had:

Col. Philip Aylett, of King William Co., Va.

ROBERT BRUCE, King of Scotland, had:

Margery, *m.* Walter, High Steward, and had:

Robert II., King of Scotland, who had:

Robert III., King of Scotland, who had:

James I., King of Scotland, who had:

James II., King of Scotland, who had:

Margery, *m.* William, Lord Crichton, and had:

Sir James Crichton, of Fendraught, who had:

Margaret, *m.* John Robertson, and had:

Gilbert Robertson, of Muirton, who had:

David Robertson, of Muirton, who had:

William Robertson, of Muirton, who had:

William Robertson, of Gladney, who had:

Rev. William Robertson, of Edinburgh, who had:

Jean, *m.* Alexander Henry, and had:

Col. John Henry, of Va., who had:

Gov. Patrick Henry, of Va., who had:

m. Elizabeth Henry, of "Red Hill," Va.

Mary Macon Aylett⸗Philip Fitzhugh, of Va.

Lucy Fitzhugh⸗John Robertson Redd, of Va.

Lucy Redd, member of the National Society of⸗William Jacqueline Holliday, of Indianapolis,
the Colonial Dames of America | Ind., also of Royal Descent.

Ariana Ambler Holliday,
member of the National
Society of the Colonial
Dames of America,
m.
Henry W. Bennett.
Issue.

Jaqueline S. Holliday,
m.
Florence Baker.
Issue.

Lucy Fitzhugh Holliday,
m.
George E. Hume.

PEDIGREE XXXVIII.

CHARLEMAGNE, Emperor of the West, had by his third wife, Lady Hildegarde, *d.* 783, daughter of Childebrand, Duke of Suabia:

PEPIN, KING OF LOMBARDY and Italy, who *m.* Lady Bertha, daughter of William, Count of Thoulouse, and had:

BERNARD, KING OF LOMBARDY, who had by his wife, Lady Cunegonde:

PEPIN, COUNT OF VERMANDOIS and Peronne, 840, who had:

HERBERT I., COUNT DE VERMANDOIS, *d.* 902, who had:

HERBERT II., COUNT DE VERMANDOIS, *d.* 943, who had:

ALBERT I., THE PIOUS, COUNT DE VERMANDOIS, *d.* 987, who *m.* Princess Gerberga, daughter of Louis IV., King of France, and had:

HERBERT III., COUNT DE VERMANDOIS, who had:

OTHO, COUNT DE VERMANDOIS, 1021–1045, who had:

HERBERT IV., COUNT DE VERMANDOIS, 1045–1080, who *m.* Lady Hildebrante, daughter of Raoul III., Count de Valois, and had:

ADELHEID, COUNTESS OF VERMANDOIS, who *m.* (his third wife) Hugh Magnus, Duke of France and Burgundy, Marquis of Orleans, Count of Paris, Valois and Vermandois, son of Henry I., of France, and had:

LADY ISABEL DE VERMANDOIS, who *m.*, first, Robert, first Baron de Bellomont, Earl of Mellent, created, in 1103, Earl of Leicester, and had:

ROBERT, second Earl of Leicester, justiciary of England, *d.* 1168, who had by his wife, Lady Aurelia, daughter of Ralph de Waer, Earl of Norfolk, Suffolk and Cambridge, 1066:

ROBERT, third Earl of Leicester, steward of England, *d.* 1196, who had by his wife, Petronella, daughter of Hugh de Grentemaisnill:

LADY MARGARET DE BELLOMONT, who *m.* Saier de Quincy, created, 1207, Earl of Winchester, a surety for the Magna Charta of King John, *d.* 1219 (*see* "The Magna Charta Barons and their American Descendants"), and had:

ROGER DE QUINCY, second Earl of Winchester, constable of Scotland. *d.* 1264, who had by his wife, Lady Helen, daughter of Alan McDonal, Lord of Galloway:

LADY MARGARET DE QUINCY, who *m.* (his second wife) William de Ferrers, seventh Earl of Derby, *d.* 1254, and had:

WILLIAM DE FERRERS, Lord of Groby, second son by second wife, *d.* 1287, who *m.* Lady Joan, sister of Hugh, Earl of Winchester, executed in 1336, and daughter of Hugh le Despencer, *k.* 1265, and had:

LADY ANNE DE FERRERS, who *m.* (his first wife) John, second Lord Grey de Ruthyn, *d.* 1323, and had:

LADY MAUD DE GREY, who *m.* Sir John de Norville, lord of Norton, Yorkshire, and had:

JOHN DE NORTON, of Sharpenhow, in Bedfordshire, father of:

JOHN NORTON, of Sharpenhow, who had by his second wife, Jane, daughter of John Cooper, or Cowper:

RICHARD NORTON, second son (brother of Thomas, father of Thomas Norton, the Elizabethan poet, who *d.* 1532), who *m.* Margery Wingate, of Sharpenhow, will proved in 1572, and had:

WILLIAM NORTON, of Sharpenhow, who had by his first wife, Margery, daughter of William Hawes, and widow of —— Hamon:

WILLIAM NORTON, of Storford, (*see* the Hertfordshire and Bedfordshire Visitations), who *m.* Alice, daughter of John Browest, and had:

REV. WILLIAM NORTON, of Ipswich, Massachusetts, *b.* 1610, *d.* 30 April, 1694 (*see* Mather's "Magnalia," vol. i., 286; "New England Historical Genealogical Register," xiii., 225; "American Heraldic Journal," January, 1886; "Herald and Genealogist," part xv., 276), who *m.* Lucy, sister of Sir George Downing, and daughter of Emanuel Downing and his wife, Lucy Winthrop, a sister of Governor John Winthrop, and had:

REV. JOHN NORTON, of Hingham, who *m.* Mary Mason, and had:

ELIZABETH NORTON, *m.* Colonel John Quincy, of Braintree, and had:

ELIZABETH QUINCY, *m.* Rev. William Smith, of Weymouth, and had:

ABIGAIL SMITH, *b.* 22 November, 1744, *d.* 28 October, 1818, who *m.*, 25 October, 1764, John Adams, of Quincy, Massachusetts, second President of the United States, *b.* 30 October, 1735, *d.* 4 July, 1826, and had:

JOHN QUINCY ADAMS, of Quincy, Massachusetts, sixth President of the United States, *b.* 11 July, 1767, *d.* 29 February, 1848, who *m.* in London, 27 July, 1797, Louisa Catharine, *b.* 12 February, 1775, *d.* 15 May, 1852, daughter of Joshua Johnson, of London and Nantes, a grandson of Thomas and Mary (Baker) Johnson, of Maryland, 1660, and had:

CHARLES FRANCIS ADAMS, of Quincy, Massachusetts, *b.* 18 August, 1809, *d.* 21 November, 1886; United States Minister to Great Britain, 1861–68, *etc.*, and always a prominent candidate for the Presidency of the United States. He *m.*, 3 September, 1820, Abigail Brown Brooks, of Boston, also of Royal Descent, and had:

MARY ADAMS, a member of the Massachusetts Society of the Colonial Dames of America, who *m.* Henry P. Quincy, of Boston, and had: *Dorothy* and *Eleanor.*

PEDIGREE XXXIX.

EDWARD III., **King of England,** had by his wife, Philippa, daughter of William, Count of Hainault and Holland :

SIR EDMUND PLANTAGENET, surnamed *de Langley*, K.G., Duke of York ; Earl of Cambridge, who had by his first wife, Princess Isabel, daughter and co-heiress of Peter, King of Castile and Leon :

LADY CONSTANCE PLANTAGENET, who *m.* Thomas, second Baron le Despencer, of Glamorgan, created, 1337, Earl of Gloucester, beheaded in 1400, also of Royal Descent, and had :

LADY ISABEL LE DESPENCER, who *m.*, first, Richard Beauchamp, Lord Bergavenny ; created, 1421, Earl of Worcester, and had :

LADY ELIZABETH BEAUCHAMP, 1415–1447, who *m.*, 1435, Sir Edward Nevill, K.G., Baron Bergavenny, *d.* 1476, also of Royal Descent, and had :

SIR GEORGE NEVILL, Baron Bergavenny and Latimer, 1440–1492, who had by his first wife, Margaret, *d.* 1485, daughter of Sir Hugh Fenn, subtreasurer of England :

SIR EDWARD NEVILL, of Aldington Park, Kent, beheaded for treason 9 January, 1538, who had by his wife, Lady Eleanor, also of Royal Descent, daughter of Andrew, Lord Windsor of Stamwell :

LADY KATHERINE NEVILL, widow of —— Royden (*see* Foster's " Royal Lineages," p. 5), who *m.*, secondly, Clement Throckmorton, of Haseley, Warwick, sewer to the Queen ; commander at siege of Bologne (*see* Nicolas's " Testamenta Vetusta," p. 560, and Burke's " Royal Families," ii., Ped. 124), *d.* 1594–99, and had :

KATHERINE THROCKMORTON, (*see* Burke's " Royal Families," i., Ped. 83), who *m.* Thomas Harby, of Alveston, Northamptonshire, *d.* 1592, and had :

KATHERINE HARBY, sister of Sir Job Harby, Bart. (*see* Burke's " Royal Families," ii., Ped. 116), who *m.* Dr. Daniel Oxenbridge, of Daventry, Northamptonshire, *d.* 1642, son of Rev. John Oxenbridge, of Southam (*see* Burke's " History of the Commoners," under " Beckford of Fonthill "), and had :

1.—REV. JOHN OXENBRIDGE,* pastor of the First Church, Boston,

---

* MRS. GEORGE S. HALE, a member of the Massachusetts State Society of the National Society of the Colonial Dames of America, is also of Royal Descent through Rev. John Oxenbridge.

Massachusetts, *b.* at Daventry, 30 January, 1609, *d.* 28 December, 1674. He had by his third wife, Susannah :

THEODORA OXENBRIDGE, *b.* 1659, *d.* 1697 ; *m.*, 21 November, 1677 (his first wife), Rev. Peter Thacher, of Milton, Massachusetts, and had :

REV. OXENBRIDGE THACHER, of Milton, *m.* Sarah Kent, and had :

BATHSHEBA THACHER, *m.*, 1769, Jeremiah Dummer Rogers, of Charlestown, Massachusetts, *d.* 1784, and had :

MARGARET ROGERS, *m.* Jonathan Chapman, and had :

JONATHAN CHAPMAN, mayor of Boston, Massachusetts, *m.* Lucinda Dwight, and had :

FLORENCE CHAPMAN, a member of the Massachusetts Society of the Colonial Dames of America, who *m.* Henry Rogers Dalton, of Boston, Massachusetts, and had : *Alice, Philip Spalding, Susan Dexter, Florence, d.* 1890, and *Ellen Bancroft.*

2.—ELIZABETH OXENBRIDGE, who *m.* Caleb Cockercraft (or "Cockroft"), *d.* 1644, and had :

ELIZABETH COCKERCRAFT, who *m.* Nathaniel Hering, *d.* 1678, and had :

OLIVER HERING, who *m.* Elizabeth Hughes, and had :

OLIVER HERING, JR., who *m.* Anna Maria Morris, and had :

CAPTAIN JULINES HERING, of Jamaica, who *m.*, 2 April, 1761, Mary, daughter of Captain John Inglis, of Philadelphia, and his wife, Catherine, daughter of George McCall, of Philadelphia, and had :

MARY HELEN HERING, who *m.* Henry Middleton, of Charleston, South Carolina, Governor of South Carolina, member of Congress, minister to Russia, *etc.*, son of Arthur Middleton, a signer of the Declaration of Independence, and had :

ELIZA MIDDLETON, who *m.* Joshua Francis Fisher, of Philadelphia, also of Royal Descent, 1807–1873, and had :

MARIA MIDDLETON FISHER, a member of the Society of the Colonial Dames, who *m.* Brinton Coxe, of Philadelphia. *Issue.*

PEDIGREE XL.

EDWARD I., King of England, *m.*, first, 1254, Lady Eleanor, daughter of Ferdinand III., King of Castile, and had by her:

PRINCESS JOANE OF ACRE, *m.*, first, 1290, Gilbert de Clare, third Earl of Gloucester and seventh Earl of Hertford, *d.* 1295, and had:

LADY ELIZABETH DE CLARE, widow of John de Burgh and of Theobald de Verdon, *m.*, third, Sir Roger d'Amory, *d.* 1322, and had:

LADY ELIZABETH D'AMORY, who *m.* John, third Baron Bardolf, of Wormegay, *d.* 1363, and had:

WILLIAM, fourth Baron Bardolf, *d.* 1385; *m.* Agnes, *d.* 1403, daughter of Sir Michael, second Baron Poynings (her first husband), and had:

LADY CECELIA BARDOLF, *d.* 1432; *m.* Sir Brian Stapylton, Knt., of Ingham, Norfolk, *d.* 1438, and had:

SIR MILES STAPYLTON, Knt., of Ingham, *d.* 1466; *m.*, secondly, Lady Katherine, daughter of Sir Thomas de la Pole, Knt. (first husband), son of Michael de la Pole, second Earl of Suffolk, also of Royal Descent (*see* Burke's "Royal Families," Ped. 117), and had:

LADY ELIZABETH STAPYLTON, heiress, who *m.*, first, Sir William Calthorpe, Knt., of Burnham and Ingham, Norfolk, *d.* 1494, and had:

LADY ELIZABETH CALTHORPE, *m.* Francis Hassylden, of Gilden Morden, Cambridgeshire, and Little Chesterford, Essex; sheriff of Cambridgeshire in 1509, *d.* 1522, and had:

FRANCES HASSYLDEN, heiress, *d.* 1581; *m.*, 1515, Sir Robert Peyton, Knt., of Iselham, Cambridgeshire; sheriff of Cambridgeshire and Huntingdonshire, 17 and 27 Henry VIII. and 1 Mary, *d.* 1550 (*see* Hayden's "Virginia Genealogies," p. 464), and had:

ROBERT PEYTON, of Iselham, 1523–1590, M.P., high sheriff of Cambridgeshire, *m.* Elizabeth, *d.* 1591, daughter of Richard, Lord Rich, of Letze, lord high chancellor of England, 1548, and had:

SIR JOHN PEYTON, Knt. and Baronet, of Iselham, lord of Peyton Hall, in Boxford; M.P. 1593, high sheriff of Cambridgeshire; created a Baronet and knighted by James I., *d.* 1616; *m.*, 1580, Lady Alice, *d.* 1626, daughter of Sir Edward Osborne, Knt., lord mayor of London, 1583, and had:

SIR EDWARD PEYTON, second Baronet, of Iselham, 1578–1656; knighted 4 February, 1610; *m.*, secondly, 1614, Jane, daughter of Sir James Cal-

thorpe, of Norfolk, Knt., and widow of Sir Henry Thymelthorp, and
had by her:

THOMAS PEYTON, of Wicken and Rougham, Norfolk, 1616–1687, who
m., first, Elizabeth, *d.* 1668, daughter of Sir William Yelverton, of
Rougham, second Baronet, and his wife, Lady Ursula, daughter of Sir
Thomas Richardson, Knt.; speaker of House of Commons and lord
chief justice of King's Bench, 1626, and had:

MAJOR ROBERT PEYTON, of Gloucester county, Virginia, "living in Virginia, 1693" (*see* Hayden's "Virginia Genealogies"); "left no male
issue" (*see* Kimber's, 1771, and Betham's "Baronetage," 1800).

ELIZABETH PEYTON, his daughter, *m.*, 168–, Colonel Peter Beverley, of
Gloucester county, Virginia, *d.* 1728, son of Robert Beverley, of "Bever-
ley Park," King and Queen and Caroline counties, Virginia, who *d.* 1687.
He was clerk of Virginia House of Burgesses, 1691–96; speaker, 1700–
14; surveyor-general and member of the council, 1719–28; treasurer of
Virginia Colony, 1719–1723, and had by Elizabeth Peyton:

ELIZABETH BEVERLEY, 1691–1723, who *m.*, 1709, William Randolph,
of "Chatsworth," 1681–1742, and had:

PETER RANDOLPH, of "Chatsworth," surveyor of customs of North
America, 1749; member of the Virginia House of Burgesses, *etc.*, *d.*
1767; *m.* Lucy, daughter of Robert Bolling, of "Bollingbrook," a descendant of the Indian Princess Pocahontas, of Virginia, and had:

COLONEL ROBERT RANDOLPH, of "Eastern View," Fauquier county, Virginia, 1760–1825; *m.* Elizabeth Hill Carter, of "Shirley," *d.* 1832, also
of Royal Descent, and had:

CAPTAIN CHARLES CARTER RANDOLPH, of "The Grove," who *m.* Mary
Anne Fauntleroy Mortimer, of Fredericksburg, Virginia, and had:

LANDONIA RANDOLPH, who *m.* Robert Dabney Minor, United States
Navy, of Fredericksburg, Virginia, and had:

LANDONIA RANDOLPH MINOR, a member of the Virginia Society of the
Colonial Dames of America, who *m.* William Sparrow Dashiell, of Richmond, Virginia, and had: *Robert Minor* and *Thomas Grayson.*

PEDIGREE XLI.

DAVID I., King of Scotland, 1124, had by his wife, Lady Matilda, widow of Simon de St. Liz, Earl of Huntingdon, *d.* 1115, and daughter of Waltheof, Earl of Northumberland, beheaded in 1075:

PRINCE HENRY OF SCOTLAND, eldest son, Earl of Northumberland, eldest son, *d. v. p.* 1159; *m.*, 1139, Lady Ada, *d.* 1178, daughter of William de Warren, second Earl of Surrey, and had:

PRINCESS MARJORY (sister of King Malcolm IV., and King William I., of Scotland), who *m.* Gilchrist, Earl of Angus, and had:

LADY BEATRIX, who *m.* Walter Stewart, generally called of Dondonald, high steward and justiciary of Scotland, *d.* 1241, and had:

LADY MARGARET STEWART, who *m.* Colin Fitzgerald, who for bravery in the battle of Large, on the part of King Alexander III., in 1263, received the charter of free barony of Kintail, in Rosshire, and *d.* in 1278, at the Castle of Island Donan, and had:

KENNETH, second lord of Kintail, who *m.* Lady Morba Macdonald, daughter of Alexander, lord of Lorn, and *d.* in 1304, had:

KENNETH MACKENNETH, third lord of Kintail, *d.* 1378, who *m.* Lady Margaret, daughter of David de Strathbogie, Earl of Athol, and had:

KENNETH MACKENZIE, fourth lord of Kintail, who *m.* Fynvola, daughter of Roderick Macleod, of Lewes, and had:

MURDOCK MACKENZIE-DON, fifth lord of Kintail, *d.* 1375, who *m.* Isabel, daughter of Murdoch Macaula, of Lochbroom, and had:

MURDOCH MACKENZIE, sixth lord of Kintail, *d.* 1416, who *m.* Fynvola, daughter of Macleod, of Harris, and had:

ALEXANDER MACKENZIE, seventh lord of Kintail, *d.* 1488, who *m.*, first, Lady Agnes, daughter of Colin Campbell, first lord of Argyle, and had:

SIR KENNETH MACKENZIE, eighth lord of Kintail, *d.* 1507, who *m.*, secondly, Lady Agnes, daughter of Hugh, Lord Lovat, and had by her:

JOHN MACKENZIE, ninth lord of Kintail, *d.* 1556-57, who *m.* Elizabeth Grant, and had:

KENNETH MACKENZIE, tenth lord of Kintail, *d.* 6 June, 1568, who *m.* Lady Isabel Stewart, daughter of John, third Earl of Atholl, and had:

LADY AGNES MACKENZIE, who *m.*, 1567, Lachlan-Mohr MacIntosh, of Dunachtane and Knocknagail, the sixteenth chief of Clan Chattan (*see*

11 (169)

Douglas's "Peerage of Scotland," ii., 480; Buchanan's "Ancient Scottish Surnames;" Shaw's "MacIntoshes and Clan Chattan"), and had:

WILLIAM MACINTOSH, of Essick and Borlum, second son, d. 1630, who m., 1594, Elizabeth, daughter of Robert Innes, of Invermarkie, grandson of Robert Innes, of Innerbrakie, and his wife, Elspeth, daughter of Sir John Stewart, of Balveny, first Earl of Athol, also of Royal Descent, and had:

LACHLAN MACINTOSH, of Borlum and Bolkeskine, who m., first, Anne, widow of Sir Lachlan McIntosh, of MacIntosh, and had:

CAPTAIN JOHN-MOHR MACINTOSH,* eldest son, b. Bolkeskine 24 March, 1700; came to America in 1733, and settled in that part of Georgia now called McIntosh county. He entered actively upon the defence of the colony against the Spaniards, and was captain of the first company of Highlanders organized in America, and at Fort Moosa was severely wounded and taken prisoner, sent to Madrid, and exchanged at the treaty of Aix la Chapelle; a delegate to the Provincial Assembly of Georgia, 1751, etc. He m., 4 March, 1725, Marjory, b. 1701, daughter of John Frazer, of Garthmore, and his wife, Elizabeth Frazer, of Errogy, and d. at "Borlum," near Darien, Georgia, 1761, having issue:

1.—COLONEL WILLIAM MCINTOSH, of Darien, b. at "Borlum," 27 January, 1726, d. 1796. He took an active part in the Revolutionary War, and commanded the first regiment of cavalry in the Georgia Continental Line, and was a delegate to the first Provincial Congress at Savannah, July, 1775. He m. Jane Maccoy, and had:

MAJOR-GENERAL JOHN MCINTOSH, of "Fairhope," near Darien, Georgia, where he d. 12 November, 1826. He served with distinction in the Revolutionary War and the War of 1812. He m., 17 June, 1781, Sarah, daughter of William Swinton, and had:

COLONEL JAMES SIMMONS MCINTOSH, United States Army, b. 19 June, 1787. He served in the American Army in the War of 1812; in the Seminole War and in the Mexican War, and was mortally wounded at El Molino del Rey, and died in the City of Mexico, 26 September, 1847. He m., 29 December, 1815, Mrs. Eliza (Matthews) Shumate, d. 1833, and had:

MARY ELIZA MCINTOSH, a member of the California Society of the Colonial Dames of America, who m., first, Colonel Charles Clark Keeney, M.D., United States Army, and had: Charles McI. and James Ward, and m., secondly, William Alvord, of San Francisco. No issue.

---

* MRS. ROBERT E. BROWN, a member of the Georgia State Society of the National Society of the Colonial Dames of America, is also of Royal Descent through John MacIntosh.

2.—GEORGE McINTOSH, a member of the Provincial Congress which met at Savannah 4 July, 1775, who had by his wife, Lady Anne, daughter of Sir Patrick Houstoun, 1735–1762, president of the King's Council in Georgia:

JOHN HOUSTON McINTOSH, of Darien, Georgia, who *m.*, 30 April, 1791, Eliza Bayard, *d.* 1846, also of Royal Descent, and had:

I.—JOHN HOUSTON McINTOSH, JR., 1802–1852, who *m.*, 13 September, 1832, Mary Randolph Higbee, of Trenton, New Jersey, and had:

MARY RANDOLPH McINTOSH, a member of the Georgia Society of the Colonial Dames of America, who *m.*, 12 March, 1861, John Kilgour, of Cincinnati, Ohio, and had: *Charles, Bayard Livingston, Elizabeth, Louise,* and

1.—MARY KILGOUR, a member of the New York Society of the Colonial Dames of America, who *m.*, 16 April, 1890, Edmund E. Miller, of Cincinnati, and had: *Mary Kilgour, b.* 4 April, 1891.

2.—CHARLOTTE KILGOUR, a member of the New York Society of the Colonial Dames of America, who *m.*, 21 April, 1896, Captain Ashton B. Hyle, M.D., United States Army, and had: *John Kilgour, b.* 21 March, 1897.

II.—ELIZA BAYARD McINTOSH, who *m.* Duncan L. Clinch, United States Army, and had:

ELIZA BAYARD CLINCH, who *m.* General Robert Anderson, United States Army, of Fort Sumter fame, and had:

ELIZA McINTOSH CLINCH ANDERSON, a member of the New York Society of the Colonial Dames of America, who *m.* James M. Lawton, of New York City.

THE ROYAL DESCENTS

OF

MR. AND MRS. CHARLES COLLINS,

OF NEW YORK CITY.

ALFRED THE GREAT, King of England⹂Ethelbith, daughter of Ethelan the Great.

Edward the Elder, King of England⹂Edgiva, daughter of Earl Sigelline.

Edmund I., King of England⹂Elgiva, granddaughter of Alfred the Great.

Edgar the Peaceful, King of England⹂Elfrida, daughter of Ordgar, Earl of Devon.

Ethelred the Unready, King of England⹂Elgifa, daughter of Earl Thorad.

Edmund Ironsides, King of England⹂Algitha of Denmark.

Prince Edward the Exile, of England⹂Agatha of Germany.

Princess Margaret, of England⹂Malcolm Canmore, King of Scotland.

David I., King of Scotland⹂Lady Matilda of Northumberland.

Henry, Earl of Huntingdon⹂Lady Ada de Warren.

David, Earl of Huntingdon⹂(Name uncertain).

Lady Margaret de Huntingdon⹂Alan McDonald, lord of Galloway.

Lady Helen McDonald⹂Roger, 2d Earl of Winchester.

Lady Elizabeth de Quincey⹂Alexander, 2d Earl of Buchan.

Lady Agnes Cumyn⹂Gilbert, 8th Earl of Angus.

Robert, 9th Earl of Angus⹂Alianore ———.

Sir Thomas de Umfraville, of Harbottle⹂Joan de Rodam.

Sir Thomas de Umfraville, of Riddesdale⹂Agnes ———.

Lady Joan de Umfraville⹂Sir William Lambert, of Owlton.

Robert Lambert, of Owlton⹂(Name unknown).

Henry Lambert, of Ongar⹂(Name unknown).

Elizabeth Lambert⹂Thomas Lyman, of Navistoke.

Henry Lyman, of High Ongar⹂Alicia Hyde, of Westersfield.

John Lyman, of High Ongar⹂Margaret Gérard, of Beauchamp.

Henry Lyman, of High Ongar⹂Phillis Scott, of Navistoke.

Richard Lyman, d. Hartford, Ct., 1640⹂Sarah Osborne.

Lieut. John Lyman, of Northampton, Mass.⹂Dorcas Plum.

Moses Lyman, of Northampton, Mass.⹂Anne ———.

Moses Lyman⹂Mindwell Sheldon.　　Mary Lyman⹂Samuel Dwight.

Moses Lyman⹂Sarah Hayden.　　Mary Dwight⹂Daniel Hall, Jr.

Moses Lyman⹂Mary Judd.　　Mary Hall⹂Eliphalet Terry.

Mary Lyman⹂Amos M. Collins.　　Eliphalet Terry⹂Lydia Coit.

Charles Collins, 1817–1891⹂Mary Hall Terry, 1820–1900.

Lydia Coit Collins⹂William P. Ketcham.	Clarence Lyman Collins⹂Marie Louise Clark.	Louise Terry Collins⹂William Allen Butler, Jr.

Arthur Collins Ketcham⹂Margaret Bruce Allen.　Mary Van W. Ketcham⹂Thomas Hunt Talmadge.　Ethel Miriam Ketcham.　Edith Lyman Collins⹂Richid Bey, Comte Butler. Czaykowski.　Wm. Allen Butler.　Lyman Collins Butler.　Charles Terry Butler.　Lydia Coit Butler.　Louise Tracy Butler.

William T. Ketcham. Thomas H. Talmadge.
Margaret B. Ketcham. Lillian Talmadge.
Arthur C. Ketcham.

Vladimer.　　Stanislaus.

PEDIGREE XLII.

JAMES I., King of Scotland, had by his wife, Lady Joan de Beaufort, daughter of Sir John, Earl of Somerset, a grandson of Edward III., King of England :

PRINCESS JANET STEWART (sister of King James II.), who *m.* George Gordon, second Earl of Huntley, also of Royal Descent, and had :

ALEXANDER GORDON, third Earl of Huntley, who *m.* Lady Janet Stewart, daughter of John, Earl of Athol, also of Royal Descent, and had :

LADY JOAN GORDON, who *m.* Colin Campbell, third Earl of Argyle, *d.* 1533, also of Royal Descent, and had :

ARCHIBALD CAMPBELL, fourth Earl of Argyle, *d.* 1558, who *m.*, secondly, Lady Margaret, daughter of William Græm, Earl of Monteith, also of Royal Descent, and had by her :

SIR COLIN CAMPBELL, sixth Earl of Argyle, *d.* 1584, who *m.* Lady Agnes, daughter of William Keith, marshal of Scotland, also of Royal Descent, and widow of James, Earl of Moray, the regent of Scotland, and had :

ARCHIBALD CAMPBELL, seventh Earl of Argyle, who *m.* Lady Anne, daughter of William Douglas, Earl of Morton, also of Royal Descent, and had :

LADY MARY CAMPBELL, who *m.* Robert Montgomery, Jr., of Skelmurlie, *d. v. p.* (*see* Wood's Douglas's " Peerage of Scotland," i., pp. 74, 509), also of Royal Descent, and had :

SIR ROBERT MONTGOMERY, of Skelmurlie, Bart., *d.* 7 February, 1684, who *m.* Antonia, daughter of Sir James Scott, of Rossie, Fifeshire, and had :

LADY MARGARET MONTGOMERY, who *m.* Godfrey Macalester, laird of Loup, and chief of Clan Alester, in Kintyre (*see* Gregory's " History of the Western Islands," and Burke's " Royal Families," i., Ped. 106), and had :

JOHN MACALESTER, of Ardnakill and Torrisdale Glen, *d.* aged 96 years, who *m.* Miss McNeill, of Terfergus, *d.* aged 98 years, and had :

MARGARET MACALESTER, *b.* 1712, who *m.*, first, Charles MacQuarrie, of Campbelltown (of MacQuarrie, of Ulva family), and *m.*, secondly, Duncan Macalester, of Tarbert, and had by her first husband :

ISABELLA MACQUARRIE, 1740–1807, who *m.* Charles Macalester, of Tarbert, master of Campbelltown, lost at sea in 1797, and had:

CHARLES MACALESTER, JR., *b.* Campbelltown, Kintyre, 1766, *d.* Philadelphia, Pennsylvania, 1832, who *m.* Anna Sampson, of Perth, and had:

EMILY MACALESTER, who *m.* Nicholas Hopkins, of Philadelphia, and had, besides other issue (*see* "Americans of Royal Descent," fourth edition, vol. ii., p. 627):

EDWARD MACALESTER HOPKINS, of Philadelphia, who *m.*, first, Lydia, daughter of Samuel N. Lewis, of Philadelphia, and had by her:

EMILY MACALESTER HOPKINS, of Philadelphia, a member of the Pennsylvania Society of the Colonial Dames of America.

PEDIGREE XLIII.

EDWARD III., King of England, *m.*, 1327, Lady Philippa, daughter of William, Count of Hainault and Holland, and had:

SIR LIONEL PLANTAGENET, K.G., Duke of Clarence, Earl of Ulster, *etc.*, 1338–1368; *m.*, first, 1352–54, Lady Elizabeth, 1332–1363, daughter of Sir William de Burgh, third Earl of Ulster, murdered in Ireland 6 June, 1333, also of Royal Descent, and his wife, Lady Maud Plantagenet, also of Royal Descent, and had :

LADY PHILIPPA PLANTAGENET, only child, who *m.*, in 1368, when only 13 years of age, Edmund de Mortimer, third Earl of March, lord-lieutenant of Ireland, Earl of Ulster, *d.* 1381, and had:

LADY ELIZABETH DE MORTIMER, 1371–1417, who *m.*, first, Sir Henry Percy, K.G., the renowned Hotspur, *k.* at Shrewsbury in 1403, son of Henry, fourth Lord Percy, of Alnwick, created, 1377, Earl of Northumberland, also of Royal Descent, and had :

SIR HENRY PERCY, K.G., second Earl of Northumberland, *b.* 1393, *k.* at St. Albans in 1455. He *m.* Lady Eleanor Nevil (her second husband), daughter of Ralph, first Earl of Westmoreland, and Lady Joan de Beaufort, also of Royal Descent, and had :

HENRY PERCY, third Earl of Northumberland, *k.* at Towton, in 1461. He *m.* Lady Eleanor, only child of Richard Poynings, *d. v. p.* 1430, eldest son of Robert, fifth Lord Poynings, *k.* 1446, and had :

SIR HENRY PERCY, K.G., fourth Earl of Northumberland, who was murdered, 28 April, 1489, by order of King Henry VII., having issue by his wife, Lady Matilda, sister of William, second Earl of Pembroke and Huntingdon, and daughter of Sir William de Herbert, K.G., of Ragland, created Earl of Pembroke in 1468 :

SIR HENRY ALGERNON PERCY, K.G., fifth Earl of Northumberland, *d.* 1527. He *m.* Lady Catherine, daughter of Sir Robert Spencer, Knt., of Spencer-Combe, Devonshire, by Eleanor, Countess of Ormond and Wiltshire, his wife, also of Royal Descent, and had :

LADY MARGARET PERCY, who *m.* Sir Henry Clifford, K.G., eleventh Baron Clifford, created, 1525, Earl of Cumberland, also of Royal Descent, and had :

LADY CATHERINE CLIFFORD, widow of John, Baron Scroope, of Bolton, who *m.*, secondly, Sir Richard Cholmoneley, Knt., of Roxby, and had by him :

(175)

SIR HENRY CHOLMONELEY, Knt., of Grandmount, Whitby, and Roxby, *d.* 1641, who had by his wife, Margaret, daughter of Sir William de Babthorpe:

MARY CHOLMONELEY, *b.* 1593, *d.* 1649, who *m.* the Hon. Rev. Henry Fairfax, of Oglethorpe, rector of Bolton-Percy, in Yorkshire, *b.* 1588, *d.* 1665 (second son of Sir Thomas, created Baron Fairfax, of Cameron, *d.* 1640, who 'purchased the title for £1500 from King James I. (*see* Wood's Douglas's "Peerage of Scotland," i., 560; Lodge's "Peerage of Ireland," v., 1789; Neill's "Fairfaxes of England and America," *etc.*), and had:

HENRY FAIRFAX, of Oglethorpe, who succeeded as fourth Lord Fairfax, of Cameron, in 1671, *b.* 1631, *d.* 1688 (*see* Burke's "Royal Families," ii., Ped. 147); *m.* Frances, daughter of Sir Robert Berwick, of Tolston, Yorkshire, and had:

HON. HENRY FAIRFAX, of Denton and Tolston, sheriff of Yorkshire, 1691, *d.* 1708; *m.* Anne, daughter of Richard Harrison, of Yorkshire, and had:

HON. WILLIAM FAIRFAX, of "Belvoir," in Virginia, fourth son, *b.* 1691, *d.* 1757; president of the Council of Virginia; *m.*, first, Sarah, daughter of Major Walker, of the Bahamas, and had by her:

SARAH FAIRFAX, who *m.* Major John Carlyle, of Alexandria, Virginia, and had:

SARAH CARLYLE, who *m.* William Herbert, of Alexandria, Virginia, and had:

WILLIAM HERBERT, who *m.* Maria Dulany, and had:

ARTHUR HERBERT, who *m.* Alice Gregory, and had:

MARY HERBERT, a member of the Virginia Society of the Colonial Dames of America, who *m.* 4 June, 1890, John D. Hooe, of Warrenton, Virginia, and had: *Bernard* (deceased).

HON. WILLIAM FAIRFAX, of "Belvoir," *m.*, secondly, Deborah, daughter of Francis Clarke, of Salem, Massachusetts, and had by her:

HON. REV. BRYAN FAIRFAX, of Alexandria, Virginia, who succeeded as eighth Lord Fairfax, *d.* 1802. He *m.*, first, Elizabeth, daughter of Wilson Cary, of Virginia, and had by her:

1.—THOMAS FAIRFAX, of "Vacluse," Fairfax county, Virginia, ninth Baron Fairfax, of Cameron, 1762–1846, who had by his third wife, Margaret, daughter of William Herbert, of Alexandria, Virginia:

HON. ORLANDO FAIRFAX, M.D., of Richmond, Virginia, who had by his wife, Mary Randolph Cary:

MONIMIA FAIRFAX, who *m.* George Davis, and had:

I.—MARY FAIRFAX DAVIS, a member of the North Carolina Society of the Colonial Dames of America, the Order of the Crown, etc., who *m.* Minor Fairfax Heiskell Gouverneùr, of Wilmington, North Carolina.

II.—CARY DAVIS, who *m.* Donald MacRae, of Wilmington, North Carolina.

2.—HON. FERNANDO FAIRFAX, of Alexandria, *b.* 1763, who *m.* Elizabeth Cary, and had:

FLORETTA FAIRFAX, who *m.* Rev. Samuel Haggins, and had:

REV. JOHN HAGGINS, of Bath county, Kentucky, who *m.* Margery Mildred, daughter of Colonel William and Elizabeth (Carr) Johnson, and had:

COLONEL GEORGE WASHINGTON FAIRFAX HAGGINS, who *m.* Sarah, daughter of Cornelius and Mary (Norman) Beebe, and had:

NANCY JOHNSON HAGGINS, who *m.* Joseph Kling, of Seymour, Indiana, and had:

VIRGINIA LYNDALL KLING, of Cincinnati, Ohio, who *m.* Horace Bernard Dunbar, of Boston, Massachusetts, and had: *Dorothy, b.* 1 April, 1894.

THE ROYAL DESCENTS

OF

MRS. KELLER ANDERSON,

AND

MRS. THOMAS DAY.

EDWARD I., King of England=Princess Eleanor of Castile.

Princess Joan Plantagenet=Gilbert de Clare, Earl of Gloucester and Hertford.

Lady Margaret de Clare=Hugh de Audley, Earl of Gloucester.

Lady Margaret de Audley=Sir Ralph de Stafford, K.G., Earl of Stafford.

Sir Hugh de Stafford, K.G., Earl of Stafford=Lady Philippa de Beauchamp.

Lady Margaret de Stafford=Sir Ralph de Neville, K.G., Earl of Westmoreland.

Ralph de Neville, of Oversley, Warwickshire=Lady Mary de Ferrers.

John de Neville, of Wymersley, Yorkshire=Lady Elizabeth de Newmarch.

Joan de Neville=Sir William Gascoigne, of Gawthrope, Yorkshire.

Sir William Gascoigne, of Gawthrope, York=Lady Margaret de Percy.

Lady Elizabeth Gascoigne=Gilbert de Talboys, of Kyme.

Sir George de Talboys, of Kyme=(Name unknown.)

Lady Anne de Talboys=Sir Edward Dymoke, of Scrivelsby, Lincolnshire.

Lady Frances Dymoke=Thomas Windebank, of Haines Hill, Berkshire.

Mildred Windebank=Robert Reade, Linkenholt Manor, Southampton.

Col. George Reade, of Gloucester Co., Va.=Elizabeth Martian.

Mildred Reade=Col. Augustine Warner, Jr., of "Warner's Hall."

Elizabeth Warner=Col. John Lewis, Gloucester Co., Va.

Col. Charles Lewis=Mary Howell.

Anne Lewis=Edmund Taylor, Caroline Co., Va.

Frances Taylor=Rev. Nathaniel Moore, Granville Co., N. C.

Anne Lewis Moore=Edward Washington Dale, Columbia, Tenn.

Anne Lewis Dale=James Robertson, of Ayrshire, Scotland.

Jean Robertson=Col. Keller Anderson, United States Army.   Mary Robertson=Capt. Thomas Day, of Memphis, Tenn.

Claude Desha Anderson, of Memphis, Tenn.=Mary Simmons.   Jean Keller Anderson, of Memphis, Tenn.   Mary Louise Day.

Claude Desha Anderson, Jr.

PEDIGREE XLIV.

EDWARD III., King of England, *m.*, 1327, Lady Philippa, daughter of William, Count of Hainault and Holland, and his wife, Joanna, daughter of Charles de Valois, younger son of **Philip III.**, **King of France,** and had :

EDMUND PLANTAGENET Earl of Cambridge and Duke of York, who *m.*, first, Lady Isabel, daughter of **Peter, King of Castile and Leon,** and had by her :

RICHARD PLANTAGENET, Earl of Cambridge, beheaded in 1415, who *m.* Lady Anne, daughter of Edward de Mortimer, Earl of March, and his wife, Lady Philippa, daughter of Lionel, Duke of Clarence, second son of **Edward III.**, **King of England,** and had :

RICHARD PLANTAGENET, Earl of Cambridge and Duke of York, the Protector, starter of the War of Roses, *k.* in the final battle of Wakefield, 1460. He *m.* Lady Cecily, daughter of Ralph de Nevill, Earl of Westmoreland, also of Royal Descent, and had :

SIR GEORGE PLANTAGENET, K.G., Duke of Clarence (brother of Kings Richard III. and Edward IV., father of King Edward V. and Richard, Duke of York, both murdered in the Tower of London, and Elizabeth, consort of King Henry VII.), who *m.* Lady Isabel de Nevill, daughter of Richard Earl of Salisbury and Warwick, also of Royal Descent (her sister, Anne, *m.*, first, Edward, only son of King Henry VII., and *m.*, secondly, King Richard III.). He was attainted of treason and drowned in a butt of Malmsey wine in the Tower of London, in 1477, and his honors were forfeited. His only daughter :

LADY MARGARET PLANTAGENET, Countess of Salisbury, beheaded for high treason, when 72 years old, 27 May, 1541 (sister of Edward, "the last of the Plantagenets," who was executed in 1499 on London Tower Hill), *m.* Sir Richard Pole, K.G., and had :

SIR HENRY POLE, first Lord Montagu, beheaded in 1539, on London Tower Hill, for high treason. He *m.* Lady Jean, daughter of George Neville, Lord Abergavenny, also of Royal Descent, and had :

LADY WINIFRED POLE, widow of Sir Thomas Hastings, who *m.* (his second wife) Thomas Barrington, high sheriff of Hertford and Essex, in 1562, and had :

SIR FRANCIS BARRINGTON, Bart., M.P. for Essex, 1601, *etc.*, knighted at Theobald's, 7 May, 1607, created a baronet in 1611, *d.* 3 July, 1629 ; *m.*, first, Lady Joan, daughter of Sir Henry Cromwell (*alias* Williams), of Hinchingbrook, and had by her:

LADY JOAN BARRINGTON, who *m.* Sir Richard Everard, of Much-Waltham, Essex, created a baronet in 1628 (see Banks's "Extinct Baronage," 1808; Brown's "·Genesis of the United States," page 826; "New England His. Gen. Reg.," July, 1889; Kimber's "Baronetage," 1771; Meade's "Old Families and Churches of Virginia"), and had:

SIR HUGH EVERARD, Bart., second son, 1654–1705, who *m.* Mary, daughter of John Brown, M.D., of Salisbury, and had:

SIR RICHARD EVERARD, Bart., Governor of North Carolina, for the Proprietors, *d.* 1732, who *m.* Susannah, *d.* 1739, daughter of Rev. Richard Kidder, D.D., Bishop of Bath and Wells, accidentally *k.* in 1703, and had:

LADY SUSANNAH EVERARD, who *m.* (Kimber's "Baronetage," Vol. I.) David Meade, *b.* County Kerry, Ireland (*see* "Meade," in O'Hart's "Irish Landed Gentry"), who *d.* in Nansemond county, Virginia, and had:

1.—ANNE MEADE, who *m.* Richard Randolph, Jr., of "Curles," Virginia, a descendant of the Indian Princess Pocahontas, of Virginia, and had:

MARY RANDOLPH, who *m.* William Bolling, and had:

THOMAS BOLLING, who *m.* Louisa Morris, and had:

VIRGINIA RANDOLPH BOLLING, who *m.* Alex. Quarles Holladay, and had:

MARY STUART HOLLADAY, a member of the North Carolina Society of the Colonial Dames of America, who *m.* Rev. Peyton Harrison Hoge, of Louisville, Kentucky, and had: *Virginia Randolph Bolling, William Lacy, Mary Stuart, Peyton Harrison, Elizabeth Addison,* and *Evelyn Cary.*

2.—MARY MEADE, who *m.* George Walker, of Virginia, and had:

HELEN WALKER, who *m.* William Call, major in Virginia line, Continental Army, and had:

GENERAL RICHARD KEITH CALL, Governor of the Florida Territory and member of Congress from Florida, who *m.* Mary Kirkman, and had:

MARY CALL, who *m.* Theodore Brevard, of Tallahassee, Florida, Brigadier-General Confederate States Army, and had:

CAROLINE MAYS BREVARD, of Tallahassee, a member of the North Carolina Society of the Colonial Dames of America.

PEDIGREE XLV.

HENRY III., King of England, 1206–1272; *m.*, 1236, Eleanor of Provence, *d.* 1291, and had by her:

PRINCE EDMUND, Earl of Leicester, Lancaster and Chester, high steward of England, 1245–1295. He had by his second wife, Blanche, widow of Henry I., King of Navarre, *d.* 1274, and daughter of Robert, Earl of Artois, son of **LOUIS VIII., King of France,** by his wife, Blanche of Castile:

HENRY PLANTAGENET, third Earl of Lancaster, *d.* 1345; *m.* Maud, *b.* 1280, daughter of Patrick de Chaworth, 1253–1282, and had:

LADY ELEANOR PLANTAGENET, widow of John, second Baron Beaumont, *d.* 1342, who *m.*, secondly (his second wife), Sir Richard Fitz-Alan, K.G., ninth Earl of Arundel and seventh Earl of Surrey, *d.* 1375, and had by her:

JOHN FITZ-ALAN, Baron Maltravers, who *m.* Lady Eleanor, the heiress and granddaughter of John, Baron Maltravers, and had:

JOHN FITZ-ALAN, Lord Maltravers, lost at sea, in 1380, who had:

LADY JOAN FITZ-ALAN, *m.* Sir William Echyngham, *d.* 1412, and had:

SIR THOMAS ECHYNGHAM, Knt., *d.* 1444, who had:

THOMAS, Baron Echingham, *d.* 1482, who had:

LADY MARGARET ECHINGHAM, who *m.* William Blount, *d. v. p.*, eldest son of Sir Walter le Blount, K.G., *d.* 1474; treasurer of Calais, 1461; created Lord Montjoy, and his wife, Lady Anne Nevill, also of Royal Descent, and had:

ELIZABETH BLOUNT, who *m.* Sir Andrews, Baron Wyndsore, of Stanwell and Bardsley Abbey, *d.* 1549, also of Royal Descent, and had:

LADY EDITH WYNDSORE, who *m.* George Ludlow, of Hill Deverill, high sheriff of Wiltshire, 1567, *d.* 1580 (*see* Keith's "Ancestry of Benjamin Harrison"), and had:

THOMAS LUDLOW, of Dinton, *d.* 1607, who *m.* Jane, daughter of Thomas Pyle, of Bopton, Wilts, and had:

GABRIEL LUDLOW, *bapt.* 10 February, 1587, called to the Bar, 1620, *d.* 1639; *m.* Phyllis ——, and had:

SARAH LUDLOW, *d.* about 1668, who *m.* (his fourth wife) Colonel John Carter, of "Carotoman," Lancaster county, Virginia, who came to Virginia about 1643, probably from Middlesex, and became a member of the Virginia House of Burgesses from Lower Norfolk county in 1643–44; county justice and a member of the Governor's Council, 1657, d. 10 June, 1669, and had:

COLONEL ROBERT CARTER,* of "Carotoman," 1663–1732, only son by Sarah Ludlow, a member and speaker of the House of Burgesses, 1695–99; treasurer of the Colony, 1704–32, etc. (see Keith's "Ancestry of Benjamin Harrison"). He m., first, 1688, Judith, d. 1699, daughter of John Armistead, of "Hesse," Gloucester county, Virginia, and m., secondly, 1701, Elizabeth, daughter of Thomas Landon, of Middlesex county, Virginia, and widow of ——— Willis. From his wealth and authority in the colony he became known as "King Carter" (see Glenn's "Some Colonial Mansions").

COLONEL ROBERT CARTER had by his second wife:

1.—COLONEL CHARLES CARTER, of "Cleve," King George county, Virginia, 1707–1764, who m., first, Mary Walke, and had by her:

I.—ELIZABETH CARTER, who m. William Churchill, of "Wilton," Middlesex county, Virginia, and had:

HANNAH CHURCHILL, m. Benjamin Robinson, and had:

WILLIAM ROBINSON, m. Martha Stubbs, and had:

BENJAMIN NEEDLES ROBINSON, who m. Lucy Heabred Moore, also of Royal Descent, and had:

ELIZABETH TAYLOR ROBINSON, m. John Daniel Turner, M.D., and had:

LOUISE BEVERLEY TURNER, a member of the Virginia Society of the Colonial Dames of America, who m. Isaac N. Jones, of Richmond, Virginia, and had: Bernard Moore.

II.—JUDITH FRANCES CARTER, who m. William Burnet Browne, of "Elsing Green," King William county, Virginia, also of Royal Descent, and had:

MARY BURNET BROWNE, who m. Herbert Claiborne, of "Chestnut Grove," New Kent county, Virginia, also of Royal Descent, and had:

HERBERT AUGUSTINE CLAIBORNE, 1784–1841; m. Delia, daughter of John Hayes, of Richmond, Virginia, and had:

MAJOR JOHN HAYES CLAIBORNE, of Richmond, Virginia; m. Anna

---

* The following ladies, members of the National Society of the Colonial Dames of America, are also of Royal Descent, through Colonel Robert Carter:

MRS. EDWARD C. ANDERSON, Georgia State Society.

MRS. ALEXANDER R. LAWTON, Georgia State Society.

Virginia, daughter of George Washington Bassett, of "Eltham," New Kent county, Virginia, also of Royal Descent, and had: DELIA CLAIBORNE, a member of the Virginia Society of the Colonial Dames of America, who *m.*, 10 June, 1885, General Simon Bolivar Buckner, of "Glen Lily," Hart county, Kentucky, and had: *Simon B., b.* 18 July, 1886.

COLONEL CHARLES CARTER, of "Cleve," had by his second wife, Ann Byrd, also of Royal Descent:

I.—MARIA CARTER, who *m.* William Armistead, of "Hesse," Gloucester county, Virginia, and had:

ELEANOR BOWLES ARMISTEAD, who *m.* Judge William McMechen, of Baltimore, Maryland, and had:

SIDNEY JANE McMECHEN, who *m.* John Charles Van Wyck, of Baltimore, and had:

SIDNEY McMECHEN VAN WYCK, *b.* 6 April, 1830, *d.* at San Francisco, California, 27 April, 1887, who *m.* Nannie Churchill Crittenden, also of Royal Descent, and had:

LAURA SANCHEZ VAN WYCK, of San Francisco, a member of the California Society of the Colonial Dames of America.

II.—LANDON CARTER, of "Cleve," 1751–1811, *m.*, first, Mildred Willis, also of Royal Descent, and had:

LUCY LANDON CARTER, *m.* General John Minor, of Fredericksburg, Virginia, and had:

LUCIUS HORATIO MINOR, of "Edgewood," *m.* Catherine Frances Berkeley, also of Royal Descent (see p. 188), and had:

MARY WILLIS MINOR, of Baltimore, a member of the Maryland Society of the Colonial Dames of America.

2.—MARY CARTER, *b.* 1712, *d.* 17 September, 1736, who *m.* George Braxton, of "Newington," King and Queen county, Virginia, and had:

CARTER BRAXTON, of "Elsing Green," *b.* 10 September, 1736, *d.* 10 October, 1797, a member of the Continental Congress and a signer of the Declaration of Independence. He *m.*, first, 16 July, 1755, Judith, daughter of Christopher Robinson, 3d, and his wife, Judith Wormeley, and had by her, who *d.* 1757:

I.—MARY BRAXTON, *b.* 1756, *d.* about 1782, who *m.*, 1779, Robert Page, Jr., of "Broad Neck," *b.* 15 June, 1752, *d.* 1794, and had:

SARAH WALKER PAGE, *b.* about 1784, *d.* 1833, who *m.*, about 1800, Humphrey Brooke, of Spottsylvania county, Virginia, *b.* about 1757, *d.* 1843–4, and had:

ANNA AYLETTE BROOKE, *b.* 16 January, 1808, *d.* 2 June, 1845, who *m.*, 27 December, 1825, Oliver Abbott Shaw, of Lexington,

Massachusetts, also of Royal Descent, *b.* May, 1799, *d.* March, 1855, and had:

1.—SARAH COLUMBIA BRAXTON SHAW, *b.* 4 July, 1837, *d.* May, 1872; *m.*, 1 January, 1869, Albert Henry Rose, and had:

> ANNA BROOKE ROSE, of Alameda, California, a member of the Virginia and California Societies of the Colonial Dames of America.

2.—JOANNA MAYNARD SHAW, *b.* 26 May, 1830, a member of the Virginia and California Societies of the Colonial Dames of America, who *m.*, 15 October, 1846, Selden Stuart Wright, of Essex county, Virginia, 1822–1893, and had:

I.—MARY STUART WRIGHT, 1847–1878; *m.*, 1867, William B. Hooper, and had, besides other issue:

> MARY STUART HOOPER, a member of the Virginia and California Societies of the Colonial Dames of America, who *m.*, 1889, Cavalier Hamilton Jouett, of San Francisco. *Issue.*

II.—COLONEL STUART SELDEN WRIGHT, of Fresno, California, who *m.*, 1873, Maria Byrd Hopkins, also of Royal Descent, a member of the Virginia and California Societies of the Colonial Dames of America, and had:

> LOUISE KIMBALL WRIGHT, a member of the Virginia and California Societies of the Colonial Dames of America, who *m.*, 1895, John M. McClure, of Oakland, California. *Issue.*

III.—ANN AYLETTE BROOKE WRIGHT, a member of the Virginia and California Societies of the Colonial Dames of America.

IV.—ELIZA SHAW WRIGHT, a member of the Virginia and California Societies of the Colonial Dames of America, who *m.*, 1881, John D. Tallant, of San Francisco. *Issue.*

II.—JUDITH BRAXTON, who *m.* John White, and had:

MARY PAGE WHITE, who *m.* (his first wife) Andrew Stevenson, of Blenheim, Albemarle county, Virginia, member and Speaker of the House of Representatives and United States Minister to England, and had:

JOHN WHITE STEVENSON, of Covington, Kentucky, former Governor of Kentucky and United States Senator, who *m.* Sibella Winston, and had:

JUDITH WHITE STEVENSON, a member of the Virginia Society of the Colonial Dames of America, who *m.* John Flack Winslow, of Cincinnati, Ohio, and had: *John W. Stevenson, b.* Covington, Kentucky, 3 April, 1893.

3.—ANNE CARTER, who *m.*, 1722, Benjamin Harrison, of " Berkeley," Charles City county, Virginia, a member of the House of Burgesses, *d.* 1745, also of Royal Descent (p. 34), and had :

I.—BENJAMIN HARRISON, of " Berkeley," member of the Continental Congress, a signer of the Declaration of Independence, Governor of Virginia, *b.* 1726, *d.* 24 April, 1791, who *m.*, 13 December, 1730, Elizabeth Bassett, also of Royal Descent, and had :

GENERAL WILLIAM HENRY HARRISON, of Ohio, the ninth President of the United States, *b.* 9 February, 1773, *d.* Washington City, 4 April, 1841. He *m.*, 22 November, 1795, Ann, *d.* 25 February, 1864, aged 88 years, daughter of John Cleves Symmes, of Ohio, 1742–1814, associate justice of the Supreme Court of New Jersey, United States district judge for the Northwest Territory, one of the founders of the city of Cincinnati, and had :

1.—JOHN SCOTT HARRISON, of Cleves, Ohio, *b.* 4 October, at Vincennes, 1804, *d.* 1878, a member of Congress. He *m.*, secondly, 12 August, 1831, Elizabeth Irwin, and had by her :

GENERAL BENJAMIN HARRISON, of Indianapolis, Indiana, *b.* 20 August, 1833, the twenty-third President of the United States. He *m.*, first, Caroline, daughter of Rev. John Witherspoon Scott, of Ohio, and his wife, Mary, daughter of John Neal, of Philadelphia, Pennsylvania, and had by her, who *d.* 25 October, 1892 :

MARY SCOTT HARRISON, a member of the Virginia Society of the Colonial Dames of America, who *m.*, 5 November, 1884, James Robert McKee, of Indianapolis, Indiana, and had issue : *Benjamin H.* and *Mary Lodge.*

2.—LUCY SINGLETON HARRISON, 1800–1826, who *m.*, 1819 (his first wife), Judge David K. Este, of Cincinnati, also of Royal Descent, and had :

LUCY ANNE HARRISON ESTE, who *m.* Joseph F. Reynolds, of Baltimore, Maryland, and had :

ANNA HARRISON REYNOLDS, who *m.* John Law Crawford, and had :

LUCY CRAWFORD, a member of the Maryland Society of the Colonial Dames of America, who *m.* George C. Woodruff, of Litchfield, Connecticut. *No issue.*

II.—NATHANIEL HARRISON, a member of the Virginia State Senate, 1780, who *m.* Mary, daughter of Edmund Ruffin, of Prince George county, Virginia, and had :

12

EDMUND HARRISON, of Amelia county, Virginia, 1761–1826, member of the House of Delegates, member of the Council, 1793, *etc.*, who *m.* Martha Wayles Skipwith, also of Royal Descent, and had:

WILLIAM HENRY HARRISON, of Amelia county, Virginia, 1812–1884, who *m.* Lucy A. Powers, and had:

PROFESSOR EDMUND HARRISON, A.M., *b.* 17 February, 1843, president of Bethel Female College, Kentucky; *m.* Kate Steger, and had:

1.—LULIE HARRISON, a member of the Virginia Society of the Colonial Dames of America, who *m.* Dana Henry Rucker, of Richmond, Virginia, and had: *Edmund Harrison, b.* 18 February, 1898.

2.—JENNIE HARRISON, a member of the Virginia Society of the Colonial Dames of America, who *m.* Charles H. Chalkley, of Hopkinsville, Kentucky.

3.—LELIA SKIPWITH HARRISON, a member of the Virginia Society of the Colonial Dames of America, who *m.* Howard D. Hoge, of Richmond.

III.—CARTER HENRY HARRISON, of "Clifton," who *m.* Susan, daughter of Isham Randolph, of "Dungeness," who *d.* 1742, and had:

ROBERT CARTER HARRISON, who had by his first wife, Ann Cabell:

1.—MARY HOPKINS HARRISON, who *m.* Samuel Q. Richardson, and had:

ROBERT CARTER RICHARDSON, who *m.* Marie Louise Harris, and had:

MARY CABELL RICHARDSON, of Covington, Kentucky, a member of the Virginia Society of the Colonial Dames of America, a founder of the Order of Colonial Governors, *etc.*

2.—VIRGINIA HARRISON, who *m.* David Castleman, and had:

HUMPHREYS CASTLEMAN, of Columbus, Georgia, who *m.* Eva Garrard, a member of the Georgia Society of the Colonial Dames of America, and had:

ISABEL GARRARD CASTLEMAN, a member of the Georgia Society of the Colonial Dames of America (also of Royal Descent through Elizabeth Burwell, p. 34), who *m.* Samuel Harrison McAfee.

4.—COLONEL LANDON CARTER, of "Sabine Hall," Richmond county, Virginia, who had by his second wife, Maria Byrd, also of Royal Descent:

I.—MARIA BYRD CARTER, who *m.* Robert Beverley, of " Wakefield," Culpeper county, Virginia, *d.* 1800, also of Royal Descent, and had :

EVELYN BYRD BEVERLEY, widow of George Lee, who *m.*, secondly, Patrick Hume Douglas, M.D., of Loudoun county, Virginia, *d.* 1837, and had :

WILLIAM BYRD DOUGLAS, *b.* 1815, *d.* Nashville, Tennessee, 13 December, 1882 ; *m.*, first, Martha Rebecca Bright, and had :

MARY MARGARET DOUGLAS, a member of the Virginia Society of the Colonial Dames of America, who *m.*, first, James R. Buckner, and had : *James R.*, and *m.*, secondly, Edward D. Richards, and had : *Evelyn B.* (see p. 58), all of Nashville, Tennessee.

II.—LANDON CARTER, of Pittsylvania county, Virginia ; *m.* Judith Fauntleroy, also of Royal Descent, and had :

WORMELEY CARTER, who *m.* Sarah Edwards, and had :

WORMELEY CARTER, who *m.* Lucinda Washington Alexander, and had :

JUDGE WILLIAM ALEXANDER CARTER, who *m.* Mary Eliza Hamilton, and had :

MARY ADA CARTER, a member of the Pennsylvania Society of the Colonial Dames of America, who *m.*, 1874, Joseph K. Corson, M.D., surgeon United States Army, also of Royal Descent, and had : *Mary Carter, b.* 1876, *d.* 1890, and *Edward Foulke, b.* 1883.

LANDON CARTER, of " Sabine Hall ;" *m.*, thirdly, Elizabeth Wormeley, and had by her :

1.—ROBERT CARTER, of " Sabine Hall ;" *m.* Winifred Beale, and had :

I.—LANDON CARTER, of " Sabine Hall," 1756–1820 ; *m.*, secondly, Mary, daughter of John Armistead, and had by her :

FRANCES CARTER, who *m.* Major Rozier Dulany, United States Army, also of Royal Descent, and had :

REBECCA DULANY, who *m.* Colonel Richard H. Dulany, of " Welborne," Virginia, also of Royal Descent, and had :

FRANCES ADDISON CARTER DULANY, a member of the Maryland Society of the Colonial Dames of America, who *m.* J. Southgate Lemmon, of Baltimore.

II.—FRANCES CARTER, who *m.* Thomas Ludlow Lee, and had :

WINIFRED BEALE LEE, who *m.* William Brent, of " Richland,' and had :

THOMAS LEE BRENT, *m.* Jane Duncan Wilkins, and had :

WINIFRED LEE BRENT, a member of the Maryland Society of the Colonial Dames of America, who *m.* Henry F. Le H. Lyster, of Detroit, Michigan, and had: 1. *Dr. William J.*, United States Army; 2. *Eleanor Carroll*, wife of Edward H. Parker, of Detroit; 3. *Henry Lawrence;* 4. *Florence Murray;* 5. *Thomas Lee Brent.*

2.—ELIZABETH WORMELEY CARTER, *m.* Nelson Berkeley, of "Airwell," Hanover county, Virginia, and had:

DR. CARTER BERKELEY, of " Edgewood ;" *m.* Mrs. Frances (Page) Nelson, also of Royal Descent (see pp. 34, 133 and 134), and had:

CATHERINE FRANCES BERKELEY, *m.* Lucius Horatio Minor, of " Edgewood," also of Royal Descent (see p. 183), and had:

MARY WILLIS MINOR, of Baltimore, a member of the Maryland Society of the Colonial Dames of America.

THE ROYAL DESCENTS

OF

MRS. THOMAS LEE ALFRIEND,

AND

MRS. HERBERT DALE LAFFERTY.

ALFRED THE GREAT, of England, had:

Edward the Elder, King of England, who had :

Edmund I., King of England, who had :

Edgar the Peaceful, King of England, who had :

Ethelred II., King of England, who had :

Edmund II., King of England, who had :

Edward the Exile, Prince of England, who had:

Margaret, m. Malcolm III., of Scotland, and had:

David I., King of Scotland, who had :

Prince Henry of Scotland, who had :

David, Earl of Huntingdon, who had :

Isabella, m. Robert, Earl of Annandale, and had:

Robert Bruce, Earl of Annandale, who had:

Robert Bruce, Earl of Carrick, who had :

Robert Bruce, King of Scotland, who had :

Margery, m. Walter, High Steward, and had :

Robert II., King of Scotland, who had :

Catherine, m. Sir David Lindsay, and had :

Alexander, Earl of Crawford, who had :

Walter Lindsay, of Beaufort, who had :

Sir David Lindsay, of Edzell, who had :

Walter Lindsay, of Edzell, who had :

Alexander Lindsay, of Edzell, who had :

Rev. David Lindsay, Bishop of Ross, who had :

Rachel, m. Rev. Dr. John Spottiswood, and had :

Sir Robert Spottiswood, of New Abbey, who had:

Surgeon Robert Spottiswood, who had :

Gen. Alexander Spotswood, of Va., who had :

ALFRED THE GREAT, of England, had :

Ethelwida, m. Baldwin II., of Flanders, and had :

Arnolph the Great, Count of Flanders, who had :

Baldwin III., Count of Flanders, who had :

Arnolph II., Count of Flanders, who had :

Baldwin IV., Count of Flanders, who had :

Baldwin V., Count of Flanders, who had :

Maud, m. William the Conqueror, and had :

Henry I., King of England, who had :

Maud, m. Geoffrey, Count of Anjou, and had :

Henry II., King of England, who had :

John, King of England, who had :

Henry III., King of England, who had :

Edmund, Earl of Lancaster, who had :

Henry, Earl of Lancaster, who had :

Joan, m. John de Mowbray, and had :

John, 4th Baron de Mowbray, who had :

Eleanor, m. Roger de la Warr, and had :

Joan, m. Sir Thomas de West, and had :

Sir Reginald, Baron de la Warr, who had :

Sir Richard, Baron de la Warr, who had :

Sir Thomas, Baron de la Warr, who had :

Sir George West, Knt., who had :

Sir William, Baron de la Warr, who had :

Sir Thomas, Baron de la Warr, who had :

Gov. John West, of Va., who had :

Col. John West, of " West Point," Va., who had :

Capt. Nathaniel West, of Va., who had :

Unity, m. William Dandridge, R. N., and had :

John Spotswood, of Virginia, m. Mary Dandridge, of "Elsing Green," Va.

Anne Spotswood ⊤ Lewis Burwell.

Spotswood Burwell ⊤ Mary Marshall.

Mary Ann Spotswood Burwell ⊤ Otis F. Manson, M.D.

Eliza Sanger Manson, member of the National ⊤ Thomas Lee Alfriend, of Richmond, Va.
Society of the Colonial Dames of America.

Mary Burwell Alfriend, = Herbert Otis	Sally	Maria
member of the Na- Dale Manson	Spotswood	Lee
tional Society of the Lafferty. Alfriend.	Alfriend.	Alfriend.
Colonial Dames of		
America. *No issue.*		

PEDIGREE XLVI.

EDWARD I., **King of England,** had by his first wife, Princess Eleanor, daughter of Ferdinand III., King of Castile and Leon:

PRINCESS ELEANOR PLANTAGENET, who m. Henri, Count de Barr, and had:

LADY ELEANOR DE BARR, who m. Llewelyn ap Owen ap Merededd, of Royal Descent from Rhys ap Tudor, Prince of South Wales, and had:

THOMAS AP LLEWELYN, who m. Lady Eleanor, also of Royal Descent, daughter of Philip ap Iver ap Cadivor, and had:

ELEANOR V. PHILIP, who m. Griffith Vychan, lord of Glyndyfrdwy, and had:

LOWRY VAUGHN (sister of Owen Glendower), who m. Robert Puleston, of Emral, and had:

JOHN PULESTON, of Emral, who m. Angharad, daughter of Griffith Hanmer, of Hanmer, and had:

MARGARET PULESTON (*see* Dwnn's "Visitations of Wales"), m. David ap Ievan ap Einion, constable of Harlech Castle, 1468, and had:

EINION AP DAVID, of Cryniarth, in Edermon, who had:

LLEWELYN AP EINION, who had:

GRIFFITH AP LLEWELYN, who m. Mary, daughter of Howell ap Harry, and had:

CATHERINE VCH GRIFFITH, who m. Edward ap Ievan, of Llanwddyn parish, Montgomeryshire, and had:

ELLEN VCH EDWARD, who m. Lewis ap Griffith, of Yshute (Ysputty-Ievan) Denbighshire, 1525-1600, also of Royal Descent, and had:

ROBERT AP LEWIS, of Rhiwlas, near Bala, Merionethshire, 1555-1645, who m. Gwyrryl (Gwervyl), daughter of Hewelyn (Llewelyn) ap David, of Llan Rwst, Denbighshire, and had:

EVAN AP ROBERT AP LEWIS,* of Rhiwlas and Vron Gôch, Merionethshire, 1585-1662 (*see* Glenn's "Merion in the Welsh Tract"), m. Jane ———, and had:

1.—OWEN AP EVAN, of Fron Gôch farm, near Bala, d. 1669; m. Gainor John, d. 14 December, 1678, and had:

---

* MRS. HENRY SHIPPEN HUIDEKOPER, a member of the Pennsylvania Society of the National Society of the Colonial Dames of America, is also of Royal Descent through Evan Robert Lewis.

(190)

JANE OWEN, *b.* at Fron Gôch, 1653–54, *d.* Merion, Pennsylvania, 1 September, 1686; *m.* in Wales, 1672–73, Hugh Roberts, of Kiltalgarth township, Merionethshire, a minister among the Friends, *d.* 1702. They removed to Chester county, Pennsylvania, in 1683, and in 1692 he was a member of the Provincial Council, and had:

ROBERT ROBERTS, *b.* 7 January, 1673, who had by his second wife, Priscilla Jones:

ELIZABETH ROBERTS, who *m.* Isaac Parrish, and had:

ISAAC PARRISH, who *m.* Sarah Mitchell, and had:

JOSEPH PARRISH, who *m.* Susanna Cox, and had:

WILLIAM DILLWYN PARRISH, who *m.* Elizabeth W. Miller, and had:

MARY PARRISH, a member of the Pennsylvania Society of the Colonial Dames of America, who *m.* Louis Starr, M.D., of Philadelphia, and had: *Louis, b.* 5 June, 1882; *Dillwyn P., b.* 3 October, 1883, and *Elizabeth Parrish, b.* 29 April, 1889.

2.—EVAN AP EVAN, of Vron Gôch, who *m.* twice, and had:

THOMAS AP EVAN, *alias* THOMAS EVANS, *b.* at Vron Gôch, 1651, came to Pennsylvania 1698, lived in Gwynedd, and *d.* at Goshen in 1738. He had by his first wife, Ann, *d.* at Gwynedd, 26 March, 1716:

HUGH EVANS, of Merion, Pennsylvania, *d.* Philadelphia, 6 April, 1772, aged 90 years, a member of the Provincial Assembly, 1722, 1746–54. He *m.*, thirdly, 13 February, 1716, Lowry, widow of Robert Lloyd, and daughter of Reese John William, also of Royal Descent, and had (*see* Jenkins's "History of Gwynedd," p. 152):

SUSANNA EVANS, 1719–1801, who *m.*, 30 May, 1740, Owen Jones, Sr., of Merion, 1711–1793, the last Provincial treasurer of Pennsylvania, also of Royal Descent (p. 160), and had:

1.—HANNAH JONES, 1749–1829, who *m.*, 1779, Amos Foulke, of Philadelphia, 1740–1791, also of Royal Descent, and had:

EDWARD FOULKE, of Gwynedd, 1784–1851; *m.*, 1810, Tacy, daughter of Isaac and Gainor Jones, and had, besides other issue:

I.—ANNE JONES FOULKE, 1811–1888, *m.*, 1833, Hiram Corson, M.D., of Conshohocken, and had:

SUSAN FOULKE CORSON, a member of the Pennsylvania Society of the Colonial Dames of America, who *m.*, 26 November, 1868, Jawood Lukens, of Conshohocken. *No issue.*

II.—PRISCILLA FOULKE, 1821–1882, *m.*, 22 November, 1849, Thomas Wistar, Jr., of Philadelphia, and had:

SUSAN FOULKE WISTAR, a member of the Pennsylvania Society of the Colonial Dames of America, who *m.*, 27 May, 1872,

Howard Comfort, of Philadelphia, and had: *William Wistar, b*
27 May, 1874.

III.—REBECCA JONES FOULKE, *b.* 18 May, 1829, a member of the
Pennsylvania Society of the Colonial Dames of America, who *m.*,
8 October, 1857, Robert R. Corson, of New Hope, Pennsylvania. ·*No
issue.*

2.—LOWRY JONES, who *m.*, 5 July, 1760, Daniel Wister, of Philadelphia, 1738–1805, and had:

I.—JOHN WISTER, of Philadelphia, 1776–1862; *m.* Elizabeth Harvey,
and had:

LOUIS WISTER, of Ardmore, Pennsylvania, *m.* Elizabeth Emlen
Randolph, and had: *Sara Edythe,* and

ELIZABETH HARVEY WISTER, a member of the Pennsylvania So-
ciety of the Colonial Dames of America, who *m.* Charles Penrose
Keith, of Philadelphia, author of " The Provincial Councillors of
Pennsylvania and their Descendants," "Ancestry of Benjamin
Harrison," *etc. No issue.*

II.—CHARLES JONES WISTER, of Philadelphia, 1782–1865, who *m.* Rebecca Bullock, and had:

WILLIAM WYNNE WISTER, of Philadelphia, *m.* Hannah Lewis Wilson, and had:

RACHAEL WILSON WISTER, who *m.*, 12 November, 1862, William
Barton Rogers, and had:

MABEL ROGERS, a member of the Pennsylvania Society of the Colonial Dames of America, who *m.* Edgar W. Baird, of Philadelphia,
and had: *Edgar W.* and *Gainor Owen.*

THE ROYAL DESCENT

OF

MRS. BYRON COLEMAN DICK,

OF OAKLAND, CAL.

HUGH CAPET, King of France, had :

Robert the Pious, King of France, who had :

Henry I., King of France, who had :

Hugh Magnus, Duke of France, who had :

Isabel, *m.* Robert, Earl of Mellent, and had :

Robert, second Earl of Leicester, who had :

Robert, third Earl of Leicester, who had :

Margaret, *m.* Saier de Quincey, and had :

Roger, Earl of Winchester, who had :

Elizabeth, *m.* Alexander Cumyn, and had :

Agnes, *m.* Gilbert de Umfraville, and had :

Robert, second Earl of Angus, who had :

Thomas de Umfraville, of Harbottle, who had :

Sir Thomas de Umfraville, of Kyme, who had :

Joan, *m.* Sir William Lambert, and had :

Robert Lambert, of Owlton, who had :

Henry Lambert, of Ongar, who had :

Elizabeth, *m.* Thomas Lyman, and had :

Henry Lyman, of Navistoke, who had :

John Lyman, of High Ongar, who had :

Henry Lyman, of High Ongar, who had :

Richard Lyman, of Hartford, Conn., who had :

John Lyman, of Northampton, Mass., who had :

Benjamin Lyman, of Northampton, who had :

Mary, *m.* Oliver Pomeroy, and had :

HUGH CAPET, King of France, had :

Robert the Pious, King of France, who had :

Henry I., King of France, who had :

Hugh Magnus, Duke of France, who had :

Isabel, *m.* William, Earl of Surrey, and had :

William, Earl of Warren and Surrey, who had :

Isabel, *m.* Hameline Plantagenet, and had :

Isabel, *m.* Roger, Earl of Norfolk, and had :

Hugh Bigod, Earl of Norfolk, who had :

Sir Hugh Bigod, Knt., who had :

Sir John Bigod, Knt., who had :

Roger Bigod, of Settington, who had :

Joan, *m.* Sir William de Chauncy, and had :

John Chauncy, of Stepney, who had :

John Chauncy, of Sawbridgeworth, who had :

John Chauncy, of Sawbridgeworth, who had :

John Chauncy, of Pishobury, who had :

Henry Chauncy, of New Place, who had :

George Chauncy, of Yardleybury, who had :

Rev. Charles Chauncy, D.D., who had :

Sarah, *m.* Rev. Gershom Bulkeley, and had :

Edward Bulkeley, of Wethersfield, who had :

Rachel Lyman Pomeroy *m.* Brig.-Major Edward Bulkeley.

Col. Selah Francis⹋Roxa Lyman Bulkeley.

Judge Jesse Booth, of New York⹋Roxa Bulkeley Francis.

Byron Coleman Dick, of Oakland, Cal.=Ellen Cordelia Bulkeley Booth, member of the
Conn. Society of the Colonial Dames of America.
No issue.

PEDIGREE XLVII.

DAVID I., King of Scotland, had by his wife, Lady Matilda, daughter of Waltheof, Earl of Northumberland :

HENRY, Prince of Scotland, eldest son, Earl of Northumberland, *d. v. p.*, 1152, who *m.*, 1139, Lady Ada de Warren, *d.* 1178, daughter of William, second Earl of Warren and Surrey, and had :

PRINCESS MARGARET, widow of Conan le Petit, Earl of Brittany and Richmond, *d.* 20 February, 1171, who *m.*, secondly, Humphrey, fourth Baron de Bohun, constable of England, and had :

LADY —— DE BOHUN, who *m.* (his first wife) Reginald, sixth Baron de Mohun, of Dunster, *d.* 1256, and had :

JOHN DE MOHUN, Baron de Mohun, of Dunster, *d.* 1278 ; *m.* Joan, daughter of Sir Reginald Fitz-Piers, òf Blewleveny, and had :

SIR JOHN DE MOHUN, first Lord Mohun of Dunster Castle, by writ, *d.* 1330 ; *m.* Auda, daughter of Sir Richard Tibetot, Knt., and had :

LADY MARGARET DE MOHUN, who *m.* Sir John Cantilupe, Knt., grandson of John Cantilupe, of Smithfield, and had :

ELEANOR CANTILUPE, who *m.* Sir Thomas de West, Knt., of Roughcombe, Wiltshire, Governor of Christ Church Castle ; summoned to Parliament, 1333, for Warwickshire as Baron West, *d.* 1344, and had :

SIR THOMAS DE WEST, Knt., second Baron West, of Hampston-Cantilupe, and Great Torrington, Devonshire ; *m.* Lady Alice, daughter of Reginald Fitz-Piers, Baron of Wolverly, and had :

SIR THOMAS DE WEST, third Baron West, Knt., *d.* in 1405 ; *m.* Lady Joan, half-sister and heiress of Thomas, Lord de la Warr, and daughter of Roger de la Warr, *d.* 1371, and his second wife, Lady Eleanor de Mowbray, also of Royal Descent, and had :

SIR REGINALD DE WEST, second son, who, on the death of Lord de la Warr, had livery of the lands of his mother's inheritance, and was summoned to Parliament as Lord de la Warr (*see* Doyle's " Official Baronage "). He *d.* 27 August, 1451, possessed of vast estates, having had issue by his wife, Margaret, daughter of Robert Thorley :

RICHARD DE WEST, Lord de la Warr, *d.* 10 March, 1475 ; *m.* Catherine, daughter of Robert, Baron de Hungerford, and had :

SIR THOMAS DE WEST, K.B., K.G., Lord de la Warr, *d.* 1524 ; *m.*, first, Elizabeth, daughter of Hugh Mortimer, of Mortimer Hall, Hants, and

(194)

m., secondly, Alianor, daughter of Sir Roger Copley, of Gatton, and had:

SIR GEORGE WEST, Knt., second son, *d.* 1538; *m.* Lady Elizabeth, daughter of Sir Anthony Moreton, of Lechdale, Gloucestershire, and had:

SIR WILLIAM WEST, *b. ante* 1520, *d.* 30 December, 1595, created Baron de la Warr, 5 February, 1570 (*see* Foster's " Peerage ''); *m.*, 1554, Elizabeth, daughter of Thomas Strange, of Chesterton, Gloucestershire, and had:

SIR THOMAS WEST, only son, second Lord de la Warr (*see* Dugdale's " Baronage " of 1676; Brown's " Genesis of the United States," p. 1045), *d.* April, 1602; *m.* Anne Knowles, and had:

LADY PENELOPE WEST, *b.* 9 September, 1582, who *m.*, 1599, Herbert Pelham, of Boston, Lincolnshire, *d.* July, 1624 (*see* " American Heraldic Journal," iii., p. 84; Berry's "Sussex Pedigrees "), and had:

HERBERT PELHAM,* of Boston, Lincolnshire, eldest son, *b.* 1600, *d.* in July, 1674. He removed with some of his children, his wife being dead, to Cambridge, Massachusetts, in 1638, and was treasurer of Harvard College in 1643, and was chosen an assistant in 1645. In 1647 he returned to England, and became a member of Parliament in 1654 (*see* " Mass. His. Col.," third ser., iii.). He *m.*, first, 1626, Jemima, daughter of Thomas Waldegrave, of Bures, Essex, and *m.*, secondly, Elizabeth, daughter of Godfrey Bosville, of Gunthwaite, Yorkshire, and widow of Roger Harlakenden, who *d.* in New England, in 1638, and had by her:

PENELOPE PELHAM, *bapt.* at Bures, in 1633, *d.* 7 December, 1703; *m.*, 1657, in New England, Josiah Winslow, of Marshfield, who was *b.* at Plymouth, 1629, and *d.* at Careswell, 18 December, 1680; was commander of the military of Plymouth Colony and of that of the United Colonies in the King Philip War, 1675, and Governor of Plymouth Colony, 1673–80. He was son of Edward Winslow, of Droitwich, Worcestershire, one of the Pilgrims to New England, and Governor of Plymouth Colony. Governor Winslow and Penelope had:

JUDGE ISAAC WINSLOW, of Marshfield, *b.* 1670, *d.* 6 December, 1738. Commander of the Colony's militia; member of the council twenty years; chief justice of Court of Common Pleas and judge of probate; *m.*, 11 July, 1700, Sarah, *d.* 1753, aged 80, daughter of John Wensley, of Boston, and had:

PENELOPE WINSLOW, *b.* 27 December, 1704, *d.* 1737; *m.*, June 30, 1724,

---

* MRS. GEORGE S. HALE, a member of the Massachusetts State Society of the National Society of the Colonial Dames of America, is of Royal Descent through Herbert Pelham.

James, *b.* 14 April, 1700, *d.* July, 1757, son of James (of Nathaniel of Richard the Pilgrim) and Sarah (Doty) Warren, and had :

SARAH WARREN, *b.* 13 May, 1730; *d.* 15 March, 1797; *m.*, 2 December, 1755, William, *b.* 12 October, 1729, *d.* 15 June, 1809, son of Nicholas and Sarah (Warren) Sever, and had :

WILLIAM SEVER, *b.* 23 June, 1759, *d.* 27 October, 1798 ; *m.*, 29 October, 1785, Mary, *b.* 21 December, 1759, *d.* 15 January, 1821, daughter of John and Mary (Church) Chandler, and had :

PENELOPE WINSLOW SEVER, *b.* 21 July, 1786, *d.* 2 April, 1872 ; *m.*, 6 September, 1807, Levi, *b.* 25 October, 1782, *d.* 29 May, 1868, son of Levi and Martha (Waldo) Lincoln, and had :

DANIEL WALDO LINCOLN, *b.* 19 January, 1813, *d.* 1 July, 1880, who *m.*, 30 November, 1841, Frances Fiske, *b.* 15 October, 1819, *d.* 8 April, 1873, daughter of Francis Taliaferro Merrick, 1792–1863, and had :

1.—FRANCES MERRICK LINCOLN, of Worcester, Massachusetts, a member of the Massachusetts Society of the Colonial Dames of America.

2.—MARY WALDO LINCOLN, a member of the Massachusetts Society of the Colonial Dames of America, who *m.* Joseph Estabrook Davis, of Boston, and had: *Lincoln, b.* 31 March, 1872, and *Mabel, b.* 25 March, 1875.

3.—WALDO LINCOLN, of Worcester, Massachusetts, *m.*, 24 June, 1873, Fanny Chandler (daughter of George and Josephine Rose Chandler, of Worcester), a member of the Massachusetts Society of the Colonial Dames of America, and had: *Merrrick, b.* 25 May, 1875; *Josephine Rose, b.* 28 February, 1878; *Daniel Waldo, b.* 2 September, 1882; *George Chandler, b.* 6 August, 1884, and *Dorothy, b.* 4 March, 1890.

PEDIGREE XLVIII.

HENRY I., **King of France,** had by his wife, Anne of Russia:

HUGH THE GREAT, Duke of France and Burgundy, Marquis of Orleans, Count of Paris, Valois and Vermandois, who had by his third wife, Lady Adelheid, daughter of Herbert IV., Count de Vermandois, also of Royal Descent:

LADY ISABEL DE VERMANDOIS, *d.* 1131, who *m.*, first, Robert de Beaumont, or Bellomont, Earl of Mellent, created, in 1103, Earl of Leicester, *d.* 1118 (*see* " L'Art de Verifier les Dates," xii.), and had:

LADY ELIZABETH DE BELLOMONT, who *m.* Gilbert Fitz-Gilbert de Clare, created, in 1138, Earl of Pembroke, *d.* 1149, and had:

RICHARD DE CLARE, " the Strongbow," second Earl of Pembroke, lord justice of Ireland, *d. s. p. m.* 1176, who *m.* Lady Eva, daughter of Dermot MacMurcha, the last King of Leinster, and had:

LADY ISABEL DE CLARE, who *m.*, 1189 (his first wife), William le Marshal, Earl of Pembroke, Protector of England during the nonage of Henry III., *d.* 1219, and had:

LADY ISABEL MARSHALL, who *m.*, first, Gilbert de Clare, Earl of Clare, Hertford and Gloucester, a surety for the Magna Charta, *d.* 1229, and had:

LADY ISABEL DE CLARE, who *m.* Robert Bruce, fifth Earl of Annandale, 1210–1295, and had:

ROBERT BRUCE, Earl of Annandale and Carrick, 1245–1304 ; *m.*, 1271, Margaret, Countess of Carrick, widow of Adam Kilconcath, *d.* 1270, and daughter and heiress of Neil, second Earl of Carrick, *d.* 1256, and had:

LADY MARY BRUCE (sister of Robert Bruce, King of Scotland), widow of Sir Neil Campbell, who *m.*, secondly, Sir Alexander Fraser, lord chamberlain of Scotland, 1323, *k.* 1332, and had:

SIR JOHN FRASER, of Aberbothnot, eldest son, whose only child:

LADY MARGARET FRASER, *m.* Sir William Keith, great marshal of Scotland, *d.* 1406–8, and had:

LADY ELIZABETH KEITH, who *m.* Sir Adam de Gordon, of Huntley, *k.* at Homildon, and had:

LADY ELIZABETH DE GORDON, only child, who *m.*, before 27 March, 1408, Alexander de Seton, and had:

ALEXANDER DE SETON, of Gordon and Huntly, created, in 1445, Earl of Huntly, *d.* 1470, who had by his fourth wife, " The Fair Maid of Moray," a daughter of Comyn of Altyre :

LADY MARGARET DE GORDON, *b. ante* 1460, *d.* 1506, who *m.* (the obligation for the marriage of his half-sister signed by George de Gordon, Earl of Huntly, 26 June, 1484) Hugh Rose, eighth laird of Kilravock and Geddes (his second wife), *d.* 17 March, 1517 (*see* " Rose of Kilravock," 1683, reprint by the Spalding Club, Edinburgh, 1848), and had :

JOHN ROSE, of Bellivat, second son, who *m.* (contract dated "at Elgin the penult daye of Aprill in yᵉ yeir of God IᴹVᶜ and xxvj yeirs ") Marjory, daughter of James Dunbar, of Cunzie, also of Royal Descent, and had :

JOHN ROSE, of Bellivat, who *m.* a daughter of Alexander Urquhart, of Burdsyards, and had :

JOHN ROSE, of Bellivat, who *m.*, first, a daughter of —— Falconar, of Hawkerton, and had :

HUGH ROSE, second son, who *m.* Katherine, daughter of —— Ord, of Finachty, and had :

PATRICK ROSE, of Lochihills, eldest son, *d.* 31 March, 1727, who *m.* Isabel Falloch, of Bogtown, and had :

JOHN ROSE, of Wester Alves, *d. v. p.,* 13 April, 1724, who *m.*, *ante* 1704, Margaret Grant, of Whitetree, *d.* 1774, and had (*see* W. G. Stanard's " Rose Chart-Pedigree," 1895) :

REV. ROBERT ROSE, third son, *b.* at Wester Alves, 12 February, 1704 ; came to Virginia in 1725, was rector of St. Anne's parish, Essex county, 1728–1747, and of Albemarle parish, 1747–1751 ; *d.* at Richmond, 30 June, 1751. He had by his second wife, *m.* 6 November, 1740, Anne, daughter of Henry Fitzhugh, of " Bedford," King George county, Virginia, 1720–1789 :

COLONEL HUGH ROSE, of " Geddes," Amherst county, Virginia, 1743–1797, a member of the Amherst county committee of safety ; county lieutenant ; member of the House of Delegates ; high sheriff of Amherst county, 1775 ; *m.* Caroline, daughter of Colonel Samuel Jordan, of " Seven Islands," Buckingham county, Virginia, *d.* 1789, and had :

1.—ROBERT H. ROSE, M.D., *d.* 1835 ; *m.* Frances Taylor, daughter of Colonel James and Nelly (Conway) Madison, of " Montpelier," Virginia, and sister of President Madison, and had :

NELLY CONWAY ROSE, *m.* John Francis Newman, and had :

I.—ELLEN ROSE NEWMAN, *d.* 1869, who *m.* Rev. John Ambrose Wheelock, *d.* 1866, and had :

ELIZABETH JOSEPHINE WHEELOCK, of Grand Rapids, Michigan, a member of the Order of the Crown, *etc.*

II.—MARY FRANCES NEWMAN, *m.* James Rose, and had:
NELLIE CONWAY ROSE, a member of the Order of the Crown, who
m. William T. Baggett, of San Francisco, and had *Nellie Rose.*

2.—GUSTAVUS ADOLPHUS ROSE, M.D., of Lynchburg, Virginia, *b.* Nelson county, Virginia, 13 March, 1789, *d.* at La Porte, Indiana, 20 January, 1860; *m.,* 4 January, 1816, Ann Shepherd, *b.* 9 September, 1797, *d.* 5 July, 1856, daughter of Hon. David S. Garland, member of Congress, of Lynchburg, Virginia, and had:

I.—JUDITH CABELL ROSE, of Richmond, Virginia, a member of the Virginia Society of the Colonial Dames of America, who *m.,* at La Porte, Indiana, 21 July, 1846, Benjamin Powell Walker, *b.* Hartford, Indiana, 30 January, 1817, *d.* New York, 14 February, 1887, and had:

1.—JOHN GARLAND; 2. GUSTAVUS A.; 3. FREDERICK, *d. inf.,* 1862.

4.—WILLIAM JAMES WALKER, of Richmond, Virginia, *m.,* first, Josephine Irvine, daughter of Dr. R. T. Coleman, of Richmond, and had: *Robert C.;* and *m.,* secondly, Columbia Stanard Hayes, a member of the Virginia Society of the Colonial Dames of America.

5.—BENJAMIN POWELL WALKER, *m.* Lillie Mackie, of New Bedford, Massachusetts, and had: *Bradford Mackie.*

6.—FRANCES MARIA, *m.* Clarendon Harris, of Cambridge, Massachusetts, and had: *Clarendon, Edward Doubleday* and *Katherine Holbrook.*

7.—LANDON ROSE WALKER, of Richmond, Virginia.

8.—ANNIE FITZHUGH ROSE WALKER, of Richmond, a member of the Virginia Society of the Colonial Dames of America, the Order of the Crown, *etc.*

II.—DAVID GARLAND ROSE, who *m.* Maria Louisa, daughter of John and Frances (Allen) Walker, and had:

MARIA LOUISA ROSE, a member of the Virginia Society of the Colonial Dames of America, who *m.* Samuel J. Filer, of Springfield, Massachusetts.

III.—CAROLINE MATILDA ROSE, of Chicago, a member of the Virginia and Illinois Societies of the Colonial Dames of America, *b.* Lynchburg, Virginia, *m.* William James Walker, of La Porte, Indiana, and had:

1.—MARTHA GARLAND WALKER, member of the Virginia and Illinois Societies of the Colonial Dames of America, who *m.* Sylvanus Landor Trippe, of New York, and had: *Carolyn Rose Walker.*

2.—JOHN CRAWFORD; 3. WILLIAM JAMES; 4. FRANCES M.

5.—CAROLINE M. WALKER, who *m.* George Fisher, of Harrisburg, Pennsylvania, and had: *Carolyn* and

ROSE FISHER, a member of the Virginia Society of the Colonial Dames of America, who *m.* Madison B. Kennedy, of New York.

THE ROYAL DESCENTS

OF

MR. AND MRS. WM. J. HOLLIDAY,

OF INDIANAPOLIS, IND.

ALFRED THE GREAT, of England, had :	ALFRED THE GREAT, of England, had :
Ethelwida, *m.* Baldwin II., of Flanders, and had:	Edward the Elder, King of England, who had :
Arnolph, Count of Flanders, who had :	Edmund I., King of England, who had :
Baldwin III., Count of Flanders, who had :	Edgar, King of England, who had :
Arnolph II., Count of Flanders, who had :	Ethelred, King of England, who had :
Baldwin IV., Count of Flanders, who had :	Edmund Ironsides, King of England, who had :
Baldwin V., Count of Flanders, who had :	Edward, the Exile, Prince of England, who had :
Matilda, *m.* William the Conqueror, and had :	Margaret, *m.* Malcolm, King of Scots, and had :
Henry I., King of England, who had :	Matilda, *m.* Henry I., King of England, and had :
Maud, *m.* Geoffrey, of Anjou, and had :	Maud, *m.* Geoffrey, Count of Anjou, and had :
Henry II., King of England, who had :	Henry II., King of England, who had :
John, King of England, who had :	John, King of England, who had :
Henry III., King of England, who had :	Henry III., King of England, who had :
Edward I., King of England, who had :	Edmund, Earl of Lancaster, who had :
Edward II., King of England, who had :	Henry, Earl of Lancaster, who had :
Edward III., King of England, who had :	Joan, *m.* John de Mowbray, and had :
Lionel, Duke of Clarence, who had :	John, Baron de Mowbray, who had :
Philippa, *m.* Edmund de Mortimer, and had :	Eleanor, *m.* Roger de la Warr, and had :
Elizabeth, *m.* Sir Henry Percy, K.G., and had :	Joan, *m.* Sir Thomas de West, and had :
Henry, Earl of Northumberland, who had :	Sir Reginald, Lord de la Warr, who had :
Henry, Earl of Northumberland, who had :	Sir Richard, Lord de la Warr, who had :
Margaret, *m.* Sir William Gascoigne, and had :	Sir Thomas, Lord de la Warr, who had :
Elizabeth, *m.* Gilbert de Talboys, and had :	Sir George West, Knt., who had :
Sir George de Talboys, Knt., who had :	Sir William, Lord de la Warr, who had :
Anne, *m.* Sir Edward Dymoke, and had :	Sir Thomas, Lord de la Warr, who had :
Frances, *m.* Sir Thomas Windebank, and had :	Col. John West, of Va., who had :
Mildred, *m.* Robert Reade, and had :	Col. John West, Jr., of Va., who had :
Col. George Reade, of Va., who had :	Nathaniel West, of Va., who had :
Mildred, *m.* Augustine Warner, and had :	Unity, *m.* William Dandridge, of Va., and had :
Mary, *m.* John Smith, of "Purton," and had :	Martha, *m.* Philip Aylett, of Va., and had :
Augustine Smith, of Va., who had :	Col. William Aylett, of Va., who had :
John Smith, of "Shooter's Hill," who had :	Col. Philip Aylett, of Va., who had :
Edward Smith, of Va., who had :	Mary, *m.* Philip Fitzhugh, of Va., and had :
Ariana, *m.* William D. Holliday, and had :	Lucy, *m.* John Robertson Redd, and had :

William Jaquelin Holliday *m.* Lucy Redd.

Ariana Ambler=Henry W. Holliday Bennett.	Jaquelin S. Holli-=Florence day Baker.	Lucy Fitzhugh Holliday, *m.* George E. Hume.
Edward Jaquelin Louise Bennett. Bennett.	William Jaquelin Frederick Taylor Holliday. Holliday.	

THE ROYAL DESCENT

OF

MRS. BRITTON DAVIS,

OF EL PASO, TEXAS.

HUGH CAPET, King of France, 987, had by his wife, Lady Adela (or Alisa), daughter of William, Duke of Aquitaine, by his wife, Lady Adelheid, daughter of Otto I., Emperor of Saxony:

PRINCESS HEDEWIGE (or Havide), sister of King Robert the Pious, who *m.* Rynerius (or Raginerus) IV., eleventh Count of Hainault, and had:

LADY BEATRIX, *m.* Eblo I., Count de Rouci and de Reimes, and had:

LADY ADELA (or Alexandria), Countess de Rouci, who *m.* Hildwin IV., Count de Montdidier and de Rouci, and had:

LADY MARGARET DE ROUCI, who *m.* Hugh, first Count de Clermont (*see* " L'Art de Verifier les Dates," xii., 282), and had:

LADY ADELIZA DE CLERMONT, who *m.* Gilbert de Tonsburg, in Kent, second Earl of Clare, and had:

GILBERT DE CLARE, created, in 1138, Earl of Pembroke, *d.* 1149, who *m.* Lady Elizabeth de Bellomont, daughter of Robert, Earl of Mellent and Leicester, and had:

RICHARD DE CLARE, " the Strongbow," second Earl of Pembroke, lord justice of Ireland, *d.* 1176, who had by his wife, Lady Eva, daughter of Dermot Mac Murcha, King of Leinster:

LADY ISABEL DE CLARE, who *m.*, 1189 (his first wife), William le Marshal, Earl of Pembroke, protector of England during the nonage of Henry III., *d.* 1219, and had:

LADY MAUD MARSHALL, who *m.*, first, Hugh Bigod, third Earl of Norfolk, one of the sureties for the Magna Charta of King John, *d.* 1225, and had:

SIR RALPH BIGOD, Knt., third son, who *m.* Lady Berta de Furnival, and had:

LADY ISABEL BIGOD, who *m.*, first, Gilbert de Lacy, *d. v. p.*, son of Walter, sixth Baron de Lacy, of Trim, *d.* 1241, and had:

LADY MARGARET DE LACY, who *m.* (his first wife) John, sixth Baron de Verdon, *k.* 1274, and had:

13   (201)

SIR THEOBALD DE VERDON, seventh Baron, lord high constable of Ireland, *d.* 1309; *m.* Lady Maud, daughter of Sir Edmund, seventh Baron de Mortimer, of Wigmore, *k.* 1303, and had:

LADY ELIZABETH DE VERDON, who *m.* Bartholomew, second Baron Burghersh, and had:

SIR BARTHOLOMEW BURGHERSH, third Baron, *d.* 1369, whose daughter:

LADY ELIZABETH BURGHERSH, *m.* Maurice Fitz-Gerald, fourth Earl of Kildare, *d.* 1390, and had:

GERALD FITZ-GERALD, fifth Earl of Kildare, lord justice of Ireland in 1405, *d.* 1410, who *m.* Lady Margery, daughter of Sir John de Rocheford, Knt., lord of Thistledown, and had:

JOHN-CAM FITZ-GERALD, sixth Earl of Kildare, *d.* 1427, who had by his wife, Margaret de la Herne:

THOMAS FITZ-GERALD, seventh Earl of Kildare, lord deputy of Ireland in 1454, and in 1493, lord chancellor, who, dying 25 March, 1478, left issue by his wife, Lady Joan, who *d.* 1486, daughter of James Fitz-Gerald, seventh Earl of Desmond, also of Royal Descent:

GERALD FITZ-GERALD, eighth Earl of Kildare, lord deputy of Ireland, who *m.* Lady Allison, daughter of Sir Rowland Eustace, Baron of Portlester, lord chancellor and treasurer of Ireland, and had:

LADY ELEANOR FITZ-GERALD, who *m.*, first, Donnel Mac Fineere Mac Carthy-Reagh, prince of Carberry, in Ireland, and had:

LADY JULIA MAC CARTHY, who *m.* Dermod O'Sullivan, eleventh Lord Beare and Bantry, who was *k.*, 1549, by an accident, at his castle of Dunboy, and had:

SIR PHILIP O'SULLIVAN-BEARE, who as tanist to his brother Sir Owen's son, Dermond, held the Castle of Ardea, county Kerry. He *m.* a daughter of Cormack O'Brien, Earl of Thomond, also of Royal Descent, and had:

DANIEL O'SULLIVAN-BEARE, of Ardea Castle, who *m.* Lady Margaret, daughter of the Earl of Clancarthy, by his wife, Lady Margaret, daughter of Donogh O'Brien, fourth Earl of Thomond, and had:

PHILIP O'SULLIVAN-BEARE, of Ardea, who *m.* Lady Honora, daughter of Donogh, Earl of Clancarthy, *d.* 1666, and his wife, Lady Ellen, daughter of Thomas Butler, Lord Thurles, governor of Kilkenny, *d.* 1619, also of Royal Descent, and had:

DANIEL O'SULLIVAN-BEARE, of Ardea, who *m.* Lady Ellen, daughter of Daniel O'Sullivan-Mor, tenth lord of Dunkerron, who *d.* 1699, also of Royal Descent, and had:

OWEN O'SULLIVAN, of Ardea, who *m.* Mary, daughter of Colonel Owen Mac Sweeney, of Muskerry, and had:

MAJOR PHILIP O'SULLIVAN, of Ardea, who *m*. Joanna, daughter of Dermod McCarthy-Mor, of Killoween, county Kerry, and had:

JOHN SULLIVAN, *b*. Ardea, county Kerry, 17 June, 1690, came to America in 1723, and *d*. at South Berwick, Maine, 20 June, 1795, aged 105 years (*see* "N. E. Historical and Genealogical Register," October, 1865), and had by his wife, Margaret Browne, a native of County Kerry, who *d*. in 1801, aged 87 years:

MARY SULLIVAN, 1752–1827; *m*. Theophilus Hardy, of Durham, New Hampshire, and had:

MARGERY HARDY, who *m*. Edward Wells, of Durham, and had:

CHARLES WELLS, of New York City, who *m*. Mary Wiggin, and had:

MARIE ANTOINETTE WELLS, who *m*. Levi Steele, and had:

ANTOINETTE WELLS STEELE, a member of the New York and Texas Societies of the Colonial Dames of America, who *m*. Britton Davis, of El Paso, Texas, and had: *Newton, b*. New York, 22 March, 1890; *Antoinette, b*. Orange, N. J., 13 November, 1892; and *Britton, b*. El Paso, 5 October, 1896.

THE ROYAL DESCENT

OF

MRS. LOUIS C. WASHBURN,

OF ROCHESTER, NEW YORK.

EDWARD III., King of England⹋Lady Philippa of Hainault.

Lionel, Duke of Clarence⹋Lady Elizabeth de Burgh.

Lady Philippa Plantagenet⹋Edmund Mortimer, Earl of Marche.

Lady Elizabeth Mortimer⹋Sir Henry Percy, " Hotspur."

Henry, Earl of Northumberland⹋Lady Eleanor Neville.

Henry, Earl of Northumberland⹋Lady Eleanor Poynings.

Lady Margaret Percy⹋Sir William Gascoigne.

Lady Dorothy Gascoigne⹋Sir Ninian Markenfield.

Lady Alice Markenfield⹋Robert Mauleverer.

Dorothy Mauleverer⹋John Kaye, of Woodsome.

Robert Kaye, of Woodsome⹋Ann Flower, of Whitewell.

Grace Kaye⹋Sir Richard Saltonstall, of Huntwick.

Richard Saltonstall, of Ipswich, Mass.⹋Muriel Gurdon.

Nathaniel Saltonstall, of Haverhill, Mass.⹋Elizabeth Ward.

Gurdon Saltonstall, Governor of Connecticut⹋Elizabeth Rosewell.

General Gurdon Saltonstall⹋Rebecca Winthrop.

Rebecca Saltonstall⹋David Mumford, New London, Ct.

Thomas Mumford⹋Mary Sheldon Smith.

George Huntington Mumford⹋Anne Elizabeth Hart.

Henrietta Saltonstall Mumford, a member of⹋Louis Cope Washburn, Rochester, N. Y.
the National Society of the Colonial Dames
of America,

| Henrietta Mumford Washburn. | Helen Carpenter Washburn. | Louis Mumford Washburn. |

PEDIGREE L.

EDWARD III., King of England, had by his wife, Lady Philippa, daughter of William, Count of Hainault, also of Royal Descent:

SIR LIONEL PLANTAGENET, K.G., Duke of Clarence, Earl of Ulster, who *m.*, first, Lady Elizabeth de Burgh, daughter of William, Earl of Ulster, also of Royal Descent, and had:

LADY PHILIPPA PLANTAGENET, who *m.* Edmund de Mortimer, third Earl of Marche, also of Royal Descent, and had:

LADY ELIZABETH DE MORTIMER, who *m.* Sir Henry de Percy, the renowned " Hotspur," also of Royal Descent, and had:

HENRY DE PERCY, second Earl of Northumberland, *k.* at St. Albans, 1455 ; *m.* Lady Eleanor Neville, daughter of Ralph, first Earl of Westmoreland, by his second wife, both of Royal Descent, and had:

HENRY DE PERCY, third Earl of Northumberland, *k.* at Towton, 1461 ; *m.* Lady Eleanor, daughter of Richard, Baron Poynings, and had:

LADY MARGARET DE PERCY, who *m.* Sir William Gascoigne, of Gawthrope, Yorkshire, also of Royal Descent, and had:

LADY DOROTHY GASCOIGNE, who *m.* Sir Ninian de Markenfield, also of Royal Descent, and had:

LADY ALICE MARKENFIELD, who *m.* Robert Mauleverer, second son of Sir William Mauleverer, of Wothersome, Yorkshire, also of Royal Descent (*see* " Magna Charta Barons and their Descendants "), and had:

DOROTHY MAULEVERER, who *m.* John Kaye, of Woodsome, Yorkshire, also of Royal Descent, and had:

ROBERT KAYE, of Woodsome, *temp.* 1612, who *m.* Ann, daughter of John Flower, of Whitewell, and had:

GRACE KAYE,* who *m.* Sir Richard Saltonstall, of Huntwick, *b.* 1586, lord of the manor of Ledsham, near Leeds, England. He was one of the first-named associates of the original patentees of Massachusetts Bay in charter granted 4 May, 1628, also first named among the assist-

---

* The following ladies, members of the National Society of the Colonial Dames of America, are also of Royal Descent, through Grace Kaye :

MRS. FLEMING G. BAILEY, Georgia State Society.

MRS. ROBERT RANTOUL, Minnesota State Society.

MRS. NEAL RANTOUL, Massachusetts State Society.

MRS. EDMUND M. WHEELRIGHT, Massachusetts State Society.

ants appointed thereby, and also one of the original patentees of Connecticut, and came to America in April, 1630, and was founder of Watertown, Massachusetts. He returned to England, and was appointed ambassador to Holland, and was also a member of the high court of justice held to try the Duke of Hamilton and others for high treason. His eldest son by Grace Kaye:

RICHARD SALTONSTALL, of Ipswich, Massachusetts, *b.* at Woodsome, Yorkshire, 1610, *d.* at Hulme, England, 29 April, 1694; graduate of Emmanuel College, Cambridge; came to New England in 1630 with his father; was deputy to general court, 1635–7; assistant, 1637–49–64–80–82; was appointed by the general court sergeant-major in Colonel Endicott's Regiment, October, 1641. He *m.* Muriel, daughter of Brampton Gurdon, of Assington, County Suffolk, England; member of Parliament from Sudbury, 1620; high sheriff, 1629; and Muriel Sedley, his wife, also of Royal Descent, and had:

COLONEL NATHANIEL SALTONSTALL, of Haverhill, Massachusetts, eldest son, *b.* Ipswich, 1639, *d.* Haverhill, Massachusetts, 21 May, 1707; Colonel of the Essex Regiment; was assistant 1679–92; member of council under Sir Edmund Andros, also member of their Majesties' council under charter of William and Mary, 1689; judge of oyer and terminer court, 1692, but resigned, refusing to serve in witchcraft trials. He *m.*, 28 December, 1663, Elizabeth, daughter of Rev. John and Alice Ward, of Haverhill, and had:

1.—GOVERNOR GURDON SALTONSTALL, eldest son, *b.* 27 March, 1666, *d.* 20 September, 1724. He was ordained to the ministry and settled at New London, Connecticut, and was the governor of the Connecticut colony, 1707–24. He had by his first wife ("Early Connecticut Marriages," ii., 1), Jerusha, *d.* Boston, 25 July, 1697, daughter of James Richards, of Hartford:

I.—ELIZABETH SALTONSTALL, *b.* 1 May, 1690, who *m.* Richard Christophers, and had:

RICHARD CHRISTOPHERS, who *m.* Lucretia Bradley, and had:

ELIZABETH CHRISTOPHERS, who *m.* Captain Joseph Hurlburt and had:

HANNAH HURLBURT, *b.* 12 December, 1769, *d.* 1855, who *m.* Rev. William Patten, and had:

WILLIAM SAMUEL PATTEN, who *m.* Eliza Williams Bridgham, and had:

ELIZABETH BRIDGHAM PATTEN, *b.* 1831, who *m.*, 1860, Arthur Fenner Dexter, 1830–1886, and had:

ELIZABETH BRIDGHAM DEXTER, of Providence, a member of the Rhode Island Society of the Colonial Dames of America.

II.—SARAH SALTONSTALL, *b.* 8 April, 1694, who *m.*, first, John Gardiner, Jr., of New London, Connecticut (son of John Gardiner, third lord of Gardiner's Island manor), *d.* 15 January, 1725, and had:

JERUSHA GARDINER, who *m.*, 7 March, 1742, John Christophers, of New London ("Early Connecticut Marriages," ii., 19), and had: LUCRETIA CHRISTOPHERS, who *m.* John Mumford, Jr., of New London, and had:

CATHERINE MUMFORD, who *m.*, 5 January, 1800, Isaac Thompson, M.D., of Stratford and New London, Connecticut, and had:

ELLEN DOUGLAS THOMPSON, who *m.*, 16 April, 1833, Frederick Lennig, of Philadelphia, Pennsylvania, *b.* in Germany, only son of John Frederick and Margaret Antoinette (Geyger) Lennig, and had:

1.—MARGARET ANTOINETTE LENNIG, a member of the Pennsylvania Society of the Colonial Dames of America, Daughters of the American Revolution Society, Society of the Colonial Governors, the Mary Washington Memorial Association, Society of Mayflower Descendants, Society Daughters of the Cincinnati, who *m.*, 30 May, 1878, Joseph Henry Oglesby (son of Joseph Henry and Elizabeth (Hite) Oglesby, of Louisville, Kentucky), and had: *Joseph Henry*, *b.* 1 July, 1881.

2.—LUCRETIA CHRISTOPHERS LENNIG, of Philadelphia, a member of the Pennsylvania Society of the Colonial Dames of America.

GOVERNOR GURDON SALTONSTALL, 1666–1724, had by his second wife, Elizabeth, daughter of William Rosewell:

GENERAL GURDON SALTONSTALL, JR., of New London, fourth son, *b.* 22 December, 1708. He served as delegate to several colonial conventions; was a member of several committees of New London conducting Revolutionary affairs, and was appointed a brigadier general in 1776. He *m.*, 15 March, 1732, Rebecca, daughter of John Winthrop, F.R.S., *d.* London, 1747 (a son of Chief Justice Waite Still Winthrop, son of John Winthrop, governor of the Connecticut and New Haven Colonies, 1657–1676, son of John Winthrop, the "Father of the Massachusetts Colony," governor of Massachusetts Bay Colony, 1629–1649), and his wife, Anne, daughter of Joseph Dudley, president of the Colony of Massachusetts, New Hampshire and Maine, 1686, governor of Massachusetts Colony, *etc.*, son of Major-General Thomas Dudley, governor of Massachusetts Colony, 1634–1650, *etc.*, and had:

REBECCA SALTONSTALL, *b.* 31 December, 1734, who *m.*, 1 January, 1758, David Mumford, of New London, and had:

THOMAS MUMFORD, *b.* 13 July, 1770, *m.*, 20 January, 1795, Mary Sheldon Smith, of Litchfield, Connecticut, and had:

George Huntington Mumford, *b.* 21 July, 1805, *m.*, 24 May, 1836, Anne Elizabeth, daughter of Truman Hart, of Palmyra, New York, and had:

I.—Henrietta Saltonstall Mumford, a member of the New York Society of the Colonial Dames of America, who *m.*, April, 1890, Louis Cope Washburn, of Rochester, New York, and had: *Henrietta Mumford, Helen Carpenter,* and *Louis Mumford.*

II.—Helen Elizabeth Mumford, a member of the New York Society of the Colonial Dames of America, whq *m.*, 10 November, 1870, William L. Halsey, of Rochester, New York. *No issue.*

III.—George Hart Mumford, *m.*, 10 December, 1867, Sarah Dana, and had: *Gurdon S.* and *George Dana Mumford,* who *m.*, 25 April, 1894, Ethel Watts, and had: *George Hart, b.* January, 1895.

IV.—Mary Louise Mumford, who *m.*, 2 January, 1873, Edward Payson Fowler, M.D., of New York, and had: *Edward M.* and *Louise Mumford,* who *m.* Robert Miles Gignoux, and had: *Louise M.* and *Mildred.*

2.—Elizabeth Saltonstall, *d.* 1726, *m.*, secondly, 1692, Rev. Roland Cotton, of Sandwich, Massachusetts, 1667–1721–2, and had:

I.—Rev. John Cotton, D.D., the founder of Newton, Massachusetts, *m.*, 19 February, 1719, Mary Gibbs, and had:

Mary Cotton (widow of Rev. Mr. Cheny), who *m.*, secondly, 13 October, 1748, Rev. Dr. Joseph Pynchon, of Boston, 1705–1756, and had:

Margaret Pynchon, who *m.*, 28 April, 1779, Stephen Keeler, of Norwalk, Connecticut, and had:

I.—Mathers Keeler, who *m.*, 20 August, 1832, Serena Howard, and had:

Eugenia Mary Keeler, who *m.*, 19 September, 1866, Julius Frank Caulkins, and had:

Edith Serena Caulkins, a member of the Order of the Crown, who *m.* Lyman Francis Gray, of Buffalo, New York:

II.—Margaret Keeler, who *m.* Dr. Erastus Sergeant, Jr., of Lee and Stockbridge, Massachusetts, and had:

Mary Ann Sergeant, who *m.* Rev. Samuel Newbury, of Middlebury, Vermont, and had: *Samuel Sergeant, Katherine Sedgwick* (Mrs. Robb), *Egbert,* and

1.—Mary Ann Newbury, a member of the Massachusetts and Iowa Societies of the Colonial Dames of America, the Order of the Crown, *etc.,* who *m.* Judge Austin Adams, of Dubuque, Iowa, and had: *Annabel, Eugene, Herbert,* and *Cecilia.*

2.—FRANCES E. NEWBURY, a member of the Massachusetts and Michigan Societies of the Colonial Dames of America, who *m.* John J. Bagley, of Detroit, Michigan.

II.—JOANNA COTTON, 1694–1772, *m.* Rev. John Brown, *d.* 1742, and had: ABIGAIL BROWN, *m.* Rev. Edward Brooks, 174--1781, and had:

1.—PETER CHARDON BROOKS, of Boston, who *m.* Ann Gorham, and had: ABIGAIL BROWN BROOKS, *d.* 6 January, 1889, who *m.*, 3 September, 1829, Charles Francis Adams, of Quincy, Massachusetts, *b.* 18 August, 1809, *d.* 21 November, 1886, United States Minister to Great Britain, 1861–68, *etc.*, also of Royal Descent, son of John Quincy Adams, President of the United States, and a grandson of John Adams, President of the United States (p. 164), and had:

MARY ADAMS, a member of the Massachusetts Society of the Colonial Dames of America, who *m.* Henry Parker Quincy, of Boston, and had *Dorothy* and *Elinor.*

2.—JOANNA COTTON BROOKS, *m.* Nathaniel Hall, of Medford, Massachusetts, *b.* 1761, and had:

CAROLINE HALL, *m.* (his second wife) Rev. Francis Parkman, D.D., of Boston, 1788–1852, and had:

I.—FRANCIS PARKMAN, of Boston, 1823–1893, the historian, who *m.* Catherine Scollay, daughter of Dr. Jacob and Mary (Scollay) Bigelow, of Boston, and had:

GRACE PARKMAN, a member of the Massachusetts Society of the Colonial Dames of America, who *m.* Charles P. Coffin, of Longwood, Massachusetts, and had: *Francis Parkman, Miriam,* and *Mary Bigelow.*

II.—CAROLINE HALL PARKMAN, *b.* 30 June, 1825, who *m.* Rev. John Cordner, LL.D., of Boston, 1816–1894, and had:

CAROLINE PARKMAN CORDNER, of Boston, a member of the Massachusetts Society of the Colonial Dames of America.

THE ROYAL DESCENT

OF

MRS. ERASTUS GAYLORD PUTNAM,

OF ELIZABETH, NEW JERSEY.

CHARLEMAGNE, Emperor of the West=Lady Hildegarde of Savoy.

Louis I., King of France=Lady Judith of Bavaria.

Charles II., King of France=Lady Richildis (second wife).

Princess Judith of France=Baldwin I., Count of Flanders.

Baldwin II., Count of Flanders=Ethelwida, dau. Alfred the Great of England.

Arnoul, Count of Flanders=Lady Alix of Vermandois.

Baldwin III., Count of Flanders=Lady Matilda of Saxony.

Arnoul II., Count of Flanders=Lady Susanna d'Inree of Italy.

Baldwin IV., Count of Flanders=Lady Agiva of Luxemberg.

Baldwin V., Count of Flanders=Adela, gr. dau. of Hugh Capet.

Lady Matilda of Flanders=William I., King of England.

Henry I., King of England=Matilda, dau. Malcolm III., of Scotland.

Maud, Empress of Germany=Geoffroi, Count of Anjou.

Henry II., King of England=Eleanor, Duchess of Aquitaine.

John, King of England=Lady Isabel de Tailléfer.

Henry III., King of England=Lady Eleanor of Provence.

Edward I., King of England=Eleanor, dau. of Ferdinand III., of Castile.

Princess Joan Plantagenet=Ralph, Earl of Gloucester.

Thomas de Monthermer=(Name unknown.)

Lady Margaret de Monthermer=Sir John, Baron de Montacute.

John, Earl of Salisbury=Lady Maud Buxhull.

Thomas, Earl of Salisbury=Lady Eleanor de Holland.

Lady Alice de Montacute=Richard, Earl of Salisbury.

Lady Alice de Neville=Henry, Lord Fitzhugh.

Lady Elizabeth Fitzhugh=Sir William Parr, K.G.

William, Lord Parr, of Horton=Lady Mary Salisbury.

Lady Elizabeth Parr=Sir Nicholas de Woodhull, Bedfordshire.

Fulke Woodhull, of Thenford=Alice Coles.

Lawrence Woodhull, of Thenford=(Name unknown.)

Mary Woodhull=William Nicolls, of Islippe.

John Nicolls, of Islippe=Joane Grafton.

Rev. Matthias Nicolls, of Islippe=Martha Oakes.

Judge Matthias Nicolls, of New York=Abigail Johns.

William Nicoll, of Islip, L. I., N. Y.=Anne Van Rensselaer.

Benjamin Nicoll, of Islip, L. I., N. Y.=Charity Floyd.

Benjamin Nicoll, Jr., of N. York=Mary Magdelen Holland.

Prof. Samuel Nicoll, M.D., of N. York=Anne Fargie.

Frances Mary Nicoll=George Bloom Evertson, of Poughkeepsie.

Frances Mary Evertson, member of the National=William Amos Woodward, of New York.
Society of the Colonial Dames of America,

Mary Nicoll Woodward, member of the National=Erastus Gaylord Putnam, of Elizabeth, N. J.
Society of the Colonial Dames of America.
(Issue d. young.)

PEDIGREE LI.

HENRY III., King of England, had by his wife, Lady Eleanor, daughter of Raymond de Berenger, Count of Provence:

EDMUND PLANTAGENET, Earl of Leicester, Lancaster, and Chester, lord high steward, who had by his second wife, Lady Blanche, granddaughter of Louis VIII., King of France:

HENRY PLANTAGENET, Earl of Lancaster and Leicester, who m. Lady Maud, also of Royal Descent, daughter of Patrick de Chaworth, 1253–1282, and had:

LADY ELEANOR PLANTAGENET, who m., secondly (his second wife), Sir Richard Fitz-Alan, K.G., Earl of Arundel and Surrey, and had:

LADY ALICE FITZ-ALAN, who m. Sir Thomas de Holland, K.G., second Earl of Kent, marshal of England, also of Royal Descent, and had:

LADY ELEANOR DE HOLLAND, who m. (his first wife) Thomas de Montacute, last Earl of Salisbury, also of Royal Descent, and had:

LADY ALICE DE MONTACUTE, who m. Sir Richard de Nevill, K.G., created Earl of Salisbury, 4 May, 1442; lord great chamberlain of England, who was beheaded for siding with the Yorkists in 1461, and his head was fixed upon a gate of the city of York, also of Royal Descent, and had:

LADY ALICE DE NEVILLE (sister of Richard Neville, K.G., Earl of Salisbury and Warwick, the renowned " king maker "), who m. Henry, fifth Baron Fitzhugh, of Ravensworth, steward of the honor of Richmond and Lancaster, also of Royal Descent, d. 1472, and had:

LADY ELIZABETH FITZ-HUGH, who m. Sir William Parr, K.G., constable of England, also of Royal Descent, and had:

WILLIAM, LORD PARR, of Horton, Northampton, d. 1546, who was uncle of Katherine Parr, last wife of Henry VIII., of England. He was chamberlain to her Majesty, and was advanced to the peerage 23 December, 1543. He m. Lady Mary, daughter of Sir William Salisbury, and had:

LADY ELIZABETH PARR (she is also called Alice), who m. (his second wife) Sir Nicholas Woodhull, lord of Woodhull, county Bedford, d. 1532, and had by her (see the Northamptonshire Visitations, 1564 and 1618; the Yorkshire Visitations, 1584, and Dugdale's " Baronage "):

FULKE WOODHULL, of Thenford Manor, Northamptonshire, second son and heir, and eldest son by his father's second wife, who m. Alice, daughter of William Coles, or Colles, of Lye, or Leigh, county Worcester, and had·

LAWRENCE WOODHULL, younger son (brother of Nicholas, eldest son and heir apparent in 1618, who had five sons then living, his apparent heir being son Gyles, *b.* 1582, *see* "Miscellanæ Geneal. et Heraldica," iv., 417), father of:

1.—MARY WOODHULL, who *m.* (his second wife) William Nicolls, of Islippe, Northamptonshire, and had:

JOHN NICOLLS, who *m.* Joane, daughter and heir of George Grafton, and had:

REV. MATTHIAS NICOLLS, who *m.*, 1630, Martha Oakes, of Leicestershire, and had:

MATTHIAS NICOLLS, *b.* at Islippe, Northamptonshire, 1621, was a graduate of Cambridge University and a lawyer of the Inner Temple. He was appointed secretary of the commission "to visit the colonies and plantations known as New England," and commissioned captain of the military force, before leaving England, 1664; was secretary of the province of New York, 1664–87; member of the King's council, 1667–80; speaker of Provincial Assembly, 1683–4; judge of the court of admiralty, 1686; mayor of New York, 1672, and *d.* 22 December, 1687, and was buried at Cow Neck, Long Island. He *m.* Abigail Johns, who administered on his estate 22 July, 1693, and had:

WILLIAM NICOLL, commonly called "the Patentee," *b.* 1657, at Islippe, Northamptonshire, and educated for the bar. He came to America with his father in 1664, and was a lawyer of great prominence at New York. He was member of the Governor's council, New York, 1691–8; attorney-general of the province, 1687; member of the Provincial Assembly, 1701–23, and speaker, 1702–18. He purchased, 29 November, 1683, from Winnequaheagh, Sachem of Connectquut, a tract of land on Long Island, embracing originally one hundred square miles, but in consequence of sales made the quantity now owned by the family does not exceed forty thousand acres, comprising the Nicoll Manor, at Islip, Long Island. He also owned one-half of Shelter Island. He was vestryman of Trinity Church, New York, 1698–1702, and *d.* at Nicoll Manor in May, 1723. He *m.*, 1693, Anne, daughter of Jeremias Van Rensselaer, and widow of her cousin, Kiliaen Van Rensselaer, of Watervliet, New York, patroon of the lordship and manor of Rensselaerswyck, and had:

BENJAMIN NICOLL, *b.* at Islip, Long Island, 1694, who inherited from his father the Islip estate, known as Nicoll Manor, and devoted himself to its care, and *d.* in 1724. He *m.*, 1714, Charity, his first cousin, daughter of his aunt, Margaret Nicoll, and Richard Floyd, of Setaulket, Long Island (who *m.*, secondly, September 26, 1725, Rev. Dr. Samuel Johnson, first president of King's, afterwards Columbia, College, New York, and their son, Dr. William Samuel Johnson, was first president of Columbia College, New York), and had:

BENJAMIN NICOLL, JR., *b.* at Islip, Long Island, 17 March, 1718, graduated at Yale College in 1734. He was a lawyer, and successively incorporator, trustee, and governor of King's College, New York, a founder and trustee of the Society Library, New York, 1754, and a vestryman of Trinity Church, New York, 1751–60, and *d.* 15 April, 1760. He *m.* Mary Magdalen, daughter of Edward Holland, mayor of the city of New York, and had:

DR. SAMUEL NICOLL, *b.* 19 August, 1754, *d.* 2 February, 1796. He was a graduate of the Edinburgh University, 1776, and completed his medical studies in Paris, and was professor of chemistry in Columbia College, 1792–96. He *m.*, first, 1 June, 1782, Anne, his second cousin, daughter of Captain Winter Fargie, of the British army, and Eve, his wife, daughter of Henry Holland and his wife, Alida Beeckman, and had by her:

FRANCES MARY NICOLL, *b.* at Stratford, Connecticut, 17 December, 1785, *d.* 24 March, 1861; *m.*, 13 April, 1809 (his second wife), George Bloom Evertson, son of Jacob Evertson (descended from Admiral John Evertson, lieutenant-admiral of Zeeland, *k.* in battle against the English, 1666), and his wife, Margaret, daughter of George Bloom, and had:

FRANCES MARY EVERTSON, a member of the New Jersey Society of the Colonial Dames of America, Daughters of the American Revolution, Daughters of Holland Dames of New York, and hereditary life member of the National Mary Washington Memorial Association, *b.* at Poughkeepsie, New York, 26 April, 1811, *d.* in New York City, 15 March, 1899; *m.*, 4 December, 1828, William Amos Woodward, *b.* in New London, Connecticut, 21 March, 1801, *d.* at Keewaydin, Orange county, New York, 19 September, 1883, and had:

I.—GEORGE EVERTSON WOODWARD, *m.* Eliza Bethia Deodata Mortimer. *Issue.*

II.—FRANCIS WILLIAM WOODWARD, a member of the Society of Colonial Wars, who *m.*, 1 October, 1862, Anne Jay (daughter of General George Patton Delaplaine, of Madison, Wisconsin), a member of the New Jersey Society of the Colonial Dames of America, a descendant of Governor William Livingston, of New Jersey, and had:

HARRIET B. WOODWARD, a member of the New Jersey Society of the Colonial Dames of America, who *m.*, at Eau Claire, Wisconsin, 18 October, 1899, Caleb Forbes Davis, of Keokuk, Iowa.

III.—MARY NICOLL WOODWARD, a member of the New Jersey Society of the Colonial Dames of America, Society Daughters of the American Revolution, Huguenot Society of America, Daughters of Holland Dames, and hereditary life member of the National Mary Washington Memorial Association, who *m.*, 30 January, 1867, Erastus Gaylord Putnam, of Elizabeth, New Jersey, descended from John and Priscilla Putnam, who settled in Salem, Massachusetts, in 1634, and had four children, who died young.

IV.—HARRIET BOWEN WOODWARD, *m.* John Wylie Barrow. *Issue.*

2.—RICHARD WOODHULL, *b.* at Thenford, 13 September, 1620, removed to Long Island, New York, about 1647, and purchased, in 1665, 108,000 acres, now the site of Brookhaven. (*See* Thompson's " History of Long Island," iii., 399 ; " N. Y. Geneal. and Biog. Record," iii., 10 ; iv., 54–8.) He was made justice of the Court of Assizes in 1666, and dying in October, 1690, left issue by his wife Deborah :

RICHARD WOODHULL, of Setauket, *b.* 9 October, 1649, *d.* 18 October, 1699, a justice of the Court of Assizes in 1678. He *m.*, 19 August, 1680, Temperance, daughter of Rev. Jonah Fordham, of Southampton, Long Island (*see* Pelletreau's " Early Long Island Wills," his wife, " Temperance Topping," was executrix to his will, proved 28 May, 1700), and had :

NATHANIEL WOODHULL, of Mastic, Long Island, second son, *d.* 9 March, 1760 ; *m.*, 1716, Sarah, daughter of Richard Smith, of Smithtown, Long Island, and had : *Hannah* (who *m.*, 7 October, 1740, Selah Strong, of Brookhaven, Long Island, and had : *Major Nathaniel Strong*, *m.* Amy Brewster, and had : *Selah*), and

1.—CAPTAIN EBENEZER WOODHULL, *d.* 4 October, 1803, who *m.* Abigail, *d.* 21 November, 1829, daughter of Hezekiah Howell, and had :

RUTH WOODHULL, 1770–1810, who *m.* Selah Strong, aforesaid, and had :

SCHUYLER STRONG, who *m.* Frances Cruger, and had :

RUTH WOODHULL STRONG, a member of the Pennsylvania Society of the Colonial Dames of America, who *m.* Benjamin Dorrance, of Dorrancetown, Luzerne county, Pennsylvania, and had : *Anne, Frances,* and *Ruth, d.* 13 February, 1895.

2.—GENERAL NATHANIEL WOODHULL, of Mastic, eldest son, *b.* 30 December, 1722, *d.* in a prison-ship, 20 September, 1776. Prior to the Revolution he had served under both Amherst and Abercrombie during the war with France. At the breaking out of the American Revolution he was chosen president of the Provincial Congress of New York, and was twice re-elected. After the battle of Long Island he was made a prisoner, and was assassinated because he refused to say " God save the King." He *m.*, 1761, Ruth, *d.* 1822, daughter of Nicoll Floyd, of Mastic (and sister of General William Floyd, a signer of the Declaration of Independence), and had :

ELIZABETH WOODHULL, only child, *b.* 30 November, 1762, *d.* 14 September, 1839, who *m.*, first, Henry Nicoll, of New York, and had :

ELIZA WILLETTS NICOLL, who *m.* Richard Smith, 5th, and had :

JOHN LAWRENCE SMITH, who *m.* Mary Nicoll Clinch, and had :

1.—CORNELIA STEWART SMITH, a member of the New York Society of the Colonial Dames of America, who *m.* Prescott Hall Butler, of New York City, and had : *Lawrence Smith, Charles Stewart,* and *Susan Louisa.*

2.—LOUISA NICOLL SMITH, who *m.* F. S. Osborne.

3.—KATE ANNETTE SMITH, who *m.* J. B. Wetherill.

4.—ELLA BATAVIA SMITH, a member of the New York Society of the Colonial Dames of America, who *m.* Devereux Emmet, of New York.

5.—BESSIE SMITH, a member of the New York Society of the Colonial Dames of America, who *m.* Stanford White, of St. James, Long Island, New York, and had : *Lawrence Grant.*

ELIZABETH WOODHULL, 1762–1839; *m.*, secondly, General John Smith, of St. George's Manor, Suffolk, Long Island, New York, member of Congress, United States Senator, *etc.*, and had :

SARAH AUGUSTA TANGIER SMITH, only daughter, *b.* May 19, 1794, *d.* 13 November, 1877 ; *m.*, 2 June, 1816, John L. Lawrence, member of the New York State Senate, comptroller of New York City, minister to Sweden, *etc.*, and had :

1.—JUDGE ABRAHAM R. LAWRENCE, of New York City, fifth son, a justice of the Supreme Court of the State of New York for over twenty-five years. He *m.* Eliza, only daughter of William Miner, M.D., of New York City, and had :

RUTH LAWRENCE, of New York City, only daughter, a member of the New York Society of the Colonial Dames of America.

2.—ELIZABETH LAWRENCE, who *m.*, 1837, Alfred Newbold Lawrence, of New York, *b.* 1813, also of Royal Descent, and had :

HANNAH NEWBOLD LAWRENCE, of New York City, a member of the New York Society of the Colonial Dames of America.

3.—LYDIA LAWRENCE, who *m.* William Thurston Horn, of New York, and had :

ANNIE L. HORN, of New York City, a member of the New York Society of the Colonial Dames of America.

THE ROYAL DESCENT

OF

MRS. SELDEN STUART WRIGHT,

OF SAN FRANCISCO, CAL.

EDWARD I., King of England꞊Princess Eleanor of Castile.

Princess Elizabeth Plantagenet꞊Humphrey de Bohun, Earl of Hereford.

Lady Margaret de Bohun꞊Hugh de Courtenay, Earl of Devon.

Lady Elizabeth de Courtenay꞊Sir Andrew Luttrell, of Chilton.

Lady Elizabeth Luttrell꞊John Stratton, of Weston.

Elizabeth Stratton꞊John Andrews, of Stoke.

Elizabeth Andrews꞊Thomas Wyndsore.

Sir Andrews Wyndsore, of Stanwell꞊Lady Elizabeth Blount.

Lady Edith Wyndsore꞊George Ludowe, of Hill Deverill.

Thomas Ludlow, of Dinton꞊Jane Pyle, of Bopton, Wilts.

Gabriel Ludlow, 1587-1639꞊Phyllis ——.

Sarah Ludlow (fourth wife)꞊John Carter, of Gloucester Co., Va.

Robert Carter, of " Carotoman "꞊Elizabeth (Landon) Willis.

Mary Carter꞊George Braxton, of King and Queen Co., Va.

Carter Braxton, of " Elsing Green," Va.꞊Judith Robinson.

Mary Braxton꞊Robert Page, of " Broad Neck," Va.

Sarah Walker Page꞊Humphrey Brooke, of Spottsylvania Co., Va.

Anne Aylett Brooke꞊Oliver Abbott Shaw, Lexington, Mass.

Joanna Maynard Shaw, member of the National꞊Selden Stuart Wright, of Essex Co., Va.
Society of the Colonial Dames of America, the
Order of the Crown, etc. *Issue* (see pp. 184, 219).

PEDIGREE LII.

HENRY I., King of **France**, had by his third wife, Anne of Russia, of Royal Descent:

Hugh the Great, Duke of France and Burgundy, *etc.*, who had by his wife, Lady Adelheid de Vermandois, also of Royal Descent:

Lady Isabel de Vermandois, *d.* 1131, widow of Robert de Beaumont, Earl of Mellent and Leicester, *d.* 1118, who *m.*, secondly, William de Warren, second Earl of Surrey, and had:

Lady Gundreda de Warren, who *m.*, first, Roger de Bellomont de Newburg, second Earl of Warwick, *d.* 1153, and had:

Waleran de Newburg, fourth Earl of Warwick, *d.* 1205, who *m.*, secondly, Lady Alice, daughter of John d'Harcourt, Knt., and widow of John de Limsey, and had by her:

Lady Alice de Newburg, *m.* William, Baron de Mauduit, of Hanslape, heritable chamberlain of the Exchequer, *d.* 1256, and had:

Lady Isabel de Mauduit, who *m.* William, fifth baron of Beauchamp of Elmly, *d.* 1268, and had:

Walter de Beauchamp, first baron of Alcester and Powyke, third son (brother of William, created Earl of Warwick), steward to the household of King Edward I., *d.* 1306. He *m.* Lady Alice, daughter of Ralph, Baron de Toni, of Flamsted, Herts, and his wife, Lady Alice de Bohun, also of Royal Descent, and had:

Giles de Beauchamp, fourth baron of Alcester, in Warwickshire and Powyke, in Gloucestershire, *temp.* 14 Edward III., third son, who had:

Roger de Beauchamp, second son, first Baron Beauchamp, of Bletsho, chamberlain to the household of King Edward III., *d.* 1379, who had by his first wife, Sybil, daughter of Sir William de Patshull:

Roger, second Baron Beauchamp, of Bletsho and Lydiard-Tregoze, who had:

Sir John, third Baron Beauchamp, of Bletsho, *d.* 1413, who had:

Lady Margaret de Beauchamp, who *m.*, first, Sir Oliver de St. John, Knt., of Penmark, in Glamorganshire. (Her second husband was John de Beaufort, Duke of Somerset, by whom she had: Lady Margaret, who *m.* Edward Tudor, Earl of Richmond, and had: Henry VII., King of England.) By her first husband, Lady Margaret had:

14   (217)

SIR JOHN DE ST. JOHN, K.B., of Penmark, eldest son, who *m.* Lady Alice, daughter of Sir Thomas Bradshaw, and had:

SIR JOHN DE ST. JOHN, of Bletsho, Bedfordshire, who *m.* Lady Sybil, daughter of Morgan ap Jenkyns ap Philip, and had:

SIR JOHN DE ST. JOHN, Knt., who *m.* Lady Margaret, daughter of Sir William Walgrave,. Knt., and had by her:

OLIVER ST. JOHN, created, in January, 1559, Lord St. John, of Bletsho, who had by his wife, Agnes Fisher:

THOMAS ST. JOHN, of Bletsho, younger son, who had:

SIR OLIVER ST. JOHN, Knt., member of Parliament, of Caysho, Bedfordshire, who *m.* Sarah, daughter of Edward Bulkley, of Odell, Bedfordshire, and had:

LADY ELIZABETH ST. JOHN,* *b.* 1605, *d.* at Lyme, Connecticut, 3 March, 1677, who *m.*, 6 August, 1629 (his second wife), Rev. Samuel Whiting, D.D., *b.* 20 November, 1597, at Boston, Lincolnshire (*see* Thompson's "History of Boston"). They came to America in 1636, and settled at Lynn, Massachusetts, where he *d.* 11 December, 1679 (*see* "Memoir of Rev. Samuel Whiting, D.D.," by William Whiting, of Boston; "American Heraldic Journal," i., 58, and Drake's "History of Boston"). Rev. Samuel Whiting had by Elizabeth, his wife:

1.—REV. SAMUEL WHITING, of Billerica, Massachusetts, *b.* Shirbeck, England, 1630, *d.* 1713; *m.*, 12 November, 1656, Dorcas, *b.* 1 November, 1637, daughter of Leonard Chester, of Wethersfield, and had:

I.—OLIVER WHITING, *b.* 1665, *d.* 1736; *m.*, 1690, Anne Danforth, *b.* 8 March, 1668, *d.* 13 August, 1737, and had:

DORCAS WHITING, *d.* 21 May, 1763, *m.*, 17 March, 1720 (his third wife), Joshua Abbott, *b.* 16 June, 1685, *d.* 11 February, 1769, and had:

OLIVER ABBOTT, *b.* 26 March, 1727, *d.* 10 April, 1796; *m.*, 13 February, 1752, Joanna French, and had:

JOANNA ABBOTT, *b.* 24 July, 1755, *m.* 21 May, 1776, Simon Winship, *b.* 2 November, 1749, *d.* 4 January, 1813, and had:

JOANNA WINSHIP, *b.* 5 May, 1777, *d.* 10 March, 1848; *m.*, about 1798, Darius Shaw, and had:

OLIVER ABBOTT SHAW, *b.* May, 1799, *d.* March, 1855; *m.*, 27 De-

---

* The following ladies, members of the National Society of the Colonial Dames of America, are also of Royal Descent, through Elizabeth St. John:

MRS. MANNING F. FORCE, Ohio State Society.

MRS. JOHN C. GRAY, Massachusetts State Society.

MISS JULIA LOUISE ROBINSON, Pennsylvania State Society.

cember, 1825, Ann Aylett Brooke, also of Royal Descent, *b.* 16 January, 1808, *d.* 2 June, 1845, and had:

1.—SARAH COLUMBIA BRAXTON SHAW, *b.* 4 July, 1837, *d.* May, 1872; *m.*, 1 January, 1869, Albert Henry Rose, and had:

ANNA BROOKE ROSE, of Alameda, California, a member of the Virginia and California Societies of the Colonial Dames of America.

2.—JOANNA MAYNARD SHAW, of San Francisco, *b.* 26 May, 1830, member of the Virginia and California Societies of the Colonial Dames of America, who *m.*, 15 October, 1846, Selden Stuart Wright, of Essex county, Virginia, *b.* 7 March, 1822, *d.* 26 February, 1893, and had:

I.—MARY STUART WRIGHT, *b.* Lexington, Holmes county, Mississippi, 17 August, 1847, *d.* San Rafael, California, 7 September, 1878; *m.*, 21 November, 1867, William B. Hooper, *b.* 1835, and had:

1.—MARY STUART HOOPER, *b.* 15 August, 1868, a member of the Virginia and California Societies of the Colonial Dames of America, who *m.*, March, 1889, Cavalier Hamilton Jouett, of San Francisco, *d.* 9 October, 1898, and had: *William Hooper, b.* 9 December, 1889, and *John Hamilton, b.* 14 May, 1892.

2.—CATHERINE BURCHELL HOOPER, *b.* 26 November, 1869, *d.* April, 1888.

3.—GEORGE KENT HOOPER, *b.* 22 April, 1871.

4.—EULALIE HOOPER, *b.* 1873, *d.* 1877.

5.—SELDEN STUART, *b.* 6 November, 1874; 6. ROSA, *b.* 19 July, 1876.

II.—ROBERT WALKER WRIGHT, *b.* 27 September, 1848, Lexington, Mississippi, *d.* 11 July, 1850.

III.—COLONEL STUART SELDEN WRIGHT, of Fresno, California, *b.* Yazoo City, Mississippi, 5 November, 1850; *m.*, 30 April, 1873, Maria Byrd Hopkins, a member of the Virginia and California Societies of the Colonial Dames of America, also of Royal Descent (p. 57), and had:

LOUISE KIMBALL WRIGHT, *b.* 6 December, 1874, a member of the Virginia and California Societies of the Colonial Dames of America, who *m.*, 7 June, 1895, John Mannen McClure, of Oakland, California, and had: *Wright Mannen, b.* 7 April, 1896.

IV.—ANN AYLETTE BROOKE WRIGHT, of Haywards, Alameda county, California, *b.* 9 January, 1853, Yazoo City, Mississippi, a member of the Virginia and California Societies of the Colonial Dames of America.

V.—GEORGE THOMAS WRIGHT, of San Francisco, California, *b.* Yazoo county, Mississippi, 22 March, 1855; *m.* Sophie Landsburger, and had : *Cedrie, b.* 9 April, 1889.

VI.—SARAH MAYNARD WRIGHT, *b.* Carroll county, Mississippi, 26 May, 1857, *d.* in San Francisco, California, 10 August, 1860.

VII.—ELIZA SHAW WRIGHT, *b.* Carroll county, Mississippi, 12 June, 1859, a member of the Virginia and California Societies of the Colonial Dames of America, who *m.*, in San Francisco, in April, 1881, John Drury Tallant, of San Francisco, and had :

> 1.—ELISE, *b.* 15 April, 1883 ; 2. DRURY, *b.* November, 1885 ; 3. SELDEN S., *b.* 1 March, 1887, *d.* 20 January, 1897 ; 4. JOHN D., *b.* 17 April, 1888.

VIII.—PAGE BRAXTON WRIGHT, *b.* San Francisco, 27 January, 1863, *d.* 12 May, 1864.

IX.—RALPH KIRKHAM WRIGHT, *b.* San Francisco, 24 April, 1865.

X.—ROBERTA EVELYN LEE WRIGHT, *b.* 30 January, 1868, *m.*, 26 November, 1892, George H. Hillmann, of Alameda, California, and had :

> 1.—MARY SELDEN, *b.* 6 December, 1893 ; 2. KATHERINE, *b.* March, 1897.

XI.—WILLIAM HAMMOND WRIGHT, *b.* 4 November, 1871.

XII.—BROOKE MAYNARD WRIGHT, *b.* Geneva, Switzerland, 30 January, 1877.

II.—SAMUEL WHITING, who had by his wife, Elizabeth :

ELIZABETH WHITING, who *m.* Rev. Samuel Ruggles, of Billerica, and had :

ELIZABETH RUGGLES (widow of Samuel Dummer, of Wilmington), *b.* 21 June, 1707, who *m.*, secondly, 29 May, 1739 (*see* "N. E. His. Geneal. Reg.," xii., 339), Rev. Daniel Rogers, of Littleton, Massachusetts, *b.* at Ipswich, Massachusetts, 17 October, 1706, *d.* 22 November, 1782, a descendant of Governor Thomas Dudley, Major-General Daniel Dennison, Rev. Dr. John Rogers, president of Harvard College, 1676, *etc.*, and had :

1.—JEREMIAH DUMMER ROGERS, of Charlestown, 1743–1784, who *m.*, 25 December, 1769, Bathsheba Thatcher, also of Royal Descent, and had :

> MARGARET ROGERS, 1778–1858, who *m.*, 1804, Jonathan Chapman, of Boston, *d.* 1832, and had :

JONATHAN CHAPMAN, 1807–1848, mayor of the city of Boston, 1840–42, who *m.*, 25 April, 1832, Lucinda, daughter of Jonathan Dwight, and had:

FLORENCE CHAPMAN, *b.* 1847, a member of the Massachusetts Society of the Colonial Dames of America, who *m.*, 1872, Henry Rogers Dalton, of Boston, and had: *Alice, Philip Spalding, Susan Dexter, Florence, d.* 1890, and *Ellen Bancroft.*

2.—SARAH ROGERS, *b.* February, 1755, *d.* 5 July, 1835, who *m.*, 8 May, 1784 (his second wife), Samuel Parkman, of Boston, *b.* 22 August, 1751, *d.* 11 June, 1824, and had:

I.—REV. FRANCIS PARKMAN, D.D., of Boston, *b.* 3 June, 1788, *d.* 12 November, 1852, who *m.*, secondly, Caroline Hall, *d.* August, 1871, also of Royal Descent, and had by her:

1.—FRANCIS PARKMAN, of Boston, 1823–1893, the historian, who *m.* Catherine Bigelow, and had: *Francis, Katherine S.*, and

GRACE PARKMAN, a member of the Massachusetts Society of the Colonial Dames of America, who *m.* Charles P. Coffin, of Longwood, Massachusetts. *Issue.*

2.—CAROLINE HALL PARKMAN, *b.* 30 June, 1825, who *m.* Rev. John Cordner, LL.D., of Boston, 1816–1894, and had: *Mary Agnes, Elizabeth P.*, and

CAROLINE PARKMAN CORDNER, of Boston, a member of the Massachusetts Society of the Colonial Dames of America.

II.—ELIZABETH WILLARD PARKMAN, *b.* 31 March, 1785, *d.* 14 April, 1853, who *m.*, 2 February, 1809, Robert Gould Shaw, *d.* 3 May, 1853, and had:

SAMUEL PARKMAN SHAW, *b.* 19 November, 1813, *d.* 7 December, 1869, who *m.* Hannah Buck, and had eleven children, of whom:

I.—HANNAH BLAKE SHAW, a member of the Massachusetts Society of the Colonial Dames of America.

II.—MRS. GRANT WALKER, of Boston, Massachusetts, a member of the Order of the Crown.

2.—ELIZABETH WHITING, 1645–1733, who *m.* Rev. Jeremiah Hobart, of Haddam, Connecticut, *b.* Haverhill, England, 6 April, 1630, *d.* 1715–16, son of Rev. Peter Hobart, 1604–1679, and had:

DOROTHY HOBART, 1679–1733, who *m.*, first, 19 April, 1704, Daniel Mason, of Norwich, Connecticut, *d. ante* 1707, and had:

JEREMIAH MASON, of Norwich, Connecticut, 1705–1779; *m.*, 1727, Mary, 1704–1799, daughter of Thomas Clark, of Haddam, and had:

COLONEL JEREMIAH MASON, of Lebanon, 1730–1813; *m.*, 1754, his cousin, Elizabeth, daugther of James and Anna Fitch, and had:

ELIZABETH MASON, *m.*, 1786, her cousin, Judge John Griswold Hillhouse, of Montville, Connecticut, *d.* 1806, and had:

MARIAN HILLHOUSE, who *m.* Elias W. Williams, and had:

MARY ELIZABETH WILLIAMS, *b.* 23 January, 1825, *d.* 12 July, 1897, who *m.*, 14 October, 1857, William Fitch, of Fitchville, Connecticut, and had:

SARAH GRISWOLD FITCH, a member of the New York Society of the Colonial Dames of America, who *m.*, 14 July, 1897, Francis Hillhouse, of New Haven, Connecticut, and had: *Mary Fitch, b.* 15 April 1898.

DOROTHY HOBART, 1679–1733, *m.*, secondly, 1 October, 1707, Hezekiah Brainerd, of Haddam, *b.* 24 May, 1680, *d.* 24 May, 1727, a member of the governor's council of Connecticut, 1723, *etc.*, and had: *Rev. Nehemiah Brainerd*, 1712–1744 (*m.* Elizabeth Fiske), and

I.—DOROTHY BRAINERD, *b.* 23 February, 1710, who *m.* Lieutenant David Smith, and had:

JERUSHA SMITH, *m.* Ezra Brainerd, of Haddam, Connecticut, *b.* 17 August, 1744, a member of the general assembly, 1777–1818, and had:

CALVIN BRAINERD, of Haddam, *b.* 23 September, 1778, *m.* Sarah, daughter of Captain Nehemiah Brainerd (son of the aforesaid Rev. Nehemiah Brainerd), *b.* 1741, a member of the general assembly, and Sarah Brainerd, his wife, and had:

CORDELIA BRAINERD, *b.* 30 March, 1814, *m.* Rev. Eleazar Cady Thomas, D.D., and had:

MARY HALSEY THOMAS, *b.* Gates, Monroe county, New York, 29 August, 1842, a member of the California Society of the Colonial Dames of America, who *m.*, in San Francisco, 25 October, 1880, John R. Jarboe, of Santa Cruz, California.

II.—MARTHA BRAINERD, *b.* Haddam, 1 September, 1716, *d.* 11 October, 1754, who *m.*, 2 August, 1738, Major-General Joseph Spencer, *b.* 3 October, 1714, *d.* 13 January, 1789, and had:

JOSEPH SPENCER, *d.* Vienna, West Virginia, 11 May, 1824; *m.*, 1777, Deborah Selden, *b.* Lynn, Connecticut, 29 December, 1753, *d.* Vienna, 25 August, 1825, and had:

ELIZABETH SPENCER, *b.* Vienna, 17 September, 1786, *d.* Detroit, Michigan, 31 March, 1853; *m.* Lewis Cass, Governor of Michigan, *etc.*, *b.* Exeter, New Hampshire, 9 October, 1782, *d.* Detroit, 17 June, 1866, and had:

MATILDA FRANCES CASS, *b.* Detroit, 11 July, 1818, *d.* London, England, 16 November, 1898, who *m.*, 19 September, 1839, Henry Ledyard, *b.* New York, 5 March, 1812, *d.* London, England, 7 June, 1880, son of Benjamin Ledyard, 1779–1811, and his wife, Susan French, daughter of Henry Brockholst Livingston, of New York, 1757–1823, and had :

ELIZABETH CASS LEDYARD, of Colorado Springs, Colorado, a member of the Rhode Island Society of the Colonial Dames of America, *b.* 1 October, 1840, who *m.*, 9 April, 1862, Francis Wayland Goddard, *b.* 5 May, 1833, *d.* 16 May, 1889, who was also of Royal Descent, as follows: *William Arnold*, of Rhode Island, 1587–1676 (see p. 13) had *Joanna Arnold*, who *m.* Zachariah Rhodes (see p. 15), and had : *Rebecca Rhodes*, who *m.*, first, 3 February, 1672, Nicholas Power, *d.* Providence, 19 December, 1675, and had: *Nicholas Power, Jr.*, *d.* Providence, 18 May, 1734; *m.* Mary Tillinghast, *d.* 13 November, 1769, and had: *Hope Power*, *b.* 4 January, 1701, *d.* 8 June, 1792; *m.* James Brown, *d.* Providence, 27 April, 1739, and had: *Nicholas Brown*, of Providence, *b.* 28 July, 1729, *d.* 29 May, 1791; *m.* 2 May, 1762, Rhoda Jenckes, *d.* 16 December, 1783, and had : *Hope Brown*, *b.* 22 February, 1773, *d.* 21 August, 1855 ; *m.* Thomas Pointer Ives, *d.* Providence, 30 April, 1835, and had : *Charlotte Rhoda Ives*, who *m.*, 22 May, 1821, William Giles Goddard, *d.* Providence, 16 February. 1846, and had : *Francis Wayland Goddard*, 1833–89, who had by his wife, Elizabeth Cass Ledyard, aforesaid :

1.—CHARLOTTE IVES GODDARD, *b.* 1 March, 1863, a member of the Rhode Island Society of the Colonial Dames of America, who *m.*, 12 October, 1887, Amos Lockwood Danielson, of Providence, Rhode Island, and had : *Henry Ledyard*, *b.* 21 July, 1888.

2.—HENRY LEDYARD GODDARD, *b.* at Providence, Rhode Island, 23 November, 1866, *d.* at Colorado Springs, Colorado, 30 August, 1893.

3.—REV. JOSEPH WHITING, of Southampton, Long Island, New York, *b.* Lynn, 6 April, 1641, *d.* 7 April, 1723. He *m.*, first, 11 November, 1646, Sarah, daughter of Judge Thomas Danforth, deputy governor of Massachusetts, 1678–84, and president of Maine, 1692, and had by her :

I.—REV. JOHN WHITING, of Concord, Massachusetts, *b.* 20 January, 1681, *d.* 4 May, 1752. He *m.*, 1712, Mary, *d.* at Concord, 29 May, 1731, aged 42 years, daughter of Rev. John Cotton, of Hampton, New Hamp, shire, *d.* 1710 son of Rev. Seaborn Cotton, and grandson of Rev. John Cotton, of Boston, Mass., and his wife, Anne, daughter of Captain Thomas Lake, of Boston, and a descendant of Governor Simeon Bradstreet and Governor Thomas Dudley, of Massachusetts, and had :

JUDGE THOMAS WHITING, of Concord, Massachusetts, *b.* 25 June, 1717, *d.* 1776 ; *m.*, 25 March, 1742, Lydia, daughter of Rev. Thomas and Lydia (Richardson) Parker, of Dracut, Massachusetts, and had :

1.—MARY WHITING, *b.* 5 July, 1743, who *m.*, first, 17 April, 1766, Captain William Barron, of Concord, who served under General Amherst in Canada, and in the Northeast Provinces, 1755–63, *d.* at Petersham, Massachusetts, and had:

MARY AUGUSTA BARRON, who *m.*, 27 February, 1800, Stalham Williams, of Dalton, Massachusetts, and Utica, New York, and had:

1.—FRANCES LUCRETIA WILLIAMS, *d.* 29 February, 1884, *m.*, 3 January, 1821, Captain Richard Winslow Sherman, of Vergennes, Vermont, *d.* 22 March, 1868, and had:

CORNELIA FRANKLIN SHERMAN, a member of the New York Society of the Colonial Dames of America, who *m.*, first, 2 January, 1853, William Thomas Mumford, of Rochester, New York, *d.* 10 April, 1856, and *m.*, secondly, 29 January, 1877, William Bennett Jackson, of Utica, New York, *d.* 28 December, 1890.

2.—SARAH TILESTON NEWTON WILLIAMS, who *m.*, first, 22 February, 1846, David Scoville, of Rochester, New York, *d.* 1847, and *m.*, secondly, June, 1852, Thomas H. Wood, of Utica, *d.* Paris, France, 1874, and had:

SARAH ELIZABETH SCOVILLE, a member of the New York Society of the Colonial Dames of America, who *m.*, 30 November, 1875, Wallace Clarke, M.D., of Montreal, Canada, and Utica, New York, and had: *Wallace Roxburgh* and *Thomas Wood.*

2.—JOHN LAKE WHITING, *b.* Concord, 22 July, 1755, *d.* Lancaster, Massachusetts; *m.*, 1782, Olive, 1762–1842, daughter of Ross Wyman, and had:

RELIEF WHITING, *b.* Shrewsbury, Massachusetts, 11 July, 1783, *d.* 7 December, 1851; *m.*, 24 February, 1805, at Carlisle, Massachusetts, Reuben Foster Blood, and had:

CAROLINE BLOOD, *b.* Carlisle, 4 December, 1805, *d.* Davenport, Iowa, 1 October, 1890; *m.*, 2 December, 1835, Rev. Julius Alexander Reed, D.D., *b.* Windsor, Connecticut, 16 January, 1809, *d.* Davenport, Iowa, 27 August, 1890, and had:

1. ANNA REED, *b.* Wyeth, Illinois, 30 August, 1836, member of the Society of the Mayflower Descendants, the Order of the Crown, *etc.*, who *m.*, at Grinnell, Iowa, 16 December, 1861, Henry Washington Wilkinson, of Providence, Rhode Island, *b.* Manville, Rhode Island, 20 August, 1835, *d.* Franklin, Massachusetts, 6 May, 1898, and had: I. *Henry Lawrence, b.* 10 August, 1865, *m.*, 4 June, 1896, Bertha Sandfred, of Bridgeport, Connecticut; II. *Alfred Hall, b.* 29 May, 1868,

m., 19 November, 1895, Elizabeth Burrows Kenyon, of Providence, Rhode Island; III. *Anna Reed, b.* 10 January, 1870, *m.*, 9 October, 1895, Edward Harris Rathburn, of Woonsocket, Rhode Island, and had: *Rachel Harris, b.* 13 September, 1897.

2.—ROSANNA REED, *b.* 11 August, 1839, *d.* 24 April, 1840.

3. MARY REED, *b.* Fairfield, Iowa, 9 February, 1843, a member of the Massachusetts and Iowa Societies of the Colonial Dames of America, Society of Mayflower Descendants, *etc.*, who *m.*, 17 August, 1863, Samuel Francis Smith, Jr., of Davenport, Iowa, *b.* Waterville, Maine, 5 September, 1836, son of Rev. Samuel Francis Smith, D.D., of Boston, Massachusetts, the author of the national anthem, "America," and had: *Anna Reed, b.* Davenport, 15 September, 1870.

II.—BENJAMIN WHITING, *b.* 1694, *d.* at Wallingford, Connecticut, 2 October, 1773; *m.*, 30 May, 1723, Rebecca, daughter of John and Mary (Mason) Parmlee, and had:

ABIGAIL WHITING, *b.* 7 September, 1736, who *m.*, 11 May, 1757, Dringon Andrews, *b.* Meriden, Connecticut, 27 August, 1730, *d.* 1 June, 1807, and had:

WHITING ANDREWS, *b.* Meriden, 23 March, 1764, *d.* Claramount, New Hampshire, 18 December, 1811; *m.* Lucy, daughter of Benjamin Curtis, of Meriden, and had:

ABIGAIL ANDREWS, *b.* 25 January, 1792, *d.* at Hampton, New York, 26 July, 1856, who *m.*, 1816, Mason Hulett, Jr., *b.* Belcherstown, Massachusetts, 19 February, 1775, *d.* Hampton, New York, 5 October, 1847, also of Royal Descent, and had:

HANNAH LUCY HULETT, *b.* at Hampton, 4 July, 1817; *d.* at Rutland, 28 January, 1892, who *m.*, 23 June, 1837, Henry Hitchcock, of Rutland, Vermont, 1805–71, also of Royal Descent, and had:

ABIGAIL JANE HITCHCOCK, *b.* Clarendon Springs, Vermont, 3 May, 1843, a member of the Massachusetts Society of the Colonial Dames of America, the Order of the Crown, *etc.*, who *m.*, 15 February, 1866, Horace Hoxie Dyer, of Rutland, Vermont, and had: *Captain Horace Edward*, a member of the Order of Runnemede, *etc.*, *b.* 16 April, 1870.

THE ROYAL DESCENT

OF

MRS. WILLIAM ALVORD,

OF SAN FRANCISCO, CAL.

PHILIP III., King of France⊤Princess Isabella of Arragon.

EDWARD I., King of England⊤Princess Margaret of France.

Edmund, Earl of Kent⊤Margaret de Wake.   ROBERT BRUCE,⊤Elizabeth de Burgh.
King of Scots

Lady Joan Plantagenet⊤Thomas, Earl of Kent.   Matilda of Scotland⊤Thomas Isaac, Esq.

Thomas, Earl of Kent⊤Alice Fitzalan.   Joanna Isaac⊤John, Lord of Lorn.

Margaret de Holland⊤John, Earl of Somerset.   Isabel d'Ergadia⊤Sir John Stewart.

Joan, widow of King James I.⊤James Stewart, the "Black Knight of Lorn."

Sir John Stewart, Earl of Athol⊤Eleanor, dau. William, Earl of Orkney.

Sir John Stewart, Earl of Athol⊤Mary, dau. Archibald, Earl of Argyle.

Lady Isabel Stewart⊤Kenneth Mackenzie, Lord of Kintail.

Lady Agnes Mackenzie⊤Lachlan MacIntosh, Chief of Clan Chattan.

William MacIntosh, of Essick and Borlum⊤Elizabeth Innes.

Lachlan MacIntosh, of Borlum⊤Ann, widow of Sir Lachlan McIntosh.

Capt. John MacIntosh, of "Borlum," Ga.⊤Marjory Frazer, of Garthmore.

Col. William McIntosh, of Darien, Ga.⊤Jane Maccoy.

Gen. John McIntosh, of "Fairhope," Ga.⊤Sarah Swinton.

Col. James S. McIntosh, U. S. Army⊤Mrs. Eliza (Matthews) Shumate.

Col. Charles C. Keeney, M.D.,⊤Mary Eliza McIntosh,⸺William Alvord,
U. S. Army,   member of the Cali-   of San Francisco,
fornia Society of the   (second husband).
Colonial Dames of   *No issue.*
America.

Charles McIntosh Keeney.   James Ward Keeney.

PEDIGREE LIII.

HENRY I., King of France, had by his wife, Lady Anne, daughter of Jaroslaus, Grand Duke, or Czar, of Russia:

HUGH THE GREAT, Duke of France and Burgundy, Count de Vermandois, who *m.*, thirdly, Adela, Countess de Vermandois, and had by her:

LADY ISABEL DE VERMANDOIS, *d.* 1131, who *m.*, first, in 1096, Robert, Baron de Bellomont, Earl of Mellent and Leicester, and had:

ROBERT DE BELLOMONT, second Earl of Leicester, justiciary of England, *d.* 1168, who *m.* Lady Amicia de Waer, daughter of Ralph, Earl of Norfolk, Suffolk and Cambridge, and had:

ROBERT DE BELLOMONT, third Earl of Leicester, lord high steward of England, *d.* 1196, who *m.*, 1167, Lady Petronella, daughter of Hugh, Baron de Grentesmaismil, and had:

LADY MARGARET DE BELLOMONT, who *m.* Saher de Quincey, one of the twenty-five trustees of the Magna Charta, created, 1207, Earl of Winchester, *d.* 1219, and had:

LADY HAWISE DE QUINCEY, who *m.* Hugh de Vere, fourth Earl of Oxford, great high chamberlain, *d.* 1263, and had:

ROBERT DE VERE, fifth Earl of Oxford, *d.* 1296; *m.* Alice, daughter of Gilbert de Saundford, chamberlain in fee to Queen Eleanor, 1250, and had:

ALPHONSUS DE VERE, second son, *d. v. p.*, who *m.* Jane, daughter of Sir Richard Foliot, and had:

JOHN DE VERE, seventh Earl of Oxford, who fought at Cressy, commanded at Poictiers, and was *k.* at Rheims, 14 June, 1360. He *m.* Lady Maud, widow of Robert Fitzpayne and daughter of Bartholomew, Baron de Badlesmere, executed in 1322, and his wife, Lady Margaret de Clare, also of Royal Descent, and had:

LADY MARGARET DE VERE, widow of Henry de Beaumont, *d.* 1369, who *m.*, secondly, Sir John Devereux, and had:

SIR WILLIAM DEVEREUX, who *m.* Anne, daughter of Sir John Barre, and had:

SIR WALTER DEVEREUX, *k.* 1402, who *m.* Agnes Crophull, and had:

ELIZABETH DEVEREUX, who *m.* Sir John Milbourne, and had:

SIMON MILBOURNE, who *m.* Jane, daughter of Sir Ralph Baskerville, of Erdisley, Hereford, also of Royal Descent, and had:

(227)

BLANCHE MILBOURNE, who m. James Whitney, of Newport in the Marches, and had:

SIR ROBERT WHITNEY, K.B., a Gloucestershire magistrate, who m. Margaret Wye, and had:

SIR ROBERT WHITNEY, knighted 2 October, 1553, d. 5 August, 1567; m. Sybil, daughter of Sir James Baskerville, also of Royal Descent, and had:

ROBERT WHITNEY, who m. Elizabeth Morgan, and had:

THOMAS WHITNEY, of Lambeth Marsh, London, d. April, 1637, m., 12 May, 1583, Mary, buried 25 September, 1629, daughter of John Bray, and had:

JOHN WHITNEY, b. 1589, bapt. 20 July, 1592, came from Islesworth parish, near London, with his wife Elinor and five sons, to New England in June, 1635, and d. at Watertown, Massachusetts, 1 June, 1673. He m., first, in London, Elinor ———, who d. at Watertown, 11 May, 1659, aged 60 years (see Pierce's "John Whitney of Watertown," W. L. Whitney's "Whitney Family," Henry Melville's "Ancestry of John Whitney," "Magna Charta Barons and Their American Descendants," p. 181, etc.), and had by her:

1.—JOHN WHITNEY, b. 1620, bapt. Islesworth parish, 14 September, 1621, came with his parents to New England, d. at Watertown, Massa. chusetts, 12 October, 1692. In 1642 he m. Ruth, daughter of Robert and Mary Reynolds, of Wethersfield, and had:

I.—BENJAMIN WHITNEY, b. Watertown, 28 June, 1660, d. 1736; m., first, 30 March, 1687, Abigail, daughter of William and Mary (Bemis) Hagar, and m., secondly, Elizabeth ———, and had:

ENSIGN DANIEL WHITNEY, b. Watertown, 17 July, 1700, d. Watertown, 1775; m. Dorothy, b. 1706, daughter of Simon and Joanna (Stone) Taintor, and had by her, who d. 7 August, 1788:

MARY WHITNEY, b. 10 September, 1731, d. August, 1805; who m., 10 June, 1762, Major John Woodbridge, of Continental Army, b. Windsor, Connecticut, 24 July, 1732, d. South Hadley, Massachusetts, 27 December, 1782, son of Rev. John, 1702–1783; son of Rev. John, 1678–1718; son of Rev. John, 1644–1691; son of Rev. John, b. 1613 at Stenton, England, d. at Newbury, Massachusetts, 1695, and had:

MARTHA WOODBRIDGE, b. 8 January, 1771, d. 12 July, 1830, who m., 1794, John Dunlap, of Huntingdon, Massachusetts, and had:

SAMUEL DUNLAP, b. 6 March, 1801, d. Amherst, Massachusetts,

29 July, 1872; *m.*, 1 November, 1836, Sarah Electa, daughter of Roswell and Peace (Cook) Field, and had :

SARAH ALMIRA DUNLAP, a member of the New Hampshire Society of the Colonial Dames of America, the Order of the Crown, *etc.*, who *m.*, 1 May, 1876, Professor David Pearce Penhallow, of Montreal, Canada, and had: *Dunlap Pearce, b.* 9 August, 1880.

II.—NATHANIEL WHITNEY, of Weston, Massachusetts, 1646–1732; *m.*, 1673, Sarah Hagar, and had :

NATHANIEL WHITNEY, of Watertown, Massachusetts, 1675–1730; *m.*, 1695, Mary Robinson, and had :

ISRAEL WHITNEY, of Killingby, Connecticut, 1710–1746; *m.* Hannah ————, and had :

SYBIL WHITNEY, 1733–1812, who *m.* Captain Oliver Cummings, of Dunstable, Massachusetts, *d.* 1810, and had :

CAPTAIN JOSIAH CUMMINGS, of Dunstable, 1763–1834; *m.*, 1785, Sarah Taylor, and had :

SALLY CUMMINGS, who *m.*, 1806, John Cummings, of Tyngsboro, Massachusetts, 1779–1886, also of Royal Descent (*see* " Magna Charta Barons and Their American Descendants "), and had :

WILLARD CUMMINGS, of Tyngsboro, *b.* 1811, who *m.*, 1835, Mary Ann Pollard, and had :

ELLEN MARIA CUMMINGS, who *m.*, 1853, Joshua Flagg Davis, of Chalmsford, Massachusetts, *b.* 1822, and had :

ANNA MARIA DAVIS, *b.* 20 March, 1856, a member of the Order of the Crown, *etc.*, who *m.*, 30 June, 1886, Lord Karl von Rydingsvärd, of Sweden and Boston, Massachusetts.

2.—RICHARD WHITNEY, *bapt.* Islesworth parish, 6 January, 1623–24, who *m.*, 7 May, 1651, Martha Credam, and had :

RICHARD WHITNEY, who *m.* Elizabeth Sawtell, and had :

RICHARD WHITNEY, who *m.*, at Lancaster, Massachusetts, Hannah Whitcomb, and had :·

DANIEL WHITNEY, who *m.*, at Lancaster, 9 February, 1744, Dorothy Goss, and had :

SILAS WHITNEY, who *m.*, at Stow, Massachusetts, 3 September, 1780, Patience Goodnow, and had :

JOHN WHITNEY, who *m.*, at Waltham, Massachusetts, 1 July, 1804, Susannah Piles, and had :

GEORGE H. WHITNEY, of Ithaca, New York, who *m.*, at Providence, Rhode Island, 13 April, 1852, Priscilla Gallup, and had :

ISABEL WHITNEY, a member of the New York Society of the Colonial Dames of America, who *m.*, 9 April, 1898, William H. Sage, of "Uplands," Albany, New York.

3.—BENJAMIN WHITNEY, *b.* Watertown, 6 June, 1643, *d.* 1723; *m.*, first, at York, Maine, Jane ——, *d.* 14 November, 1690, and had:

JONATHAN WHITNEY, of Sherborn, Milford, *etc.*, Massachusetts, *b.* 1680, *d.* January, 1754; *m.*, about 1700, Susanna ——, and had:

MARY WHITNEY, *b.* 28 May, 1710, *d.* 9 July, 1788; *m.* Joseph Jones, of Milford, Massachusetts, *b.* 27 December, 1709, *d.* 3 April, 1796, and had:

JOSEPH JONES, JR., of Milford, *b.* 29 September, 1737, *d.* 22 August, 1799; *m.* Ruth, *b.* 10 November, 1743, *d.* 1825, daughter of Nehemiah Nelson, and had:

ALEXANDER JONES, *b.* 8 August, 1764, *d.* 19 March, 1840; *m.*, in Charleston, South Carolina, 28 January, 1790, Mary, *b.* Milledgeville, Georgia, 24 December, 1773, *d.* Providence, Rhode Island, 5 September, 1835, daughter of George Farquhar, 1745–1779, and had:

REV. ALEXANDER JONES, *b.* Charleston, South Carolina, 8 November, 1796, *d.* Perth Amboy, New Jersey, in 1874; *m.* Anne Northey, daughter of Captain Benjamin King Churchill, of Bristol, Rhode Island, and had:

CLARA CHURCHILL JONES, *b.* 31 May, 1820, *d.* 29 December, 1881; *m.* Alexander Parker Crittenden, *b.* 14 January, 1816, *d.* at San Francisco, California, 5 November, 1870, son of Thomas Turpin and Mary Howard (Parker) Crittenden, of Kentucky, and had:

NANNIE CHURCHILL CRITTENDEN, *b.* Brazoria, Texas, 19 January, 1843, who *m.* Sidney McMechen Van Wyck, *b.* Baltimore, Maryland, 6 April, 1830, *d.* San Francisco, California, 27 April, 1887, also of Royal Descent, and had:

I.—LAURA SANCHEZ VAN WYCK, of San Francisco, *b.* Oakland, California, 5 September, 1879, a member of the California Society of the Colonial Dames of America, the Order of the Crown, *etc.*

II.—SIDNEY MCMECHAN VAN WYCK, JR., of San Francisco.

THE ROYAL DESCENT

OF

MRS. VIRGINIA LYNDALL. DUNBAR,

OF CINCINNATI, OHIO.

EDWARD III., King of England⹋Lady Philippa of Hainault.

  Lionel, Duke of Clarence⹋Lady Elizabeth de Burgh.

  Lady Philippa Plantagenet⹋Edmund de Mortimer, Earl of Marche.

  Lady Elizabeth de Mortimer⹋Sir Henry de Percy, called "Hotspur."

Henry de Percy, Earl of Northumberland⹋Lady Eleanor de Neville.

Henry de Percy, Earl of Northumberland⹋Lady Eleanor de Poynings.

Henry de Percy, Earl of Northumberland⹋Lady Matilda de Herbert.

Henry de Percy, Earl of Northumberland⹋Lady Catherine Spencer.

  Lady Margaret de Percy⹋Henry de Clifford, Earl of Cumberland.

  Lady Catherine de Clifford⹋Sir Richard Cholmoneley, of Roxby.

Sir Henry Cholmoneley, of Roxby⹋Lady Margaret de Babthorpe.

  Lady Mary Cholmoneley⹋Rev. Henry Fairfax, of Bolton-Percy.

  Henry, Lord Fairfax, of Cameron⹋Lady Frances Berwick.

  Henry Fairfax, of Denton⹋Anne Harrison, of Yorkshire.

  William Fairfax, of "Belvoir," Va.⹋Deborah Clarke.

Rev. Bryan, Lord Fairfax of Cameron⹋Elizabeth Cary.

Fernando Fairfax, of Alexandria, Va.⹋Elizabeth Cary.

  Mercy Floretta Fairfax⹋Rev. Samuel Haggins.

Rev. John Haggins, of Bath Co., Ky.⹋Margery Mildred Johnson.

Col. George Washington Fairfax Haggins⹋Sarah Ann Beebe.

  Nancy Johnson Haggins⹋Joseph Kling, of Seymour, Indiana.

  Virginia Lyndall Kling⹋Horace Bernard Dunbar, of Boston, Mass.

Dorothy Dunbar, b. 1 April, 1894.

PEDIGREE LIV.

HENRY III., King of England, had by his wife, Lady Eleanor, daughter of Raymond, Count of Provence, also of Royal Descent:

EDMUND PLANTAGENET, 1245–1295, Earl of Leicester. He *m.*, secondly, Blanche, widow of Henry, King of Navarre, and daughter of Robert, Earl of Artois, son of Louis VIII., King of France, and had by her:

HENRY PLANTAGENET, Earl of Leicester and Lancaster, *d.* 1345. He *m.* Lady Maud, daughter of Patrick de Chaworth and Lady Isabel de Beauchamp, also of Royal Descent, and had:

LADY JOAN PLANTAGENET, who *m.*, first, John, third Baron de Mowbray, of Axholme, *d.* 1361, also of Royal Descent, and had:

JOHN DE MOWBRAY, fourth Baron Mowbray, of Axholme, *d.* 1368. He *m.* Lady Elizabeth, only child of John, third Lord Segrave, by his wife, Lady Margaret Plantagenet, also of Royal Descent, and had:

LADY MARGERY DE MOWBRAY, who *m.* John, second Baron de Welles, *d.* 1422, also of Royal Descent, and had:

EUDO DE WELLES, eldest son, *d. v. p.*, who *m.* Lady Maud, daughter of Ralph, Baron de Greystock, also of Royal Descent, and had:

SIR LIONEL DE WELLES, Baron Welles, of Gainsby, lord lieutenant of Ireland, *k.* in the battle of Towton Field, 1461. He had by his first wife, Lady Joan, daughter of Sir Robert Waterton, Knt.:

LADY MARGARET DE WELLES, who *m.* Sir Thomas Dymoke, Knt., of Scrivelsby, Lincolnshire, and had:

SIR LIONEL DYMOKE, Knt., of Scrivelsby, high sheriff of Lincolnshire, *d.* 1519; *m.* Joan, daughter of Richard Griffith, of Stockford, and had:

LADY ALICE DYMOKE, who *m.* (his second wife) Sir William Skipwith, Knt., of Ormsby, sheriff of Lincolnshire, also of Royal Descent (*see* Burke's "Royal Families," Ped. cii.), and had:

SIR WILLIAM HENRY SKIPWITH, Knt., of Ormsby and Prestwould, Leicestershire, only son, who had by his wife, Anne, daughter of John Tothby (or his wife Jane, daughter of Francis Hall, of Grantham):

SIR WILLIAM SKIPWITH, Knt., of Prestwould, who *m.* Margaret, daughter of Roger Cave, of Stamford, and had:

SIR WILLIAM SKIPWITH, Bart., of Prestwould, eldest son, who sold Prestwould in 1653, and was created, 20 December, 1622, a baronet, and had issue by his wife, a daughter of Sir Thomas Kempe:

SIR GREY SKIPWITH, of Virginia, third Bart., brother of Sir Henry, second Bart., who *d. s. p.* He had by his wife, Bridget:

SIR WILLIAM SKIPWITH, of Virginia, fourth Bart., who *m.* Sarah, daughter of John Peyton, of Virginia, and had:

SIR WILLIAM SKIPWITH, of "Prestwould," Mecklenburg county, Virginia (brother of Sir Grey, of Virginia, fifth Bart., *b.* 2 August, 1705), who succeeded as sixth Bart., *b.* 1707, *d.* 1764; *m.*, 1733, Elizabeth, only daughter of John Smith, sheriff of Middlesex county, and had:

1.—SIR PEYTON SKIPWITH, of "Prestwould," seventh Bart., *d.* 1805; *m.*, first, Ann, and *m.*, secondly, Jean, both daughters of Hugh Miller, of Blandford, Virginia, *d.* London, 13 February, 1762, and had by Ann:

PEYTON SKIPWITH, second son, brother of Sir Grey Skipwith, of "Prestwould," Warwickshire, England, eighth Bart., 1771–1852, in whose line the baronetcy is continued. He removed from "Prestwould" to Maury county, Tennessee, where he *m.* Cornelia, daughter of Major-General Nathaniel Greene, of the Continental Army, and dying at his seat "Coates," in Georgia, had:

GEORGE GREENE SKIPWITH, *b.* at "Prestwould," *d.* at "Estoteville," Hinds county, Mississippi, 24 December, 1853. He *m.* Mary Ann, daughter of William Newsum and his wife, Sallie, daughter of Wilson Cary and Jean B., daughter of Dabney Carr, and his wife, a sister of President Jefferson, and had:

MARY SKIPWITH, a member of the Virginia Society of the Colonial Dames of America, who *m.*, in December, 1860, Percy Roberts, of New Orleans. *No issue.*

2.—COLONEL HENRY SKIPWITH, of Williamsburg, Virginia, 1751–1815, an officer in the Virginia Line, Continental Army, who *m.*, 1772, a daughter of John Wayles, of "The Forest," Charles City county, Virginia, and his wife, Martha, daughter of Francis Eppes, and had:

MARTHA WAYLES SKIPWITH, who *m.* Edmund Harrison, of Amelia county, Virginia, 1761–1826, member of the House of Delegates and of the Council, 1793, also of Royal Descent (pp. 35, 186), and had:

WILLIAM HENRY HARRISON, of Amelia county, Virginia, 1812–1884, who *m.* Lucy A. Powers, and had:

PROFESSOR EDMUND HARRISON, of Louisville, *m.* Kate Steger, and had:

1.—LULIE HARRISON, a member of the Virginia Society of the Colonial Dames of America, who *m.* Dana Henry Rucker, of Richmond, Virginia, and had: *Edmund Harrison, b.* 18 February, 1898.

2.—JEANIE HARRISON, a member of the Virginia Society of the Colonial Dames of America, who *m.* Charles H. Chalkley, of Hopkinsville.

3.—LELIA SKIPWITH HARRISON, a member of the Virginia Society of the Colonial Dames of America, who *m.* Howard D. Hoge, of Richmond.

PEDIGREE LV.

JAMES II., King of Scotland, had by his wife, Lady Mary, daughter of Arnold of Egmond, Duke of Guelders:

PRINCESS MARY STEWART, who had by her second husband, Sir James, first Lord Hamilton, of Cadyou:

JAMES HAMILTON, second Lord Hamilton, created Earl of Arran, who had by his third wife, Lady Janet, daughter of Sir David Betoun, of Creich:

JAMES HAMILTON, second Earl of Arran, created Duke of Chatel-herault, who had by his wife, Lady Margaret, daughter of James Douglas, third Earl of Morton:

SIR CLAUD HAMILTON, third son, created Lord Hamilton, of Paisley, who had by his wife, Lady Margaret, daughter of George, sixth Lord Seton:

JAMES HAMILTON, created, 10 July, 1606, Earl of Abercorn, eldest son, *d. v. p.* 16 March, 1617, who had by his wife, Lady Marion, daughter of Sir Thomas, fifth Lord Boyd:

SIR GEORGE HAMILTON, Bart., of Donalong, county Tyrone, Ireland fourth son, who *m.*, in 1629, Lady Mary Butler, daughter of Walter, Viscount Thurles, and had:

LADY MARGARET HAMILTON, who *m.*, in 1688, Matthew Forde, M.P., of Coolgreany, county Wexford, Ireland, *d.* 1713 (*see* Wood's Douglas's "Peerage of Scotland," ii., 8), son of Nicholas Forde, of Killyleagh, county Down, and had:

MATTHEW FORDE, M.P., of Seaforde, county Down, *d.* 1729, who *m.*, in 1698, Anne (will probated at Dublin, 12 March, 1768), daughter of Rev. William Brownlowe, rector of Lurgan parish, county Armagh, and had:

STANDISH FORDE, fourth son (refer to his sister Margaret Forde's will, probated at Dublin, May, 1773), who came to Maryland in 1730, and settled in Philadelphia in 1734, where he *d.* in 1766. He *m.*, first, Hannah ———, and *m.*, secondly, Parthenia ——— (*see* "Phila. Adm.," 1766, Lib. H., fo. 15, and "Phila. Wills," 1766, Lib. N., fo. 506), and had by the latter, who *d.* in 1766:

STANDISH FORDE, JR., *b.* Philadelphia, 8 April, 1759; *d.* 28 April, 1806 (*see* "Philadelphia Wills," Lib. 1, fo. 487). He *m.*, at Christ Church,

Philadelphia, 5 December, 1795, Sarah, *b.* 16 January, 1775, daughter of John and Eleanor (Waters) Britton, of Philadelphia, and had, besides others:

1.—ELINOR FORDE, *b.* 9 October, 1796, *d.* 19 February, 1868; *m.*, 14 October, 1812, William Sutton Hansell, *b.* 9 November, 1787, *d.* 22 December, 1872, and had: *Mary Sutton, William Forde, Henry Holcombe, Sarah Forde, Standish F., Barnett, John Forde, Theophilus Brantley, Robert, Edward, Susan Budd, Samuel Robb, George* and

I.—ANNE SUTTON HANSELL, who *m.*, 8 June, 1852, Alexander Thomas Lane, of Philadelphia, and had:

ANNE HANSELL LANE, who *m.*, 30 April, 1883, John Scollay, of Philadelphia, and had: *Edith Anne* (deceased), *Anna Lane,* and *Elinor Gertrude.*

II.—ELLEN FORDE HANSELL, who *m.*, 16 October, 1845, Joseph French Page, of Philadelphia, and had: *Joseph French, Edward Delano, Henry Hansell, William Hansell, Louise Rodman, Robert Hansell,* and

1.—ELLEN HANSELL PAGE, a member of the Pennsylvania Society of the Colonial Dames of America, who *m.* Henry C. Butcher, of Philadelphia, and had:

I.—LAURA PAGE BUTCHER, a member of the Pennsylvania Society of the Colonial Dames of America.

II.—HENRY C. BUTCHER, JR., of Philadelphia.

III.—ALICE TYSON, wife of George Brinton Roberts, of Philadelphia.

IV.—ELEANOR PAGE BUTCHER.

2.—FRANCES PAGE, a member of the New York Society of the Colonial Dames of America, who *m.* Winthrop Burr, of Boston.

2.—MARGARET LAMB FORDE, *b.* 3 February, 1799, who *m.*, 8 September, 1820, Benjamin Poultney Smith, and had, besides others:

JOHN JAMES SMITH, who *m.*, 17 September, 1844, Mary Ann Atkinson, and had:

SARAH FORDE SMITH, a member of the Pennsylvania Society of the Colonial Dames of America, who *m.* Charles Benjamin Wilkinson, and had: *Mary Elizabeth* and *J. Atkinson.*

THE ROYAL DESCENT

OF

MRS. FREDERICK C. POISSON,

OF LONDON, ENGLAND.

EDWARD I., King of England=Princess Eleanor of Castile.

Princess Joan Plantagenet=Gilbert de Clare, Earl of Gloucester and Hertford.

Lady Margaret de Clare=Hugh de Audley, Earl of Gloucester.

Lady Margaret de Audley=Sir Ralph de Stafford, K.G., Earl of Stafford.

Sir Hugh de Stafford, K.G., Earl of Stafford=Lady Philippa de Beauchamp.

Lady Margaret de Stafford=Sir Ralph de Neville, K.G., Earl of Westmoreland.

Ralph de Neville, of Oversley, Warwickshire=Lady Mary de Ferrers.

John de Neville, of Wymersley, Yorkshire=Lady Elizabeth de Newmarch.

Joan de Neville=Sir William Gascoigne, of Gawthrope, Yorkshire.

Sir William Gascoigne, of Gawthrope, York=Lady Margaret de Percy.

Lady Elizabeth Gascoigne=Gilbert de Talboys, of Kyme.

Sir George de Talboys, of Kyme=(Name unknown.)

Lady Anne de Talboys=Sir Edward Dymoke, of Scrivelsby, Lincolnshire.

Lady Frances Dymoke=Thomas Windebank, of Haines Hill, Berkshire.

Mildred Windebank=Robert Reade, Linkenholt Manor, Southampton.

Col. George Reade, of Gloucester Co., Va.=Elizabeth Martian.

Mildred Reade=Col. Augustine Warner, Jr., of "Warner's Hall."

Mildred Warner=Lawrence Washington, Westmoreland Co., Va.

Augustine Washington, Stafford Co., Va.=Mary Ball, of "Epping Forest," Va.

Betty Washington=Col. Fielding Lewis, of "Kenmore," Va.

Howell Lewis, Kanawha Co., W. Va.=Ellen Pollard.

Frances Fielding Lewis=Humphrey B. Gwathmey, of Richmond, Va.

Virginia Gwathmey, member of the National=Adam Empie, of Wilmington, N. C.
Society of the Colonial Dames of America,

Herbert Russell Latimer= died in 1887,	Frances Fielding= Lewis Empie, member of the Order of the Crown, National Society of the Colonial Dames of America, etc.	Frederick C. Poisson, of Hyde Park Gate, London, England. No issue.	Annie Empie, mem-= ber of the Order of the Crown, So- ciety of the Colo- nial Dames of America, etc.	Edward Bailey.
Herbert Russell Latimer.	Empie Latimer.			Edward. Virginia. Karin D. Frances F. L.

PEDIGREE LVI.

ROBERT III., King of Scotland, had by his wife, Lady Annabella, daughter of Sir John Drummond:

PRINCESS MARY STEWART, second daughter, who *m.* George Douglas, Earl of Angus, also of Royal Descent, and had:

LADY ELIZABETH DOUGLAS, who *m.* Sir Alexander Forbes, first Lord Forbes, and had:

JAMES, second Lord Forbes, *d.* 1460, who *m.* Lady Egidia, or Geiles Keith, also of Royal Descent, daughter of Sir William de Keith, created 4 July, 1458, the first earl marshal of Scotland, and had:

DUNCAN FORBES, second son, who *m.* Lady Christiana Mercer, daughter of the laird of Ballar, and had:

WILLIAM FORBES, of Corsindae, who *m.* Margaret, daughter of Lumsden of Cullon, and widow of the laird of Caskieben, and had:

DUNCAN FORBES, of Monymusk, who *m.* Agnes, daughter of William Gray, and had:

WILLIAM FORBES, of Monymusk, who *m.* Lady Margaret Douglas, daughter of the ninth Earl of Angus, and had:

JOHN FORBES, of Leslie, who *m.*, secondly, Lady Margaret, daughter of the laird of Skeene, and had:

ALEXANDER FORBES, of Auchinhamper and Auchorties, who *m.* Anne, daughter of William Seaton, of Minnues, and had:

JOHN FORBES, of Auchorties, Aberdeenshire, who *m.* Barbara, daughter of William Johnstoun, of Aberdeenshire, and had:

ALEXANDER FORBES, of Auchorties, and afterwards of London (*see* Playfair's "British Family Antiquity," "The Barclays of Ury," and Jaffray's Diary), who *m.* Jean, youngest daughter of Robert Barclay, of Ury, the celebrated Apologist for the Quakers, 1648–1690, also of Royal Descent, and had:

CHRISTIANA FORBES, *b.* 6 February, 1714–15, *d.* 9 March, 1733–4, who *m.*, 10 September, 1732, William Penn, the third, of London, *b.* 21 March, 1702–3, *d.* February, 1746, son of William Penn, Jr., and grandson of William Penn, the founder of Pennsylvania, and had:

CHRISTIANA GULIELMA PENN, *b.* 22 October, 1733, *d.* 1803, heiress of the Penn estates in England and Ireland, and of the Springetts, in Sussex, who *m.*, 1761, Peter Gaskell, of Bath, England, *d.* 1785, and had:

(237)

PETER PENN-GASKELL, of Shaunagary and of "Ashwood," *b.* 9 May, 1763, *d.* 16 July, 1831, who *m.*, 5 November, 1793, Elizabeth, daughter of Nathan Edwards, of Montgomery county, Pennsylvania, and had:

CHRISTIANA GULIELMA PENN-GASKELL, *b.* 27 May, 1805, *d.* 1830, who *m.*, 2 January, 1827, William Swabric Hall, of Laventhorpe Hall and London, *b.* 1799, *d.* 26 September, 1862, and had:

COLONEL PETER PENN-GASKELL HALL, of Philadelphia, paymaster United States Army (retired), *b.* 16 March, 1830, who *m.*, first, 24 December, 1861, Anne, daughter of Philip Mixsell, of Easton, Pennsylvania, and had:

1.—CHRISTIANA GULIELMA PENN-GASKELL HALL, of Philadelphia, a member of the Society of Colonial Dames.

2.—ELIZA PENN-GASKELL HALL, a member of the Society of Colonial Dames, who *m.*, 1 June, 1892, Henry James Hancock, of Philadelphia, also of Royal Descent, a member of the Order of Runnemede, and had: *Jean Barclay Penn-Gaskell, b.* 24 March, 1893.

COLONEL HALL, *m.*, secondly, November, 1871, Amelia, sister of his first wife, and had by her: *William, Peter Penn-Gaskell, Amelia,* and *Philip M.*

PEDIGREE LVII.

ROBERT II., King of Scotland, had by his first wife, Lady Elizabeth, daughter of Sir Adam Mure, of Rowallan:

ROBERT STEWART, 1399–1419, Duke of Albany, regent of Scotland, who *m.*, first, Margaret, Countess of Monteith, and had by her:

LADY MARJORY STEWART, who *m.* (his first wife) Sir Duncan Campbell, of Lochow, created, in 1445, Lord Campbell, *d.* 1453, also of Royal Descent, and had:

ARCHIBALD CAMPBELL, second son, *d. v. p.*, who *m.* Lady Elizabeth, daughter of Sir John Somerville, of Carnwarth, and had:

SIR COLIN CAMPBELL, second Lord Campbell, of Lochow, created, in 1457, Earl of Argyle, lord high chancellor of Scotland, 1483, *d.* 1493, who *m.* Lady Isabel Stewart, daughter of John, second Lord Lorn, and had:

LADY HELEN CAMPBELL, who *m.* Hugh, third Lord Montgomery, created, 1507, Earl of Eglinton, also of Royal Descent, and had:

SIR NEIL MONTGOMERY, of Lainshaw, Knt., third son, *k.* 1547; *m.* Margaret, daughter of Quintin Mure, laird of Skeldon, and had:

SIR NEIL MONTGOMERY, of Lainshaw, Knt., second son, *m.* Lady Jean, daughter of John, fourth and last Lord of Lyle, and had:

SIR NEIL MONTGOMERY, of Lainshaw, Knt., *d. ante* 1613; *m.* Elizabeth, daughter of John Cunningham, of Aiket, and had:

WILLIAM MONTGOMERY, second son, *d.* 16 November, 1659; *m.*, 1602, Jean, daughter and heiress of John Montgomery, of Brigend, and had:

JOHN MONTGOMERY, of Brigend, *d. ante* 7 December, 1647; *m.*, 1626, Elizabeth, daughter of Thomas Baxter, of Shirnston, and had:

HUGH MONTGOMERY, of Brigend, *d.*, Glasgow, 6 May, 1710, aged 80 years. He *m.*, 1653, Lady Katherine, daughter of Sir William Scott, of Clerkington, a senator of the College of Justice, and had:

WILLIAM MONTGOMERY, who disposed of his interest in the manor of Brigend, in 1692, and removed with his family, in 1701, to America, and purchased a farm, in 1706, called "Eglington," in Monmouth county, New Jersey. He *m.*, 8 January, 1684, in Edinburgh, Isabel, daughter of Robert Burnet, of Lethintie, one of the original proprietors of East, or New Jersey, and had:

1.—ROBERT MONTGOMERY, of "Eglington," Monmouth county, New

Jersey, 1687–1766; *m.*, 1710, Sarah Stacy, of Burlington, New Jersey, and had:

JAMES MONTGOMERY, of "Eglington," 1720–1760; *m.*, 1746, Esther, daughter of John Wood, of Burlington county, New Jersey, and had:

WILLIAM MONTGOMERY, of Philadelphia, 1752–1831; *m.*, 1781, Rachel, daughter of Sampson Henry, of Philadelphia, and had:

MARY MONTGOMERY, *b.* 1794, who *m.*, 1815, Professor Charles Delucena Meigs, M.D., of Philadelphia, and had:

EMILY MEIGS, who *m.* J. Williams Biddle, of Philadelphia, and had:

CHRISTINE BIDDLE, a member of the Society of the Colonial Dames of America, who *m.* Richard M. Cadwalader, of Philadelphia, also of Royal Descent. *Issue.*

2.—JAMES MONTGOMERY, of Upper Freehold, Monmouth county, New Jersey, third son, who *m.* Mary ——, and had:

ALEXANDER MONTGOMERY, of Allentown, Pennsylvania, second son, 1735–1798, who *m.* Eunia West, of Eatonton, New Jersey, 1733–1796, and had:

THOMAS WEST MONTGOMERY, M.D., of New York, 1764–1820; *m.*, 1788, Mary, daughter of Judge John Berrien, of Rocky Hill, a justice of the Supreme Court of New Jersey, and had:

JULIA MONTGOMERY, *b.* 1797, *d.* 1882, who *m.*, 1825, William M. Biddle, of Philadelphia, *d.* 1855, and had:

JULIA MONTGOMERY BIDDLE, *b.* 1840, a member of the Pennsylvania Society of the Colonial Dames of America, who *m.*, 1863, Charles Stuart Huntington, of New York, *d.* 1890, and had:

FLORENCE HUNTINGTON, *b.* New York, 1864, who *m.*, first, William M. Biddle, and *m.*, secondly, Owen A. Conner, *d.* 1897.

PEDIGREE LVIII.

HENRY III., King of England, *m.*, 1236, Lady Eleanor Berenger, daughter of Raymond, Count de Provence, and had:

EDMUND PLANTAGENET, Earl of Lancaster, who *m.*, secondly, Lady Blanche, widow of Henry, King of Navarre, and daughter of Robert, Earl of Artois, *k.* 1247, son of Louis VIII., King of France, and had by her:

HENRY PLANTAGENET, Earl of Lancaster and Leicester, who *m.* Lady Maud, daughter of Sir Patrick de Chaworth, Knt., and his wife, Lady Isabel de Beauchamp, also of Royal Descent, and had:

LADY JOAN PLANTAGENET, who *m.* John, third Baron Mowbray, also of Royal Descent, and had:

JOHN, fourth Baron Mowbray, who *m.* Lady Elizabeth Segrave, also of Royal Descent, and had:

LADY ELEANOR MOWBRAY, *m.* Roger, Baron de la Warr, and had:

LADY JOAN DE LA WARR, who *m.* Sir Thomas, third Baron West, *d.* 1405, also of Royal Descent, and had:

SIR REGINALD DE WEST, second son, Baron de la Warr, *d.* 27 August, 1451, *m.* Margaret, daughter of Robert Thorley, and had:

SIR RICHARD WEST, second Baron de la Warr, 1432–1476, *m.* Lady Catherine, daughter of Robert, Baron de Hungerford, and had:

SIR THOMAS WEST, K.G., third Baron de la Warr, *d.* 1524, who *m.*, secondly, Eleanor, daughter of Sir Roger Copley, of Gatton, and had:

SIR GEORGE WEST, second son, *d.* 1538, who *m.* Lady Elizabeth, daughter of Sir Anthony Moreton, of Lechdale, and had:

SIR WILLIAM WEST, who was disabled from all honors in 1549, but restored in the blood in 1563, and was created, 5 February, 1570, Lord de la Warr, and *d.* 30 December, 1595. He *m.*, 1554, Elizabeth, daughter of Thomas Strange, of Chesterton, Gloucestershire, and had:

SIR THOMAS WEST, only son, second Lord de la Warr, knighted in Dublin, 12 July, 1599, by the Earl of Essex, *d.* April, 1602; *m.* Anne Knowles, and had:

HON. COLONEL JOHN WEST,* *b.* 14 December, 1590; B.A., Oxford, 1 December, 1613; brother of Thomas West, third Lord de la Warr, and Francis West, both Governors of Virginia. He came to Virginia, and was a member of the House of Burgesses and the Council, 1631–59, and Governor of the Virginia Colony, 1635–37, Muster-Master General of Virginia, 1641, and dying in 1659, he left issue by his wife, Anne ——— (*see* "Virginia Historical Magazine," vol. i., p. 423):

HON. COLONEL JOHN WEST, JR., of "West Point," King William county, only child, 1632–1689, a member of the Virginia House of Burgesses, 1685, and colonel under Berkeley in Bacon's rebellion. He *m.* Unity, daughter of Joseph Croshaw, of York county, member of the House of Burgesses, 1658, and had:

1.—ANNE WEST, who *m.* Henry Fox, of King William county, Virginia, and had:

ANNE FOX, *b.* 20 May, 1684, *d.* 4 May, 1733, who *m.* (his third wife) Captain Thomas Claiborne, of "Sweet Hall," King William county, 1680–1732, also of Royal Descent, and had:

I.—NATHANIEL CLAIBORNE, *m.* Jane Cole, and had:

WILLIAM CLAIBORNE, of Manchester, Virginia, *d.* 1809; *m.* Mary, daughter of Ferdinand Leigh, of King William county, and had:

NATHANIEL HERBERT CLAIBORNE, 1777–1859, *m.*, 1815, Elizabeth Archer Binford, and had:

ELIZABETH HERBERT CLAIBORNE, 1829–1855, who *m.*, 1851, James Coleman Otey, of Bedford county, and had:

LULIE LEIGH OTEY, a member of the Virginia Society of the Colonial Dames of America, who *m.*, 1870, Hervey Darneal, of Alameda, California, and had: *Susan Cole, Herbert Claiborne,* and *Hervey Otey.*

II.—DANIEL CLAIBORNE, of King William county, who had:

MARY ANN CLAIBORNE, who *m.* John Butts, and had:

GENERAL DANIEL CLAIBORNE BUTTS, who *m.* Elizabeth Randolph Harrison, also of Royal Descent, and had:

DANIEL CLAIBORNE BUTTS, who *m.* Ariadne Smith, and had:

MARIE ELOISE BUTTS, who *m.* Robert Dunlop, and had:

---

* The following ladies, members of the National Society of the Colonial Dames of America, are also of Royal Descent, through John West:

MISS MARY M. LYONS, Virginia State Society.

MRS. WILLIAM L. ROYALL, Virginia State Society.

MISS ANNA S. DANDRIDGE, Maryland State Society.

1. AGNES DUNLOP, a member of the Virginia Society of the Colonial Dames of America, who *m.* William H. Wight, of Cockeysville, Maryland, and had: *Robert D.*

2.—MARIE DUNLOP, a member of the Virginia Society of the Colonial Dames of America, who *m.* Warner Moore, of Richmond, Virginia, and had: *Marie Jean* and *Warner.*

III.—COLONEL AUGUSTINE CLAIBORNE, of "Windsor," King William county, 1721–1787, *m.* Mary Herbert, of "Puddlecock," Dinwiddie county, Virginia, and had:

HERBERT CLAIBORNE, of "Chestnut Grove," New Kent county, Virginia, *b.* 7 August, 1746, who had by his wife, Mary Burnet Browne, also of Royal Descent:

HERBERT AUGUSTINE CLAIBORNE, of Richmond, Virginia, 1784–1841, *m.* Delia, daughter of James Hayes, of Richmond, and had:

MAJOR JOHN HAYES CLAIBORNE, of Richmond, Virginia, *m.* Anna Virginia Bassett, of "Eltham," also of Royal Descent, and had:

DELIA CLAIBORNE, a member of the Virginia Society of the Colonial Dames of America, who *m.*, 10 June, 1885, General Simon B. Buckner, of Hart county, Kentucky, and had: *Simon Bolivar, b.* 18 July, 1886.

2.—CAPTAIN NATHANIEL WEST, of King William county, Virginia, a member of the House of Burgesses, 1702, who had:

UNITY WEST, only child, who *m.*, 1719, Captain William Dandridge, of "Elsing Green," King William county, a member of the Governor's council, 1727, Captain Royal Navy, 1737–41, *d.* 1743, and had:

I.—COLONEL NATHANIEL WEST DANDRIDGE, of King and Queen county, Virginia, *b.* 7 September, 1729, *d.* 16 January, 1789, who *m.*, 1747, Dorothea, daughter of Major-General Alexander Spotswood, also of Royal Descent, and had:

1.—DOROTHEA DANDRIDGE, who *m.* (his second wife) Patrick Henry, first Governor of Virginia, also of Royal Descent, and had:

JOHN HENRY, who *m.* Elvira Bruce McClelland, and had:

WILLIAM WIRT HENRY, of Richmond, Virginia, who *m.* Lucy Gray Marshall, a member of the Virginia Society of the Colonial Dames of America, and had:

1.—LUCY GRAY HENRY, a member of the Virginia Society of the Colonial Dames of America, who *m.* Matthew Bland Harrison, of Richmond, Virginia.

2.—ELIZABETH HENRY, a member of the Virginia Society of the Colonial Dames of America, who *m.* James Lyons, of Richmond, Virginia.

2.—MAJOR ALEXANDER SPOTSWOOD DANDRIDGE, of "The Bower," Jefferson county, Virginia, *b.* 1753, an aide-de-camp to General Washington, *m.* Ann, daughter of Major-General Adam Stephen, of the Virginia Line, and had:

ADAM STEPHEN DANDRIDGE, of "The Bower," *b.* 5 December, 1782, *d.* 20 November, 1821, *m.*, 1 January, 1805, Sarah, daughter of Philip Pendleton, and had:

ALEXANDER SPOTSWOOD DANDRIDGE, M.D., of Cincinnati, Ohio, *b.* 2 November, 1819, *d.* 29 April, 1889; *m.*, 4 May, 1843, Martha, daughter of Colonel Nathaniel Pendleton, of Cincinnati, member of Congress, and had:

1.—SUSAN BOWLER DANDRIDGE, a member of the New York Society of the Colonial Dames of America, who *m.* John M. Bowers, of New York City.

2.—MARY EVELYN DANDRIDGE, of Cincinnati, a member of the Virginia Society of the Colonial Dames of America.

II.—MARTHA DANDRIDGE, who *m.* Philip Aylett, of Virginia, and had:

COLONEL WILLIAM AYLETT, *m.* Mary, daughter of Colonel James Macon and his wife, Elizabeth Moore, also of Royal Descent, and had:

1.—COLONEL PHILIP AYLETT, *m.* Elizabeth, daughter of Governor Patrick Henry, of Virginia, also of Royal Descent, and had:

MARY MACON AYLETT, *m.* Philip Fitzhugh, and had:

LUCY FITZHUGH, *m.* John Robertson Redd, and had:

LUCY REDD, a member of the Indiana Society of the Colonial Dames of America, who *m.* William J. Holliday, of Indianapolis, Indiana, also of Royal Descent, and had:

1.—ARIANA AMBLER HOLLIDAY, a member of the Indiana Society of the Colonial Dames of America, who *m.* Henry W. Bennett, of Indianapolis.

2.—JAQUELIN S. HOLLIDAY, *m.* Florence Baker.

3.—LUCY FITZHUGH HOLLIDAY, *m.* George E. Hume.

2.—ELIZABETH AYLETT, *b.* 1769, who *m.*, 17 July, 1787, Alexander Spotswood Moore, of King William county, also of Royal Descent, and had:

MILDRED WALKER MOORE, *b.* 1788, *m.*, 1806, Rev. John Wilson Campbell, of Virginia, and had:

ELIZABETH CAMPBELL, who *m.* John Maben, of Richmond, Virginia, and had:

1.—MARY MABEN, a member of the Maryland Society of the Colonial Dames of America, who *m.* Frank Peyton Clark, of Baltimore, and had : *Bessie Campbell* and *William Lawrence.*

2.—JANE MABEN, who *m.* J. Dorsey Cullen, of Richmond, and had : ELIZABETH CAMPBELL CULLEN, a member of the Virginia Society of the Colonial Dames of America, who *m.* John F. T. Anderson, of Ashland, Virginia.

III.—ELIZABETH DANDRIDGE, *m.* Philip Whitehead Claiborne, also of Royal Descent, and had :

PHILADELPHIA CLAIBORNE, *m.* Abner Waugh, and had :

SARAH SPOTSWOOD WAUGH, *m.* James Lyons, and had :

LUCY LYONS, *m.* John Hopkins, and had :

JOHN HOPKINS, *m.* Abby Byrd Page, also of Royal Descent, and had :

WILLIAM EVELYN HOPKINS, 1821–1894, Commodore United States Navy, who *m.* Louise Kimball, and had :

MARIA BYRD HOPKINS, a member of the California Society of the Colonial Dames of America, who *m.* Colonel Stuart Selden Wright, of Fresno, California, also of Royal Descent, and had :

LOUISE KIMBALL WRIGHT, a member of the Virginia Society of the Colonial Dames of America, who *m.*, 7 June, 1895, John M. McClure, of Oakland, California, and had : *Mannen Wright, b.* 7 April, 1896.

IV.—MARY DANDRIDGE, who *m.*, 1745, John Spotswood, *d.* 1759, also of Royal Descent, and had :

1.—CAPTAIN JOHN SPOTSWOOD, who *m.* Sallie Rowsee, and had :

ROBERT SPOTSWOOD, who *m.* Louisa Bott, and had :

REV. JOHN SPOTSWOOD, D.D., of Petersburg, Virginia, who *m.* Sarah Peters, daughter of William Shippen Willing, of Philadelphia, and had :

LUCY SPOTSWOOD, a member of the Pennsylvania Society of the Colonial Dames of America, who *m.* George Peirce, of Philadelphia.

2.—ANN SPOTSWOOD,·who *m.* Lewis Burwell, and had :

SPOTSWOOD BURWELL, who *m.* Mary Marshall, and had :

MARY ANN SPOTSWOOD BURWELL, who *m.* Dr. Otis F. Manson, and had :

ELIZA SANGER MANSON, a member of the Virginia Society of the Colonial Dames of America, who *m.* Thomas Lee Alfriend, of Richmond, Virginia, and had : *Sallie Spotswood, Anna Lee, Otis Manson,* and

MARY BURWELL ALFRIEND, a member of the Virginia Society of the Colonial Dames of America, who *m.* Herbert Dale Lafferty, of Richmond, Virginia. *No issue.*

THE ROYAL DESCENT

OF

MISS ISA GARTEREY URQUHART GLENN,
OF ATLANTA, GA.

	THE EMPEROR CHARLEMAGNE, had :
ALFRED THE GREAT, of England, had :	Louis I., King of France, who had :
Edward the Elder, King of England, who had :	Charles II., King of France, who had :
Edmund I., King of England, who had :	Judith, *m.* Baldwin I., of Flanders, and had :
Edgar the Peaceful, King of England, who had :	Baldwin II., Count of Flanders, who had :
Ethelred II., King of England, who had :	Arnoul the Great, Count of Flanders, who had
Edmund II., King of England, who had :	Baldwin III., Count of Flanders, who had :
Prince Edward the Exile, of England, who had :	Arnoul II., Count of Flanders, who had :
Margaret, *m.* Malcolm III., of Scotland, and had :	Baldwin IV., Count of Flanders, who had :
Matilda, *m.* Henry I., of England, and had :	Baldwin V., Count of Flanders, who had :
Maud, *m.* Geoffrey, Count of Anjou, and had :	Maud, *m.* William the Conqueror, and had :
Henry II., King of England, who had :	Henry I., King of England, who had :
John, King of England, who had :	Maud, *m.* Geoffrey, Count of Anjou, and had :
Henry III., King of England, who had :	Henry II., King of England, who had :
Edward I., King of England, who had :	John, King of England, who had :
Joan, *m.* Gilbert, Earl of Clare, and had :	Henry III., King of England, who had :
Margaret, *m.* Hugh, Lord d'Audley, and had :	Edward I., King of England, who had :
Margaret, *m.* Sir Ralph Stafford, K.G., and had :	Thomas, Earl of Norfolk, who had :
Hugh, Earl of Stafford, K.G., who had :	Margaret, *m.* John de Segrave, and had :
Margaret, *m.* Sir Ralph Neville, K.G., and had :	Elizabeth, *m.* John de Mowbray, and had :
Margaret, *m.* Richard, Lord le Scrope, and had :	Margery, *m.* Sir John de Welles, and had :
Sir Henry, Lord le Scrope, of Bolton, who had :	Eudo de Welles, heir, *d. v. p.,* who had :
Margaret, *m.* John Bernard, and had :	Sir Lionel, Baron Welles of Gainsby, who had :
John Bernard, of Abingdon, who had :	Margaret, *m.* Sir Thomas Dymoke, and had :
John Bernard, of Abingdon, who had :	Sir Robert Dymoke, of Scrivelsby, who had :
Francis Bernard, of Abingdon, who had :	Sir Edward Dymoke, of Scrivelsby, who had :
Francis Bernard, of Kingsthorpe, who had :	Frances, *m.* Sir Thomas Windebank, and had :
Col. William Bernard, of Va., who had :	Mildred, *m.* Robert Reade, and had :
Lucy, *m.* Dr. Edmund Gwynne, and had :	George Reade, of Va.=Elizabeth Martian.

Lucy Gwynne, of Gloucester Co., Va.=Thomas Reade.   Augustine=Mildred Warner, Jr., Reade.

John Smith=Mary Warner.   John Lewis=Elizabeth Warner.

Augustine Smith=Sarah Carver.   Charles Lewis=Mary Howell.

Mildred Reade=Philip Rootes. John Smith=Mary Jacquelin.   Howell Lewis=Mary Willis.

Thomas Reade Rootes=Maria Smith.   Mildred Lewis=John Cobbs.

Thomas Reade Rootes, Jr.=Sarah Ryng Battaile.

Sarah Robinson Rootes=John Addison Cobb.

Mildred Lewis Rootes Cobb=Luther Judson Glenn.

John Thomas Glenn=Helen Augusta Garrard.

Isa Garterey Urquhart Glenn, of Atlanta,
member of the National Society of the
Colonial Dames of America.

PEDIGREE LIX.

EDWARD III., King of England, had by his wife, Lady Philippa, daughter of William, Count of Hainault and Holland :

Sir Lionel Plantagenet, K.G., Duke of Clarence, Earl of Ulster, *etc.*, who had by his first wife, Lady Elizabeth, daughter of Sir William de Burgh, Earl of Ulster, murdered in Ireland 6 June, 1333, and his wife, Lady Maud Plantagenet, both of Royal Descent:

Lady Philippa Plantagenet, only child, who *m.*, in 1368, when she was only 13 years of age, Edmund de Mortimer, third Earl of Marche, lord-lieutenant of Ireland, Earl of Ulster, *d.* at Cork, 26 December, 1381, and had :

Lady Elizabeth de Mortimer, *b.* 12 February, 1371, *d.* 20 April, 1417, who *m.*, in 1380, first, Sir Henry de Percy, K.G., the renowned "Hotspur," *k.* at Shrewsbury in 1403, son of Henry, Baron Percy, of Alnwick, created, 1377, Earl of Northumberland, also of Royal Descent, and had :

Sir Henry de Percy, K.G., second Earl of Northumberland, *b.* 3 February, 1393, *k.* at St. Albans in 1455.   He *m.* Lady Eleanor Neville (her second husband), daughter of Sir Ralph, first Earl of Westmoreland, K.G., and his second wife, Lady Joan de Beaufort, both of Royal Descent, and had :

Henry de Percy, third Earl of Northumberland, *k.* at Towton in 1461, who *m.* Lady Eleanor, only child of Richard Poynings, *d. v. p.* 1430, eldest son of Robert, fifth Lord Poynings, *k.* 1446, and had:

Lady Margaret de Percy, who *m.* Sir William Gascoigne, of Gawthrope, Yorkshire, also of Royal descent, and had :

Lady Elizabeth Gascoigne, who *m.* Gilbert, Baron de Talboys, of Kyme, *d.* 1566, and had :

Sir George de Talboys, Knt., son and heir, whose daughter :

Lady Anne de Talboys, who *m.* Sir Edward Dymoke, of Scrivelsby, Lincolnshire, hereditary champion of England, high sheriff of Lincolnshire, officiated as "champion" at the coronations of Edward VI., Queen Mary, and Queen Elizabeth, also of Royal Descent, and had:

Lady Frances Dymoke, who *m.* Sir Thomas Windebank, of Haines Hill, Hurst parish, Berkshire, clerk of the signet to Queen Elizabeth and King James I., *d.* 24 October, 1607, and had :

(247)

LADY MILDRED WINDEBANK, who *m.*, in 1600 (his third wife), Robert Reade, of Linkenholt Manor, Southamptonshire, will dated 10 December, 1626, and had:

COLONEL GEORGE READE,* named in the will of his grandfather, Andrew Reade, 1619. He came to the Virginia Colony about 1637, and was burgess for James City county, 1644–49, and Gloucester county, 1656; secretary of the colony *pro tem.*, in 1640; a member of the council, 1657 till decease; will proved 20 November, 1671. He *m.*, before 1657, Elizabeth, daughter of Captain Nicholas Martian, of York county, Virginia, a justice, 1633–1657, will probated 24 April, 1657, and had:

1.—THOMAS READE, of Gloucester county, Virginia, will executed 4 January, 1694; *m.* Lucy, daughter of Dr. Edmund Gwynne, and his wife, Lucy Bernard, also of Royal Descent (*see* p. 38), and had:

    I.—MILDRED READE, who *m.* Major Philip Rootes, of "Rosewell," Virginia, and had:

        1.—THOMAS READE ROOTES, who had by his wife, Maria Smith, also of Royal Descent (*see* p. 251).

        THOMAS READE ROOTES, JR., of "Whitemarsh," who had by his wife, Sarah Ryng Battaile:

        SARAH ROBINSON ROOTES, who *m.* John Addison Cobb, son of John Cobbs, of "The Sand Hills," Augusta, and his wife, Mildred Lewis, also of Royal Descent (*see* p. 257), and had:

        I.—MARY WILLIS COBB, who *m.* first (his second wife), Colonel Frank H. Erwin, and had:

            LUCY COBB ERWIN, a member of the Georgia Society of the Colonial Dames of America, who *m.* Abner Welborn Hill, of Atlanta, and had: *Lamar, Ashby, Abner W.,* and *Thomas Cobb.*

        MARY WILLIS COBB *m.*, secondly, John A. Johnson, M.D., and had:

            SARAH COBB JOHNSON, a member of the Georgia Society of the Colonial Dames of America, who *m.* Hugh Hagan, M.D., of Atlanta, and had: *Hugh* and *Willis Cobb.*

---

* The following ladies, members of the National Society of the Colonial Dames of America, are also of Royal Descent, through George Reade:

MRS. DANIEL H. BUELL, Maryland State Society.

MISS EVELYN BYRD MCCANDLISH, Maryland State Society.

MISS SUSETTE G. STEWART, Kentucky State Society.

MRS. HAMPTON L. FERRILL, Georgia State Society.

II.—MILDRED LEWIS ROOTES COBB, who *m.* Luther Judson Glenn, descended from Dr. John Glenn, of Dublin, N. C., son of Andrew Glenn, of Longcroft, Linlithgow, and had:

JOHN THOMAS GLENN, of Atlanta, who *m.* Helen Augusta, a member of the Georgia Society of the Colonial Dames of America, daughter of William Waters Garrard and his wife, Frances Isabella Garterey Urquhart, also of Royal Descent, and had: *Garrard, Helen Mildred Lewis, William Louis,* and

ISA GARTEREY URQUHART GLENN, of Atlanta, a member of the Georgia Society of the Colonial Dames of America.

III.—SARAH MARTHA COBB, who *m.* Major John Charles Whitner, of Atlanta, and had:

1.—SARAH ROOTES WHITNER, a member of the Georgia Society of the Colonial Dames of America, who *m.* Warren Howard, of Atlanta, and had: *Martha Cobb, Whitner,* and *Mary Ann.*

2.—MARY ANN WHITNER, a member of the Georgia Society of the Colonial Dames of America, who *m.* Benjamin Charles Milner, Jr., of Atlanta, and had: *Charles Whitner, Benjamin Charles, 3d, Jean Shepard,* and *John Cobb.*

3.—ELIZA SPANN WHITNER, of Atlanta, a member of the Georgia Society of the Colonial Dames of America.

4.—MARTHA MILDRED WHITNER, a member of the Georgia Society of the Colonial Dames of America, who *m.* Willis J. Milner, of Atlanta, and had: *Willis J., Spann Whitner* and *Benjamin C.*

IV.—GENERAL THOMAS READE ROOTES COBB, who *m.* Marian Lumpkin, and had:

MARIAN THOMAS COBB, a member of the Georgia Society of the Colonial Dames of America, who *m.* Hoke Smith, of Atlanta, and had: *Marion, Mary Brent, Lucy,* and *Callie.*

2.—ELIZABETH ROOTES, who *m.* (his second wife) Rev. John Thompson, of Culpeper county, Virginia, *d.* 1772, and had:

PHILIP ROOTES THOMPSON, of Culpeper, who had by his second wife, Sally Slaughter, of Culpeper:

JUDGE ROBERT AUGUSTINE THOMPSON, of San Francisco, who had by his first wife:

Sarah Elizabeth Thompson, a member of the Virginia Society of the Colonial Dames of America, who *m.* G. W. Huie, of San Francisco, and had:

Sallie Helena Huie, a member of the Virginia Society of the Colonial Dames of America, who *m.*, 1899, her cousin, William Thompson.

Judge Robert Augustine Thompson had by his second wife, Elizabeth Jane Early:

1.—Ruth Hairston Thompson, a member of the Virginia and California Societies of the Colonial Dames of America, who *m.* William Craig, of San Francisco, California.

2.—Roberta Thompson, of San Francisco, a member of the Virginia and California Societies of the Colonial Dames of America.

II.—Mary Reade, who *m.* Captain Mordecai Throckmorton, 1696–1768, also of Royal Descent, and had:

Lucy Throckmorton, *m.* Robert Throckmorton, and had:

Frances Throckmorton, *m.* General William Madison, and had:

Rebecca Conway Madison, *m.* Reynolds Chapman, and had:

Judge John Madison Chapman, *m.* Susannah Digges Cole, also of Royal Descent, and had:

I.—Susie Ashton Chapman, a member of the Tennessee Society of the Colonial Dames of America, the Order of the Crown, *etc.*, who *m.* Calvin Perkins, of Memphis, Tennessee. *Issue.*

II.—Belle Chapman, a member of the Virginia Society of the Colonial Dames of America, the Order of the Crown, *etc.*, who *m.* William Moncure, of Richmond, Virginia. *Issue.*

III.—Ashton Alexander Chapman.

2.—John Reade, who *m.* Mary Lilly, and had:

Margaret Reade, *m.* Thomas Nelson, of Yorktown, Virginia, and had:

Mary Nelson, who *m.* Edmund Berkeley, of "Barn Elms," and had:

Nelson Berkeley, of "Airwell," who *m.* Elizabeth Wormeley Carter, also of Royal Descent, and had:

Dr. Carter Berkeley, of "Edgewood," who *m.* Mrs. Frances (Page) Nelson, also of Royal Descent, and had:

Catherine Frances Berkeley, who *m.* Lucius Horatio Minor, of "Edgewood," also of Royal Descent, (*see* pp. 56, 183, 255), and had:

Mary Willis Minor, of Baltimore, a member of the Maryland Society of the Colonial Dames of America.

3.—MILDRED READE, who *m.*, before 1671, Colonel Augustine Warner, Jr., of Warner's Hall, Gloucester county, Virginia, *b.* 3 July, 1642, *d.* 19 June, 1681, a member and speaker of the Virginia House of Burgesses, 1658–77, a member of the Council from 10 May, 1680 (son of Captain Augustine Warner, of Warner's Hall, 1610–1674, a burgess for York county, 1652, Gloucester county, 1655, a member of the Council, 1659–74, *etc.*), and had:

I.—MARY WARNER, who *m.*, 17 February, 1688, John Smith, of "Purton," Gloucester county, Virginia, son of Major John Smith, of Warwick county, Virginia, and had:

AUGUSTINE SMITH, *b.* 16 June, 1687, *d.* 30 December, 1756; *m.*, 9 November, 1711, Sarah, daughter of Captain William Carver, a justice for Lower Norfolk county, 1665; high sheriff, 1670; a member of the House of Burgesses, 1665–72; general surveyor of highways, who took a prominent part in Bacon's rebellion, and was executed, and had by her:

JOHN SMITH, of "Shooter's Hill," Middlesex county, Virginia, *b.* 13 November, 1715, *d.* 19 November, 1771, a member of the House of Burgesses; *m.*, 17 November, 1737, Mary, daughter of Edward and Martha (Cary) Jacquelin, of Jamestown, Virginia, and had: *Maria*, wife of Thomas Reade Rootes (*see* p. 248), and

1.—MARY SMITH, who *m.* Rev. Thomas Smith, and had:

SARAH SMITH, who *m.* Benjamin Dabney, and had:

THOMAS SMITH GREGORY DABNEY, who *m.* Sophia Hill, and had:

SOPHIA DABNEY (Mrs. Thurmond, of Sewanee, Tennessee), a member of the Virginia Society of the Colonial Dames of America. Issue: *Sophia Dabney.*

2.—EDWARD SMITH, who *m.* Elizabeth Bush, and had:

ARIANA AMBLER SMITH, who *m.* William D. Holliday, and had:

WILLIAM JAQUELIN HOLLIDAY, of Indianapolis, who *m.* Lucy Redd, also of Royal Descent, a member of the Virginia and Indiana Societies of the Colonial Dames of America, and had:

1.—ARIANA AMBLER HOLLIDAY, a member of the Virginia and Indiana Societies of the Colonial Dames of America, who *m.* Henry W. Bennett, of Indianapolis, and had: *Edward Jaquelin* and *Louise.*

2.—JAQUELIN S. HOLLIDAY, who *m.* Florence Baker, and had: *William J.* and *Frederick Taylor.*

3.—LUCY FITZHUGH HOLLIDAY, who *m.* George E. Hume, and had: *William Manser.*

3.—Augustine Smith, of "Shooter's Hill," b. 3 August, 1738, d. 1774, m. (his second wife) Margaret, daughter of David Boyd, of Northumberland county, Virginia, and had:

Mary Jacquelin Smith, b. 12 February, 1773, d. 31 October, 1846; m. John Cripps Vowell, of Alexandria, Virginia, and had:

Sarah Gosnelle Vowell, b. 6 October, 1813, a member of the Virginia Society of the Colonial Dames of America, who m. Francis Lee Smith, of Fauquier county, Virginia, and had:

1.—L. Jacquelin Smith, b. 2 October, 1837, d. Morristown, New Jersey, 19 February, 1895. He served four years in the Confederate army, was aide-de-camp to General R. E. Lee, and was lieutenant-colonel of artillery at the end of the Civil War. He m. Mary, daughter of John and Sarah Poythress (Smith) Campbell, of New York City, and had: *John Campbell, Augustine Jacquelin, Sarah Poythress*, and *Gladys*.

2.—Margaret Vowell Smith, of Alexandria, Virginia, b. 2 March, 1839, a member of the Virginia Society of the Colonial Dames of America, the Order of the Crown, etc., author of "Governors of Virginia."

3.—Clifton Hewitt Smith, of New York City, b. 19 August, 1841. He served four years in the Confederate army, was captain and assistant adjutant-general on General Beauregard's staff, was taken prisoner at Fort Morgan and confined in Fort Lafayette.

4.—Mary Jacquelin Smith, b. 4 October, 1843, d. 7 September, 1884.

5.—Francis Lee Smith, Jr., of Alexandria, Virginia, b. 6 October, 1845. When a cadet at the Virginia Military Institute he took part with the cadet corps in the battle at New Market, 15 May, 1864, where he was twice severely wounded; a member of the Virginia Senate, 1879–83; was captain of the Alexandria Light Infantry, and lieutenant-colonel Third Regiment Virginia Volunteers. He m. Jannie L., daughter of Major W. T. Sutherlin, of Danville, Virginia, and had: *Jannie S.* and *Sarah Vowell, d.*

6.—Alice Corbin Smith, a member of the Virginia Society of the Colonial Dames of America, b. 15 June, 1848, m. William E. Strong, of New York City, and had: *Francis Lee, d., Annie Massie*, and *Alice Everard*.

7.—Major Courtland Hawkins Smith, of Alexandria, Virginia, b. 29 August, 1850, d. 22 July, 1892; was mayor of Alexandria, 1879, assistant adjutant-general of Virginia, and an aide-de-camp and chief of staff to Governor Fitzhugh Lee. He m., 15 December, 1875, Charlotte E. Rossiter, of New York City, and had: *Francis Lee, d.*, and *Cortland H., b.* 21 January, 1878.

8.—SARAH VOWELL SMITH, *b.* 23 March, 1853 ; *m.* Edward L. Daingerfield, of Alexandria, Virginia, and had: *Sarah Vowell, John Bathurst, d., Mary Helen, Francis Lee,* and *Edward Lonsdale, d.*

9.—ROBERT WOODLEIGH SMITH, *b.* 2 November, 1856, *d.* 6 August, 1857.

II.—MILDRED WARNER, who *m.*, first, 1690, Lawrence Washington (eldest son of Colonel John Washington, 1627–1677, by his second wife, Anne Pope, of Charles county, Maryland, *m.* 1660), *b.* Bridge's Creek, Westmoreland county, Virginia, 166–, *d.* at Bridge's Creek in 1697, and had :

1.—JOHN WASHINGTON (uncle of President Washington), *b.* Bridge's Creek, 1692, *d.* in Gloucester county, Virginia, *m.* Catherine Whiting, and had :

WARNER WASHINGTON, *b.* Bridge's Creek, 1717, *d.* Frederick county, Virginia, 1791, *m.*, first, Elizabeth, daughter of Colonel William Macon, of New Kent county, Virginia, and had by her :

WARNER WASHINGTON, JR., *b.* Gloucester county, Virginia, 15 April, 1751, *d.* Clark county, Virginia. He *m.*, secondly, at Elmington, Gloucester county, Virginia, 13 June, 1795, Sarah Warner Rootes, and had by her :

READE WASHINGTON, *b.* at "Audley," in Virginia, 18 May, 1796, *d.* at Pittsburgh, Pennsylvania. He *m.*, in 182–, Elizabeth Crawford, of Chambersburg, Pennsylvania, and had :

AUGUSTUS WASHINGTON, *b.* about 1823, who *m.*, April 6, 1852, Susan T. Fulton, of Pittsburgh, Pennsylvania, and had :

1.—WILLIAM HERBERT WASHINGTON, Philadelphia, *d.* 14 July, 1900, aged 45; *m.*, November 14, 1885, Constance L. Bowden, of New York, and had : *Bowden, b.* 16 July, 1892.

2.—ELIZABETH CRAWFORD WASHINGTON, a member of the Pennsylvania Society of the Colonial Dames of America.

2.—AUGUSTINE WASHINGTON, of Stafford county, Virginia, *d.* 12 April, 1743, aged about 50 years, who *m.*, 6 March, 1730–1 (his second wife), Mary, *d.* at "Mt. Vernon," 25 August, 1789, aged about 80 years (*see* Hayden's "Virginia Genealogies," p. 81), daughter of Colonel Joseph Ball, of "Epping Forest," Lancaster county, Virginia, and had :

I.—COLONEL CHARLES WASHINGTON (brother of President Washington), *b.* 2 May, 1738; *m.* Mildred, daughter of Colonel Francis Thornton, and had :

COLONEL GEORGE AUGUSTINE WASHINGTON, *m.* Frances Bassett, and had :

ANNA MARIA WASHINGTON, *m.* Rubin Thornton, and had:

CHARLES AUGUSTINE THORNTON, *m.* Cornelia Randolph, and had:

ANNA MARIA WASHINGTON THORNTON, a member of the North Carolina Society of the Coloniel Dames of America, who *m.* Philip Barton Key, of Statesville, North Carolina.

II.—BETTY WASHINGTON (sister of President Washington), *b.* at "Wakefield," Westmoreland county, Virginia, 20 June, 1733, who *m.*, in May, 1750 (his second wife), Colonel Fielding Lewis, of "Kenmore," Spottsylvania county, Virginia, and had:

1.—HOWELL LEWIS, of Kanawha county, West Virginia, who *m.* Ellen Pollard, and had:

FRANCES FIELDING LEWIS, who *m.* Humphrey Brooke Gwathmey, of Richmond, Virginia, and had:

VIRGINIA GWATHMEY, a member of the North Carolina Society of the Colonial Dames of America, who *m.* Adam Empie, of Wilmington, North Carolina, and had: *Swift Miller, Brooke Gwathmey, Virginia* (deceased); *Adam* (deceased); *Ellen* (deceased); *Theodore Gwathmey* (who *m.* Evelyn Pearson); *Adam,* and

I.—ANNIE EMPIE, a member of the North Carolina Society of the Colonial Dames of America, the Order of the Crown, *etc.,* who *m.* Edward Bailey, and had: *Edward, Virginia, Karin Dohlstrome,* and *Frances Fielding Lewis.*

II.—FRANCES FIELDING LEWIS EMPIE, a member of the North Carolina Society of the Colonial Dames of America, the Order of the Crown, *etc.,* who *m.,* first, Herbert Russell Latimer, *d.* 1887, and had: *Herbert Russell* and *Empie,* and *m.,* secondly, in 1890, Frederick C. Poisson, of London, England. *No issue.*

2.—ROBERT LEWIS, private secretary to his uncle, General George Washington, who *m.* Judith Walker Browne, also of Royal Descent, and had:

ELIZABETH BURNET LEWIS, who *m.* George Washington Bassett, of "Eltham," New Kent county, Virginia, 1800–1878, also of Royal Descent, and had:

I.—ANNA VIRGINIA BASSETT, who *m.* Major John Hayes Claiborne, of Richmond, Virginia, also of Royal Descent, and had:

DELIA CLAIBORNE, a member of the Virginia Society of the Colonial Dames of America, who *m.* General Simon B. Buckner, of Hart county, Kentucky, and had: *Simon B.*

II.—ELLA BASSETT, a member of the Virginia Society of the Colonial Dames of America, *d.* 1898, who *m.* Lewis William Washington. *Issue.*

3.—MILDRED WASHINGTON, widow of Roger Gregory, who *m.*, secondly (his third wife), Colonel Henry Willis, and had:

COLONEL LEWIS WILLIS, who *m.* Mary Champe, and had:

MILDRED WILLIS, who *m.* Landon Carter, of "Cleve," also of Royal Descent, and had:

LUCY LANDON CARTER, *m.* General John Minor, of "Hazel Hill," and had:

LUCIUS HORATIO MINOR, of "Edgewood," *m.* Catherine Frances Berkeley, also of Royal Descent (p. 250), and had:

MARY WILLIS MINOR, of Baltimore, a member of the Maryland Society of the Colonial Dames of America.

III.—ELIZABETH WARNER, *b.* 24 November, 1672, *d.* 5 February, 1720, who *m.* at "Cheesecake," before 1692, Colonel John Lewis, of "Warner Hall," of Gloucester county, Virginia, *b.* 30 November, 1669, *d.* 14 November, 1725, colonel of county militia; a councillor in 1715; member and speaker of the House of Burgesses, and had:

1.—COLONEL CHARLES LEWIS, of "The Byrd," Gloucester county, will proved 20 December, 1779; colonel of county militia, commissioned 20 March, 1753, and 18 August, 1761. He *m.*, 17 May, 1717, Mary, 1700–1779, daughter of John Howell, and had:

I.—ANNE LEWIS, *b.* 2 March, 1732, *d.* 1809 or 1810, who *m.* Edmund Taylor, of Caroline county, Virginia, *b.* 5 July, 1723, *d.* 1808, will dated 10 January, 1807, son of John Taylor (and Catherine, daughter of Philip Pendleton, 1650–1721), son of James Taylor, *d.* 1698, and had:

FRANCES TAYLOR, *d.* 26 January, 1815, aged 62, who *m.*, 15 January, 1789, Rev. Nathaniel Moore, *b.* in Granville county, North Carolina, 10 December, 1757, *d.* at Columbia, Tennessee, 23 June, 1829, and had:

1.—MARY MOORE, *b.* 18 August, 1794, *d.* 28 June, 1884; *m.*, 26 July, 1814, William Porter, *d.* 28 December, 1843, aged 70, and had:

WILLIAM TAYLOR PORTER, *b.* 21 April, 1828, *d.* 21 March, 1864; *m.*, 17 February, 1857, Mary Pillow, *b.* 6 March, 1838, and had:

LOUISE PORTER, *b.* 30 January, 1858, a member of the Tennessee Society of the Colonial Dames of America, the Order of the Crown, *etc.*, who *m.*, 11 December, 1880, William Keeling Phillips, of Nashville, *b.* 20 January, 1854.

2.—ANNE LEWIS MOORE, *b.* 3 November, 1796, *d.* 13 February, 1828; *m.*, 22 May, 1815, Edward Washington Dale, *b.* 11 November, 1790, in Worcester county, Maryland, *d.* 7 July, 1840, at Columbia, and had: *Mary F.*, wife of Archibald Williams; *Thomas, Nathaniel,* and

I.—ELVIRA H. DALE, who *m.* Jerome Bonaparte Pillow, of Tennessee, son of Gideon Pillow, and his wife, Anne, daughter of Josias Payne, Jr., and had: *Mrs. Anne Lewis Ridley, Mrs. Martha Woodson Long, Mrs. Frances Parker, Edward Dale, Jerome B.*, and

    1.—ELVIRA DALE PILLOW, a member of the Virginia Society of the Colonial Dames of America, the Order of the Crown, *etc.*, who *m.* John Maffitt Gray, of Nashville, and had:

       I.—ANNIE PAYNE GRAY, *m.* J. W. Madden, M.D., of Nashville, and had: *Annie Gray.*

       II.—JOHN M. GRAY, JR., of Nashville, *m.* Rebecca Wilson, and had: *Rebecca.*

    2.—CYNTHIA SAUNDERS PILLOW, a member of the Virginia Society of the Colonial Dames of America, the Order of the Crown, *etc.*, who *m.* Captain William Decatur Bethell, of Memphis, Tennessee, and Denver, Colorado, and had:

       I.—BESSIE BETHELL, *m.* John M. Foster, M.D., of Denver, and had: *Bethell, Pinckney,* and *John M.*

       II.—JEROME PILLOW BETHELL, *d. s. p.*, who *m.* Lucy Watts.

       III.—CHARLES C. PINCKNEY BETHELL, *d. unm.*

       IV.—HATTIE BETHELL, *d.* young.

       V.—JENNIE BETHELL, *m.* John P. Edrington, of Memphis, and had: *William Bethell, Cynthia,* and *John Price, Jr.*

       VI.—WILLIAM DECATUR BETHELL, JR., of Memphis, *m.* Helen Worden, of Denver, and had: *William Decatur, 3d,* and *Charles Worden.*

II.—ANNE LEWIS DALE, *b.* 14 May, 1821, *d.* 17 February, 1888; *m.*, 9 October, 1845, James Robertson, *b.* Ayrshire, Scotland, 8 December, 1816, *d.* at Memphis, Tennessee, 26 May, 1898, and had: *Mrs. Elvira Gray, Edward H., John Nathaniel, Edward Dale, James T., Jerome Pillow,* and

    1.—JEAN ROBERTSON, *b.* Maury county, Tennessee, 1 September, 1846, a member of the Virginia Society of the Colonial Dames of America, the Order of the Crown, *etc.*, who *m.*, 11 February, 1869, Colonel Keller Anderson, United States Army, of Memphis, *b.* Cynthiana, Kentucky, 21 September, 1842, and had:

I.—CLAUDE DESHA ANDERSON, of Memphis, *b.* 1871; *m.*, 1896, Mary Simmons, and had: *Claude Desha, b.* 11 August, 1897.

II.—JEAN KELLER ANDERSON, of Memphis.

2.—MARY ROBERTSON, a member of the Virginia Society of the Colonial Dames of America, the Order of the Crown, *etc.*, who *m.* Captain Thomas Day, of Memphis, and had: *Mary Louise.*

II.—JOHN LEWIS, 1720–1794, who *m.*, 1741, Jane Lewis, *b.* 1727, and had:

MARY LEWIS, *d.* 1813, who *m.* Captain William Williams, *d.* 1813, and had:

FIELDING LEWIS WILLIAMS, 1794–1845, who *m.*, 1827, Frances P. Boyd, *d.* 1833, and had:

FIELDING LEWIS WILLIAMS, JR., 1832–1898, who *m.*, 1863, Abby Louisa Miller, of Bristol, Rhode Island, *b.* 1842, and had:

1.—LOUISE MILLER WILLIAMS, a member of the Rhode Island Society of the Colonial Dames of America, who *m.* John Taylor Lewis, of Virginia, also of Royal Descent.

2.—MILDRED LEWIS WILLIAMS, a member of the Rhode Island Society of the Colonial Dames of America, who *m.*, 1891, William Frederick Williams, of Bristol, Rhode Island, and had: *William Frederick, b.* 3 April, 1896.

III.—HOWELL LEWIS, of "The Byrd," who *m.* Mary, daughter of Colonel Henry Willis and his first wife, Mrs. Mildred (Howell) Brown, and had:

MILDRED LEWIS, who *m.* John Cobbs, of the "Sand Hills," Augusta, Georgia, and had: *John Addison Cobb* (p. 248), and

I.—MARY WILLIS COBBS, who *m.* Colonel Robert W. Flournoy, and had:

MARY MILDRED FLOURNOY, who *m.* Nathaniel Alexander Adams, and had:

MARY WILLIS ADAMS, who *m.* William Bullock Jackson, and had:

MARY VIRGINIA JACKSON, a member of the Georgia Society of the Colonial Dames of America, who *m.* Richard Wylly Thiot, of Savannah, and had: *Florence King, Richard Wylly, Edith Nowlan,* and *Mary Mildred Bryan.*

II.—MILDRED COBBS, *m.* William H. Jackson, and had:

MILDRED LEWIS COBB JACKSON, *m.* Colonel John D. Grant, and had:

WILLIAM DANIEL GRANT, *m.* Sarah Francis Reid, and had:

SARAH FRANCES GRANT, a member of the Georgia Society of the Colonial Dames of America, who *m.* John Marshall Slaton, of Atlanta.

2.—COLONEL ROBERT LEWIS, of " Belvoir," Albemarle county, Virginia, *d.* 1757, who *m.* Jane, daughter of Nicholas and Mildred (Thompson) Meriwether, and had [besides other issue, from whom is descended MRS. JOHN B. GORDON (*nee* Frances R. Haralson), of "Kirkwood," Atlanta, a member of the Georgia Society of the Colonial Dames of America, mother of MRS. BURTON-SMITH (*nee* Frances Gordon) and CAROLINE LEWIS GORDON, of Atlanta, both members of the Georgia Society of the Colonial Dames of America]:

I.—JANE LEWIS, who *m.*, first, Major Thomas Meriwether, and had:

MARY MERIWETHER, who *m.* Captain Richard P. White, and had:

MALINDA LEWIS WHITE, who *m.* Pleasant Moore Benning, and had:

JUDGE HENRY LEWIS BENNING, of Muscogee county, Georgia, brigadier-general Confederate States Army, *m.* Mary Howard Jones, and had:

1.—LOUISE VIVIAN BENNING, a member of the Georgia Society of the Colonial Dames of America, who *m.* Samuel Spencer, of New York City.

2.—ANNA CAROLINE BENNING, of Columbus, Georgia, a member of the Georgia Society of the Colonial Dames of America, a member of the Order of the Crown, *etc.*

II.—NICHOLAS LEWIS, *b.* 1742, who *m.* Mary, daughter of Dr. Thomas and Mildred Thornton (Meriwether) Walker, of " Castle Hill," Virginia, and had:

NICHOLAS MERIWETHER LEWIS, *b.* 1767, who *m.* his cousin, Mildred, daughter of Joseph Hornby, and his wife, Mildred, daughter of Dr. Thomas Walker, of " Castle Hill," and had:

ANNAH HORNSBY LEWIS, who *m.*, 31 August, 1814 (his second wife), Hancock Taylor, *b.* 29 January, 1781, *d.* 29 March, 1841, and had:

MARY LOUISE TAYLOR, *b.* 20 May, 1824, who *m.*, 2 May, 1843, Archibald Magill Robinson, of Louisville, Kentucky, and had:

ANNAH WALKER ROBINSON, *b.* 5 November, 1848, a member of the Mississippi Society of the Colonial Dames of America, who *m.*, 5 October, 1870, James Henry Watson, of Memphis, Tennessee, *b.* 3 January, 1848, and had: *John William Clark, b.* 5 October, 1871, *d.* 27 June, 1872; *Archibald R., b.* 27 December,

1872; *James Henry, b.* 5 July, 1874; *Louise Taylor, b.* 23 December, 1875, *d.* 3 September, 1876; *Catherine Davis, b.* 25 November, 1877, and *Elizabeth Lee, b.* 8 October, 1880.

3.—JOHN LEWIS, of "Warner's Hall," 1644-1754, had by his wife, Frances Fielding:

COLONEL CHARLES LEWIS, who had by his wife, Lucy Taliaferro:

MARY WARNER LEWIS, who *m.*, first, Philip Lightfoot, and had:

PHILIP LIGHTFOOT, *m.* Sallie Savigne Bernard, and had:

WILLIAM BERNARD LIGHTFOOT, *m.* Sarah Bee Ross, and had:

I.—NORA MEADE LIGHTFOOT, a member of the Maryland Society of the Colonial Dames of America, who *m.* William Reynolds, of Baltimore, and had: *Eleanor Tarleton* and *Nora Lightfoot.*

II.—SALLIE BERNARD LIGHTFOOT, a member of the Maryland Society of the Colonial Dames of America, who *m.* Robert Tarleton, of Baltimore, and had:

1.—SARAH LIGHTFOOT TARLETON, a member of the Maryland Society of the Colonial Dames of America, who *m.* Alexander B. Colvin, M.D., of Canada.

2.—ROBERT MELVIN TARLETON, of Baltimore, *unm.*

3.—MARGARET, wife of Marshall Winchester, of Baltimore.

THE ROYAL DESCENT

OF

MRS. FRANKLIN R. CARPENTER,

OF DENVER, COLORADO.

Princess Eleanor of Castile=**EDWARD I.**, King of England=Princess Margaret of France.

Humphrey, Earl of Here-=Elizabeth Plantag- Thomas, Earl of Norfolk=Alice Halys.
ford   enet.

Eleanor de Bohun=James, Earl of Ormond. Margaret Plantagenet=John de Segrave.

Petronella Butler=Gilbert de Talbot.   Elizabeth de Segrave=John de Mowbray.

Richard de Talbot=Ankeretta le Strange. Jane de Mowbray=Thomas de Grey.

John, Earl of Shrewsbury=Maud de Neville. Thomas de Grey=Alice de Neville.

Thomas de Talbot=(Name unknown.)   Elizabeth de Grey=Philip d'Arcy.

Elizabeth de Talbot=Henry de Grey.

Lady Margaret de Grey=John, Baron d'Arcy.

Philip, Baron d'Arcy=Lady Eleanor Fitz-Hugh.

Lady Margaret d'Arcy=Sir John Conyers, of Hornby, Yorkshire.

Richard Conyers, of Horden=Lady Elizabeth Claxton, of Horden, Durham.

Robert Conyers, of Horden=Margaret Bamforth, of Seham, Durham.

Christopher Conyers, of Horden=Elizabeth Jackson, of Bedale, Durham.

Richard Conyers, of Horden=Mabel Lumley, of Ludworth, Durham.

Christopher Conyers, of Horden=Anne Hedsworth, of Harraton, Durham.

Mary Conyers=William Wilkinson, of Lanchester, Durham.

Lawrence Wilkinson, Providence, R. I.=Susannah Smith, of Providence, R. I.

Samuel Wilkinson, Providence, R. I.=Plain Wickenden, of Providence, R. I.

Joseph Wilkinson, of Scituate, R. I.=Martha Pray, of Smithfield, R. I.

Prudence Wilkinson=Isaiah Angell.

Prudence Angell=Gideon Austin.

Ruth Austin=James Cranston.

Martha Cranston=Silas Bingham, Jr.

Hannah Bingham=James Fuller Howe, M.D.

Annette Howe=Franklin R. Carpenter, M.A., Ph.D., F.G.S.A., etc.,
of Denver, Colorado.

Arthur Howe Carpenter, b. Oct. 19, 1877.	Harold Howe Carpenter, b. Jan. 26, 1881; d. Oct. 20, 1890.	Cranston Howe Carpenter, b. Oct. 10, 1882.	Malcolm Howe Carpenter, b. Aug. 7, 1884.	Grace Howe Carpenter, b. Oct. 21, 1887; d. Aug. 27, 1899.	Annette Howe Carpenter, b. Aug. 15, 1892.	Talbot Howe Carpenter, b. Jan. 19, 1896.

PEDIGREE LX.

ETHELRED II., King of England, called the Unready, *d.* 1016, had by his first wife, Lady Elgiva, *d.* 1003, daughter of Earl Thorad :

PRINCESS ELGIVA, who *m.* Uthrea, Earl of Northumbria, and had:

LADY AGATHA, or Aldigitha, who *m.* Maldred, son of Crynan, lord of the Isles, and grandson of Malcolm II., King of Scotland, and had :

COSPATRICK, Earl of Northumberland and Dunbar, who had :

COSPATRICK, first Earl of Dunbar, *d.* 1139, who had :

COSPATRICK, second Earl of Dunbar, *d.* 1147, who had :

COSPATRICK, third Earl of Dunbar, *d.* 1166, who had :

WALDEVE, fourth Earl of Dunbar, *d.* 1182, who had :

PATRICK, fifth Earl of Dunbar, who had :

PATRICK, sixth Earl of Dunbar, who *m.* Lady Euphemia, daughter of Walter Stewart, the fifth hereditary high steward of Scotland, and had :

LADY —— DUNBAR, who *m.* her cousin, James Stewart, the seventh hereditary lord high steward of Scotland, and had :

WALTER STEWART, the eighth hereditary lord high steward of Scotland, 1293–1326, who had by his third wife, Lady Isabel, daughter of Sir John Graham, of Abercorn :

LADY EGIDIA STEWART, half-sister of King Robert II., of Scotland, and widow of James Lindsay, Earl of Crawford, who *m.*, secondly, Sir Hugh de Eglintoun, of that Ilk, justiciary of Lothian, 1361, lord of Ardrossan, *d.* 1376, and had :

LADY ELIZABETH DE EGLINTOUN, sole heiress, who *m.* John de Montgomery, laird of Eglintoun and Ardrossan, in right of his wife, who signalized himself in the battle of Otterburn by capturing Henry de Percy, whose ransom built the Castle of Polnone, *d.* after 8 October, 1392, and had :

SIR JOHN DE MONTGOMERY, laird of Eglisham, Eglintoun and Ardrossan, a hostage for the Earl of Douglas in 1408; one of the jury which tried the Duke of Albany in 1425, *d. ante* 10 August, 1430. He *m.* Lady Margaret, daughter of Robert Maxwell, laird of Caerlaverock, and had :

LADY ANNE DE MONTGOMERY, who *m.* (contract dated 16 June, 1425) Sir Robert Cunyngham, laird of Kilmures, one of the hostages for James I., and knighted by him (the eldest son of Sir William, *d.* 1418, the

(261)

second son of Sir William Cunyngham, by his first wife, name unknown, *see* Paterson's " His. of Ayr and Wigton," viii., 470, and Douglas's " Peerage," i., 321), and had :

ALEXANDER CUNYNGHAM, created Lord Kilmures in 1450, and Earl of Glencairn in 1488, *k.* at Bannockburn, who *m.* Lady Margaret, daughter of Sir Adam Hepburn, second lord of Hales, and had :

WILLIAM CUNYNGHAM, laird of Craigends, second son, *m.* Elizabeth, daughter of Walter Stewart, of Arthurly and Wester-Patrick, and had :

WILLIAM CUNYNGHAM, laird of Craigends, *m.* Egidia, daughter of John Campbell, of Killoch, and had :

GILBERT CUNYNGHAM, third laird of Craigends, *k.* 1547, who *m.* Margaret (or Elizabeth), daughter of William Livingston, fourth laird of Kilsyth, *d.* 1540, and had :

JAMES CUNYNGHAM, of Ashenyeard, second son, who *m.* Margaret Fleming, daughter of the laird of Barrochan, and had :

WILLIAM CUNYNGHAM, of Glengarnock, second son, who *m.* Rebecca Muirland, daughter of the laird of Lenhouse, and had :

RICHARD CUNYNGHAM, of Glengarnock, who *m.*, 3 October, 1654, Elizabeth, daughter of James Heriot, of Trabroun, and had :

ROBERT CUNYNGHAM, *b.* 24 March, 1669; removed to the Island of St. Christopher, and *d.* 1749; *m.*, 26 September, 1693, Judith Elizabeth, daughter of Daniel de Bonneson, of Morlais, France, and had :

MARY CUNYNGHAM, *b.* 4 April, 1699, *d.* 13 March, 1771, who *m.*, 1723 Isaac Roberdeau, who removed from Rochelle, France, to the Island of St. Christopher, in 1685, and *d.* before 1743, and had :

DANIEL ROBERDEAU, of Philadelphia, only son, *b.* St. Christopher, 1727. He was a member of the Pennsylvania Assembly, 1756–60; of the Council of Safety, 1775–76; general commanding the Pennsylvania troops in the Revolutionary War; member of the Continental Congress, 1777–79, and signer of the Articles of Confederation. He *m.*, first, 3 October, 1761, Mary Bostwiek, and had :

MARY ROBERDEAU, *b.* Philadelphia, May, 1774, who *m.* Thomas Patten, of Alexandria, Virginia, and had :

SELINA BLAIR PATTEN, *b.* Alexandria, 12 September, 1805, who *m.* Rev. John T. Wheat, D.D., of Virginia, and had :

JOSEPHINE MAY WHEAT, *b.* 22 February, 1833, who *m.* Francis E. Shober, sometime member of Congress from North Carolina, and had :

MAY SHOBER, a member of the North Carolina Society of the Colonial Dames of America, the Order of the Crown, *etc.*, who *m.* Archibald Boyden, of Salisbury, and had : *May Wheat* and *Jane Henderson.*

THE ROYAL DESCENT

OF

MRS. HOMER HINE STUART,

OF NEW YORK CITY.

HUGH CAPET, King of France=Adela, dau. William, Duke of Aquitaine.

Robert I., the Pious,=Lady Constance King of France | of Provence.

Princess Havide=Rynerius IV., Count or Hedewige | of Hainault.

Henry I., King of=Lady Anne of Russia. France

Lady Beatrix=Eblo de Rouci.

Hugh Magnus,=Lady Adelheid of Duke of France | Vermandois.

Countess Adela=Hildwin de Montdider.

Lady Margaret de Rouci=Hugh de Clermont.

William de Warren,=Lady Isabel de=Robert de Bellomont, Lady Adeliza=Gilbert de Tonsburg, Earl of Surrey | Vermandois | Earl of Leicester. de Clermont | Earl of Clare.

William de Warren,=Lady Alice de Talvas, Lady Elizabeth de Bellomont=Gilbert de Clare, Earl Earl of Surrey | also of Royal Descent. of Pembroke.

Lady Isabella de=Hameline Plantagenet, Richard "the Strongbow,"=Eva, dau. Dermot, Warren | Earl of Surrey. 2d Earl of Pembroke | King of Leinster.

Lady Isabella de=Roger Bigod, Earl of Lady Isabel de Clare=William le Marshal, Warren | Norfolk. Protector of England.

Hugh Bigod, second Earl of Norfolk=Lady Maud Marshall.

Sir Hugh Bigod, Justiciary of England=Joan, dau. of Robert Burnet.

Sir John Bigod, Knt.=(Name unknown.)

Sir Roger Bigod, of Settington=(Name unknown.)

Lady Joan Bigod=Sir William de Chauncy, of Skirpenbeck.

John Chauncy, of Stepney=Margaret Gifford, of Gedleston.

John Chauncy, of Sawbridgeworth=Anne Leventhorp, of Shingey.

John Chauncy, of Sawbridgeworth=Daughter of Thomas Boyce.

John Chauncy, of Pishobury=Elizabeth (Proffit) Mansfield.

Henry Chauncy, of Newplace Giffords=Lucy ——.

George Chauncy, of Yardleybury=Anne Welsh, of Great Wymondley.

Rev. Charles Chauncy, D.D., 1592-1671, second=Catherine Eyre, of New Sarum. President of Harvard College

Rev. Nathaniel Chauncy, of Hatfield, Mass.=Abigail Strong, of Northampton, Mass.

Rev. Nathaniel Chauncy, of Durham, Ct.=Sarah Judson, of Stratford, Conn.

Col. Elihu Chauncy, of Durham, Mass.=Mary Griswold, of Killingworth.

Catherine Chauncy=Rev. Elizur Goodrich, D.D., of Durham, Mass.

Rev. Samuel Goodrich, of Ridgefield, Conn.=Elizabeth Ely, of Pachog.

Catherine Chauncy Goodrich=David Dunbar, of Berlin, Conn.

Margaret Elizabeth Dunbar, member of the So-=Homer Hine Stuart, of New York, b. 1 April, 1810, ciety of Colonial Dames of the State of New | d. 5 October, 1885. York

Katharine Dunbar Stuart=John G. Dunscomb, member of the Society | of New York. of the Colonial Dames of the State of New York

Homer Hine Stuart,=Margaret Inglis Stuart, Jr., of Philadel- | Beck- of New York phia, Penna. | with City. *Unm.* | Kenny.

Margaret Stuart Cecil John Carol Godefroi Dunscomb, b. Dunscomb, Dunscomb, Dunscomb, Jan. 26, 1886. b. Sept. 20, b. Oct. 27, b. Jan. 23, 1887. 1889. 1893.

Homer Howland Stuart, b. July 5, 1890.

PEDIGREE LXI.

EDWARD I., King of England, *m.*, secondly, 1299, Margaret, daughter of Philip III., King of France, and had by her:

EDMOND, Earl of Kent, beheaded in 1329. He *m.* Lady Margaret, daughter of John, Baron de Wake, also of Royal Descent, and had:

LADY JOAN PLANTAGENET, "the Fair Maid of Kent" (divorced wife of William de Montacute, Earl of Salisbury), who *m.*, secondly, Sir Thomas de Holland, K.G., Earl of Kent, *d.* 1360, also of Royal Descent (she *m.*, third, Edward, "the Black Prince," son of King Edward III., and by him was the mother of King Richard II.), and had:

SIR THOMAS DE HOLLAND, K.G., 1350–1397, second Earl of Kent, marshal of England, who *m.* Lady Alice Fitz-Alan, daughter of Richard, K.G., Earl of Arundel and Surrey, and his wife, Lady Eleanor Plantagenet, also of Royal Descent, and had:

LADY MARGARET HOLLAND, *d.* 31 December, 1440, who *m.*, first, Sir John de Beaufort, K.G., Marquis of Dorset, Earl of Somerset, *d.* 1418, also of Royal Descent, and had:

LADY JOAN DE BEAUFORT, who *m.*, first, James I., King of Scotland, and had James II., King of Scotland, and *m.*, secondly, in 1439, Sir James Stewart, "the Black Knight of Lorn," also of Royal Descent, and had:

SIR JOHN STEWART, created, in 1457, Earl of Athol, *d.* 1512, who *m.*, secondly, Lady Eleanor, daughter of William Sinclair, Earl of Orkney and Caithness, also of Royal Descent, and had:

LADY ELIZABETH STEWART, who *m.* (his second wife) Andrew, third Lord Gray (*see* Playfair's "British Family Antiquity," iii.), and had:

LADY JEAN GRAY, who *m.*, first, Sir Alexander Blair, of Balthyock (*see* Wood's Douglas's "Peerage of Scotland," i., 669, ii., 156), and had:

SIR THOMAS BLAIR, Knt., of Balthyock, Perthshire, who had:

LADY EUPHAME BLAIR, *m.* Andrew Scott, the second son of Sir William Scott, of Balweary and Innertiel, by his wife, Lady Isabel Lindsay, the daughter of Patrick, fourth Lord Lindsay, of the Byres, also of Royal Descent (*see* Douglas's "Peerage of Scotland," i., 384), and had:

ANDREW SCOTT, of Kirkstyle, who *m.* Lady Margaret, daughter of Sir Patrick Ogilvie, of Inchmartin, and had by her an only son:

GEORGE SCOTT, of Kirkstyle, who *m.* Catherine, daughter of Hugh Montcrief, of Rind, and had:

PATRICK SCOTT, who sold the lands of Kirkstyle, and acquired the lands and Barony of Ancrum, in Roxburgshire. He *m.*, first, Elizabeth, daughter of Simson, of Monturpie, in Fife, and had by her:

SIR JOHN SCOTT, Bart., of Ancrum, created a baronet of Nova Scotia 27 October, 1671, *d.* 1712 (*see* Playfair's "British Family Antiquity," viii., App. 308), who *m.*, first, Elizabeth, daughter of Francis Scott, of Mangerton, and had by her:

JOHN SCOTT, third son, who came to New York about 1702, and was appointed commandant of Fort Hunter, on the Mohawk. He *m.*, 1702, Magdalen, daughter of John Vincent, of New York, and had:

JOHN SCOTT, of New York, *b.* 1702, *d.* 30 April, 1733, eldest son, who *m.* Marian Morin, who *d.* 5 September, 1755, and had:

BRIGADIER-GENERAL JOHN MORIN SCOTT, 1730–1784, only son; secretary of State of New York, member of the Provincial and of the Continental Congress, and a member of the Society of the Cincinnati. He *m.* Helena Rutgers, of New York, and had:

LEWIS ALLAIRE SCOTT, only son, secretary of State of New York, *b.* 11 February, 1759, *d.* 17 March, 1798. He *m.*, 18 January, 1785, Juliana, daughter of William Sitgreaves, of Easton, Pennsylvania, and had:

JOHN MORIN SCOTT, of Philadelphia, Pennsylvania, only son, elected mayor of Philadelphia in 1841, and twice re-elected, *b.* in New York City, 25 October, 1789. He *m.*, 15 May, 1817, Mary, daughter of George Emlen, of Philadelphia, and dying 3 April, 1858, had issue:

1.—SARAH EMLEN SCOTT, who *m.* Joseph Dennie Meredith, of Philadelphia, and had:

MARY EMLEN MEREDITH, a member of the New York Society of the Colonial Dames of America, who *m.* J. Montgomery Hare, of New York City. *Issue.*

2.—LEWIS ALLAIRE SCOTT, of Philadelphia, *b.* 10 August, 1819, who *m.*, 27 June, 1857, Frances Anna, daughter of Richard Wistar, Jr., of Philadelphia, 1790–1863, also of Royal Descent, had, besides other children:

HANNAH LEWIS SCOTT, of Philadelphia, a member of the Pennsylvania Society of the Colonial Dames of America.

3.—JULIA SCOTT, a member of the Pennsylvania Society of the Colonial Dames of America, who *m.* Robert Waln Leaming, of Philadelphia, *d.* 1884, and had, besides other children:

I.—MARY EMLEN LEAMING, a member of the Pennsylvania Society of the Colonial Dames of America, who *m.* Richard Francis Wood, of Philadelphia. *Issue.*

II.—JULIA LEAMING, a member of the Pennsylvania Society of the Colonial Dames of America, who *m.* Nicholas Lennig, of Philadelphia, also of Royal Descent.

17

PEDIGREE LXII.

EDWARD I., King of England, had by his first wife, Princess Eleanor of Castile:

PRINCESS JOAN D'ACRE, who *m.*, first, Gilbert de Clare, Earl of Hertford and Gloucester, and had:

LADY MARGARET DE CLARE, widow of Piers de Gavestone, Earl of Cornwall, who *m.*, secondly, Hugh, second Baron d'Audley, created, 1337, Earl of Gloucester, *d.* 1347, and had:

LADY MARGARET D'AUDLEY, who *m.* Sir Ralph Stafford, K.G., second Baron Stafford, created, 1351, Earl of Stafford, *d.* 1372, also of Royal Descent, and had:

SIR HUGH DE STAFFORD, K.G., second Earl of Stafford, *d.* 1268, who *m.* Lady Philippa de Beauchamp, daughter of Sir. Thomas, Earl of Warwick, also of Royal Descent, and had:

LADY MARGARET DE STAFFORD, who *m.* Sir Ralph de Neville, K.G., created, 1397, Earl of Westmoreland, earl marshal of England, also of Royal Descent, and had:

LADY PHILIPPA DE NEVILLE, who *m.* Thomas de Dacre, sixth Baron de Dacre, of Gillesland, who *d.* 1457, and had:

THOMAS DE DACRE, of Gillesland *d. v. p.*, who *m.* Elizabeth, daughter of Sir Richard Bowet, *d.* 1423, and his wife, Amy d'Ufford, also of Royal Descent, and had:

LADY JOAN DE DACRE, heiress, will proved 14 July, 1486, who *m.*, *ante* 1457, Sir Richard Fienes, also of Royal Descent, constable of the Tower of London; lord chamberlain to the household of King Edward IV., and Baron Dacre, of the South, in right of his wife, 1459–84, *d.* 1484, and had:

SIR JOHN FIENES, eldest son, *d. v. p. ante* 1484, who *m.* Lady Alice, daughter of Henry, Baron Fitzhugh, of Ravensworth, *d.* 1472, and Lady Alice de Neville, also of Royal Descent, and had:

SIR THOMAS FIENES, heir to his grandfather, Sir Richard, Baron Dacre, of the South, made a Knight of the Bath by Henry VII.; will proved in 1534. He *m.* Anne, daughter of Sir Humphrey Bouchier, *k. v. p.* at Barnetfield fighting under the royal banner, also of Royal Descent, and had:

LADY CATHERINE DE FIENES, sister of Thomas, heir, *d. v. p.* before

1531, father of Thomas, who succeeded to the title, and was hanged for treason in 1541, aged 24 years. Her sister Mary *m.* Henry, Lord Norreys, who was hanged in 1537. She *m.* (*see* Horsfield's " History of Sussex," ii., p. 484, and the "Sussex Arch. Coll.," viii., pp. 214 and 233; Sussex "Visitations," 1634, and the Haynes chart pedigree, prepared in 1860 by Judge Nathaniel Chauncey, of Philadelphia, and Rev. Henry Jones of Bridgeport, Connecticut) Richard Loudenoys, of Briade, Sussex, and had :

MARY LOUDENOYS, heiress, who *m.* (*see* Kent "Visitations," 1574; Berry's "Kent Pedigrees," Essex "Visitations," 1612 and 1634, and Nichol's "Topographer," i., p. 228) Thomas Harlakenden, of Worthon, Kent, will dated 1562, proved in 1564, and had :

ROGER HARLAKENDEN, of Earl's Colne, Essex, and Kenardiston and Woodchurch, Kent, third son, 1535–1603. He signed the Harlakenden-Loudenoys pedigree in the Herald's "Visitation of Kent," 1574, and was the steward to the Earl de Vere, from whom he purchased the manor of Earl's Colne in 1583 (*see* Brayley's "History of Essex"). He had by his first wife, Elizabeth, daughter of Thomas Hardres, and widow of George Harlakenden, of Woodchurch :

RICHARD HARLAKENDEN, of Earl's Colne, heir, *d.* 24 August, 1631, aged 66 years (*see* Nichol's "Topog. et Geneal.," i., 25). He *m.* Margaret (or Mary), daughter of Edward Hubbart (or Hobart), of Stanstead-Montifichet, and had :

MABEL HARLAKENDEN,* *b.* Earl's Colne, 27 September, 1614, *d.* 1655. She came to New England in 1635 with her brother Roger, brother of Richard, the heir (*see* " N. E. His. Geneal. Reg.," x., 129 ; xiv., 319 ; xv., 327, and xvi., 167, 194. Morant's "His. of Essex," Porter's "Historical Notices," *etc.*). She *m.*, first (his second wife), in 1636, Colonel John

---

* The following ladies, members of the National Society of the Colonial Dames of America, are also of Royal Descent, through Mabel Harlakenden :

MISS MELISSA D. ATTERBURY, New York State Society.

MRS. CHARLES DEERING, Pennsylvania State Society.

MRS. HENRY S. HOWE, Massachusetts State Society.

MRS. JOHN F. MAYNARD, New York State Society.

MRS. ALFRED P. ROCKWELL, Massachusetts State Society.

MRS. DANIEL STIMSON, New York State Society.

MRS. KILIAEN VAN RENSSELAER, New York State Society.

MISS JULIA C. WELLS, New York State Society.

MRS. ALEXANDER D. JONES, South Carolina State Society.

MISS CORNELIA L. NEVINS, New York State Society.

MISS LOUISE E. NEVINS, New York State Society.

Haynes, *b.* Coddicot, Hertfordshire, 1597, Governor of the Massachusetts colony, 1635, and first Governor of the Connecticut Colony, 1639,
d. at Hartford, 1 March, 1653–54, and had :

RUTH HAYNES, 1639–1688, who *m.*, 1654–55, Samuel Wyllys, of Hartford, 1632–1709 (son of George Wyllys, Governor of the Connecticut
Colony, 1645, *see* Talcott's " Wyllys Family "), and had :

1.—RUTH WYLLYS, 1656–1729, *m.*, 1692 (his second wife), Rev. Edward Taylor, *b.* at Sketchley, Leicestershire, 1642, arrived in New England 26 April, 1668, *d.* 24 June, 1729, at Westfield, Massachusetts, and
had :

ELDAD TAYLOR, *b.* Westfield, 10 April, 1708, *d.* 21 May, 1777, at
Boston ; was a Representative, 1762–64, and member of the Governor's Council ; he had by his second wife, Thankful Day, *d.* 1803 :

I.—ELIZABETH TAYLOR, who *m.* Andrew Perkins, of Norwich, Connecticut, and had :

CHARLES PERKINS, of Norwich, who *m.* Clarissa Deming, and
had :

LUCRETIA DEMING PERKINS, who *m.* (his second wife) John
Williams Quincy, Jr., of New York, and had :

MARY PERKINS QUINCY, of New Haven, a member of the
Connecticut Society of the Colonial Dames of America.

II.—MAJOR EDWARD TAYLOR, of the Massachusetts Line, Continental Army, who *m.* Sarah, daughter of Jonathan Ingersoll, a captain in the Hampshire regiment, in the Crown Point expedition,
1755, *k.* in battle, and his wife, Eunice Mosely, and had :

PAMELIA TAYLOR, who *m.*, 1800, Archippus Morgan, of West Springfield, and had :

FRANCIS MORGAN, of New York, who *m.* Semphronia Antoinette
Converse, and had :

FRANCES WEBB MORGAN, who *m.* George Anson Starkweather, of
New York, and had :

ANTOINETTE CONVERSE STARKWEATHER, *b.* New York City, 10 March,
1864, a member of the Massachusetts Society of the Colonial Dames
of America, who *m.* John K. Burgess, of Dedham, Massachusetts.
No issue.

2.—HEZEKIAH WYLLYS, *b.* 3 April, 1672, *d.* 24 December, 1741. He
held many municipal offices in Hartford, and was secretary of the
Connecticut colony, 1712–34.   He *m.*, 2 May, 1704, Elizabeth, *d.* 1762,
daughter of Rev. Jonathan Hobart, of East Haddam, Connecticut, and
his wife, Elizabeth Whiting, also of Royal Descent, and had :

COLONEL GEORGE WYLLYS, of Hartford, 1710–1796, secretary of the

Connecticut colony for 66 years; *m.* his cousin, Mary, 1715–1774, daughter of Rev. Timothy Woodbridge, of Simsbury, and had:

MARY WYLLYS, *b.* 1742, *m.*, 8 March, 1764, Eleazer Pomeroy, of Middletown, Connecticut, *d.* 1783, and had:

SAMUEL WYLLYS POMEROY, of Pomeroy, Ohio, 1764–1841; *m.*, 1793, Clarissa, daughter of Richard and Mary (Wright) Alsop, of Middletown, Connecticut, and had:

CLARA ALSOP POMEROY, who *m.*, 1833, Valentine B. Horton, of Pomeroy, Ohio, and had:

FRANCES DABNEY HORTON, of Sandusky, Ohio, a member of the Ohio Society of the Colonial Dames of America, who *m.* Brigadier-General and Judge Manning F. Force, LL.D., of Cincinnati, Ohio.

3.—MEHITABLE WYLLYS, 1658–1697, who *m.*, first, 1676, Rev. Daniel Russell, of Charlestown, Massachusetts, 1658–1680 (son of Richard Russell, treasurer of the Massachusetts colony, 1644–74), and had:

MABEL RUSSELL, 1677–1722, who *m.*, first, 12 June, 1701, Rev. John Hubbard, *b.* 1679, *d.*, Jamaica, Long Island, 1705, and had:

    1.—COLONEL JOHN HUBBARD, of New Haven, who *m.*, 30 August, 1724, Elizabeth Stevens, and had:

        COLONEL LEVERETT HUBBARD, M.D., of New Haven, who *m.*, 22 May, 1746, Sarah Whitehead, and had:

        SARAH HUBBARD, who *m.*, 1776, Judge John Trumbull, LL.D., of Hartford, and had:

        JULIANA TRUMBULL, who *m.*, 29 June, 1806, William Woodbridge, of Detroit, 1780–1861, first Governor of Michigan, and had:

        DUDLEY B. WOODBRIDGE, of Detroit, who *m.*, 28 October, 1861, Martha J. Lee, and had:

        MATTIE WOODBRIDGE, a member of the Michigan Society of the Colonial Dames of America, the Order of the Crown, *etc.*, who *m.*, 27 October, 1886, Charles Horton Metcalf, of Detroit, and had: *Woodbridge, b.* 23 June, 1888; *Marjorie Woodbridge, b.* 9 February, 1891; *Elizabeth Woodbridge, b.* 27 May, 1893, and *Marian Woodbridge, b.* 18 September, 1895.

    2.—DANIEL HUBBARD, of New Haven, Connecticut, *b.* 3 April, 1706, *d.* 24 March, 1741; *m.* Martha Coit, of New London, Connecticut, *b.* 1706, and had:

        I.—RUSSELL HUBBARD, *b.* 1732, *m.*, 1755, Mary Gray, of Wyndham, Connecticut, and had:

MARY HUBBARD, who *m.*, 1777, Lieutenant David Nevins, of Norwich, Connecticut, *b.* 1747, *d.*, New York, 21 January, 1838, and had:

JAMES NEVINS, of Philadelphia, *b.* 1 August, 1790, *d.* 11 March, 1866; *m.* Achsah Willis, *b.* 27 May, 1792, *d.* 23 August, 1847, and had:

1.—JONATHAN WILLIS NEVINS, of Philadelphia, *b.* 26 March, 1826, *d.* 21 August, 1861; *m.*, April, 1848, Adaline Tichenor, *b.* 2 May, 1824, and had:

> KATHERINE NEVINS, a member of the Pennsylvania Society of the Colonial Dames of America, who *m.*, 30 September, 1885, Thomas Hewson Bradford, M.D., of Philadelphia, and had: *Mary Hewson, b.* 26 July, 1886; *Katherine Nevins, b.* 12 May, 1888, and *William, b.* 19 January, 1890.

2.—ISABELLA NEVINS, who *m.*, 26 April, 1838, Edward Siddons Whelen, of Philadelphia, also of Royal Descent (*see* "Americans of Royal Descent," ped. ii.), *b.* 22 August, 1813, and had:

> ISABELLA NEVINS WHELEN, a member of the Pennsylvania Society of the Colonial Dames of America, who *m.*, 2 September, 1871, Prof. Persifor Frazer, M.D., of Philadelphia, and had: *Persifor, m.* Mary, daughter of John Lowber Welsh, of Philadelphia; *Lawrence* (deceased), *John* and *Charlotte.*

3.—CORNELIA NEVINS, who *m.* Joseph Reese Fry, and had:

> ELIZABETH FRY, a member of the Pennsylvania Society of the Colonial Dames of America, who *m.*, 14 November, 1867, John Jacob Ridgway, of Philadelphia, and had: *Thomas, Mabel,* wife of Edward F. Coward, of New York, and *Violet.*

II.—DANIEL HUBBARD, JR., *m.* Mary Greene, and had:

HENRY HUBBARD, *m.* Mary Chadwell, and had:

MARY GREENE HUBBARD, *m.* William Scollay Whitwell, and had:

ELIZABETH WHITWELL, a member of the Massachusetts Society of the Colonial Dames of America, who *m.* William Tudor, of Boston (a grandson of Colonel William Tudor, Judge Advocate General, Continental Army), and had: *Henry D., b.* Paris, 30 October, 1874; *William, b.* Boston, 14 June, 1876, who served with the "Rough-Riders" regiment during the American-Spanish war; *Elizabeth, b.* Boston, 27 November, 1878; *Delia*

Aimée, b. Marietta, Georgia, 22 April, 1880, and *Mary, b.* Paris, 30 July, 1886.

MABEL RUSSELL, 1677–1722, *m.*, secondly, 1707 (his first wife), Rev. Samuel Woodbridge (son of Rev. Benjamin, *d.* 1710, son of Rev. John, 1634–1695, and his wife Mercy, daughter of Thomas Dudley, Governor of Massachusetts Colony), *b.* about 1683, *d.* at East Hartford, Connecticut, 1746, and had:

1.—RUSSELL WOODBRIDGE, *b.* 8 May, 1719, *d.* East Hartford, 1782; *m.*, 1741, Anna Olmsted, and had:

DEODATUS WOODBRIDGE, *b.* 6 September, 1757, *d.* East Hartford, 1836; *m.*, first, 1780, Esther Willis, and had by her:

ELECTA WOODBRIDGE, *b.* 2 January, 1781, *d.* 1858; *m.*, 1798, George Cheney, of Manchester, Connecticut, *b.* 20 December, 1771, *d.* 1829, and had:

CHARLES CHENEY, *b.* South Manchester, Connecticut, 26 December, 1803, *d.* 20 June, 1874; *m.*, at Providence, Rhode Island, 21 October, 1829, Waitstill Dexter Shaw, *b.* Providence, Rhode Island, October 17, 1809, *d.* Mt. Pleasant, Ohio, April 6, 1841, and had:

KNIGHT DEXTER CHENEY, *b.* Mt. Pleasant, Ohio, 9 October, 1837, *m.*, at Exeter, New Hampshire, 4 June, 1862, Ednah Dow Smith, *b.* at South Berwick, Maine, 12 May, 1841, and had:

EDNAH PARKER CHENEY, of South Manchester, Connecticut, a member of the Connecticut Society of the Colonial Dames of America.

2.—ELIZABETH WOODBRIDGE, 1714–1754, who *m.*, 1737, Rev. Ephraim Little, 1707–1787, and had:

FAITH LITTLE, *b.* 1754, who *m.*, 1781, Rev. Lemuel Parsons, 1753–1791, and had:

NANCY WOODBRIDGE PARSONS, 1787–1882, who *m.*, 1807, Quartus Knight, 1783–1827, and had:

LEMUEL PARTRIDGE KNIGHT, 1815–1891, who *m.*, 1845, Julia Jane Judson, 1822–1897, and had:

FANNY JUDSON KNIGHT, a member of the Michigan Society of the Colonial Dames of America, the Order of the Crown, *etc.*, who *m.*, 1876, William Addison Butler, of Detroit, and had: *Edith Knight, b.* 1877, and *Lawrence Knight, b.* 1879.

MEHITABLE WYLLYS, 1658–1697, had by her third husband, *m.* in 1676, Rev. Timothy Woodbridge, of Hartford, *d.* 30 April, 1732:

MARY WOODBRIDGE, *b.* 19 June, 1692, *d.* 17 February, 1766, who *m.*, 7 May, 1724, Judge William Pitkin, of East Hartford, Connecticut, judge of the superior court and Governor of the Connecticut Colony, *b.* 30 April, 1694, *d.* 1 October, 1769, and had:

REV. TIMOTHY PITKIN, of Farmington, Connecticut, *b.* 13 January, 1727, *d.* 8 July, 1812; *m.*, 9 August, 1753, Temperance, *b.* 29 April, 1732, *d.* 19 May, 1772, daughter of Rev. Thomas Clap, D.D., of Windham, Connecticut, president of Yale College, *d.* 1767, and his first wife, Mary Whiting, daughter of Rev. Samuel and Elizabeth (Adams) Whiting, and had:

I.—TIMOTHY PITKIN, *m.*, 6 June, 1801, Elizabeth Hubbard, and had:

REV. THOMAS CLAP PITKIN, *m.*, 19 May, 1841, Harriet Louisa Starr, and had: *Mary Caswell, Louisa Burr*, and

ANNA DENIO PITKIN, a member of the Michigan Society of the Colonial Dames of America.

II.—CATHERINE PITKIN, *b.* 22 February, 1757, *d.* 13 September, 1837, *m.*, 17 November, 1774, Rev. Nathan Perkins, D.D., of West Hartford, Connecticut, *b.* 12 May, 1748, *d.* 18 January, 1838, and had:

CATHERINE PERKINS, *b.* 20 January, 1782, *d.* 19 February, 1848, who *m.*, 20 December, 1803, Charles Seymour, of Hartford, Connecticut, *b.* January 17, 1777, *d.* 21 January, 1852, and had:

MARY SEYMOUR, *b.* 1 November, 1820, *d.* 18 April, 1883, who *m.*, 28 October, 1846, Russell Goodrich Talcott, of Hartford, Connecticut, *b.* 15 August, 1818, *d.* March 3, 1863, and had:

MARY KINGSBURY TALCOTT, of Hartford, a member of the Connecticut Society of the Colonial Dames of America, the Order of the Crown, *etc.*

4.—MARY WYLLYS, 1656–1729, who *m.*, 1684 (his second wife), Rev. Joseph Eliot, of Guilford, Connecticut, 1638–1694 (son of Rev. John Eliot, the apostle to the Indians), and had:

I.—REV. JARED ELIOT, M.D., of Killingworth, Connecticut, 1685–1763, who *m.*, 1710, Elizabeth, daughter of Samuel Smithson, and had:

AARON ELIOT, of Killingworth (Clinton), 1718–1785, who *m.* Mary, daughter of Rev. William Worthington, and had:

BENJAMIN ELIOT, 1762–1848, *m.*, in Virginia, Frances Panca, and had:

MARY WORTHINGTON WATKINS ELIOT, 1798–1865, who *m.*, 1821, Chester Ashley, of Little Rock, Ark., *b.* Amherst, Massachusetts; was United States Senator from Arkansas when he *d.*, in Washington City, in 1878, also of Royal Descent, and had:

1.—WILLIAM ELIOT ASHLEY, of Little Rock, Arkansas, *d.* 1868, who *m.* at Little Rock, in 1846, Frances E. Grafton, also of Royal Descent, and had:

FRANCES ANN ASHLEY, a member of the Massachusetts and Arkansas Societies of the Colonial Dames of America, who *m.* Clifton Sidney Gray, M.D., of Little Rock, *d. s. p.* 14 February, 1899.

2.—FRANCES ANN ASHLEY, 1825–1851, who *m.* at Little Rock, 1850, Rev. Andrew Fields Freeman, of Little Rock, *b.* Warrenton, North Carolina, and had:

MARY ASHLEY FREEMAN, a member of the Massachusetts and Arkansas Societies of the Colonial Dames of America, the Order of the Crown, *etc.*, who *m.*, 1872, Judge Sterling R. Cockrill, of Little Rock, chief justice of the supreme court of Arkansas, also of Royal Descent, and had: *Ashley, Ann McDonald, Sterling R., Mary Freeman, Emmet, Garland,* and *Freeman.*

II.—ABIAL ELIOT, who *m.* Mary Leete, and had:

NATHANIEL ELIOT, who *m.* Beulah Parmalee, and had:

WILLIAM ELIOT, who *m.* Ruth Rossiter, and had:

WILLIAM HORACE ELIOT, who *m.* Mary Law, and had:

WILLIAM HORACE ELIOT, who *m.* Sarah Sawyer, and had:

WILLEMENA ELIOT, a member of the Massachusetts and Michigan Societies of the Colonial Dames of America, who *m.*, 26 December, 1877, Dr. Justin Edwards Emerson, of Detroit, Michigan, and had: *Paul Eliot, Filip Law,* and *Ralf de Pomeroy.*

THE ROYAL DESCENT

OF

MISS ANNIE FITZHUGH ROSE WALKER,

OF RICHMOND, VA.

ALFRED THE GREAT, of England, had :

Edward the Elder, King of England, who had :

Edmund I., King of England, who had :

Edgar the Peaceful, King of England, who had :

Ethelred II., King of England, who had :

Edmund II., King of England, who had :

Prince Edward the Exile, of England, who had :

Margaret, m. Malcolm III., of Scotland, and had :

St. David, King of Scotland, who had :

Henry, Prince of Scotland, who had :

David, Earl of Huntingdon, who had :

Isabel, m. Robert, Earl of Annandale, and had :

Robert Bruce, Lord of Annandale, who had :

Robert Bruce, Earl of Carrick, who had :

Robert Bruce, King of Scotland, who had :

Margery, m. Walter, High Steward, and had :

Robert II., King of Scotland, who had :

Egidia, m. William Douglas, and had :

Egidia, m. Henry, Earl of Orkney, and had :

William, Earl of Orkney and Caithness, who had :

Eleanor, m. John Stewart, Earl of Athol, and had :

Isabel, m. Alexander Robertson, and had :

John Robertson, of Muirton, who had :

Gilbert Robertson, of Muirton, who had :

David Robertson, of Muirton, who had :

William Robertson, of Muirton, who had :

William Robertson, of Gladney, who had :

Rev. William Robertson, of Edinburgh, who had:

Jean, m. Alexander Henry, of Aberdeen, and had:

Col. John Henry, of Hanover Co., Va., who had :

Jane, m. Col. Samuel Meredith, and had :

Jane, m. David S. Garland, and had :

THE EMPEROR CHARLEMAGNE, had :

Pepin, King of Italy, who had :

Bernard, King of Italy, who had :

Pepin, Count de Vermandois, who had :

Herbert I., Count de Vermandois, who had :

Herbert II., Count de Vermandois, who had :

Albert I., Count de Vermandois, who had :

Herbert III., Count de Vermandois, who had :

Otho, Count de Vermandois, who had :

Herbert IV., Count de Vermandois, who had :

Adelheid, m. Hugh, Count de Vermandois, and had:

Isabel, m. William, Earl of Surrey, and had :

Ada, m. Henry, Prince of Scotland, and had :

David, Earl of Huntingdon, who had :

Isabel, m. Robert, Lord of Annandale, and had :

Robert Bruce, Lord of Annandale, who had :

Robert Bruce, Earl of Carrick, who had :

Mary, m. Sir Alexander Fraser, and had :

Sir John Fraser, of Aberbothnot, who had :

Margaret, m. Sir William de Keith, and had :

Elizabeth, m. Sir Adam de Gordon, and had :

Elizabeth, m. Alexander de Seton, and had :

Alexander Seton, Earl of Huntley, who had :

Margaret, m. Hugh Rose, of Kilravock, and had :

John Rose, of Bellivat, who had :

John Rose, of Bellivat, who had :

John Rose, of Bellivat, who had :

Hugh Rose, who had :

Patrick Rose, of Lochihills, who had :

John Rose, of Wester Alves, who had :

Rev. Robert Rose, d. Richmond, Va., who had :

Col. Hugh Rose, of Amherst Co., Va., who had :

Ann Shepherd Garland m. Dr. Gustavus A. Rose, of Lynchburg, Va.

Judith Cabell Rose, of Richmond, Va., member of the Virginia Society of the Colonial Dames of America. ┬ Benjamin Powell Walker, of Hartford, Indiana, d. New York City, 14 Feb., 1887.

Annie Fitzhugh Rose Walker, of Richmond, Va., member of the Virginia Society of the Colonial Dames of America, the Order of the Crown, etc.

PEDIGREE LXIII.

EDWARD I., King of England, had by his first wife, Princess Eleanor of Castile:

PRINCESS ELIZABETH PLANTAGENET, widow of John de Vere, who *m.*, secondly, 1306, Humphrey de Bohun, fourth Earl of Hereford and Essex, and had:

LADY ELEANOR DE BOHUN, who *m.*, first, 1327, James Butler, second Earl of Carrick, created Earl of Ormond, 1328, and had:

LADY PETRONELLA BUTLER, who *m.* (his first wife) Gilbert, third Baron Talbot, of Goodrich Castle, 1332–1387, and had:

RICHARD, fourth Baron Talbot, of Goodrich Castle, and, in the right of his wife, sixth Baron le Strange, *d.* 1396. He *m.* Lady Ankeretta, daughter of John, fourth Baron le Strange, of Blackmere, and had:

GENERAL SIR JOHN DE TALBOT, K.G., lord of Furnival, second son, created, 1448, Earl of Shrewsbury, lord-lieutenant of Ireland, Earl of Waterford and Wexford, in Irish Peerage, lord chancellor of Ireland, *k.* in battle in France in 1453, aged 80 years. He *m.*, first, 1408, Lady Maud, daughter of Thomas de Neville, baron of Furnival, *d.* 1406, also of Royal Descent, and had:

LORD THOMAS DE TALBOT, eldest son, *d. v. p.* in France, 145–, who had:

LADY ELIZABETH TALBOT, who *m.* Sir Henry de Grey, of Wilton, and had:

LADY MARGARET DE GREY, *d.* 144–, who *m.*, first, John D'Arcy, fifth Baron D'Arcy, *b.* 1377, *d.* 1411, and had:

PHILIP, sixth Baron D'Arcy, *d.* 1418, who had by his wife, Lady Eleanor, daughter of Henry, third Baron Fitz-Hugh:

LADY MARGARET D'ARCY, who *m.* Sir John Conyers, of Hornby Castle, Yorkshire, and had:

RICHARD CONYERS, of Horden, Durham, who *m.* Lady Elizabeth, daughter of Sir Robert Claxton, Knt., of Horden, and had:

ROBERT CONYERS, of Horden, who *m.* Margaret Bamforth, of Seham, Durham, and had:

CHRISTOPHER CONYERS, of Horden, who *m.* Elizabeth, daughter of John Jackson, of Bedale, and had:

RICHARD CONYERS, of Horden, who *m.* Isabel, daughter of Robert Lumley, of Ludworth, and had:

CHRISTOPHER CONYERS, of Horden, who *m.*, secondly, 1586, Lady Anne, daughter of Sir John Hedsworth, Knt., of Harraton, Durham (*see* Durham "Visitations," 1575), and had :

MARY CONYERS, who *m.* William Wilkinson, of Lanchester, Durham, son of Lawrence Wilkinson, of Harperley House, Durham, and had :

LAWRENCE WILKINSON,* a lieutenant in the army of Charles I.; taken prisoner at the surrender of Newcastle, 22 October, 1644; his estates having been sequestered and sold by Parliament, 1645, he came, with his wife and a son to Providence, Rhode Island, in 1646; was a commissioner, 1659, 1667; deputy, 1667, 1673, *etc.; d.* 9 August, 1692. He *m.* Susannah, *d.* 1692, daughter of Christopher and Alice Smith, of Providence, and had :

1.—JOHN WILKINSON, of Providence, *b.* Smithfield, 2 March, 1654, *d.* 10 April, 1708; *m.*, 16 April, 1689, Deborah Whipple, *b.* 1 August, 1670, *d.* 24 June, 1748, and had :

JOHN WILKINSON, of Providence, *b.* 16 March, 1690, *d.* 25 September. 1756; *m.*, 20 March, 1718, Rebecca Scott, of Smithfield, *b.* 11 February, 1699, *d.* after 1756, and had :

JOHN WILKINSON, of Smithfield, *b.* 20 March, 1724, *d.* 23 June, 1804; *m.* Ruth Angell, of Providence, and had :

OZIEL WILKINSON, of Pawtucket, *b.* 30 January, 1744, *d.* 22 October, 1815; *m.*, 8 April, 1766, Lydia Smith, of Smithfield, *b.* 11 February, 1747, and had :

ISAAC WILKINSON, of Pawtucket, *b.* 10 October, 1768, *d.* 2 March, 1843; *m.* Lois Marsh, of Pawtucket, and had :

MARY WILKINSON, *b.* 11 October, 1804, *d.* 27 February, 1883; *m.*, 13 December, 1821, Benjamin Fessenden, of Pawtucket, *b.* 13 June, 1797, *d.* 6 January, 1881, and had :

MARY WILKINSON FESSENDEN, *b.* 24 October, 1827, *d.* 20 September, 1886; *m.*, 30 October, 1849, William Francis Sayles, of Pawtucket, *b.* 20 September, 1824, *d.* 7 May, 1894, also of Royal Descent, and had :

MARY FESSENDEN SAYLES, a member of the Rhode Island Society of the Colonial Dames of America, *b.* 29 September, 1850, who *m.*, 21 May, 1872, Roscoe Stetson Washburn, of Providence, and had : *Maurice King, Roscoe Clifton, William F. S.* (deceased), and *John Fessenden* (deceased).

2.—CAPTAIN SAMUEL WILKINSON, of Providence, Rhode Island, eldest

---

* MRS. EDWIN A. DAMON, a member of the Pennsylvania State Society in the National Society of the Colonial Dames of America, is also of Royal Descent through Lawrence Wilkinson.

son, a justice of the peace, *d.* 27 August, 1727; *m.*, 1672, Plain, daughter of Rev. William Wilkenden, of Providence, and had:

I.—JOSEPH WILKINSON, *m.* Martha Pray, and had:

PRUDENCE WILKINSON, *m.* Isaiah Angell, and had:

PRUDENCE ANGELL, *m.* Gideon Austin, and had:

RUTH AUSTIN, *m.* James Cranston, and had:

MARTHA CRANSTON, *m.* Silas Bingham, Jr., and had:

HANNAH BINGHAM, *m.* Dr. James Fuller Howe, and had:

ANNETTE HOWE, who *m.* Franklin R. Carpenter, Ph.D., of Denver, Colorado. *Issue,* see p. 260.

II.—RUTH WILKINSON, 1685–86–1738, who *m.* William Hopkins, of Providence, Rhode Island, and had:

STEPHEN HOPKINS, of Providence, Rhode Island, *b.* 7 March, 1707, *d.* 13 July, 1785; member of the Continental Congress, a signer of the Declaration of Independence, Governor of Rhode Island, *etc.* He *m.*, 9 October, 1726, Sarah, 1707–1753, daughter of Sylvanus Scott, of Providence, and had:

LYDIA HOPKINS, 1733–1793, who *m.*, 1763, Colonel Daniel Tillinghast, of Providence, 1732–1803, and had:

JOHN TILLINGHAST, of Uxbridge, Massachusetts, *b.* 1766, at Providence, *d.* 1839, at Newport, Indiana; *m.*, 1803, Hannah (Sherman) Russell, 1769–1837, and had:

SARAH SCOTT TILLINGHAST, 1806–1880, who *m.*, 1832, Griffin Clark, of Norwich and Hampton, Connecticut, and Oregon, Wisconsi 1801–1876, and had:

ANNAH RUSSELL CLARK, a member of the Rhode Island Society of the Colonial Dames of America, who *m.*, 6 May, 1868, Shepard Leach Sheldon, of Madison, Wisconsin, and had: *Georgiana Russell* and *Henry Tillinghast.*

THE ROYAL DESCENT

OF

MRS. GEORGE INNES, JR.,

OF NEW YORK CITY.

HUGH CAPET, King of France=Adela, dau. William, Duke of Aquitaine.

Robert I., the Pious,=Lady Constance
King of France | of Provence.

Princess Havide=Rynerius IV., Count
or Hedewige | of Hainault.

Henry I., King of=Lady Anne of Russia.
France

Lady Beatrix=Eblo de Rouci.

Hugh Magnus,=Lady Adelheid of
Duke of France | Vermandois.

Countess Adela=Hildwin de Montdider.

Lady Margaret de Rouci=Hugh de Clermont.

William de Warren,=Lady Isabel de=Robert de Bellomont,
Earl of Surrey | Vermandois | Earl of Leicester.

Lady Adeliza=Gilbert de Tonsburg,
de Clermont | Earl of Clare.

William de Warren,=Lady Alice de Talvas,
Earl of Surrey | also of Royal Descent.

Lady Elizabeth de Bellomont=Gilbert de Clare, Earl
of Pembroke.

Lady Isabella de=Hameline Plantagenet,
Warren | Earl of Surrey.

Richard "the Strongbow,"=Eva, dau. Dermot,
2d Earl of Pembroke | King of Leinster.

Lady Isabella de=Roger Bigod, Earl of
Warren | Norfolk.

Lady Isabel de Clare=William le Marshal,
Protector of England.

Hugh Bigod, second Earl of Norfolk=Lady Maud Marshall.

Sir Hugh Bigod, Justiciary of England=Joan, dau. of Robert Burnet.

Sir John Bigod, Knt.=(Name unknown.)

Sir Roger Bigod, of Settington=(Name unknown.)

Lady Joan Bigod=Sir William de Chauncy, of Skirpenbeck.

John Chauncy, of Stepney=Margaret Gifford, of Gedleston.

John Chauncy, of Sawbridgeworth=Anne Leventhorp, of Shingey.

John Chauncy, of Sawbridgeworth=Daughter of Thomas Boyce.

John Chauncy, of Pishobury=Elizabeth (Proffit) Mansfield.

Henry Chauncy, of Newplace Giffords=Lucy ——.

George Chauncy, of Yardleybury=Anne Welsh, of Great Wymondley.

Rev. Charles Chauncy, D.D., 1592-1671, second=Catherine Eyre, of New Sarum.
President of Harvard College

Rev. Nathaniel Chauncy, of Hatfield, Mass.=Abigail Strong, of Northampton, Mass.

Rev. Nathaniel Chauncy, of Durham, Ct.=Sarah Judson, of Stratford, Conn.

Col. Elihu Chauncy, of Durham, Mass.=Mary Griswold, of Killingworth.

Catherine Chauncy=Rev. Elizur Goodrich, D.D., of Durham, Mass.

Judge Elizur Goodrich, LL.D., of New Haven, Ct.=Anne Willard Allen.

Nancy Goodrich, 1793-1847=Henry Leavitt Ellsworth, of Hartford, son of
Oliver Ellsworth, Chief Justice of the United
States Supreme Court.

Annie Goodrich Ellsworth. She was a member=Roswell Smith, b. Lebanon, Ct., 30 March, 1829 ; d.
of the Society of the Colonial Dames of the | New York, 19 April, 1892.
State of New York. When her father was
Chief of the U. S. Patent Office she had the
honor of sending the first telegram, May 24,
1844, at the request of Mr. Morse, which read,
"What hath God wrought." She d. in New
York, 21 January, 1900, aged 73 years.

Julia Goodrich Smith, m. 23 April, 1879=George Innes, Jr., of New York City.

Elizabeth Innes,	Juliet Innes,	George Ellsworth Innes,
b. New York, 22	b. Montclair, N. Y.,	b. Montclair, N. Y., 10
March, 1880.	17 June, 1881.	October, 1882.

PEDIGREE LXIV.

EDWARD III., **King of England**, had by his wife, Lady Philippa, daughter of William, Count of Hainault and Holland:

THOMAS PLANTAGENET, Duke of Gloucester, who had by his wife, Lady Alianore, daughter of Humphrey de Bohun, last Earl of Hereford and Essex, Earl of Northampton, also of Royal Descent:

LADY ANNE PLANTAGENET (widow of Thomas and Edmund, Earls of Stafford), who *m.*, thirdly, William de Bouchier, Earl of Ewe, and had:

SIR JOHN DE BOUCHIER, K.G., fourth son, *d.* 1474, *m.* Lady Margery, daughter and heiress of Richard de Berners, of West Horsley, Surry, and had:

SIR HUMPHREY DE BOUCHIER, eldest son, *k. v. p.* at Barnetfield, whose daughter:

LADY ANNE DE BOUCHIER, *m.* Sir Thomas Fienes, K.B., Baron Dacre of the South, 1470–1534, and had:

LADY CATHERINE FIENES (*see* p. 267), who *m.* Richard Loudenoys, of Briade, Sussex, and had:

MARY LOUDENOYS, sole heir, who *m.* Thomas Harlakenden, of War-horn, Kent (*see* "Visitations of Essex," 1612 and 1634, and Berry's "Kent Pedigrees"), *d.* 1564, and had:

ROGER HARLAKENDEN, of Kenardiston, Kent, 1535–1603 (*see* "Visitations of Kent," 1574), who *m.*, first, Elizabeth, daughter of Thomas Hardres, and widow of George Harlakenden, of Woodchurch, Kent (*see* Braley's "History of Essex"), and had:

THOMAS HARLAKENDEN, of Earl's Colne, Essex, third son, who *m.* Dorothy Cheney, of Drayton, Berks, and had:

DOROTHY HARLAKENDEN,* *bapt.* 12 December, 1596, *bur.* Toppesfield, 3 August, 1636; *m.*, 2 April, 1617 (his first wife), Samuel Symonds, *b.* at Great Yeildham, Essex, *bapt.* 9 June, 1595; came to New England in 1637, and was provincial councillor and deputy-governor of the Massa-

---

* The following ladies, members of the National Society of the Colonial Dames of America, are also of Royal Descent through Dorothy Harlakenden :

MRS. CHARLES DEERING, Pennsylvania State Society.

MRS. DANIEL STIMSON, New York State Society.

MISS MARIAN F. HARRIS, Pennsylvania State Society.

MISS ELIZABETH W. WHITE, New Hampshire State Society.

chusetts Bay Colony, 1673–78, *d.* at Ipswich, in October, 1678 (*see* " The Ancestry of Priscilla Baker," " The Ancestry of Ebenezer Greenough," Symonds " Heraldic Collection of Essex," in the Camden Society Publications, and the " American Heraldic Journal," January, 1865), and had :

I.—WILLIAM SYMONDS, of Ipswich, Massachusetts, *m.* Mary, daughter of Jonathan Wade, of Ipswich, and had :

DOROTHY SYMONDS, *b.* 21 October, 1670, *m.*, 19 December, 1695, Cyprian, *b.* 17 January, 1671, son of John Whipple, of Ipswich, 1632–1695, and had :

SAMUEL WHIPPLE, of Stonington, Connecticut, *b.* 13 September, 1702, *m.*, 20 June, 1726, Bethiah Patch, and had :

AMOS WHIPPLE, of Stonington, *b.* 16 March, 1739, *m.*, 26 January, 1769, Ann Hewitt, *b.* 26 May, 1746, and had :

MALACHI WHIPPLE, of Albany, New York, *b.* 20 June, 1770, *d.* 12 December, 1836 ; *m.* Priscilla Brown, 1777–1860, and had :

LUCY WHIPPLE, *b.* 21 November, 1817, *d.* 26 May, 1884 ; *m.*, 7 August, 1834, at Berne, New York, Chauncy Hulburt, of Philadelphia, *b.* 15 August, 1813, *d.* 31 August, 1896, and had :

1.—JOANNA CROMBIE HULBURT, deceased.

2.—HELEN AMELIA HULBURT, a member of the New York Society of the Colonial Dames of America, Society of " Mayflower " Descendants, *etc.*, who *m.* Elijah Warrington Murphey, of Albany, New York, and had : *Harriet Louise,* wife of Henry Otis Chapman, of New York; *Lucy Whipple, d.; Helen Virginia, d.; Martha, Virginia Hulburt, Chauncy Hulburt,* and *Elijah Warrington.*

3.—DAYTON WHIPPLE HULBURT, of Philadelphia, who *m.* Elizabeth Gundaker, of Philadelphia.

4.—HARRIET LOUISE HULBURT, who *m.* Thomas Fraley Baker, of Philadelphia.

5.—ISABELLA VIRGINIA HULBURT, who *m.* Ellis Hughes Hanson, of Philadelphia.

6.—LUCY MATILDA HULBURT, who *m.*, first, Ferdinand Heiskill, of Philadelphia, and had : *Florence M.,* wife of John Mickle Okie, of Berwyn, and *m.*, secondly, Edward Hughes Hanson, of Bala, Pennsylvania, and had : *Richard Edward* and *Helen Louise.*

7.—MARY VINCENT HULBURT, deceased.

8.—LEWIS CHEESMAN HULBURT, of Los Angeles, California, who *m.* Charlotte Smith, of Orange, New Jersey.

9.—ANNA BARNET HULBURT, who *m.* Henry W. Peacock of Philadelphia.

II.—ELIZABETH SYMONDS, *b.* Topperfield, 1624, *d.* Salem, 7 May, 1685; *m.*, at Ipswich, 24 May, 1644, Daniel Epes, of Salem, *d.* 8 January, 1693 (*see* Platt's "Ancestry of Ebenezer Greenough") and had:

MARTHA EPES, 1654–1686; *m.*, 1679 (his first wife), Robert Greenough, of Rowley, Massachusetts, *d.* 30 March, 1718, and had:

DANIEL GREENOUGH, *b.* 22 February, 1686, *d.* Bradford, Massachusetts, 25 April, 1746; *m.*, first, 25 January, 1722, Elizabeth Hatch, of Portsmouth, New Hampshire, and had:

SYMONDS GREENOUGH, *b.* New Castle, New Hampshire, 1724, *d.* at Haverhill, Massachusetts; *m.* Abigail, *b.* 24 November, 1725, daughter of John Chadwick, of Watertown, and had:

EBENEZER GREENOUGH, *b.* Haverhill, 18 February, 1753, *d.* Chester, New Hampshire, 15 December, 1827; *m.* Mary, 1759–1842, daughter of Rev. Ebenezer Flagg, of Chester, 1704–1796, and had:

EBENEZER GREENOUGH, JR., of Sunbury, Pennsylvania, *b.* 11 December, 1783, *d.* 1847; *m.*, 5 March, 1814, Abigail, *b.* 12 December, 1791, *d.* 14 August, 1868, daughter of Joseph and Susanna (Pusey) Israel, of New Castle county, Delaware, and had:

1.—MARY GREENOUGH, *b.* 26 April, 1816, *d.* 23 August, 1854; *m.*, 28 November, 1838, George Lippincott, of Philadelphia, and had:

EMILY ABIGAIL LIPPINCOTT, of Philadelphia, a member of the Pennsylvania Society of the Colonial Dames of America, *d. unm.*, 23 July, 1898.

2.—CLARA ANN GREENOUGH, *b.* 16 December, 1817, who *m.* Franklin Platt, of Philadelphia, and had:

CLARA GREENOUGH PLATT, a member of the Pennsylvania Society of the Colonial Dames of America, who *m.* James B. Canby, of Wilmington, Delaware, and Philadelphia, and had: *Clara G. Franklin P.*, and *James Benjamin.*

3.—MARIAN GREENOUGH, *b.* 13 April, 1829, widow of William Taylor Dilworth, who *m.*, secondly, James Seguin de Benneville, M.D., of Philadelphia, and had:

MARIE MATHILDE DE BENNEVILLE, of Philadelphia, a member of the Pennsylvania Society of the Colonial Dames of America.

THE ROYAL DESCENT

OF

MRS. EDWARD HUGHES HANSON,

OF BALA, PENNA.

ALFRED THE GREAT, King of England⹋Ethelbith, daughter of Ethelan the Great.

Edward the Elder, King of England⹋Edgiva, daughter of Earl Sigelline.

Edmund I., King of England⹋Elgiva, gr. dau. of Alfred the Great.

Edgar the Peaceful, King of England⹋Elfrida, daughter of Ordgar, Earl of Devon.

Ethelred the Unready, King of England⹋Elgifa, daughter of Earl Thorad.

Edmund Ironsides, King of England⹋Lady Algitha of Denmark.

Prince Edward the Exile, of England⹋Lady Agatha of Germany.

Princess Margaret, of England⹋Malcolm III., King of Scotland.

Princess Matilda, of Scotland⹋Henry I., King of England.

Empress Maud, of Germany⹋Geoffrey-Plantagenet, Count of Anjou.

Henry II., King of England⹋Lady Eleanor of Aquitaine.

John, King of England⹋Lady Isabel de Taillefer.

Henry III., King of England⹋Lady Eleanor of Provence.

Edward I., King of England⹋Princess Eleanor of Castile.

Edward II., King of England⹋Princess Isabella of France.

Edward III., King of England⹋Lady Philippa of Hainault.

Thomas, Duke of Gloucester⹋Lady Alianore de Bohun.

Lady Anne Plantagenet⹋William de Bouchier, Earl of Eu.

Sir John de Bouchier, K.G.⹋Lady Margery de Berners.

Sir Humphrey de Bouchier, Knt.⹋(Name unknown.)

Lady Anne de Bouchier⹋Sir Thomas Fienes, K.B., Baron Dacre.

Lady Catherine Fienes⹋Richard Loudenoys, of Briade, Sussex.

Mary Loudenoys⹋Thomas Harlakenden, of Warhorn, Kent.

Roger Harlakenden, of Kenardiston, Kent⹋Elizabeth Hardres, of Woodchurch, Kent.

Thomas Harlakenden, of Earl's Colne, Essex⹋Dorothy Cheney, of Drayton, Berks.

Dorothy Harlakenden⹋Samuel Symonds, Gov. of Mass. Colony, 1673-8.

William Symonds, of Ipswich, Mass.⹋Mary Wade, of Ipswich, Mass.

Dorothy Symonds⹋Cyprian Whipple, of Ipswich, Mass.

Samuel Whipple, of Stonington, Conn.⹋Bethia Patch.

Amos Whipple, of Stonington, Conn.⹋Ann Hewitt.

Malachi Whipple, of Albany, N. Y.⹋Priscilla Brown.

Lucy Whipple⹋Chauncy Hulburt, of Philadelphia, Pa.

Ferdinand Heiskill, of Philadelphia (first husband),⹋Lucy Matilda Hulburt⹋Edward Hughes Hanson, of Philadelphia and Bala, Pa.

Florence M. Heiskill⹋John M. Okie, of Berwyn, Pa.

Richard Edward Hanson.

Helen Louise Hanson.

PEDIGREE LXV.

ROBERT II., King of Scotland, had by his first wife, Lady Elizabeth, daughter of Sir Adam Mure, of Rowallan:

LADY MARGARET STEWART, who *m.* (his second wife) Eoin-Mor, or John MacDonald, lord of the Isles, and had:

DONALD MACDONALD, lord of the Isles, who *m.* Lady Margaret, daughter of Sir Walter Leslie and his wife, Euphemia, Countess of Ross, and had:

ALEXANDER MACDONALD, lord of the Isles and Earl of Ross, *d.* 1448–9, who *m.* Lady Elizabeth, daughter of Alexander de Seton, lord of Gordon and Huntley, and had:

HUGH MACDONALD, lord of the Isles, second son, *d.* 1498, who had by his second wife, Lady Mary, daughter of the chieftain of clan Gun:

DONALD-GALLOCH MACDONALD, lord of the Isles, *d.* 1506, who had by his wife, a daughter of the MacDonalds in Ireland:

DONALD-GRAMMACH MACDONALD, lord of the Isles, *d.* 1534, who *m.* Margaret, daughter of MacDonald of Moydert, and had:

DONALD-GORME MACDONALD. As eldest son of his father he claimed the title of lord of the Isles, but King James V. opposed him, and in the war which ensued Donald was slain, in 1537, leaving issue by his wife, Margaret, daughter of John Roderick McLeod, of Lewis:

DONALD-GORME MACDONALD, of Slate, who was restored in his honors by Queen Mary, in 1567, and *d.* 1585. His second son:

ARCHIBALD MACDONALD, had by his wife, Margaret, daughter of Angus MacDonald, of Dunivaig and Glynnis, in Argyle:

SIR DONALD MACDONALD, of Slate, created a baronet of Nova Scotia, 14 July, 1625, *d.* 1643–4. He *m.* Lady Janet, daughter of Kenneth, first Lord Mackenzie, of Kintail, and sister of the second Earl of Seaforth, and had:

SIR JAMES MACDONALD, of Slate, 2d Bart., *d.* 8 December, 1678, in the Isle of Skye. He fought under Montrose in 1645, and had by his second wife, Mary, daughter of John MacLeod, of that Ilk:

LADY MARIAN MACDONALD, who *m.* Patrick MacGregor, who commanded his clansmen under Montrose in support of the royal cause, 1644–5, and was outlawed, and had John, his heir, who changed his

(283)

name to "John Murray," and was the ancestor of Sir John Murray, Bart., 1795, and

JAMES MACGREGOR, second son, who changed his name to "Thomas MacGehee" when his clan was outlawed, and was an officer in the English army. He removed to Virginia, and resided in St. John's parish, King William county, where his will, dated 27 July, 1727, was probated, and had issue:

EDWARD MACGEHEE, who *m.* Katherine de Jarnette, and had:

DANIEL MACGEHEE, who *m.* Jane Brooke Hodnet, and had:

KATHERINE BROOKE GARTEREY MACGEHEE, who *m.* David Urquhart, and had: 1. *Katherine Louisa Banks,* who *m.* Jesse Ansley, *issue;* 2. *Jane Eliza Brooks,* who *m.* William Weeden, of Alabama, *issue;* 3. *Dr. John A.,* no *issue;* 4. *Sarah Ann,* who *m.* John Garner, *issue;* 5. *David W., d. unm.;* 6. *Mary Matilda,* who *m.* (his first wife) William Waters Garrard, *issue;* 7. *Caroline Lucy,* who *m.* Lemuel Tyler Downing, *issue;* and

FRANCES ISABELLA GARTEREY URQUHART, 1818–1890, who *m.,* 1843 (his second wife) William Waters Garrard, of "Hilton," Muscogee county, Georgia, 1818–1866, also of Royal Descent, and had:

1.—WILLIAM URQUHART GARRARD, *m.* Mary Lawton, and had: *William, Guilielma, Emily,* and *Cecilia.*

2.—EVA MATILDA GARRARD, a member of the Georgia Society of the Colonial Dames of America, who *m.* Humphreys Castleman, of Columbus, also of Royal Descent (see p. 186), and had: *Louis* and

MARY ISABELLA GARRARD CASTLEMAN, a member of the Georgia Society of the Colonial Dames of America, who *m.* Samuel Harrison McAfee, of West Point, Georgia.

3.—LOUIS FORD GARRARD, *m.* Anna Leonard, and had: *Louis Ford, Francis Urquhart, Anna Leonard, Guy Castleman, Van de Van, Helen Glenn,* and *Isabel.*

4.—HELEN AUGUSTA GARRARD, *b.* 28 August, 1850, a member of the Georgia Society of the Colonial Dames of America, who *m.,* 23 April, 1873, John Thomas Glenn, of Atlanta, captain in Confederate States Army, *d.* 14 March, 1899, also of Royal Descent, and had: *Garrard, Helen Mildred Lewis, William Louis, John Thomas* (deceased), *Luther Judson* (deceased), and

ISA GARTEREY URQUHART GLENN, a member of the Georgia Society of the Colonial Dames of America, the Order of the Crown, *etc.*

5.—GERTRUDE KATE GARRARD, a member of the Georgia Society of the Colonial Dames of America, who *m.* James Watson Harris, of Meriden, Mississippi, and had: *Garrard, Isabel* (wife of William H. Hall), *Helen Glenn, Eva Castleman,* and *David Urquhart.*

PEDIGREE LXVI.

ROBERT II., King of Scotland, had by his second wife, Lady Euphemia, Countess of Moray, daughter of Hugh, Earl of Ross:

DAVID, Earl of Caithness and Strathern, who had by his wife, Lady Euphemia:

LADY EUPHEMIA STEWART, Countess of Strathern, who *m.* (his second wife) Sir Patrick Graham, Earl of Strathern, *jure uxoris*, and had:

LADY EUPHEMIA GRAHAM, who *m.* Archibald, Earl of Douglas and second Duke of Touraine, son of Archibald, Earl of Douglas and his wife, Princess Margaret, daughter of Robert III., King of Scotland, by his wife, Lady Annabella Drummond, and had:

LADY MARGARET DOUGLAS, "the Fair Maid of Galloway," who *m.* John Stewart, first Earl of Athol, uterine brother of King James II., and son of Sir James Stewart, "the Black Knight of Lorn," by his wife, Lady Joan, widow of King James I., and daughter of Sir John de Beaufort, K.G., Marquis of Dorset, *etc.*, and his wife, Lady Margaret de Holland, both descendants of kings of England and France, and had:

LADY CATHERINE STEWART, who *m.* John, sixth Lord Forbes, son of Lord William, son of Lord James Forbes (son of Sir Alexander Forbes and his wife, Lady Elizabeth, daughter of George Douglas, first Earl of Angus and his wife, Princess Mary, daughter of Robert III., King of Scotland, by his wife, Lady Annabella Drummond) and his wife, Lady Egidia, daughter of William de Keith, Earl Marshal of Scotland, and his wife, Lady Mary, daughter of James, Lord Hamilton, and his wife, Princess Mary, daughter of James II., King of Scotland, by his wife, Lady Mary, daughter of Arnold, Duke of Guilders, and had:

LADY ELIZABETH FORBES, who *m.* (*see* Douglas's " Baronage," p. 341, and Wood's Douglas's " Peerage," i., 592) John Grant, of Grant ·and Freuchie, and had:

JAMES DE GRANT, of Freuchie, heir, baillie of Kinloss Abbey, 1539, who had by his second wife, Lady Barbara Erskine:

ARCHIBALD GRANT, second son, who *m.* Lady Isabella Comyn, of Erneside, and had:

HELEN GRANT, *d.* 1694, who *m.* Alexander MacDuff, of Keithmore, *d.* 1700, and had:

ELEANOR DUFF, who *m.* William Green, of the bodyguard to William of Orange, and had:

ROBERT GREEN, of Orange (Culpeper) county, Virginia (*see* Slaughter's "St. Mark's Parish"), member of the House of Burgesses, 1695–1747, who *m.* Eleanor Dunn, and had:

NICHOLAS GREEN, of Kentucky, who *m.* Elizabeth, daughter of Ajalon and Joyce (Barbour) Price, of Culpeper, and had:

NICHOLAS GREEN, who had by his wife, Lucy:

ELIZABETH GREEN, who *m.*, 1777, Anthony Garrard, of Stafford county, Virginia, *bapt.* 12 February, 1756, in Overwharton parish, *d.* 1807, and had:

JACOB GARRARD, of Wilkes county, Georgia, who *m.*, 1813, Martha Newsom Hardin, and had:

WILLIAM WATERS GARRARD, of "Hilton," near Columbus, Georgia, 1818–1866, who *m.*, 1843, Frances Isabella Garterey Urquhart, also of Royal Descent, and had, besides other issue:

1.—HELEN AUGUSTA GARRARD, of Atlanta, *b.* 28 August, 1850, a member of the Georgia Society of the Colonial Dames of America, who *m.*, 23 April, 1873, Captain John Thomas Glenn, *b.* 21 March, 1844, *d.* 14 March, 1899, also of Royal Descent, an aide-de-camp to his uncle, General Howell Cobb, Confederate States Army, son of Luther J. Glenn, Colonel Confederate States Army, and had, besides other issue:

ISA GARTEREY URQUHART GLENN, of Atlanta, a member of the Georgia Society of the Colonial Dames of America, the Order of the Crown, the Society Daughters of the American Revolution, *etc.*

2.—EVA MATILDA GARRARD, a member of the Georgia Society of the Colonial Dames of America, who *m.* Humphreys Castleman, of Columbus, also of Royal Descent, and had: *Louis*, and

MARY ISABELLA GARRARD CASTLEMAN, a member of the Georgia Society of the Colonial Dames of America, who *m.* Samuel Harrison McAfee, of West Point, Georgia.

3.—GERTRUDE KATE GARRARD, a member of the Georgia Society of the Colonial Dames of America, who *m.* James Watson Harris, of Jackson, Mississippi. *Issue.*

PEDIGREE LXVII.

HENRY III., King of England, had by his wife, Lady Eleanor, daughter of Raymond de Berenger, Count of Provence:

EDMUND PLANTAGENET, Earl of Lancaster, *etc.*, lord ,high steward of England, who had by his second wife, Lady Blanche, widow of Henry I., King of Navarre, and daughter of Robert, Count of Artois, son of Louis VIII., King of France:

HENRY PLANTAGENET, Earl of Lancaster, who *m.* Lady Maud, also of Royal Descent, daughter of Patrick de Chaworth, and had:

LADY JOAN PLANTAGENET, who *m.* John, third Baron de Mowbray, of Axholm, also of Royal Descent, and had:

JOHN DE MOWBRAY, fourth Baron, who had by his wife, Lady Elizabeth, daughter of John, third Baron de Segrave, and his wife, Margaret Plantagenet, Duchess of York, also of Royal Descent:

LADY MARGERY DE MOWBRAY (sister of Thomas, Duke of Norfolk), who *m.* John, second Baron de Welles, and had:

EUDO DE WELLES, eldest son, *d. v. p.*, who *m.* Lady Maud, also of Royal Descent, daughter of Ralph, fifth Baron de Greystock, and had:

SIR LIONEL DE WELLES, sixth Baron, Governor of Ireland, *k.* 1461, whose daughter

LADY CICELY DE WELLES, *m.* Sir Robert Willoughby, a grandson of Sir William, Baron Willoughby de Eresby, and his wife, Lady Lucy le Strange, also of Royal Descent, and had:

SIR CHRISTOPHER WILLOUGHBY, K.B., 1453–1499, who *m.* Lady Margaret, daughter of Sir William Jenney, of Knottishall, Suffolk, and had:

CHIEF JUSTICE SIR THOMAS WILLOUGHBY, will proved 5 November, 1545, who *m.* Lady Bridget, daughter of Sir Robert Reade, of Bore Place, Kent, chief justice, *etc.*, and had:

CHRISTOPHER WILLOUGHBY, will proved 11 January, 1586; *m.* Margery Tottishurst, and had:

CHRISTOPHER WILLOUGHBY, of Chiddingstone, Kent, *d. ante* 1633, who had by his wife, Martha ———:

COLONEL WILLIAM WILLOUGHBY, of London and Portsmouth, an officer in the Parliamentary Army, in the Civil War; commissioner of the Royal Navy, *etc.*, *d.* 1651, who had by his wife, Elizabeth (her will dated in 1662), " who was an Eaton " (*see* " N. E. His. Gen. Reg.,'' October, 1899):

FRANCIS WILLOUGHBY, who came to New England in 1638; returned to England and was commissioner of the Royal Navy, 1652; member of Parliament, 1659; came to New England again in 1662, and was deputy-governor of Massachusetts Colony, 1665–71 (*see* Salisbury's " Family Histories "). He *m.*, thirdly, about 1659, Mrs. Margaret Taylor, daughter of William Locke, of Merton, county Surry, England, and had by her :

SUSANNAH WILLOUGHBY, 1664–1710, who *m.* (his first wife) Judge Nathaniel Lynde, of Saybrook, Connecticut, 1659–1729, also of Royal Descent, and had :

ELIZABETH LYNDE, 1688–1778, who *m.* Judge Richard Lord, of Lyme, Connecticut, 1690–1776, and had :

CAPTAIN ENOCH LORD, of Lyme, 1726–1814 ; *m.* Hepzibah Mervin, and had :

RICHARD LORD, of Lyme, 1752–1818 ; *m.* Ann Mitchell, and had :

SARAH ANN LORD, 1799–1835, who *m.* Judge Charles Johnson McCurdy, LL.D., of Lyme, also of Royal Descent, and had :

EVELYN McCURDY, only child, a member of the Connecticut Society of the Colonial Dames of America, who *m.* Professor Edward Elbridge Salisbury, of New Haven, Connecticut. *No issue.*

THE ROYAL DESCENT

OF

MRS. WILLIAM WASHINGTON GORDON,

OF SAVANNAH, GA.

EMPEROR CHARLEMAGNE⊤Hildegarde de Suabia.

Louis I., King of France. — Pepin, King of Italy.

Charles II. **ALFRED THE GREAT.** — Bernard, King of Italy.

Louis II. Edward the Elder. — Pepin de Peronne.

Charles III.⊤Egiva, of England. — Herbert I. de Vermandois.

Louis IV., King of France. — Herbert II. de Vermandois.

Gerberga, Princess of France⊤Albert I. de Vermandois.

Herbert III. de Vermandois. **HUGH CAPET, of France.**

Otho de Vermandois. Robert I., King of France.

Herbert IV. de Vermandois. Henry I., King of France.

Adelheid de Vermandois⊤Hugh Magnus, of France.

William, Earl of Surrey⊤Isabel. **WILLIAM THE CONQUEROR.**

Henry, Earl of Northumberland⊤Ada. Henry I., King of England.

Humphrey, Earl of Hereford⊤Margaret. Maud, Empress of Germany.

Henry, Earl of Hereford and Essex. Henry II., King of England.

Humphrey, Earl of Hereford and Essex. John, King of England.

Humphrey de Bohun. Henry III., King of England.

Humphrey, Earl of Hereford and Essex. Edward I., King of England.

Humphrey, Earl of Hereford and Essex⊤Elizabeth Plantagenet.

Lady Margaret de Bohun⊤Sir Hugh, Earl of Devon.

Edward Courtenay, of Goderington⊤Emeline d'Auney, of Modeford.

Sir Hugh Courtenay, of Haccomb⊤Maud Beaumont, of Shirwill.

Lady Margaret Courtenay⊤Sir Theobald Grenville, of Stowe.

Sir William Grenville, of Bideford⊤Philippa Bonville, of Chuton.

Thomas Grenville, of Stowe⊤Elizabeth Gorges.

Sir Thomas Grenville, of Stowe⊤Elizabeth Gilbert, of Compton.

Sir Roger Grenville, of Stowe⊤Margaret Whitleigh, of Efford.

Lady Amy Grenville⊤John Drake, of Ashe, Devon.

Robert Drake, of Wiscombe, Devon⊤Elizabeth Prideaux, of Thewboro.

William Drake, of Wiscombe Park⊤Philippa Dennys, of Holcombe.

John Drake, d. Windsor, Ct., 1659⊤Elizabeth Rodgers.

Job Drake, d. Windsor, Ct., 1689⊤Mary Wolcott.

Job Drake, d. Windsor, Ct., 1171⊤Elizabeth (Clarke) Cook.

Sarah Drake, 1686-1747⊤Gen. Roger Wolcott, Gov. of Conn., d. 1767.

Alexander Wolcott, M.D., of New London⊤Mary Richards (third wife).

Alexander Wolcott, d. Boston, 1828⊤Frances Burbank.

Frances Wolcott⊤Arthur W. Magill, of Middletown, Ct.

Juliette A. Magill⊤John H. Kinzie, d. Chicago, 1870.

Eleanor Lytle Kinzie, vice-president of the Na-⊤Gen. William Washington Gordon, of Savannah, tional, and president of the Georgia Society of Georgia. *Issue (see* p. 107). the Colonial Dames of America.

PEDIGREE LXVIII.

ROBERT II., **King of Scotland**, had by his first wife, Lady Elizabeth, daughter of Sir Adam Mure, of Rowallan:

LADY CATHERINE STEWART, who *m.* Sir David Lindsay, of Glenesk, created Earl of Crawford, and had:

ALEXANDER LINDSAY, second Earl of Crawford, who *m.* Lady Mariotta, only child of Sir David Dunbar, of Cockburn, also of Royal Descent, and had:

SIR WALTER LINDSAY, of Beaufort, third son, who *m.* (*see* "Wood's Douglas's Peerage of Scotland," I., 164, 376) Sophia, or Isabella, Livingston, and had:

SIR DAVID LINDSAY, of Edzell and Beaufort, *d.* 1527, who had by his first wife, Catherine Fotheringham, of Powrie:

WALTER LINDSAY, of Edzell, eldest son, *k. v. p.* at Flodden, 9 September, 1513, who *m.* a daughter of Erskine, of Dun, and had:

ALEXANDER LINDSAY (younger brother of Sir David Lindsay, of Edzell, eighth Earl of Crawford), who *m.* a daughter of Barclay, of Mathers, and had:

RIGHT REV. DAVID LINDSAY, D.D., of Leith, 1531–1613, Bishop of Ross in 1600, Chaplain to King James I., who had by his wife, whose name has not been preserved:

RACHEL LINDSAY, who *m.* the Most Rev. John Spottiswood, of that Ilk, *b.* 1565, Archbishop of St. Andrews, in 1615; Lord High Chancellor of Scotland, in 1635. He crowned King Charles I., at Holyrood, in 1639, and dying in London, 2 December, 1639, was buried by the King's command in Westminster Abbey (*see* Playfair's "British Family Antiquity," VIII., 305). Archbishop Spottiswood had by Rachel, his wife:

SIR ROBERT SPOTTISWOOD, Knt., of New Abbey, Kent, second son, *b.* 1596 (*see* the "Spottiswood Miscellany," 1844, Vol. I.). He was a member of the Privy Council to James VI., of Scotland, and was appointed by King Charles I. lord president of the college of justice and secretary for Scotland in 1636. He *m.*, 1629, Lady Bethia, eldest daughter of Sir Alexander Morrison, of Preston Grange, a senator in the college of justice, and his wife, Eleanor Maule, also of Royal Descent, and was executed for political reasons by the Covenanters, 20 January, 1646, having had issue:

ROBERT SPOTTISWOOD, surgeon to the Governor and garrison of Tangier (*see* Campbell's "Spottiswood Genealogy," 1868, and Fontaine's "Spottiswood Genealogy," 1881). He *m.* Catharine Elliott, widow, and dying at Tangier, in 1680, had by her:

MAJOR-GENERAL ALEXANDER SPOTSWOOD,* of "Porto Bello," James City county, Virginia, only son, *b.* at Tangier, 1676, *d.* 7 June, 1740; aide-de-camp to the Duke of Marlborough; arrived in Virginia 20 June, 1710, in the man-o'-war *Deptford;* lieutenant-governor and commander-in-chief of the Virginia colony, *etc.* (*see* Douglas's "Baronage of Scotland," 1798). He *m.*, 1724, ——— Butler, daughter of Richard and Ann Brayne, of Westminster (*see* "Virginia Historical Magazine," II., 340), and had:

1.—JOHN SPOTSWOOD, of Virginia, eldest son, *d.* 1759; *m.*, 1745, Mary Dandridge, of "Elsing Green," also of Royal Descent, and had:

I.—ANN SPOTSWOOD, who *m.* Lewis Burwell, and had:

SPOTSWOOD BURWELL, who *m.* Mary Marshall, and had:

MARY ANN SPOTSWOOD BURWELL, who *m.* Otis F. Manson, M.D., and had:

ELIZA SANGER MANSON, a member of the Virginia Society of the Colonial Dames of America, who *m.* Thomas Lee Alfriend, of Richmond, Virginia, and had:

1.—MARY BURWELL ALFRIEND, a member of the Virginia Society of the Colonial Dames of America, who *m.* Herbert Dale Lafferty, of Richmond. *No issue.*

2. OTIS MANSON; 3. SALLY SPOTSWOOD; 4. ANNA LEE.

II.—CAPTAIN JOHN SPOTSWOOD, who *m.* Sallie Rouze, and had:

ROBERT SPOTSWOOD, who *m.* Louisa Bott, and had:

REV. JOHN SPOTSWOOD, D.D., of Petersburg, Virginia, who *m.* Sarah Peters, daughter of William Shippen Willing, of Philadelphia, and had:

LUCY SPOTSWOOD, *b.* New Castle, Delaware, a member of the Pennsylvania Society of the Colonial Dames of America, who *m.* George Peirce, of Philadelphia.

2.—DOROTHEA SPOTSWOOD, who *m.*, 1747, Colonel Nathaniel West Dandridge, of Virginia, also of Royal Descent, and had:

I.—MAJOR ALEXANDER SPOTSWOOD DANDRIDGE, of "The Bower," Jefferson county, Virginia, *m.* Ann Stephen, and had:

ADAM STEPHEN DANDRIDGE, of "The Bower," 1782–1821, *m.*, 1805, Sarah Pendleton, and had:

---

* MISS ANNA SPOTSWOOD DANDRIDGE, a member of the Maryland Society Colonial Dames of America, is also of Royal Descent through Alexander Spotswood.

ALEXANDER SPOTSWOOD DANDRIDGE, M.D., of Cincinnati, Ohio, 1819–1889; *m.*, 1843, Martha, daughter of Colonel Nathaniel Pendleton, of Cincinnati, and had, besides other children:

1.—SUSAN BOWLER DANDRIDGE, a member of the New York Society of the Colonial Dames of America, who *m.* John M. Bowers, of New York City.

2.—MARY EVELYN DANDRIDGE, of Cincinnati, a member of the Virginia Society of the Colonial Dames of America.

II.—DOROTHEA DANDRIDGE, who *m.* (his second wife) Patrick Henry, of " Red Hill," Virginia, first Governor of Virginia, also of Royal Descent, and had:

JOHN HENRY, who *m.* Elvira Bruce McClelland, and had:

WILLIAM WIRT HENRY, of Richmond, Virginia, who *m.* Lucy Gray Marshall, a member of the Virginia Society of the Colonial Dames of America, and had:

1.—LUCY GRAY HENRY, a member of the Virginia Society of the Colonial Dames of America, who *m.* Matthew Bland Harrison, of Richmond, Virginia.

2.—ELIZABETH HENRY, a member of the Virginia Society of the Colonial Dames of America, who *m.* James Lyons, of Richmond, Virginia.

3.—ANN CATHERINE SPOTSWOOD, 1726–1802, who *m.*, 1745, Colonel Bernard Moore, of "Chelsea," King William county, Virginia, and had:

I.—ALEXANDER SPOTSWOOD MOORE, *b.* 1763, who *m.*, 19 July, 1787, Elizabeth, *b.* 1769, daughter of Colonel William Aylett, of " Fairfield," also of Royal Descent, and had:

MILDRED WALKER MOORE, *b.* 17 June, 1788, who *m.*, 17 June, 1806, Rev. John Wilson Campbell, of Virginia, and had:

ELIZABETH CAMPBELL, who *m.* John Maben, of Richmond, and had:

1.—MARY MABEN, a member of the Maryland Society of the Colonial Dames of America, who *m.* Frank Peyton Clark, of Baltimore, and had: *Bessie Campbell* and *William Lawrence*.

2.—JANE MABEN, who *m.* J. Dorsey Cullen, of Richmond, and had:

ELIZABETH CAMPBELL CULLEN, a member of the Virginia Society of the Colonial Dames of America, who *m.* John F. T. Anderson, of Ashland, Hanover county, Virginia.

II.—LUCY MOORE, who *m.*, 1774, Rev. Henry Skyren, of Hampton, Virginia, *b.* at White Haven, England, and had:

ELIZABETH SKYREN, who *m.* Robert Temple, of "Ampthill" and Fredericksburg, Virginia, and had :

MARY TEMPLE, who *m.* Thomas Crouch, of Richmond, and had :

ELIZABETH SKYREN CROUCH, who *m.*, 7 July, 1857, Howson Hooe Wallace, of Richmond, Virginia, *b.* 1 April, 1830, and had :

BESSIE BROWN WALLACE, *b.* Fredericksburg, 19 February, 1860, a member of the Virginia Society of the Colonial Dames of America, who *m.* Charles Armistead Blanton, M.D., of Richmond, Virginia, and had : *Wyndham Bolling, Howson Wallace,* and *Elizabeth Skyren.*

III.—BERNARD MOORE, of "Chelsea," *m.*, first, Lucy Ann Heabred Leiper, of Chester county, Pennsylvania, and had by her :

1.—ELIZABETH MOORE, *m.* Colonel James Macon, and had :

MARY MACON, *m.* Colonel William Aylett, and had :

COLONEL PHILIP AYLETT, who *m.* Elizabeth, daughter of Governor Patrick Henry, of Virginia, also of Royal Descent, and had :

MARY MACON AYLETT, who *m.* Philip Fitzhugh, and had :

LUCY FITZHUGH, who *m.* John Robertson Redd, of Virginia, and had :

LUCY REDD, a member of the Indiana Society of the Colonial Dames of America, who *m.* William J. Holliday, of Indianapolis, and had :

I.—ARIANA AMBLER HOLLIDAY, a member of the Indiana Society of the Colonial Dames of America, who *m.* Henry W. Bennett, of Indianapolis. *Issue.*

II.—JAQUELIN S. HOLLIDAY, *m.* Florence Baker. *Issue.*

III.—LUCY FITZHUGH HOLLIDAY, *m.* George E. Hume. *Issue.*

2.—ANDREW LEIPER MOORE, *m.* Ann Fitzhugh, sister of Governor Thomas Nelson and daughter of Robert Nelson, son of William Nelson and his wife, Elizabeth Burwell, also of Royal Descent, and had :

LUCY HEABRED MOORE, who *m.* Benjamin Needles Robinson, also of Royal Descent, and had :

ELIZABETH TAYLOR ROBINSON, who *m.* John Daniel Turner, M.D., and had :

LOUISE BEVERLEY TURNER, a member of the Virginia Society of the Colonial Dames of America, who *m.* Isaac N. Jones, of Richmond, Virginia, and had : *Bernard Moore.*

PEDIGREE LXIX.

JOHN, King of England, who had by his second wife (*m.* 1200), Lady Isabel, daughter of Aymer de Taillefer, Count of Angueleme:

PRINCESS ELEANOR PLANTAGENET, who *m.* Simon de Montfort, second Earl of Leicester, *k.* 1264, also of Royal Descent, and had:

LADY ELEANOR DE MONTFORT, who *m.* Llewelyn ap Gryffth, Prince of North Wales, and had:

LADY CATHERINE, who *m.* Philip ap Ivor ap Cadivor, and had:

LADY ELEANOR, who *m.* Thomas ap Llewelyn, of Trefgarned, lord of South Wales, also of Royal Descent, and had:

LADY ELEANOR, who *m.* Griffith Vychan IV., lord of Glyndyfrdwy, also of Royal Descent, and had:

TUDOR, lord of Gwyddelwern (brother of the celebrated Owen Glendower), *b.* 1345, *k.* 15 May, 1405, who *m.* Maud v. Ieuf ap Howell ap Adar, and had:

LADY LOWRY, heiress, who *m.* Gruffydd ap Einion, of Cors-y-Gedol, Merionethshire, and had:

ELLISSAU AP GRUFFYDD, *m.* Margaret v. Jenkin ap Ievan, also of Royal Descent, and had:

LOWRY, *m.* Reinaullt ap Gruffydd ap Rhys, of Branas Uchaf, and had:

MARY, *m.* Robert Lloyd ap David Lloyd, of Gwern y Brychdwyn, and had:

THOMAS LLOYD, *b.* 1515–20, *d.* 1612; *m.* Catherine v. Robert ap Griffith. and had:

MARY LLOYD, *m.* Richard, of Tyddyn Tyfod, and had:

RHYS AP RICHARD, who had:

GRIFFYTH AP RHYS, *alias* Griffith Price, who had:

RICHARD PRICE, of Glanlloidiogin, Llanfawr parish, Merionethshire, will dated 26 January, 1685–86, proved in 1686, who had:

HANNAH PRICE, 1656–1741, who *m.* Rees ap John ap William, *d.* 26 May, 1697 (*see* Glenn's "Merion in the Welsh Tract," p. 73). They came from Iscregenan, Merionethshire, bearing a certificate of removal from the Society of Friends, dated 4 April, 1684, to Pennsylvania, and took up land in the "Welsh Tract," near Philadelphia, and had:

Lowry Jones, 1680–1762, widow of Robert Lloyd, *d.* at Merion, Pennsylvania, 1714, who *m.*, secondly, 13 February, 1716, at Merion Meeting House (his third wife), Hugh Evans, of Philadelphia, 1682–1772, and had:

Susannah Evans, *b.* 25 January, 1719–20, *d.* 4 July, 1801; *m.*, 30 July, 1740, Owen Jones, *b.* 19 November, 1711, *d.* 9 October, 1793, the last provincial treasurer of Pennsylvania, also of Royal Descent, and had:

Hannah Jones, 1749–1829; *m.*, 1779, Amos Foulke, of Philadelphia, 1740–1791, also of Royal Descent (p. 118), and had:

Edward Foulke, of Gwynedd, Pennsylvania, 1784–1851; *m.*, 1810, Tacy Jones, and had, besides other issue:

1.—Anne Jones Foulke, 1811–1888; *m.*, 1833, Hiram Corson, M.D., of Conshohocken, and had:

Susan Foulke Corson, a member of the Pennsylvania, Society of the Colonial Dames of America, who *m.*, 26 November, 1868, Jawood Lukens, of Conshohocken. *No issue.*

2.—Priscilla Foulke, 1821–1882; *m.*, 1849, Thomas Wistar, Jr., of Philadelphia, and had:

Susan Foulke Wistar, a member of the Pennsylvania Society of the Colonial Dames of America, who *m.*, 27 May, 1872, Howard Comfort, of Philadelphia, and had: *William Wistar, b.* 27 May, 1874.

3.—Rebecca Jones Foulke, *b.* 18 May, 1829, a member of the Pennsylvania Society of the Colonial Dames of America, who *m.*, 8 October, 1857, Robert R. Corson, of New Hope, Pennsylvania. *No issue.*

PEDIGREE LXX.

EDWARD I., **King of England**, had by his first wife, Princess Eleanor, daughter of Ferdinand III., King of Castile and Leon:

PRINCESS JOAN PLANTAGENET, who had by her first husband, Gilbert de Clare, Earl of Hertford and Gloucester:

LADY MARGARET DE CLARE, who had by her second husband, Hugh d'Audley, first Earl of Gloucester:

LADY MARGARET D'AUDLEY, who *m.* Sir Ralph, second Baron de Stafford, K.G., first Earl of Stafford, and had:

SIR HUGH DE STAFFORD, K.G., second Earl of Stafford, who *m.* Lady Philippa, daughter of Sir Thomas de Beauchamp, K.G., Earl of Warwick, also of Royal Descent, and had:

LADY MARGARET DE STAFFORD, who *m.* (his first wife) Sir Ralph Neville, K.G., first Earl of Westmoreland, earl marshal of England, also of Royal Descent, and had:

LADY ALICE DE NEVILLE, who *m.* Sir Thomas de Grey, of Heton, beheaded 5 August, 1415, also of Royal Descent, and had:

LADY ELIZABETH DE GREY, who *m.* Sir Philip d'Arcy, fourth Baron d'Arcy, Admiral of the Royal Navy, also of Royal Descent, and had:

JOHN D'ARCY, fifth Baron d'Arcy, who *m.* Lady Margaret, daughter of Sir Henry, fifth Baron de Grey, of Wilton, also of Royal Descent, and had:

PHILIP D'ARCY, sixth Baron d'Arcy, *m.* Lady Eleanor, daughter of Henry, fourth Baron Fitzhugh, also of Royal Descent, and had:

LADY MARGERY D'ARCY, who *m.* Sir John Coniers, K.G., of Hornby, and had:

LADY ELEANOR CONIERS, who *m.* Sir Thomas de Markenfield, will dated 8 April, 1497, and had:

SIR NYAN MARKENFIELD, who *m.* Lady Dorothy, daughter of Sir William Gascoigne, *d.* 4 March, 1486, also of Royal Descent, and had:

LADY ALICE MARKENFIELD, who *m.*, 16 October, 1524, Robert Mauleverer, of Worthersome, York, also of Royal Descent, and had:

DOROTHY MAULEVERER, who *m.*, 1542, John Kaye, of Woodersome, Yorkshire, and had:

EDWARD KAYE, of Woodersome, *m.* Anne, daughter of Robert Tirwhitt, of Ketelby, Lincolnshire, and had:

Lucia Kaye, who *m.* John Pickering, of Techmersh, Northampton-shire, and had:

Elizabeth Pickering, who *m.* Robert Throckmorton, of Ellington, Huntingdonshire (*see* " The Magna Charta Barons and their American Descendants," p. 199), and had:

Gabriel Throckmorton, of Ellington, 1577-1626, *m.* Alice, daughter of William Bedles, of Bedfordshire, and had:

Robert Throckmorton, of Ellington, 1608-1662, will proved at London, 21 June, 1664; *m.* Judith Bromsall, and had:

John Throckmorton, of Ellington, 1633-1678, *m.* ——— Mason, and had:

Gabriel Throckmorton, second son, *b.* 1665. He came to Virginia before 1684, and inherited under will of his brother Robert, of Peyton Pawa, Huntingdonshire, proved 3 May, 1699, a plantation in New Kent County, Virginia. He was the presiding justice of Gloucester county, Virginia, and dying in January, 1737, had by his wife, *m.* in 1690, Frances, daughter of Mordecai Cooke, of " Mordecai's Mount," Gloucester county, Virginia:

Major Robert Throckmorton, of Ware parish, Gloucester county, Virginia, who *m.*, first, 14 August, 1730, Mary Lewis, also of Royal Descent, and had:

Robert Throckmorton, of Culpeper county, Virginia, *b.* 20 November, 1736, who *m.*, 16 June, 175-, Lucy, daughter of Captain Mordecai Throckmorton (brother of the aforesaid Major Robert Throckmorton), 1696-1767, high sheriff of King and Queen county, Virginia, 1740, and his wife, Mary Reade, also of Royal Descent, and had:

Frances Throckmorton, *m.* General William Madison, and had:

Rebecca Conway Madison, *m.* Reynolds Chapman, and had:

Judge John Madison Chapman, *m.* Susannah Digges Cole, also of Royal Descent, and had:

1.—Susie Ashton Chapman, a member of the Tennessee Society of the Colonial Dames of America, who *m.* Calvin Perkins, of Memphis. *Issue.*

2.—Belle Chapman, a member of the Virginia Society of the Colonial Dames of America, who *m.* William Moncure, of Richmond, Virginia. *Issue.*

3.—Ashton Alexander Chapman.

PEDIGREE LXXI.

RHYS AP TEWDWR, Prince of South Wales, who was defeated and slain by the Normans, *temp.* William Rufus, had by his wife, Lady Gwenllian, daughter of **Gruffydd ap Cynan, Prince of North Wales :**

PRINCESS ELIZABETH, who *m.* Edmund, Baron Carew, and had:

SIR EDGAR DE CAREW, Baron of Carew, or Cayrowe, who had:

JOHN (ST. ANDREW) DE CAREW, Baron of Carew, who had:

ANNE (NESTA) DE CAREW, who *m.* Thomas Awbrey, son of William Awbrey, of Aberkynfrig and Slough, Brecknockshire, a descendant of Stiant Awbrey, brother of Baron de Awbrey, Earl of Bullen and Earl Marshal of France, 1066, and had :

THOMAS AWBREY, of Aberkynfrig, constable and ranger of the forest of Breçon, who *m.* Johan, daughter of Trahaerne ap Einion, lord of Comond, and had :

THOMAS AWBREY-GÔCH, of Aberkynfrig, who *m.* Nesta, daughter of Owen Gethyn, of Glyn Taway, and had :

RICHARD AWBREY, of Aberkynfrig, who *m.* Creislie, daughter of Philip ap Elidor (or Phe ap Eledr), and had :

GWALTER (WALTER) AWBREY, of Aberkynfrig, who *m.* Johan, daughter of Rees Morgan ap Einion, of Carmarthen, and had :

MORGAN AWBREY, of Aberkynfrig, who *m.* Alice, daughter of Watkin Thomas ap David Lloyd, and had :

JENKIN AWBREY, of Aberkynfrig, who *m.* Gwenlliam, daughter of Owain ap Griffith, of Tal y Llyn, and had :

HOPKIN AWBREY, of Aberkynfrig, who *m.* Anne, daughter of John ap Griffith, of Gwyn, and had :

WILLIAM AWBREY, of Aberkynfrig, *d.* 27 June, 1547; *m.*, secondly, Jane, widow of Thomas Lloyd, and daughter of Sir Richard Herbert, Knt., of Montgomery Castle, a gentleman usher to Henry VIII., by his second wife, Jane, daughter of Gwilim ap Rees Phillip, of Llwynhowell, and had by her :

RICHARD AWBREY, of Aberkynfrig, eldest son, *d.* 1580, who sold his paternal estate. He *m.* Margaret, daughter of Thomas Gunter, of Gileston, and had :

RICHARD AWBREY, of Llanelyw, *d.* 23 September, 1646, buried in the church of Llanelyw; a stone recites his wife's parentage and children; he *m.* Anne, daughter of William Vaughan, of Llanelyw, and had:

THOMAS AWBREY, third son, who had:

WILLIAM AWBREY, of Llanelyw, Brecknock, *b.* 1626, *d.* 16 December, 1716, buried in the church; a stone recites his parentage, marriage and issue. He *m.*, 1646, his cousin, Elizabeth, daughter of William, eldest son of Richard Awbrey, *d.* 1646, aforesaid, and obtained the Llanelyw estate, and had:

MARTHA AWBREY,* *b. ante* 1662, *d.* 7 February, 1726-7, who joined the Society of Friends, and, "being engaged to be married to one Rees Thomas, who had gone to Pennsylvania, accompanied by her relatives, John and Barbara Bevan, of Treverigg, Glamorganshire, to Philadelphia," was *m.*, 18 April, 1692, at Haverford Meeting, Pennsylvania, to the said Rees Thomas, who became a justice of the peace and member of the assembly; will proved 12 February, 1742-3 (*see* Glenn's "Merion in the Welsh Tract," p. 305, *etc.*), and had:

WILLIAM THOMAS, *m.*, 12 May, 1724, Elizabeth Harry, and had:

REES THOMAS, *m.*, 13 November, 1758, Priscilla Jerman, and had:

WILLIAM THOMAS, *m.*, 5 April, 1786, Naomi Walker, and had:

REES THOMAS, *m.*, 29 March, 1810, Rebecca Brooke, and had:

WILLIAM B. THOMAS, *m.*, 22 January, 1836, Emily W. Holstein, and had:

1.—ANNA ELIZABETH THOMAS, a member of the Pennsylvania Society of the Colonial Dames of America, who *m.*, 3 February, 1858, Nathan Brooke, of Media, Pennsylvania, *d.* 1888, and had:

   I.—WILLIAM THOMAS BROOKE, *m.*, 11 May, 1881, Rebecca Chapman, and had: *Ida Lewis, Josephine Atmore,* and *Gertrude Chapman.*

   II.—IDA LONGMIRE BROOKE, *m.*, 14 December, 1881, J. Howard Lewis, Jr., and had: *John Crozer, Sarah Fallon, Helen Brooke, Emily Thomas,* and *Mildred Irwin.*

   III.—HUGH JONES BROOKE, *m.*, 25 April, 1893, Harriet Boyer Weand.

   IV.—HUNTER, JR.; V. EMILY THOMAS.

2.—MARY A. THOMAS, a member of the Pennsylvania Society of the Colonial Dames of America, who *m.*, 25 February, 1874, Hunter Brooke, of Philadelphia, and had: *Helen* and *Marie Thomas.*

---

* The following ladies, members of the National Society of the Colonial Dames of America, are also of Royal Descent through Martha Awbrey:

MRS. CHARLES RICHARDSON, Pennsylvania State Society.
MRS. GEORGE B. ROBERTS, Pennsylvania State Society.
MRS. HENRY K. DILLARD, Pennsylvania State Society.
MISS MARY WILLIAM PEROT, Pennsylvania State Society.

3.—REBECCA BROOKE THOMAS, a member of the Pennsylvania Society of the Colonial Dames of America, who *m.*, 20 November, 1867, George Hamilton Colket, of St. Davids, Pennsylvania, and had:

I.—EMILY THOMAS COLKET, *m.*, 30 October, 1889, Harrison Koons Caner, and had: *Harrison Koons, George Colket, William John,* and *Gerald Wayne.*

II.—MARY WALKER; III. TRISTRAM COFFIN; IV. GEORGE H.

PEDIGREE LXXII.

ROBERT BRUCE, King of Scotland, had by his second wife, Lady Elizabeth de Burgh, of Royal Descent:

LADY MATILDA BRUCE, who *m.* Thomas Isaac, Esquire, and had:

JOANNA ISAAC, who *m.* John d' Ergadia, lord of Lorn, and had:

ISABEL D' ERGADIA, who *m.* Sir John Stewart, lord of Innermeth, and had:

ROBERT STEWART, created, in 1439, Lord Lorn and Innermeth, who *m.* Lady Margaret, daughter of Robert Stewart, Duke of Albany, son of **Robert II., King of Scotland,** and had:

LADY MARGARET STEWART, who *m.* Robert, eighth Lord Erskine, *d.* 1453, also of Royal Descent, and had:

LADY MARGARET ERSKINE, who *m.*, *ante* 1457, James Rutherford, of Edgarston, son of James Rutherford, of Lethbertshiels, and had:

THOMAS RUTHERFORD, of Edgarston, who had:

ROBERT RUTHERFORD, of Edgarston, who had:

THOMAS RUTHERFORD, of Edgarston, who had:

RICHARD RUTHERFORD, of Edgarston, who had by his wife, a granddaughter of the laird of Buccleugh:

ROBERT RUTHERFORD, of Edgarston, who *m.* Margaret, daughter of Andrew Riddle, of that Ilk, and his wife Violet, daughter of William Douglas, of Pompherston (*see* Douglas's " Baronage of Scotland "), and had by her:

JOHN RUTHERFORD, of Edgarston, who *m.* Barbara Abernethy, daughter of the Bishop of Caithness, and had by her:

THOMAS RUTHERFORD, of Edgarston, who, dying in 1720, had issue by his wife, Susannah, daughter of Riddle, of Minto:

SIR JOHN RUTHERFORD, Knt., who *m.*, 1710, Elizabeth Cairncross, of Colmslie, and had by her nineteen children, of whom:

WALTER RUTHERFURD, captain in 62d Foot, English Army, who *m.*, first, Catherine, daughter of James Alexander, of New York, also of Royal Descent, and had:

JOHN RUTHERFURD, of Edgarston, New Jersey, *b.* 1760, *d.* 23 February, 1840; Presidential elector and United States Senator from New Jersey, 1791–98. He *m.*, 1781, Magdalena, daughter of General Lewis Morris,

chief justice and Governor of New Jersey, a member of the Continental
Congress, and a signer of the Declaration of Independence, and had:

ROBERT WALTER RUTHERFURD, of New York, 1778–1851, who *m.* his
cousin, Sabina E., daughter of Colonel Lewis Morris, Jr., and had:

JOHN RUTHERFURD, of New York, *d.* 1871; *m.* Charlotte, daughter of
James Kane Livingston, of New York, and had:

1. HELENA RUTHERFURD, a member of the New York Society of the
Colonial Dames of America, who *m.* Alfred Ely, of Newton, Massachusetts, and New York City.

2. LIVINGSTON RUTHERFURD.

3. ARTHUR ELLIOTT RUTHERFURD.

4. MORRIS RUTHERFURD.

PEDIGREE LXXIII.

CONN CEADCATHA (" Conn of the Hundred Battles "), **King of all Ireland,** A.D., 123–157, had:

LADY SABINA, who *m.*, secondly, Olioll Olum, 'first king of United Munster, and had:

CIAN, third son, founder of Clan Cian in Ormond, the chief family of the Sept being O'Cearbhaill, anglicized O'Carroll. Cian's descendant (*see* O'Hart's " Irish Pedigrees," third edition, 107):

EILE RIGH DHEARG, or " Eile the red," after whom the territory possessed by the O'Carrolls in Leinster was called Duiche Eiligh, or Ele, " the estates of Ely," whereof his posterity were styled kings, then princes, and finally chiefs and barons. The fourteenth son and heir from him was:

MONACH O'CARROLL, who was the first to use this surname. His descendant and heir in the eighth generation was:

FIONN II., " King of Ely," *k.* in 1205, who had:

TEIGE O'CARROLL, chief of Ely, who had:

DONAL, who had:

DONOUGH DHEARG, *d.* 1306, who had:

WILLIAM ALAINN, who had:

DONOUGH, *d.* 1377 (these were chieftains of Ely), who had:

RODERIC, of Ely, who had:

DANIEL [who had: *Roderic,* who had: *Donough*], who had (according to O'Clery's " Linea Antiqua "):

TEIGE COACH, of Litterlouna, created " lord baron of Ely " in 1552, *d.* 1554, who had:

DONOUGH (whose brother Roger succeeded to Ely), who had:

DANIEL, of Litterlouna, who had:

ANTHONY, of Litterlouna, who had:

DANIEL O'CARROLL, of Litterlouna, Kings county, who had (besides possibly *Anthony,* of Lishlenboy, County Tipperary, will proved 1724, to whose son, Captain James Carroll, of Lord Dongan's Regiment of Dragoons, Daniel Carroll, of Rock Creek, wrote an interesting genealogical letter about their relations in America, 20 December, 1762, preserved in the Catholic archives at Notre Dame, Indiana):

CHARLES CARROLL,* of Litterlouna and the Inner Temple, London, who arrived in Maryland, 1 October, 1688, and received large grants of land in the Province, was a magistrate, register of the land office, agent and receiver general of rents, for the Calverts. He was commissioned attorney-general 18 July, 1688. He *m.* Mary Darnall, and had:

1.—DANIEL CARROLL, of "Duddington," who had by his wife, Anne Rosier:

　I.—ELIZABETH CARROLL, *m.* Daniel Carroll, of Rock Creek, Upper Marlboro, Maryland, 1762, also of Royal Descent, and had:

　　DANIEL CARROLL, *b.* 1752, *m.* Eleanor Digges, and had:

　　WILLIAM CARROLL, *m.* Henrietta Maria Williamson, and had:

　　DAVID WILLIAMSON CARROLL, *m.* Melanie Scull, and had:

　　MELANIE CARROLL, a member of the Maryland Society of the Colonial Dames of America, who *m.* Daniel A. Boone, of Baltimore, and had: *Carroll J., d.; William C., R. Sanchez, Charles Louis, Melanie,* wife of Ferdinand C. Dugan; *Clara,* and *Ellen Theresa.*

　II.—CHARLES CARROLL, who had by his second wife, Ann Sprigg:

　　WILLIAM THOMAS CARROLL, who *m.,* 14 October, 1828, Sally Sprigg, and had:

　　ALIDA CATHERINE CARROLL, who *m.,* in Washington, District of Columbia, 18 December, 1866, John Marshall Brown, of Portland, Maine, and had:

　　SALLY CARROLL BROWN, a member of the Maryland Society of the Colonial Dames of America, who *m.,* 5 April, 1893, Herbert Payson, of Portland, Maine, and had: *Alida, b.* 27 January, 1895; *Anne Carroll, b.* 14 October, 1896; *John Brown, b.* 1 October, 1897, and *Charles Shipman, b.* 16 October, 1898.

2.—CHARLES CARROLL, of "Doughoregan Manor," Howard county, Maryland, 1702–1782, attorney-general of Maryland, *m.* Elizabeth Brooke, and had:

　CHARLES CARROLL of "Carrollton," 1737–1832, a member of the Continental Congress and a signer of the Declaration of Independence, United States Senator, *etc.; m.,* 1768, Mary, daughter of Henry Darnall, Jr., and had:

　　COLONEL CHARLES CARROLL of "Carrollton," only son, *d.* 1861, who *m.,* 1799, Harriet, *d.* 1861, daughter of Benjamin Chew, of Philadelphia, chief justice of Pennsylvania, and had:

---

* The following ladies, members of the National Society of the Colonial Dames of America, are also of Royal Descent through Charles Carroll:

MRS. OUTERBRIDGE HORSEY (deceased), Maryland State Society.

MRS. RICHARD S. HILL, Maryland State Society.

MARY SOPHIA CARROLL, 1804–1886, who *m.* Richard Henry Bayard, *d.*, Philadelphia, 1868, United States Senator from Delaware, son of James A. Bayard, United States Senator from Delaware, and his wife Ann, daughter of Richard Bassett, Governor of Delaware, and brother of James A. Bayard, Jr., United States Senator from Delaware, and had :

I.—CAROLINE BAYARD, who *m.* Henry Baring Powel, of Philadelphia, *d.* 1852, and had :

MARY DE VAUX POWEL, a member of the Society of the Colonial Dames of America, who *m.* Rev. George Woolsey Hodge, of Philadelphia. *Issue.*

II.—RICHARD BASSETT BAYARD, of Baltimore, *d.* 1878, *m.*, 1860, his cousin, Ellen Gilmor Howard, and had : *Richard H.*, and

ELLEN HOWARD BAYARD, of Baltimore, a member of the Maryland Society of the Colonial Dames of America.

THE ROYAL DESCENT

OF

MRS. PHILIP H. COOPER,

OF MORRISTOWN, NEW JERSEY.

HUGH CAPET, King of France⹋Adela, dau. William, Duke of Aquitaine.

Robert I., the Pious,⹋Lady Constance
King of France | of Provence.

Princess Havide⹋Rynerius IV., Count
or Hedewige | of Hainault.

Henry I., King of⹋Lady Anne of Russia.
France

Lady Beatrix⹋Eblo de Rouci.

Hugh Magnus,⹋Lady Adelheid of
Duke of France | Vermandois.

Countess Adela⹋Hildwin de Montdider.

Lady Margaret de Rouci⹋Hugh de Clermont.

William de Warren,⹋Lady Isabel de⹋Robert de Bellomont,
Earl of Surrey | Vermandois | Earl of Leicester.

Lady Adeliza⹋Gilbert de Tonsburg,
de Clermont | Earl of Clare.

William de Warren,⹋Lady Alice de Talvas,
Earl of Surrey | also of Royal Descent.

Lady Elizabeth de Bellomont⹋Gilbert de Clare, Earl
of Pembroke.

Lady Isabella de⹋Hameline Plantagenet,
Warren | Earl of Surrey.

Richard "the Strongbow,"⹋Eva, dau. Dermot,
2d Earl of Pembroke | King of Leinster.

Lady Isabella de⹋Roger Bigod, Earl of
Warren | Norfolk.

Lady Isabel de Clare⹋William le Marshal,
Protector of England.

Hugh Bigod, second Earl of Norfolk⹋Lady Maud Marshall.

Sir Hugh Bigod, Justiciary of England⹋Joan, dau. of Robert Burnet.

Sir John Bigod, Knt.⹋(Name unknown.)

Sir Roger Bigod, of Settington⹋(Name unknown.)

Lady Joan Bigod⹋Sir William de Chauncy, of Skirpenbeck.

John Chauncy, of Stepney⹋Margaret Gifford, of Gedleston.

John Chauncy, of Sawbridgeworth⹋Anne Leventhorp, of Shingey.

John Chauncy, of Sawbridgeworth⹋Daughter of Thomas Boyce.

John Chauncy, of Pishobury⹋Elizabeth (Proffit) Mansfield.

Henry Chauncy, of Newplace Giffords⹋Lucy ——.

George Chauncy, of Yardleybury⹋Anne Welsh, of Great Wymondley.

Rev. Charles Chauncy, D.D., 1592-1671, second⹋Catherine Eyre, of New Sarum.
President of Harvard College

Sarah Chauncy, 1631-1699⹋Rev. Gershom Bulkeley, 1636-1713.

Rev. John Bulkeley, of Colchester, Conn.⹋Patience Prentice, of New London, Conn.

Gershom⹋Abigail
Bulkeley | Robbins.

Patience⹋Ichabod
Bulkeley | Lord.

Sarah⹋John
Bulkeley | Taintor.

Abigail⹋Enos
Lord | Hosford.

John Taintor, of Windham, Conn.⹋Sarah Hosford.

Sarah Taintor, 1787-1827⹋Israel Foote, of New York, 1783-1871.

John Taintor Foote, of Morristown, N. J.⹋Jordena Cannon Harris.

Katharine Jordena Foote, member of the Na-⹋Philip H. Cooper, Captain in the United States
tional Society of the Colonial Dames of Amer- | Navy.
ica

Dorothy B. Cooper, b. 9 March, 1889.

Leslie B. Cooper, b. 24 March, 1894.

PEDIGREE LXXIV.

ALFRED THE GREAT, King of England, had by his wife, Lady Elswitha, daughter of Ethelan the Great, Earl of Mercia:

EDWARD THE ELDER, King of England, who had by his third wife, Lady Egiva, daughter of the Saxon Earl, Sigelline:

PRINCESS EGIVA, who *m.*, first (his second wife), Charles III., King of France, a lineal descendant of the Empeřor Charlemagne, and had:

LOUIS IV., King of France, who *m.* Lady Gerberga de Saxe, daughter of Henry I., Emperor of Germany, and widow of Giselbert I., Duke of Lorraine, and had:

PRINCESS MATHILDE (or "Mahaut de France"), who *m.* Conrad le Pacifique, King of Arles, and had:

LADY BERTHA, who *m.* Eudes I., second Count of Blois, son of Thibaut I., Count of Blois, and his wife, Lady Leutgarde (widow of William, *Lougue Epee*, Duke of Normandy (*see* "L'Art," xiii., p. 6), daughter of Herbert II., Count de Vermandois, a lineal descendant of the Emperor Charlemagne (*see* p. 163), and had:

EUDES II., fourth Count de Blois and Champagne, second son, who had by his second wife, Lady Ermengarde, daughter of Robert, first Count d'Auvergne:

LADY BERTHE DE BLOIS, who *m.*, first, Alain III., Duke of Bretagne, *d.* 1 October, 1040, eldest son of Geoffroi I., Duke of Bretagne, *d.* 1008, and his wife, Lady Havois, or Hawiga, daughter of Richard I., Duke of Normandy, and his second wife, Lady Gonnor (*see* Anderson's "Royal Genealogies"), and had:

LADY HAVOIS DE BRETAGNE, who *m.* ("L'Art," xiii., 202), Hoel V., Duke of Bretagne, *d.* 13 April, 1084, and had:

ALAIN, Duke of Bretagne, *d.* 13 October, 1119, who had by his second wife (*see* "L'Art," xiii., 62), Lady Ermengarde, the divorced wife of William IX., Duke of Aquitaine, and daughter of Foulques IV., Count d'Anjou:

CONAN III., Duke of Bretagne, Prince of Rennes and Nantes, *d.* 17 September, 1148, who had by his wife, Lady Mathilde (*see* "L'Art," xiii., 203):

LADY BERTHA DE BRETAGNE, only child, who *m.*, first (*see* "L'Art," xiii., 249), Alain II., Count de Penthievre, Duke of Bretagne, and fourth

(307)

Earl of Richmond (*see* Dugdale's " Baronage," and " L'Art," xiii., 205, 247), and had :

LADY CONSTANCE DE BRETAGNE (sister of Conan IV., Duke of Bretagne and Earl of Richmond, *d.* 1171, who *m.* Margaret, sister of William, King of Scots, and had *Constance*, only child, who *m.*, first, Geoffroi, son of Henry II., of England, who *m.*, after 1160, Alain III., Viscount de Rohan (*see* " L'Art," xiii., 206, 273, and " Dictionnaire de la Noblesse "), and had :

ALAIN IV., Viscount de Rohan, Count of Brittainy, feudal Baron le Zouche, of Ashby, who *m.* (*see* " L'Art," xiii., 274) Lady Mabilla, daughter of Raoul II., lord of Fougeres, a crusader, *d.* 1196 (*see* the authorities and particulars for this genealogy cited in " L'Art de Verifier les Dates des Faits Historiques "), and had :

ROGER LE ZOUCHE, feudal Baron le Zouche, of Ashby (*see* Nicolas's " Historic Peerage "), father of

ROGER LE ZOUCHE, feudal Baron le Zouche, of Ashby (brother of Williom, Baron le Zouche, *d.* 1199, who in confirming grants made by his father to the Abbey of St. Segius, in Anjou, in a deed to the monks of Swaverey, in Cambridgeshire, calls Roger le Zonche his father, and Alan le Zouche, Earl of Brittany, his grandfather (Burke's " Extinct Peerages "). Roger le Zouche was an adherent of King John, and for his fidelity received the gift of many manors of the rebel barons, and was sheriff of Devonshire in 1229. He had by his wife, Lady Margaret :

LADY ALICE LE ZOUCHE, who *m.* (*see* Dugdale's " Baronage," 1675) Sir William Harcourt, of Stanton-Harcourt, Oxford, and had :

LADY ARABELLA HARCOURT (widow of Sir Fluke Pembrugge), who *m.*, secondly, Sir John de Digby, *d.* 1267, both buried at Tilton (*see* Nichol's " Leicestershire," iii., Pt. I., 471–72, and Salisbury's " Genealogies "), and had :

JOHN DE DIGBY, of Tilton, Leicestershire (*see* Leland's " Itinerary," iii., Pt. I., 462), eldest son, had by his wife, Margaret (Wake ?) :

JOHN DE DIGBY, second son, who *m.* Elizabeth, daughter of William d'Oseville, and had :

ROBERT DE DIGBY, of Tilton, only son, *d.* before 1412 ; *m.* Catherine, daughter of Simon de Pakeman, in Leicestershire, and had :

SIMON DE DIGBY, of Tilton and of Drystoke, Rutlandshire, eldest son, *d.* before 1440 ; *m.* Jean, daughter of Sir James Beler, or Bellaire, of Kirby Bellers, Leicestershire, and had :

SIR EVERARD DE DIGBY, of Drystroke, eldest son high sheriff of Rutlandshire, 1459 ; member of Parliament, 1446 ; *k.* at Towton, with his three brothers, 29 March, 1461 (*see* Nichol's " Leicestershire," iii., Pt. I., p. 463, and Hutchins' " Dorsetshire," iii. 475) ; *m.* Anne, daughter of Sir Francis Clarke, of Whyssendom, Rutland, and had :

EVERARD DE DIGBY, of Tilton, eldest son, high sheriff of Rutland, 1459, *etc.*; member of Parliament for Rutland; buried at Tilton; will proved 12 February, 1508–9. He *m.* Jacquetta, *d.* 29 June, 1496, buried at Drystoke, daughter of Sir John Elys (*see* Nichols' "Topog. et Geneal.," iii., 284), and had:

SIR JOHN DE DIGBY, of Eye Kettleby, Leicestershire, third son, high sheriff of Rutland, 1491, *etc.*, and Warwick and Leicestershire, 1515; knighted on Bosworth Field by Henry VII., and appointed knight-marshal to the King and captain of Calais (*see* Leland's "Itinerary," iv., 19); will dated 1 August, 1529, was proved 30 October, 1546, but his epitaph at Melton states he *d.* in 1533 (*see* Hutchins' "Dorset," iv., 475). He *m.*, first, Catherine, daughter of Nicholas (or John) Griffin, of Brabrooke, Northamptonshire (*see* Warwickshire "Visitations," 1619), and had by her, who *d.* before 1517:

WILLIAM DIGBY, of Kettleby, eldest son, *d. ante* 1 August, 1529, who had by his first wife, Rose, daughter of William Perwich, or Prestwith, of Luffenham (*see* Leicestershire "Visitations," 1619, and Salisbury's "Genealogies," vol. i., Pt. 2, pp. 438–445, and authorities there cited):

SIMON DIGBY, of Beadale, Rutland, who was attainted and executed for being a rebel in March, 1570 (*see* "Calendar of Eng. State Papers," Dom. ser., addenda). He *m.* Anne, daughter of Reginald Grey, and had:

EVERARD DIGBY, second son, who *m.* Catherine, daughter of Magistri Stockbridge de van der Shaff, Theodor de Newkirk, and had:

ELIZABETH DIGBY,* only child, 1584–1669. She was educated a Protestant in Holland in her mother's family, and *m.*, at St. John's, Hackney, London, 25 October, 1614, Enoch Lynde, of St. Andrew's parish, Hubbard, London, *d.* 23 April, 1636 (letters to administer his estate granted to his widow, 7 October, 1637), and had:

JUDGE SIMON LYNDE, of Boston, Massachusetts, third son, *bapt.* at St. Andrew's, June, 1624, *d.* 22 November, 1687; came to Boston in 1650 (*see* Salisbury's "Genealogies" and the "Lynde Diaries"), and *m.*, February, 1652–53, Hannah, *b.* 28 June, 1635, *d.* 20 December, 1684,

---

* The genealogy of "the renowned family of Digby," preserved at Sherbourne Castle, Dorsetshire, was prepared from the Digby archives by the order Sir Kenelm Digby, at a cost of $6000. It is a folio volume of 589 vellum leaves, the first 165 ornamented with the illuminated coats of arms, and crests of the family and its allies. It contains also sketches of family monuments, and memorial windows and portraits, besides transcripts of family wills, grants, patents, deeds, *etc.*; funeral entries, marriage and baptismal records, *etc.*; to illustrate and prove the history of this distinguished family. The genealogy of the Lynde and allied families was compiled and printed in seven large volumes, by Professor and Mrs. Salisbury, of New Haven, at a cost of $22,000.

daughter of John Newgate, or Newdigate, *d.* 4 September, 1665, aged 84 years, and had :

I.—JUDGE SAMUEL LYNDE, of Boston, Massachusetts, *b.* 1 December, 1653, *d.* October, 1721 ; *m.*, 20 October, 1674, Mary, 1657–1697, daughter of Jarvis Ballord, of Boston, and had :

> MARY LYNDE, *b.* 16 November, 1680, *d.* 26 March, 1732 ; *m.*, 6 April, 1702, John Valentine, of Boston, *d.* 1742, advocate-general of the province of Massachusetts Bay and New Hampshire and Rhode Island, and had:

> > THOMAS VALENTINE, of Hopkinton, Massachusetts, *b.* 3 August, 1713, *d.* 17 April, 1783 ; *m.*, 17 July, 1735, Elizabeth, daughter of James Gooche and his wife Elizabeth, daughter of Sir Charles Hobby, Knt., of Boston, and had :

> > > I.—ELIZABETH VALENTINE, *b.* 18 May, 1739, *d.* 26 March, 1807 ; *m.* Zaccheus Ballord, *b.* 21 March, 1731, *d.*, at Thompson, Connecticut, 1800, and had :

> > > > LYNDE BALLORD, of Thompson, *b.* 15 May, 1774, *d.* 7 June, 1825 ; *m.*, 4 December, 1794, Polly, 1777–1816, daughter of John and Chloe (Fuller) Bates, and had :

> > > > > REV. JOHN BATES BALLORD, *b.* 25 October, 1795, *d.* New York, 29 January, 1856 ; *m.*, 28 May, 1824, Augusta Maria Gilman, *b.* Gilmanton, New Hampshire, 26 June, 1804, *d.* 17 May, 1890, at Colchester, Connecticut, and had :

> > > > > > ESEK STEERE BALLORD, of Davenport, Iowa, *b.* Bloomfield, Connecticut, 26 July, 1830, a founder of the Order of Runnemede; *m.*, 4 September, 1862, Frances A. Webb, and had, besides other issue (*see* " The Magna Charta Barons and Their American Descendants ") :

> > > > > > > KATHARINE AUGUSTA BALLORD, *b.* 5 August, 1864, a member of the Iowa Society of the Colonial Dames of America, who *m.*, 26 June, 1888, Leon M. Allen, of Davenport, Iowa, and had : *Leon Ballord, b.* 9 January, 1891 ; *Frances Priscilla, b.* 17 April, 1894, and *Allerton, b.* 6 February, 1898.

II.—SAMUEL VALENTINE, of Hopkinton, *b.* 7 December, 1745, *d.* 10 March, 1834 ; *m.*, 17 December, 1771, Elizabeth, daughter of Colonel John and Hannah (Simpson) Jones, and had :

> 1.—SAMUEL VALENTINE, JR., of Hopkinton, *b.* 14 February, 1773, *d.* 19 February, 1823 ; *m.*, secondly, January 1, 1809, Mary, *b.* 29 January, 1783, *d.* 13 August 1861, daughter of Captain Richard Fiske, of Framingham, Massachusetts, *b.* 25 February, 1750, *d.* 9 January, 1824, and had by her:

Eliza Fiske Valentine, *b.* Hopkinton, 10 November, 1813, a member of the Massachusetts and Michigan Societies of the Colonial Dames of America, the Order of the Crown, *etc.*, who *m.* Benjamin Stow Farnsworth, of Boston, Massachusetts, *b.* 9 August, 1804, *d.* at Detroit, 30 November, 1893, and had :

I.—Harriet Eliza Prescott Farnsworth, of Detroit, a member of the Massachusetts and Michigan Societies of the Colonial Dames of America, the Order of the Crown, *etc.*

II.—Henrietta Lynde Farnsworth, of Detroit, a member of the Massachusetts and Michigan Societies of the Colonial Dames of America, *etc.*, and founder of the Order of the Crown.

III.—Mary Susan Farnsworth, a member of the Order of the Crown, *m.* 14 February, 1867, William Wirt Smith, of Chicago, and had :

Edna Valentine Smith, a member of the Order of the Crown.

2.—Colonel Joseph Valentine, of Hopkinton, *b.* 18 November, 1776, *d.* 26 March, 1845 ; *m.*, first, Fanny Haven, *d.* 1841, and had :

Harriet Jones Valentine, 1800–1870; *m.*, first, 1806, Abraham Harrington, of Hopkinton, 1792–1828, and had :

Frances A. Harrington, *b.* 26 May, 1817, *d.* 22 October, 1886 ; *m.*, 1838, Norman Cutter, of St. Louis, Missouri, and had :

Mary Webber Cutter, a member of the Massachusetts and Missouri Societies of the Colonial Dames of America, who *m.*, 24 January, 1859, Hugh McKittrick, of St. Louis, Missouri, and had :

1.—Thomas Harrington McKittrick, *b.* 17 April, 1864; *m.*, 9 May, 1888, Hildegarde Sterling, and had : *Thomas H., Jr., b.* 14 March, 1889; *Margaret, b.* 8 January, 1891, and *Edward Sterling, b.* 3 November, 1897.

2.—Martha McKittrick, *b.* 12 January, 1866, *d.* 5 November, 1892 ; *m.*, 6 November, 1889, William C. Stribling, and had : *Mildred Clarkson, b.* 23 August, 1890, and *William C., Jr., b.* 27 January, 1892.

3.—Hugh McKittrick, Jr., *b.* 16 August, 1868 ; *m.*, 9 May, 1895, Grace Kennett, and had : *Hugh, b.* 27 March, 1896, *d.* 7 February, 1899 ; *William Kennett, b.* 1 August, 1897, and *Mary, b.* 3 September, 1898.

4.—Alan, *b.* 17 July, 1871, *d.* 5 December, 1886; 5. Walter, *b.* 19 March, 1873 ; 6. Mary, *b.* 22 February, 1875 ; 7. Ralph, *b.* 17 August, 1877.

II.—Nathaniel Lynde, *b.* 22 November, 1659, *d.*, Saybrook, Connecticut, 5 October, 1729, the first treasurer of Yale College ; *m.*, in Boston,

1683, Susannah, 1664–1709, daughter of Francis Willoughby, deputy-governor of Massachusetts Colony, 1665–71, and had:

I.—HANNAH LYNDE, *b.* 2 December, 1694, *d.* before 1736; *m.*, 22 June, 1725, Rev. George Griswold, *b.* 13 August, 1692, *d.* Lyme, Connecticut, 14 October, 1761, and had:

ELIZABETH GRISWOLD, *b.* 16 July, 1729, *d.* 16 January, 1779; *m.*, 1747, John Raymond, *b.* 18 January, 1725, *d.*, Montville, Connecticut, 7 May, 1789; second lieutenant in Captain Chapman's Company at the battle of Bunker's Hill, and had:

ANNA RAYMOND, *b.* 13 December, 1758, *d.*, Salem, Connecticut, 28 July, 1842; *m.*, 24 May, 1787, Stephen Billings, *b.* 8 December, 1750, *d.* Salem, 29 January, 1798; captain in 7th Regiment Connecticut Line; a member of the Society of the Cincinnati, and had:

NANCY BILLINGS, *b.* 23 December, 1792, *d.* 2 January, 1858, at Berlin, Ohio; *m.*, 13 March, 1815, Joseph Otis, *b.* 24 September, 1792, *d.*, at Berlin, 16 April, 1844, and had:

JOSEPH EDWARD OTIS, of Chicago, *b.* 30 April, 1830; *m.*, 3 May, 1859, Ellen Maria Taylor, *b.* 30 August, 1837, and had:

MARY TAYLOR OTIS, a member of the Massachusetts and Illinois Societies of the Colonial Dames of America, *b.* 24 November, 1860, who *m.*, 19 November, 1885, John Elias Jenkins, of Chicago, Illinois, *b.* 18 October, 1849, and had: *John Elliott, b.* 30 December, 1890.

II.—ELIZABETH LYNDE, 1684–1778, who *m.* Judge Richard Lord, of Lyme, Connecticut, 1690–1776, and had:

1.—ELIZABETH LORD, *b.* 1735, who *m.*, 1760, Jared Eliot, Jr., of Killingworth, Connecticut, 1728–1811, also of Royal Descent, and had:

JARED ELIOT, of Killingworth, 1761–1841, who *m.*, 1785, Clarissa, daughter of John Lewis, and had:

MARY ELIOT, 1792–1838 (widow of Henry Eliot), who *m.*, secondly, Joseph Dana Grafton, of St. Genevieve, Missouri, and had:

FRANCES E. GRAFTON, 1829–1898, who *m.*, at Little Rock, in 1846, William Eliot Ashley, of Little Rock, Arkansas, *d.* 1868, also of Royal Descent, and had: *Chester Grafton, Francis Freeman, Harriet Eliza, William Eliot,* and

FRANCES ANNE ASHLEY, a member of the Massachusetts and Arkansas Societies of the Colonial Dames of America, who *m.* Clifton Sidney Gray, M.D., *b.* Missouri, and *d. s. p.*, Little Rock, Arkansas, 14 February, 1899.

2.—CAPTAIN ENOCH LORD, of Lyme, 1726–1814, who *m.* Hepzibah, daughter of Joseph Mervin, of Lyme, and had:

RICHARD LORD, of Lyme, 1752–1818, who *m.* Anne, daughter of Captain William Mitchell, and had:

SARAH ANN LORD, 1799–1835, who *m.* Judge Charles Johnson McCurdy, LL.D., of Lyme, also of Royal Descent (p. 106), and had:

EVELYN McCURDY, only child, a member of the Connecticut Society of the Colonial Dames of America, who *m.* Professor Edward Elbridge Salisbury, of New Haven, Connecticut. *No issue.*

III.—ELIZABETH LYNDE, *b.* 25 March, 1662, *d.* June, 1746, who *m.* George Pordage, of Boston, and had:

HANNAH PORDAGE, who *m.*, secondly, 1714, James Bowdoin, of Boston, 1676–1747, member of the Colonial Council, and had:

ELIZABETH BOWDOIN, 1717–1771 (sister of Governor James Bowdoin), who *m.*, 26 October, 1732, James Pitts, of Boston, 1710–1776, member of the Colonial Council, and had:

SAMUEL PITTS, 1745–1805; *m.*, 1776, Johanna Davis, and had:

THOMAS PITTS, 1779–1836; *m.*, 9 November, 1802, Elizabeth Mountfort, and had:

I.—EMELINE PITTS, 1812–1893, who *m.* Benjamin Sanborn, M.D., 1800–1846, and had:

NANCY MERRILL SANBORN, of Detroit, a member of the Massachusetts and Michigan Societies of the Colonial Dames of America, the Order of the Crown, *etc.*

II.—SAMUEL MOUNTFORT PITTS, 1810–1886, who *m.*, 24 June, 1836, Sarah Bradford Merrill, and had:

1.—FRANCES PITTS, a member of the Massachusetts and Michigan Societies of the Colonial Dames of America, the Order of the Crown, *etc.*, who *m.* General Henry M. Duffield, of Detroit, and had: *Henry Martyn, Pitts, Divie Bethune, Dr. Francis, Morse Stewart,* and *Graham.*

2.—THOMAS PITTS, of Detroit, who *m.* Louise Strong Chapin, and had: *Samuel Lendall,* and

HELEN STRONG PITTS, a member of the Massachusetts and Michigan Societies of the Colonial Dames of America, who *m.*, 19 June, 1900, Arthur M. Parker, of Detroit.

3.—JULIA PITTS, a member of the Massachusetts and Michigan Societies of the Colonial Dames of America, the Order of the Crown, *etc.*, who *m.* Thomas Cranage, of Bay City, Michigan, and had: *Samuel Pitts,* and

20

MARY HILL CRANAGE, a member of the Massachusetts and Michigan Societies of the Colonial Dames of America, the Order of the Crown, *etc.*

IV.—CHIEF JUSTICE BENJAMIN LYNDE, of Salem, who *m.*, 27 April, 1699, Mary Browne, also of Royal Descent (p. 138), and had:

CHIEF JUSTICE BENJAMIN LYNDE, JR., of Salem, who *m.*, 1 November, 1731, Mary Goodrich, daughter of Major John Bowles, of Roxbury, and had:

LYDIA LYNDE, who *m.* Rev. William Walter, of Boston, and had:

HARRIOT TYNGE WALTER, who *m.* John Odin, and had:

ESTHER ODIN, who *m.* Rev. Benjamin Dorr, D.D., and had:

I.—ESTHER ODIN DORR, a member of the Pennsylvania Society of the Colonial Dames of America, who *m.* William Hewitt Webb, of Philadelphia, and had:

ANNIE GRISCOM WEBB, a member of the Pennsylvania Society of the Colonial Dames of America, who *m.* Albert Ripley Leeds, of Hoboken, New Jersey.

II.—MARY WARREN DORR, a member of the Pennsylvania Society of the Colonial Dames of America, who *m.* William L. Schäffer, of Philadelphia.

III.—HARRIOT ODIN DORR, a member of the Pennsylvania Society of the Colonial Dames of America, who *m.*, 17 October, 1867, Major James Edward Carpenter, of Philadelphia, also of Royal Descent (*see* "Americans of Royal Descent," ii., 639), and had: *Edward, Helen, Grace, d. young; William Dorr,* and *Lloyd Preston.*

PEDIGREE LXXV.

EDWARD I., King of England, had by his first wife, *m.*, 1254, Eleanor, *d.* 1290, daughter of Ferdinand III., King of Castile and Leon: PRINCESS ELIZABETH PLANTAGENET, 1282–1316, widow of Sir John de Vere, who *m.*, secondly, 14 November, 1302, Humphrey de Bohun, Earl of Hereford and Essex, lord high constable, *k.* at Boroughbridge in 1321, also of Royal Descent, and had:

SIR WILLIAM DE BOHUN, K.G., fifth son, created, 1337, Earl of Northampton, *d.* 1360, who *m.* Lady Elizabeth, *d.* 1356, daughter of Bartholomew, first Baron de Badlesmere, executed in 1322, and his wife, Lady Margaret de Clare, also of Royal Descent, and had:

LADY ELIZABETH DE BOHUN, who *m.* (his first wife) Sir Richard Fitz-Alan, K.G., tenth Earl of Arundel, beheaded in 1398, also of Royal Descent, and had:

LADY ELIZABETH FITZ-ALAN, *d.* 8 July, 1425, who had by her third husband, Sir Robert Goushill, of Hault Hucknall, county Derby (*see* Glover's "History of Derby," ii., 78):

LADY JOAN GOUSHILL, who *m.* Sir Thomas Stanley, K.G., Baron Stanley, *d.* 12 January, 1458, and had:

LADY ELIZABETH STANLEY (a sister of Sir William Stanley, who crowned Henry VII. on Bosworth Field), who *m.* Sir Richard Molineux, of Sefton, county Lancaster, *k.* at Bloreheath in 1459, and had:

SIR THOMAS MOLINEUX, of Sefton, knight-banneret, who *m.* Lady Anne, daughter of Thomas de Dutton, and had:

SIR WILLIAM MOLINEUX, of Sefton, *d.* 1548; *m.* Lady Jane, daughter of Sir Richard Rigge, and had:

SIR RICHARD MOLINEUX, of Sefton, *d.* 1568; *m.* Lady Eleanor, daughter of Sir Alexander Ratcliffe, of Ordsall, and had:

LADY MARGARET MOLINEUX, *d.* 1617, who *m.* John Warren, Esqr., of Poynton, Baron of Stockport, high sheriff of Cheshire, *d.* 1588, second son, and appointed heir of Sir Edward Warren, of Poynton, Baron of Stockport, *d.* 1568 (*see* Watson's "Ancient Earls of Warren and Surrey," and Ormerod's "History of Cheshire"), and had:

SIR EDWARD WARREN, Knt., of Poynton, heir, Baron of Stockport, *bapt.* at Prestbury, 9 April, 1563, high sheriff of Cheshire; knighted while serving with the army in Ireland; *bur.* at Stockport, 14 November,

1609. He *m.*, secondly, at Prestbury, 16 October, 1581, Anne, daughter of Sir William Davenport, of Bramall, Cheshire, and had by her, who was *bur.* at Stockport, 13 July, 1597 :

JOHN WARREN, of Poynton, heir, admitted to Gray's Inn, London, 4 March, 1609–10, *d.* 20 June, 1621 (Inqui. P. M. at Chester, 30 April, 1622). He *m.* (covenant dated 11 February, 1593; contract, 28 October, 1594), Anne Ognal, of Bylkesley, Warwickshire, *bur.* at Stockport, May, 1652, and had :

EDWARD WARREN, of Poynton, heir, *b.* 10 May, *bapt.* 19 May, 1605, *bur.* at Stockport, 10 September, 1687, will dated 26 January, 1683, proved at Chester in 1687. He was a royalist, and his estates were sequestered, but was pardoned in 1647. He gave the Herald his pedigree for the "Visitation," 17 September, 1663. He had by his first wife, Margaret Arderne, *bur.* at Stockport, 20 April, 1644, ten children, of whom :

HUMPHREY WARREN, of Charles county, Maryland, third child, *b.* at Poynton, 7 July, 1632. "He was reared as a merchant" (*see* Herald's Cheshire "Visitations," 1663; Watson's "Ancient Earls of Warren and Surrey and their Descendants," and Ormerod's "History of Cheshire"), and came to Maryland as a "merchant" with his young son Humphrey, one of his head-rights (Maryland Land Records, lib. v., fo. 235), and was granted, 12 February, 1662–3, a tract of 300 acres of land, called "Frailty," in Charles county, surveyed for him 22 June, 1663, and patented to him 4 August, 1664. He was an active Protestant, and was appointed a commissioner of the peace, 16 September, 1670. He *d.* intestate in 1673, at his seat, "Halton's Point," Charles county, and 9 May, 1673, his estate was administered and committed to Thomas Howell, who *m.* his widow (Maryland Testa. Proc., v., 439). He was twice married in England, and had by his first wife, *d. ante* 1652, whose name has not been found :

COLONEL HUMPHREY WARREN, of Charles county, Maryland, *b.* about 1652. He was appointed a commissioner of the peace, 2 March, 1675, and was an active Protestant in 1689, and 4 September, 1689, was appointed colonel of foot in Charles county. He was one of the committee of seven of the Protestant freemen which seized the government of Maryland from the representative of the Proprietary, 1 August, 1689, and was a justice of the quorum and a coroner for Charles county, 1689. By his will, dated 14 August, 1689, proved Charles county, 25 February, 1694–5, he devised a large estate. He was twice married, and had by his second wife, Margery, *m. ante* 1681, whose surname is unknown, who survived him :

JOHN WARREN, of Charles county, third son, *b.* 18 June, 1687, will dated 12 August, 1713, proved 13 February, 1713–14.

He left a large estate. He had by his wife, Judith, whose surname is unknown, who survived him:

ANN WARREN, who *m.* William Dent, of Charles county, and had:

ANN DENT, who *m.* Samuel Briscoe, and had:

WILLIAM DENT BRISCOE, who *m.* Sarah Stone, and had:

WALTER HANSON STONE BRISCOE, who *m.* Emeline Wellmore Dallam, and had:

JEANNETTE ELEANOR BRISCOE, who *m.* James Richard Thomas, and had:

JEANNETTE BRISCOE THOMAS, a member of the Maryland Society of the Colonial Dames of America, who *m.* James Bourne Parran, of Baltimore, and had: *Jeannette Briscoe.*

HUMPHREY WARREN, of Charles county, Md., 1632–1673, had by his second wife, Eleanor, whose surname is unknown:

THOMAS WARREN, of Charles county, Maryland (*see* Testa. Proc., Md. Archives, xvii., 122), who was brought to Maryland in 1663 (*see* "Maryland Immigrants," Land Office, Annapolis). He received from his father's estate the farm called "Frailty" (*see* Calvert's Rent Roll), where he resided at the time of his decease, and which he devised to his second wife, Jane, by his will dated 6 January, 1705–6; proved 23 November, 1710. He *m.*, first, before 13 June, 1688 (at this date his father-in-law conveyed a farm called "Strife," in Charles county, to his daughter Mary and her husband, Thomas Warren), Mary, a daughter of Capt. William Barton, Jr., of Port Tobacco parish, Charles county, who was appointed, 4 September, 1689, Captain of Foot, in Charles county, and for several terms was a Commissioner for the Peace, and was recommended by Lord Baltimore, October, 1691, for a seat in the Council, and had by her *Thomas,* a minor in 1705, living in 1757, *Sarah, Elizabeth,* and:

BARTON WARREN, of Charles county, Maryland, a minor in 1705. He inherited from his father's estate the farms "Frailty" and "Strife" (*see* Calvert's Rent Roll, 13 June, 1736), which he devised by will, dated 3 February, proved 9 March, 1757, to his sons and his wife Elizabeth ——, by whom he had (all named in his will), *Notley, John, Edward,* of Georgia; *Robert, b.* 6 September, 1742, *d.* in Tennessee, 26 October, 1826, having nineteen married children alive; *Susannah, Mrs. Jane Hungerford,* and

1.—WILLIAM BARTON WARREN, who removed to Lancaster county, Virginia, and then to Woodford county, Kentucky, and *d.* at Georgetown in 1809, aged 71 years. He *m.*, at Port Tobacco, Maryland, Mary Jane Yates, and had, besides other issue:

WILLIAM MONROE WARREN, of Georgetown, Kentucky, b. 1 July,
1775, d. 22 February, 1824; m., at Georgetown, Maria F. Fauntleroy, b. 17 July, 1780, also of Royal Descent, and had: *Anne E.*
(who m. E. L. Johnson, *issue*), *Margaret L.* (who m. Thornton F.
Johnson, *issue*), *John F., Maria*, and

WILLIAM BARTON WARREN, of Jacksonville, Illinois, b. 1 March,
1802, m. Ann Dorsey Price, and had, besides others who d. young:

I.—WILLIAM MONROE WARREN, m. Priscilla Hitt, and had: *Maria,
William Barton, Sarah Hitt, Robert, Samuel, Mary, Annie, Margaret.*

II.—PHIL WARREN, of Springfield, Illinois, m. Cordelia Birchal, and
had: *Caleb Birchal, Phil Barton, Adele, Louise*, wife of J. E. T. Butler, *Lillian*, wife of O. B. Caldwell, *Cordelia, Maria*, and *Florence.*

III.—MARIA WARREN, who m. William A. Turney, and had: *Annie*,
wife of T. J. Baird; *William, John A., Maria*, and *Maud*, wife of J.
A. Kimber.

IV.—MARY LOUISA WARREN, a member of the Order of the Crown,
etc., who m. Thomas Booth, of St. Louis. *Issue d.* young.

V.—AGNES WARREN, who m. V. M. Kenney, of Berlin, Illinois, and
had: *Dr. Joseph B.*, of Colorado Springs; *Dr. W. Warren*, of St.
Louis; *Annie*, wife of C. W. Nelson, of St. Louis; *Lou Booth*, and
Sallie Warren.

2.—MARY WARREN (she removed in 1779 to Pittsylvania county, Virginia, with her children), who m., first, Harrison Musgrave, of Charles
county, Maryland, who d. *ante* 29 April, 1760, intestate (the date of her
bond, filed in Charles county, 14 June, by his widow, as administratrix,
with her brothers, Notley and John Warren, as securities; *see* "Testa-
mentary Proceedings," vol. xxxvii., fo. 377, and "Inventories," vol. lxx.,
Register of Wills office, Annapolis). She m., secondly (his second wife),
John Stone, of Port Tobacco, Maryland, will dated 6 August, probated
in Charles county by his widow, 12 September, 1775, and had by him:
John, Matthew, Elizabeth and *Warren*, and

REV. BARTON WARREN STONE, youngest child, "b. near Port Tobacco,
24 December, 1772," d. at Hannibal, Missouri, 6 November, 1844. He
was a Christian minister (*see* his "Biography," published in 1847).
He m., first, 2 July, 1801, Elizabeth, daughter of Colonel William
Campbell, of Muhlenburg county, Kentucky, and his wife, Tabitha,
daughter of General William Russell, Jr., of Culpeper county, Virginia
(*see* "Americans of Royal Descent," pp. 862–863), and had by her, who
d. May 30, 1810:

MARY ANNE HARRISON STONE, b. Bourbon county, Kentucky, 21 September, 1805, d. 31 August, 1872, who m., 5 September, 1821, Captain

Charles Chilton Moore, of " Forest Retreat," Fayette county, Kentucky, who served in the army in the War of 1812, *b.* Culpeper county, Virginia, 1 December, 1789, *d.* 8 August, 1860, and had :

HANNAH A. RANSDELL MOORE, *b.* 25 April, 1825, *d.* 11 May, 1890, who *m.*, 25 October, 1845, John de Lafayette Grissim, M.D., of Georgetown, Kentucky, *b.* Tennessee, 27 January, 1818, *d* 16 April, 1869, and had :

1.—MARY GRISSIM, *m.* Charles Oscar Kenney, of Georgetown. *No issue.*

2.—LIDA CAMPBELL GRISSIM, a member of the Virginia Society of the Colonial Dames of America, the Order of the, Crown, *etc.*, who *m.*, 15 December, 1874, Judge Samuel Franklin Leib, of " Liebheim," San José, California, and had : *Lida Campbell*, a member of the Order of the Crown, *etc.*, *Elna Warren, Franklin Allen, Roy Chilton,* and *Earl Warren.*

3.—BARTON WARREN, *d. inf.* 4. CHARLES CHILTON, drowned, aged 13.

5. ANNAH WARREN GRISSIM, of Georgetown, *unm.*

6.—JEANETTE DE LAFAYETTE GRISSIM, a member of the Order of the Crown, *etc., m.* William B. Gano, of Dallas, Texas. *Issue : Allene Stone, Marcus D., d. inf. ; Vera, d. inf. ; Richard Chilton, Annette Warren,* and *Martha Moore.*

7.—EVELYN MOORE GRISSIM, *m.* Paul Fürst, of Dallas, Texas, and had : *Hannah Moore, Elise Campbell,* and *Franklin Leib.*

8.—JOHN DE LAFAYETTE GRISSIM, M.D., of San José, California, *unm.*, a member of the Order of Runnemede, *etc.*

THE ROYAL DESCENT

OF

MRS. MARY NEWBURY ADAMS,

OF DUBUQUE, IOWA.

WILLIAM I., King of England, had:	**HUGH CAPET**, King of France, had:
Henry I., King of England, who had:	Robert the Pious, King of France, who had:
Maud, *m.* Geoffrey, Count of Anjou, and had:	Henry I., King of France, who had:
Henry II., King of England, who had:	Philip I., King of France, who had:
John, King of England, who had:	Louis VI., King of France, who had:
Henry III., King of England, who had:	Louis VII., King of France, who had:
Edward I., King of England, who had:	Philip II., King of France, who had:
Thomas, Earl of Norfolk., *etc.*, who had:	Louis VIII., King of France, who had:
Margaret, *m.* John de Segrave, and had:	Louis IX., King of France, who had:
Elizabeth, *m.* John de Mowbray, and had:	Philip III., King of France, who had:
Margery, *m.* John de Welles, and had:	Philip IV., King of France, who had:
Margery, *m.* Sir Stephen le Scrope, and had:	Isabel, *m.* Edward II., King of England, and had:
Sir Henry, Baron le Scrope, of Marham, who had:	Edward III., King of England, who had:
Joan, *m.* Henry, Baron Fitzhugh, and had:	Thomas, Duke of Gloucester, who had:
Henry, third Baron Fitzhugh, who had:	Anne, *m.* Sir William, Earl of Ewe, and had:
Eleanor, *m.* Philip, Baron d'Arcy, and had:	Sir John Bouchier, K.G., Baron Berners, who had:
Margery, *m.* Sir John Conyers, K.G., and had:	Sir Humphrey Bouchier, Knt., who had:
Eleanor, *m.* Sir Thomas Markenfield, and had:	Sir John Bouchier, Baron Berners, who had:
Sir Nyan de Markenfield, Knt., who had:	Jane, *m.* Edmund Knyvett, and had:
Alice, *m.* Robert Mauleverer, and had:	John Knyvett, of Plumstead, Norfolk, who had:
Dorothy, *m.* John Kaye, of Woodsome, and had:	Sir Thomas Knyvett, of Plumstead, who had:
Robert Kaye, of Woodsome, Yorkshire, who had:	Abigail, *m.* Sir Martin Sedley, and had:
Grace, *m.* Sir Richard Saltonstall, Knt., and had:	Muriel, *m.* Brampton Gurdon, M.P., and had:

Richard Saltonstall, of Ipswich, Mass., *m.* Muriel Gurdon, of Assington, Suffolk.

Col. Nathaniel Saltonstall, of Haverhill Elizabeth Ward, of Haverhill, Mass.

Elizabeth Saltonstall Rev. Roland Cotton, of Sandwich, Mass.

Rev. John Cotton, D.D., of Newton, Mass. Mary Gibbs.

Mary Cotton Rev. Joseph Pynchon, D.D., of Boston, Mass.

Margaret Pynchon Stephen Keeler, of Norwalk, Conn.

Margaret Keeler Dr. Erastus Sergeant, Jr., of Lee, Mass.

Mary Ann Sergeant Rev. Samuel Newbury, of Middlebury, Vt.

Mary Keeler Newbury, member of the Conn. and Judge Austin Adams, of Dubuque, Iowa.
Mich. Societies of the Colonial Dames of America, the Order of the Crown, *etc.*

Annabel Adams	O. S. Goan.	Eugene Adams	Anna Plaister.	Cecilia Adams. *Unm.*	Herbert Adams	Elsie Payne.

Adelaide Goan.	Emily Goan.	Percival Goan.	Elizabeth Goan.	Donald, *d. inf.*	Adele Adams.	Waldo Adams.	Olive Adams.	Harlon Adams.	Philip Adams.

PEDIGREE LXXVI.

ROBERT THE PIOUS, King of France, had by his second wife, Lady Constance, daughter of William, Count of Provence:

ROBERT, DUKE OF BURGUNDY, *d.* 1075, whose eldest son

HENRY OF BURGUNDY, *d. v. p.*, was the father of

EUDES, DUKE OF BURGUNDY, *d.* 1102, whose daughter :

LADY ALIX (widow of Bertrand, Count of Tripoli), *m.*, secondly, William de Talvas III., Count of Alençon and Ponthieu, and had :

LADY ADELA DE TALVAS, *d.* 1174, who *m.*, first, William de Warren, third Earl of Surrey, *d.* 1148, also of Royal Descent (*see* pp. 11–12), and had :

LADY ISABELLA DE WARREN, who *m.*, secondly, Hameline Plantagenet, fifth Earl of Warren and Surrey, and had :

LADY ISABELLA DE WARREN, who *m.* (his first wife) Roger Bigod, created Earl of Norfolk, also of Royal Descent, and had :

HUGH BIGOD, second Earl of Norfolk, *m.* Lady Maud Marshall, daughter of William, Earl of Pembroke, protector of England, and had :

SIR RALPH BIGOD, third son, who *m.* Berta de Furnival, and had :

LADY ISABEL BIGOD, who *m.*, secondly, John Fitzgeoffrey, of Barkhampstead, justiciary of Ireland in 1246, and had :

JOHN FITZJOHN, justiciary of Ireland, *d.* in 1258, father of :

MAUD FITZJOHN, who *m.*, secondly, William de Beauchamp, created Earl of Warwick, *d.* 1298, also of Royal Descent, and had :

LADY SARAH DE BEAUCHAMP, who *m.* Richard, sixth Baron de Talbot, of Goodrich, *d.* 1306, also of Royal Descent, and had :

LADY GWENTHELLEAN DE TALBOT, who *m.* Sir Payne de Turberville, custos of Glamorganshire, 134–, and had :

LADY SARAH DE TURBERVILLE, who *m.* William de Gamage, sheriff of Gloucestershire in 1325, and had :

GILBERT DE GAMAGE, of Rogiad, who *m.* Lettice, daughter of Sir William Seymour, of Penhow, and had :

SIR WILLIAM GAMAGE, of Rogiad and Coyty, who *m.* Mary, daughter of Sir Thomas de Rodburg, and had :

SIR THOMAS GAMAGE, of Rogiad and Coyty, who *m.* Matilda, daughter of Sir John Dennis, and had:

LADY JANE GAMAGE, who m. Roger ap Arnold ap Arnholt-Vychan, of Llanthony Manor, in Monmouthshire, also of Royal Descent, and had :

THOMAS ARNOLD, eldest son, succeeded to Llanthony Manor. He m. Agnes, daughter of Sir Richard Wairnstead, and had :

RICHARD ARNOLD, second son, of Street parish, Somersetshire, m. Emmote, daughter of Pearce Young, of Damerham, Wilts, and had:

RICHARD ARNOLD, eldest son, of Bagbere Manor, Dorsetshire; will dated 15 May, 1593, was proved 9 July, 1595; buried in July, 1595, in the Milton Church. He had by his first wife, whose name has not been preserved :

THOMAS ARNOLD, of Melcombe Horsey and Cheselbourne Manors, Dorsetshire. He m., first, Alice Gully (see p. 13). He had by his second wife (whose name has not been preserved) an only son (see Austin's " Genealogical Dictionary of Rhode Island," " Ralph Earle and His Descendants," the " N. E. His. Geneal. Reg.," vol. xxxiii., p. 432) :

THOMAS ARNOLD, bapt. 18 April, 1599. He m., first, in England, about 1623-4, came to New England, and m., secondly, about 1638-9, Phebe, daughter of George Parkhurst, of Watertown, Massachusetts. He removed to Providence, Rhode Island, from Watertown, in 1654, and was a deputy in 1666-67, 1670-72, and town councillor, 1672 ; d. September, 1674, and had by his second wife, who d. in 1688 :

1.—ELIZABETH ARNOLD, d. 20 October, 1747, who m., 22 November, 1678, Captain Samuel Comstock, d. 27 May, 1727, and had: Hassadiah (see below) and :

JOHN COMSTOCK, b. 26 March, 1693, d. 12 June, 1750; m. Esther Jenks, and had :

SAMUEL COMSTOCK, d. 16 January, 1765, m., 1 January, 1738, Anna Brown, d. 16 November, 1776, and had:

BENJAMIN COMSTOCK, b. 7 March, 1747, d. 30 September, 1828; m., 28 January, 1776, Mary Winsor, b. 2 April, 1755, d. 9 November, 1825, and had :

WILLIAM COMSTOCK, b. 20 January, 1786, d. 27 October, 1873; m., 19 September, 1824, Harriet Pearson, b. 16 October, 1803, d. 26 August, 1882, and had :

ANNA LOUISE COMSTOCK, b. 20 April, 1836, m., 13 May, 1853, Edward Augustus Balch, b. 2 April, 1833, d. 14 January, 1871, and had :

ANNA AUGUSTA BALCH, b. 29 October, 1858, a member of the Rhode Island Society of the Colonial Dames of America, who m., 6 May, 1886, Charles Value Chapin, of Providence, Rhode Island, and had : Howard Miller, b. 11 May, 1887.

2.—ELEAZER ARNOLD, of Providence, Rhode Island, b. 17 June, 1651, *d.* 29 August, 1722; *m.* Eleanor, *d.* 1722, daughter of John and Elizabeth Smith, of Providence, and had:

JOSEPH ARNOLD, of Smithfield, Rhode Island, *d.* 4 November, 1746, who *m.*, 20 June, 1716, Mercy Stafford, *b.* 27 September, 1694, *d.* 175-, and had:

I.—CALEB ARNOLD, of Gloucester, Rhode Island, *m.*, 26 January, 1746, Patience Brown, and had:

NEHEMIAH ARNOLD, of Providence, *b.* 15 March, 1748, *d.* 12 March, 1835; *m.*, 1774, Alice Brown, *b.* 12 August, 1754, *d.* 18 May, 1822, and had:

AMY ARNOLD, who *m.*, 19 September, 1796, Governor Caleb Earle, of Providence, and had:

MARY ANN EARLE, who *m.*, 1828, William Robinson Watson, of Providence, and had:

WILLIAM H. WATSON, *b.* 8 November, 1829, *m.*, 1 May, 1854, Sarah Thompson Carlile, of Providence, and had:

LUCY CARLILE WATSON, of Utica, New York, *b.* 10 February, 1855, a member of the New York Society of the Colonial Dames of America.

II.—SAMUEL ARNOLD, ·*b.* 12 July, 1736, *m.* Elizabeth ———, and had: *Israel,* and

ELIZABETH ARNOLD, *b.* 29 March, 1775, who *m.* Christopher Brown, *b.* 26 December, 1769, and had:

NABBY BROWN, *b.* 7 September, 1799, *d.* 24 July, 1877; *m.* Israel Arnold, Jr., *b.* 8 May, 1792, *d.* 16 November, 1864 (son of the aforesaid Israel Arnold, 1755–1840, and his wife Deborah Olney), and had:

CHARLOTTE B. ARNOLD, *b.* 22 May, 1833, who *m.* 1 January, 1856, William Bibby, *b.* 10 June, 1829, and had:

MAUD BELLE BIBBY, a member of the New Hampshire Society of the Colonial Dames of America, the Order of the Crown, *etc.*, who *m.*, 4 June, 1890, Samuel de Wolf Lewis, of Newport, New Hampshire.

3.—RICHARD ARNOLD, of Providence, *b.* 22 March, 1642, *d.* 22 April, 1710; will probated 10 May; member of the Town Council, 1700, and speaker of the House of Deputies, 1707–8. He *m.*, first, Mary Angell, and had by her, who *d.* in 1695:

I.—MARY ARNOLD, who *m.* Thomas Steere, *d.* 27 August, 1735, and had:

PHEBE STEERE, *b.* 26 October, 1699, *d.* 1 August, 1767; *m.* John Matthewson, *b.* 6 October, 1699, and had:

ELIZABETH MATTHEWSON, *b.* 4 November, 1742, *d.* 9 April, 1822; *m.*, first, 23 October, 1763, Mason Hulett, of Belcherstown, Massachusetts, and had:

MASON HULETT, JR., of Hampton, New York, 1775–1847; *m.* Abigail Andrews, also of Royal Descent, and had:

HANNAH LUCY HULETT, *b.* 4 July, 1817, *d.* 28 January, 1893; *m.*, 23 June, 1837, Henry Hitchcock, of Rutland, Vermont, also of Royal Descent (p. 149), and had:

ABIGAIL JANE HITCHCOCK, *b.* 3 May, 1843, a member of the Massachusetts Society of the Colonial Dames of America, *etc.*, who *m.*, 15 February, 1866, Horace Hoxie Dyer, of "Dyer Place," Rutland, Vermont, *b.* 2 April, 1820, and had: *Captain Horace Edward.*

II.—THOMAS ARNOLD, *b.* 24 March, 1675, *d.* 3 February, 1727; *m.*, 6 December, 1706, Elizabeth Burlingame, *b.* 9 January, 1684, *d.* 5 May, 1752, and had:

JONATHAN ARNOLD, *b.* 18 November, 1708, *d.* 29 December, 1796; *m.* Abigail Smith, *b.* 10 June, 1714, *d.* 29 June, 1801, and had:

WELCOME ARNOLD, *b.* 25 March, 1745, *d.* 30 September, 1797; *m.*, 11 February, 1773, Patience Greene, *b.* 13 May, 1754, *d.* 2 November, 1809, and had:

RICHARD JAMES ARNOLD, *b.* 5 October, 1796, *d.* 10 March, 1873; *m.* Louisa Caroline Gindrat, *b.* 8 April, 1804, *d.* 15 October, 1871, and had:

MARY CORNELIA ARNOLD, *b.* 22 January, 1841, a member of the Rhode Island Society of the Colonial Dames of America, who *m.*, 27 June, 1861, William Richmond Talbot, of Providence, Rhode Island, and had: *Mary Cornelia, b.* 9 November, 1862; *Charlotte Richmond, b.* 16 September, 1864, *d.* 28 February, 1865; *Arnold Gindrat, b.* 19 December, 1865; *Helen, b.* 1 June, 1872; *Harriet, b.* 28 August, 1873, and *William de Peyster, b.* 27 April, 1877, *d.* 28 October, 1878.

III.—CAPTAIN RICHARD ARNOLD, of Smithfield, Rhode Island, 1668–1745, who *m.*, first, Mary, daughter of Joseph and Mary (Pray) Woodward, and had by her:

1.—RICHARD ARNOLD, who *m.*, 19 May, 1722, Ruth Aldrich, and had:

RUTH ARNOLD, who *m.*, 3 March, 1738–9, Gideon Comstock, son of Hassadiah (and his first wife, Catherine Pray), son of Captain Samuel Comstock and his wife Elizabeth, a daughter of the aforesaid Thomas Arnold, 1599–1674, and had:

COLONEL ADAM COMSTOCK, of the Rhode Island Line, Continental Army, *b.* Smithfield, January, 1740, *d.* Saratoga, New

York, 10 April, 1819. After the war was a New York judge, assemblyman, and State senator. He *m.*, 10 April, 1763, Margaret McGregor, *b.* 8 September, 1745, *d.* Saratoga, 3 March, 1807, and had:

RUTH COMSTOCK, *b.* 31 December, 1763, *d.* 16 August, 1800, who *m.*, at Schenectady, 11 February, 1787, Rev. Nicholas Van Vranken, of Fishkill, New York, *b.* 24 May, 1762, *d.* 20 May, 1804, and had:

MARGARET MATILDA VAN VRANKEN, *b.* 23 November, 1795, *d.* 12 September, 1850, who *m.*, at Schenectady, 29 September, 1819, Phinehas Prouty, a captain in the War of 1812, *b.* Langdon, New Hampshire, 14 January, 1788, *d.* Geneva, New York, 21 February, 1862, and had:

I.—HARRIET PROUTY, *b.* Geneva, 28 May, 1823, a member of the New York Society of the Colonial Dames of America, who *m.*, at Geneva, 11 December, 1844, General Thomas Hillhouse, *b.* Watervliet, Albany county, New York, 10 March, 1816, *d.* Yonkers, 31 July, 1897, and had:

   1.—MARGARET PROUTY HILLHOUSE, of New York City, *b.* at "Walnut Grove," Watervliet, 5 January, 1846, a member of the New York Society of the Colonial Dames of America, the Society of Daughters of the Cincinnati, the Society of Daughters of the Holland Dames, the Mary Washington Association, the Daughters of the American Revolution Society, *etc.*

   2.—HARRIET AUGUSTA HILLHOUSE, a member of the New York Society of the Colonial Dames of America, the Society of Daughters of the Cincinnati, *etc.*, who *m.* Walter Wood Adams, of Dobb's Ferry-on-Hudson, New York.

   3.—ADELAIDE HILLHOUSE, of New York.

II.—SARAH AUGUSTA PROUTY, who *m.* Alexander de Lafayette Chew, of Geneva, New York, also of Royal Descent, and had:

   CATHERINE ALEXANDER CHEW, a member of the New Jersey Society of the Colonial Dames of America, who *m.* Samuel Winship, of Morristown, New Jersey. *Issue.*

III.—PHINEHAS PROUTY, JR., *m.* Adelaide Cobleigh, and had:

   ADELAIDE ALEXANDER PROUTY, of Geneva, New York, a member of the Pennsylvania Society of the Colonial Dames of America, who *m.* Walter Chrystie, of High Bridge, New Jersey, and had: *Phinehas Prouty, Margaret Harlan,* and *Walter.*

2.—THOMAS ARNOLD, of Smithfield, *d.* 11 December, 1765,*m.*, thirdly, Patience Cook, and had by her:

LYDIA ARNOLD, *b.* 16 October, 1749, *d.* 10 July, 1828, who *m.* William Buffum, of Smithfield, *b.* 20 December, 1741, *d.* 27 August, 1829, and had:

PATIENCE BUFFUM, who *m.* Pliny Earle, of Leicester, Massachusetts, and had:

THOMAS EARLE, of Philadelphia, who *m.* Mary Hussey, of Nantucket, Massachusetts, and had:

1.—GEORGE H. EARLE, of Philadelphia, who *m.* Ellen Frances Von Leer, and had:

FLORENCE EARLE, a member of the Pennsylvania Society of the Colonial Dames of America, who *m.* Edward Hornor Coates, of Philadelphia.

2.—CAROLINE EARLE, a member of the Pennsylvania Society of the Colonial Dames of America, who *m.* Richard P. White, of Philadelphia. *Issue.*

3.—FRANCES EARLE, a member of the Pennsylvania Society of the Colonial Dames of America, who *m.* Edward Hine Johnson, of Philadelphia.

CAPTAIN RICHARD ARNOLD, of Smithfield, 1668–1745; *m.*, secondly, 14 November, 1715, Dinah, daughter of John and Dinah (Steere) Thornton, and had by her:

JOSIAH ARNOLD, 1717–1745; *m.* Amy Phillips, and had:

JONATHAN ARNOLD, *b.* 3 December, 1741, *d.* 1 February, 1793; *m.*, first, 19 January, 1763, Molly Burr, *b.* 23 November, 1743, *d.* 18 October, 1781, and had:

SALLY ARNOLD, *b.* 22 November, 1777, *d.* 17 July, 1814; *m.*, 8 October, 1797, James Burrill, *b.* 25 April, 1772, *d.* 25 December, 1820, and had:

SARAH PERKINS BURRILL, *b.* 8 February, 1812, *d.* 4 January, 1852; *m.*, 16 November, 1829, William Sedley Fearing, *b.* 12 October, 1802, *d.* 8 April, 1843, and had:

KATE SEDLEY FEARING, *b.* 25 December, 1842, a member of the Massachusetts Society of the Colonial Dames of America, who *m.*, first, 18 January, 1872, Alexander Carter, of The Spring, Kenilworth, England, and *m.*, secondly, 12 October, 1880, Edwin Cely Trevilian, of Midelney Place, Curry Rivel, Somerset, England, and had: *Maurice Fearing Cely Trevilian, b.* 22 October, 1881.

PEDIGREE LXXVII.

ROBERT BRUCE, King of Scotland, had by his second wife, Lady Elizabeth, daughter of Richard de Burgh, Earl of Ulster, of Royal Descent:

LADY MARGARET BRUCE, who *m.*, 1344 (his first wife), William, Earl of Sutherland, *d.* 1370, and had:

WILLIAM, EARL OF SUTHERLAND, *d.* 1389 (his wife's name unknown), who had:

ROBERT, EARL OF SUTHERLAND, *d.* 1442, who had by his wife, Lady Mabilla, daughter of John Dunbar, Earl of Moray, son of Patrick, Earl of Dunbar and March, and his first wife, Lady Agnes Randolph, both of Royal Descent:

ALEXANDER SUTHERLAND, of Dunbeath, third son, will executed 12 November, 1456, who *m.* Lady Mariot McDonnell, daughter of Donald, lord of the Isles, *d.* 1427, and his wife, Margaret, Countess of Ross (*see* Wood's Douglas's "Peerage of Scotland," vol. ii., 8, 339, 573), and had:

LADY MARJORY SUTHERLAND, Countess of Caithness, who *m.*, November, 1456 (his second wife), William Sinclair, of Roslyn, third Earl of Orkney and Earl of Caithness (in right of his second wife), chancellor of Scotland, also of Royal Descent, and had:

LADY ELEANOR SINCLAIR, who *m.* (his second wife) Sir John Stewart, of Balveny and Lorn, first Earl of Athol, *d.* 1512, also of Royal Descent, and had:

LADY ISABEL STEWART, who *m.* (his second wife, *see* Wood's Douglas's "Peerage of Scotland," i., 141 and 549) Alexander Robertson, fifth baron of Strowan, and had:

JOHN ROBERTSON, first laird of Muirton, in Elgin, second son, who *m.* Margaret, daughter of Sir James Crichton, of Fendraught, eldest son of William, third Lord Chrichton (*see* Wood's Douglas's "Peerage," i., 610; ii., 716), and had:

GILBERT ROBERTSON, of Muirton, who *m.* Janet, daughter of John Reid, of Ackenhead, and had:

DAVID ROBERTSON, of Muirton, who *m.* —— Innes, and had:

WILLIAM ROBERTSON, of Muirton, who *m.* Isabel Petrie, and had:

WILLIAM ROBERTSON, of Gladney, who *m.* —— Mitchell, and had:

REV. WILLIAM ROBERTSON, of Edinburgh (*see* Burke's "Royal Families," ii., ped. 190), who *m.* a daughter of Pitcairn, of Dreghorn, and had :

JEAN ROBERTSON, who *m.* Alexander Henry, of Aberdeen, and had :

COLONEL JOHN HENRY, of Hanover county, Virginia, who *m.* Sarah, widow of John Syme, and daughter of Isaac Winston, of Hanover county, *d.* 1760, and had, besides other issue (*see* p. 116) :

JANE HENRY, who *m.* Colonel Samuel Meredith, and had :

JANE HENRY MEREDITH, who *m.* David S. Garland, of Lynchburg, Virginia, member of Congress, and had :

ANN SHEPHERD GARLAND, 1797–1856, who *m.*, 4 January, 1816, Gustavus Adolphus Rose, M.D.. of Lynchburg, 1789–1860, also of Royal Descent, and had :

1.—JUDITH CABELL ROSE, of Richmond, Virginia, a member of the Virginia Society of the Colonial Dames of America, who *m.*, 21 July, 1846, Benjamin Powell Walker, *d.*, New York, 14 February, 1887, son of John, of Hartford, Indiana, 1787–1844, son of Benjamin, 1758–1846, son of John Walker, who was slain by Indians, in Northumberland county, Pennsylvania, in August, 1782, and had, besides other issue (*see* p. 199) :

ANNIE FITZHUGH ROSE WALKER, a member of the Virginia Society of the Colonial Dames of America, the Order of the Crown, *etc.*

2.—DAVID GARLAND ROSE, who *m.* Maria Louisa, daughter of John Walker, 1787–1844, aforesaid, and had :

MARIA LOUISA ROSE, a member of the Virginia Society of the Colonial Dames of America, who *m.* Samuel J. Filer, of Springfield, Massachusetts, and had : *Rose, Helen,* and *Edith.*

3.—CAROLINE MATILDA ROSE, of Chicago, a member of the Illinois Society of the Colonial Dames of America, who *m.* William James Walker, of La Porte, Indiana, son of John Walker, 1787–1844, aforesaid, and had :

I.—MARTHA GARLAND WALKER, of Chicago, a member of the Illinois Society of the Colonial Dames of America, who *m.* Sylvanus L. Trippe, of New York, and had : *Carolyn Rose Walker.*

II.—CAROLINE M. WALKER, a member of the Illinois Society of the Colonial Dames of America, who *m.* George Fisher, of Harrisburg, Pennsylvania, and had : *Carolyn,* and

ROSE FISHER, a member of the Virginia Society of the Colonial Dames of America, who *m.* Madison B. Kennedy, of New York, and had : *Jane.*

PEDIGREE LXXVIII.

ROBERT III., **King of Scotland**, had by his wife, Lady Annabella, daughter of Sir John Drummond, of Stobhall:

PRINCESS ELIZABETH STEWART, who *m.* Sir James Douglas, Lord of Dalkeith and Morton, and had:

SIR JAMES DOUGLAS, third Lord of Dalkeith, who *m.* Lady Agnes Keith, daughter of the earl marshal of Scotland, and had:

SIR JOHN DOUGLAS, second son (brother of James, first Earl of Morton), who *m.* the heiress of Hawthornden, of Abernethy, and had:

DAVID DOUGLAS, of Tilquhille, or Tiliwhilly, 1479, who *m.* Janet, daughter of Thomas Ogston, and had:

JAMES DOUGLAS, of Tiliwhilly, who *m.* Christian Forbes, of Tolquhoun, and had:

ARTHUR DOUGLAS, of Tiliwhilly, 1535, who *m.* Janet, daughter of Auchenleck of Balmanno, and had:

JOHN DOUGLAS, of Tiliwhilly, 1576, who *m.* Giles, daughter of Robert Erskine, of Dun, and had:

JOHN DOUGLAS, of Tiliwhilly, 1594, who *m.* Mary, daughter of Sir Peter Young, and had:

JAMES DOUGLAS, of Tiliwhilly and Inchmarlo, fourth son and eventually heir, *d.* 1672, who *m.* Isabel, a granddaughter of Sir John Ramsay, Lord Bothwell, of Balmain, and had:

JOHN DOUGLAS, of Inchmarlo and Tiliwhilly, who *m.* Grizel, daughter of Thomas Forbes, of Watertown, and his wife Jean, daughter of David Ramsay, of Balmain, and had:

JOHN DOUGLAS, of Tiliwhilly, 1723–1749, who *m.* Agnes, daughter of Rev. James Horn, of Westhall, minister of Elgin, and his wife Isabel, daughter of David Ramsey, of Balmain, and had:

EUPHEMIA DOUGLAS, *d.* 21 December, 1766, aged 55, who *m.*, 1733, Charles Irvine, of Cults, near Aberdeen, *d.* 28 March, 1779, aged 83, both buried at Cults (*see* "American Historical Register," p. 308, November, 1895, for his ancestry), and had:

JOHN IRVINE, M.D., *b.* 15 September, 1742. He came to Georgia about 1765, and was a member of the last royal assembly of 1780; went to England and was physician to the Admiralty, and subsequently returned to Georgia and *d.* at Savannah, 15 October, 1808. He *m.*, first, at

Sunbury, Georgia, 5 September, 1765, Ann Elizabeth, daughter of Colonel Kenneth Baillie, ensign in the Darien Rangers 1735, *d.* July, 1766 (*see* " Am. His. Register," vol. iii., p. 311, for an account of his family), and had:

ANNE IRVINE, *b.* 14 January, 1770, who *m.*, first, 13 April, 1786, Captain James Bulloch (son of Archibald Bulloch, 1750–1777, president of Georgia, 1776, and Mary, daughter of Judge James de Veaux, of Georgia, 1750–1785), and had :

JOHN IRVINE BULLOCH, M.D., clerk of the federal court, *d.*, Cedar Hill, Liberty county, Georgia, 1827, who *m.*, 1 January, 1814, Charlotte, daughter of John Glenn, Chief Justice of Georgia, 1776–78, and had :

WILLIAM GASTON BULLOCH, M.D., *b.* 3 August, 1815, deceased ; *m.*, 6 November, 1851, Mary Eliza Adams, a member of the Georgia Society of the Colonial Dames of America, daughter of John Lewis, of Cobb county, Georgia, and had :

1.—JOSEPH GASTON BULLOCH, M.D., of the United States Indian service, a member of the Aryan Order of St. George, etc., *m.* Eunice Helena Bailey, and had: *Archibald Irvine de Veaux, William Gaston Glenn,* and *Douglas Eugene St. Cloud.*

2.—ROBERT HUTCHINSON BULLOCH, of Savannah.

3.—EMMA HAMILTON BULLOCH, of Savannah, a member of the Georgia Society of the Colonial Dames of America.

PEDIGREE LXXIX.

ALFRED THE GREAT, King of England, had by his wife, Lady Alswitha, daughter of Ethelan the Great, Earl of Mercia, lineally descended from Crida, first king of Marcia, *d.* A.D. 594 (*see* Dr. James Anderson's "Royal Genealogies," 1732; and Betham's "Genealogical Tables"):

LADY ETHELFLEDA, *d.* 15 June, 919, who *m.* Ethelred, Earl of Mercia, 895, *d.* 912, son of Hugh the Great, Earl of Mercia, and had:

LADY ELFWINA, co-heiress of Mercia (sister of Algiva, queen consort of Edmund I.), who *m.* Edulf (son of Ordgar, Earl of Devon), brother of Lady Alfrida, wife of King Edgar, and had:

LEOFWINE, appointed by Ethelred II. Earl of Mercia, 1005, who *m.* Lady Alward, daughter of Athelstan, the Danish Duke of the East Angles, and had:

LEOFRIC THE GREAT, Earl of Mercia, or Chester and Leicester, 1016, *d.* 31 August, 1027, who *m.* the celebrated Lady Godiva, of Coventrytown, daughter of the Earl of Lincoln, and had:

ALGAR, Earl of Mercia, 1053, who *m.* Lady Alversa Malet, and had:

EDWYN, the last Saxon Earl of Mercia, *k.* 1071, brother-in-law of Harold, King of England. His son:

EDWYN DE TEMPLE, a feudal baron, sometimes styled Earl of Leicester and Coventry, took his surname from his manor, in Sparkenhoe Hundred, Leicestershire (*see* Barton's "Leicestershire," and Lodge's "Irish Peerages," 1754, under Palmertson). His presumed descendant:

HENRY DE TEMPLE, feudal Baron of Temple Manor and Little–Shepey, Leicestershire, *temp.* 3 Edward I., *m.* Lady Maud, or Matilda, daughter of Sir John Ribbesford, Knt., and had:

RICHARD DE TEMPLE, Baron of Temple-Manor, 24 Edward I., who *m.* Catherine, daughter of Thomas de Langley, and had:

NICHOLAS DE TEMPLE,* 16 Edward II., who *m.* Lady Margery, daughter

---

* NICHOLAS DE TEMPLE, 16 Edward II. (according to a pedigree in the Leicestershire "Visitations"), had: NICHOLAS DE TEMPLE, who *m.* Maria, daughter of Robert Dabernon, and had: THOMAS DE TEMPLE, who *m.* Joan, daughter of John Brasbridge, and had: ROBERT DE TEMPLE, who *m.* Maria, daughter of William Ringescote, and had: THOMAS TEMPLE, of Witney, Oxfordshire.

See also Nicholl's "Herald and Genealogist," vol. viii. ; "American Heraldic Journal," January, 1865, and October, 1866, and Baker's "Northamptonshire," vol. i.

of Sir Roger Corbet, of Sibton (or Isabella, daughter of William Bar-
well), and had:

RICHARD DE TEMPLE, of Shepey, 20 Edward III., who *m.* Lady Agnes,
daughter of Sir Ralph Stanley, Knt., and had:

NICHOLAS DE TEMPLE, 46 Edward III., who *m.* Maud, daughter of
John Burguillon, of Newton, in Leicestershire, and had:

RICHARD DE TEMPLE, buried in All Saint's, Shepey Magna, who *m.*
Joan, daughter of William de Shepey, of Shepey Magna, Leicestershire,
and had:

THOMAS TEMPLE, of Whitney, Oxfordshire (either third son of Richard aforesaid, or second son of Robert, *see* Note, p. 331), who *m.* Maria,
or Mary, daughter of Thomas Gedney, and had:

WILLIAM TEMPLE, of Witney, who *m.* Isabel, daughter and heiress of
Henry Everton, and had:

THOMAS TEMPLE, of Witney, who *m.* Alice, daughter and heiress to
John Heritage, of Burton-Dorset, Warwickshire, and had:

PETER TEMPLE, of Stowe, Buckinghamshire and Burton-Dorset, who
had a grant of the Manor of Marston-Boteler, in Warwickshire, second
son, *d.* 28 May, 1577. He *m.* Millicent, daughter of William Jykett, or
Jekyle, of Newington, in Middlesex, and had:

JOHN TEMPLE, of Stowe, eldest son, 1542–1603; *m.* Susan, daughter of
Thomas Spencer, of Everton, in Northampton, and had:

SIR THOMAS TEMPLE, of Stowe, created a baronet, 29 June, 1611, *d.*
1637. He *m.* Esther, daughter of Miles Sandys, of Latimers (or Eaton),
Bucks, and had: SIR PETER TEMPLE, second Bart., *b.* 1592, and:

SIR JOHN TEMPLE, Knt., of Biddleson and Stanton-Bury (*see* "The
National Cyclo. of Useful Knowledge," xi., 938; Nicholl's "Herald and
Genealogist," viii.; Burke's; Kimber's, etc., "Baronetages;" Lodge's
"Peerage of Ireland," 1754; Baker's "Northamptonshire," i.; the
"American Heraldic Journal," January, 1865, October, 1866). He *m.*,
first, Dorothy, daughter of Edmund Lee, of Stanton-Bury, and had:

DOROTHY TEMPLE,* who *m.*, at Odell, 4 January, 1634, John Alston,

---

* The following ladies, members of the National Society of the Colonial Dames of
America, are also of Royal Descent through Dorothy Temple:

MRS. FRANK GAINES, Alabama State Society.
MISS MARY McGAW FISKE, Massachusetts State Society.
MRS. JAMES J. MAYFIELD, Alabama State Society.
MRS. FREDERICK G. MARTIN, Arkansas State Society.
MRS. GEORGE W. VAN HOOSE, Alabama State Society.
MRS. WARREN B. WATKINS, Alabama State Society.
MRS. SAMUEL G. WOOLF, Alabama State Society.
MRS. ANNIE J. WARING, Georgia State Society.
MRS. JOSEPH B. SOLOMON, North Carolina State Society.
MISS MARY E. FITTS, Alabama State Society.

of Parvenham, Bedfordshire; entered at the Inner Temple; buried at Parvenham, 15 August, 1687 (his mother was the second wife of Sir John Temple, his father-in-law; *see* Kimber and Johnson's "Baronetages," 1771, i., 457), and had:

JOHN ALSTON, of Parvenham, fourth son, *d.* 1704, who *m.* Anne Willis, and had:

MAJOR JOHN ALSTON, *bapt.* at Filmersham, Bedfordshire, 5 December, 1673, came to North Carolina before 1720, and was associate justice of the colony, 1724–30; *d.* in Chowan county, North Carolina, 1758, having issue by his wife, Mary Clark, who survived him:

MAJOR JAMES ALSTON, of New Berne, North Carolina, *d.* 1761, *m.* Christine, daughter of Colonel George Lillington, of North Carolina, and had:

1.—COLONEL JAMES ALSTON, *d.* 1815, *m.*, 1774, Grizeal Yancey, 1752–1845, and had:

I.—SARAH ALSTON, 1779–1861, who *m.* Joseph Groves, 1768–1850, and had:

REV. JOHN JOSEPH GROVES, 1800–1885; *m.* Mary Louisa Harvie, and had:

JOSEPH ASBURY GROVES, M.D., of Selma, Alabama, *b.* 1830, *m.* Elizabeth Royall Robertson, and had:

ELIZABETH ROYALL GROVES, a member of the North Carolina and Alabama Societies of the Colonial Dames of America, the Order of the Crown, *etc.*

II.—NATHANIAL ALSTON, 1775–1852; *m.*, 1800, Mary Grey Jeffreys, and had:

JUDGE WILLIAM JEFFREYS ALSTON, *b.* 31 December, 1800, *d.* June, 1876; member United States Congress and Alabama State Senate; *m.*, 26 August, 1824, Martha Cade, of Marengo county, Alabama, and had:

MARY GREY ALSTON, *b.* 26 August, 1837, who *m.*, 1 March, 1855, James Kent, M.D., of Petersburg, Virginia, *b.* 8 January, 1830, *d.* 22 May, 1881, colonel of the Forty-fourth Regiment of Alabama, Confederate States Army, during the Civil War, and had:

MARY ROSALINE KENT, *b.* 1 March, 1856, a member of the North Carolina and Alabama Societies of the Colonial Dames of America, the Order of the Crown, *etc.*, who *m.*, 8 September, 1875, Edward Taylor Fowlkes, of Selma, Alabama, *b.* 19 May, 1848, *d.* 3 June, 1886, and had: *Grace Byrd, b.* 17 August, 1876, *d.* 22 August, 1876, and *Ethel Edward, b.* 2 November, 1879.

2.—WILLIAM ALSTON, lieutenant-colonel North Carolina Line, Continental Army, member of the Provincial Congress, *etc.*, who *m.* his cousin, Charity Alston, and had:

MAJOR JAMES ALSTON, of Abbeville, South Carolina, an officer under General Jackson in the Florida war, *m.* Catherine, daughter of Major Andrew Hamilton, of Abbeville, who served under General Pickens in the Revolutionary war; a member of the South Carolina Assembly, *etc.*, and had:

JANE ALSTON, who *m.* Colonel Henry Coalter Cabell, of Richmond, Virginia (son of Governor William H. Cabell, of Virginia), chief of artillery in the Confederate States army of the peninsula, and of McLaw's Division, Confederate States army of Northern Virginia, and had:

KATHERINE HAMILTON CABELL, a member and the president of the Virginia Society of the Colonial Dames of America, who *m.* Herbert A. Claiborne, Jr., of Richmond, Virginia, also of Royal Descent (*see* " Americans of Royal Descent," ii., 689), and had: *Jennie Alston.*

PEDIGREE LXXX.

EDWARD I., King of England, had by his first wife, Princess Eleanor of Castile:

PRINCESS JOAN, who *m.*, first, Gilbert de Clare, Earl of Clare, Hertford and Gloucester, *d.* 1295, and had:

LADY MARGARET DE CLARE, who *m.*, secondly, Hugh, Baron d'Audley, created, 1337, Earl of Gloucester, *d. s. p.*, *m.*, 1347, and had:

LADY MARGARET D'AUDLEY, who *m.* Sir Ralph de Stafford, K.G., second Baron Stafford, created, 1351, Earl of Stafford, *d.* 1372, and had:

HUGH DE STAFFORD, second Earl of Stafford, *d.* 1386, who *m.* Lady Phillippa de Beauchamp, daughter of Sir Henry, third Earl of Warwick, one of the original Knights of the Garter, *d.* 1369, and had:

LADY MARGARET DE STAFFORD, who *m.* (his first wife) Sir Ralph, K.G., fourth Baron Nevill, of Raby, earl marshal of England, created, 1399, Earl of Westmoreland, *d.* 1425, and had:

LADY MARGARET DE NEVILL, who *m.* Sir Richard le Scrope, of Bolton, *d.* 1420, and had:

SIR HENRY LE SCROPE, of Bolton, *d.* 1459, *m.* Elizabeth, daughter of John le Scrope, of Masham and Upsal, and had:

RICHARD LE SCROPE, second son, who *m.* Eleanor Washburne, and had:

ELEANOR LE SCROPE, who *m.* Sir Thomas Wyndham, *d.* 1522, and had:

MARY WYNDHAM, who *m.* Erasmus Paston, *d.* 1540, and had:

SIR WILLIAM PASTON, *d.* 1610, who *m.* Frances Clere, and had:

GERTRUDE PASTON, who *m.* Sir William Reade, son of William Reade, of London, *d.* 1522, and had:

SIR THOMAS READE, who *m.* Mildred, daughter of Sir Thomas Cecil, first Earl of Exeter, and had:

THOMAS READE, of Barton, *m.* Ann, daughter of Thomas Hooe, and had:

THOMAS READE, who *m.* Mary Stoneham, and had:

SIR THOMAS READE, Bart., *m.* Mary, daughter of John Brockett, and had:

SIR THOMAS READE, *m.* Mary, daughter of Sir Thomas Cornwall, of Burford, Sulop, and had:

WILLIAM READE, of Woburn, Massachusetts, *d.*, at New-Castle-on-Tyne, 1656. He *m.* Mabel Kendall, *d.* 5 June, 1690, and had:

RALPH READE, of Woburn, 1630–1711; *m.* Mary Peirce, 1636–1701, and had:

JOSEPH READ, of Woburn, *m.*, 1692, Phœbe Walker, and had:

NATHANIEL REED, *b.* 28 March, 1704, *m.*, 3 October, 1773, Hannah, *b.* 1 October, 1716, daughter of Ebenezer Flagg, 1678–1700, and had:

CAPTAIN JOSHUA REED, 1739–1805; *m.*, 28 November, 1759, Rachel, 1737–1818, daughter of Joshua Wyman, of Woburn, 1639–177–, and had:

MARY REED, 1760–1796, who *m.*, 1779, Eleaser Flagg Poole, of Woburn, 1761–1790, also of Royal Descent (*see* Browning's "Magna Charta Barons," p. 184), and had:

MARY POOLE, 1780–1857, who *m.*, 1798, Joshua Davis, of Springfield, Vermont, and had:

JOSHUA DAVIS, of Boston, Massachusetts, 1805–1873, who *m.*, 1827, Catherine Parkhurst, and had:

JOSHUA FLAGG DAVIS, of Boston and Chelmsford, Massachusetts, *m.*, 1853, Ellen Maria Cummings, also of Royal Descent (*see* p. 351), and had:

ANNA MARIA DAVIS; a member of the Vermont Society of the Colonial Dames of America, the Order of the Crown, *etc.*, who *m.*, 30 June, 1886, Lord Karl von Rydingsvärd, of Sweden and Boston, Massachusetts.

PEDIGREE LXXXI.

ROBERT II., King of Scotland, had by his wife, Lady Elizabeth, daughter of Sir Adam Muir, of Rowallan:

ROBERT STUART, Duke of Albany, Regent of Scotland, who *m.* Lady Margaret, daughter of Murdoch, Earl of Monteith, and had:

LADY MARGARET STUART, who *m.* Sir Duncan Campbell, of Lochow, first Lord Campbell of Argyll, and had:

SIR COLIN CAMPBELL, of Glenurchy, *d.* 1478, who had by his fourth wife, Margaret, daughter of Luke Stirling, of Keir:

HELEN CAMPBELL, who *m.* William Stuart, of Balendivan (Baldowran) and Balquhidder, and had:

JOHN STUART, of Glenbucky, second son, who *m.* a daughter of Buchanan of MacCorthe, and had:

DUNCAN STUART, of Glenbucky, who *m.* a daughter of McLarin of Achleskin, and had:

ALEXANDER STUART, of Glenbucky, "who *m.* a second cousin" (a Stuart), and had:

PATRICK STUART, eldest son, who sold the right and title of Glenbucky to his brother Duncan. He *m.* Christian, daughter of Sir John Drummond, of Niganer, and had:

WILLIAM STUART, of Ledcreich and Translarry, who *m.* Mary, daughter of Duncan Macgregor, and had:

PATRICK STUART, of Ledcreich, an officer in the army of Charles I., and suffered greatly on account of his loyalty. He *m.* Margaret, daughter of Robert Buchanan, of Drumlain, and had:

ALEXANDER STUART, of Ledcreich, who *m.* Catherine, daughter of Alexander Stewart, "brother of Robert Stewart, of Glenogle," and had:

PATRICK STUART, eldest son and heir, laird of Ledcreich, in Balgheider, Perthshire, a staunch supporter of Prince Charles Edward. "He came, in company with six Argylshire gentlemen and his brother William, and above three hundred common people, from Scotland to Cape Fear, in North Carolina, in 1739" (*see* "American Historical Register," i., 441), and *d.* about 1772 at Cheraws, South Carolina. He *m.*, in Perthshire, Elizabeth, daughter of Dr. Duncan Menzies, and had:

CATHERINE STUART, who *m.*, first, 25 December, 1764, William Little,

Jr., of Cheraws (son of Chief Justice Little, of Edenton, North Carolina), *b.* 27 September, 1728, *d.* October, 1766, and had:

ELIZABETH LITTLE, *b.* 24 November, 1765, *d.* 26 April, 1829, who *m.*, at Cheraws, 22 January, 1784, Morgan Brown, 4th, *b.* on Grassy Island, Pee Dee river, South Carolina, in January, 1758, *d.* in Tennessee, 23 February, 1840, and had:

ELIZABETH LITTLE BROWN, *b.* 6 February, 1792, *d.* 10 December, 1854, who *m.*, first, in 1807, Samuel Vance, of Clarksville, Tennessee, 1784–1823, and had:

ELIZABETH LITTLE VANCE, *b.* 18 June, 1818, who *m.*, 27 April, 1837, Robertson Topp, of Memphis, *b.* 20 April, 1807, *d.* June, 1876, and had:

FLORENCE TOPP, a member of the Tennessee Society of the Colonial Dames of America, who *m.*, 8 August, 1867, William Martin Farrington, of Memphis, and had: *Florence, d.* 27 April, 1875; *William M.,* and *Valerie.*

PEDIGREE LXXXII.

HENRY I., King of France, had by his wife, Anne of Russia:

HUGH THE GREAT, Count of Vermandois, who had by his third wife, Lady Adelheid, daughter of Herbert IV., Count of Vermandois, also of Royal Descent:

LADY ISABEL DE VERMANDOIS, who *m.*, first, Robert de Bellomont, Earl of Mellent, created, in 1103, Earl of Leicester, and had:

LADY ELIZABETH DE BELLOMONT, who *m.* Gilbert Fitz-Gilbert de Clare, created, in 1138, Earl of Pembroke, *d.* 1149, and had:

RICHARD DE CLARE, "the Strongbow," second Earl of Pembroke, lord justice of Ireland, *d. s. p. m.* 1176, who *m.* Lady Eva, daughter of Dermot MacMurcha, the last King of Leinster, Ireland, and had:

LADY ISABEL DE CLARE, who *m.*, 1189 (his first wife), William le Marshal, Earl of Pembroke, protector of England, *d.* 1219, and had:

LADY SYBIL MARSHALL, who *m.* William de Ferrers, Earl of Derby and Nottingham, *d.* 1191, and had:

LADY MAUD DE FERRERS, widow of William de Kyme, who *m.*, secondly, William de Vyvon, son of Hugh de Vivonia and Mabel, daughter of William Malet, a surety for the Magna Charta, and had:

LADY CICELY DE VYVON, who *m.* John, Baron de Beauchamp, of Hache, Somerset, *d.* 1283, and had:

JOHN DE BEAUCHAMP, of Hache, first baron by writ, *d.* 1336, who *m.* Lady Joan d'Audley, and had:

JOHN DE BEAUCHAMP, of Hache, second Baron, *d.* 1343, who had by his wife, Lady Margaret:

LADY CICELY DE BEAUCHAMP, *m.* Sir Roger de St. Maur, and had:

SIR WILLIAM DE SEYMOUR, *m.* Margaret de Brockburn, and had:

ROGER DE SEYMOUR, *m.* Maud d'Esturmê, and had:

SIR JOHN DE SEYMOUR, *m.* Isabel MacWilliams, and had:

JOHN DE SEYMOUR, *m.* Elizabeth Coker, and had:

JOHN DE SEYMOUR, *m.* Elizabeth Darrell, and had:

SIR JOHN SEYMOUR, Knight banneret, of Wolf Hall, Wilts, *d.* 21 December, 1536, who *m.* Lady Margaret, *d.* 1550, daughter of Sir Henry Wentworth, of Nettlested, Suffolk, also of Royal Descent, and had:

SIR HENRY SEYMOUR, of Marvel, Hants, second son, made a Knight of the Bath at the coronation of his nephew, Edward VI. He was a brother of Edmund Seymour, first Duke of Somerset; Lady Jane Seymour, a queen consort of Henry VIII.; and Thomas, Lord Seymour, who *m.* Queen Catherine Parr, widow of Henry VIII. He *m.* Barbara, daughter of Thomas Morgan, Esq'r, and had *Sir John* and

LADY JANE SEYMOUR, who *m.* (*see* Collins's " Peerage ") Sir John Rodney, of Stoke-Rodney and Pilton, Somerset, *b.* 1557, *d.* 6 August, 1612, and had sixteen children (*see* Thomas Sadler's pedigree of their descendants, 1765), of whom:

WILLIAM RODNEY, *b.* 1610, who *d.* at Hantsfield, Somersetshire, 12 June, 1699; *m.* Lady Alice, daughter of Sir Thomas Cæsar, a baron of the Exchequer, and had:

WILLIAM RODNEY, who came to Pennsylvania with Penn, in 1682, and became a member and first Speaker of the Assembly of Delaware; sheriff of Sussex county, and a member of Penn's Council in 1698, *d.* 8 April, 1708, aged 56. He *m.*, first, in Philadelphia, 1688, Mary, daughter of Thomas and Sarah Hollyman, and had by her, who *d.* 20 December, 1692:

WILLIAM RODNEY, *b.* 27 October, 1689, *d.* 26 June, 1732; sheriff of Kent county, Delaware; *m.* Ruth, daughter of John Curtis, of New Castle, Delaware, and had:

JOHN RODNEY, of Lewes, Delaware, *b.* 7 September, 1725, *b.* 23 November, 1792; *m.*, 1752, Ruth Hunn, and had:

JUDGE DANIEL RODNEY, of Lewes, *b.* 10 September, 1764, *d.* 2 September, 1846; Governor of Delaware, 1814–17; United States Senator from Delaware, 1826–27; *m.*, 1788, Sarah, daughter of Major Henry Fisher, of Lewes, and had:

REV. JOHN RODNEY, of Germantown, Philadelphia, *b.* 20 August, 1796, *d.* 188–, who *m.* Sarah, daughter of James S. Duval, of Philadelphia, and had:

JOHN DUVAL RODNEY, of Philadelphia, who had:

LOUISE CHASZOURNE RODNEY, of Philadelphia, a member of the Pennsylvania Society of the Colonial Dames of America.

THE ROYAL DESCENT

OF

MRS. JOHN J. BAGLEY,

OF DETROIT, MICH.

WILLIAM I., King of England, had:

Henry I., King of England, who had:

Maud, m. Geoffrey, Count of Anjou, and had:

Henry II., King of England, who had:

John, King of England, who had:

Henry III., King of England, who had:

Edward I., King of England, who had:

Thomas, Earl of Norfolk, etc., who had :

Margaret, m. John de Segrave, and had :

Elizabeth, m. John de Mowbray, and had :

Margery, m. John de Welles, and had :

Margery, m. Sir Stephen le Scrope, and had:

Sir Henry, Baron le Scrope, of Marham, who had:

Joan, m. Henry, Baron Fitzhugh, and had :

Henry, third Baron Fitzhugh, who had :

Eleanor, m. Philip, Baron d'Arcy, and had :

Margery, m. Sir John Conyers, K.G., and had :

Eleanor, m. Sir Thomas Markenfield, and had :

Sir Nyan de Markenfield, Knt., who had :

Alice, m. Robert Mauleverer, and had :

Dorothy, m. John Kaye, of Woodsome, and had :

Robert Kaye, of Woodsome, Yorkshire, who had:

Grace, m. Sir Richard Saltonstall, Knt., and had:

HUGH CAPET, King of France, had :

Robert the Pious, King of France, who had :

Henry I., King of France, who had :

Philip I., King of France, who had :

Louis VI., King of France, who had:

Louis VII., King of France, who had :

Philip II., King of France, who had :

Louis VIII., King of France, who had :

Louis IX., King of France, who had :

Philip III., King of France, who had :

Philip IV., King of France, who had :

Isabel, m. Edward II., King of England, and had :

Edward III., King of England, who had:

Thomas, Duke of Gloucester, who had :

Anne, m. Sir William, Earl of Ewe, and had :

Sir John Bouchier, K.G., Baron Berners, who had :

Sir Humphrey Bouchier, Knt., who had :

Sir John Bouchier, Baron Berners, who had :

Jane, m. Edmund Knyvett, and had :

John Knyvett, of Plumstead, Norfolk, who had :

Sir Thomas Knyvett, of Plumstead, who had :

Abigail, m. Sir Martin Sedley, and had :

Muriel, m. Brampton Gurdon, M.P., and had :

Richard Saltonstall, of Ipswich, Mass., m. Muriel Gurdon, of Assington, Suffolk.

Col. Nathaniel Saltonstall, of Haverhill═Elizabeth Ward, of Haverhill, Mass.

Elizabeth Saltonstall═Rev. Roland Cotton, of Sandwich, Mass.

Rev. John Cotton, D.D., of Newton, Mass.═Mary Gibbs.

Mary Cotton═Rev. Joseph Pynchon, D.D., of Boston, Mass.

Margaret Pynchon═Stephen Keeler, of Norwalk, Conn.

Margaret Keeler═Dr. Erastus Sergeant, Jr., of Lee, Mass.

Mary Ann Sergeant═Rev. Samuel Newbury, of Middlebury, Vt.

Frances E. Newbury, member of the Mass. and Mich. Societies of the Colonial Dames of America, etc.═Gov. John Judson Bagley, of Detroit, Mich.

Florence Bagley.═R. M. Sherman.	Katherine Sherman.	John Bagley, d. unm.	Esther Newbury Bagley.═Cutler.	Frances Bagley.	Dr. F. Brown.═Frances Bagley.	Margaret Bagley.═George Hosmer.	Olive Butterick.═Stedman
Mary Sherman.	Harold Sherman.	Mary Bagley.	John Bagley.	Dwight Bagley.	Philip Brown.	Marjorie Brown.	Dorothy Hosmer. Margaret Hosmer.	Frances Butterick.	Helen Butterick.

Paul Bagley, unm.   Helen Bagley═James Anderson.

Helen Anderson.

PEDIGREE LXXXIII.

DAVID I., **King of Scotland**, had by his wife, Lady Matilda, widow of Simon de St. Liz, *d.* 1115, and daughter of Waltheof, Earl of Northumberland, beheaded in 1075:

HENRY, Earl of Northumberland, eldest son, *d. v. p.*, 1152, who *m.*, 1139, Lady Ada de Warren, *d.* 1178, daughter of William, second Earl of Warren and Surry, and had:

DAVID, Earl of Huntingdon (brother of King William the Lion), who *m.* Lady Maud, daughter of Hugh, Earl of Chester, and had:

LADY ISABEL DE HUNTINGDON, who *m.* Robert de Bruce, Earl of Annandale, and had:

ROBERT DE BRUCE, Earl of Annandale, a claimant to the crown of Scotland, who *m.* Lady Isabel de Clare, daughter of Gilbert, Earl of Clare and Gloucester, also of Royal Descent, and had:

ROBERT DE BRUCE, Earl of Annandale and Carrick, 1245–1304, who *m.*, 1271, Margaret, Countess of Carrick, and had:

LADY ISABEL BRUCE (sister of King Robert I., of Scotland), who *m.*, first, Sir Thomas Randolph, of Strathwith, high chamberlain of Scotland, 1296, and had:

THOMAS RANDOLPH, created, in 1314, Earl of Moray; regent of Scotland; *m.* Lady Isabel, daughter of Sir John Stewart, of Bonkyl, and had:

LADY AGNES RANDOLPH, known as "Black Agnes." During the absence of her husband she defended the castle of Dunbar for nineteen weeks against the English, in 1337–8. She *m.* Patrick, ninth Earl of Dunbar and Marche, and Earl of Moray, 1285–1369, also of Royal Descent, and had:

LADY AGNES DUNBAR, who *m.*, about 1372 (his first wife), Sir James Douglas, lord of Dalkeith and Liddesdale, *d.* 1420, and had:

LADY JANET DOUGLAS, who *m.* Sir John Hamilton, of Cadyow, *d.* before 28 July, 1397, and had:

SIR JAMES HAMILTON, of Cadyow, one of the hostages for the ransom of King James I. in 1424, and a member of His Majesty's Privy Council, who *m.*, before 20 October, 1422, Lady Janet, daughter of Sir Alexander Livingston, of Callendar, governor to young King James II., justice-general of Scotland in 1449, and ambassador to England, *d.* 145-, and his wife, a daughter of Dundas, of Dundas, and had :

GAVIN HAMILTON, provost of the Collegiate Church of Bothwell (*see* Wood's Douglas's " Peerage of Scotland," i., 311, 695), who *m.* Jean Muirhead, " the Fair Maid of Lechbrunnock," and had :

JOHN HAMILTON, of Orbiston, who *m.* Jean, daughter of Hamilton, of Woodhall, and had :

GAVIN HAMILTON, of Orbiston and Raplock, 1512-1540, commendator of Kilwinning, who *m.* Helen, daughter of Wallace, of Cairnhill, and had :

JOHN HAMILTON, of Orbiston, killed in the battle of Langsyde, who *m.* Margaret, daughter of Hamilton, of Haggs, and had :

MARJORY HAMILTON, who *m.* David Dundas, of Duddingston, and had :

JAMES DUNDAS, of Duddingston, eldest son (*see* Burke's " Landed Gentry," 1858), who had :

BETHIA DUNDAS, who *m.* James Hume, manager of the estates of James, Earl of Moray (son of Sir Patrick Hume, of Fastcastle, and his wife Elizabeth, daughter of Sir Neil Montgomery, of Lainshaw, *k.* 1547, also of Royal Descent, and sister of Isabel, wife of Robert Logan, of Restalrig), and had :

ISABEL HUME, who *m.* Patrick Logan, *b.* Ormiston, East Lothian, about 1630, a member of the Society of Friends, " an apt schoolmaster," employed in Ireland and in Bristol, England, by the Friends, after 1690 (*see* " Early History of the Society of Friends in Bristol," by William Tanner), who, it is believed, was a son of Robert Logan, aforesaid, eldest son of Sir Robert Logan, of Fastcastle, the last laird of Restalrig, *d.* 1602 (*see* " Americans of Royal Descent," vol. i., p. 226), and had :

JAMES LOGAN,* of " Stenton," Philadelphia county, Pennsylvania, *b.* Lurgan, County Armagh, Ireland, 20 October, 1674, *d.* 31 December, 1751. He succeeded his father as the schoolmaster at Bristol till 1699, when he came to Pennsylvania with William Penn as his secretary, and became chief justice of Pennsylvania and president of the Provincial Council, *etc.* He *m.*, 1714, Sarah, daughter of Charles Read, of Philadelphia, a Provincial assemblyman and alderman, and had :

1.—WILLIAM LOGAN, of " Stenton," Philadelphia county, Pennsylvania, 1718-1776, a Provincial councillor (*see* Keith's " Provincial Councillors of Pennsylvania "), who *m.*, 24 March, 1740, Hannah, 1722-1777, daughter of George Emlen, of Philadelphia, and had :

---

* MISS HETTY SMITH, a member of the Pennsylvania State Society of the National Society of the Colonial Dames of America, is of Royal Descent through James Logan.

I.—SARAH LOGAN, 1751-1796, who *m.*, 17 March, 1772, Thomas Fisher, of Philadelphia, 1741-1810 (*see* p. 16, Keith's " Provincial Councillors of Pennsylvania "), and had:

    1.—WILLIAM LOGAN FISHER, of "Wakefield," Philadelphia county, Pennsylvania, 1781-1862; *m.*, first, 25 November, 1802, Mary, daughter of Samuel Rodman, of New Bedford, Massachusetts, and had:

        THOMAS RODMAN FISHER, of Philadelphia, who *m.*, 18 November, 1829, Letitia, daughter of Jonathan Ellicott, of Ellicott's Mills, Maryland, and had:

        MARY RODMAN FISHER, a member of the Pennsylvania Society of the Colonial Dames of America, who *m.*, 1 February, 1860, George W. Carpenter, of Germantown, Philadelphia, and had:

        1.—LETITIA E. CARPENTER, *m.*, 18 April, 1881, William Redwood Wright, of Philadelphia.

        2.—ELIZABETH RODMAN FISHER CARPENTER, a member of the Pennsylvania Society of the Colonial Dames of America, who *m.* Robert E. Glendinning, of Philadelphia.

    2.—JOSHUA FISHER, of "Wakefield," Philadelphia, 1775-1806; *m.*, 1807, Elizabeth Powell, daughter of Tench and Ann (Willing) Francis, and had:

        JOSHUA FRANCIS FISHER, of "Alverthorpe," Philadelphia, 1806-1873; *m.* Eliza Middleton, *d.* 1890, also of Royal Descent, and had:

        MARIA MIDDLETON FISHER, a member of the Society of the Colonial Dames of America, who *m.* Brinton Coxe, of Philadelphia, and had: *Charlotte, Eliza, Marie,* and *Edmund.*

II.—CHARLES LOGAN, M.D., of "Belle Mead," Powhatan county, Virginia, *d.* 1794, *m.*, in 1779, by Friends' ceremony in Philadelphia, Mary Pleasants, and had:

    SARAH PLEASANTS LOGAN, *b.* Philadelphia, 23 November, 1781, *m.*, at the residence of Samuel Pleasants, "Fine Creek," Powhatan county, 28 June, 1800, James Carter, M.D., of Prince Edwards county, Virginia, *b.* 3 May, 1769, and had:

    MARY PLEASANTS CARTER, *b.* 16 August, 1807, *d.* 8 August, 1877; *m.*, 15 September, 1818, Thomas Radford Bolling, of Petersburg, Virginia, and had:

    SALLY LOGAN BOLLING, *b.* 9 June, 1839, *d.* 25 April, 1892; *m.*, 7 April, 1858, Thomas Cowles Shearer, of Mobile, Alabama, and had:

MARTHA COWLES SHEARER, a member of the Pennsylvania and Texas Societies of the Colonial Dames of America, who *m.* George F. Pendexter, of Austin, Texas, son of George W. and Clara (Drew) Pendexter, of Dover, New Hampshire, and had: *George.*

III.—DR. GEORGE LOGAN, of "Stenton," 1753–1821; United States Senator, 1801–07; *m.*, 1781, Deborah, daughter of Charles Norris, of "Fairhill," Philadelphia county, Pennsylvania, and had:

DR. ALBANUS CHARLES LOGAN, of "Stenton," *m.* Maria Dickinson, also of Royal Descent, and had:

GUSTAVUS GEORGE LOGAN, of "Stenton," *m.* Anna Armatt, and had:

FRANCES ARMATT LOGAN, a member of the Pennsylvania Society of the Colonial Dames of America, *d.* 8 May, 1898.

2.—HANNAH LOGAN, 1719–1761; *m.*, 7 October, 1748, John Smith, of "Franklin Park," Burlington county, New Jersey, 1722–1771, a member of the Pennsylvania Assembly, and of the Governor's Council in New Jersey, and had:

I.—JOHN SMITH, of "Green Hill," Burlington county, New Jersey, 1761–1803; *m.*, 8 April, 1784, Gulielma Maria Morris, 1766–1826, also of Royal Descent, and had:

JOHN JAY SMITH, of "Ivy Lodge," Philadelphia county, Pennsylvania, 1798–1881; *m.*, 1821, Rachel C. Pearsall, and had:

ELIZABETH PEARSALL SMITH, of Germantown, Philadelphia, a member of the Pennsylvania Society of the Colonial Dames of America.

II.—JAMES SMITH, of Burlington county, New Jersey, 1750–1833; *m.*, 13 January, 1772, Esther, daughter of William Heulings, of Burlington, New Jersey, and had:

1.—HANNAH SMITH, 1773–1830, who *m.* 11 December, 1794, Henry S. Drinker, of Philadelphia, *d.* 1824, and had:

ESTHER DRINKER, *b.* 1 November, 1798, who *m.* Israel Pemberton Pleasants, and had:

NANCY PEMBERTON PLEASANTS, a member of the Pennsylvania Society of the Colonial Dames of America, who *m.* Samuel S. Hollingsworth, of Philadelphia, and had: *Esther D. P., Samuel S., Mary E., d.* 1883; *Israel P. P., Roger P., John V. P.,* and *Nancy P.*

2.—JAMES LOGAN SMITH, of Chambersburg, Pennsylvania, *b.* 14 September, 1793, *d.* 6 March, 1843; *m.*, secondly, 11 September, 1838, Mary daughter of James Couper, M.D., and had:

ANNIE COUPER SMITH, who *m.* Rev. Alexander Proudfit, and had:

MARY COUPER PROUDFIT, of Springfield, Ohio, a member of the Maryland and Ohio Societies of the Colonial Dames of America.

PEDIGREE LXXXIV.

ROBERT THE PIOUS, King of France, had by his second wife, Lady Constance, daughter of William, Count of Provence:

LADY ADELA, who *m.*, first, Richard III., Duke of Normandy, (she *m.*, secondly, Baldwin V., of Flanders, and by him was the mother of Maud, queen consort of William the Conqueror), and had:

LADY ALIX, who *m.* Ranulf, viscount of Bayeux, and had:

RANULF DE MESCHINES, viscount of Bayeux, created, 1119, Earl Palatine of Chester; *m.* Lady Maud, daughter of Rubard, Viscount de Auveranches, created, 1086, Earl of Chester, and had:

RANULF DE MESCHINES, Earl Palatine of Chester, *d.* 1153; *m.* Lady Maud, daughter of Robert, Earl of Mellent and Gloucester, and had:

HUGH DE MESCHINES, Earl Palatine of Chester, *d.* 1181, who had by his wife, Lady Bartred, daughter of Simon, Earl of Evereux:

LADY ——— DE MESCHINES, who *m.* Reginald Bacon (*see* pp. 30–31), and had:

RICHARD BACON, who *m.* Alice de Multon, and had:

SIR ROBERT BACON, of Baconsthorp, Norfolk, who *m.* the daughter of Sir Richard d'Ingham, and had:

SIR THOMAS BACON, who *m.* Elizabeth ———, living 1249, and had:

SIR HENRY BACON, 1270, who had:

SIR HENRY BACON, who *m.* Margaret Ludham, and had:

SIR ROGER BACON, who *m.* Felicia Kirton, and had:

BEATRICE BACON, heiress, who *m.* Sir William Thorpe, and had:

WILLIAM THORPE, *m.* Margery, daughter of John Quadlop, and had:

JOHN THORPE, whose daughter and heiress:

MARGERY THORPE, *m.* John Bacon, of Drinkstone, and·had:

EDMUND BACON, of Drinkstone, who *m.* Elizabeth Crofts, and had:

JOHN BACON, of Drinkstone, who *m.* Agnes Cockfield, and had:

ROBERT BACON, of Drinkstone, who *m.* Isabel Cage, and had:

ALDERMAN JAMES BACON, of London, *d.* 15 June, 1573, *bur.* St. Dunstan's (a brother of Sir Nicholas Bacon, lord keeper of the Great Seal, 1509–1579, whose son was the celebrated Sir Francis, Lord Verulam), who had by his second wife, Margaret, daughter of William Rawlings, of London, and widow of Richard Gouldston:

SIR JAMES BACON, of Friston Hall, Suffolk, knighted in 1604 at White Hall, *d.* 17 January, 1618; *m.* Elizabeth, daughter of Francis Bacon, of Hessett, *d.* 14 December, 1580, and had: *Rev. James* (*see* p. 32 and " Va. His. Mag.," ii., 125), and:

NATHANIEL BACON, of Friston Hall, eldest son, *b.* 15 May, 1593, *bur.* 7 August, 1644, at Friston Church; *m.* Anne, daughter of Sir Thomas le Grosse, of Crostwick, Norfolk, and had:

THOMAS BACON, of Friston (*see* " Va. His. Mag.," i., 430), who had by his first wife, Elizabeth, *d.* 2 January, 1647, aged 25 years, daughter of Sir Robert Brooke, of Cockfield Hall, Suffolk :

MAJOR-GENERAL NATHANIEL BACON,* the younger, "the Rebel Patriot of 1676 " (*see* " Va. His. Mag.," i., p. 170), only son, *b.* 2 January, 1647, *d.* in Gloucester county, Virginia, 26 October, 1666 (*see* " N. E. His. Geneal. Reg.," vol. xxxvii.; Keith's " Ancestry of Benjamin Harrison," and Brown's " Genesis of the United States "). He *m.* Elizabeth, *bapt.* 17 December, 1650, daughter of Sir Edward Duke, Bart., of Burhall Lodge, Suffolk (*see* Suckling's " His. of Suffolk," ii., 186; Burke's " Extinct Baronetages "), and had: *Elizabeth* (called also Mary) *bapt.* Friston parish, 12 April, 1674, *m.* Dr. Hugh Chamberlain, physician to Queen Anne, and (according to pedigrees accepted by the Georgia Society of the Colonial Dames):

NATHANIEL BACON (called also " John "), *b.* in Virginia 1675-6. After his father's death he was adopted in the family of Mrs. Frances Izard. In 1725 he petitioned the Virginia Council for confirmation to him of the grant of 1030 acres of land in Henrico county, which he inherited from Mrs. Izard. His will, dated in 1743, probated in Henrico county, mentions his children by his wife Elizabeth Parke, of whom :

1.—NATHANIEL PARKE BACON, of Henrico county, Virginia, father of:

CAPTAIN JOHN BACON, of Georgia, *m.* Agnes Hobson, and had:

I.—JOHN BACON, of Savannah, Georgia, *d.* April, 1812, aged 46; *m.*

---

* The following ladies, members of the National Society of the Colonial Dames of America, are also of Royal Descent, through General Nathaniel Bacon :

MRS. ANN BARRETT PHINIZY, Georgia State Society.

MRS. MARY E. WARE CHARBONNIER (deceased), Georgia State Society.

MRS. FRANK H. MILLER, JR., Georgia State Society.

MRS. JAMES F. MCGOWAN, Georgia State Society.

MRS. SAMUEL H. MCAFEE, Georgia State Society.

MRS. MARY K. ADAMS BULKLEY, Georgia State Society.

MRS. PLEASANT A. STOVALL, Georgia State Society.

MRS. ALEXANDER J. PERRY, Georgia State Society.

MRS. SARAH D. ADAMS MCWHORTER, Georgia State Society.

Eliza Ruffin, daughter of Nathaniel Cocke, of Fauquier county, Virginia, and had:

JOHN EDMUND BACON, *b.* Augusta, Georgia, 1812, *d.* Columbus, Georgia, 1882; *m.*, first, Clementina, daughter of Robert West Alston, of Halifax county, North Carolina, and had by her:

1.—ROBERT ALSTON BACON, of Graysville, Georgia, *unm.*

2.—HENRIETTA ALSTON BACON, of Alexander City, Alabama, who *m.*, 1858, Joseph Bibb McDonald, and had:

I.—JOHN BACON MCDONALD, a graduate of the United States Military Academy, Captain in the 3d Cavalry, United States Army, *b.* 1859; *m.*, 1888, Kate Murphy, and had: *Joseph Robert, d. inf.; Joseph Edmund, b.* 1890; *Robert Dyer, b.* 1892; *Lila Mary, b.* 1894; and *John Bacon, b.* 1897.

II.—MARY MALONE MCDONALD, *b.* 1860; *m.*,1885, Hiram Donald Barr, M.D., of Anniston, Alabama, and had: *Roberta Bacon, d. inf.*, and *Henrie Lynn, b.* 1889.

III.—JOSEPH STERLING MCDONALD, 1862–1898; *m.*, 1888, Lula Penny, *d.* 1897.

IV.—CLEMENTINA ALSTON MCDONALD, *b.* 1865; *m.*, 1887, James Elbert Pearson, M.D., of Sylacauga, Alabama, and had: *Katie May, b.* 1889; *Leslie Alston, b.* 1891, and *McDonald, b.* 1893.

V.—ROBERTA BACON MCDONALD, *b.* 1878; *m.*, 1899, Benjamin Russell.

II.—EDMUND BACON, *m.* Elizabeth Cocke, and haa .

SARAH BACON, *m.* Sherwood Bugg, and had:

OBEDIENCE BUGG, *m.* Colonel James Maitier, and had:

KEZIA PARIS MAITIER, *m.* Major George Golphin Yoville McMurphy, and had:

SARAH SUSANNAH MCMURPHY, *m.* John Marsh Adams, and had:

ELIZABETH BACON ADAMS, a member of the Georgia and Michigan Societies of the Colonial Dames of America, who *m.* Joshua Henry Rathbone, M.D., of Ann Arbor, Michigan.

2.—NATHANIEL BACON, of Henrico county, 1705–1779, who had:

I.—AGNES BACON, *m.* Matthew Hobson, of Virginia, and had:

AGNES HOBSON, *m.* John Langston Bacon, and had:

MARY BACON, *m.* General Thomas Glascock, of Richmond county, Georgia, and had:

GENERAL THOMAS GLASCOCK, JR., *m.* Harriet Hatcher Hayes, and had:

MARY SAVANNAH GLASCOCK, *m.* Thomas Barrett, and had:

HARRIET GLASCOCK BARRETT, *m.* James Gardner Gould, son of Judge William Tracy Gould, son of Judge James Gould, of Litchfield, Connecticut, and Sally McCurdy, a daughter of Major-General Uriah Tracy, a descendant of Deputy-Governor William Bradford, son of Governor William Bradford, and had:

HARRIET GOULD, of Augusta, a member of the Georgia Society of the Colonial Dames of America, Society of " Mayflower " Descendants, Society of Descendants of Colonial Governors, *etc.*, who *m.* Richard Sims Jefferies (deceased), and had : *James Gould.*

II.—SARA BACON, *d.* 26 January, 1816, aged 76, who *m.*, before 1760, Charles Edwin Crenshaw, of Hanover county, Virginia, and had :

MARY TEMPERANCE CRENSHAW, *d.* 26 March, 1807, who *m.* William Rice, M.D., of Charlotte, Virginia, and had :

SAMUEL BLAIR RICE, of Halifax, Virginia, who *m.* Lucinda Walton, daughter of Rev. William Leftwich, of Bedford, Virginia, and had :

SARA AGNES RICE, a member of the Virginia Society of the Colonial Dames of America, who *m.* Roger A. Pryor, LL.D., judge of supreme court, New York City, Brigadier-General Confederate States Army; *b.* Dinwiddie county, Virginia, 19 July, 1828, and had :

1.—MARIE GORDON PRYOR, a member of the Virginia Society of the Colonial Dames of America, *m.* Henry Crenshaw Rice, of Charlotte, Virginia, and had : *Mary Blair, Henry Izard Bacon, Roger Pryor* and *Theodorick Bland.*

2.—THEODORICK BLAND PRYOR, *unm.* 1871.

3.—ROGER A. PRYOR, JR., of New York.

4.—MARY BLAIR PRYOR, a member of the Virginia Society of the Colonial Dames of America, who *m.* Francis T. Walker of Charlottesville, Virginia, and had : *Roger Pryor, Lindsay Howell, Frances Theodora Bland, Francis Thomas* and *Mary Blair.*

5.—WILLIAM RICE PRYOR, M.D., of New York, *m.* Louise Gabrielle, daughter of John Allan, of Richmond, Virginia, and had : *Hoffman Allan* and *Louise Gabrielle.*

6.—LUCY ATKINSON PRYOR, a member of the Virginia Society of the Colonial Dames of America, who *m.* Arthur Page Brown, of San Francisco, California, and had : *Katrina Trask, Agnes,* and *Lucy.*

7.—FRANCES THEODORA BLAND PRYOR, of New York, a member of the Virginia Society of the Colonial Dames of America, *m.* William de Leftwich Dodge, of Paris, France, and had : *Roger Pryor.*

THE ROYAL DESCENT

OF

MRS. JOHN FLICK WINSLOW,

OF CINCINNATI, OHIO.

EDWARD I., King of England⹂Princess Eleanor of Castile.

Princess Elizabeth Plantagenet⹂Humphrey de Bohun, Earl of Hereford.

Lady Margaret de Bohun⹂Hugh de Courtenay, Earl of Devon.

Lady Elizabeth de Courtenay⹂Sir Andrew Luttrell, of Chilton.

Lady Elizabeth Luttrell⹂John Stratton, of Weston.

Elizabeth Stratton⹂John Andrews, of Stoke.

Elizabeth Andrews⹂Thomas Wyndsore.

Sir Andrews Wyndsore, of Stanwell⹂Lady Elizabeth Blount.

Lady Edith Wyndsore⹂George Ludowe, of Hill Deverill.

Thomas Ludlow, of Dinton⹂Jane Pyle, of Bopton, Wilts.

Gabriel Ludlow, 1587-1639⹂Phyllis ———.

Sarah Ludlow (fourth wife)⹂John Carter, of Gloucester Co., Va.

Robert Carter, of " Carotoman "⹂Elizabeth (Landon) Willis.

Mary Carter⹂George Braxton, of King and Queen Co., Va.

Carter Braxton, of " Elsing Green," Va.⹂Judith Robinson.

Judith Braxton⹂John White, of Va.

Mary Page White⹂Andrew Stevenson, of " Blenheim," Va.

John W. Stevenson, of Covington, Ky.⹂Sibella Winston.

Judith White Stevenson⹂John F. Winslow, of Cincinnati.

John W. S. Winslow, *b.* 3 April, 1893.

PEDIGREE LXXXV.

EDWARD III., **King of England,** had by his wife, Lady Philippa, daughter of William, Count of Hainault and Holland:

SIR LIONEL PLANTAGENET, K.G., Duke of Clarence, who *m.*, first, Lady Elizabeth, daughter of Sir William de Burgh, third'Earl of Ulster, and his wife, Lady Maud, daughter of Henry Plantagenet, Earl of Lancaster, both of Royal Descent, and had:

LADY PHILIPPA PLANTAGENET, who *m.* Edmund de Mortimer, Earl of Marche, *d.* 1381, also of Royal Descent, and had:

LADY ELIZABETH DE MORTIMER, who *m.* Sir Henry Percy, called Hotspur, *k.* 1403, also of Royal Descent, and had:

LADY ELIZABETH PERCY, who *m.* John de Clifford, Baron Clifford, *d.* 1432, also of Royal Descent, and had:

THOMAS DE CLIFFORD, Baron Clifford, *k.* 1454, *m.* Lady Joan, daughter of Thomas de Dacre, first Baron Dacre, also of Royal Descent, and had:

JOHN DE CLIFFORD, Baron Clifford, *k.* 1461, father of

JOHN DE CLIFFORD, Baron Clifford, *d.* 1485, *m.* Lady Margaret, daughter of Sir Henry de Bromflete, of Vesci, Yorkshire, also of Royal Descent, and had:

LADY MARY DE CLIFFORD, who *m.* Sir Philip Wentworth, of Nettlested, Suffolk, and had:

SIR HENRY WENTWORTH, of Nettlested, who *m.* Lady Anne, daughter of Sir John de Say, and had:

LADY ELIZABETH WENTWORTH, who *m.* Sir John Seymour, of Wolf Hall, Wilts, *d.* 1536, also of Royal Descent, and had:

SIR EDWARD DE SEYMOUR, K.G., first Duke of Somerset, beheaded in 1552; *m.*, first, Lady Catherine, daughter of Sir William Fillol, of Woodlands, Dorset, and his wife Elizabeth Wingfield, also of Royal Descent, and had:

SIR EDWARD DE SEYMOUR, Lord Seymour, *d.* 1593, *m.* Mary, or Margaret, daughter of Judge John Welsh, and had:

SIR EDWARD SEYMOUR, Bart., of Berry-Pomeroy, who *m.* Elizabeth, daughter of Sir Arthur Champernon, of Darlington, Devon, also of Royal Descent, and had:

LADY MARY SEYMOUR, *m.* Sir George Farwell, of Hill-Bishop, Somerset, *d.* 1647, and had:

JOHN FARWELL, of Hill-Bishop, who *m.* Dorothy, daughter of Sir John Routh, and had:

HENRY FARWELL, *d.*, at Chelmsford, Massachusetts, 1 August, 1670, *m.* Olive ——, *d.* 1 March, 1691-2, and had:

JOSEPH FARWELL, of Dunstable, Massachusetts, 1642-1722; *m.*, 25 December, 1666, Hannah Learned, of Woburn, and had:

SARAH FARWELL, *m.*, 5 September, 1707, Jonathan Howard, of Chelmsford, 1675-1758, and had:

JACOB HOWARD, of Chelmsford, Massachusetts, 1719-1798; *m.*, 1745, Rachel Fletcher, and had:

SARAH HOWARD, *m.*, 1776, John Cummings, of Tyngsboro, Massachusetts, 1753-1837, and had:

JOHN CUMMINGS, of Tyngsboro, who *m.*, 1806, Salla Cummings, also of Royal Descent (*see* p. 229), and had:

WILLARD CUMMINGS, who *m.* Mary Anne Pollard, and had:

ELLEN MARIA CUMMINGS, who *m.* Joshua Flagg Davis, of Boston and Chelmsford, also of Royal Descent (*see* p. 336), and had:

ANNA MARIA DAVIS, a member of the Vermont Society of the Colonial Dames of America, the Order of the Crown, *etc.*, who *m.*, 30 June, 1886, Lord Karl von Rydingsvärd, of Sweden and Boston, Massachusetts.

ADDENDA.

Page 16.—*Mrs. Julia Sweet Weir, d.* 19 March, 1900. She had only one child, *Laura, d.* 5 August, 1865, aged 12 years.

Page 22.—Mrs. John Kilgour is a member of the Georgia and Ohio Societies of the Colonial Dames of America.

Page 24.—Mrs. Maria Denning King Van Rensselaer was a member and founder of "the original" Society of the Colonial Dames.

Page 24.—Mr. Frederic Bronson *d.* in March, 1900.

Page 26.—*Matthew Allyn*, 1605–1670, and his wife Margaret Wyatt, of Royal Descent, had :
Mary Allyn, m. 11 June, 1646, Captain Benjamin Newberry, and had :
Sarah Newberry, m., 4 June, 1668, Captain Preserved Clapp, and had :
Roger Clapp, m., 20 November, 1706, Elizabeth Bartlett, and had :
Aaron Clapp, m., 1747, Jemima Bartlett, and had :
Achsah Clapp, m., 16 September, 1780, John Dewey, and had :
Sarah Dewey, m., 19 December, 1804, Gurdon Lord, and had :
Sarah Naomi Lord, m., 12 June, 1849, Renel Kimball, Jr., of Leyden, New York, and had :
Lucy Lord Kimball, a member of the New York Society of the Colonial Dames of America, the Order of the Crown, *etc.*, who *m.*, 29 August, 1877, Henry Gilbert Hart, of Utica, New York, and had : *Henry Gilbert, b.* 25 January, 1879; *Merwin Kimball, b.* 25 June, 1881, and *Richard Seymour, b.* 13 March, 1887.

Page 32.—Abigail Smith, the first wife of Major Lewis Burwell, Jr., was heir to Colonel Bacon, her uncle. She was *bapt.* at St. James's Church, Colchester, Virginia.

Page 32.—Rev. James Bacon had apparently two wives, and it is uncertain which was the mother of Colonel Nathaniel Bacon, who *d.* 16 March, 1692, and Mrs. Martha Smythe, or Smith (*see* Keith's "Ancestry of Benjamin Harrison," p. 22). His second wife was Martha, daughter of George Woodward and his second wife, Elizabeth Honeywood.

Page 33.—Mrs. Thomas Marshall Colston was Miss Eliza Jacqueline Fisher.

Page 33.—Mary Eloise Howard, *m.* Francis Eliot Shoup.

Page 38.—*Judge R. Augustine Thompson's* daughter (by his first wife), *Sarah Elizabeth, m.* G. W. Huie, and had : *Sallie Helena Huie*, who *m.*, in 1899, William Thompson. Judge Thompson's daughter (by his second wife), *Ruth Hairston Thompson, m.* William Craig.

Page 39.—Belle Chapman, *m.* William Moncure on 12 December, 1878.

Page 40.—The mother of Princess Joan Plantagenet was Princess Eleanor of Castile.

Page 42.—*Miss Augusta Dearborn Boyd*, of Portland, Maine, is a member of the Order of the Crown.

Page 47.—The *m.*, in September, 1293, of Henry III., Comte de Bar, and Princess Eleanor Plantagenet, and the pedigree which follows, are from Burke's "Royal Families," Ped. XXXI. in Vol. i., and his "Royal Descents," Ped. CX. But "L'Art de Verifier les Dates," vol. xiii., p. 457, mentions only one daughter of this marriage: "Jeanne, femme de Jean de Varennes, Comte de Sussex." However, Burke's "Royal Families," vol. i., Ped. LII., gives the following royal descent for Eleanor, wife of Gryffyth Vychan, fourth Lord of Glyndfrdwy: JOHN, KING OF ENGLAND, had by his wife Isabel: ELEANOR, who had by her second husband, Simon de Montfort, Earl of Leicester, *d.* 1238: ELEANOR, *d.* 1280, who *m.* Llewelyn ap Gryffyth, Prince of North Wales, and had: CATHERINE, heiress, who *m.* Philip ap Ivor, lord of Cardigan, and had: ELEANOR, heiress, who *m.* Thomas ap Llewelyn, and had: ELEANOR, wife of the aforesaid Gryffyth Vaughn.

Page 48.—Mr. John Hone resides at Red Bank, New Jersey.

Page 48.—The wife of Archibald McCall, Jr., of Philadelphia, was Elizabeth Cadwalader, 1773–1824.

Page 63.—Christopher Curwen and his son Thomas were both knighted, and were high sheriffs. Sir Christopher was one of the truce commissioners between England and Scotland, in 1438. He *d.* 17 July, 1450, aged 46. His wife was a daughter of Sir John Huddleston, of Millom.

Page 64.—Lieutenant-Colonel Thomas Claiborne, 1647-1683 ; *m.* Sarah Fenn.

Page 71.—*Mrs. Roswell Smith,* who *d.* 21 January, 1900, aged 73 years. Sent the first telegram for Mr. Morse, the inventor, which was, "What hath God wrought?" Her daughter, Julia Smith, *m.,* 23 April, 1879, George Innes, Jr., of New York, and had : *Elizabeth, b.* New York City, 22 March, 1880; *Juliet, b.* Montclair, New Jersey, 17 June, 1881, and *George Ellsworth, b.* at Montclair, 10 October, 1882.

Page 72.—*Mrs. Katharine Stuart Dunscomb's* son, Cecil, was *b.* 20 September, 1887.

Page 72.—*Homer Hine Stuart, Jr., m.* Margaret Beckwith Kenny.

Page 77.—*Mrs. Peterfield Trent, d.* before May, 1900.

Page 84.—Mary Sage was *b.* 9 April, 1699, at Cromwell, Connecticut.

Page 85.—Cephas Smith, Sr., resided at Sandisfield, Massachusetts.

Page 85.—Names of children of *Judge Jesse and Roxa (Francis) Booth : Walter Bulkeley, m.* Eliza Banner ; *Pembroke Somerset ; George Washington, m.* Hester Look; *Mary Elizabeth, m.* Hugh Beatie Cochran ; *Roxa Lyman, m.* L. R. Slade; *Thyrza Angeline, m.* Julius Austin ; *Flora Sylvia, m.* Selah Look; *Julia Portia, m.* Earl Hollingsworth, and *Ella Cordelia,* a member of the Connecticut and California Societies of the Colonial Dames of America, who *m.* Byron Coleman Dick.

Page 87.—William Henry Bulkeley, *m.,* September, 1863, Emma Gurney.

Page 87.—The issue of *Mrs. Sarah T. (Bulkeley) Macauley : Richard Bulkeley, Frances Gurney, b.* 1 December, 1897, and *Sally.*

Page 88.—It is only a tradition that Horatio T. Harris was ever connected with United States Navy, and the statement has not been verified.

Page 90.—Richard Wood, *b.* 1755, resided at Greenwich, New Jersey. His wife Elizabeth, *b.* 1776, was the daughter of John Bacon, *b.* 1725 (*see* "Family Sketches," by Mrs. Richard D. Wood).

Page 92.—*Miss Susan Kidder Meares* is a member of the North Carolina Society of the Colonial Dames of America.

Page 92.—*James Claypoole,* 1634-1687, of Royal Descent; had :

Nathaniel Claypoole, of Philadelphia, 1672-172- ; *m.* Elizabeth ——, and had :

James Claypoole, m. Mary Hood, and had :

James Claypoole, m. Mary Kemp, and had :

James Claypoole, m. Elizabeth Morrison, and had :

John Claypoole, m. Martha Ann Browne, and had :

Julia Ann Claypoole, d. 1899, a member of the Order of the Crown, who *m.* Isaac Freeman Rasin, of Baltimore, Maryland, and had :

1.—*Helen Ringgold Rasin,* a member of the Order of the Crown, *m.* Hugo Albert Rennert.

2.—*Julia Angela Rasin,* of Baltimore, a member of the Order of the Crown.

3.—*Gertrude Browne Rasin,* of Baltimore, a member of the Order of the Crown.

Page 94.—*Rebecca Wallace,* 1778-1867, of Royal Descent, *m.* Judge Jacob Burnet, and had :

William Burnet, of Cincinnati, who had by his second wife, Susan M. Clark :

Josephine Clark Burnet, a member of the Order of the Crown, who *m.* (his second wife) Peter Rudolph Neff, of Cincinnati, and had : *Rudolph, Robert Burnet, Rebecca,* and

Susan Clark Neff, of Cincinnati, a member of the Order of the Crown.

Page 95.—*Lucy Wortham James* was *b.* at St. James, Missouri, 13 September, 1880.

Page 98.—*Mrs. Nannie Jenifer Triplett,* of Richmond, had also : 1. *John Richards Triplett, m.* Sallie Ross, of Mobile, and had : *Mary Amanda, Sallie Ross, Nannie T.,* and *Helen Lyons.* 2. *Mary Jenifer,* wife of Philip Haxall, of Richmond. *No issue.* Mrs. Lizzie Campbell Price was the second child and Mrs. Montague the fourth child of Mrs. Nannie O. J. Triplett.

Page 104.—Count John Delafield, 1786-1853 ; *m.,* first, at the Hillingdon Church, in Middlesex county, England, 22 January, 1812. His eldest son, John, *b.* in East Street, St. George's, Bloomsbury, London, 21 October, 1812, *d.* 12 December, 1866; *m.,* 14 June, 1833, Edith Wallace, and had : Count Wallace Delafield, of St. Louis, Missouri, a member of the Order of Runnemede, *etc.*

Page 106.—*Ursula Wolcott,* 1724-1788, of Royal Descent, *m.* Governor Matthew Griswold, of Connecticut, and had :

Governor Roger Griswold, of Connecticut, who *m.* Fanny Rogers, and had :

Eliza Woodbridge Griswold, who *m.* Charles Leicester Boalt, and had :

Fanny Griswold Lane Boalt, a member of the Connecticut Society of the Colonial Dames of America, the Order of the Crown, *etc.,* who *m.* Jay Osborne Moss, of Sandusky, Ohio, and had:

1.—*Cornelia Emily Moss,* a member of the New York Society of the Colonial Dames of America, who *m.* George Hunter Brown, Jr., and had : *Ursula Wolcott.*

2.—*Augustus Leicester Moss, m.* Carrie Babcock Curtiss, of Hartford, Connecticut, and had : *Wolcott Griswold.*

Page 107.—Dr. Elijah F. Reed, *m.* 6 January, 1792.

Page 108.—Mary Reed, *m.,* 17 August, 1863, Samuel Francis Smith.

Page 136.—Emily Slaughter was the second wife of Samuel K. Bradford, Jr.

Page 136.—*Mrs. Mary Wright Wootton's* son is *Herbert Wright Wootton.*

Page 139.—Harriot Tynge Walter, *m.* John Odin.

Page 140.—Gilbert de Clare was Earl of Hertford.

Page 149.—*Arthur Collins Ketcham, m.,* New York City, Margaret Bruce Allen, and had : *Margaret Bruce* and *Arthur Collins.*

Page 149.—*Charles* and *Mary Hall (Terry) Collins,* of New York City, also had issue ; *Charles Terry Collins, d.* 1883, second child, who *m.* Mary A. Wood, and had : 1. *Charles.* 2. *Clarence Lyman, 2d.* 3. *Mary Terry.* 4. *Arthur Morris,* and *Arthur Morris Collins,* fourth child, who *d.* young, *unm.*

Page 150.—*Clarence L. Collins,* also had *Maude, d. inf.*

Page 150.—*Mrs. William Allen Butler, Jr.,* was the fifth child.

Page 152.—General William Lyman, *d.,* at Cheltenham, 22 September, 1811. He did not *m.,* on 11 *June,* 1803, Jerusha Welles.

Page 152.—James S. Cox was *b.* 13 February, 1822.

Page 171.—*Charlotte Kilgour, m.* Captain Ashton B. Heyl, surgeon, United States army.

Page 177.—Mercy Floretta Fairfax, *m.* Rev. Samuel Haggings.

Page 177.—Mr. and Mrs. M. F. H. Gouverneur had issue : *Fairfax Heiskell.* Mr. and Mrs. Donald MacRae have no issue.

Pages 177, 231.—*Mrs. Virginia Dunbar* is a member of the Order of the Crown.

Page 188.—*Mrs. Henry F. Le H. Lyster,* of Detroit, is also of Royal Descent through *Colonel William Digges,* deputy-governor of Maryland, and his wife, Elizabeth Sewell (p. 76), who had : *Anne,* who *m.* Governor Henry Darnall, and had :

Eleanor, who *m.* Daniel Carroll, *d.* 1751, and had :

Eleanor, who *m.* William Brent, of "Richland," Stafford county, Virginia, and had : *Daniel Carroll Brent,* who *m.* Anne Fenton Lee, and had : *William Brent,* who *m.* his cousin, Winifred Beale Lee (also of Royal Descent, *see* p. 187), and had : *Thomas Lee Brent,* father of *Mrs. Lyster,* whose daughter, *Mrs. Edward H. Parker,* of Detroit, is a member of the Michigan Society of the Colonial Dames of America.

Page 189.—Anna Lee is the name of Mrs. Alfriend's daughter, and not Maria Lee.

Page 193.—Brigadier-Major Edward Bulkeley was the son of Charles, son of Edward, of Wethersfield, 1673-1748, as on pp. 84, 85.

Page 198.—*Rev. Robert Rose,* of Virginia, 1704-1751, of Royal Descent, had by his wife, Anne Fitzhugh :

Charles Rose, of "Bellivat," Nelson county, Virginia, third son, who *m.* —— Jordan, and had :

Dr. Joseph Rose, 1776-1849, who had by his second wife, Nancy Armstrong :

U —— M. Rose, b. 5 March, 1834, *m.* Margaret Gibbs, and had :

Fanny Rose, b. 5 November, 1863, a member of the Virginia and Arkansas Societies of the Colonial Dames of America, who *m.,* 1 January, 1884, Wallace W. Dickinson, of Little Rock, and had : *Wallace W., b.* 15 January, 1885; *Rose, b.* 18 April, 1886, and *Benjamin F., b.* 23 July, 1888.

Page 198.—*Colonel Hugh Rose,* of "Geddes," had by his wife, Caroline Jordan :

Anne Fitzhugh Rose, m. Samuel Irvine, and had :

Mary Fleming Irvine, m. Samuel Anthony, and had :

Samuel Irvine Anthony, m. Nancy B. Emery, and had :

Mary Jeanette Anthony, a member of the Virginia Society of the Colonial Dames of America, the Order of the Crown, *etc.*, who *m.* Charles Gifford Dyer, and had :

Stella Dyer, a member of the Order of the Crown.

Page 199.—Benjamin Powell Walker's son is Bradford Hastings.

Page 199.—*Mrs. Maria Rose Fisher* had issue : *Rose, Helen,* and *Edith.*

Page 199.—*Mrs. Caroline Walker Fisher* is a member of the Virginia and Illinois Societies of the Colonial Dames of America.

Page 199.—*Mrs. Rose Fisher Kennedy* has issue : *Jane.*

Page 199.—*Mrs. William James Walker* (Columbia Stanard Hayes), of Richmond, a member of the Virginia Society of the Colonial Dames of America, is of Royal Descent through Colonel Robert Carter, page 132, she being a sister of Mrs. Eaches, page 136.

Page 208.—Samuel Sergeant Newbury was *k.* in battle in 1865.

Page 208.—*Mrs. Katherine Sedgewick (Newbury) Robb* has issue : *Marion* and *Russell.*

Page 208.—Egbert Starr Newbury *m.* F. Kellogg, and had : *Egbert, George, Katherine,* and *Sergeant.*

Page 208.—*Mrs. Mary Newbury Adams* is a member of the Connecticut and Iowa Societies of the Colonial Dames of America, Order of Colonial Governors, Order of the Crown, *etc.*

Pages 209, 341.—Mrs. John Judson Bagley died at Colorado Springs, Colorado, 7 February, 1897.

Page 215.—"The Long Island Lawrences " are descendants of "Thomas Lawrence, of St. Albans," Herts, 1588–1624. It has long been presumed by these descendants that they were of Royal Descent through the Lawrences of Lancashire, but recently the particular pedigree connecting these two branches has been found so defective the claim of Royal Descent is suspended.

Page 216.—Lady Edith Wyndsor *m.* George Ludlowe, of Hill Deverill.

Page 220.—*Roberta E. Lee Wright m.* George H. Hellman, and had : *Mary S., Katherine,* and *Roberta Lee Wright, b.* July, 1899.

Page 224.—*Mrs. Anna Reed Wilkinson* is also of Royal Descent through John Drake, p. 105, being a sister of Mrs. Samuel Francis Smith, p. 108.

Page 229.—*Lady Anna von Rydingsvärd* is a member of the Vermont Society of the Colonial Dames of America.

Page 239.—*Mrs. Paul Wayland Bartlett,* a member of the Order of the Crown, is of Royal Descent through William Montgomery.

Page 248.—*Mrs. Burton Smith* (Frances Gordon), *Mrs. John B. Gordon* (Frances R. Haralson), and *Miss Caroline Lewis Gordon,* of "Kirkwood," Atlanta, members of the Georgia Society of the Colonial Dames of America, are of Royal Descent through Colonel George Reade.

Page 251.—Mary Warner *m.,* 17 February, 1680, John Smith, of "Purton," Gloucester county, Virginia.

Page 267.—*Mrs. James Henry Parker,* of New York City, a member of the New York Society of the Colonial Dames of America, the Order of the Crown, *etc.*, is of Royal Descent through Mabel Harlakenden.

Page 304.—*Colonel Charles Carroll,* of "Homewood," *d.* 1861, had :

Charles Carroll, of Donghoregan Manor, only son, 1801–1862, who *m.*, 1825, Mary Digges, daughter of John Lee, of Needwood, Frederick county, Maryland, son of Thomas S. Lee, Governor of Maryland, and had :

Albert Henry Carroll, Confederate States army, *k.* in battle in 1862 ; *m.* Mary Cornelia, daughter of William George Read, and his wife, Sophia Catherine, daughter of Colonel John Eager Howard, thrice Governor of Maryland, United States Senator, *etc.*, and had : *Mary Sophia, Mary Elinor,* and

Agnes Carroll, Countess Henssenstamm, of Matzleinsdorf, Austria, a member of the Order of the Crown.

Page 315–319.—This royal descent is a revise and correction of Mrs. Samuel F. Leib's pedigree printed in " Americans of Royal Descent," vol. ii., pp. 859–863.

INDEX TO AMERICANS OF ROYAL DESCENT.

(357)